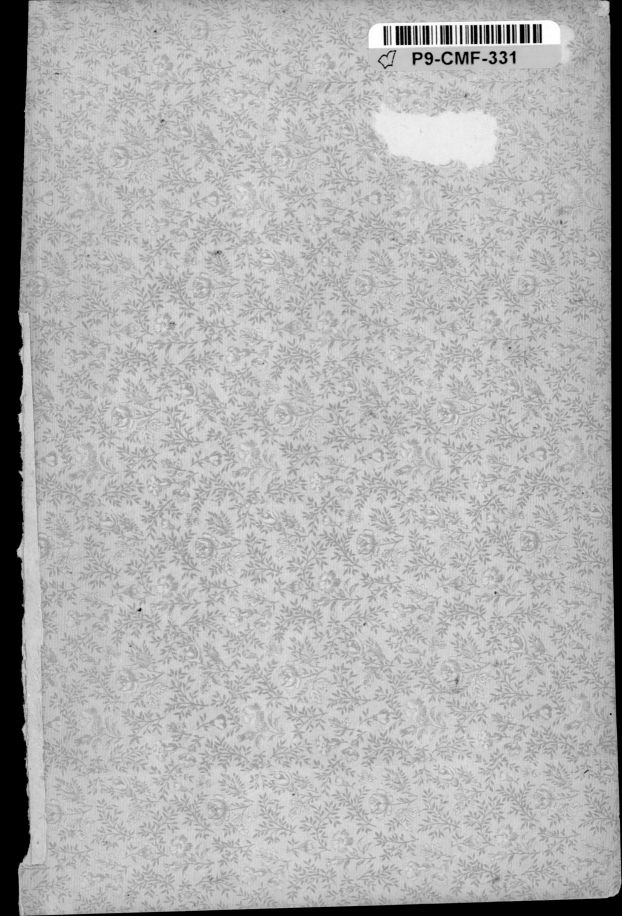

TWENTY YEARS OF CONGRESS:

FROM

LINCOLN TO GARFIELD.

WITH A REVIEW OF

THE EVENTS WHICH LED TO THE POLITICAL
REVOLUTION OF 1860.

BY

JAMES G. BLAINE.

VOLUME I.

NORWICH, CONN.:
THE HENRY BILL PUBLISHING COMPANY.
1884.

ELECTROTYPED AND PRINTED

BY RAND, AVERY, AND COMPANY,

BOSTON, MASS.

CONTENTS OF VOLUME I.

CHAPTER I.

A REVIEW OF THE EVENTS WHICH LED TO THE POLITICAL REVOLUTION OF 1860.

CHAPTER II.

CHAPTER III.

CHAPTER IV.

CHAPTER V.

CHAPTER VI.

CHAPTER VII.

CHAPTER VIII.

CHAPTER IX.

CHAPTER X.

CHAPTER XI.

CHAPTER XII.

CHAPTER XIII.

CHAPTER XIV.

CHAPTER XV.

CHAPTER XVI.

CHAPTER XVII.

CHAPTER XVIII.

CHAPTER XIX.

CHAPTER XX.

CHAPTER XXI.

CHAPTER XXII.

CHAPTER XXIII.

CHAPTER XXIV.

CHAPTER XXV.

CHAPTER XXVI.

LIST OF STEEL PORTRAITS.

TWENTY YEARS OF CONGRESS.

CHAPTER I.

A REVIEW OF THE EVENTS WHICH LED TO THE POLITICAL REVOLUTION OF 1860.

ORIGINAL COMPROMISES BETWEEN THE NORTH AND THE SOUTH EMBODIED IN THE CONSTITUTION. — EARLY DISSATISFACTION WITH NATIONAL BOUNDARIES. — ACQUISITION OF LOUISIANA FROM FRANCE BY PRESIDENT JEFFERSON. — BONAPARTE'S ACTION AND MOTIVE IN CEDING LOUISIANA. — STATE OF LOUISIANA ADMITTED TO THE UNION AGAINST OPPOSITION IN THE NORTH. — AGITATION OF SLAVERY QUESTION IN CONNECTION WITH THE ADMISSION OF MISSOURI TO THE UNION. — THE TWO MISSOURI COMPROMISES OF 1820 AND 1821. — ORIGIN AND DEVELOPMENT OF THE ABOLITION PARTY. — STRUGGLE OVER THE RIGHT OF PETITION.

THE compromises on the Slavery question, inserted in the Constitution, were among the essential conditions upon which the Federal Government was organized. If the African slave-trade had not been permitted to continue for twenty years, if it had not been conceded that three-fifths of the slaves should be counted in the apportionment of representatives in Congress, if it had not been agreed that fugitives from service should be returned to their owners, the Thirteen States would not have been able in 1787 "to form a more perfect union." These adjustments in the Constitution were effected after the Congress of the old Confederation had dedicated the entire North-west Territory to freedom. The ancient commonwealth of Virginia had, for the good of all, generously and patriotically surrendered her title to the great country north of the Ohio and east of the Mississippi, which to-day constitutes five prosperous and powerful States and a not inconsiderable portion of a sixth. This was the first territory of which the General Government had exclusive control, and the prompt prohibition of slavery therein by the Ordinance of 1787 is an important and significant fact. The

1

anti-slavery restriction would doubtless have been applied to the territory south of the Ohio had the power existed to impose it. The founders of the government not only looked to the speedy extinction of slavery, but they especially abhorred the idea of a geographical line, with freedom decreed on one side, and slavery established on the other. But the territory south of the Ohio belonged to the Southern States of the Union, — Kentucky to Virginia; Tennessee to North Carolina; Alabama and Mississippi to Georgia, with certain co-extensive claims put forth by South Carolina. When cessions of this Southern territory were made to the General Government, the States owning it exacted in every case a stipulation that slavery should not be prohibited. It thus came to pass that the Ohio River was the dividing-line. North of it freedom was forever decreed. South of it slavery was firmly established. Within the limits of the Union as originally formed the slavery question had therefore been compromised, the common territory partitioned, and the Republic, half slave, half free, organized and sent forth upon its mission.

The Thirteen States whose independence had been acknowledged by George III., occupied with their outlying territories a vast area, exceeding in the aggregate eight hundred thousand square miles. Extended as was this domain, the early statesmen of the Union discovered that its boundaries were unsatisfactory, — hostile to our commercial interests in time of peace, and menacing our safety in time of war. The Mississippi River was our western limit. On its farther shore, from the Lake of the Woods to the Balize, we met the flag of Spain. Our southern border was the 31st parallel of latitude; and the Spanish Floridas, stretching across to the Mississippi, lay between us and the Gulf of Mexico. We acquired from Spain the right of deposit for exports and imports at New Orleans, but the citizens of the Union who lived west of the Alleghanies were discontented and irritated to find a foreign power practically controlling their trade by intercepting their access to the sea. One of the great problems imposed upon the founders of the Union was to remove the burdens and embarrassments which obstructed the development of the Western States, and thus to render their inhabitants as loyal by reason of material prosperity as they already were in patriotic sympathy. The opportunity for relief came from remote and foreign causes, without our own agency; but the courageous statesmanship which discerned and grasped the opportunity, deserved, as it has received, the commemoration of three generations. The boundaries of the Union were vastly enlarged, but the geographical change was not greater than the effect produced upon the political and social condition of the people. The ambitions developed by the acquisition of new territory led to serious conflicts of opinion between North and South, — conflicts which steadily grew in intensity until, by the convulsion of war, slavery was finally extinguished.

A great European struggle, which ended twelve years before our Revolution began, had wrought important changes in the political control of North America. The Seven Years' War, identical in time with the French and Indian War in America, was closed in 1763 by numerous treaties to which every great power in Europe was in some sense a party. One of the most striking results of those treaties on this side of the Atlantic was the cession of Florida to Great Britain by Spain in exchange for the release of Cuba, which the English and colonial forces under Lord Albemarle had wrested from Spanish authority the preceding year. England held Florida for twenty years, when among the disasters brought upon her by our Revolution was its retrocession to Spain in 1783, — a result which was accounted by our forefathers a great gain to the new Republic. Still more striking were the losses of France. Fifty years before, by the Treaty of Utrecht, France had surrendered to England the island of Newfoundland, Nova Scotia (then including New Brunswick), and the Hudson-bay Territory. She now gave up Canada and Cape Breton, acknowledged the sovereignty of Great Britain in the original thirteen Colonies as extending to the Mississippi, and, by a separate treaty, surrendered Louisiana on the west side of the Mississippi, with New Orleans on the east side, to Spain. Thus, in 1763, French power disappeared from North America. The last square mile of the most valuable colonial territory ever possessed by a European sovereign was lost under the weak and effeminate rule of Louis XV., a reign not fitted for successful war, but distinguished only, as one of its historians says, for "easy-mannered joyance, and the brilliant charm of fashionable and philosophical society."

The country which France surrendered to Spain was of vast but indefinite extent. Added to her other North-American colonies, it gave to Spain control of more than half the continent. She continued in possession of Louisiana until the year 1800, when, during some European negotiations, Bonaparte concluded a treaty at San Ildefonso with Charles IV., by which the entire territory was retroceded to France. When the First Consul acquired Louisiana, he appeared to look forward to a career of peace, — an impression greatly strengthened by the conclusion of the treaty of Amiens the ensuing year. He added to his prestige as a ruler when he regained from Spain the American empire which the Bourbons had weakly surrendered thirty-seven years before, and he expected a large and valuable addition to the trade and resources of France from this vast colonial possession. The formal transfer of so great a territory on a distant continent was necessarily delayed; and, before the Captain-general of France reached New Orleans in 1803, the Spanish authorities, still in possession, had become so odious to the inhabitants of the western section of the Union by their suspension of the right of deposit at New Orleans, that there was constant danger of an armed collision. Mr. Ross of Pennsylvania, an able and conservative statesman, moved in the Senate of the United States that the government be instructed to seize New Orleans. Gouverneur Morris, a statesman of the Revolutionary period, then a senator from New York, seconded Mr. Ross. So intense was the feeling among the people that a large army of volunteers could have been easily raised in the Mississippi valley to march against New Orleans; but the prudence of Mr. Jefferson restrained every movement that might involve us in a war with Spain, from which nothing was to be gained, and by which every thing would be risked.

Meanwhile Mr. Robert R. Livingston, our minister at Paris, was pressing the French Government for concessions touching the free navigation of the Mississippi and the right of deposit at New Orleans, and was speaking to the First Consul, as a French historian observes, in a tone which "arrested his attention, and aroused him to a sense of the new power that was growing beyond the sea." Mr. Livingston was re-enforced by Mr. Monroe, sent out by President Jefferson as a special envoy in the spring of 1803, in order to effect some adjustment of the irritating questions which were seriously endangering the relations between France and the United States. The instructions of Mr. Madison, then secretary of State, to Mr. Monroe, show that the utmost he expected was to acquire from France the city of New Orleans and the Floridas, of which he believed France either then was, or was about to become, the actual owner. Indeed, the treaty by which France had acquired Louisiana was but imperfectly understood; and, in the slowness and difficulty of communication, Mr. Madison could not accurately know the full extent of the cession made at San Ildefonso. But Mr. Jefferson did not wait to learn the exact provisions of that treaty. He knew instinctively that they deeply concerned the United States. He saw with clear vision that by the commercial disability upon the western section of the Union its progress would be obstructed, its already attained prosperity checked; and that possibly its population, drawn first into discontent with the existing order of things, might be seduced into new and dangerous alliances. He determined, therefore, to acquire the control of the left bank of the Mississippi to its mouth, and by the purchase of the Floridas to give to Georgia and the Mississippi territory (now constituting the States of Alabama and Mississippi) unobstructed access to the Gulf.

But events beyond the ocean were working more rapidly for the interest of the United States than any influences which the government itself could exert. Before Mr. Monroe reached France in the spring of 1803, another war-cloud of portentous magnitude was hanging over Europe. The treaty of Amiens had proved only a truce. Awkwardly constructed, misconstrued and violated by both parties, it was about to be formally broken. Neither of the plenipotentiaries who signed the treaty was skilled in diplomacy. Joseph Bonaparte acted for his brother; England was represented by Lord Cornwallis, who twenty years before had surrendered the British army at Yorktown. The wits of London described him afterwards as a general who could neither conduct a war nor conclude a peace.

Fearing that, in the threatened conflict, England, by her superior naval force, would deprive him of his newly acquired colonial empire, and greatly enhance her own prestige by securing all the American possessions which France had owned prior to 1763, Bonaparte, by a dash in diplomacy as quick and as brilliant as his tactics on the field of battle, placed Louisiana beyond the reach of British power. After returning to St. Cloud from the religious services of Easter Sunday, April 10, 1803, he called two of his most trusted advisers, and, in a tone of vehemence and passion, said, —

"I know the full value of Louisiana, and have been desirous of repairing the fault of the French negotiators who lost it in 1763. A few lines of a treaty have restored it to me, and now I must expect to lose it. . . . The English wish to take possession of it, and it is thus they will begin the war. . . . They have already twenty ships of the line in the Gulf of Mexico. . . . The conquest of Louisiana would be easy. I have not a moment to lose in putting it out of their reach. . . . The English have successively taken from France the Canadas, Cape Breton, Newfoundland, Nova Scotia, and the richest portions of Asia. But they shall not have the Mississippi, which they covet."

The discussion went far into the night. The two ministers differed widely in the advice which they gave the First Consul; one was in favor of holding Louisiana at all hazards; the other urged its prudent cession rather than its inevitable loss by war. They both remained at St. Cloud for the night. At daybreak the minister who had advised the cession was summoned by Bonaparte to read dispatches from London, that moment received, which certainly foreshadowed war, as the English were making military and naval preparations with extraordinary rapidity. After reading the dispatches, the First Consul said,

"Irresolution and deliberation are no longer in season. I renounce Louisiana. It is not only New Orleans that I will cede, it is the whole colony without any reservation. I know the value of what I abandon. I renounce it with the gravest regret. To attempt obstinately to retain it would be folly. I direct you to negotiate this affair with the envoy of the United States. Do not even wait the arrival of Mr. Monroe. Have an interview this very day with Mr. Livingston. . . . But I require a great deal of money for this war. I will be moderate. I want fifty millions for Louisiana."

The minister, who was opposed to the sale, interposed, in a subsequent interview, some observations "upon what the Germans call the *souls*, as to whether they could be the subject of a contract or sale." Bonaparte replied with undisguised sarcasm, —

"You are giving me the ideology of the law of nature. But I require money to make war on the richest nation in the world. Send your maxims to London. I am sure they will be greatly admired there."

The First Consul afterwards added, "Perhaps it will be objected that the Americans will be found too powerful for Europe in two or three centuries; but my foresight does not embrace such remote fears. Besides, we may hereafter expect rivalries among the members of the Union. The confederations, which are called perpetual, only last till one of the contracting parties finds it to his interest to break them."

Two days after this conversation Mr. Monroe opportunely arrived, and on the 30th of April the treaty ceding Louisiana to the United States was formally concluded. Mr. Monroe and Mr. Livingston had no authority to negotiate for so vast an extent of territory; but the former was fully possessed of President Jefferson's views, and felt assured that his instructions would have been ample if the condition of France had been foreseen when he sailed from America. Communication with Washington was impossible. Under the most favorable circumstances, an answer could not be expected in less than three months. By that time British ships would probably hold the mouths of the Mississippi, and the flag of St. George be waving over New Orleans. Monroe and Livingston both realized that hesitation would be fatal; and they boldly took the responsibility of purchasing a territory of unknown but prodigious extent, and of pledging the credit of the government for a sum which, rated by the ability to pay, was larger than a similar pledge to-day for five hundred millions of dollars.

The price agreed upon was eleven million two hundred and fifty thousand dollars in six per cent United States bonds, the interest of which was made payable in London, Amsterdam, and Paris, and the principal at the treasury in Washington in sums of three millions per annum, beginning fifteen years after the bonds were issued. In a separate treaty made the same day, the United States agreed to pay twenty million francs additional, to be applied by France to the satisfaction of certain claims owed to American citizens. Thus the total cost of Louisiana was eighty millions of francs, or, in round numbers, fifteen millions of dollars.

No difficulty was experienced in putting the United States in possession of the territory and of its chief emporium, New Orleans. The French Government had regarded the possession of so much consequence, that Bernadotte, afterwards King of Sweden, was at one time gazetted as Captain-general; and, some obstacles supervening, the eminent General Victor, afterwards Marshal of France and Duke of Belluno, was named in his stead. But all these plans were brushed aside by one stroke of Bonaparte's pen; and the United States, in consequence of favoring circumstances growing out of European complications, and the bold and competent statesmanship of Jefferson, obtained a territory larger in area than that which was wrested from the British crown by the Revolutionary war.

It seems scarcely credible that the acquisition of Louisiana by Jefferson was denounced with a bitterness surpassing the partisan rancor with which later generations have been familiar. No abuse was too malignant, no epithet too coarse, no imprecation too savage, to be employed by the assailants of the great philosophic statesman who laid so broad and deep the foundations of his country's growth and grandeur. President of a feeble republic, contending for a prize which was held by the greatest military power of Europe, and whose possession was coveted by the greatest naval power of the world, Mr. Jefferson, through his chosen and trusted agents, so conducted his important negotiation that the ambition of the United States was successfully interposed between the necessities of the one and the aggressive designs of the other. Willing to side with either of those great powers, for the advantage of his own country, not under-rating the dangers of war, yet ready to engage in it for the control of the great water-way to the Gulf, the President made the largest conquest ever peacefully achieved and at a cost so small that the total sum expended for the entire territory does not equal the reve-nue which has since been collected on its soil in a single month in time of great public peril. The country thus acquired forms to-day the States of Louisiana, Arkansas, Missouri, Iowa, Kansas, Nebraska, Minnesota west of the Mississippi, Colorado north of the Arkansas, besides the Indian Territory and the Territories of Dakota, Wyoming, and Montana. Texas was also included in the transfer, but the Ore-gon country was not. The Louisiana purchase did not extend beyond the main range of the Rocky Mountains, and our title to that large area which is included in the State of Oregon and in the Territories of Washington and Idaho rests upon a different foundation, or, rather, upon a series of claims, each of which was strong under the law of nations. We claimed it first by right of original discovery of the Co-lumbia River by an American navigator in 1792; second, by original exploration in 1805; third, by original settlement in 1810, by the enterprising company of which John Jacob Astor was the head; and, lastly and principally, by the transfer of the Spanish title in 1819, many years after the Louisiana purchase was accomplished. It is not, however, probable that we should have been able to maintain our title to Oregon if we had not secured the intervening country. It was certainly our purchase of Louisiana that enabled us to secure the Spanish title to the shores of the Pacific, and without that title we could hardly have maintained our claim. As against England our title seemed to us to be perfect, but as against Spain our case was not so strong. The purchase of Louisiana may therefore be fairly said to have carried with it and secured to us our possession of Oregon.

The acquisition of Louisiana brought incalculable wealth, power, and prestige to the Union, and must always be regarded as the master-stroke of policy which advanced the United States from a comparatively feeble nation, lying between the Atlantic and the Mississippi, to a continental power of assured strength and boundless promise. The *coup d'état* of the First Consul was an overwhelming surprise and disappointment to the English Government. Bonaparte was right in assuming that prompt action on his part was necessary to save Louisiana from the hands of the English. Twelve days after the treaty ceding Louisiana to the United States was signed, the British ambassador at Paris, Lord Whitworth, demanded his passports. At Dover he met the French ambassador to England, General Andreossy, who had likewise demanded his passports. Lord Whitworth loaded General Andreossy with tokens of esteem, and conducted him to the ship which was to bear him back to France. According to an eminent historian, "the two ambassadors parted in the presence of a great concourse of people, agitated, uneasy, sorrowful. On the eve of so important a determination, the warlike passion subsided; and men were seized with a dread of the consequences of a desperate conflict. At this solemn moment the two nations seemed to bid each other adieu, not to meet again till after a tremendous war and the convulsion of the world."

England's acquisition of Louisiana would have proved in the highest degree embarrassing, if not disastrous, to the Union. At that time the forts of Spain, transferred to France, and thence to the United States, were on the east side of the Mississippi, hundreds of miles from its mouth. If England had seized Louisiana, as Bonaparte feared, the Floridas, cut off from the other colonies of Spain, would certainly have fallen into her hands by easy and prompt negotiation, as they did, a few years after, into the hands of the United States. England would thus have had her colonies planted on the three land-sides of the Union, while on the ocean-side her formidable navy confronted the young republic. No colonial acquisition ever made by her on any continent has been so profitable to her commerce, and so strengthening to her military position, as that of Louisiana would have proved. This fact was clearly seen by Bonaparte when he hastily made the treaty ceding it to the United States. That England did not at once attempt to seize it, in disregard of Bonaparte's cession, has been a source of surprise to many historians. The obvious reason is that she dreaded the complication of a war in America when she was about to assume so heavy a burden in the impending European contest. The inhabitants of the Union in 1803 were six millions in number, of great energy and confidence. A large proportion of them were accustomed to the sea and could send swarms of privateers to prey on British commerce. Independent citizens would be even more formidable than were rebellious colonists in the earlier struggle with the mother country, and, acting in conjunction with France, could effectively maintain a contest. Considerations of this nature doubtless induced the Addington ministry to acquiesce quietly in a treaty whose origin and whose assured results were in every way distasteful, and even offensive, to the British Government.

The extent and boundaries of the territory thus ceded by France were ill-defined, and, in fact, unknown. The French negotiator who conferred with Monroe and Livingston, declared a large portion of the country transferred to be no better known at the time "than when Columbus landed at the Bahamas." There was no way by which accurate metes and bounds could be described. This fact disturbed the upright and conscientious Marbois, who thought that "treaties of territorial cession should contain a guaranty from the grantor." He was especially anxious, moreover, that no ambiguous clauses should be introduced in the treaty. He communicated his troubles on this point to the First Consul, advising him that it seemed impossible to construct the treaty so as to free it from obscurity on the important matter of boundaries. Far from exhibiting any sympathy with his faithful minister's solicitude on this point, Bonaparte quietly informed him that, "if an obscurity did not already exist, it would perhaps be good policy to put one in the treaty." In the possibilities of the First Consul's future, the acquisition of Spanish America may have been expected, or at least dreamed of, by him; and an ill-defined, uncertain boundary for Louisiana might possibly, in a few years, be turned greatly to his advantage.

There was certainly obscurity enough in the transfer to satisfy the fullest desire of Bonaparte. France ceded Louisiana to the United States "with all its rights and appurtenances," as acquired by the retrocession from Spain under the treaty of San Ildefonso, Oct. 1, 1800; and by that treaty Spain had "transferred it to France with the same extent it then had in the hands of Spain, and that it had when France previously possessed it, and such as it should be with the treaties subsequently entered into between Spain and other

States." This was simply giving to us what Spain had given to France, and that was only what France had before given to Spain, — complicated with such treaties as Spain might have made during the thirty-seven years of her ownership. It was evident, therefore, from the very hour of the acquisition, that we should have abundant trouble with our only remaining neighbors in North America, Spain and Great Britain, in adjusting the boundaries of the vast country which we had so successfully acquired from France.

Fortunately for the United States, the patriotic and far-seeing administration of Mr. Jefferson was as energetic in confirming as it had been in acquiring our title to the invaluable domain. As soon as the treaty was received the President called an extra session of Congress, which assembled on the 17th of October, 1803. Before the month had expired the treaty was confirmed, and the President was authorized to take possession of the territory of Louisiana, and to maintain therein the authority of the United States. This was not a mere paper warrant for exhibiting a nominal supremacy by floating our flag, but it gave to the President the full power to employ the army and navy of the United States and the militia of the several States to the number of eighty thousand. It was a wise and energetic measure for the defense of our newly acquired territory, which in the disturbed condition of Europe, with all the Great Powers arming from Gibraltar to the Baltic, might at any moment be invaded or imperiled. The conflict of arms did not occur until nine years after; and it is a curious and not unimportant fact, that the most notable defeat of the British troops in the second war of Independence, as the struggle of 1812 has been well named, occurred on the soil of the territory for whose protection the original precaution had been taken by Jefferson.

With all these preparations for defense, Mr. Jefferson did not wait to have our title to Louisiana questioned or limited. He set to work at once to proclaim it throughout the length and breadth of the territory which had been ceded, and to the treaty of cession he gave the most liberal construction. According to the President, Louisiana stretched as far to the northward as the Lake of the Woods; towards the west as far as the Rio Grande in the lower part, and, in the upper part, to the main chain of the mountains dividing the waters of the Pacific from the waters of the Atlantic. To establish our sovereignty to the shores of the Pacific became a matter of instant solicitude with the watchful and patriotic President. In the previous session he had obtained from Congress an appropriation of two millions of dollars "for the purpose of defraying any extraordinary expenses which may be incurred in the intercourse between the United States and foreign nations." In the confidential message which so promptly secured the money, the President suggested that the object to be accomplished was a better understanding with the Indian tribes, and the fitting out of an exploring and scientific expedition across the continent, though our own domain at the time was terminated on the west by the Mississippi. It was believed, that, between the lines of the message, Congress could read that our negotiations with France and Spain touching the free navigation of the Mississippi might soon reach a crisis. Hence the prompt appropriation of a sum of money which for the national treasury of that day was very large.

The two men selected to conduct the expedition across the continent, Meriwether Lewis and William Clarke, were especially fitted for their arduous task. Both were officers in the army, holding the rank of captain. Lewis had been private secretary to the President, and Clarke was brother to the heroic George Rogers Clarke, whose services were of peculiar value in the Revolutionary struggle. Before they could complete the preparations for their long and dangerous journey, the territory to be traversed had been transferred to the United States, and the expedition at once assumed a significance and importance little dreamed of when Jefferson first conceived it. The original design had been a favorite one with Mr. Jefferson for many years. When he resided in Paris as our minister, before the Federal Government was organized, he encouraged a similar expedition, to be fitted out in Kamtchatka, to sail to our western coast, and thence to come eastward across the continent. This design was to be executed by the somewhat noted John Ledyard, a roving and adventurous man from Connecticut, who had accompanied Captain Cook on his famous voyage to the Pacific, and whom Jefferson afterwards met in Paris. The necessary authority was obtained from the Russian Government; but, after Ledyard had reached the borders of Kamtchatka, he was suddenly recalled, driven with speed day and night in a closed carriage, on a return journey of several thousand miles, and set down in Poland, penniless, and utterly broken in health. This strange action was the offspring of jealousy on the part of the Empress Catharine, who feared that the energy of the young and vigorous government of the United

States would absorb the north-west coast of America, upon which the Russian Government had already set its ambition.

The success of the Lewis and Clarke expedition aided greatly in sustaining our title to the Oregon country. The joint leaders of it became celebrated by their arduous achievement, and were rewarded accordingly. Lewis was appointed governor of Louisiana territory in 1807, and held the position until his death in 1809; while Clarke was for a long period governor of the territory of Missouri, serving in that capacity when the State was admitted to the Union. But while the Lewis and Clarke expedition largely increased our knowledge of the country, and added to the strength of our title, it did not definitely settle any disputed question. With Spain we had constant trouble in regard to the boundaries of Louisiana, both on the west in the direction of Texas, and on the east along the confines of Florida. She had always been dissatisfied with Bonaparte's transfer of Louisiana to the United States. If that result could have been foreseen, the treaty of San Ildefonso would never have been made. The government of the United States believed that Louisiana, as held by France, had bordered on the Rio Grande, and that, by the treaty with Bonaparte, we were entitled to territory in the direction of Florida as far as the Perdido. In the vexatious war with the Seminoles, General Jackson did not hesitate to march across the line, capture Pensacola, and seize the Barancas. The comments, official and personal, which were made on that rash exploit, led to controversies and estrangements which affected political parties for many years after. Jackson's hostility to John Quincy Adams, his exasperating quarrel with Clay, his implacable hatred for Calhoun, all had their origin in events connected with the Florida campaign of 1818.

To compose the boundary troubles with Spain, a treaty was negotiated in 1819, which, with many gains, entailed some signal losses upon the United States. The whole of Florida was ceded by Spain, an acquisition which proved of great value to us in every point of view. As Florida had become separated from the other Spanish colonies by the cession of Louisiana, the government at Madrid found difficulty in satisfactorily administering its affairs and guarding its safety. South of the United States, to the Straits of Magellan, the Spanish flag floated over every foot of the continent except the Empire of Brazil and some small colonies in Guiana. The cession of Louisiana to Bonaparte involved the loss of Florida which was now formally transferred to the United States. But Spain received more than an equivalent. The whole of Texas was fairly included in the Louisiana purchase, — if the well-studied opinion of such eminent statesmen as Clay, John Quincy Adams, Van Buren, and Benton may be accepted, — and we paid dearly for Florida by agreeing to retreat from the Rio Grande to the Sabine as our southwestern frontier, thus surrendering Texas to Mexico. The western boundary of the Louisiana territory was defined as beginning at the mouth of the Sabine (which is the boundary of the State of Louisiana to-day), continuing along its western bank to the 32° of north latitude, thence by a line due north to the Red River, thence up the Red River to the 100th meridian west from Greenwich, or the 23d west from Washington, thence due north to the Arkansas, thence following the Arkansas to its source in latitude 42°, and thence by that parallel to the Pacific Ocean. Should the Arkansas fall short of the 42°, a due north line to that parallel was to be taken. The United States solemnly renounced all claim to territories west or south of the line just mentioned, and Spain renounced all claim to territory east or north of it. Thus all boundary disputes with Spain were ended, and peace was secured, though at a great cost; as events in after years so fully proved.

Meanwhile territorial government had been established over a large section of the country acquired from France; and it was rapidly peopled by an enterprising emigration, almost wholly from the Southern States. Louisiana sought to enter the Union in 1811, and then for the first time occurred an agitation in Congress over the admission of a slave State. Opposition to it was not, however, grounded so much upon the existence of slavery as upon the alleged violation of the Constitution in forming a State from territory not included in the original government of the Union. Josiah Quincy of Massachusetts made a violent speech against it, declaring that if Louisiana were admitted, "the bonds of this Union are virtually dissolved; that the States which compose it are free from their moral obligations; and that, as it will be the right of all, so it will be the duty of some, to prepare definitely for a separation, amicably if they can, violently if they must." Mr. Quincy was disquieted at the mere thought of extending the Union beyond its original limits. He had "heard with alarm that six States might grow up beyond the Mississippi, and that the mouth of the Ohio might be east of the centre of a contemplated empire." He declared that "it was not for these men that our fathers fought, not for them that the Constitution was adopted. Our fathers were not madmen: they had not taken degrees at the hospital of idiocy." He maintained with great vehemence that there was "no authority to throw the rights and liberties of this people into 'hotchpot' with the wild men of the Missouri, nor with the mixed, though more respectable, race of Anglo-Hispano-Gallo-Americans who bask on the sands in the mouth of the Mississippi." Mr. Quincy's sentiments were far more radical than those held by the mass of Northern or New-England people, yet there was undoubtedly a strong opposition to the admission of Louisiana. Many Northern men had opposed the purchase of the territory from France, believing it to be unconstitutional; and they dreaded the introduction of senators and representatives from territory which they considered foreign. Nevertheless the bill admitting the State passed the House by a vote of two-thirds of the members. The opposition was wholly from the North, and largely from New England. The contest was confined to Congress — the issue failing to excite popular interest. A majority of the people, both North and South, were convinced that the ownership of the mouth of the Mississippi was of inestimable value to the Union, and that it could not be permanently secured except by admitting as a State the territory which included and controlled it. This conclusion was strengthened by the near approach of war with Great Britain, soon after formally declared. The advantage of a loyal and devoted population at New Orleans, identified in interest and in sympathy with the government, was too evident to need argument. If the weight of reason had not already been on the side of admitting Louisiana, the necessities of war would have enforced it.

Six years after Louisiana entered the Union, Missouri applied for admission as a slave State. A violent agitation at once arose, continued for two years, and was finally allayed by the famous compromise of 1820. The outbreak was so sudden, its course so turbulent, and its subsidence so complete, that for many years it was regarded as phenomenal in our politics, and its repetition in the highest degree improbable if not impossible. The "Missouri question," as it was popularly termed, formally appeared in Congress in the month of December, 1818; though during the preceding session petitions for a State government had been received from the inhabitants of the territory. When the bill proposing to admit the State came before the House, Mr. James Tallmadge, jun., of New York, moved to amend it by providing that "the further introduction of slavery be prohibited in said State of Missouri, and that all children born in the State after its admission to the Union shall be free at the age of twenty-five years." The discussion which followed was able, excited, and even acrimonious. Mr. Clay took an active part against the amendment, but his great influence was unavailing in the face of the strong anti-slavery sentiment which was so suddenly developed in the North. Both branches of Mr. Tallmadge's amendment were adopted and the bill was passed. In the Senate the anti-slavery amendment encountered a furious opposition and was rejected by a large majority. The House refuse to recede; and, amid great excitement in the country and no little temper in Congress, each branch voted to adhere to its position. Thus for the time Missouri was kept out of the Union.

On the second day after the opening of the next Congress, December, 1819, Mr. John Holmes presented a memorial in the House of Representatives from a convention which had been lately held in the District of Maine, praying for the admission of said district into the Union "as a separate and independent State, on an equal footing with the original States." On the same day, and immediately after Mr. Holmes had taken his seat, Mr. John Scott, territorial delegate, brought before the House the memorial presented in the previous Congress for the admission of Missouri on the same terms of independence and equality with the old States as prayed for by Maine. From that hour it was found impossible to consider the admission of Maine and Missouri separately. Geographically remote, differing in soil, climate, and products, incapable of competing with each other in any pursuit, they were thrown into rivalry by the influence of the one absorbing question of negro slavery. Southern men were unwilling that Maine should be admitted unless the enabling Act for Missouri should be passed at the same time, and Northern men were unwilling that any enabling Act should be passed for Missouri which did not contain an anti-slavery restriction. Mr. Clay, then an accepted leader of Southern sentiment, — which in his later life he ceased to be, — made an earnest, almost fiery, speech on the question. He declared that before the Maine bill should be finally acted on, he wanted to know "whether certain doctrines of an alarming character, with respect to a restriction on the admission of new States west of the Mississippi, were to be sustained on this floor." He wanted to know "what conditions Congress could annex to the admission of a new State; whether, indeed, there could be a partition of its sovereignty."

Despite the eloquence and the great influence of the Speaker, the Southern representatives were overborne and the House adopted the anti-slavery restriction. The Senate refused to concur, united Maine and Missouri in one bill, and passed it with an entirely new feature, which was proposed by Mr. Jesse B. Thomas, a senator from Illinois. That feature was simply the provision, since so widely known as the Missouri Compromise, which forever prohibited slavery north of 36° 30′ in all the territory acquired from France by the Louisiana purchase. The House would not consent to admit the two States in the same bill, but finally agreed to the compromise; and in the early part of March, 1820, Maine became a member of the Union without condition. A separate bill was passed, permitting Missouri to form a constitution preparatory to her admission, subject to the compromise, which, indeed, formed one section of the enabling Act. Missouri was thus granted permission to enter the Union as a slave State. But she was discontented with the prospect of having free States on three sides, — east, north, and west.

Although the Missouri Compromise was thus nominally perfected, and the agitation apparently ended, the most exciting, and in some respects the most dangerous, phase of the question was yet to be reached. After the enabling Act was passed, the Missouri Convention assembled to frame a constitution for the new State. The inhabitants of the Territory had become angered by the long delay imposed upon them, caused, as they believed, by the introduction of a question which concerned only themselves, and which Congress had no right to control. In this resentful mood they were led by the extremists of the convention to insert a provision in the constitution, declaring that "it shall be the duty of the General Assembly, as soon as may be, to pass such laws as may be necessary to prevent free negroes or mulattoes from coming to or settling in this State under any pretext whatsoever." As soon as the constitution with this obnoxious clause was transmitted to Congress by the President, the excitement broke forth with increased intensity and the lines of the old controversy were at once re-formed.

The parliamentary struggle which ensued was bitter beyond precedent; threats of dissolving the Union were frequent, and apprehension of an impending calamity was felt throughout the country. The discussion continued with unabated vigor and ardor until the middle of February, and the Congress was to terminate on the ensuing fourth of March. The House had twice refused to pass the bill admitting Missouri, declaring that the objectionable clause in her organic law was not only an insult to every State in which colored men were citizens, but was in flat contradiction of that provision in the Federal Constitution which declares that "the citizens of each State shall be entitled to all the privileges and immunities of citizens in the several States."

The defeat, apparently final, of the admission of Missouri, created intense indignation. Southern senators and representatives charged that they were treated unjustly by the North, and dealt with unfairly in Congress. In pursuance of the compromise of the year before, Maine had been admitted and her senators were in their seats. The organs of Southern opinion accused the North of overreaching the South in securing, under the name of a compromise, the admission of Maine, while still retaining the power to exclude Missouri. A feeling that bad faith has been practiced is sure to create bitterness, and the accusation of it produces increased bitterness in return. The North could easily justify itself by argument, but the statement without argument apparently showed that the South had been deceived. The course pursued by the senators from Maine, — John Holmes and John Chandler, — in voting steadily for the admission of Missouri, tended greatly to check recrimination and relieve asperity of feeling. Mr. Holmes was a man of ability, of experience in public affairs, and of eminent distinction at home. With a rare gift of humor, and with conversational talent almost unrivaled, he exerted an influence over men in private and social intercourse which gave him singular power in shaping public questions. He was an intimate friend and political supporter of Mr. Clay, and their cordial co-operation at this crisis evoked harmony from chaos, and brought a happy solution to a question that was troubling every patriotic heart. They united in a final effort, and through the instrumentality of a joint committee of seven senators and twenty-three representatives, — of which Mr. Holmes was chairman on the part of the Senate, and Mr. Clay on the part of the House, — a second and final compromise was effected, and the admission of Missouri secured. This compromise declared that Missouri should be admitted to the Union upon the fundamental condition that no law should ever be passed by her Legislature enforcing the objectionable provision in her constitution, and that by a solemn public act the State should declare and record her assent to this condition, and transmit to the President of the United States an authentic copy of the Act. Missouri accepted the condition promptly but not cheerfully, feeling that she entered the Union under a severe discipline, and with hard and humiliating conditions. It was in this compromise, not in the one of the preceding session, that Mr. Clay was the leading spirit. Though the first was the more important, and dealt with larger questions of a more enduring nature, it did not at the time create so great an impression on the public mind as the second, nor did its discussion produce so much antagonism between the North and the South. Thirty years after these events Mr. Clay called attention to the fact that he had received undeserved credit for the Missouri Compromise of 1820, which he had supported but not originated. On the other hand, he had received only the slightest mention for his agency in the second compromise, which he had really originated and carried through Congress. The second compromise had passed out of general recollection before Mr. Clay's death, though it had made him a Presidential candidate at forty-three years of age.

The most remarkable fact connected with the excitement over the Missouri question, which engrossed the country for more than two years, was the absence of any premonition of its coming. There had been no severe political struggle in the nation since the contest between Madison and De Witt Clinton in 1812. Monroe had been chosen almost without opposition in 1816, and, even while the Missouri controversy was at its height, he was re-elected in 1820 by a practically unanimous vote, the North and the South being equally cordial in supporting him. In the House of Representatives, where the battle was so fierce, and the combatants were so evenly divided, Mr. Clay had been chosen speaker with only eight adverse votes, and these were given by men who acted from personal prejudice, and not from political difference. But the outbreak indicated, and indeed heralded, the re-forming of old party lines. The apparent unanimity only concealed a division that was already fatally developed. The party of Jefferson by its very success involved itself in ruin. Its ancient foe, the eminent and honorable party of Federalists, made but a feeble struggle in 1816, and completely disappeared from the national political field four years later, and even from State contests after the notable defeat of Harrison Gray Otis by William Eustis for governor of Massachusetts in 1823. But no political organization can live without opposition. The disappearance of the

Federalists was the signal for factional divisions among their opponents; and the old Republican party, which had overthrown the administration of John Adams in 1800, which had laid the embargo, and forced a war with England, was now nearing its end. It divided into four parts in the Presidential election of 1824, and with its ancient creed and organization never re-appeared in a national contets. Jefferson had combined and indeed largely created its elements. He beheld it everywhere victorious for a quarter of a century, and he lived to see it shattered into fragments by the jealousy of its new leaders. The Democratic and Whig parties were constructed upon the ruins of the old organizations. In each were to be found representatives of the Republicanism of Jefferson and the Federalism of Hamilton. The ambition of both to trace their lineage to the former was a striking proof of its popular strength.

The Missouri question marked a distinct era in the political thought of the country, and made a profound impression on the minds of patriotic men. Suddenly, without warning, the North and the South, the free States and the slave States, found themselves arrayed against each other in violent and absorbing conflict. During the interval between the adoption of the Federal Constitution and the admission of Missouri, there had been a great change in the Southern mind, both as to the moral and the economic aspects of slavery. This revolution of opinion had been wrought in large degree by the cotton-plant. When the National Government was organized in 1789, the annual export of cotton did not exceed three hundred bales. It was reckoned only among our experimental products. But, stimulated by the invention of the gin, production increased so rapidly, that, at the time of Missouri's application for admission to the Union, cotton-planting was the most remunerative industry in the country. The export alone exceeded three hundred thousand bales annually. But this highly profitable culture was in regions so warm that outdoor labor was unwelcome to the white race. The immediate consequence was a large advance in the value of slave-labor, and in the price of slaves. This fact had its quick and decisive influence, even in those slave-holding States which could not raise cotton. The inevitable and speedy result was a consolidation of the political power necessary to protect an interest at once so vast and so liable to assault.

It was not unnatural that this condition should lead to a violent outburst on the slavery question, but it was nevertheless wholly unexpected. The causes which led to it had not been understood and analyzed. The older class of statesmen, who had come down from the period of the Revolution, from the great work of cementing the Union and framing the Constitution, deplored the agitation, and viewed the results with the gravest apprehension. The compromise by a geographical line, dividing the slave States from the free, was regarded by this class of patriots as full of danger, — a constant menace to the peace and perpetuity of the Union. To Mr. Jefferson, still living in vigorous old age, the trouble sounded like an alarm-bell rung at midnight. While the measure was pending in Congress, he wrote to a member of the House of Representatives, that "the Missouri question is the most portentous one which has ever threatened the Union. In the gloomiest hour of the Revolutionary war I never had any apprehensions equal to those which I feel from this source." Men on both sides of the controversy began to realize its significance and to dread its probable results. They likened the partition of the country by a geographical line unto the ancient agreement between Abraham and Lot, where one should go to the right, and the other to the left, with the certainty of becoming aliens, and the possibility of becoming enemies.

With the settlement of the Missouri question, the anti-slavery agitation subsided as rapidly as it had arisen. This was a second surprise to thinking men. The result can, however, be readily explained. The Northern States felt that they had absolutely secured to freedom a large territory west and north of Missouri. The Southern States believed that they had an implied and honorable understanding, — outside and beyond the explicit letter of the law, — that new States south of the Missouri line could be admitted with slavery if they desired. The great political parties then dividing the country accepted the result and for the next twenty years no agitation of the slavery question appeared in any political convention, or affected any considerable body of the people.

Within that period, however, there grew up a school of anti-slavery men far more radical and progressive than those who had resisted the admission of Missouri as a slave State. They formed what was known as the Abolition party, and they devoted themselves to the utter destruction of slavery by every instrumentality which they could lawfully employ. Acutely trained in the political as well as the ethical principles of the great controversy, they clearly distinguished between the powers which Congress might and might not exercise under the limitations of the Constitution. They began, therefore, by demanding the abolition of slavery in the District of Columbia, and in all the national forts, arsenals, and dock-yards, where, without question or cavil, the exclusive jurisdiction belonged to Congress; they asked that Congress, under its constitutional authority to regulate commerce between the States, would prohibit the inter-State slave-trade; and they prayed that our ships sailing on the high-seas should not be permitted by the government to carry slaves as part of their cargo, under the free flag of the United States, and outside the local jurisdiction that held them in bondage. They denied that a man should aid in executing any law whose enforcement did violence to his conscience and trampled under foot the Divine commands. Hence they would not assist in the surrender and return of fugitive slaves, holding it rather to be their duty to resist such violation of the natural rights of man by every peaceful method, and justifying their resistance by the truths embodied in the Declaration of Independence, and, still more impressively, by the precepts taught in the New Testament.

While encountering, on these issues, the active hostility of the great mass of the people in all sections of the Union, the Abolitionists challenged the respect of thinking men, and even compelled the admiration of some of their most pronounced opponents. The party was small in number, but its membership was distinguished for intellectual ability, for high character, for pure philanthropy, for unquailing courage both moral and physical, and for a controversial talent which has never been excelled in the history of moral reforms. It would not be practicable to give the names of all who were conspicuous in this great struggle, but the mention of James G. Birney, of Benjamin Lundy, of Arthur Tappan, of the brothers Lovejoy, of Gerrit Smith, of John G. Whittier, of William Lloyd Garrison, of Wendell Phillips, and of Gamaliel Bailey, will indicate the class who are entitled to be held in remembrance so long as the possession of great mental and moral attributes gives enduring and honorable fame. Nor would the list of bold and powerful agitators be complete or just if confined to the white race. Among the colored men — often denied the simplest rights of citizenship in the States where they resided — were found many who had received the gift of tongues, orators by nature, who bravely presented the wrongs and upheld the rights of the oppressed. Among these Frederick Douglass was especially and richly endowed not only with the strength but with the graces of speech; and for many years, from the stump and from the platform, he exerted a wide and beneficent influence upon popular opinion.

In the early days of this agitation, the Abolitionists were a proscribed and persecuted class, denounced with unsparing severity by both the great political parties, condemned by many of the leading churches, libeled in the public press, and maltreated by furious mobs. In no part of the country did they constitute more than a handful of the population, but they worked against every discouragement with a zeal and firmness which bespoke intensity of moral conviction. They were in large degree recruited from the society of Friends, who brought to the support of the organization the same calm and consistent courage which had always distinguished them in upholding before the world their peculiar tenets of religious faith. Caring nothing for prejudice, meeting opprobrium with silence, shaming the authors of violence by meek non-resistance, relying on moral agencies alone, appealing simply to the reason and the conscience of men, they arrested the attention of the nation by arraigning it before the public opinion of the world, and proclaiming its responsibility to the judgment of God.

These apostles of universal liberty besieged Congress with memorials praying for such legislative measures as would carry out their designs. Failure after failure only served to inspire them with fresh courage and more vigorous determination. They were met with the most resolute resistance by representatives from the slave-holding States, who sought to deny them a hearing, and declared that the mere consideration of their propositions by Congress would not only justify, but would inevitably precipitate, a dissolution of the Union. Undaunted by any form of opposition, the Abolitionists stubbornly maintained their ground, and finally succeeded in creating a great popular excitement by insisting on the simple right of petition as inseparable from free government and free citizenship. On this issue John Quincy Adams, who had entered the House of Representatives in 1831, two years after his retirement from the Presidency, waged a memorable warfare. Not fully sympathizing with the Abolitionists in their measures or their methods, Mr. Adams maintained that they had the right to be heard. On this incidental issue he forced the controversy until it enlisted the attention of the entire country. He finally drove the opponents of free discussion to seek shelter under the adoption of an odious rule in the House of

Representatives, popularly named the "Atherton gag," from Mr. Charles G. Atherton, a Democratic representative from New Hampshire, who reported it to the House in December, 1838. The rule was originally devised, however, in a caucus of Southern Democratic members. In the light of the present day, when slavery no longer exists in the land, when speech is absolutely free, in and out of Congress, it is hard to believe that during the Presidency of Mr. Van Buren, and under the speakership of Mr. Polk, the House of Representatives voted that "every petition, memorial, resolution, proposition, or paper, touching or relating in any way or to any extent whatever to slavery or the abolition thereof, shall on presentation, without any further action thereon, be laid upon the table, without being debated, printed, or referred."

The Southern representatives, both Democrats and Whigs, and the Northern Democrats, sustained this extraordinary resolution, which became widely known as the 21st Rule of the House. The Northern Whigs, to their honor be it said, were steadily against it. The real design of the measure was to take from Mr. Adams the power of precipitating a discussion on the slavery question, but the most unskilled should have seen that in this it would fail. It resembled in its character the re-actionary and tyrannical edicts so frequently employed in absolute governments, and was unsuited to the temper, ran counter to the judgment, and proved offensive to the conscience, of the American people.

Profoundly opposed as were many citizens to a denial of the right of petition, very few wished to become identified with the cause of the Abolitionists. In truth it required no small degree of moral courage to take position in the ranks of that despised political sect forty-five years ago. Persecutions of a petty and social character were almost sure to follow, and not infrequently grievous wrongs were inflicted, for which, in the absence of a disposition among the people to see justice done, the law afforded no redress. Indeed, by an apparent contradiction not difficult to reconcile, many of those who fought bravely for the right of the Abolitionists to be heard in Congress by petition, were yet enraged with them for continually and, as they thought, causelessly, raising and pressing the issue. They were willing to fight for the right of the Abolitionists to do a certain thing, and then willing to fight the Abolitionists for aimlessly and uselessly doing it. The men who were governed by these complex motives were chiefly Whigs. They felt that an increase of popular strength to the Abolitionists must be at the expense of the party which, continuing to make Clay its idol, was about to make Harrison its candidate. The announcement, therefore, on the eve of the national contest of 1840, that the Abolitionists had nominated James G. Birney of Michigan for President, and Francis J. Le Moyne of Pennsylvania for Vice-President, was angrily received by the Whigs, and denunciations of the movement were loud and frequent. The support received by these candidates was unexpectedly small, and showed little ground, in the judgment of the Whigs, for the course taken by the Abolitionists. Their strength was almost wholly confined to New England, Western New York, and the Western Reserve of Ohio. It was plainly seen, that, in a large majority of the free States, the Abolitionists had as yet made no impression on public opinion.

Any less earnest body of men would have been discouraged, but the Abolition party was composed of devotees possessing the true martyr spirit, and, instead of being appalled by defeat, they were inspired with fresh zeal, and incited to new effort. They had not failed to observe, that, while few were disposed to unite in extreme anti-slavery measures, there was a growing number whose conscience was aroused on the general subject of human bondage. The emancipation of negroes with a view to their settlement in Africa, as advocated by the Colonization Society, received the support of conservative opponents of slavery, the sympathy of the Churches, and the patronage of leading men among the slave-holders of the Border States. The National Government was repeatedly urged to give its aid to the scheme; and, during the excitement on the Missouri question, Congress appropriated $100,000, nominally for the return of Africans who had been unlawfully landed in the United States after the slave trade was prohibited, but really as an indirect mode of promoting the project of colonization. As a scheme for the destruction of domestic slavery it was ridiculed by the Abolitionists, who in the end violently opposed it as tending to deaden the public conscience to the more imperative duty of universal emancipation. The philanthropic efforts of the Society were abundantly rewarded, however, by the establishment of the Republic of Liberia, whose career has been eminently creditable and advantageous to the African race.

CHAPTER II.

SOON after the failure of the Abolitionists to exhibit popular strength, the slavery question was forced upon public attention independently of their efforts, and by causes whose operation and effect were not distinctly foreseen by those who set them in motion. The Americans who, in a spirit of adventure, migrated to Texas after that province had revolted from Mexico, became the controlling power in the young republic, and under the lead of General Sam Houston, in the month of April, 1836, won a memorable victory over the Mexican army at San Jacinto. Thenceforward, in differing degrees of earnestness, the annexation of Texas became a subject of consideration in the United States, but it was never incorporated in the creed of either of the great parties until the Presidential canvass of 1844. Not long after the death of President Harrison in April, 1841, his successor, John Tyler, had serious disagreements with the leading Whigs, both in his cabinet and in Congress, respecting the establishment of a national bank. Mr. Clay led the attack upon him openly and almost savagely, arraigning him as a traitor to the principles upon which he had been elected, and pursuing the quarrel so violently, that in September, five months after Tyler's accession, every member of his cabinet resigned except Mr. Webster. He lingered, unwelcome if not distrusted, until July, 1843, for the purpose of conducting the negotiations in regard to the North-eastern boundary, which he brought to a termination by the Ashburton Treaty. The new secretary of State, Abel P. Upshur of Virginia,

26

— who had been at the head of the Navy Department for a few months, — was a man of strong parts and brilliant attainments, but not well known outside of his own commonwealth, and subject therefore to disparagement as the successor of a man so illustrious as Mr. Webster. He grasped his new duties, however, with the hand of a master, and actively and avowedly pursued the policy of acquiring Texas. His efforts were warmly seconded by the President, whose friends believed with all confidence that this question could be so presented as to make Mr. Tyler the Democratic candidate in the approaching Presidential election. What Mr. Upshur's success might have been in the difficult field of negotiation upon which he had entered, must be left to conjecture, for his life was suddenly destroyed by the terrible accident on board the United-States steamer "Princeton," in February, 1844, but little more than seven months after he had entered upon his important and engrossing duties.

Mr. Tyler's administration being now fully committed to the scheme of Texas annexation, the selection of a new secretary of State was matter of extreme importance. The President had been finally separated from all sympathy with the party that elected him, when Mr. Webster left the cabinet the preceding summer. But he had not secured the confidence or the support of the Democracy. The members of that party were willing to fill his offices throughout the country, and to absorb the honors and emoluments of his administration; but the leaders of positive influence, men of the grade of Van Buren, Buchanan, Cass, Dallas, and Silas Wright, held aloof, and left the government to be guided by Democrats who had less to risk, and by Whigs of the type of Henry A. Wise of Virginia and Caleb Cushing of Massachusetts, who had revolted from the rule of Mr. Clay. It was the sagacity of Wise, rather than the judgment of Tyler, which indicated the immense advantage of securing Mr. Calhoun for the head of the cabinet. The great Southern leader was then in retirement, having resigned from the Senate the preceding year. By a coincidence worth noting, Webster, Clay, and Calhoun were all at that moment absent from the Senate, each having voluntarily retired. In later life, chastened by political adversity, they returned to the chamber where, before their advent and since their departure, there have been no rivals to their fame.

Naturally, Mr. Calhoun would have been reluctant to take office under Tyler at any time, and especially for the brief remainder of an administration which had been continually under the ban of public opinion, and which had not the slightest prospect of renewal. With quick observation and keen insight, however, he perceived a great opportunity to serve the South, and to serve the South was with him not only a principle, but a passion. He realized, moreover, that the hour was at hand for an historic revenge which the noblest of minds might indulge. He saw intuitively that the Texas question was one of vast importance, with untold possibilities. He saw with equal clearness that it had never been presented in such manner as to appeal to the popular judgment, and become an active, aggressive issue in the struggle for the Presidency. A large section of the Democratic party had looked favorably upon annexation ever since 1836, but the leaders had not dared to include the scheme in the avowed designs of party policy. They had omitted it purposely in making up the issues for the Van Buren campaign of 1840, and, up to the hour when Mr. Calhoun entered the State Department, the intention of the managers was to omit it in the contest of 1844 against Mr. Clay. Mr. Tyler's advocacy of Texas annexation had injured rather than promoted it in the estimation of the Democratic party; but when Mr. Calhoun, with his astute management, and his large influence in the slave-holding States, espoused it, the whole tenor of Southern opinion was changed, and the Democracy of that section received a new inspiration.

Mr. Van Buren, aspiring again to the Presidency, desired to avoid the Texas issue. Mr. Calhoun determined that he should meet it. He had every motive for distrusting, opposing, even hating, Van Buren. The contest between them had been long and unrelenting. When Van Buren, as secretary of State, was seized with the ambition to succeed Jackson, he saw Calhoun in the Vice-Presidency, strongly intrenched as heir-apparent; and he set to work to destroy the friendship and confidence that existed between him and the President. The rash course of Jackson in the Seminole campaign of 1818 had been severely criticised in the cabinet of Monroe, and Mr. Calhoun, as secretary of War, had talked of a court of inquiry. Nothing, however, was done and the mere suggestion had been ten years forgotten, when Jackson entered upon the Presidency, entertaining the strongest friendship, both personal and political, for Calhoun. But the damaging fact was unearthed and the jealousy of Jackson was aroused. Calhoun was driven into a deadly quarrel, resigned the Vice-Presidency, and went back to South Carolina to engage in the nullification contest. Van Buren quietly usurped his place in the regard and confidence of Jackson, and succeeded to the Presidency. Calhoun, denounced in every paper under the control of the administration, was threatened with prosecution, and robbed for a time of the confidence of the Democratic party. By the strangely and rapidly changing fortunes of politics, it was now in his power to inflict a just retribution upon Van Buren. He did not neglect the opportunity.

Mr. Calhoun urged the scheme of annexation with intense earnestness. Taking up the subject where Mr. Upshur had left it, he conducted the negotiation with zeal and skill. His diplomatic correspondence was able and exhaustive. It was practically a frank avowal that Texas must be incorporated in the Union. He feared that European influence might become dominant in the new republic, and, as a consequence, that anti-slavery ideas might take root, and thence injuriously affect the interests, and to some extent the safety, of the Southern States. In an instruction to William R. King, our minister at Paris, Mr. Calhoun called his attention to the fact that England regarded the defeat of annexation "as indispensable to the abolition of slavery in Texas." He believed that England was "too sagacious not to see what a fatal blow abolition in Texas would give to slavery in the United States." Then, contemplating the effect of the general abolition of slavery, he declared that "to this continent it would be calamitous beyond description." It would "destroy in a great measure the cultivation and production of the great tropical staples, amounting annually in value to nearly $300,000,000." It is a suggestive commentary on Mr. Calhoun's evil foreboding, that the great tropical staple of the South has steadily increased in growth under free labor, and that the development of Texas never fairly began until slavery was banished from her soil.

Discussing the right of Texas to independence, in an instruction to Wilson Shannon, our minister to Mexico, Mr. Calhoun averred that "Texas had never stood in relation to Mexico as a rebellious province struggling to obtain independence. The true relation between them is that of independent members of a federal government, the weaker of which has successfully resisted the attempts of the stronger to conquer and subject her to its power." This was applying to the constitution of Mexico the same construction which he had so long and so ably demanded for our own. It was, indeed, but a paraphrase of the State-sovereignty and State-rights theory, with which he had persistently indoctrinated the Southern mind. Ten years after Mr.

Calhoun was in his grave, the same doctrine, in almost the same form of expression, became familiar to the country as the Southern justification for resorting to civil war.

The prompt result of Mr. Calhoun's efforts was a treaty of annexation which had been discussed but not concluded under Mr. Upshur. It was communicated to the Senate by the President on the 12th of April, 1844. The effect which this treaty produced on the political fortunes of two leading statesmen, one in each party, was extraordinary. Prior to its negotiation, the Democrats throughout the Union were apparently well united in support of Mr. Van Buren as their Presidential candidate. Mr. Clay was universally accepted by the Whigs, — his nomination by a national convention being indeed but a matter of form. Relations of personal courtesy and confidence, if not of intimate friendship, had always subsisted between Mr. Clay and Mr. Van Buren during their prolonged public service. It was now believed that they had come to an understanding, through the negotiation of friends, to eliminate the Texas question from the campaign of 1844 by defeating the Tyler-Calhoun treaty, and agreeing to a general postponement of the subject, on the ground that immediate annexation would plunge the country into war. Very soon after the treaty was sent to the Senate by the President, Mr. Clay published in the "National Intelligencer" his famous Raleigh letter against annexation. The "Globe" of the same day contained a more guarded communication from Mr. Van Buren, practically taking the same ground. Considering the widely different characteristics of the two men, the letters were singularly alike in argument and inference. This fact, in connection with the identical time of publication, strengthened the suspicion, if not the conclusion, that there was a pre-arranged understanding between the eminent authors.

The letter of Mr. Van Buren was fatal to his prospects. He was caught in the toils prepared by Mr. Calhoun's diplomacy. His disastrous defeat four years before by General Harrison had not injured him within the lines of his own party, or shorn him of his prestige in the nation. He still retained the undiminished confidence of his old adherents in the North, and a large support from the Southern Democracy outside of the States in which Mr. Calhoun's influence was dominant. But the leading Democrats of the South, now inflamed with the fever of annexation, determined upon Van Buren's defeat as soon as his letter opposing the acquisition of Texas appeared. They went to work industriously and skillfully to compass that end. It was not a light task. The force of New York, as has been so frequently and so signally demonstrated, is difficult to over-come in a Democratic National Convention; and New York was not only unanimously, but enthusiastically, for Mr. Van Buren. Hitherto New York and the South had been in alliance, and their joint decrees were the rule of action inside the Democratic party. They were now separated and hostile, and the trial of strength that ensued was one of the most interesting political contests ever witnessed in the country. The Democratic masses had so long followed Southern lead that they were bewildered by this new and unexpected develop-ment. From the organization of the Federal Government to that hour, a period of fifty-six years, Mr. Van Buren was the only North-ern man whom the Democracy had supported for the Presidency; and Mr. Van Buren had been forced upon the party by General Jackson. His title to his political estate, therefore, came from the South. It remained strong because his supporters believed that Jackson was still behind him. One word from the great chief at the Hermitage would have compelled Mr. Van Buren to retire from the field. But the name of Jackson was powerful with the Democratic masses. Against all the deep plots laid for Van Buren's overthrow, he was still able, when the national convention assembled at Balti-more in May, 1844, to count a majority of the delegates in favor of his nomination.

The Texas treaty of annexation was still pending in the Senate with a decided majority committed against its confirmation, both upon public and partisan grounds. The Whig senators and the friends of Van Buren had coalesced for its defeat after their respec-tive chiefs had pronounced against it. Mr. Crittenden of Kentucky and Colonel Benton were the leaders under whose joint efforts the work of Calhoun was to be set at naught. But, in fact, the work of Calhoun had already been effectually done and he could afford to disregard the fate of the treaty. He had consolidated the Demo-cratic delegates from the slave-holding States against Mr. Van Buren, and the decree had gone forth for his political destruction. Mr. Van Buren, with the aid of the more populous North, had indeed secured a majority of the convention, but an instrumentality was at hand to overcome this apparent advantage. In the two preceding national conventions of the Democratic party, the rule requiring a two-thirds vote of all the delegates to make a nomination had been adopted at the instance of Mr. Van Buren's friends in order to insure his victory. It was now to be used for his defeat. Foreseeing this result, the same zealous and devoted friends of Mr. Van Buren resisted its adoption. Romulus M. Sanders of North Carolina introduced the rule, and was sustained with great vigor by Robert J. Walker of Mississippi, and George W. Hopkins of Virginia. The leading opponents of the rule were Marcus Morton of Massachusetts, Nathan Clifford of Maine, and Daniel S. Dickinson of New York. The discussion was conducted by Southern men on one side, and by Northern men on the other, — the first division of the kind in the Democratic party. Slavery was the ominous cause! The South triumphed and the rule was fastened upon the convention.

Immediately after this action Mr. Van Buren received a majority of the votes on the first ballot, and it was not unnaturally charged that many of those supporting him must have been insincere, inasmuch as they had the full right, until self-restrained by the two-thirds rule, to declare him the nominee. But this conclusion does not necessarily follow. Mr. Van Buren had been nominated in the National Democratic Conventions of 1835 and 1839 with the two-thirds rule in operation; and now to force his nomination for a third time by a mere slender majority was, in the judgment of wise and considerate party leaders among his own friends, a dangerous experiment. They instinctively feared to disregard a powerful and aggressive minority stubbornly demanding that Mr. Van Buren should be subjected to the same test which his friends had enforced in previous conventions. Their argument was not satisfactorily answered, the rule was adopted, and Mr. Van Buren's fate was sealed.

The Southern men who insisted upon the rule had the courage to use it. They had absolute control of more than one-third of the convention; and, whatever might come, they were determined that Mr. Van Buren should not be nominated. As the most effective mode of assailing his strength, they supported a Northern candidate against him, and gave a large vote for General Cass. This wrought the intended result. It demoralized the friends of Mr. Van Buren and prepared the way for a final concentration upon Mr. Polk, which from the first had been the secret design of the Southern managers. It was skillfully done, and was the direct result of the Texas policy which Mr. Calhoun had forced the Democratic party to adopt. To Mr. Van Buren it was a great blow, and some of his friends were indisposed to submit to a result which they considered unfair. For the first time in the history of any convention, of either party, a candidate supported by a majority of the delegates failed to be nominated. The two-thirds rule, as Colonel Benton declared, had been originally framed, "not to thwart a majority, but to strengthen it." But it was remorselessly used to defeat the majority by men who intended, not only to force a Southern policy on the government, but to intrust that policy to the hands of a Southern President. The support of Cass was not sincere, but it served for the moment to embarrass the friends of Van Buren, to make the triumph of what Benton called the Texas conspiracy more easy and more sure, and in the end to lay up wrath against the day of wrath for General Cass himself. Calhoun's triumph was complete. Politically he had gained a great victory for the South. Personally he had inflicted upon Mr. Van Buren a most humiliating defeat, literally destroying him as a factor in the Democratic party, of which he had so long and so successfully been the leader.

The details of Mr. Van Buren's defeat are presented because of its large influence on the subsequent development of anti-slavery strength in the North. He was sacrificed because he was opposed to the immediate annexation of Texas. Had he taken ground in favor of annexation, he would in all probability have been nominated with a fair prospect of election; though the general judgment at the time was that Mr. Clay would have defeated him. The overthrow of Mr. Van Buren was a crisis in the history of the Democratic party, and implanted dissensions which rapidly ripened into disaster. The one leading feature, the forerunner of important political changes, was the division of delegates on the geographical line of North and South. Though receiving a clear majority of the entire convention on the first ballot, Mr. Van Buren had but nine votes from the slave States; and these votes, singularly enough, came from the northern side of the line of the Missouri Compromise. This division in a Democratic National Convention was, in many of its relations and aspects, more significant than a similar division in the two Houses of Congress.

Though cruelly wronged by the convention, as many of his supporters thought, Mr. Van Buren did not himself show resentment, but effectively sustained his successful competitor. His confidential friend, Silas Wright, had refused to go on the ticket with Mr. Polk, and George M. Dallas was substituted by the quick and competent management of Mr. Robert J. Walker. The refusal of Mr. Wright led the Whigs to hope for distraction in the ranks of the New-York Democracy; but that delusion was soon dispelled by Wright's acceptance of the nomination for governor, and his entrance into the canvass with unusual energy and spirit. It was widely believed that Jackson's great influence with Van Buren was actively exerted in aid of Polk's election. It would have cruelly embittered the few remaining days of the venerable ex-president to witness Clay's triumph, and Van Buren owed so much to Jackson that he could not be indifferent to Polk's success without showing ingratitude to the great benefactor who had made him his successor in the Executive chair. Motives of this kind evidently influenced Mr. Van Buren; for his course in after years showed how keenly he felt his defeat, and how unreconciled he was to the men chiefly engaged in compassing it. The cooler temperament which he inherited from his Dutch ancestry enabled him to bide his time more patiently than men of Scotch-Irish blood, like Calhoun; but subsequent events plainly showed that he was capable of nursing his anger, and of inflicting a revenge as significant and as fatal as that of which he had been made the victim, — a revenge which would have been perfect in its gratification had it included Mr. Calhoun personally, as it did politically, with General Cass.

Mr. Clay's letter opposing the annexation of Texas, unlike the letter of Mr. Van Buren, brought its author strength and prestige in the section upon which he chiefly relied for support in the election. He was nominated with unbounded manifestations of enthusiasm at Baltimore, on the first of May, with no platform except a brief extract from one of his own letters embraced in a single resolution, and containing no reference whatever to the Texas question. His prospects were considered most brilliant, and his supporters throughout the Union were absolutely confident of his election. But the nomination of Mr. Polk, four weeks later, surprised and disquieted Mr. Clay. More quickly than his ardent and blinded advocates, he perceived the danger to himself which the candidacy of Mr. Polk inevitably involved; and he at once became restless and dissatisfied with the drift and tendency of the campaign. The convention which nominated Mr. Polk took bold ground for the immediate re-annexation of Texas and re-occupation of Oregon. This peculiar form of expression was used to indicate that Texas had already belonged to us under the Louisiana purchase, and that Oregon had been wholly ours prior to the treaty of joint occupancy with Great Britain. It further declared, that our title to the whole of Oregon, up to 54° 40′ north latitude, was "clear and indisputable"; thus carrying our claim to the borders of the Russian possessions, and utterly denying and defying the pretension of Great Britain to the ownership of any territory bordering on the Pacific.

By this aggressive policy the Democratic party called forth the enthusiasm of the people, both North and South, in favor of territorial acquisition, — always popular with men of Anglo-Saxon blood, and appealing in an especial manner to the young, the brave, and the adventurous, in all sections of the country. Mr. Clay, a man of most generous and daring nature, suddenly discovered that he was on the timid side of all the prominent questions before the people, — a position occupied by him for the first time. He had led public sentiment in urging the war of 1812 against Great Britain; had served with distinction in negotiating the Treaty of Peace at Ghent; had forced the country into an early recognition of the South-American republics at the risk of war with Spain; had fiercely attacked the Florida Treaty of 1819, for surrendering our rightful claim to Texas as part of the Louisiana purchase; and had, when secretary of State, held high ground on the Oregon question in his correspondence with the British Government. With this splendid record of fearless policy throughout his long public career, a defensive position, suddenly thrust upon him by circumstances which he had not foreseen, betrayed him into anger, and thence naturally into imprudence. All his expectations had been based upon a contest with Mr. Van Buren. The issues he anticipated were those of national bank, of protective tariff, of internal improvements, and the distribution of the proceeds from the sale of the public lands, — on all of which he believed he would have the advantage before the people. The substitution of Mr. Polk changed the entire character of the contest, as the sagacious leaders of the Southern Democracy had foreseen. To extricate himself from the embarrassment into which he was thrown, Mr. Clay resorted to the dangerous experiment of modifying the position which he had so recently taken on the Texas question. Apparently underrating the hostility of the Northern Whigs to the scheme of annexation, he saw only the disadvantage in which the Southern Whigs were placed, especially in the Gulf region, and, in a less degree, in the northern tier of slave-holding States. Even in Kentucky — which had for years followed Mr. Clay with immense popular majorities — the contest grew animated and exciting as the Texas question was pressed. The State was to vote in August; and the gubernatorial canvass between Judge Owsley, the Whig candidate, and General William O. Butler, the nominee of the Democrats, was attracting the attention of the whole nation. This local contest not only enlisted Mr. Clay's interest, but aroused his deep personal feeling. In a private letter, since made public, he urged the editors of the Whig press "to lash Butler" for some political shortcomings which he pointed out. In a tone of unrestrained anger, he declared that "we should have a pretty time of it with one of Jackson's lieutenants at Washington, and another at Frankfort, and the old man in his dotage at the Hermitage dictating to both." To lose Kentucky was, for the Whigs, to lose every thing. To reduce the Whig majority in Mr. Clay's own State would be a great victory for the Democracy, and to that end the leaders of the party were straining every nerve.

Mr. Clay realized that it was his position on the Texas question, as defined in the Raleigh letter, which was endangering his prestige in Kentucky. This fact, added to the pressure upon him from every other slave-holding State, precipitated him into the blunder which probably cost him his election. A few weeks after the nomination of Mr. Polk, on the first day of July, 1844, Mr. Clay, while resting quietly at Ashland, wrote to Stephen Miller of Tuscaloosa what has since been known as his Alabama letter. It was written to relieve the Southern Whigs, without anticipation of its effect upon the fortunes of Northern Whigs. Mr. Clay was surrounded by men of the South only, breathed their atmosphere, heard their arguments; and, unmindful of the unrepresented Northern sentiment, he took the fatal step. He declared, that, "far from having any personal objection to the annexation of Texas," he "would be glad to see it annexed, without dishonor, without war, with the common consent of the Union, and upon just and fair terms." This letter received the popular designation of Mr. Clay's political "death-warrant," from the disastrous effect it produced on his prospects in certain free States where before its appearance he had been considered irresistibly strong.

The immediate and palpable effect of the Alabama letter in the North was an increase of power and numbers to the Abolitionists. To Mr. Clay this was its most destructive result. Prior to 1840 the Abolitionists had been so few and so scattered that they had not attempted a national organization, or taken any part in the political

contests of the country. In that year, however, they named James
G. Birney as their candidate for the Presidency, and cast for him
only 6,745 votes out of a total of 2,410,778. In 1844 the Abolitionists again named Mr. Birney as their Presidential candidate; and,
until the appearance of the Alabama letter, the general impression
was that their vote would not be larger than in 1840. Indeed,
so long as Mr. Clay held firmly to his opposition to Texas annexation, the tendency of the Abolitionists was to prefer him to Mr.
Polk. But the moment the letter of surrender appeared thousands
of anti-slavery Whigs who had loyally supported Mr. Clay went over
at once to the Abolitionists. To the popular apprehension, Mr. Clay
had changed his ground, and his new position really left little difference between himself and his opponent on the absorbing question
of Texas annexation, but it still gave to Mr. Polk all the advantage
of boldness. The latter was outspoken for the annexation of Texas,
and the former, with a few timid qualifications, declared that he
would be glad to see Texas annexed. Besides this, Mr. Polk's position on the Oregon question afforded some compensation by proposing
to add a large area of free territory to offset the increase of slave
territory in Texas. Under such arguments the Abolition party grew
rapidly and steadily until, at the election, they polled for Mr. Birney
58,879 votes. This vast increase over the vote of 1840 was very
largely at the expense of the Whig party, and its specific injury to
Mr. Clay is almost a matter of mathematical demonstration. In
New York the vote stood for Polk 237,588, for Clay 232,482, for
Birney, 15,812. The plurality for Mr. Polk was only 5,106. In
1840 the vote for Mr. Birney in New York was 2,798.[1] But for the
Alabama letter it has always been believed that Mr. Clay would
have received a sufficient number of the Birney votes to give him a

---

[1] Total vote cast for James G. Birney, Abolition candidate for President, in 1840
and in 1844 : —

	1840.	1844.		1840.	1844.
Connecticut	179	1,943	New York	2,798	15,812
Illinois	—	149	Ohio	903	8,050
Indiana	—	2,106	Pennsylvania . . .	343	3,138
Maine	194	4,836	Rhode Island . . .	42	107
Massachusetts . . .	1,621	10,860	Vermont	319	3,954
Michigan	321	3,632			
New Hampshire . . .	126	4,161		6,745	58,879
New Jersey . . .	69	131			

plurality. The election hinged on the result in New York. One hundred and thirty-eight electoral votes were necessary to a choice. With New York, Mr. Clay would have had a total of one hundred and forty-one. Mr. Polk, with New York added to his vote, received a total of one hundred and seventy, and was elected President of the United States.

No contest for the Presidency, either before or since, has been conducted with such intense energy and such deep feeling. Mr. Clay's followers were not ordinary political supporters. They had the profound personal attachment which is looked for only in hereditary governments, where loyalty becomes a passion, and is blind and unreasoning in its adherence and its devotion. The logical complement of such ardent fidelity is an opposition marked by unscrupulous rancor. This case proved no exception. The love of Mr. Clay's friends was equaled by the hatred of his foes. The zeal of his supporters did not surpass the zeal of his opponents. All the enmities and exasperations which began in the memorable contest for the Presidency when John Quincy Adams was chosen, and had grown into great proportions during the long intervening period, were fought out on the angry field of 1844. Mr. Polk, a moderate and amiable man, did not represent the acrimonious character of the controversy. He stood only as the passive representative of its principles. Behind him was Jackson, aged and infirm in body, but strong in mind, and unbroken in spirit. With him the struggle was not only one of principle, but of pride; not merely of judgment, but of temper; and he communicated to the legions throughout the country, who regarded him with reverence and gratitude, a full measure of his own animosity against Clay. In its progress the struggle absorbed the thought, the action, the passion, of the whole people. When its result was known, the Whigs regarded the defeat of Mr. Clay, not only as a calamity of untold magnitude to the country, but as a personal and profound grief, which touched the heart as deeply as the understanding. It was Jackson's final triumph over Clay. The iron-nerved old hero died in seven months after this crowning gratification of his life.

For twenty years these two great, brave men headed the opposing political forces of the Union. Whoever might be candidates, they were the actual leaders. John Quincy Adams was more learned than either; Mr. Webster was stronger in logic and in speech; Calhoun more acute, refined, and philosophic; Van Buren better skilled in combining and directing political forces; but to no one of these was given the sublime attribute of leadership, the faculty of drawing men unto him. That is natural, not acquired. There was not in the whole country, during the long period of their rivalry, a single citizen of intelligence who was indifferent to Clay or to Jackson. For the one without qualification, against the other without reservation, was the rule of division from the northernmost township of New England to the mouths of the Mississippi. Both leaders had the highest courage; physical and moral, in equal degree. Clay held the advantage of rare eloquence; but Jackson had a splendid military record, which spoke to the hearts of the people more effectively than words. Members for twenty years of the same party, they differed slightly, if at all, in political principles when the contest began; but Jackson enjoyed the prestige of a more lineal heirship to the creed of Jefferson, Madison, and Monroe; while Clay, by his imprudence in becoming secretary of State, incurred not only the odium of the "bargain and sale," but a share of the general unpopularity which at that time attached to the name of Adams. It is not in retrospect difficult to measure the advantages which Jackson possessed in the long contest, and to see clearly the reasons of his final triumph over the boldest of leaders, the noblest of foes. Still less is it difficult to see how largely the personality of the two men entered into the struggle, and how in the end the effect upon the policies and prosperity of the country would have been nearly the same had the winner and the loser exchanged places. In each of them patriotism was a passion. There never was a moment in their prolonged enmity and their rancorous contests when a real danger to the country would not have united them as heartily as in 1812, when Clay in the House and Jackson on the field co-operated in defending the national honor against the aggressions of Great Britain.

The election of Mr. Polk was an unquestionable verdict from the people in favor of the annexation of Texas. Mr. Clay and Mr. Van Buren had been able to defeat the treaty negotiated by Mr. Calhoun; but the popular vote overruled them, and pronounced in favor of the Democratic position after full and fair hearing. Mr. Tyler was anxious that the scheme so energetically initiated by him should be fully accomplished during his term. The short method of joint resolution was therefore devised by the ever fertile brain of Mr. Calhoun, and its passage through Congress intrusted to the skillful management of Robert J. Walker, then a senator from Mississippi, and already indicated for the portfolio of the Treasury in the new administration. Mr. Polk was in consultation with Mr. Tyler during the closing weeks of the latter's administration, and the annexation by joint resolution had his full concurrence. It was passed in season to receive the approval of President Tyler on the first day of March, three days before the eventful administration of Mr. Polk was installed in power. Its terms were promptly accepted by Texas, and at the next session of Congress, beginning December, 1845, the constitution of the new State was approved. Historic interest attached to the appearance of Sam Houston and Thomas J. Rusk as the first senators from the great State which they had torn from Mexico and added to the Union.

The lapse of forty years and the important events of intervening history give the opportunity for impartial judgment concerning the policy of acquiring Texas. We were not guiltless towards Mexico in originally permitting if not encouraging our citizens to join in the revolt of one of the States of that Republic. But Texas had passed definitely and finally beyond the control of Mexico, and the practical issue was, whether we should incorporate her in the Union or leave her to drift in uncertain currents — possibly to form European alliances which we should afterwards be compelled, in self-defense, to destroy. An astute statesman of that period summed up the whole case when he declared that it was wiser policy to annex Texas, and accept the issue of immediate war with Mexico, than to leave Texas in nominal independence to involve us probably in ultimate war with England. The entire history of subsequent events has vindicated the wisdom, the courage, and the statesmanship with which the Democratic party dealt with this question in 1844.

CHAPTER III.

THE annexation of Texas being accomplished, the next step was looked for with absorbing interest. In the spring of 1845 the Democratic party stood victor. Its policy had been approved by the people, its administration was in power. But success had brought heavy responsibilities, and imposed upon the statesmanship of Mr. Polk the severest of tasks. Texas came to us with undefined boundaries, and with a state of war at that moment existing between herself and Mexico. We had annexed a province that had indeed maintained a revolt for years against the central government of a neighboring republic; but its independence had never been conceded, the hope of its subjugation had never been abandoned. When Congress passed the joint resolution of annexation, the Mexican minister entered a formal protest against the proceeding, demanded his passports, and left the United States. By this course, Mexico placed herself in an unfriendly, though not necessarily hostile, attitude. The general apprehension however was that we should drift into war, and the first message of Mr. Polk aroused the country to the impending danger. He devoted a large space to the Texas question, informing Congress that "Mexico had been marshaling and organizing armies, issuing proclamations, and avowing the intention to make war on the United States, either by open declaration, or by invading Texas." He had therefore "deemed it proper, as a precautionary measure, to order a strong squadron to the coast of Mexico, and to concentrate an efficient military force

41

on the western frontier of Texas." Every one could see what this
condition of affairs portended, and there was at once great excitement throughout the country. In the North, the belief of a large
majority of the people was that the administration intended to precipitate war, not merely to coerce Mexico into the acknowledgment
of the Rio Grande as the boundary of Texas, but also to acquire
further territory for the purpose of creating additional slave States.
As soon as this impression, or suspicion, got abroad, the effect was
an anti-slavery revival which enlisted the feelings and influenced
the political action of many who had never sympathized with the
Abolitionists, and of many who had steadily opposed them.

These men came from both the old political parties, but the larger
number from the Whigs. Indeed, during almost the entire period of
the anti-slavery agitation by the Abolitionists, there had existed a
body of men in the Whig ranks who were profoundly impressed
with the evils of slavery, and who yet thought they could be more
influential in checking its progress by remaining in their old party,
and, in many sections of the country, maintaining their control of it.
Of these men, John Quincy Adams stood undeniably at the head;
and with him were associated, in and out of Congress, Mr. Seward,
Mr. Benjamin F. Wade, Mr. Fessenden, Mr. Giddings, Mr. Thaddeus
Stevens, besides a large number of able and resolute men of less
public distinction, but of equal earnestness, in all parts of the
North. Subsequent events have led men to forget that Millard
Fillmore, then a representative from New York, was one of Mr.
Adams's early co-laborers in the anti-slavery cause, and that in the
important debate on the admission of Arkansas, with a constitution
making slavery perpetual, Caleb Cushing of Massachusetts led the
radical free sentiment of New England. A large number of distinguished Democrats in the North also entertained the strongest anti-
slavery convictions, and were determined, at the risk of separating
from their party associates, to resist the spread of slavery into free
territory. Among the most conspicuous of these were Salmon P.
Chase, John P. Hale, Hannibal Hamlin, Preston King, John M.
Niles, David Wilmot, David K. Cartter, and John Wentworth.
They had many co-laborers and a band of determined and courageous followers. They were especially strong in the State of New
York, and, under the name of Barnburners, wrought changes which
affected the political history of the entire country.

The two great parties on the eve of the Mexican war were thus somewhat similarly situated. In the South all the members of both were, by the supposed necessity of their situation, upholders of slavery, though the Democrats were on this question more aggressive, more truculent, and more menacing, than the Whigs. The Southern Whigs, under the lead of Mr. Clay, had been taught that slavery was an evil, to be removed in some practicable way at some distant period, but not to be interfered with, in the States where it existed, by outside influence or force. The Democrats, under the lead of Mr. Calhoun, defended the institution of slavery as right in itself, as scripturally authorized, as essential in the economy of labor, and as a blessing to both races. In the North both parties were divided on the question; each had its anti-slavery wing and its pro-slavery wing, with many local names to distinguish them. Between the two a relentless controversy began, — a controversy marked as much by epithet as by argument, and conducted with such exasperation of feeling as clearly foreshadowed a break of existing party lines, and the formation of new associations, through which, in the phrase of that day, "men who thought alike could act together."

This being the condition of the two great parties which divided the country, it was evident that the acquisition of territory from Mexico must lead to an agitation of the slavery question, of which no man could measure the extent, or foresee the consequences. It was the old Missouri struggle renewed, with more numerous combatants, a stronger influence of the press, a mightier enginery of public opinion. It arose as suddenly as the agitation of 1820, but gave indications of deeper feeling and more prolonged controversy. The able and ambitious men who had come into power at the South were wielding the whole force of the national administration, and they wielded it with commanding ability and unflinching courage. The Free-soil sentiment which so largely pervaded the ranks of the Northern Democracy had no representative in the cabinet, and a man of pronounced anti-slavery views was as severely proscribed in Washington as a Roundhead was in London after the coronation of Charles II.

The policy of maintaining an equality of slave States with free States was to be pursued, as it had already been from the foundation of the government, with unceasing vigilance and untiring energy. The balancing of forces between new States added to the Union had been so skillfully arranged, that for a long period two States were admitted at nearly the same time, — one from the South, and one

from the North.   Thus Kentucky and Vermont, Tennessee and
Ohio, Mississippi and Indiana, Alabama and Illinois, Missouri and
Maine, Arkansas and Michigan, Florida and Iowa, came into the
Union in pairs, not indeed at precisely the same moment in every
case, but always with reference each to the other in the order named.
On the admission of Florida and Iowa, Colonel Benton remarked
that "it seemed strange that two territories so different in age, so distant from each other, so antagonistic in natural features and political
institutions, should ripen into States at the same time, and come
into the Union by a single Act; but these very antagonisms — that
is, the antagonistic provisions on the subject of slavery — made the
conjunction, and gave to the two young States an inseparable admission."   During the entire period from the formation of the Federal
Government to the inauguration of Mr. Polk, the only variation from
this twin birth of States — the one free, the other slave — was in the
case of Louisiana, which was admitted in 1812, with no corresponding State from the North.   Of the original Thirteen States, seven
had become free, and six maintained slavery.   Of the fifteen that
were added to the Union, prior to the annexation of Texas, eight
were slave, and seven were free; so that, when Mr. Polk took the
oath of office, the Union consisted of twenty-eight States, equally
divided between slave-holding and free.   So nice an adjustment had
certainly required constant watchfulness and the closest calculation
of political forces.   It was in pursuit of this adjustment that the
admission of Louisiana was secured, as an evident compensation for
the loss which had accrued to the slave-holding interest in the
unequal though voluntary partition of the Old Thirteen between
North and South.

The more rapid growth of the free States in population made
the contest for the House of Representatives, or for a majority in the
Electoral colleges, utterly hopeless to the South; but the constitutional equality of all the States in the Senate enabled the slave
interest to defeat any hostile legislation, and to defeat also any nominations by the President of men who were offensive to the South
by reason of their anti-slavery character.   The courts of the United
States, both supreme and district, throughout the Union, including
the clerks and the marshals who summoned the juries and served the
processes, were therefore filled with men acceptable to the South.
Cabinets were constituted in the same way.   Representatives of
the government in foreign countries were necessarily taken from the

class approved by the same power. Mr. Webster, speaking in his most conservative tone in the famous speech of March 7, 1850, declared that, from the formation of the Union to that hour, the South had monopolized three-fourths of the places of honor and emolument under the Federal Government. It was an accepted fact that the class interest of slavery, by holding a tie in the Senate, could defeat any measure or any nomination to which its leaders might be opposed; and thus, banded together by an absolutely cohesive political force, they could and did dictate terms. A tie-vote cannot carry measures, but it can always defeat them; and any combination of votes that possesses the negative power will in the end, if it can be firmly held, direct and control the positive action of the body to which it belongs. A strong minority, so disciplined that it cannot be divided, will, in the hands of competent leaders, annoy, distract, and often defeat, the majority of a parliamentary body. Much more can one absolute half of a legislative assembly, compactly united, succeed in dividing and controlling the other half, which has no class interest to consolidate it, and no tyrannical public opinion behind it, decreeing political death to any member who doubts or halts in his devotion to one supreme idea.

With one-half the Senate under the control of the slave-holding States, and with the Constitution declaring that no amendment to it should ever destroy the equality of the States in the Senate, the Southern leaders occupied a commanding position. Those leaders constituted a remarkable body of men. Having before them the example of Jefferson, of Madison, and of George Mason in Virginia, of Nathaniel Macon in North Carolina, and of the Pinckneys and Rutledges in South Carolina, they gave deep study to the science of government. They were admirably trained as debaters, and they became highly skilled in the management of parliamentary bodies. As a rule, they were liberally educated, many of them graduates of Northern colleges, a still larger number taking their degrees at Transylvania in Kentucky, at Chapel Hill in North Carolina, and at Mr. Jefferson's peculiar but admirable institution in Virginia. Their secluded mode of life on the plantation gave them leisure for reading and reflection. They took pride in their libraries, pursued the law so far as it increased their equipment for a public career, and devoted themselves to political affairs with an absorbing ambition. Their domestic relations imparted manners that were haughty and sometimes offensive; they were quick to take affront, and they

not infrequently brought needless personal disputation into the discussion of public questions; but they were, almost without exception, men of high integrity, and they were especially and jealously
careful of the public money. Too often ruinously lavish in their
personal expenditures, they believed in an economical government,
and, throughout the long period of their domination, they guarded
the Treasury with rigid and unceasing vigilance against every
attempt at extravagance, and against every form of corruption.

Looking into the future, the Southern men took alarm lest the
equality of their section should be lost in the Senate, and their long
control of the Federal Government ended. Even with Texas added
to the Union, this equality was barely maintained, for Wisconsin
was already seeking admission; and the clause in the articles of
annexation providing that four new States might be carved out
of the territory of Texas whenever she asked it, gave no promise of
speedy help to the South. Its operation would, in any event, be
distant, and subject to contingencies which could not be accurately
measured. There was not another foot of territory south of 36° 30′,
save that which was devoted to the Indians by solemn compact, from
which another slave State could be formed. North of 36° 30′ the
Missouri Compromise had dedicated the entire country to freedom.
In extent it was, to the Southern view, alarmingly great, including
at least a million square miles of territory. Except along its river
boundaries it was little known. Its value was underrated, and a
large portion was designated on our maps as the Great American
Desert. At the time Texas was annexed, and for several years afterwards, not a single foot of that vast area was organized under any
form of civil government. Had the Southern statesmen foreseen
the immense wealth, population, and value of this imperial domain
in the five great States and four Territories into which it is to-day
divided, they would have abandoned the struggle for equality. But
the most that was hoped, even in the North, within any near period,
was one State north of Iowa, one west of Missouri, and one from the
Oregon country.. The remainder, in the popular judgment, was
divided among mountain gorges, the arid plains of the middle, and
the uninviting region in the north, which the French *voyageurs* had
classed under the comprehensive and significant title of *mauvaises
terres*. With only three States anticipated from the great area in
the north-west, it was the evident expectation of the Southern men
who then had control of the government, that, if war with Mexico

should ensue, the result would inevitably be the acquisition of sufficient territory to form slave States south of the line of the Missouri Compromise as rapidly as free States could be formed north of it; and that in this way the ancient equality between North and South could be maintained.

But the scheme of war did not develop as rapidly as was desired by the hot advocates of territorial expansion. A show of negotiation for peace was kept up by dispatching Mr. John Slidell as minister to Mexico upon the hint that that government might be willing to renew diplomatic relations. When Mr. Slidell reached the city of Mexico he found a violent contest raging over the Presidency of the republic, the principal issue being between the war and anti-war parties. Mr. Slidell was not received. The Mexican Government declared, with somewhat of reason and consistency, that they had been willing to listen to a special envoy who would treat singly and promptly of the grave question between the two republics, but they would not accept a minister plenipotentiary who would sit down near their government in a leisurely manner, as if friendly relations existed, and select his own time for negotiation, — urging or postponing, threatening or temporizing, as the pressure of political interests in the United States might suggest. Mr. Slidell returned home; but still the conflict of arms, though so imminent, was not immediately precipitated. Mr. Polk's cautious and somewhat timid course represented the resultant between the aggressive Democrat of the South who was for war regardless of consequences, and the Free-soil Democrat of the North who was for peace regardless of consequences; the one feeling sure that war would strengthen the institution of slavery, the other confident that peace would favor the growth of freedom. As not infrequently happens in the evolution of human events, each was mistaken in the final issue. The war, undertaken for the extension of slavery, led in the end to its destruction.

The leading influence in Mr. Polk's cabinet was divided between Mr. Buchanan, secretary of State, and Mr. Marcy, secretary of War. Both were men of conservative minds, of acute judgment in political affairs, of long experience in public life; and each was ambitious for the succession to the Presidency. Neither could afford to disregard the dominant opinion of the Southern Democracy; still less could either countenance a reckless policy, which might seriously embarrass our foreign affairs, and precipitate a dangerous crisis in our relations with England. These eminent statesmen quickly perceived that the long-standing issue touching our north-western boundary, commonly known as the Oregon question, was surrounded with embarrassments which, by mismanagement, might rapidly develop into perils of great magnitude in connection with the impending war with Mexico.

The Oregon question, which now became associated, if not complicated, with the Texas question, originated many years before. By our treaty with Spain in 1819, the southern boundary of our possessions on the Pacific had been accurately defined. Our northern boundary was still unadjusted, and had been matter of dispute with Great Britain ever since we acquired the country. By the treaty of Oct. 20, 1818, the 49th parallel of north latitude was established as the boundary between the United States and British America, from the Lake of the Woods to the Stony Mountains, as the Rocky Mountains were then termed. In the same treaty it was agreed that any country claimed by either the United States or Great Britain westward of the Stony Mountains should, with its harbors, bays, and rivers, be open for the term of ten years to the vessels, citizens, and subjects of either power. This agreement was entered into solely for the purpose of preventing disputes pending final settlement, and was not to be construed to the prejudice of either party. This was the beginning of the joint occupancy of the Oregon country, England having with prompt and characteristic enterprise forced her way across the continent after she had acquired Canada in 1763. Stimulated by certain alleged discoveries of her navigators on the north-west coast, Great Britain urged and maintained her title to a frontage on the Pacific, and made a bold claim to sovereignty, as far south as the mouth of the Columbia River, nearly, indeed, to the northern border of California.

Nothing had been done towards an adjustment during the ten years of joint occupancy, and when the term was about to expire, the arrangement was renewed by special convention in 1827, for an indefinite period, — each power reserving the right to terminate the convention by giving twelve-months' notice to the other. The President, John Quincy Adams, made the briefest possible reference to the subject in his message to Congress, December, 1827 ; speaking of it as a temporary compromise of the respective rights and claims of Great Britain and the United States to territory westward of the Rocky Mountains. For many years thereafter, the subject, though languidly pursued in our diplomatic correspondence, was not alluded to in a President's message, or discussed in Congress. The contracting parties rested content with the power to join issue and try titles at any time by simply giving the required notice. The subject was also overshadowed by more urgent disputes between Great Britain and the United States, especially that relating to the Northeastern boundary, and that touching the suppression of the African slave-trade. The latter involved the old question of the right of search. The two governments came to an agreement on these differences in 1842 by the negotiation of the convention known as the Ashburton Treaty. In transmitting the treaty to Congress, President Tyler made, for the first time since the agreement for a joint occupancy was renewed in 1827, a specific reference to the Oregon question. He informed Congress, that the territory of the United States commonly called the Oregon country was beginning to attract the attention of our fellow-citizens, and that "the tide of our population, having reclaimed from the wilderness the more contiguous regions, was preparing to flow over those vast districts which stretch from the Rocky Mountains to the Pacific Ocean;" that Great Britain "laid claim to a portion of the country and that the question could not be well included in the recent treaty without postponing other more pressing matters." He significantly added, that though the difficulty might not for several years involve the peace of the two countries, yet he should urge upon Great Britain the importance of its early settlement.

As this paragraph was undoubtedly suggested and probably written by Mr. Webster, it attracted wide attention on both sides of the Atlantic; and from that moment, in varying degrees of interest and urgency, the Oregon question became an active political issue. Before the next annual meeting of Congress, Mr. Upshur had succeeded Mr. Webster in the State department; and the message of the President took still more advanced ground respecting Oregon. For political reasons, there was an obvious desire to keep the action of the government on this issue well abreast of its aggressive movements in the matter of acquiring Texas. Emboldened by Mr. Webster's position of the preceding year, Mr. Upshur, with younger blood, and with more reason for a demonstrative course, was evidently disposed to force the discussion of the question with the British Government. Under his influence and advice, President Tyler declared, in his message of December, 1843, that "after the most rigid, and, as far as practicable, unbiased, examination of the subject, the United States have always contended that their rights appertain to the entire region of country lying on the Pacific, and embraced between latitude 42° and 54° 40′." Mr. Edward Everett, at that time our minister in London, was instructed to present these views to the British Government.

Before the President could send another annual message to Congress, Mr. Calhoun had been for several months at the head of the State Department, engaged in promoting, with singular skill and ability, his scheme for the annexation of Texas. With his quick perception, he discerned that if the policy apparently indicated by Mr. Webster and aggressively proclaimed by Mr. Upshur, on the Oregon question, should be followed, and that issue sharply pressed upon Great Britain, complications of a most embarrassing nature might arise, involving in their sweep the plans, already well matured, for acquiring Texas. In order to avert all danger of that kind, Mr. Calhoun opened a negotiation with the British minister in Washington, conducting it himself, for the settlement of the Oregon question; and at the very moment when the Democratic National Convention which nominated Mr. Polk was declaring our title to the whole of Oregon as far as 54° 40′ to be "clear and unquestionable," the Democratic secretary of State was proposing to Her Majesty's representative to settle the entire controversy by the adoption of the 49th parallel as the boundary!

The negotiation was very nearly completed, and was suspended only by some dispute in regard to the right of navigating the Columbia River. It is not improbable that Mr. Calhoun, after disclosing to the British Government his willingness to accept the 49th parallel as our northern boundary, was anxious to have the negotiation temporarily postponed. If the treaty had been concluded at that time, it would have seriously interfered with the success of Mr. Polk's candidacy by destroying the prestige of the " Fifty-four forties," as Colonel Benton termed them. In Mr. Polk's election, Mr. Calhoun was deeply and indeed doubly interested; first, because of his earnest desire to defeat Mr. Clay, with whom he was at swords' points on all public issues; and again, because, having assumed the responsibility of defeating the nomination of Mr. Van Buren, he was naturally desirous that his judgment should be vindicated by the election of the candidate whom his Southern friends had put forward. Urgently solicitous for the annexation of Texas, those friends were indifferent to the fate of the Oregon question, though willing that it should be made a leading issue in the North, where it was presented with popular effect. The patriotic spirit of the country was appealed to, and to a considerable extent aroused and inflamed by the ardent and energetic declaration of our title to the whole of Oregon. "Fifty-four forty or fight" became a Democratic watchword; and the Whigs who attempted to argue against the extravagance or inexpediency of the claim continually lost ground, and were branded as cowards who were awed into silence by the fear of British power. All the prejudice against the British Government which had descended from the Revolution and from the war of 1812 was successfully evoked by the Democratic party, and they gained immeasurably by keeping an issue before the people which many of their leaders knew would be abandoned when the pressure of actual negotiation should be felt by our government.

Mr. Polk, however, in his Inaugural address, carefully re-affirmed the position respecting Oregon which his party had taken in the national canvass, and quoted part of the phrase used in the platform put forth by the convention which nominated him. The issue had been made so broadly, that it must be squarely met, and finally adjusted. The Democrats in their eagerness had left no road for honorable retreat, and had cut themselves off from the resources and convenient postponements of diplomacy. Dangerous as it was to the new administration to confront the issue, it would have been still more dangerous to attempt to avoid it. The decisive step, in the policy to which the administration was committed, was to give formal notice to Great Britain that the joint occupation of the Oregon country under the treaty of 1827 must cease. A certain degree of moral strength was unexpectedly imparted to the Democratic position by the fact that the venerable John Quincy Adams was decidedly in favor of the notice, and ably supported, in a unique and powerful speech in the House of Representatives, our title to the country up to 54° 40'. The first convention for joint occupancy had been negotiated while Mr. Adams was secretary of State, and the second while he was President; so that, in addition to the weight of authority with which he always spoke, his words seemed entitled to special confidence on a question with which he was necessarily so familiar. His great influence brought many Whigs to the support of the resolution; and on the 9th of February, 1846, the House, by the large vote of 163 to 54, declared in favor of giving the treaty notice to Great Britain.

The country at once became alarmed by the growing rumors that the resolution of the House was a direct challenge to Great Britain for a trial of strength as to the superior title to the Oregon country, and it was soon apparent that the Senate would proceed with more circumspection and conservatism. Events were rapidly tending towards hostilities with Mexico, and the aggrandizement of territory likely to result from a war with that country was not viewed with a friendly eye, either by Great Britain or France. Indeed, the annexation of Texas, which had been accomplished the preceding year, was known to be distasteful to those governments. They desired that Texas might remain an independent republic, under more liberal trade relations than could be secured from the United States with its steady policy of fostering and advancing its own manufacturing interests. The directors of the administration saw therefore more and more clearly that, if a war with Mexico were impending, it would be sheer madness to open a quarrel with Great Britain, and force her into an alliance against us. Mr. Adams and those who voted with him did not believe that the notice to the British Government would provoke a war, but that firmness on our part, in the negotiation which should ensue, would induce England to yield her pretensions to any part of Oregon ; to which Mr. Adams maintained, with elaboration of argument and demonstration, she had no shadow of right.

Mr. Adams was opposed to war with Mexico, and therefore did not draw his conclusions from the premises laid down by those who were charged with the policy of the administration. They naturally argued that a war with Great Britain might end in our losing the whole of Oregon, without acquiring any territory on our south-western border. The bare possibility of such a result would defeat the policy which they were seeking to uphold, and would at the same time destroy their party. In short, it became apparent that what might be termed the Texas policy of the administration, and what might be termed its Oregon policy, could not both be carried out. It required no prophet to foresee which would be maintained and which would be abandoned. " Fifty-four forty or fight " had been a good cry for the political campaign ; but, when the fight was to be with Great Britain, the issue became too serious to be settled by such international law as is dispensed on the stump.

A very bitter controversy over the question began in the Senate as soon as the House resolution was received. But from the outset it was apparent that those who adhered to the 54° 40′ policy, on which Mr. Polk had been elected, were in a small minority. That minority was led by General Cass; but its most brilliant advocate in debate was Edward A. Hannegan, Democratic senator from Indiana, who angrily reproached his party for playing false to the pledges on which it had won a victory over the greatest political leader of the country. He measured the situation accurately, read with discrimination the motives which underlay the change of policy on the part of the administration and its Southern supporters, and stated the whole case in a quick and curt reply to an interruption from a pro-slavery senator, — "If Oregon were good for the production of sugar and cotton, it would not have encountered this opposition. Its possession would have been at once secured." The change in the Democratic position was greatly aided by the attitude of the Whig senators, who almost unanimously opposed the resolution of notice to Great Britain, as passed by the House. Mr. Webster, for the first if not the only time in his senatorial career, read a carefully prepared speech, in which he did not argue the question of rightful boundary, but urged that a settlement on the line of the 49th parallel would be honorable to both countries, would avert hostile feeling, and restore amity and harmony. Mr. Berrien of Georgia made an exhaustive speech, inquiring into the rightfulness of title, and urged the line of 49°. Mr. Crittenden followed in the same vein, and in a reply to Senator William Allen of Ohio, chairman of Foreign Affairs, made a speech abounding in sarcasm and ridicule. The Whigs having in the campaign taken no part in the boastful demand for 54° 40', were not subjected to the humiliation of retracing imprudent steps and retracting unwise declarations.

Under the influences at work in the Senate, events developed rapidly. The House resolution of notice was defeated; and the Senate passed a substitute of a less aggressive type, in which the House, through the instrumentality of a conference committee, substantially concurred. The resolution as finally adopted authorized the President "at his discretion" to give the notice for the termination of the treaty to Great Britain. The preamble further softened the action of Congress by declaring that the notice was given in order that "the attention of the governments of both countries may be the more earnestly directed to the adoption of all proper measures for a speedy and amicable adjustment of the differences and disputes in regard to said territory."

The Southern Democrats in the House receded from their action, and the modified resolution was carried by nearly as large a vote as had been the previous one for decided and peremptory notice. In short, the great mass of the Southern Democrats in both Houses precipitately threw the Oregon issue aside. They had not failed to perceive that the hesitation of the administration in forcing an issue with Mexico was due to the apprehension of trouble with Great Britain, and they made haste to promote schemes of territorial acquisition in the South-West by withdrawing the pretensions so imprudently put forth in regard to our claims in the North-West. Only forty-six votes were given in the House against what was termed a disgraceful surrender. These were almost entirely from Northern Democrats, though a few Southern Democrats refused to recede. Among those who thus remained firm were Andrew Johnson, Stephen A. Douglas, Howell Cobb, Preston King, and Allen G. Thurman.

The passage of the modified and friendly resolution of notice dispelled all danger of trouble with Great Britain, and restored a sense of security in the United States. Immediately after its adoption, Mr. Buchanan, Secretary of State, under direction of the President, concluded a treaty with the British minister on the basis discussed by Mr. Calhoun two years before. The 49th parallel was agreed upon as the boundary between the two countries, with certain concessions for a defined period, touching the rights of the Hudson-bay Company, and the navigation of the Columbia River by the British. This treaty was promptly confirmed by the Senate, and the long controversy over the Oregon question was at rest. It had created a deep and wide-spread excitement in the country, and came very near precipitating hostilities with Great Britain. There is no doubt whatever that the English Government would have gone to war rather than surrender the territory north of the 49th parallel. This fact had made the winter and early spring of 1846 one of profound anxiety to all the people of the United States, and more especially to those who were interested in the large mercantile marine which then sailed under the American flag.

In simple truth, the country was not prepared to go to war with Great Britain in support of "our clear and unquestionable title" to the whole of Oregon. With her strong naval force on the Pacific, and her military force in Australasia, Great Britain could more readily and more easily take possession of the country in dispute than could the United States. We had no way of reaching Oregon except by doubling Cape Horn, and making a dangerous sea-voyage of many thousand miles. We could communicate across the continent only by the emigrant trail over rugged mountains and almost trackless plains. Our railway system was in its infancy in 1846. New-York City did not have a continuous road to Buffalo. Philadelphia was not connected with Pittsburg. Baltimore's projected line to the Ohio had only reached Cumberland, among the eastern foot-hills of the Alleghanies. The entire Union had but five thousand miles of railway. There was scarcely a spot on the globe, outside of the United Kingdom, where we could not have fought England with greater advantage than on the north-west coast of America at that time. The war-cry of the Presidential campaign of 1844 was, therefore, in any event, absurd; and it proved to be mischievous. It is not improbable, that, if the Oregon question had been allowed to rest for the time under the provisions of the treaty of 1827, the whole country would ultimately have fallen into our hands, and the American flag might to-day be waving over British Columbia. The course of events and the lapse of time were working steadily to our advantage. In 1826 Great Britain declined to accept the 49th parallel, but demanded the Columbia River as the boundary. Twenty years afterwards she accepted the line previously rejected. American settlers had forced her back. With the sweep of our emigration and civilization to the Pacific coast two years after the treaty of 1846, when gold was discovered in California, the tendency would have been still more strongly in our favor. Time, as Mr. Calhoun said, "would have effected every thing for us" if we could only have been patient and peaceful.

Taking the question, however, as it stood in 1846, the settlement must, upon full consideration and review, be adjudged honorable to both countries. Wise statesmen of that day felt, as wise statesmen of subsequent years have more and more realized, that a war between Great Britain and the United States would not only be a terrible calamity to both nations, but that it would stay the progress of civilization throughout the world. Future generations would hold the governing power in both countries guilty of a crime if war should ever be permitted except upon the failure of every other arbitrament. The harmless laugh of one political party at the expense of the other forty years ago, the somewhat awkward receding from pretensions which could not be maintained by the Executive of the nation, have passed into oblivion. But a striking and useful lesson would be lost if it should be forgotten that the country was brought to the verge of war by the proclamation of a policy which could not be, and was not intended to be, enforced. It was originated as a cry to catch votes; and except with the ignorant, and the few whose judgment was carried away by enthusiasm, it was from the first thoroughly insincere. If the punishment could have fallen only upon those who raised the cry, perfect justice would have been done. But the entire country suffered, and probably endured a serious and permanent loss, from the false step taken by men who claimed what they could not defend and did not mean to defend.

The Secretary of State, Mr. Buchanan, gained much credit for his conduct of the Oregon question, both diplomatically and politically. His correspondence with Mr. Pakenham, the British minister at Washington, was conspicuously able. It strengthened Mr. Buchanan at home, and gave him an enviable reputation in Europe. His political management of the question was especially adroit. His party was in sore trouble over the issue, and naturally looked to him for relief and escape. To extricate the Administration from the embarrassment caused by its ill-timed and boastful pretensions to the line of 54° 40′ was a difficult and delicate task. To accomplish it, Mr. Buchanan had recourse to the original and long disused habit of asking the Senate's advice in advance of negotiating the treaty, instead of taking the ordinary but at that time perilous responsibility of first negotiating the treaty, and then submitting it to the Senate for approval. As a leading Northern Democrat, with an established reputation and a promising future, Mr. Buchanan was instinctively reluctant to take the lead in surrendering the position which his party had so defiantly maintained during the canvass for the Presidency in 1844, and which he had, as Secretary of State, re-affirmed in a diplomatic paper of marked ability. When the necessity came to retreat, Mr. Buchanan was anxious that the duty of publicly lowering the colors should not be left to him. His device, therefore, shifted the burden from his own shoulders, and placed it on the broader ones of the Senate.

Political management could not have been more clever. It saved Mr. Buchanan in large degree from the opprobrium visited on so many leading Democrats for their precipitate retreat on the

Oregon question, and commended him at the same time to a class
of Democrats who had never before been his supporters.   General
Cass, in order to save himself as a senator from the responsibility
of surrendering our claim to 54° 40′, assumed a very warlike attitude, erroneously supposing that popularity might be gained by the
advocacy of a rupture with England.   Mr. Buchanan was wiser.
He held the middle course.   He had ably sustained our claim to
the whole of Oregon, and now, in the interest of peace, gracefully
yielded to a compromise which the Senate, after mature deliberation, had advised.   His course saved the administration, not indeed
from a mortifying position, but from a continually increasing embarrassment which seemed to force upon the country the cruel alternatives of war or dishonor.

Mr. Polk was, from some cause, incapable of judging Mr.
Buchanan generously.   He seems to have regarded his Secretary
of State as always willing to save himself at the expense of others.
He did not fail to perceive that Mr. Buchanan had come out of
the Oregon trouble with more credit, at least with less loss, than
any other man prominently identified with its agitation and settlement.   This was not pleasing to the President.   He had evidently
not concealed his distrust from the outset, and had cumbered his
offer of a cabinet position with conditions which seemed derogatory to the dignity of Mr. Buchanan, — conditions which a man of
spirit might well have resented.   He informed Mr. Buchanan that,
as he should "take no part himself between gentlemen of the
Democratic party who might become aspirants to the Presidency,"
he desired that "no member of the cabinet should do so."   He
indeed expressed himself to Mr. Buchanan in a manner so peremptory as to be offensive : "Should any member of my cabinet become
a candidate for the Presidency or Vice-Presidency of the United
States, it will be expected on the happening of such an event that
he will retire from the cabinet."   Remembering that Madison, Monroe and John Quincy Adams had each been nominated for the
Presidency while holding the position of Secretary of State in the
cabinet of his predecessor, Mr. Polk was attaching a new and
degrading condition to the incumbency of that office.

Mr. Polk did not stop with one exaction.   Addressing Mr.
Buchanan as if he were about to become a department clerk, he
informed him that he disapproved "the practice which has sometimes prevailed of cabinet officers absenting themselves for long

periods from the seat of government," and practically demanded a pledge that Mr. Buchanan would remain at his post, and be punctual in the discharge of his official duties. In reading Mr. Polk's letter, the inference seems natural that he felt under some pressing obligation to tender to Mr. Buchanan the appointment of secretary of State, but desired to accompany it with conditions which would subordinate him in the general conduct of the administration. With a spirit of docility, if not humility, altogether incomprehensible, Mr. Buchanan "accepted the position cheerfully and cordially *on the terms on which the offer was made.*"

It is not surprising that, after agreeing to enter Mr. Polk's cabinet on these conditions, Mr. Buchanan had abundant reason to complain afterwards that the President did not treat him with " delicacy and confidence." On several occasions he was on the point of resigning his position. He was especially aggrieved that the President refused to nominate him to the Supreme Bench in 1846 as the successor of Henry Baldwin. In view of Mr. Buchanan's career, both before and after that time, it seems strange that he should have desired the position. It seems stranger still that Mr. Polk, after refusing to appoint him, should have nominated George W. Woodward, a Pennsylvania Democrat, who was unacceptable to Mr. Buchanan. Mr. Polk, however, appreciated the temperament of Mr. Buchanan, and apparently knew how much he would endure without resentment. While his presence in the cabinet was evidently not a source of pleasure to the President, he realized that it brought character, strength, and power to the administration. Mr. Buchanan was an older man than Mr. Polk, was superior to him intellectually, had seen a longer and more varied public service, and enjoyed a higher personal standing throughout the country.

The timidity of Mr. Buchanan's nature made him the servant of the administration when, with boldness, he might have been its master. Had he chosen to tender his resignation in resentment of his treatment by Mr. Polk, the administration would have been seriously embarrassed. There was, at the time, no Northern Democrat of the same rank to succeed him, except General Cass, and he was ineligible by reason of his uncompromising attitude on the Oregon question. Mr. Polk could not call a Southern man to the State Department so long as Robert J. Walker was at the head of the Treasury. He could not promote Mr. Marcy from the War

Department without increasing the discontent already dangerously developed in the ranks of the New-York Democracy. Mr. Buchanan, therefore, held absolute control of the situation had he chosen to assert himself. This he failed to do, and continued to lend his aid to an administration whose policy was destroying him in his own State, and whose patronage was persistently used to promote the fortunes of his rivals and his enemies.

Mr. Polk was by singular fortune placed at the head of one of the most vigorous and important administrations in the history of the government. He had not been trained in the higher duties of statesmanship, and was not personally equal to the weighty responsibilities which devolved upon him. He was overshadowed by the ability of at least three members of his cabinet, and was keenly sensible of their superiority. He had, however, a certain aptitude for affairs, was industrious, and in personal character above reproach. Mr. Webster described him with accuracy when he spoke of him as "respectable but never eminent."

When first elected to the House of Representatives in 1824, Mr. Polk was but twenty-nine years of age. He was re-elected continuously for fourteen years. He was one of the most pronounced adherents of Jackson, and joined in the extreme and unreasonable opposition to the administration of John Quincy Adams. The period of his service in the House was distinguished by partisanship of a more bigoted and vindictive type than prevailed at any other time in the history of that body. He was Speaker during the last Congress of Jackson's Presidency and during the first under the administration of Van Buren. When the Whig members forced an inquiry into the conduct of Samuel Swartwout, the defaulting collector of customs for the port of New York, — a case which figured prominently in the exciting Presidential canvass of 1840, — they would not trust Mr. Polk with the duty of naming the committee of investigation. The House itself exercised the power of appointment, to the great disparagement of the Speaker.

When Mr. Polk closed his service in the Chair, at the end of th. Twenty-fifth Congress, no Whig member could be found who was willing to move the customary resolution of thanks, — an act of courtesy which derives its chief grace by coming from a political opponent. When the resolution was presented by a Democratic Representative from the South, it was opposed in debate by prominent Whig members. Henry A. Wise, who five years later supported Mr. Polk for the Presidency, desired to have the resolution peremptorily ruled out on a point of order. Sergeant S. Prentiss, the incomparably brilliant member from Mississippi, attacked it most violently. His impassioned invective did not stop short of personal indignity and insult to Mr. Polk. He denied with emphatic itera-tion that the Speaker had been "impartial." On the contrary he had been "the tool of the Executive, the tool of his party." He analyzed Mr. Polk's course in the appointment of committees, and with much detail labored to prove his narrowness, his unfairness, his injustice as a presiding officer. For one, he said, he was "not willing to give to Mr. Polk a certificate of good behavior, to aid him in his canvass for the governorship of Tennessee, for which he is known to be a candidate." He believed "this vote of thanks was to be used as so much capital, on which to do political business," and he declared with much vehemence that he "was not disposed to furnish it."

The opprobrious language of Prentiss did not wound Mr. Polk so seriously as did the vote of the House on the resolution of thanks. The Whigs, as a party, resisted its adoption. The Democrats could not even bring the House to a vote upon the resolution without the use of the *previous question*, and this, as a witty observer remarked, was about as humiliating as to be compelled to call the *previous question* on resolutions of respect for a deceased member. When the demand was made for "the main question to be put," the Whigs, apparently eager to force the issue to the bitter end, called for the *ayes* and *noes*. John Quincy Adams, who headed the roll, led off in the negative, and was sustained by such able and conservative mem-bers as John Bell from Mr. Polk's own State, McKennan of Pennsyl-vania, Evans of Maine, Corwin of Ohio, Menifee from the Ashland district in Kentucky, and William Cost Johnson of Maryland. The vote stood 92 to 75. Mr. Polk had been chosen Speaker by a majority of thirteen. The Whigs had thus practically consolidated their party against a vote of courtesy to the presiding officer of the House.

Mr. Polk's situation was in the highest degree embarrassing, but he behaved with admirable coolness and self-possession. He returned his thanks to the "majority of the House," which had adopted the resolution, significantly emphasizing the word "majority." He said he regarded the vote just given "as of infinitely more value than the common, matter-of-course, customary resolution which, in the courtesy usually prevailing in parliamentary bodies, is passed at the close of their deliberations." His reference "to the courtesy usually prevailing in parliamentary bodies" was made, as an eye-witness relates, with "telling accent, and with a manner that was very disconcerting to the Whigs." His address was scrupulously confined to "the majority of the House," and to the end Mr. Polk exhibited, as was said at the time, "a magnificent contempt for the insulting discourtesy of the Whigs."

The incident was made very prominent in the ensuing canvass in Tennessee, where Mr. Polk won a signal victory, and was installed as governor. The Democrats treated the action of the House as a deliberate insult, not merely to the Speaker, but to his State, and not only to his State, but to the venerable ex-president, whose residence at the Hermitage, in the judgment of his devoted followers, made Tennessee illustrious and almost sacred ground. Jackson himself was roused to intense indignation, and, though beyond threescore and ten, was active and unceasing in his efforts to insure a victory to Mr. Polk. The contest, though local in its essential character, attracted observation and interest far beyond the borders of the State.

The political importance of Mr. Polk was enhanced by the proscriptive course of his opponents in the House of Representatives. The refusal to join in the resolution of thanks operated in a manner quite contrary to the expectations of the Whigs, and was indeed effectively turned against them. The generous instincts of the people condemned an attempt to destroy the honorable fame of a public man by what they considered to be an act of spiteful persecution. It was the opinion of John Bell, who of all men had the best opportunity for impartial judgment in the premises, that the vote of himself and his fellow Whigs on the resolution was an indirect but potential cause of Mr. Polk's nomination and election to the Presidency. It gave him prominence as a friend of Jackson, and made him available as a candidate against Van Buren for the Democratic nomination. The opponents of the latter instinctively knew that it would be dangerous to defeat him with any one who did not stand well with Van Buren's powerful patron. The events of 1839 and 1844 in the life of Mr. Polk have therefore an interesting relation to each other.

CHAPTER IV.

Review (*continued*). — Relations with Mexico. — General Taylor marches his Army to the Rio Grande. — First Encounter with the Mexican Army. — Excitement in the United States. — Congress declares War against Mexico. — Ill Temper of the Whigs. — Defeat of the Democrats in the Congressional Elections of 1846. — Policy of Mr. Polk in Regard to Acquisition of Territory from Mexico. — Three-Million Bill. — The Famous Anti-slavery Proviso moved by David Wilmot. — John Quincy Adams. — His Public Service. — Robert C. Winthrop chosen Speaker. — Treaty of Guadalupe Hidalgo. — Presidential Election of 1848. — Effort of the Administration to make a Democratic Hero out of the Mexican War. — Thomas H. Benton for Lieutenant-General. — Bill defeated. — Nomination of General Taylor for the Presidency by the Whigs. — Nomination of General Cass by the Democratic Party. — Van Buren refuses to support him. — Democratic Bolt in New York. — Buffalo Convention and the Organization of the Free-soil Party. — Nomination of Van Buren and Charles Francis Adams. — Mr. Clay's Discontent. — Mr. Webster's Speech at Marshfield. — General Taylor elected. — The Barnburners of New York. — Character and Public Services of Mr. Van Buren.

BY a suggestive coincidence, the practical abandonment of the line of 54° 40′ by the administration was contemporaneous with the outbreak of the Mexican war. The modified resolution of notice to Great Britain was finally passed in both branches of Congress on the 23d of April, and on the succeeding day the first blood was shed in that contest between the two Republics which was destined to work such important results in the future and fortunes of both.

The army of occupation in Texas, commanded by General Zachary Taylor, had, during the preceding winter, been moving westward with the view of encamping in the valley of the Rio Grande. On the 28th of March General Taylor took up his position on the banks of the river, opposite Matamoras, and strengthened himself by the erection of field-works. General Ampudia, in command of the Mexican army stationed at Matamoras, was highly excited by the arrival of the American army, and on the 12th of April notified General Taylor to break up his camp within twenty-four hours, and to retire beyond the Nueces River. In the event of his failure to comply with these demands, Ampudia announced that "arms, and arms alone, must decide the question." According to the persistent claim of the Mexican Government, the Nueces River was the western boundary of Texas; and the territory between that river and the Rio Grande — a breadth of one hundred and fifty miles on the coast — was held by Mexico to be a part of her domain, and General Taylor consequently an invader of her soil. No reply was made to Ampudia; and on the 24th of April General Arista, who had succeeded to the command of the Mexican army, advised General Taylor that "he considered hostilities commenced, and should prosecute them."

Directly after this notification was received, General Taylor dispatched a party of dragoons, sixty-three in number, officers and men, up the valley of the Rio Grande, to ascertain whether the Mexicans had crossed the river. They encountered a force much larger than their own, and after a short engagement, in which some seventeen were killed and wounded, the Americans were surrounded, and compelled to surrender When intelligence of this affair reached the United States, the war-spirit rose high among the people. "Our country has been invaded," and "American blood spilled on American soil," were the cries heard on every side. In the very height of this first excitement, without waiting to know whether the Mexican Government would avow or disavow the hostile act, President Polk, on the 11th of May, sent a most aggressive message to Congress, "invoking its prompt action to recognize the existence of war, and to place at the disposition of the Executive the means of prosecuting the contest with vigor, and thus hastening the restoration of peace." As soon as the message was read in the House, a bill was introduced authorizing the President to call out a force of fifty thousand men, and giving him all the requisite power to organize, arm, and equip them. The preamble declared that "war existed by the act of Mexico," and this gave rise to an animated and somewhat angry discussion. The Whigs felt that they were placed in an embarrassing attitude. They must either vote for what they did not believe, or, by voting against the bill, incur the odium which always attaches to the party that fails by a hair's-breadth to come to the defense of the country when war is imminent.

Prominent Whigs believed, that, as an historical and geographical fact, the river Nueces was the western boundary of Texas, and that the President, by assuming the responsibility of sending an army of occupation into the country west of that river, pending negotiations with Mexico, had taken a hostile and indefensible step. But all agreed that it was too late to consider any thing except the honor of the country, now that actual hostilities had begun. The position of the Whigs was as clearly defined by their speakers as was practicable in the brief space allowed for discussion of the war bill. Against the protest of many, it was forced to a vote, after a two hours' debate. The administration expected the declaration to be unanimous; but there were fourteen members of the House who accepted the responsibility of defying the war feeling of the country by voting "no"—an act which required no small degree of moral courage and personal independence. John Quincy Adams headed the list. The other gentlemen were all Northern Whigs, or pronounced Free-Soilers.

The Senate considered the bill on the ensuing day, and passed it after a very able debate, in which Mr. Calhoun bore a leading part. He earnestly deprecated the necessity of the war, though accused by Benton of plotting to bring it on. Forty senators voted for it, and but two against it,—Thomas Clayton of Delaware and John Davis of Massachusetts. Mr. Crittenden of Kentucky and Mr. Upham of Vermont, when their names were called, responded "Ay, except the preamble." The bill was promptly approved by the President, and on the 13th of May, 1846, the two Republics were declared to be at war. In the South and West, from the beginning, the war was popular. In the North and East it was unpopular. The gallant bearing of our army, however, changed in large degree the feeling in sections where the war had been opposed. No finer body of men ever enlisted in an heroic enterprise than those who volunteered to bear the flag in Mexico. They were young, ardent, enthusiastic, brave almost to recklessness, with a fervor of devotion to their country's honor. The march of Taylor from the Rio Grande, ending with the unexpected victory against superior numbers at Buena Vista, kept the country in a state of excitement and elation, and in the succeeding year elevated him to the Presidency. Not less splendid in its succession of victories was the march of Scott from Vera Cruz to the city of Mexico, where he closed his triumphal journey by taking possession of the capital, and enabling his government to dictate terms of peace.

For the first and only time in our political history, an administration conducting a war victorious at every step, steadily lost ground in the country. The House of Representatives which declared war on the 11th of May, 1846, was Democratic by a large majority. The House, elected in the ensuing autumn, amid the resounding acclamations of Taylor's memorable victory at Monterey, had a decided Whig majority. This political reverse was due to three causes, — the enactment of the tariff of 1846, which offended the manufacturing interest of the country; the receding of the administration on the Oregon question, which embarrassed the position and wounded the pride of the Northern Democrats; and the wide-spread apprehension that the war was undertaken for the purpose of extending and perpetuating slavery. The almost unanimous Southern vote for the hasty surrender of the line of 54° 40′, on which so much had been staked in the Presidential campaign, gave the Whigs an advantage in the popular canvass. The contrast between the boldness with which the Polk administration had marched our army upon the territory claimed by Mexico, and the prudence with which it had retreated from a contest with Great Britain, after all our antecedent boasting, exposed the Democrats to merciless ridicule. Clever speakers who were numerous in the Whig party at that day did not fail to see and seize their advantage.

The Mexican war had scarcely begun when the President justified the popular suspicion by making known to Congress that one of its objects was to be the acquisition of territory beyond the Rio Grande. Perhaps it would be fairer to say that he expected such acquisition to be one of its results. He ably vindicated the policy of marching a military force into the territory between the Nueces and the Rio Grande, by the fact that he was memorialized to do so by the still existing Congress of Texas, on the urgent plea that Mexico was preparing to move upon the territory with a view to its recapture. In this Congress of Texas, the same body that completed the annexation, there were representatives from the territory in dispute beyond the Nueces; and the President felt that they were in an eminent degree entitled to the protection of our government. Events were so hurried that in three months from the formal declaration of war, and before any victory of decisive significance had been achieved, the President sent a special message to Congress, in which he suggested that "the chief obstacle to be surmounted in securing peace would be the adjustment of a boundary that would prove satisfactory and convenient to both republics." He admitted that we ought to pay a fair equivalent for any concessions which might be made by Mexico, and asked that a sum of money should be placed in his hands to be paid to Mexico immediately upon the ratification of a treaty of peace. As a precedent for this unusual request, the President cited the example of Mr. Jefferson in asking and receiving from Congress, in 1803, a special appropriation of money, to be expended at his discretion. As soon as the reading of the message was concluded, Mr. McKay of North Carolina, chairman of the committee of ways and means, introduced a bill, without preamble or explanation, directing that two millions of dollars be appropriated, to be "applied under the direction of the President to any extraordinary expenses which may be incurred in our foreign intercourse." The war was not referred to, Mexico was not named, and the simple phraseology of the Jefferson Act of 1803 was repeated word for word.

A very animated debate followed, in which Northern men took the lead. Mr. Robert C. Winthrop spoke of the administration with unwonted harshness, declaring that "it and its friends had thought fit, during the present session, to frame more than one of these important measures, so as to leave their opponents in a false position whichever way they voted." . . . He "could not and would not vote for this bill as it now stood. . . . It was a vote of unlimited confidence in an administration in which, he was sorry to say, there was very little confidence to be placed." Mr. John Quincy Adams differed from Mr. Winthrop, and could not refrain from a pardonable thrust at that gentleman for his previous vote that "war existed by act of Mexico." He differed from his colleague, Mr. Adams demurely affirmed, with a regret equal to that with which he had differed from him on the bill by which war was declared. He should now vote for this bill in any form, but suggested that it be so amended as to specify expressly that the money is granted for the purpose of negotiating peace with Mexico.

The bill was promptly modified in accordance with the desire of Mr. Adams, and at the moment when its passage seemed secure it was arrested by an amendment of momentous character, submitted by a young member from Pennsylvania. David Wilmot represented a district which had always given Democratic majorities, and was himself an intense partisan of that political school. He was a man of strong *physique* and strong common sense; of phlegmatic temperament, without any pretension to genius; a sensible speaker, with no claim to eloquence or oratory. But he had courage, determination, and honesty. He believed the time had come to arrest the progress and extension of slavery. He knew that the two-million bill was urged by the President because he wished to use the money to promote the acquisition of territory, and he determined then and there to make a stand in favor of free soil. He thereupon, on the 8th of August, 1846, moved a *proviso* to the two-million bill, declaring it to be "an express and fundamental condition to the acquisition of any territory from Mexico, that neither slavery nor involuntary servitude shall ever exist therein."

Mr. Wilmot was in the first session of his first Congress, was but thirty-three years of age, and up to that moment had not been known beyond his district. His amendment made his name familiar at once throughout the length and breadth of the Republic. No question had arisen since the slavery agitation of 1820 that was so elaborately debated. The Wilmot Proviso absorbed the attention of Congress for a longer time than the Missouri Compromise: it produced a wider and deeper excitement in the country, and it threatened a more serious danger to the peace and integrity of the Union. The consecration of the territory of the United States to freedom became from that day a rallying cry for every shade of anti-slavery sentiment. If it did not go as far as the Abolitionists in their extreme and uncompromising faith might demand, it yet took a long step forward, and afforded the ground on which the battle of the giants was to be waged, and possibly decided. The feeling in all sections became intense on the issue thus presented, and it proved a sword which cleft asunder political associations that had been close and intimate for a lifetime. Both the old parties were largely represented on each side of the question. The Northern Whigs, at the outset, generally sustained the proviso, and the Northern Democrats divided, with the majority against it. In the slave States both parties were against it, only two men south of Mason and Dixon's line voting for free soil, — John M. Clayton of Delaware in the Senate, and Henry Grider of Kentucky in the House. Mr. Grider re-entered Congress as a Republican after the war. Among the conspicuous Whigs who voted for the proviso were Joseph R. Ingersoll and James Pollock of Pennsylvania, Washington Hunt of New York, Robert C. Winthrop of Massachusetts, Robert C. Schenck of Ohio, and Truman Smith of Connecticut. Among the Democrats were Hannibal Hamlin, and all his colleagues from Maine, Simon Cameron of Pennsylvania, Preston King of New York, John Wentworth of Illinois, Allen G. Thurman of Ohio, and Robert McClelland of

Michigan, afterwards Secretary of the Interior under President Pierce.

Mr. Webster voted for the proviso, but with gloomy apprehensions. He could "see little of the future, and that little gave him no satisfaction." He spoke with portentous gravity, and arrested the attention of the country by the solemnity of his closing words: "All I can scan is contention, strife, and agitation. The future is full of difficulties and full of dangers. We appear to be rushing on perils headlong, and with our eyes all open." There was a singular disagreement between the speech and the vote of Mr. Webster. The speech indicated his real position. His vote was in deference to the opinion of Massachusetts. The most conspicuous Northern Whigs who voted against the proviso were Alexander Ramsey of Pennsylvania, since the distinguished Republican senator from Minnesota, and Secretary of War under President Hayes; and Samuel F. Vinton of Ohio, one of the oldest and ablest representatives in Congress.

The House attached the proviso to the two-million bill, and thus defeated it for the session. The Democratic Senate took it up on the day fixed for final adjournment. The majority were not willing to accept the appropriation with the anti-slavery condition upon it, and John Davis of Massachusetts, fearing if the bill went back to the House the proviso might on reconsideration be defeated, deliberately held the floor until the session expired. In the next session the two-million bill, increased to three millions, was passed without the proviso, the administration being strong enough, with the persuasions of its patronage, to defeat the anti-slavery amendment in both branches.

During the proceedings on the three-million bill, an interesting and instructive incident occurred. The venerable John Quincy Adams appeared in the House for the first time during the session, on the 13th of February (1847), having been detained by a very severe illness. As he passed inside the door the entire House voluntarily rose, business was suspended, and Mr. Andrew Johnson of Tennessee (afterwards President of the United States), addressing the Chair, said, that in compliance with the understanding with which he selected a seat at the beginning of the session, he now tendered it to the venerable member from Massachusetts, and congratulated him on being spared to return to the House. Mr. Adams, enfeebled by disease, tremulous with age, returned his thanks, regretting that he had not "voice to respond to the congratulations of his friends for the honor which had been done him." Among those who paid this unusual, indeed unprecedented, mark of respect to a fellow-member, were many from the South, who within a few years had voted to censure Mr. Adams, and had endeavored in every way to heap obloquy upon him for his persistent course in presenting anti-slavery petitions. Spontaneous in impulse, momentary in duration, simple in form, it was yet one of the most striking tributes ever paid to moral dignity and lofty character.

Mr. Adams was nearing the end of his illustrious life, and a year later was stricken down in the seat which had been so graciously tendered him. His career was in many respects remarkable. He had been minister to five different European courts, senator of the United States, appointed to the Supreme Bench, had been eight years Secretary of State, and four years President. His opportunities were great, his advantages rare, his natural abilities strong. To these he added a high standard of morality, and a love and endurance of labor possessed by few. But it may fairly be doubted whether, if his Presidency had closed his public life, his fame would have attracted special observation. He would scarcely have ranked above Monroe, and would have borne no comparison with Madison. In the Senate he had made no impression. His service abroad was one of industrious routine. His career as Secretary of State was not specially distinguished. The only two treaties of marked importance that were negotiated during his incumbency, were carried, on test questions, by the Cabinet against his judgment. His dispatches have been little quoted as precedents. His diplomatic discussions were not triumphs. Indeed, he was not felicitous with his pen, and suffers by contrast with some who preceded him and many who followed him in that office. But in his sixty-fifth year, when the public life of the most favored draws to a close, the noble and shining career of Mr. Adams began. He entered the House of Representatives in 1831, and for the remainder of his life, a period of seventeen years, he was the one grand figure in that assembly. His warfare against those who would suppress free speech, his heroic contest in favor of the right of the humblest to petition for redress of grievances, are among the memorable events in the parliamentary history of the United States. The amplitude of his knowledge, his industry, his unflagging zeal, his biting sarcasm, his power to sting and destroy without himself showing passion, made a combination of qualities as rare as it was formidable. His previous career had been one of eminent respectability, to be coldly admired and forgotten. His service in the House gave him a name as enduring as the Republic whose history he adorned.

In breadth and thoroughness of learning, Mr. Adams surpassed all his contemporaries in public life. His essays, orations, and addresses were surprisingly numerous, and upon a great variety of subjects. It cannot be said, however, that he contributed any thing to the permanent literature of the country. Nor, in a true estimate of his extraordinary career in Congress, can it be asserted that he attained the first rank as a parliamentary debater. It must be borne in mind that much of his fame in the House of Representatives was derived from the nature of the one question with which he became so conspicuously identified. It was in large degree the moral courage of his position which first fixed the attention of the country and then attracted its admiration. The men with whom he had exciting scenes in regard to the "right of petition" and its cognate issues were in no case the leading statesmen of the day. Wise, Bynum, Dromgoole, Pinckney, Lewis, Thomas F. Marshall, and the other Southern representatives with whom Mr. Adams came in conflict, were ready and brilliant men, but were far below the first rank as debaters. Indeed, with very few exceptions, the really eminent debaters were in the Senate during the period of Mr. Adams's service in the House. Mr. Clay, Mr. Webster, Mr. Calhoun, Mr. Benton, Mr. Hayne, Mr. Silas Wright, Mr. Crittenden, Mr. Ewing, Mr. Watkins Leigh, Mr. Rives, Mr. Choate, Mr. John M. Clayton, Mr. Berrien, were an altogether higher and abler class of men than those with whom Mr. Adams had his frequent wrangles in the House. The weapons which he so successfully employed against the young "fire-eaters" would have proved pointless and valueless in a contest with any one of the eminent men who in that long period gave character to the Senate.

The only time Mr. Adams ever crossed swords in the House with a man of commanding power was in the famous discussion of January, 1836, with George Evans of Maine. Mr. Adams had made a covert but angry attack on Mr. Webster for his opposition to the Fortification Bill in the preceding Congress, when President Jackson was making such energetic demonstrations of his readiness to go to war with France. To the surprise of his best friends, Mr. Adams warmly sustained Jackson in his belligerent correspondence with the government of Louis Philippe. His position probably cost him a seat in the United States Senate for which he was then a candidate. Mr. Webster preferred John Davis, who had the preceding year beaten Mr. Adams in the contest for governor of Massachusetts. These circumstances were believed at the time to be the inciting cause for the assault on Mr. Webster. The duty of replying devolved on Mr. Evans. The debate attracted general attention, and the victory of Mr. Evans was everywhere recognized. The *Globe* for the Twenty-fourth Congress contains a full report of both speeches. The stirring events of forty years have not destroyed their interest or their freshness. The superior strength, the higher order of eloquence, the greater mastery of the art of debate, will be found in the speech of Mr. Evans.

As a parliamentary debater, using that term in its true significa-tion and with its proper limitations, George Evans is entitled to high rank. He entered the House in 1829, at thirty-two years of age, and served until 1841, when he was transferred to the Senate. He retired from that body in 1847. Upon entering the Senate, he was complimented with a distinction never before or since conferred on a new member. He was placed at the head of the Committee on Finance, taking rank above the long list of prominent Whigs, who then composed the majority in the chamber. The tenacity with which the rights of seniority are usually maintained by senators enhances the value of the compliment to Mr. Evans. Mr. Clay, who had been serving as chairman of the committee, declined in his favor with the remark that "Mr. Evans knew more about the finances than any other public man in the United States." The ability and skill displayed by Mr. Evans in carrying the tariff bill of 1842 through the Senate, fully justified the high encomiums bestowed by Mr. Clay. The opposition which he led four years after to the tariff bill of 1846 gave Mr. Evans still higher reputation, though the measure was unexpectedly carried by the casting vote of the Vice-President.

When Mr. Evans's term of service drew near to its close, Mr. Webster paid him the extraordinary commendation of saying in the Senate that " his retirement would be a serious loss to the govern-ment and the country." He pronounced the speech just then deliv-ered by Mr. Evans, on the finances, to be " incomparable." The " senator from Maine," continued Mr. Webster, " has devoted him-self especially to studying and comprehending the revenue and finances of the country, and he understands that subject as well as any gentleman connected with the government since the days of Gallatin and Crawford, — nay, as well as either of those gentlemen understood it." This was the highest praise from the highest source! Of all who have represented New England in the Senate, Mr. Evans, as a debater, is entitled to rank next to Mr. Webster!

The next Congress met in December, 1847. Besides the venerable ex-president, there were two future Presidents among its members, — Abraham Lincoln and Andrew Johnson. Mr. Robert C. Winthrop was chosen Speaker. He was nominated in the Whig caucus over Samuel F. Vinton of Ohio, because he had voted for the Wilmot Proviso, and Mr. Vinton against it. Mr. Vinton was senior in age and long senior in service to Mr. Winthrop. Mr. Vinton had entered the House in 1823 and Mr. Winthrop in 1840. Mr. Vinton had moreover been selected as the Whig candidate for Speaker in the preceding Congress, when the party was in minority. The decision against him now created no little feeling in Whig circles, especially in the West where he was widely known and highly esteemed. But, while Mr. Winthrop was rewarded by this nomination for his vote in favor of the Wilmot Proviso, the more pronounced anti-slavery men were hostile to him. In the end he owed his election to timely aid from Southern Whigs. This fact, no doubt, had its effect on Mr. Winthrop's mind, and with other influences tended to separate him rapidly and conclusively from the anti-slavery wing of the Whig party.

It would, however, be unjust to Mr. Winthrop not to recognize that the chief reason for his selection as Speaker was his pre-eminent fitness for the important post. He was a young man, and, other conditions being equal, young men have been uniformly preferred for the arduous duties of the Chair. From the organization of the government the speakers, at the time of their first election, have been under forty-five years of age, - many, indeed, under forty. In only four instances have men been selected beyond the age of fifty. Mr. Clay when first chosen was but thirty-four, Mr. Polk thirty-nine, Mr. John Bell thirty-seven, Mr. Howell Cobb thirty-three, and Mr. Robert M. T. Hunter, the youngest man ever elected Speaker, was but thirty. Mr. Winthrop was thirty-eight. He was bred to the law in the office of Mr. Webster, but at twenty-five years of age entered political life as a member of the Massachusetts House of Representatives. He was soon after promoted to the speakership of that body, where he earned so valuable a reputation as a presiding officer that some of his decisions have been quoted as precedents in the National House, and have been incorporated in permanent works on Parliamentary Law. He was chosen to Congress when he was but thirty, and was in his fifth term in the House when he was advanced to the Speakership. As an orator he was always graceful and effective, but never took high rank in the House as a debater. His early life gave promise of a long public career in Massachusetts as the successor of the older Whig leaders who were passing off the stage. He followed Mr. Webster in the Senate for a brief period, when the latter became Secretary of State under Mr. Fillmore. His conservative tendencies on the Slavery question, however, were not in harmony with the demands of public opinion in Massachusetts, and in 1851 he was defeated for the governorship by George S. Boutwell, and for the senatorship by Charles Sumner. Mr. Winthrop's political career closed when he was forty-two years of age.

The events of the year 1847 had persuaded the Whig leaders, that, if they persisted in the policy embodied in the Wilmot Proviso, they would surrender all power to control the ensuing Presidential election. By clever management and the avoidance of issues which involved the slavery question, they felt reasonably sure of the votes of Delaware, Maryland, North Carolina, Kentucky, and Tennessee, with a probability of securing Georgia, Louisiana, and Florida. To throw these States away by an anti-slavery crusade was to accept inevitable defeat, and disband the Whig party. Mr. Winthrop was therefore representing the prevailing wishes of Northern Whigs when he used his influence to restrain rather than promote the development of the anti-slavery policy which had been initiated with such vigor. The result of this change was soon visible. In the preceding House, with a large Democratic majority, the Wilmot Proviso had been adopted. In the Whig House, over which Mr. Winthrop presided, it was found impossible to repeat the vote during the preparations for the national contest then impending. The treaty of Guadalupe Hidalgo, by which we acquired a vast territory from Mexico, was ratified by the Senate, and the House voted the fifteen millions demanded by it without adding a restriction of any kind on the subject of slavery. Every acre of the nine hundred thousand square miles was free territory while under the rule of Mexico, and the Commissioners of that government were extremely anxious that the United States should give a guaranty that its character in this respect should not be changed. They urged that to see slavery recognized upon soil once owned by Mexico would be as abhorrent to that government as it would be to the United States to see the Spanish Inquisition established upon it. Mr. Nicholas P. Trist, the American commissioner, gave a reply which a free Republic reads with increasing amazement. He declared that if the territory proposed to be ceded "were increased tenfold in value, and, in addition to that, covered a foot thick with pure gold, on the single condition that slavery should be forever excluded," he would not "entertain the offer for a moment, nor even think of sending it to his government. No American President would dare to submit such a treaty to the Senate."

With this suppression, if not indeed re-action, of the popular feeling in the North, on the subject of slavery, the two great parties approached the Presidential election of 1848. Each was under peculiar embarrassment in the selection of a candidate, and the presentation of the principles on which support was to be asked. The anomaly presented in the Congressional election of 1846, where an administration conducting a successful war was defeated before the people, promised to be repeated. The Democratic party had precipitated the war, had organized the military force that prosecuted it, had controlled its immense patronage, and had brought it to a victorious conclusion, yet had gained no political strength in the country. The two gallant soldiers who had so largely shared, if indeed they had not absorbed, its glory, were Whigs, and both were in ill-humor with the administration. After the battle of Buena Vista Taylor's victorious progress had been checked and his army crippled by orders from Washington, which reduced his force, and turned the Regulars over to Scott. Scott ended his brilliant campaign in a flagrant quarrel with the Secretary of War, and was summoned home peremptorily with the prospect of a court-martial. He was ordered to leave General William O. Butler, a Democratic general, in command of the army in the city of Mexico after resistance had ceased.

The administration had obviously endeavored from the first to create a Democratic hero out of the war. Authorized to appoint a large number of officers in the increased military force, raised directly by the United States, an unjust discrimination was made in favor of Democrats. Thus William O. Butler, John A. Quitman, and Gideon J. Pillow, prominent Democratic leaders in their respective States, were appointed Major-generals directly from civil life. Joseph Lane, James Shields, Franklin Pierce, George Cadwalader, Caleb Cushing, Enos D. Hopping, and Sterling Price, were selected for the high rank of Brigadier-general. Not one Whig was included, and not one of the Democratic appointees had seen service in the field, or possessed the slightest pretension to military education. Such able graduates of West Point as Henry Clay, jun., and William R. McKee, were compelled to seek service through State appointments in volunteer regiments, while Albert Sidney Johnston, subsequently proved to be one of the ablest commanders ever sent from the Military Academy, could not obtain a commission from the General Government. In the war between Mexico and Texas, by which the latter had secured her independence, Johnston had held high command, and was perhaps the best equipped soldier, both by education and service, to be found in the entire country outside the regular army at the time of the Mexican war. General Taylor urged the President to give Johnston command of one of the ten new regiments. Johnston took no part in politics; but his eminent brother, Josiah Stoddard Johnston, long a senator from Louisiana, was Mr. Clay's most intimate friend in public life, and General Taylor's letter was not even answered. The places were wanted for adherents of the administration, and Tibbatts of Kentucky, Jere Clemens of Alabama, Milledge L. Bonham of South Carolina, Seymour of Connecticut, and men of that grade, — eminent in civil life, active partisans, but with no military training, — were preferred to the most experienced soldiers. This fact disfigures the energetic record of Mr. Marcy as secretary of War, and was eminently discreditable to the President and all his advisers.

Perhaps the most inexcusable blunder of the administration was the attempt to take Thomas H. Benton from the Senate, where he was honored, eminent, and useful, make him Lieutenant-general, and send him out to Mexico to supersede both Scott and Taylor in command of the army. The bill to enable this to be done actually passed the House. When under discussion in that branch, a prominent Democratic member from Ohio declared, as one reason for passing the bill, that two of the generals are opposed politically to the Democratic party, and "by their own acts or those of their friends are candidates for the Presidency." The evident basis of this argument was, that the Mexican war being a Democratic venture, no Whig had the right to profit by it. The bill was fortunately stopped in the Senate, though that body at the time had a Democratic majority. The measure was killed by one convincing speech from Mr. Badger of North Carolina. The senators knew Colonel Benton's temper and temperament, and understood how completely unfitted he was for military command, and how his appointment would demoralize and practically destroy the army. To the end of his life, however, Colonel Benton himself believed a serious mistake had been made. He had been commissioned colonel in the war of 1812, but though of unquestioned bravery, and deeply read in military science, it had never been his fortune to engage in battle, or to see the face of an enemy. Yet in the autobiographical sketch which precedes his " Thirty Years' View," he complacently assured himself that his appointment as Lieutenant-general over Scott and Taylor " could not have wounded professional honor," as at the time of his retiring from the army he " ranked all those who have since reached its head."

But all the efforts to make a Democratic hero out of the war failed. The line-officers appointed from civil life behaved gallantly. The volunteers under their command were exceptionally excellent, — almost competent themselves to the conduct of a campaign. The political generals who vaulted from law-offices into the command of brigades and divisions were furnished by the War Department with staff-officers carefully chosen from the best educated and most skillful of the regular army. All would not suffice, however, to displace Taylor and Scott from the post of chief heroes. " Old Rough and Ready," as Taylor was called by his troops, became a popular favorite of irresistible strength, and in the Whig convention of 1848 was chosen over Mr. Clay as the standard-bearer of the party. He was placed before the people on his record as a soldier, unhampered by the political declarations which make up the modern platform. Mr. Clay had expected the nomination, and General Scott had offered to run on the same ticket as Vice-President; but against the constantly rising tide of Taylor's popularity both ordinary and extraordinary political combinations gave way. Even the Kentucky delegation divided, — in accordance with Mr. Crittenden's judgment, though not by his advice. To the overwhelming chagrin and mortification of Mr. Clay, a man unknown in political circles was preferred as the candidate of the party of which he felt himself to have been the creator. Mr. Clay was enraged by the result, and never became reconciled to it. Though he gave in the end a quiet vote at the polls for Taylor, he stubbornly refused during the campaign to open his lips or write a word in favor of his election. Mr. Webster, though without the keen personal disappointment of Mr. Clay, was equally discontented with the nomination. He had spoken in a semi-public way for several months previous to the convention, of the folly of nominating "a swearing, swaggering, frontier colonel" for the Presidency, — an allusion to General Taylor, which was scandalously unjust, and which was contradicted by his whole life. When Taylor was finally nominated, Mr. Webster resented the selection as an indignity to the statesmen of the Whig party. His only ray of comfort was the defeat of Abbott Lawrence for the Vice-Presidency by Millard Fillmore. Mr. Lawrence was a man of wealth, the most prominent manufacturer at the time in the country, of high personal character, and of wide political influence. He was the leading Taylor-Whig in New England, and his course had given offense to Mr. Webster to such an extent indeed, that on a public occasion, after the Presidential election, he referred to Mr. Lawrence in an unfriendly and discourteous manner.

The situation became still further complicated. The Whigs believed they had avoided the responsibility of positive declaration on either side of the issue embodied in the Wilmot Proviso, by selecting a military hero as their candidate. In the phrase of the day, he could make a "Star and Stripe" canvass, with fair chance of success, on both sides of Mason and Dixon's line. There was loss to be incurred by either course. The Whig managers saw plainly that an anti-slavery policy would give almost the entire South to the Democrats, and a pro-slavery policy would rend the Whig party throughout the North. They wisely concluded, if the canvass were merely a game to win votes, that the non-committal plan was the safe one. But this evasive course was not wholly successful. There was a considerable body of men in New England, and especially in Massachusetts, known as "Conscience Whigs," who had deep convictions on the subject of slavery, and refused to support General Taylor. Conspicuous among these were Henry Wilson, E. Rockwood Hoar, and Charles Francis Adams. A defection of the same kind among the Whigs of New York was prevented by the active influence of Mr. Seward, but it developed rapidly in the northern section of Ohio. Throughout the country the Whigs began to fear that a mistake had been made, and that the old leaders had been thrown overboard without due thought of the consequences. Mr. Clay's private correspondence exhibited unmistakable gratification at this aspect of affairs, for he felt assured that the influential Whigs who were now organizing against Taylor would have supported him as cordially as they had done in 1844.

These troubles in the Whig ranks tended, of course, to encourage the Democrats, and to give them for a time great promise of success. The selection of their own candidate, however, had not been unattended with difficulty and dissension. Mr. Polk was from the first out of the question, — verifying the Scripture that those who draw the sword shall perish by the sword. The war inaugurated by him had been completely successful; "a glorious peace," as it was termed, had been conquered; a vast addition to our territory had been accomplished. Yet by common consent, in which Mr. Polk had gracefully concurred in advance, it was admitted that he was not available for re-election. He had sown the dragon's teeth, and the armed men who sprang forth wrested his sceptre from him. But it would not be candid to ascribe his disability solely to events connected with the war. He had pursued the most unwise course in dealing with the New-York Democracy, and had for himself hopelessly divided the party. He made the great blunder of not recognizing the strength and leadership of Van Buren and Silas Wright. He had been led to distrust them, had always felt aggrieved that Wright refused to run on his ticket as Vice-President, and was annoyed by the fact that, as candidate for governor, Wright received several thousand votes more than the electoral ticket which represented his own fortunes. This fact came to him in a manner which deeply impressed it upon his memory. At that time, before railroad or telegraph had hastened the transmission of news beyond the Alleghanies, Mr. Polk in his Tennessee home was in an agony of doubt as to the result in New York. The first intelligence that reached him announced the certain victory of Wright, but left the electoral ticket undecided, with very unpleasant rumors of his own defeat. When at last the returns showed that he had a plurality of five thousand in New York, and was chosen President, it did not suffice to remove the deep impressions of those few days in which, either in the gloom of defeat or in the torture of suspense, he feared that he had been betrayed by the Barnburners of New York as a revenge for Van Buren's overthrow at Baltimore. As matter of fact the suspicion was absolutely groundless. The contest for governor between Silas

Wright and Millard Fillmore called out intense feeling, and the former had the advantage of personal popularity over the latter just as Mr. Clay had over Mr. Polk. Mr. Wright's plurality was but five thousand greater than Mr. Polk's, and this only proved that among half a million voters there may have been twenty-five hundred who preferred Mr. Clay for President and Mr. Wright for governor.

But there was no manifestation of feeling or apparent withholding of confidence on the part of Mr. Polk when the result was finally proclaimed. On the contrary he offered the Treasury Department to Mr. Wright, feeling assured in advance, as the uncharitable thought, that Wright could not leave the governorship to accept it. When the office was declined, Mr. Polk again wrote Mr. Wright, asking his advice as to the New-York member of the cabinet. Mr. Wright submitted the names of three men from whom wise choice could be made, — Benjamin F. Butler, who had been attorney-general under President Jackson; John A. Dix, then recently chosen to the United-States Senate; and Azariah C. Flagg, eminent in the party, and especially distinguished for his administration of financial trust. Mr. Polk, under other and adverse influence, saw fit to disregard Mr. Wright's counsel, and selected William L. Marcy, who was hostile to Wright, and distrusted by Van Buren, for Secretary of War. From that moment the fate of Mr. Polk as candidate for re-election was sealed. The cause might seem inadequate, but the effect was undeniable. The Democratic party at the outbreak of the civil war, sixteen years afterwards, had not wholly recovered from the divisions and strifes which sprung from the disregard of Mr. Van Buren's wishes at that crisis. No appointment to Mr. Polk's cabinet could have been more distasteful than that of Mr. Marcy. He had lost the State during Mr. Van Buren's Presidency in the contest for the governorship against Mr. Seward in 1838, and thus laid the foundation, as Mr. Van Buren believed, for his own disastrous defeat in 1840. The disputes which arose from Marcy's appointment in the cabinet led to Wright's defeat for re-election in 1846, when John Young, the Whig candidate, was chosen governor of New York. To three men in the cabinet the friends of Mr. Wright ascribed the Democratic overthrow, — Mr. Buchanan, Mr. Robert J. Walker, and Mr. Marcy, — each anxious for the Presidency, and each feeling that Mr. Wright was in his way. Mr. Wright died suddenly the year after his defeat, and it was supposed for a time that harmony in the New-York Democracy might be restored over his grave. But his friends survived, and their grief was the measure of their resentment.

The course of events which disabled Mr. Polk as a candidate proved equally decisive against all the members of his cabinet; and by the process of exclusion rather than by an enthusiastic desire among the people, and still less among the leaders, General Cass was selected by the Democratic Convention as candidate for the Presidency, and William O. Butler of Kentucky for the Vice-Presidency. The Democracy of New York, in consequence of the divisions arising under the governorship of Mr. Wright, sent two full delegations to the convention, bearing credentials from separate organizations. The friends of Mr. Marcy bore the name of Hunkers; the followers of Mr. Wright ranged themselves under the title of Barnburners, — distinctions which had prevailed for some years in New York. It was in fact the old division on the annexation of Texas, and now represented the pro-slavery wing and the anti-slavery wing of the Democratic party. The National Convention sought in vain to bridge the difficulty by admitting both delegations, giving to them united the right to cast the vote of the State. But the Barnburners declined thus to compromise a principle. On a question of bread, the half-loaf is preferable to starvation, but when political honor and deep personal feeling are involved, so material an adjustment is not practicable. The Barnburners retired from the convention, disclaimed all responsibility for its conclusions, and proceeded in due time to organize against the ticket of Cass and Butler. The Hunkers, left in the convention as the sole representatives of the New-York Democracy, were startled at the situation and declined to vote. They were anxious that the nomination of Cass should not appear to be forced on the Barnburners by the rival faction. It thus happened that New York, which for twenty years under the skillful leadership of Mr. Van Buren had dictated the course of the Democracy, was now so shorn of influence through the factions engendered by his defeat, that a Presidential nomination was made, not only without her lead, but without her aid or participation.

The Democratic candidate was a man of high character. He had served creditably in the early part of the war of 1812, had been governor of Michigan Territory from 1813 to 1831, had been five years Secretary of War under General Jackson, and had gone to France as minister in 1836. He remained at the court of Louis Philippe, where he received eminent consideration, for six years. When he returned to this country in 1842, at sixty years of age, he undoubtedly intended to re-enter political life. He landed at Boston, and was received with enthusiasm by the New-England Democrats, especially of that class who had not been in special favor during the long rule of Jackson and his successor. Popular ovations were arranged for him as he journeyed westward, and, by the time he reached his home in Detroit, General Cass was publicly recognized as a candidate for the Presidency. These facts did not escape the jealous and watchful eye of Mr. Van Buren. He was aggrieved by the course of General Cass, feeling assured that its direct effect would be to injure himself, and not to promote the political fortunes of the General. But the rivalry continued to develop. Cass remained in the field, a persistent candidate for nomination, and in the end proved to be, perhaps, the most powerful factor in the combination which secured the triumph of Polk. He had deeply wounded Mr. Van Buren, and, as the latter thought, causelessly and cruelly. He had disregarded a personal and political friendship of thirty years' duration, and had sundered ties which life was too short to re-unite. Cass had gained no victory. He had only defeated old friends, and the hour of retribution was at hand.

When the delegation of Barnburners withdrew from the Baltimore Convention of 1848, they were obviously acting in harmony with Mr. Van Buren's wishes. Had they been admitted, according to their peremptory demand, as the sole delegation from New York, they could have defeated Cass in the convention, and forced the nomination of some new man unconnected with the grievances and enmities of 1844. But when the demand of the Barnburners was denied, and they were asked to make common cause with the assassins of Wright, as James S. Wadsworth had denominated the Hunkers, they indignantly shook the dust of the city from off their feet, returned to New York, and forthwith called a Democratic convention to meet at Utica on the 22d of June.

Before the time arrived for the Utica Convention to assemble, the anti-slavery revolt was widely extended, and was, apparently, no less against Taylor than against Cass. There was agitation in many States, and the Barnburners found that by uniting with the opposition against both the old parties, a most effective combination could be made. It was certain to profit them in New York, and it promised the special revenge which they desired in the defeat of

Cass. The various local and State movements were merged in one great convention, which met at Buffalo on the 9th of August, with imposing demonstrations. Many of those composing it had held high rank in both the old parties. Salmon P. Chase of Ohio was selected as president. The convention represented a genuine anti-slavery sentiment, and amid excitement and enthusiasm Martin Van Buren was nominated for President, and Charles Francis Adams for Vice-President. The Barnburners, the anti-slavery Whigs, and the old Abolitionists, co-operated with apparent harmony under the general name of the Free-soil party; and the impression with many when the convention adjourned was, that Mr. Van Buren would have a plurality over both Cass and Taylor in the State of New York. The management of the popular canvass was intrusted to Democratic partisans of the Silas Wright school, and this fact had a significant and unexpected influence upon the minds of anti-slavery Whigs.

In the first flush of the excitement, the supporters of the regular Democratic nominee were not alarmed. They argued, not illogically, that the Free-soil ticket would draw more largely from the Whigs than from the Democrats, and thus very probably injure Taylor more than Cass. But in a few weeks this hope was dispelled. The Whigs of the country had been engaged for a long period in an earnest political warfare against Mr. Van Buren. In New York the contest had been personal and acrimonious to the last degree, and ordinary human nature could hardly be expected to bury at once the grievances and resentments of a generation. Nor did the Whigs confide in the sincerity of Mr. Van Buren's anti-slavery conversion. His repentance was late, and even the most charitable suspected that his desire to punish Cass had entered largely into the motives which suddenly aroused him to the evils of slavery after forty years of quiet acquiescence in all the demands of the South. Mr. Seward, who possessed the unbounded confidence of the anti-slavery men of New York, led a most earnest canvass in favor of General Taylor, and was especially successful in influencing Whigs against Van Buren. In this he was aided by the organizing skill of Thurlow Weed, and by the editorial power of Horace Greeley. Perhaps in no other Na-tional election did three men so completely control the result. They gave the vote of New York to General Taylor, and made him President of the United States.

At an opportune moment for the success of the Whigs, Mr.

Webster decided to support General Taylor. He thoroughly distrusted Cass, — not in point of integrity, but of discretion and sound judgment as a statesman. He had rebuked Cass severely in a diplomatic correspondence touching the Treaty of Washington, when he was Secretary of State and Cass minister to France. The impression then derived had convinced him that the Democratic candidate was not the man whom a Whig could desire to see in the Presidential chair. In Mr. Van Buren's anti-slavery professions, Mr. Webster had no confidence. He said pleasantly, but significantly, that "if he and Mr. Van Buren should meet under the Free-soil flag, the latter with his accustomed good-nature would laugh." He added, with a touch of characteristic humor, " that the leader of the Free-spoil party suddenly becoming the leader of the Free-soil party is a joke to shake his sides and mine." Distrusting him sincerely on the anti-slavery issue, Mr. Webster showed that on every other question Mr. Van Buren was thoroughly objectionable to the Whigs.

The Marshfield speech, as this effort was popularly known at the time, had great influence with the Northern Whigs. Mr. Webster did not conceal his belief that General Taylor's nomination was "one not fit to be made," but by the clearest of logic he demonstrated that he was infinitely to be preferred to either of his competitors. Mr. Webster at that time had the confidence of the anti-slavery Whigs in a large degree ; he had voted for the Wilmot Proviso, and his public course had been that of a just and conservative expositor of their advanced opinion. From the day of the Marshfield speech, the belief was general that Van Buren would draw far more largely from the Democrats than from the Whigs ; that his candidacy would give the State of New York to Taylor, and thus elect him President. The loss of Whig votes was not distasteful to Mr. Van Buren after the prospect of his securing the electors of New York had vanished. Had he drawn in equal proportion from the two parties, his candidacy would have had no effect. It would have neutralized itself, and left the contest between Cass and Taylor as though he had not entered the race. By a rule of influence, whose working is obvious, the tenacity of the Democratic adherents of Van Buren increased as the Whigs withdrew. The contest between Cass and Van Buren finally became in New York, in very large degree, a struggle between Democratic factions, in which the anti-slavery profession was an instrumentality to be temporarily used, and not a principle to be permanently upheld. As the Whigs left Van Buren, the Democrats left Cass, and the end of the canvass gave a full measure of satisfaction, not only to the supporters of Taylor, but to the followers of Van Buren, who polled a larger vote for him than was given to Cass. New York, as in 1844, decided the contest. The friends of Van Buren had not simply beaten Cass at the polls, they had discredited him as a party leader. In the pithy phrase of John Van Buren, they had exposed him to the country as the candidate " powerful for mischief, powerless for good."

The total vote of New York was, for Taylor, 218,603 ; for Cass, 114,318 ; for Van Buren, 120,510. The canvass for the governorship was scarcely less exciting than that for the Presidency. Hamilton Fish was the Whig candidate ; John A. Dix, then a senator of the United States, ran as the representative of Mr. Van Buren's Free-soil party ; while the eminent Chancellor Walworth, who had recently lost his judicial position, was nominated as a supporter of Cass by the Regular Democracy. Mr. Fish had been candidate for Lieutenant-governor two years before on the Whig ticket with John Young, and was defeated because of his outspoken views against the Anti-Renters. Those radical agitators instinctively knew that the descendant of Stuyvesant would support the inherited rights of the Van Rensselaers, and therefore defeated Mr. Fish while they elected the Whig candidates for other offices. Mr. Fish now had his abundant reward in receiving as large a vote as General Taylor, and securing nearly one hundred thousand plurality over the Van Buren candidate, while he in turn received a small plurality over the representative of General Cass.

The result of the two contests left the Van Buren wing, or the Barnburners, in majority over the Hunkers, and gave them an advantage in future contests for supremacy, inside the party. Truthful history will hold this to have been the chief object of the struggle with many who vowed allegiance at Buffalo to an anti-slavery creed strong enough to satisfy Joshua R. Giddings and Charles Sumner. With Cass defeated, and the Marcy wing of the party severely disciplined, the great mass of the Van Buren host of 1848 were ready to disavow their political escapade at Buffalo. Dean Richmond, Samuel J. Tilden, John Van Buren, C. C. Cambreleng, and Sanford E. Church, forgot their anti-slavery professions, reunited with the old party, and vowed afresh their fidelity to every principle against which they had so earnestly protested. Mr. Van

Buren himself went with them, and to the end of his life maintained a consistent pro-slavery record, which, throughout a long public career was varied only by the insincere professions which he found it necessary to make in order to be revenged on Cass. But it would be unjust to include in this condemnation all the New-York Democrats who went into the Buffalo movement. Many were honest and earnest, and in after life followed the principles which they had then professed. Chief among these may be reckoned Preston King, who exerted a powerful influence in the anti-slavery advances of after years, and James S. Wadsworth, who gave his name, and generously of his wealth, to the cause, and finally sealed his devotion with his blood on the battle-field of the Wilderness.

Mr. Van Buren spent the remainder of his life in dignified retirement — surviving until his eightieth year, in 1862. In point of mere intellectual force, he must rank below the really eminent men with whom he was so long associated in public life. But he was able, industrious, and, in political management, clever beyond any man who has thus far appeared in American politics. He had extraordinary tact in commending himself to the favor and confidence of the people. Succeeding to political primacy in New York on the death of De Witt Clinton in 1828, he held absolute control of his party for twenty years, and was finally overthrown by causes whose origin was beyond the limits of his personal influence. He stood on the dividing-line between the mere politician and the statesman, — perfect in the arts of the one, possessing largely the comprehensive power of the other. His active career began in 1812, and ended in 1848. During the intervening period he had served in the Legislature of New York, had been a member of the Constitutional Convention of 1820, had been attorney-general of the State, and had been chosen its governor. In the national field he had been senator of the United States, Secretary of State, minister to England, Vice-President, and President. No other man in the country has held so many great places. He filled them all with competency and with power, but marred his illustrious record by the political episode of 1848, in which, though he may have had some justification for revenge on unfaithful associates in his old party, he had none for his lack of fidelity to new friends, and for his abandonment of a sacred principle which he had pledged himself to uphold.

CHAPTER V.

WITH the election of General Taylor, the various issues of the slavery question were left undecided and unchanged. Indeed, the progress of the canvass had presented a political anomaly. General Cass was born in New England of Puritan stock. All his mature life had been spent in the free North-West. He was a lawyer, a statesman, always a civilian, except for a single year in the volunteer service of 1812. General Taylor was born in Virginia, was reared in Kentucky, was a soldier by profession from his earliest years of manhood, had passed all his life in the South, was a resident of Louisiana, engaged in planting, and was the owner of a large number of slaves. Yet in the face of these facts General Cass ran as the distinctively pro-slavery candidate, and General Taylor received three-fourths of the votes of New England, and was supported throughout the North by the anti-slavery Whigs, who accepted William H. Seward as a leader and Horace Greeley as an exponent. But this contradiction was apparent, not real. It was soon found that the confidence of the Northern men who voted for Taylor had not been misplaced.

As his inauguration approached, the anxiety in regard to his public policy grew almost painfully intense throughout the country. There had never been a cabinet organized in which so deep an interest was felt, — an interest which did not attach so much to the persons who might compose it as to the side — pro-slavery or anti-slavery — to which the balance might incline. When the names were announced, it was found that four were from the south side of Mason and Dixon's line, and three from the north side. But a review of the political character of the members showed that the decided weight of influence was with the North. John M. Clayton of Delaware, Secretary of State, nominally from the South, had voted for the Wilmot Proviso, and had defended his action with commanding ability. William M. Meredith of Pennsylvania was one of the ablest lawyers of the country, a scholar, a wit, an orator; his training had not, however, fitted him for the Treasury Department to which he was called. Thomas Ewing of Ohio, selected to organize the Department of the Interior, just then authorized by law, was a man of intellectual power, a lawyer of the first rank, possessing a stainless character, great moral courage, unbending will, an incisive style, both with tongue and pen, and a breadth of reading and wealth of information never surpassed by any public man in America. Jacob Collamer of Vermont, Postmaster-general, was an able, wise, just, and firm man, stern in principle, conservative in action. The Attorney-general was Reverdy Johnson of Maryland, an ardent Whig partisan, distinguished in his profession, born and living in a slave State, but firmly devoted to the Union, as in later life he abundantly proved. The pronounced Southern sentiment, as represented by Toombs and Stephens, had but two representatives in the cabinet, — George W. Crawford of Georgia (nephew of the eminent William H. Crawford), Secretary of War; and William Ballard Preston of Virginia, Secretary of the Navy, — able and upright men, but less distinguished than their associates.

The country was in an expectant and restless condition. The pro-slavery leaders, who had counted upon large political gain to their section by the acquisition of territory from Mexico, were somewhat discouraged, and began to fear that the South had sown, and that the North would reap. They had hoped to establish their right by positive legislation to enter all the territories with slave property.

If they should fail in this, they believed with all confidence, and had good reason at the time for their faith, that they would be able to carry the line of 36° 30′ to the Pacific by an extension of the Missouri Compromise of 1820, and that in this way the political strength of their section would be vastly enhanced. But not long after the signing of the treaty of Guadalupe Hidalgo, an event happened which put to naught the anticipations of Southern statesmen. Gold was discovered in California late in the autumn of 1848, and by one of those marvels of emigration which the Anglo-Saxon race have more than once achieved, the Pacific slope was immediately filled with a hardy, resolute, intelligent population. In less than a year they organized a State government, adopted a constitution in which slavery was forever prohibited, and were ready by the close of 1849 to apply for admission to the Union. The inhabitants had no powers of civil government conferred by Congress; the only authority exercised by the United States being that of Colonel Bennett Riley of the regular army, who had been placed in command immediately after the Treaty of Peace by President Polk, and who was left undisturbed by President Taylor.

Congress convened on the first Monday of December, 1849, amid deep feeling, rapidly growing into excitement throughout the country. For three weeks the House was unable to organize by the choice of a speaker. The Democratic candidate was Howell Cobb; the Whig candidate, Robert C. Winthrop. The contest was finally settled on the sixty-third ballot, in accordance with a previous agreement that a plurality should elect. Mr. Cobb received one hundred and two votes; Mr. Winthrop ninety-nine, with twenty votes scattering, principally anti-slavery Whigs and Free-Soilers. It was the first time that such a step had been taken; and its constitutionality was so doubtful, that after the ballot, a resolution declaring Mr. Cobb to be speaker was adopted by general concurrence on a yea and nay vote.

The message of the President was immediately transmitted, and proved a tower of strength to the friends of the Union, and a heavy blow to the secession element, which was rampant in Congress. The President recommended that California, with her constitution, already known to be anti-slavery, be promptly admitted to the Union. He also suggested that New Mexico, already better protected in property, life, liberty, and religion than she had ever been before, be quietly left under her existing military government until she should form a State constitution, and apply for admission,— an event deemed probable in the very near future. That accomplished, as he added in a special message a few days later, the claims of Texas to a portion of New Mexico could be judicially determined, which could not be done while New Mexico remained a territory, organized or unorganized. These recommendations were intensely distasteful to the South, and grew to be correspondingly popular in the North. The sectional feeling rapidly developed and the agitation in Congress communicated itself to the entire country.

The character and eminence of the men who took part in the discussion gave it an intense, almost dramatic interest. Mr. Clay in his seventy-third year was again in the Senate by the unanimous vote of the Kentucky Legislature, in the belief that his patriotic influence was needed in the impending crisis. Webster and Cass, natives of the same New-England State, Benton and Calhoun, natives of the Carolinas, all born the same year and now approaching threescore and ten, represented in their own persons almost every phase of the impending contest. Stephen A. Douglas had entered the preceding Congress at the early age of thirty-four, and the ardent young Irish soldier, James Shields, was now his colleague. Jefferson Davis had come from Mississippi with the brilliant record of his achievements in the Mexican war, already ambitious to succeed Mr. Calhoun as the leader of the extreme South, but foiled in his Disunion schemes by his eloquent but erratic colleague, Henry S. Foote. William H. Seward of New York was for the first time taking position under the National Government, at the age of forty-nine, and Salmon P. Chase of Ohio, five years younger, was beginning his political career as the colleague of Thomas Corwin. John Bell was still honorably serving Tennessee, and John McPherson Berrien was still honoring Georgia by his service. The amiable and excellent William R. King, who had entered the Senate when Alabama was admitted in 1819, and who was Colonel Benton's senior in service by two years when he resigned in 1844 to accept the French mission, now returned, and remained until he was chosen Vice-President in 1852. Hannibal Hamlin had entered the preceding year, and was still leading a bitter fight on the slavery question against a formidable element in his own party headed at home by Nathan Clifford and represented in the Senate by his colleague, James W. Bradbury. John P. Hale, a New-Hampshire Democrat whom Franklin Pierce had attempted to discipline because as representative in Congress he had opposed the annexation of Texas, had beaten Pierce before the people, defied the Democratic party, and was promoted to the Senate an outspoken Free-Soiler.   Willie P. Mangum and George E. Badger, able, graceful, experienced statesmen, represented the steadfast Union sentiment of the "Old North State" Whigs; while Arthur P. Butler, impulsive and generous, learned and able, embodied all the heresies of the South-Carolina Nullifiers.   James M. Mason, who seemed to court the hatred of the North, and Robert M. T. Hunter, who had the cordial respect of all sections, spoke for Virginia.   Pierre Soulé came from Louisiana, eloquent even in a language he could not pronounce, but better fitted by temperament for the turbulence of a revolutionary assembly in his native land than for the decorous conservatism of the American Senate.   Sam Houston was present from Texas, with a history full of adventure and singular fortune, while his colleague, Thomas J. Rusk, was daily increasing a reputation which had already marked him in the judgment of Mr. Webster as first among the younger statesmen of the South.   Dodge of Wisconsin and Dodge of Iowa, father and son, represented the Democracy of the remotest outposts in the North-West, and, most striking of all, William M. Gwin and John C. Frémont, men of Southern birth and pro-slavery training, stood at the door of the Senate with the constitution of California in their hands to demand her admission to the Union as a free State.   At no time   before or since in the history of the Senate has its membership been so illustrious, its weight of character and ability so great.   The period marked the meeting and dividing line between two generations of statesmen.   The eminent men who had succeeded the leaders of the Revolutionary era were passing away, but the most brilliant of their number were still lingering, unabated in natural force, resplendent in personal fame.   Their successors in public responsibility, if not their equals in public regard and confidence, were already upon the stage preparing for, and destined to act in, the bloodiest and most memorable of civil struggles.

Mr. Clay had re-entered the Senate with no cordial feelings towards President Taylor's administration.   The events of the preceding year were too fresh, the wounds too deep, to be readily forgotten or quickly healed.   But he desired no quarrel and was incapable of showing petty resentment.   His mind was intent on harmonizing the serious differences between North and South, and he believed the President's plan would fall short and fail.   He desired, in the same spirit of compromise which had been so distinguishing a mark of his statesmanship in former crises, to secure "an amicable arrangement of *all* questions in controversy between the free and slave States growing out of the subject of slavery." He was so accustomed to lead, that the senators involuntarily waited for him to open the discussion and point the way. He as naturally accepted the responsibility, and in January (1850) began by submitting a series of resolutions reciting the measures which were necessary for the pacification of all strife in the country. These resolutions embraced the admission of California; governments for the territory acquired from Mexico without prohibition or permission of slavery; adjustment of the disputed boundary of Texas and the allowance of ten millions of dollars to that State for the payment of her debt; the abolition of the slave trade in the District of Columbia; more effectual provision for the restitution of fugitive slaves.

It was on these resolutions that Mr. Calhoun prepared his last formal speech. He attempted to deliver it in the Senate on the 4th of March, but was so weak that he requested Mr. Mason of Virginia to read it for him. On two or three subsequent occasions Mr. Calhoun made brief extempore remarks showing each time a gradual decay of strength. He died on the last day of March. Most touching and appreciative eulogies were delivered by Mr. Clay and Mr. Webster, after his death had been announced by his colleague, Judge Butler. Mr. Clay spoke of his "transcendent talents," of his "clear, concise, compact logic," of his "felicity in generalization surpassed by no one." He intimated that he would have been glad to see Mr. Calhoun succeed Mr. Monroe in the Presidency in 1820. Mr. Webster, who always measured his words, spoke of him as "a man of undoubted genius and commanding talent, of unspotted integrity, of unimpeached honor." Mr. Calhoun had been driven by his controversies with Jackson into a position where he was deprived of popular strength in the free States. But this very fact enhanced his power with the South, and increased his hold upon his own people. To the majority of the people in the slave-holding States he was as an inspired leader for more than twenty years. He taught the philosophy and supplied the arguments to the ambitious generation of public men who came after him, and who were prepared, as he was not, to force the issue to the arbitrament of arms. Deplorable as was the end to which his teachings led, he could not have acquired the influence he wielded over millions of men unless he had been gifted with acute intellect, distinguished by moral excellence, and inspired by the sincerest belief in the righteousness of his cause. History will adjudge him to have been single-hearted and honest in his political creed. It will equally adjudge him to have been wrong in his theory of the Federal Government, and dead to the awakened sentiment of Christendom in his views concerning the enslavement of men.

Mr. Calhoun's published works show the extent of his participation in the national councils. They exhibit his zeal, the intensity of his convictions, and at the same time the clearness and strength of his logic. His premises once admitted, it is difficult to resist the force of his conclusions. Mr. Webster assailed his premises, and in their debate of February 16, 1833, defeated him, as another senator remarked, " by the acuteness of his definitions, ' — thus meeting Mr. Calhoun on his own ground. The war and its results have in large degree remanded the theories of Mr. Calhoun to the past, but no intelligent student of the institutions of the United States can afford to neglect his elaborate, conscientious, able discussions. Taken with Mr. Webster's works they exhibit the most complete examination, the most comprehensive analysis of the often tortuous and ill-defined line which separates the powers of the National Government from the functions which properly belong to the States. Mr. Calhoun's public service may be regarded as continuous from 1810, when he was elected to Congress at twenty-eight years of age, till his death, — a period of forty years. He took his seat in the House in December, 1811, and was placed by the Speaker, Mr. Clay (with whom he was then in accord), on the Committee of Foreign Affairs. He was earnest and influential in supporting the war policy of the Madison administration, and gained so rapidly in public estimation that six years later he was appointed secretary of War by President Monroe. Thenceforward his career was illustrious. As Vice-President, as secretary of State, above all as senator from South Carolina, he gained lasting renown. His life was eminently pure, his career exceptional, his fame established beyond the reach of calumny, beyond the power of detraction.

Continuing the discussion invited by Mr. Clay's resolutions, Mr. Webster delivered, on the 7th of March, the memorable speech which cost him the loss of so many of his staunch and lifelong friends. The anti-slavery Whigs of the North, who, as the discussion went on, had waited to be vindicated by the commanding argument of Mr. Webster, were dismayed and cast down by his unex-

pected utterance. Instead of arraigning the propagandists of slavery,
he arraigned its opponents. Instead of indicting the Disunionists
of the South, he poured out his wrath upon the Abolitionists of
the North. He maintained that the North had unduly exaggerated
the dangers of slavery extension at this crisis. California was coming in as a free State. Texas, north of 36° 30′, if her boundary
should extend so far, had been declared free in the articles of annexation. In the mountainous and sterile character of New Mexico
and Utah he found a stronger prohibition of slavery than in any
possible ordinance, enactment, or proviso placed on the statute-book
by Congress. He would not, therefore, " re-enact the Law of God."
He would not force a quarrel with the South when nothing was to
be gained. He would not irritate or causelessly wound the feelings
of those who were just beginning to realize that they had lost in the
issue put at stake in the Mexican war. The speech undoubtedly
had great influence in the North, and caused many anti-slavery men
to turn back. But on the other hand, it embittered thousands who
pressed forward with sturdy principle and with a quickened zeal, not
unmixed with resentment and a sense of betrayal. In many parts
of the country, and especially in the Middle and Southern States,
the speech was received with enthusiastic approval. But in New
England, the loss of whose good opinion could not be compensated
to Mr. Webster by the applause of a world outside, he never regained his hold upon the popular affection. New friends came to
him, but they did not supply the place of the old friends, who for a
lifetime had stood by him with unswerving principle and with ever-
increasing pride.

Excitement and passion do not, however, always issue decrees
and pronounce judgments of absolute right. In the zeal of that
hour, Northern anti-slavery opinion failed to appreciate the influence
which wrought so powerfully on the mind of Mr. Webster. He
belonged with those who could remember the first President, who
personally knew much of the hardships and sorrows of the Revolutionary period, who were born to poverty and reared in privation.
To these, the formation of the Federal Government had come as a
gift from Heaven, and they had heard from the lips of the living
Washington in his farewell words, that " the Union is the edifice of
our real independence, the support of our tranquillity at home, our
peace abroad, our prosperity, our safety, and of the very liberty which
we so highly prize , that for this Union we should cherish a cordial,

habitual, immovable attachment, and should discountenance whatever may suggest even a suspicion that it can in any event be abandoned." Mr. Webster had in his own lifetime seen the thirteen colonies grow to thirty powerful States. He had seen three millions of people, enfeebled and impoverished by a long struggle, increased eightfold in number, surrounded by all the comforts, charms, and securities of life. All this spoke to him of the Union and of its priceless blessings. He now heard its advantages discussed, its perpetuity doubted, its existence threatened. A convention of slave-holding States had been called, to meet at Nashville, for the purpose of considering the possible separation of the sections. Mr. Webster felt that a generation had been born who were undervaluing their inheritance, and who might, by temerity, destroy it. Under motives inspired by these surroundings, he spoke for the preservation of the Union. He believed it to be seriously endangered. His apprehensions were ridiculed by many who, ten years after Mr. Webster was in his grave, saw for the first time how real and how terrible were the perils upon which those apprehensions were founded.

When the hour of actual conflict came, every patriot realized that a great magazine of strength for the Union was stored in the teachings of Mr. Webster. For thirty years preceding the Nullification troubles in South Carolina, the government had been administered on the States'-rights theory, in which the power of the nation was subordinated, and its capacity to subdue the revolt of seceding States was dangerously weakened. His speech in reply to Hayne in 1830 was like an amendment to the Constitution. It corrected traditions, changed convictions, revolutionized conclusions. It gave to the friends of the Union the abundant logic which established the right and the power of the government to preserve itself. A fame so lofty, a work so grand, cannot be marred by one mistake, if mistake it be conceded. The thoughtful reconsideration of his severest critics must allow that Mr. Webster saw before him a divided duty, and that he chose the part which in his patriotic judgment was demanded by the supreme danger of the hour.

Mr. Clay's resolutions were referred to a special committee of thirteen, of which he was made chairman. They reported a bill embracing the principal objects contemplated in his original speech. The discussion on this composite measure was earnest and prolonged, and between certain senators became exasperating. The Administration, through its newspapers, through the declarations of its Cabinet ministers, through the unreserved expressions of President Taylor himself, showed persistent hostility to Mr. Clay's Omnibus Bill, as it was derisively and offensively called. Mr. Clay, in turn, did not conceal his hostility to the mode of adjustment proposed in the messages of the President, and defended his own with vigor and eloquence. Reciting the measures demanded for a fair and lasting settlement, he said there were five wounds, bleeding and threatening the body politic, all needing to be healed, while the President proposed to heal but one. He described the wounds, numbering them carefully on his fingers as he spoke. Colonel Benton, who was vindictively opposed to the Omnibus Bill, made sport of the five gaping wounds, and believed that Mr. Clay would have found more wounds if he had had more fingers. This strife naturally grew more and more severe, making for the time a somewhat serious division among the Democrats, and rending the Whig party asunder, one section following Mr. Clay with great zeal, the other adhering with tenacity to the administration.

The quarrel was growing fiercer day by day, and involving all shades of political opinion, when it was suddenly arrested by the death of General Taylor on the 9th of July (1850). This sad event gave the opportunity for the success of the Compromise measures. Had General Taylor lived, their defeat was assured. As a Southern man, coming from a Gulf State, personally interested in the institution of slavery, he had a vantage-ground in the contest which a Northern President could never attain. He had, moreover, the courage and the intelligence to uphold his principles, even in a controversy with Mr. Clay. His ignorance of political and civil affairs had been grossly exaggerated. Without taking part in politics, he had been a close observer of events, and his prolonged service at frontier posts had afforded the leisure and enforced the taste for reading. He knew not only the public measures, but the public men of his time closely and appreciatively. He surprised a member of his cabinet on a certain occasion, by objecting to a proposed appointment on the ground that the man designated had voted for Benton's expunging resolution at the close of Jackson's administration, — an offense which the President would not condone. The seven members of his cabinet, actively engaged in politics all their lives, had forgotten an important fact which the President instinctively remembered.

Long before General Taylor's death it was known that Mr. Fill-

more did not sympathize with the policy of the administration.   He
had been among the most advanced of anti-slavery Whigs during
his service in the House of Representatives, and was placed on the
Taylor ticket as a conciliatory candidate, to hold to their allegiance
that large class of Whigs who resented the nomination of a Louisiana slave-holder.   But from the day he was sworn in as Vice-President his antipathy to Mr. Seward began to develop.   With the conceded ability of the latter, and with his constant opportunity on the
floor of the Senate, where he won laurels from the day of his entrance, Mr. Fillmore felt that he would himself be subordinated and
lost in the crowd of followers if he coincided with Seward.   Older
in years, long senior to Mr. Seward in the national service, he apparently could not endure to see himself displaced by a more brilliant
and more capable leader.   The two men, therefore, gradually sepa-
ated ; Mr. Fillmore using what influence he possessed as Vice-
President in favor of Mr. Clay's plan of compromise, while Mr.
Seward became the Northern leader of the Administration Whigs,
— a remarkable if not unprecedented advance for a senator in the
first session of his service.

In succeeding to the Presidency, Mr. Fillmore naturally gave the
full influence of his administration to the Compromise.   To signal-
ize his position, he appointed Mr. Webster secretary of State, and
placed Mr. Corwin of Ohio at the head of the Treasury.   Mr. Corwin,
with a strong anti-slavery record, had been recently drifting in the
opposite direction, and his appointment was significant.   It was too
late, however, to save the Omnibus Bill as a whole.   The Taylor
administration had damaged it too seriously to permit an effectual
revival in its favor.   It was finally destroyed the last week in July
by striking out in detail every provision except the bill for the
organization of the Territory of Utah.   After the Utah bill had been
enacted, separate bills followed ; — for the admission of California ;
for the organization of New Mexico, with the same condition respecting slavery which had been applied to Utah ; for the adjustment of
the Texas boundary, and the payment to that State of ten millions
indemnity ; for the more effectual recovery of fugitive slaves ; for the
abolition of the slave trade in the District of Columbia.   Congress
thus enacted separately the bills which it refused to enact together,
and the policy outlined by Mr. Clay at the beginning of the session
had triumphed.   Several Southern senators joined Jefferson Davis
in strenuous resistance to the admission of California with the bound-

aries prescribed. After seeking ineffectually to make the line of 36° 30′ the southern limit of the State, they attempted with equal lack of success to enter a solemn protest on the journal of the Senate against the wrong done to the slave-holding States in giving the entire Pacific coast to freedom. It was a last and hopeless movement of the Southern Hotspurs. The protest, at first discredited, was speedily forgotten, and California entered the Union after ten months of angry controversy, with slavery forever excluded from her imperial domain.

The session had been in all respects important and memorable. In the judgment of many it had been critical, and the dangers attending its action were increased by the death of General Taylor. The South would endure from him what they would resent and possibly resist if imposed by an anti-slavery Whig from the North. This fact had, doubtless, great influence in shaping the policy of Mr. Fillmore, both as Vice-President and President. The events of the session marred and made the reputation of many. Four senators especially, of the younger class, had laid the foundation of their prominence in the struggles of after years, — Mr. Seward as an anti-slavery Whig, Mr. Chase as a Free-Soiler, previously of Democratic affiliations, Mr. Jefferson Davis as a Southern Democrat, and Mr. Douglas as a Northern Democrat. Calhoun was dead. Clay and Webster and Cass and Benton were near the end of their illustrious careers. New men were thenceforth to guide the policy of the Republic, and among the new men in a Senate of exceptional ability these four attained the largest fame, secured the strongest constituencies, and exerted the widest influence.

Both political parties began at once to take ground in favor of the Compromise measures as a final and complete adjustment of the slavery question. The Southern Whigs under Mr. Clay's lead eagerly assumed that conclusion. Mr. Fillmore, having approved all the bills separately which taken together formed the Compromise, was of course strongly in favor of regarding these measures as a finality. Mr. Webster took the same view, though from a bill he had prepared before he left the Senate for the rendition of fugitive slaves, guaranteeing jury-trial to the fugitive, it is hardly conceivable that he would have voted for the harsh measure that was enacted. Mr. Corwin to the surprise of his friends had passed over from the most radical to the ultra-conservative side on the slavery question, and it was his change, in addition to that of Mr. Webster, which had given so brilliant an opportunity to Mr. Seward as the leader of the Northern Whigs. Mr. Corwin was irretrievably injured by a course so flatly in contradiction of his previous action. He lost the support and largely forfeited the confidence of the Ohio Whigs, who in 1848 had looked upon him as a possible if not probable candidate for the Presidency.

But against this surrender to the Compromise measures of 1850, the Whigs who followed Seward and Wade and Thaddeus Stevens and Fessenden were earnest and active. Stevens was then a member of the House and had waged bitter war against the measures. Wade and Fessenden had not yet entered the Senate, but were powerful leaders in their respective States. These men had not given up the creed which demanded an anti-slavery restriction on every inch of soil owned by the United States. They viewed with abhorrence the legislation which had placed freedom and slavery on the same plane in the Territories of Utah and New Mexico. They believed that Texas had been paid for a baseless claim ten millions of dollars, one-half of which, as a sharp critic declared, was hush-money, the other half blood-money. They regarded the cruel law for the return of fugitive slaves as an abomination in the sight of God and man. In their judgment it violated every principle of right. It allowed the personal liberty of a man to be peremptorily decided by a United-States commissioner, acting with absolute power and without appeal. For a claim exceeding twenty dollars in value, every citizen has the right to a trial by jury; but by this law the body, the life, the very soul of a man, possibly a free-born citizen, might be consigned to perpetual enslavement on the fallible judgment of a single official. An apparently slight, yet especially odious feature of the law which served in large degree to render it inoperative was that the United-States commissioner, in the event of his remanding the alleged fugitive to slavery, received a fee of ten dollars, and, if he adjudged him to be free, received only five dollars.

It soon became evident that with the Whigs divided and the Democrats compactly united upon the finality of the Compromise, the latter would have the advantage in the ensuing Presidential election. The tendency would naturally be to consolidate the slave-holding States in support of the Democratic candidate, because that party had a large, well-organized force throughout the North cherishing the same principles, co-operating for the same candidates, and controlling many, if not a majority, of the free States.

The Southern Whigs, equally earnest with the Democrats for the Compromise, were constantly injured at home by the outspoken anti-slavery principles of leading Northern Whigs. Just at that point of time and from the cause indicated began the formation of parties divided on the geographical line between North and South. But this result was as yet only foreshadowed, not developed. Both the old parties held their national conventions as usual, in 1852, with every State represented in both by full delegations. There were peculiar troubles in each. In the Democratic convention the dissensions had been in large part inherited, and had reference more to persons than to principles, more to the candidate than to the platform. While something of the same trouble was visible in the Whig ranks, the chief source of contention and of party weakness was found in the irreconcilable difference of principle between all the Southern Whigs and a large number of the Northern Whigs. In the South they were unanimous in support of the Compromise. In the North they were divided.

The Democratic National Convention met in Baltimore on the first day of June, 1852. General Cass, though he had reached his seventieth year, was again in the field. Mr. Buchanan, then sixty-one years of age, was the candidate next in strength, and Stephen A. Douglas was third. Douglas was but thirty-nine years old, the youngest man ever formally presented for the Presidency by a State delegation in a National convention. Governor Marcy was fourth in the order of strength. There were scattering votes for other candidates, but these four were seriously and hopefully urged by their respective supporters. Marcy was in many respects the fittest man to be nominated, but the fear was that the old dissensions of the New-York Democracy, now seemingly healed, would open afresh if the chief of one of the clans should be imposed on the other. Douglas was injured by his partial committal to what was known as the doctrine of "manifest destiny," — the indefinite acquisition of territory southward, especially in the direction of the West Indies. Cass was too old. Buchanan lacked personal popularity ; and, while he had the Pennsylvania delegation in his favor, a host of enemies from that State, outside the convention, warred against him most bitterly. No one of these eminent men could secure two-thirds of the delegates as required by the iron rule, and on the forty-ninth ballot Franklin Pierce of New Hampshire, who had been among the "scattering" on several preceding votes, was unanimously nominated.

The suggestion of Pierce's name was not so spontaneous and sudden as it was made to appear. The precise condition of affairs was discerned before the convention met, and some sagacious and far-seeing men, among whom the late Caleb Cushing was one, and General Benjamin F. Butler another, had canvassed the merits of Pierce before the convention met. They saw that from his record in Congress he would be entirely acceptable to the South, and at the opportune moment their plans were perfected and Pierce was nominated with a great show of enthusiasm. William R. King of Alabama was selected to run as Vice-President.

General Pierce had many qualities that rendered him a strong candidate. He had served with credit if not distinction both in the House and the Senate. He was elected to the House in 1832, when he was but twenty-eight years of age, and resigned his seat in the Senate in 1842. In the ten years which intervened before his nomination for the Presidency, he had devoted himself to the law with brilliant success, leaving it only for his short service in the Mexican war. He was still a young man when he was preferred to all the prominent statesmen of his party as a Presidential candidate. He was remarkably attractive in personal appearance, prepossessing in manner, ready and even eloquent as a public speaker, fluent and graceful in conversation. He presented thus a rare combination of the qualities which attach friends and win popular support.

The platform of principles enunciated by the convention was just what the South desired and demanded. The entire interest centred in the slavery question. Indeed, the declarations upon other issues were not listened to by the delegates, and were scarcely read by the public. Without a dissenting voice the convention resolved that "all efforts of the Abolitionists or others to induce Congress to interfere with questions of slavery or to take incipient steps in relation thereto, are calculated to lead to the most alarming and dangerous consequences." The Compromise measures, including the fugitive-slave law, which was specially named, were most heartily indorsed, and were regarded as an adjustment of the whole controversy. By way of indicating how full, complete, and final the settlement was, the convention with unrestrained enthusiasm declared that "the Democratic party will resist all attempts at renewing, in Congress or out of it, the agitation of the slavery question, under whatever shape or color the attempts may be made." Among the men who joined in these declarations were not a few who had supported Van Buren and Adams in the canvass of 1848. One of the prominent officers of the convention was the author of many of the most extreme anti-slavery declarations put forth at Buffalo.

The Whigs met at Baltimore a fortnight after the Democratic convention had adjourned. The slavery question, upon which the Democrats of all shades had so cordially coalesced, was to the Whigs a dividing sword. Mr. Fillmore was a candidate, supported with almost entire unanimity by the Southern Whigs. Mr. Webster was a candidate, and though in his fear for the Union he had sacrificed more than any other man for the South, he could secure no Southern support. General Scott was a candidate, and though born and reared in Virginia, he was supported by anti-slavery Whigs of every shade in the North, against the two men of Northern birth and Northern associations. On the first ballot, Fillmore received 133 votes, Scott 131, Webster 29. Fillmore received every Southern vote, except one from Virginia given to Scott by John Minor Botts. Scott received every Northern vote except twenty-nine given to Webster, and sixteen given to Fillmore. The friends of Mr. Webster, and Mr. Webster himself, were pained and mortified by the result. Rufus Choate was at the head of the Massachusetts delegation, and eloquently, even passionately, pleaded with Southern men to support Mr. Webster on a single ballot. But the Southern men stubbornly adhered to Fillmore, and were in turn enraged because the twenty-nine votes thrown away, as they said, on Mr. Webster, would at once renominate the President in whose cabinet Mr. Webster was at that moment serving as Premier. This threefold contest had been well developed before the convention assembled, and one feature of special bitterness had been added to it by a letter from Mr. Clay, who was on his death-bed in Washington. He urged his friends to support Mr. Fillmore. This was regarded by many as a lack of generosity on Mr. Clay's part, after the warm support which Mr. Webster had given him in his contest with Mr. Polk in 1844. But there had been for years an absence of cordiality between these Whig leaders, and many who were familiar with both declared that Mr. Clay had never forgiven Mr. Webster for remaining in Tyler's cabinet after the resignation of the other Whig members. Mr. Webster's association with Tyler had undoubtedly given to the President a measure of protection against the hot wrath of Mr. Clay in the memorable contest of 1841–2, and by natural re-action had impaired the force of Mr. Clay's attack. And now ten years after the event its memory rose to influence the Presidential nomination of 1852.

Another explanation is more in consonance with Mr. Clay's magnanimity of character. He was extremely anxious that an outspoken friend of the Compromise should be nominated. He knew when he wrote his letter that the Democrats would pledge themselves to the finality of the Compromise, and he knew the Southern Whigs would be overwhelmed if there should be halting or hesitation on this issue either in their candidate or in their platform. He felt, as the responsible author of the Compromise, that he was himself on trial, and it would be a peculiar mortification if the party which he had led so long should fail to sustain him in this final crisis of his public life. He had been sufficiently humiliated by Taylor's triumph over him in the convention of 1848. It would be an absolutely intolerable rebuke if in 1852 Taylor's policy should be preferred to his own by a Whig national convention. Taylor, indeed, was in his grave, but his old military compatriot, Scott, was a candidate for the Presidency, and the anti-Compromise Whigs under Seward's lead were rallying to his support. Mr. Clay believed that Fillmore, with the force of the national administration in his hands, could defeat General Scott, and that Mr. Webster's candidacy was a needless division of friends. Hence he sustained Fillmore, not from hostility to Webster, but as the sure and only means of securing an indorsement of the Compromise measures, and of doing justice to a Northern President who had risked every thing in support of Mr. Clay's policy.

The contest was long and earnest. Mr. Webster's friends, offended by what they considered the ingratitude of Southern Whigs, persistently refused to go over to Fillmore, though by so doing they could at any moment secure his nomination. They cared nothing for Fillmore's lead in votes, obtained as they thought in large degree from the use of patronage. They scouted it as an argument not fit to be addressed to the friends of Mr. Webster. Such considerations belonged only to men of the lower grades, struggling in the dirty pools of political strife, and were not to be applied to a statesman of Mr. Webster's rank and character. They felt, moreover, that all the popularity which Fillmore had secured in the South, and to a certain degree with the conservative and commercial classes of the whole country, had come from Mr. Webster's presence and pre-eminent service in his cabinet. In short, Mr. Webster's supporters felt that Mr. Fillmore, so far from earning their respect and deserving their applause, was merely strutting in borrowed plumage, and deriving all his strength from their own illustrious chief. This jealousy was of course stimulated with consummate art and tact by the supporters of Scott. They expressed, as they really entertained, the highest admiration for Webster, and no less frankly made known their dislike, if not their contempt, for Fillmore. Webster, as they pointed out, was supported by the voice of his own great State. Massachusetts had sent a delegation composed of her best men, with the most brilliant orator of the nation, to plead their cause at the bar of the convention. In contrast with this, Fillmore had no support from New York. The Whigs of that State had sent a delegation to impeach him before the nation for faithlessness to principle, and to demand that votes of other States should not impose on New York a recreant son to confound and destroy the party.

From this attrition and conflict the natural result was Scott's triumph. It was not reached, however, until the fifty-third ballot and until the fifth day of the convention. It was brought about by the votes of some Fillmore delegates, both in the North and the South, who felt that the long contest should be ended. The gossip of the day — with perhaps a shadow of foundation — was, that in the councils of an inner and governing circle of delegates it was finally agreed that the North might have the candidate, and the South should have the platform, and that thus a bold fight could be made in both sections. William A. Graham of North Carolina, formerly a senator in Congress from that State, subsequently its governor, and at the time secretary of the Navy in Mr. Fillmore's cabinet, was nominated for Vice-President, as a wise concession to the defeated party. The platform adopted was strongly Southern, and this fact served to confirm in the minds of many the existence of the suspected agreement for the division of honors between North and South. The convention resolved that the Compromise measures, including the fugitive-slave law (specially designated after the example of the Democratic convention), "are received and acquiesced in by the Whig party of the United States as a settlement in principle and in substance of the dangerous and exciting questions which they embrace." They further declared that this position was "essential to the nationality of the Whig party and the integrity of the Union." Alexander H. Stevens has stated that this resolution was shown to him by Mr. Webster before the convention assembled, and while Mr. Choate was his guest. The inference apparently intended was that Mr. Choate carried it to the convention as the expression of the Northern Whigs, who believed in the Compromise measures. The agreement — if one existed — that this resolution should be adopted, did not involve all the Northern Whigs. Sturdy resistance was made by many, and the final vote disclosed a powerful minority opposed to the resolutions.

For the first few weeks of the canvass the Whigs had strong hope of success. The name of General Scott evoked much enthusiasm, and his splendid military reputation, acquired in two wars, was favorably contrasted with that of General Pierce, who was one of President Polk's political brigadiers. But these indications were the bubbles and froth that floated on the surface. The personal characteristics of the candidates were lost sight of in the face of the great issues involved. The people soon perceived that if there was indeed merit in the Compromise measures, it would be wise to intrust them to the keeping of the party that was unreservedly — North and South — in favor of upholding and enforcing them. On this point there was absolutely no division in the Democratic ranks. In New York the friends of Marcy and the political heirs of Wright cordially harmonized in favor of the Compromise. Mr. Van Buren returned to Tammany Hall as fresh and buoyant as if his allegiance had never been broken ; and in a great convocation of the Democracy, the prodigal was welcomed, Pierce's nomination applauded, the platform cheered, the anti-slavery creed forsworn, the Whig party roundly abused, and word sent forth to the uttermost parts of the Union that the Empire State had resumed her place at the head of the Democratic line.

The Whigs soon found to their dismay that the platform and the candidate were inseparable. They could not make a canvass upon the one in the South and upon the other in the North. General Scott had indeed heartily assented to all the principles proclaimed at the convention, but so long as Horace Greeley was eulogizing him in the " Tribune," and Seward supporting him on the stump, it was idle to present him as an acceptable candidate to slave-holding Whigs in the South. Supporting the candidate and spitting on the platform became the expressive if inelegant watchword of many Northern Whigs, but for every Whig vote which this phrase kept to his party allegiance in the free States, it drove two over to the

Democracy in the slave States. Moreover, spitting on the platform, however effective as an indication of contempt, would not satisfy the conscience or the prejudice of large numbers of Whigs who voted directly for the candidates of the Free-soil party, John P. Hale of New Hampshire for President, and George W. Julian of Indiana for Vice-President.

Weakened by personal strife, hopelessly divided on questions of principle, the Whig party was led to the slaughter. Carrying in 1840 every State but seven for Harrison, failing to elect Mr. Clay in 1844 only by the loss of New York, triumphantly installing Taylor in 1848, the Whigs were astounded to find that their candidate had been successful in but four States of the Union, and that twenty-seven States had by large majorities pronounced for General Pierce. Massachusetts and Vermont in the North, Kentucky and Tennessee in the South, had alone remained true to the Whig standard. All the other Whig States that had stood staunch and strong in the fierce contests of the past now gave way. Connecticut and Rhode Island, which never but once failed either Federalist or Whig from the foundation of the government, now voted for a proslavery States'-rights Democrat. Delaware, which never in a single instance voted for the Democratic candidate except when Monroe had no opposition in 1820 ; which had fought against Jefferson and Madison ; which had stood firmly against Jackson and Van Buren and Polk and Cass when the Bayards were Whigs and co-operated with the Claytons, now swelled the general acclaim for Pierce. Of 296 electors Pierce received 254 and General Scott only 42. The wide sweep of the Democratic victory was a surprise to both sides, though for several weeks before the election the defeat of Scott was anticipated. He received no support from Mr. Fillmore's administration, was indeed secretly betrayed by it everywhere, and quite openly by its officials in the Southern States. He did not receive the strength of his party, and the strength of his party would have been insufficient to elect him. But overwhelming as was the defeat, it did not necessarily involve destruction. The Whigs had been beaten almost as badly when Clay ran against Jackson in 1832, and yet the party had rallied to four earnest contests and to two signal victories. The Democracy, now so triumphant, had been disastrously beaten in the contest of 1840, but in the next election had regained strength enough to defeat Mr. Clay. The precedents, therefore, permitted the Whigs to be of good cheer and bade them wait the issues of the future. They were not, however, consoled by the philosophy of defeat, and were disposed to gloomy anticipations.

As if to emphasize the disaster to the Whigs, Mr. Clay and Mr. Webster both died during the canvass; Mr. Clay in June, a few days after Scott's nomination, Mr. Webster in October, a few days before his defeat. They had both lived long enough to see the work of their political life imperiled if not destroyed. They had held the same relation to the Whigs that the elder Adams and Hamilton had held to the Federalists, that Jefferson and Madison had held to the Republicans. Comparison between them could not be fairly made, their inherent qualities and personal characteristics differed so widely. Each was superior to the other in certain traits, and in our public annals thus far each stands unequaled in his sphere. Their points of contrast were salient and numerous. Mr. Clay was born in Virginia. Mr. Webster was born in New England. Mr. Clay was a devoted follower of Jefferson. Mr. Webster was bred in the school of Hamilton. Mr. Clay was an earnest advocate of the second war with Great Britain. Mr. Webster was its steady opponent. Mr. Clay supported Madison in 1812 with great energy. Mr. Webster threw all his strength for De Witt Clinton. Mr. Clay was from the first deeply imbued with the doctrine of protection. Mr. Webster entered public life a pronounced free-trader. They were not members of the same political organization until after the destruction of the old Federal party to which Mr. Webster belonged, and the hopeless divisions of the old Republican party to which Mr. Clay belonged. They gradually harmonized towards the close of Monroe's second term, and became firmly united under the administration of John Quincy Adams. Modern political designations had their origin in the Presidential election of 1824. The candidates all belonged to the party of Jefferson, which had been called Democratic-Republican. In the new divisions, the followers of Jackson took the name of Democrats: the supporters of Adams called themselves National Republicans. They had thus divided the old name, each claiming the inheritance. The unpopularity of Mr. Adams's administration had destroyed the prospects of the National-Republican party, and the name was soon displaced by the new and more acceptable title of Whig. To the joint efforts of Mr. Clay and Mr. Webster more than to all others the formation of the Whig party was due. It was not, however, in Mr. Webster's nature to become a partisan chief. Mr. Clay on the other hand was naturally and inevitably a leader.   In all the discussions of the Senate in which constitutional questions were involved, Mr. Clay instinctively deferred to Mr. Webster.   In the parliamentary debates which concerned the position of parties and the fate of measures, which enchained the Senate and led captive the people, Mr. Clay was *facile princeps*.   Mr. Webster argued the principle.   Mr. Clay embodied it in a statute.   Mr. Webster's speeches are still read with interest and studied with profit.   Mr. Clay's speeches swayed listening senates and moved multitudes, but reading them is a disappointment.   Between the two the difference is much the same as that between Burke and Charles James Fox.   Fox was the parliamentary debater of England, the consummate leader of his party. His speeches, always listened to and cheered by a crowded House of Commons, perished with their delivery.   Burke could never command a body of followers, but his parliamentary orations form brilliant and permanent chapters in the political literature of two continents.

While Mr. Webster's name is so honorably perpetuated by his elaborate and masterly discussion of great principles in the Senate, he did not connect himself with a single historic measure.   While Mr. Clay's speeches remain unread, his memory is lastingly identified with issues that are still vital and powerful.   He advanced the doctrine of protection to the stately dignity of the American system. Discarding theories and overthrowing the dogma of strict construction, he committed the General Government irrevocably to internal improvements.   Condemning the worthless system of paper money imposed upon the people by irresponsible State banks, he stood firmly for a national currency, and he foreshadowed if he did not reach the paper money which is based to-day on the credit and the strength of the government.

Mr. Clay possessed extraordinary sagacity in public affairs, seeing and foreseeing where others were blinded by ignorance or prejudice. He was a statesman by intuition, finding a remedy before others could discover the disease.   His contemporaries appreciated his rare endowments.   On the day of his first entrance into the House of Representatives he was chosen Speaker, though but thirty-four years of age.   This was all the more remarkable because the House was filled with men of recognized ability, who had been long in the public service.   It was rendered still more striking by the fact that Mr. Clay was from the far West, from one of the only two States whose frontiers reached the Mississippi.   In the entire House there were only fifteen members from the Western side of the Alleghanies. He was re-elected Speaker in every Congress so long as he served as representative. He entered the Senate at thirty, and died a member of it in his seventy-sixth year. He began his career in that body during the Presidency of Jefferson in 1806, and closed it under the Presidency of Fillmore in 1852. Other senators have served a longer time than Mr. Clay, but he alone at periods so widely separated. Other men have excelled him in specific powers, but in the rare combination of qualities which constitute at once the matchless leader of party and the statesman of consummate ability and inexhaustible resource, he has never been surpassed by any man speaking the English tongue.

NOTE. — The Committee of Thirteen, to which reference is made on p. 94, and which attained such extraordinary importance at the time, was originally suggested by Senator Foote of Mississippi. His first proposition was somewhat novel from its distinct recognition of the sectional character of the issues involved. He proposed that the committee be chosen by ballot, that six members of it should be taken from the free States and six members from the slave States, and that the twelve thus chosen should select a thirteenth member who should be chairman of the committee. All propositions touching any of the questions at issue between the North and the South were to be referred to this committee with the view of securing a general and comprehensive compromise. The subject was debated for several weeks. Mr. Foote submitted his proposition on the 25th of February, 1850, and it was not adopted until the 18th of April. The committee was chosen on the 19th. Mr. Clay had objected to the open avowal of a division of the committee on the line of North and South, and the proposition was so modified as to simply provide for a committee of thirteen to be chosen by ballot, — the chairman to be first selected, and the other twelve members on a second ballot. The change of the resolution was one of form only; for, when the Senate came to select the members, they adhered to the plan originally suggested by Mr. Foote. Mr. Clay was made chairman, which had been the design from the first, and then six senators were taken from the free States and six from the slave States, — the first, if not the only, time this mode of appointment was adopted. The membership of the committee was highly distinguished. From the free States the Senate selected Mr. Webster, General Cass, Mr. Dickinson of New York, Mr. Bright of Indiana, Mr. Phelps of Vermont, and Mr. Cooper of Pennsylvania. From the slave States, Mr. King of Alabama, Mr. Mason of Virginia, Mr. Downs of Louisiana, Mr. Mangum of North Carolina, Mr. Bell of Tennessee, and Mr. Berrien of Georgia. The twelve were equally divided between the Whigs and the Democrats, so that, with Mr. Clay as chairman, the Whigs had the majority in numbers as they had the overwhelming superiority in weight and ability. The composition of the committee was remarkable when it is remembered that the Democrats had a majority of ten in the Senate.

CHAPTER VI.

THE Democratic party, seeing their old Whig rival prostrate, naturally concluded that a long lease of power was granted them. The victory of Pierce was so complete that his supporters could not with closest scrutiny descry an opponent worthy of the slightest consideration. If the leaders of that party, however, had deigned to look below the surface, they would have learned a fact which, if not disquieting, was at least serious and significant. This fact was contained in the popular vote, which told an entirely different story from that disclosed by the Presidential electors. From the people Pierce received a total of 1,601,274 votes, Scott 1,386,580, Hale 155,825. It will be noted that, while receiving only one-sixth as many electoral votes as Pierce, Scott received more than five-sixths as many votes at the polls. Adding the vote of Hale, it will be observed that out of a total exceeding three millions, Pierce's absolute majority was but 58,896. Thoughtful men, wise in the administration of government, skilled in the management of parties, would have found in these figures food for reflection and abundant reason for hoisting cautionary signals along the shores of the political

109

sea. The Democratic leaders were not, however, disturbed by facts or figures, but were rather made stronger in the confidence of their own strength. They beheld the country prosperous in all its material interests, and they saw the mass of the people content in both sections with the settlement of the slavery question. Since the Compromise measures were enacted in 1850, and especially since the two political parties had pledged themselves in 1852 to accept those measures as a finality, the slavery agitation had to a very large extent subsided. Disturbance was not indeed infrequently caused by the summary arrest of fugitive slaves in various parts of the North, under the stringent and harsh provisions of the new law on that subject. But though these peculiarly odious transactions exerted a deeper influence on public opinion than the Democratic leaders imagined, they were local and apparently under control. There was no national disquietude on the vexed question of slavery when Franklin Pierce was installed as President.

In his Inaugural address General Pierce pledged himself with evident zeal to the upholding of the Compromise measures and to the rigid enforcement of the laws. There is no doubt that a large majority of the people of the United States — North and South — were satisfied with the situation and bade God-speed to the popular President whose administration opened so auspiciously. The year 1853 was politically as quiet as Monroe's era of good feeling, and when Congress came together in its closing month, the President dwelt impressively upon the dangers we had passed and upon the blessings that were in store for us. In tones of solemnity he declared that when " the grave shall have closed over all who are now endeavoring to meet the obligations of duty, the year 1850 will be recurred to as a period of anxious apprehension." With high praise of the Compromise legislation of that year he said " it had given renewed vigor to our institutions and restored a sense of repose and security to the public mind." Evidently remembering the pledge given by the convention which nominated him " to resist all attempts at renewing the agitation of the slavery question in or out of Congress," the President gave emphatic assurance that this " repose " should suffer no shock during his term if he " had the power to avert it." These words were addressed to Congress on the fifth day of December, 1853, and it would be uncandid to deny that even in the North they were heartily approved by a large majority of the people, — perhaps by a majority in every State.

In precisely one month from the delivery of these words by the President an ominous movement was made in Congress. Notwithstanding all the vows of fealty to the Compromise of 1850, the pro-slavery leaders of the South were not contented with the aspect of affairs. The result of the Mexican war had deeply disappointed them. Its most striking political effect thus far was the addition to the Union of a large and imposing free State on the Pacific, — an empire indeed in prospective wealth and power. In the battle between free institutions and slave institutions, California represented a strong flank movement threatening destruction to slavery. Her vote in the Senate gave a majority of two to the free States. The equality of the sections had been steadily maintained in the Senate since the admission of Louisiana in 1812. The break now was ominous; the claim of equality had been disregarded; the superstition which upheld it was dispelled, and the defenders of slavery could see only a long procession of free States marching from the North-West to re-enforce a power already irresistibly strong. From what quarter of the Union could this anti-slavery aggression be offset? By what process could its growth be checked? Texas might, if she chose to ask for her own partition, re-enforce the slave-power in the Senate by four new States, as guarantied in the articles of annexation. But the very majesty of her dimensions protested against dismemberment. Texas was as large as France, and from the Sabine to the Rio Grande there was not a cotton-planter or a cattle-herder who did not have this fact before his eyes to inflame his pride and guide his vote against parting with a single square mile of her magnificent domain. New Mexico and Utah were mountainous and arid, inviting only the miner and the grazier and offering no inducement for the labor of the slave. The right guarantied to these territories in the Compromise of 1850 to come in as slave States was, therefore, as Mr. Webster had maintained, a concession of form and not of substance to the South. Seeing slavery thus hemmed in on all sides by nature as well as law, and sincerely believing that in such a position its final extinction was but a question of time, the Southern leaders determined to break the bonds that bound them. From their own point of reasoning they were correct. To stand still was certain though slow destruction to slavery. To move was indeed hazardous, but it gave them a chance to re-establish their equality in the administration of the government, and for this they determined to risk every thing.

To the westward and north-westward of Missouri and Iowa lay a vast territory which in 1854 was not only unsettled but had no form of civil government whatever. It stretched from the north line of Arkansas to the border of British America, — twelve and a half degrees of latitude, — and westward over great plains and across mountain ranges till it reached the confines of Utah and Oregon. It was the unorganized remainder of the territory of Louisiana, acquired from France in 1803, and in extent was ten times as large as the combined area of New York and Pennsylvania. By the Missouri Compromise every square mile of this domain had been honorably devoted to freedom. At the period named Indian tribes roamed at will throughout its whole extent and lighted their camp-fires on the very borders of Missouri and Iowa. Herds of buffalo grazed undisturbed on lands which to-day constitute the sites of large cities. Fort Leavenworth was a far-western outpost, Council Bluffs was on the frontier of civilization, and Omaha had not been named. Adventurous merchants passed over the plains to the South-West with long caravans, engaged in the Santa-Fé trade, and towards the North-West, hunters, trappers, and a few hardy emigrants penetrated the "Platte country," and through mountain passes pointed out by the trail of the Indian and the buffalo had in many instances safely crossed to Oregon. The tide of emigration which had filled Iowa and Wisconsin, and which by the gold excitement of California had for a time been drawn to the Pacific slope, now set again more strongly than ever to the Mississippi valley, demanding and needing new lands for settlement and cultivation. To answer this requirement a movement was made during the closing weeks of Mr. Fillmore's administration to establish the territory of Nebraska. A bill to that effect was passed by a two-thirds vote in the House. The slight opposition that was made came from the South, but its significance was not perceived. When the bill reached the Senate Mr. Douglas, as chairman of the committee on territories, promptly reported it, and made an apparently sincere effort to pass it. He did not succeed. Every senator from the slave-holding States, except those from Missouri, — which was locally interested in having the territory organized, — voted against it; — and the measure, antagonizing other business in which Northern senators were more immediately interested, was laid upon the table two days before President Pierce was inaugurated. The bill had fully recognized the binding force of the Missouri Compromise, and if it had passed, there could have been no pretense for the introduction of slavery in the territory of Nebraska.

Directly after the assurance so impressively given by the President that the " repose " of the country on the slavery question " should suffer no shock during his administration," the bill to organize the Territory of Nebraska was again introduced in the Senate. The motive for its defeat the preceding session was soon made apparent. Mr. Archibald Dixon of Kentucky, the last Whig governor of that State, had been chosen to succeed Mr. Clay in the Senate. But he did not succeed to Mr. Clay's political principles. He belonged to a class of men that had been recently and rapidly growing in the South, — men avowedly and aggressively pro-slavery. Mr. Dixon was the first to strike an open blow against the Missouri Compromise. Mr. Clay had been honorably identified with the pacific work of 1820, and throughout his life believed that it had been effectual in allaying the strife which in his judgment had endangered the Union. It was an alarming fact that his own successor in the Senate — less than two years after Mr. Clay's death — was the first to assail his work and to re-open a controversy which was not to cease till a continent was drenched in blood. Mr. Dixon made no concealment of his motive and his purpose, declaring that he wished the restriction removed because he was a pro-slavery man. He gave notice early in January, 1854, that when the bill to organize the Territory of Nebraska should come before the Senate, he would move that " the Missouri Compromise be repealed, and that the citizens of the several States shall be at liberty to take and hold their slaves within any of the Territories." It was very soon found that this was not a capricious movement by Mr. Dixon alone, but that behind him there was a settled determination on the part of the pro-slavery men to break down the ancient barrier and to remove the honored landmark of 1820.

The Senate had a large Democratic majority, and there was probably not one among them all who had not in the Presidential contest of 1852 publicly and solemnly vowed that the Compromise measures of 1850 were a final settlement of the slavery question, not in any event, nor upon any pretext, to be disturbed. It was specially embarrassing and perilous for Northern senators to violate pledges so recently made, so frequently repeated. It much resembled the breaking of a personal promise, and seemed to the mass of people in the free States to be a gross breach of national honor. To escape the sharp edge of condemnation, sure to follow such a transaction, a pretense was put forth that the Compromise of 1820 was in conflict with the Compromise of 1850, and that it was necessary to repeal the former in order that the doctrine of non-intervention with slavery in the Territories should become the recognized policy for all the public domain of the United States. Mr. Douglas was the first to adopt this construction. Indeed, to him may fairly be ascribed the credit or the discredit of inventing it. He had a strong hold on the South, and in his Congressional life had steadily voted on the pro-slavery side of all public questions. But he instinctively foresaw that his political future would be endangered by advocating the repeal of the Missouri Compromise on the basis and for the reason announced by Mr. Dixon. Hence the resort to the doctrine of non-intervention under which the South should get all they wished by having the right to carry their slaves into the territory, and the North could be conciliated by the presentation of another final settlement of all issues which threatened the perpetuity of the Union.

Instead of the single Territory of Nebraska, Mr. Douglas reported a measure to organize both Kansas and Nebraska; and in one of the sections of the bill the Missouri Compromise of 1820 was declared to be inoperative and void, because "inconsistent with the principle of non-intervention by Congress with slavery in the States and Territories as recognized by the Compromise measures of 1850." The bill further declared that "its true intent and meaning was not to legislate slavery into any Territory or State, and not to exclude it therefrom, but to leave the people perfectly free to regulate their domestic institutions in their own way." The North was fairly stunned by the proposition made by Mr. Douglas. Had he proposed to abolish the Constitution itself the surprise could scarcely have been greater. The acting generation had grown to manhood with profound respect and even reverence for the Missouri Compromise, and had come to regard it almost as sacredly as though it were part of the organic law of the Republic. If a Southern man talked of its repeal it was regarded as the mere bravado of an extremist. But now a Northern senator of remarkable ability, a party leader, a candidate for the Presidency, had reported the measure, and made it a test of Democratic faith, of administration fealty. The contest that followed was severe and prolonged. The bill was before Congress for a period of four months, and was finally forced through to the utter destruction of good faith between the sections. More than forty

Democratic representatives from the North flatly defied party discipline and voted against the repeal. The Democratic representatives from the slave States were consolidated in its favor, with the exception of John Millson, an able member from Virginia, and the venerable Thomas H. Benton of Missouri.

After Colonel Benton's thirty years' service in the Senate had terminated, the city of St. Louis sent him to the House in the autumn of 1852. He had entered the Senate when Missouri came into the Union as the result of the Compromise of 1820. He had remained there until after the Compromise of 1850 was adopted. He denounced the proceeding of Douglas with unsparing severity, and gave his best efforts, but in vain, to defeat the bill. He pointed out the fact that the original Compromise had been forced upon the North by the South, and that the present proposition to repeal it had been initiated "without a memorial, without a petition, without a request from any human being. It was simply and only a contrivance of political leaders, who were using the institution of slavery as a weapon, and rushing the country forward to excitements and to conflicts in which there was no profit to either section, and possibly great harm to both." Colonel Benton belonged to a class of Southern Democrats who were passing away, — of whom he, indeed, was the last in conspicuous station. He represented the Democracy of Andrew Jackson and of Nathaniel Macon, — not the Democracy of Mr. Calhoun. He placed the value of the Union above the value of slavery, and was a relentless foe to all who plotted against the integrity of the government. But his day was past, his power was broken, his influence was gone. Even in his own State he had been beaten, and David R. Atchison installed as leader of the Democratic party. His efforts were vain, his protest unheard; and amid the sorrow and gloom of thinking men, and the riotous rejoicings of those who could not measure the evil of their work, the Douglas Bill was passed. On the thirtieth of May, 1854, the wise and patriotic Compromise of March 6, 1820, was declared to be at an end, and the advocates and the opponents of slavery were invited to a trial of strength on the public domain of the United States.

No previous anti-slavery excitement bore any comparison with that which spread over the North as the discussion progressed, and especially after the bill became a law. It did not merely call forth opposition: it produced almost a frenzy of wrath on the part of thousands and tens of thousands in both the old parties, who had never before taken any part whatever in anti-slavery agitation. So conservative a statesman as Edward Everett, who had succeeded John Davis as senator from Massachusetts, pointed out the fallacy not to say the falsehood of the plea that the Compromise measures of 1850 required or involved this legislation. This plea was an after-thought, a pretense, contradicted by the discussion of 1850 in its entire length and breadth. In the North, conservative men felt that no compromise could acquire weight or sanction or sacredness, if one that had stood for a whole generation could be brushed aside by partisan caprice or by the demands of sectional necessity. The popular fury was further stimulated by the fact that from the territory included in the Louisiana purchase, three slave States had been added to the Union, and as yet only one free State; and that the solemn guaranty securing all the domain north of 36° 30′ was now to be trodden under foot when its operation was likely to prove hostile to slavery and favorable to freedom. From the beginning of the government the slave-holding interest had secured the advantage in the number of States formed from territory added to the original Union. The South had Louisiana, Arkansas, and Missouri out of the purchase from France in 1803, Florida from the purchase from Spain in 1819, and Texas, with its possibility of being divided into four additional States, from the annexation of 1845. The North had only Iowa from the Louisiana purchase and California from the territory ceded by Mexico. The North would not stop to consider its prospective advantages in the territory yet to be settled, while the South could see nothing else. The South realized that although it had secured five States and the North only two, Southern territory was exhausted, while the creation of free States in the North-West had just begun. Stripped of all the disguises with which it was surrounded by the specious cry of non-intervention by Congress, the majority in the North came to see that it was in reality nothing but a struggle between the slave States and the free States, growing more and more intense and more and more dangerous day by day.

The most striking result in the political field, produced by the repeal of the Missouri Compromise, was the utter destruction of the Whig party. Had the Southern Whigs in Congress maintained the sacredness of the work of 1820, the party throughout the country would have been able to make a sturdy contest, notwithstanding the crushing defeat of Scott two years before. Not improbably in the peculiar state of public opinion, the Whigs, by maintaining the Compromise, might have been able to carry the Presidential election of 1856. But with the exception of John Bell in the Senate and seven members of the House, the entire Whig party of the South joined the Democrats in repealing the Compromise. Of these seven, Emerson Etheridge of Tennessee and Theodore G. Hunt of Louisiana deserve especial and honorable mention for the courage with which they maintained their position. But when John M. Clayton of Delaware, who had voted to prohibit slavery in all the Territories, now voted to strike down the only legal barrier to its extension; when Badger of North Carolina, who had been the very soul of conservatism, now joined in the wild cry of the pro-slavery Democrats; when James Alfred Pearce of Maryland and James C. Jones of Tennessee united with Jefferson Davis, the Whig party of the South ceased to exist. Indeed, before this final blow large numbers of Southern Whigs had gone over to the Democracy. Toombs and Stephens and Judah P. Benjamin had been among the foremost supporters of Pierce, and had been specially influential in consolidating the South in his favor. But the great body of Whigs both in the South and in the North did not lose hope of a strong re-organization of their old party until the destruction of the Missouri Compromise had been effected. That was seen and felt by all to be the end.

Thenceforward new alliances were rapidly formed. In the South those Whigs who, though still unwilling to profess an anti-slavery creed, would not unite with the Democrats, were re-organized under the name of the American party, with Humphrey Marshall, Henry Winter Davis, Horace Maynard, and men of that class, for leaders. This party was founded on proscription of foreigners, and with special hostility to the Roman-Catholic Church. It had a fitful and feverish success, and in 1854–5, under the name of *Know-Nothings*, enrolled tens of thousands in secret lodges. But its creed was narrow, its principles were illiberal, and its methods of procedure boyish and undignified. The great body of thinking men in the North saw that the real contest impending was against slavery and not against naturalization laws and ecclesiastical dogmas. The Know-Nothings, therefore, speedily disappeared, and a new party sprang into existence composed of anti-slavery Whigs and anti-slavery Democrats. The latter infused into the ranks of the new organization a spirit and an energy which Whig traditions could never inspire. The same name was not at once adopted in all the free States in 1854, but by the ensuing year there was a general recognition throughout the North that all who intended to make a serious fight against the pro-slavery Democracy would unite under the flag of the Republican party. In its very first effort, without compact organization, without discipline, it rallied the anti-slavery sentiment so successfully as to carry nearly all the free States and to secure a plurality of the members of the House of Representatives. The indignation of the people knew no bounds. Old political landmarks disappeared, and party prejudices of three generations were swept aside in a day. With such success in the outset, the Republicans prepared for a vigorous struggle in the approaching Presidential election.

The anti-slavery development of the North was not more intense than the pro-slavery development of the South. Every other issue was merged in the one absorbing demand by Southern slave-holders for what they sincerely believed to be their rights in the Territories. It was not viewed on either side as an ordinary political contest. It was felt to be a question not of expediency but of morality, not of policy but of honor. It did not merely enlist men. Women took large part in the agitation. It did not end with absorbing the laity. The clergy were as profoundly concerned. The power of the Church on both sides of the dividing-line was used with great effect in shaping public opinion and directing political action. The Missouri Compromise was repealed in May. Before the end of the year a large majority of the people of the North and a large majority of the people of the South were distinctly arrayed against each other on a question which touched the interest, the pride, the conscience, and the religion of all who were concerned in the controversy. Had either side been insincere there would have been voluntary yielding or enforced adjustment. But each felt itself to be altogether in the right and its opponent altogether in the wrong. Thus they stood confronting each other at the close of the year 1854.

It was soon perceived by all, as the sagacious had seen from the first, that the Missouri Compromise had not been repealed merely to exhibit unity in the scope of the United-States statutes respecting slavery in the Territories. This was the euphuistic plea of those Northern senators and representatives who had given dire offense to their constituents by voting for it. It was the clever artifice of Douglas which suggested that construction. It was a deception, and it was contradicted and exposed by the logic of argument in the

North and by the logic of action in the South. No double-dealing was attempted by the Southern men. They understood the question perfectly and left the apologies and explanations to Northern men, who were hard pressed by anti-slavery constituents. Southern men knew that the repeal of the Missouri Compromise gave them a privilege which they had not before enjoyed, — the privilege of settling with their slaves on the rich plains and in the fertile valleys that stretched westward from the Missouri River. In maintaining this privilege, they felt sure of aid from the Executive of the United States, and they had the fullest confidence that in any legal controversy the Federal judiciary would be on their side.

Thus panoplied they made a desperate contest for the possession of Kansas. They had found that all the crops grown in Missouri by slave labor could be as profitably cultivated in Kansas. Securing Kansas, they would gain more than the mere material advantage of an enlarged field for slave labor. New Mexico at that time included all of Arizona; Utah included all of Nevada; Kansas, as organized, absorbed a large part of what is now Colorado, stretched along the eastern and northern boundary of New Mexico, and, crossing the Rocky Mountains, reached the confines of Utah. If Kansas could be made a slave State it would control New Mexico and Utah, and the South could again be placed in a position of political equality if not of command. The repeal of the Missouri Compromise had shown them for the first time that they could absolutely consolidate the Southern vote in Congress in defense of slavery, regardless of differences on all other issues. But this power was of no avail, unless they could regain their equality in the Senate which had been lost by what they considered the mishap of California's admission. While Clay and Benton were in the Senate with their old reverence for the Union and their desire for the ultimate extinction of slavery, California could neither be kept out nor divided on the line of 36° 30′. But the new South, the South of Jefferson Davis and Alexander H. Stephens, of Robert Toombs and Judah P. Benjamin, of James M. Mason and John C. Breckinridge, had made new advances, was inspired by new ambitions, and was determined upon the consolidation of sectional power. The one supreme need was another slave State. If this could be acquired they felt assured that so long as the Union should exist no free State could be admitted without the corresponding admission of another slave State. They would perhaps have been disappointed. Possibly they did not give sufficient heed to the influences which were steadily working against slavery in such States as Delaware and Maryland, threatening desertion in the rear, while the defenders of slavery were battling at the front. They argued, however, and not unnaturally, that prejudice can hold a long contest with principle, and that in the general uprising of the South the tendency of all their old allies would be to remain firm. They reckoned that States with few slaves would continue to stand for Southern institutions as stubbornly as States with many slaves. In all the States of the South emancipation had been made difficult, and free negroes were tolerated, if at all, with great reluctance and with constant protest.

The struggle for Kansas was therefore to be maintained and possession secured at all hazards. Although, as the Southern leaders realized, the free States had flanked them by the admission of California with an anti-slavery constitution, the Southern acquisition of Kansas would pierce the very centre of the army of freedom, and would enable the South thenceforth to dictate terms to the North. Instead of the line of 36° 30′, upon which they had so frequently offered to compromise, as a permanent continental division, they would have carried the northern boundary of slave territory to the 40th parallel of latitude and even beyond. The slave States in pursuing this policy were directed by men who had other designs than those which lay on the surface. Since the struggle of 1850 the dissolution of the Union had been in the minds of many Southern leaders, and, as the older class of statesmen passed away, this design grew and strengthened until it became a fixed policy. They felt that when the time came to strike, it was of the first importance that they should have support and popular strength beyond the Mississippi. California, they were confident, could be carried in their interest, if they could but plant supporting colonies between the Missouri and the Sierras. The Democratic party was dominant in the State, and the Democracy was of the type personated by William M. Gwin. Both her senators voted for the repeal of the Missouri Compromise, and stood by the extremists of the South as steadily as if California bordered on the Gulf of Mexico. Dissolution of the Union on the scale thus projected would, as the authors of the scheme persuaded themselves, be certain of success. From the Mississippi to the Missouri they would carry the new confederacy to the southern line of Iowa. From the Missouri to the line of Utah they would have the 40th degree of latitude; from

Utah westward they would have the 42d parallel, leaving the line of Oregon as the southern boundary of the United States on the Pacific.

This policy was not absolute but alternative. If the slave-holders could maintain their supremacy in the Union, they would prefer to remain. If they were to be outvoted and, as they thought, outraged by free-State majorities, then they would break up the government and form a confederacy of their own. To make such a confederacy effective, they must not take from the Union a relatively small section, but must divide it from ocean to ocean. They could not acquire a majority of the total population, but they aimed to secure by far the larger share of the vast domain comprised in the United States. The design was audacious, but from the stand-point of the men who were committed to it, it was not illogical. Their entire industrial system was founded upon an institution which was bitterly opposed in the free States. They could see no way, and they no longer desired to see a way, by which they might rid themselves of the servile labor which was at once their strength and their weakness. To abandon the institution was to sacrifice four thousand millions of property specially protected by law. It was for the existing generation of the governing class in the South to vote themselves into bankruptcy and penury. Far beyond this, it was in their judgment to blight their land with ignorance and indolence, to be followed by crime and anarchy. Their point of view was so radically different from that held by a large number of Northern people that it left no common ground for action, — scarcely, indeed, an opportunity for reasoning together. In the South they saw and felt their danger, and they determined at all hazards to defend themselves against policies which involved the total destruction of their social and industrial fabric. They were not mere malcontents. They were not pretenders. They did not aim at small things. They had ability and they had courage. They had determined upon mastery within the Union, or a Continental Empire outside of it.

While the South had thus resolved to acquire control of the large Territory of Kansas, the North had equally resolved to save it to freedom. The strife that ensued upon the fertile plains beyond the Missouri might almost be regarded as the opening battle of the civil war. The proximity of a slave State gave to the South an obvious advantage at the beginning of the contest. Many of the Northern emigrants were from New England, and the distance they were compelled to travel exceeded two thousand miles. There were no railroads across Iowa, none across Missouri. But despite all impediments and all discouragements, the free-State emigrants, stimulated by anti-slavery societies organized for the purpose, far outnumbered those from the slave States. Had the vexed question in the Territory been left to actual settlers it would have been at once decided adversely to slavery. But the neighboring inhabitants of Missouri, as the first election approached, invaded the Territory in large numbers, and, with boisterous disturbance and threats of violence, seized the polls, fraudulently elected a pro-slavery Legislature, and chose one of their leaders named Whitfield as delegate to Congress. Over six thousand votes were polled, of which some eight hundred only were cast by actual settlers. There were about three thousand legal voters in the Territory. The total population was somewhat in excess of eight thousand, and there were between two and three hundred slaves. The governor of the Territory, Andrew H. Reeder, a Democrat from Pennsylvania, tried faithfully and earnestly to arrest the progress of fraud and violence ; but he was removed by President Pierce, and Wilson Shannon of Ohio was sent out in his stead. The free-State settlers, defrauded at the regular election, organized an independent movement and chose Governor Reeder their delegate to Congress to contest the seat of Whitfield. These events, rapidly following each other, caused great indignation throughout the country, in the midst of which the Thirty-fourth Congress assembled in December, 1855. After a prolonged struggle, Nathaniel P. Banks was chosen Speaker over William Aiken. It was a significant circumstance, noted at the time, that the successful candidate came from Massachusetts, and the defeated one from South Carolina. It was a still more ominous fact that Banks was chosen by votes wholly from the free States, and that every vote from the slave States was given to Mr. Aiken, except that of Mr. Cullen of Delaware, and that of Henry Winter Davis of Maryland, who declined to vote for either candidate. It was the first instance in the history of the government in which a candidate for Speaker had been chosen without support from both sections. It was a distinctive victory of the free States over the consolidated power of the slave States. It marked an epoch.

The year 1856 opened with this critical, this unprecedented condition of affairs. In all classes there was deep excitement. With thoughtful men, both North and South, there was serious solicitude.

The country approached the strife of another Presidential election with the consciences of men thoroughly aroused, with their passions profoundly stirred.   Three parties were coming into the field, and it seemed impossible that any candidate could secure the approval of a majority of the voters in the Union.   In the Democratic ranks there was angry contention.   President Pierce, who had risked every thing for the South, and had received unmeasured obloquy in the North, was naturally anxious that his administration should be approved by his own party.   With all the patronage at his command, he vigorously sought a renomination.   But the party desired victory, and they feared a contest which involved an approval of the President's recreancy to solemn pledges voluntarily given.   He had been inaugurated with the applause and confidence of a nation.   He was sustained in the end by a helpless faction of a disorganized party.

The distinguished secretary of State suffered with the President. Mr. Marcy had personally disapproved the repeal of the Missouri Compromise, but he made no opposition, and the people held him equally if not doubly guilty.   It was said at the time that New-York friends urged him to save his high reputation by resigning his seat in the cabinet.   But he remained, in the delusive hope that he should receive credit for the evil he might prevent.   He was pertinently reminded that the evil he might prevent would never be be known, whereas the evil to which he consented would be read of all men.   New York had hopelessly revolted from Democratic control, and Mr. Marcy's name was not presented as a Presidential candidate, though he was at that time the ablest statesman of the Democratic party.   Mr. Douglas was also unavailable.   He had gained great popularity in the South by his course in repealing the Missouri Compromise, but he had been visited with signal condemnation in the North.   His own State, always Democratic, which had stood firmly for the party even in the overthrow of 1840, had now failed to sustain him, — had, indeed, pointedly rebuked him by choosing an opposition Legislature and sending Lyman Trumbull, then an anti-slavery Republican, as his colleague in the Senate. General Cass was seventy-four years old, and he was under the same condemnation with Pierce and Marcy and Douglas.   He had voted to repeal the Missouri Compromise, and Michigan, which had never before faltered in his support, now turned against him and embittered his declining years by an expression of popular disapproval which could not have been more emphatic.

The candidates urged for the nomination were all from the North. By a tacit but general understanding, the South repressed the ambition of its leaders and refused to present any one of the prominent statesmen from that section. Southern men designed to put the North to a test, and they wished to give Northern Democrats every possible advantage in waging a warfare in which the fruits of victory were to be wholly enjoyed by the South. If they had wished it, they could have nominated a Southern candidate who was at that moment far stronger than any other man in the Democratic party. General Sam Houston had a personal history as romantic as that of an ancient crusader. He was a native of Virginia, a representative in Congress from Tennessee, and Governor of that State before he was thirty-five. He was the intimate and trusted friend of Jackson. Having resigned his governorship on account of domestic trouble, he fled from civilized life, joined the Indians of the Western plains, roved with them for years, adopted their habits, and was made chief of a tribe. Returning to association with white men, he emigrated to Texas and led the revolt against Mexico, fought battles and was victorious, organized a new republic and was made its President. Then he turned to his native land, bearing in his hand the gift of a great dominion. Once more under the Union flag, he sat in the Capitol as a senator of the United States from Texas. At threescore years he was still in the full vigor of life. Always a member of the Democratic party he was a devoted adherent of the Union, and his love for it had but increased in exile. He stood by Mr. Clay against the Southern Democrats in the angry contest of 1850, declaring that " if the Union must be dismembered " he " prayed God that its ruins might be the monument of his own grave." He " desired no epitaph to tell that he survived it." Against the madness of repealing the Missouri Compromise he entered a protest and a warning. He notified his Southern friends that the dissolution of the Union might be involved in the dangerous step. He alone, of Southern Democrats in the Senate, voted against the mischievous measure. When three thousand clergymen of New England sent their remonstrance against the repeal, they were fiercely attacked and denounced by Douglas and by senators from the South. Houston vindicated their right to speak and did battle for them with a warmth and zeal which specially commended him to Northern sympathy. All these facts combined — his romantic history, his unflinching steadiness of purpose, his unswerving devotion to the Union — would have made him an irresistibly strong candidate had he been presented. But the very sources of his strength were the sources of his weakness. His nomination would have been a rebuke to every man who had voted for the repeal of the Missouri Compromise, and, rather than submit to that, the Southern Democrats, and Northern Democrats like Pierce and Douglas and Cass, would accept defeat. Victory with Houston would be their condemnation. But in rejecting him they lost in large degree the opportunity to recover the strength and popularity and power of the Democratic party which had all been forfeited by the maladministration of Pierce.

With Houston impracticable, other Southern candidates purposely withheld, and all the Northern candidates in Congress or of the administration disabled, the necessity of the situation pointed to one man. The Democratic managers in whose hands the power lay were not long in descrying him. Mr. Buchanan had gone to England as minister directly after the inauguration of Pierce. He had been absent from the country during all the troubles and the blunders of the Democracy, and never before was an *alibi* so potential in acquitting a man of actual or imputed guilt. He had been a candidate for the Presidency ever since 1844, but had not shown much strength. He was originally a Federalist. He was somewhat cold in temperament and austere in manners, but of upright character and blameless life. He lacked the affability of Cass, the gracious heartiness of Pierce, the bluff cordiality of Douglas. But he was a man of ability, and had held high rank as senator and as secretary of State. Above all he had never given a vote offensive to the South. Indeed, his Virginia friend, Henry A. Wise, boasted that his record was as spotless as that of Calhoun.

Buchanan's hour had come. He was a necessity to the South, a necessity to his party; and against the combined force of all the ambitious men who sought the place, he was nominated. But he had a severe struggle. President Pierce and Senator Douglas each made a persistent effort. On the first ballot Buchanan received 135 votes, Pierce 122, Douglas 33. Through sixteen ballots the contest was stubbornly maintained, Buchanan gaining steadily but slowly. Pierce was at last withdrawn, and the convention gave Buchanan 168, Douglas 121. No further resistance was made, and, amid acclamation and rejoicing, Buchanan was declared to be the unanimous choice of the convention. Major John C. Breckinridge of Kentucky, a young man of popularity and promise, was nominated for the Vice-Presidency.

Before the nomination of Buchanan and Breckinridge another Presidential ticket had been placed in the field. The pro-slavery section of the American party and the ghastly remnant of the Whigs had presented Mr. Fillmore for the Presidency, and had associated with him Andrew Jackson Donelson of Tennessee as candidate for the Vice-Presidency. On the engrossing question of the day Mr. Buchanan and Mr. Fillmore did not represent antagonistic ideas, and between them there could be no contest to arouse enthusiasm or even to enlist interest in the North. The movement for Fillmore afforded a convenient shelter for that large class of men who had not yet made up their minds as to the real issue of slavery extension or slavery prohibition.

The Republican party had meanwhile been organizing and consolidating. During the years 1854 and 1855 it had acquired control of the governments in a majority of the free States, and it promptly called a national convention to meet in Philadelphia in June, 1856. The Democracy saw at once that a new and dangerous opponent was in the field, — an opponent that stood upon principle and shunned expediency, that brought to its standard a great host of young men, and that won to its service a very large proportion of the talent, the courage, and the eloquence of the North. The convention met for a purpose and it spoke boldly. It accepted the issue as presented by the men of the South, and it offered no compromise. In its ranks were all shades of anti-slavery opinion, — the patient Abolitionist, the Free-Soiler of the Buffalo platform, the Democrats who had supported the Wilmot Proviso, the Whigs who had followed Seward.

There was no strife about candidates. Mr. Seward was the recognized head of the party, but he did not desire the nomination. He agreed with his faithful mentor, Thurlow Weed, that his time had not come, and that his sphere of duty was still in the Senate. Salmon P. Chase was Governor of Ohio, waiting re-election to the Senate, and, like Seward, not anxious for a nomination where election was regarded as improbable if not impossible. The more conservative and timid section of the party advocated the nomination of Judge McLean of the Supreme Court, who for many years had enjoyed a shadowy mention for the Presidency in Whig journals of a certain type. But Judge McLean was old and the Republican party was young. He belonged to the past, the party was looking to the future. It demanded a more energetic and attractive candidate, and John C. Frémont was chosen on the first ballot. He was forty-three years of age, with a creditable record in the Regular Army, and wide fame as a scientific explorer in the Western mountain ranges, then the *terra incognita* of the continent. He was a native of South Carolina, and had married the brilliant and accomplished daughter of Colonel Benton. Always a member of the Democratic party, he was so closely identified with the early settlement of California that he was elected one of her first senators. To the tinge of romance in his history were added the attractions of a winning address and an auspicious name.

The movement in his behalf had been quietly and effectively organized for several months preceding the convention. It had been essentially aided if not indeed originated by the elder Francis P. Blair, who had the skill derived from long experience in political management. Mr. Blair was a devoted friend of Benton, had been intimate with Jackson, and intensely hostile to Calhoun. As editor of the *Globe*, he had exercised wide influence during the Presidential terms of Jackson and Van Buren, but when Polk was inaugurated he was supplanted in administration confidence by Thomas Ritchie of the State-rights' school, who was brought from Virginia to found another paper. Mr. Blair was a firm Union man, and, though he had never formally withdrawn from the Democratic party, he was now ready to leave it because of the Disunion tendencies of its Southern leaders. He was a valuable friend to Frémont, and gave to him the full advantage of his experience and his sagacity.

William L. Dayton of New Jersey, who had served with distinction in the Senate, was selected for the Vice-Presidency. His principal competitor in the only ballot which was taken was Abraham Lincoln of Illinois. This was the first time that Mr. Lincoln was conspicuously named outside of his own State. He had been a member of the Thirtieth Congress, 1847-9, but being a modest man he had so little forced himself into notice that when his name was proposed for Vice-President, inquiries as to who he was were heard from all parts of the convention.

The principles enunciated by the Democratic and Republican parties on the slavery question formed the only subject for discussion during the canvass in the free States. From the beginning no

doubt was expressed that Mr. Buchanan would find the South practically consolidated in his favor.   Electoral tickets for Frémont were
not presented in the slave States, and Fillmore's support in that
section was weakened by his obvious inability to carry any of the
free States.   The canvass, therefore, rapidly narrowed to a contest
between Buchanan and Frémont in the North.   The Republican
Convention had declared it to be " both the right and the imperative
duty of Congress to prohibit in the Territories those twin relics of
barbarism, — polygamy and slavery."   The Democratic Convention
had presented a very elaborate and exhaustive series of resolutions
touching the slavery question.   They indorsed the repeal of the Missouri Compromise, and recognized the " right of the people of all the
Territories to form a constitution with or without domestic slavery."
The resolution was artfully constructed.   Read in one way it gave to
the people of the Territories the right to determine the question for
themselves.   It thus upheld the doctrine of "popular scvereignty "
which Mr. Douglas had announced as the very spirit of the Act
organizing Kansas and Nebraska.   A closer analysis of the Democratic declaration, however, showed that this " popular sovereignty "
was not to be exercised until the people of the Territory were sufficiently numerous to form a State constitution and apply for admission to the Union, and that meanwhile in all the Territories the
slave-holder had the right to settle and to be protected in the possession of his peculiar species of property.   In fine, the Republicans
declared in plain terms that slavery should by positive law of the
nation be excluded from the Territories.   The Democrats flatly
opposed the doctrine of Congressional prohibition, but left a margin
for doubt as to the true construction of the Constitution, and of the
Act repealing the Missouri Compromise, thus enabling their partisans to present one issue in the North, and another in the South.

The Democratic candidate in his letter of acceptance did not
seek to resolve the mystery of the platform, but left the question
just as he found it in the resolutions of the convention.   The result
was that Northern people supported Mr. Buchanan in the belief, so
energetically urged by Mr. Douglas, that the people of the Territories had the right to determine the slavery question for themselves
at any time.   The Southern people supported Mr. Buchanan in the
full faith that slavery was to be protected in the Territories until
a State government should be formed and admission to the Union
secured.   The Democratic doctrine of the North and the Demo-

cratic doctrine of the South were, therefore, in logic and in fact, irreconcilably hostile. By the one, slavery could never enter a Territory unless the inhabitants thereof desired and approved it. By the other, slavery had a foot-hold in the Territories under the Constitution of the United States, and could not be dislodged or disturbed by the inhabitants of a Territory even though ninety-nine out of every hundred were opposed to it. In the Territorial Legislatures laws might be passed to protect slavery but not to exclude it. From such contradictory constructions in the same party, conflicts were certain to arise.

The Democrats of the North sought, not unsuccessfully, to avoid the slavery question altogether. They urged other considerations upon popular attention. Mr. Buchanan was presented as a National candidate, supported by troops of friends in every State of the Union. Frémont was denounced as a sectional candidate, whose election by Northern votes on an anti-slavery platform would dissolve the Union. This incessant cry exerted a wide influence in the North and was especially powerful in commercial circles. But in spite of it, Frémont gained rapidly in the free States. The condition of affairs in Kansas imparted to his supporters a desperate energy, based on principle and roused to anger. An elaborate and exciting speech on the "Crime against Kansas," by Senator Sumner, was followed by an assault from Preston S. Brooks, a member of the House from South Carolina, which seriously injured Mr. Sumner, and sensibly increased the exasperation of the North. When a resolution of the House to expel Brooks was under consideration, he boasted that "a blow struck by him then would be followed by a revolution." This but added fuel to a Northern flame already burning to white-heat. Voters by tens of thousands declared they did not desire a Union which was held together by the forbearance or permission of any man or body of men, and they welcomed a test of any character that should determine the supremacy of the Constitution and the strength of the government.

The canvass grew in animation and earnestness to the end, the Republicans gaining strength before the people of the North every day. But Buchanan's election was not a surprise. Indeed, it had been generally expected. He received the electoral votes of every Southern State except Maryland, which pronounced for Fillmore. In the North, New Jersey, Pennsylvania, Indiana, Illinois, and California voted for Buchanan. The other eleven free States, beginning with Maine and ending with Iowa, declared for Frémont. The popular vote was for Buchanan 1,838,169, Frémont 1,341,264, Fillmore 874,534. With the people, therefore, Mr. Buchanan was in a minority, the combined opposition outnumbering his vote by nearly four hundred thousand.

The Republicans, far from being discouraged, felt and acted as men who had won the battle. Indeed, the moral triumph was theirs, and they believed that the actual victory at the polls was only postponed. The Democrats were mortified and astounded by the large popular vote against them. The loss of New York and Ohio, the narrow escape from defeat in Pennsylvania, the rebuke of Michigan to their veteran leader General Cass, intensified by the choice of Chandler as his successor in the Senate, the absolute consolidation of New England against them, all tended to humiliate and discourage the party. They had lost ten States which General Pierce had carried in 1852, and they had a watchful, determined foe in the field, eager for another trial of strength. The issue was made, the lines of battle were drawn. Freedom or slavery in the Territories was to be fought to the end, without flinching, and without compromise.

Mr. Buchanan came to the Presidency under very different auspices from those which had attended the inauguration of President Pierce. The intervening four years had written important chapters in the history of the slavery contest. In 1853 there was no organized opposition that could command even a respectable minority in a single State. In 1857 a party distinctly and unequivocally pledged to resist the extension of slavery into free territory had control of eleven free States and was hotly contesting the possession of the others. The distinct and avowed marshaling of a solid North against a solid South had begun, and the result of the Presidential election of 1856 settled nothing except that a mightier struggle was in the future.

After Buchanan's inauguration events developed rapidly. The Democrats had carried the House, and therefore had control of every department of the government. The effort to force slavery upon Kansas was resumed with increased zeal. Strafford's policy of "thorough" was not more resolute or more absolute than that now adopted by the Southern leaders with a new lease of power confirmed to them by the result of the election. The Supreme Court came to their aid, and, not long after the new administration was installed, delivered their famous decision in the Dred Scott case.

This case involved the freedom of a single family that had been held as slaves, but it gave occasion to the Court for an exhaustive treatment of the political question which was engrossing public attention.   The conclusion of the best legal minds of the country was that the opinion of the Court went far beyond the real question at issue, and that many of its most important points were to be regarded as *obiter dicta*.   The Court declared that the Act of Congress prohibiting slavery in the Territories north of 36° 30′ was unconstitutional and void.   The repeal of the Missouri Compromise was therefore approved by the highest judicial tribunal.   Not only was the repeal approved, its re-enactment was forbidden.   No matter how large a majority might be returned to Congress in favor of again setting up the old landmark which had stood in peace and in honor for thirty-four years, with the sanction of all departments of the government, the Supreme Court had issued an edict that it could not be done.   The Court had declared that slavery was as much entitled to protection on the national domain as any other species of property, and that it was unconstitutional for Congress to decree freedom for a Territory of the United States.   The pro-slavery interest had apparently won a great triumph.   They naturally claimed that the whole question was settled in their favor. But in fact the decision of the Court had only rendered the contest more intense and more bitter.   It was received throughout the North with scorn and indignation.   It entered at once into the political discussions of the people, and remained there until, with all other issues on the slavery question, it was remanded to the arbitrament of war.

Five of the judges — an absolute majority of the court — were Southern men, and had always been partisan Democrats of the State-rights' school.   People at once remembered that every other class of lawyers in the South had for thirty years been rigidly excluded from the bench.   John J. Crittenden had been nominated and rejected by a Democratic Senate.   George E. Badger of North Carolina had shared the same fate.   They were followers of Clay, and not to be trusted by the new South in any exigency where the interests of slavery and the perpetuity of the Union should come in conflict.   Instead, therefore, of strengthening the Democratic party, the whole effect of the Dred Scott decision was to develop a more determined type of anti-slavery agitation.   This tendency was promoted by the lucid and exhaustive opinion of

Benjamin R. Curtis, one of the two dissenting judges.   Judge Curtis was not a Republican.   He had been a Whig of the most conservative type, appointed to the bench by President Fillmore through the influence of Mr. Webster and the advice of Rufus Choate.   In legal learning, and in dignity and purity of character, he was unsurpassed. His opinion became, therefore, of inestimable value to the cause of freedom.   It represented the well-settled conclusion of the most learned jurists, was in harmony with the enlightened conscience of the North, and gave a powerful rallying-cry to the opponents of slavery.   It upheld with unanswerable argument the absolute right of Congress to prohibit slavery in all the Territories of the Union. Every judge delivered his views separately, but the dissenting opinion of Judge McLean, as well as of the six who sustained the views of the Chief Justice, arrested but a small share of public attention.   The argument for the South had been made by the venerable and learned Chief Justice.   The argument for the North had been made by Justice Curtis.   Perhaps in the whole history of judicial decisions no two opinions were ever so widely read by the mass of people outside the legal profession.

It was popularly believed that the whole case was made up in order to afford an opportunity for the political opinions delivered by the Court.   This was an extreme view not justified by the facts. But in the judgment of many conservative men there was a delay in rendering the decision which had its origin in motives that should not have influenced a judicial tribunal.   The purport and scope of the decision were undoubtedly known to President Pierce before the end of his term, and Mr. Buchanan imprudently announced in his Inaugural address that " the point of time when the people of a Territory can decide the question of slavery for themselves " will " be speedily and finally settled by the Supreme Court, before whom it is now pending."   How Mr. Buchanan could know, or how he was entitled to know, that a question not directly or necessarily involved in a case pending before the Supreme Court " would be speedily and finally settled " became a subject of popular inquiry.   Anti-slavery speakers and anti-slavery papers indulged in severe criticism both of Mr. Buchanan and the Court, declaring that the independence of the co-ordinate branches of the government was dangerously invaded when the Executive was privately advised of a judicial decision in advance of its delivery by the Court. William Pitt Fessenden, who always spoke with precision and never with passion, asserted in the Senate that the Court, after hearing the argument, had reserved its judgment until the Presidential election was decided.   He avowed his belief that Mr. Buchanan would have been defeated if the decision had not been withheld, and that in the event of Frémont's election " we should never have heard of a doc. trine so utterly at variance with all truth, so utterly destitute of all legal logic, so founded on error, and so unsupported by any thing resembling argument."

Mr. Lincoln, whose singular powers were beginning to be appreciated, severely attacked the decision in a public speech in Illinois, not merely for its doctrine, but for the mode in which the decision had been brought about, and the obvious political intent of the judges. He showed how the Kansas-Nebraska Act left the people of the Territories perfectly free to settle the slavery question for themselves, "subject only to the Constitution of the United States!" That qualification he said was " the exactly fitted niche for the Dred Scott decision to come in and declare the perfect freedom to be no freedom at all." He then gave a humorous illustration by asking in homely but telling phrase, " if we saw a lot of framed timbers gotten out at different times and places by different workmen, — Stephen and Franklin and Roger and James, — and if we saw these timbers joined together and exactly make the frame of a house, with tenons and mortises all fitting, what is the conclusion? We find it impossible not to believe that Stephen and Franklin and Roger and James all understood one another from the beginning, and all worked upon a common plan before the first blow was struck." This quaint mode of arraigning the two Presidents, the Chief Justice and Senator Douglas, was extraordinarily effective with the masses. In a single paragraph, humorously expressed, he had framed an indictment against four men upon which he lived to secure a conviction before the jury of the American people.

The decision was rendered especially odious throughout the North by the use of certain unfortunate expressions which in the heat of the hour were somewhat distorted by the anti-slavery press, and made to appear unwarrantably offensive. But there was no misrepresentation and no misunderstanding of the essential position of the Court on the political question. It was unmistakably held that ownership in slaves was as much entitled to protection under the Constitution in the Territories of the United States as any other species of property, and that Congress possessed no power over the subject except the power to legislate in aid of slavery. The decision was at war with the practice and traditions of the government from its foundation, and set aside the matured convictions of two generations of conservative statesmen from the South as well as from the North. It proved injurious to the Court, which thenceforward was assailed most bitterly in the North and defended with intemperate zeal in the South. Personally upright and honorable as the judges were individually known to be, there was a conviction in the minds of a majority of Northern people, that on all issues affecting the institution of slavery they were unable to deliver a just judgment; that an Abolitionist was, in their sight, the chief of sinners, deserving to be suppressed by law ; that the anti-slavery agitation was conducted, according to their belief, by two classes, — fanatics and knaves, — both of whom should be promptly dealt with; the fanatics in strait-jackets and the knaves at the cart's tail.

Chief Justice Taney, who delivered the opinion which proved so obnoxious throughout the North, was not only a man of great attainments, but was singularly pure and upright in his life and conversation. Had his personal character been less exalted, or his legal learning less eminent, there would have been less surprise and less indignation. But the same qualities which rendered his judgment of apparent value to the South, called out intense hostility in the North. The lapse of years, however, cools the passions and tempers the judgment. It has brought many anti-slavery men to see that an unmerited share of the obloquy properly attaching to the decision has been visited on the Chief Justice, and that it was unfair to place him under such condemnation, while two associate Justices in the North, Grier and Nelson, joined in the decision without incurring special censure, and lived in honor and veneration to the end of their judicial careers. While, therefore, time has in no degree abated Northern hostility to the Dred Scott decision, it has thrown a more generous light upon the character and action of the eminent Chief Justice who pronounced it. More allowance is made for the excitement and for what he believed to be the exigency of the hour, for the sentiments in which he had been educated, for the force of association, and for his genuine belief that he was doing a valuable work towards the preservation of the Union. His views were held by millions of people around him, and he was swept along by a current which with so many had proved irresistible. Coming to the

Bench from Jackson's Cabinet, fresh from the angry controversies of that partisan era, he had proved a most acceptable and impartial judge, earning renown and escaping censure until he dealt directly with the question of slavery. Whatever harm he may have done in that decision was speedily overruled by war, and the country can now contemplate a venerable jurist, in robes that were never soiled by corruption, leading a long life of labor and sacrifice, and achieving a fame in his profession second only to that of Marshall.

The aversion with which the extreme anti-slavery men regarded Chief Justice Taney was strikingly exhibited during the session of Congress following his death. The customary mark of respect in providing a marble bust of the deceased to be placed in the Supreme Court room was ordered by the House without comment or objection. In the Senate the bill was regularly reported from the Judiciary Committee by the chairman, Mr. Trumbull of Illinois, who was at that time a recognized leader in the Republican party. The proposition to pay respect to the memory of the judge who had pronounced the Dred Scott decision was at once savagely attacked by Mr. Sumner. Mr. Trumbull in reply warmly defended the character of the Chief Justice, declaring that he "had added reputation to the Judiciary of the United States throughout the world, and that he was not to be hooted down by exclamations about an emancipated country. Suppose he did make a wrong decision. No man is infallible. He was a great, learned, able judge."

Mr. Sumner rejoined with much temper. He said that "Taney would be hooted down the pages of history, and that an emancipated country would fix upon his name the stigma it deserved. He had administered justice wickedly, had degraded the Judiciary, and had degraded the age." Mr. Wilson followed Mr. Sumner in a somewhat impassioned speech, denouncing the Dred Scott decision "as the greatest crime in the judicial annals of the Republic," and declaring it to be "the abhorrence, the scoff, the jeer, of the patriotic hearts of America." Mr. Reverdy Johnson answered Mr. Sumner with spirit, and pronounced an eloquent eulogium upon Judge Taney. He said, "the senator from Massachusetts will be happy if his name shall stand as high upon the historic page as that of the learned judge who is now no more." Mr. Johnson directed attention to the fact that, whether right or wrong, the Dred Scott decision was one in which a majority of the Supreme Court had concurred, and therefore no special odium should be attached to the name of the venerable Chief Justice. Mr. Johnson believed the decision to be right, and felt that his opinion on a question of law was at least entitled to as much respect as that of either of the senators from Massachusetts, "one of whom did not pretend to be a lawyer at all, while the other was a lawyer for only a few months." He proceeded to vindicate the historical accuracy of the Chief Justice, and answered Mr. Sumner with that amplitude and readiness which Mr. Johnson displayed in every discussion involving legal questions.

Mr. Sumner's protest was vigorously seconded by Mr. Hale of New Hampshire and Mr. Wade of Ohio. The former said that a monument to Taney "would give the lie to all that had been said by the friends of justice, liberty, and down-trodden humanity," respecting the iniquity of the Dred Scott decision. Mr. Wade violently opposed the proposition. He avowed his belief that the "Dred Scott case was got up to give judicial sanction to the enormous iniquity that prevailed in every branch of our government at that period." He declared that "the greater you make Judge Taney's legal acumen the more you dishonor his memory by showing that he sinned against light and knowledge." He insisted that the people of Ohio, whose opinions he professed to represent, "would pay two thousand dollars to hang the late Chief Justice in effigy rather than one thousand dollars for a bust to commemorate his merits."

Mr. McDougall of California spoke in favor of the bill, and commented on the rudeness of Mr. Sumner's speech. Mr. Carlile of West Virginia spoke very effectively in praise of the Chief Justice. If the decision was harsh, he said, no one was justified in attributing it to the personal feelings or desires of the Chief Justice. It was the law he was expounding, and he did it ably and conscientiously. Mr. Sumner concluded the debate by a reply to Reverdy Johnson. He said that, in listening to the senator from Maryland, he was "reminded of a character, known to the Roman Church, who always figures at the canonization of a saint as the *Devil's advocate.*" He added that, if he could help it, "Taney should never be recognized as a saint by any vote of Congress." The incidents of the debate and the names of the participants are given as affording a good illustration of the tone and temper of the times. It was made evident that the opponents of the bill, under

Mr. Sumner's lead, would not permit it to come to a vote. It was therefore abandoned on the 23d of February, 1865.

Nine years after these proceedings, in January, 1874, the name of another Chief Justice, who had died during the recess, came before Congress for honor and commemoration. The Senate was still controlled by a large Republican majority, though many changes had taken place. All the senators who had spoken in the previous debate were gone, except Mr. Sumner, who had meanwhile been chosen for his fourth term, and Mr. Wilson, who had been elevated to the Vice-Presidency. Mr. Howe of Wisconsin, a more radical Republican than Mr. Trumbull, reported from the Judiciary Committee a bill originally proposed by Senator Stevenson of Kentucky, paying the same tribute of respect to Roger Brooke Taney and Salmon Portland Chase. The bill was passed without debate and with the unanimous consent of the Senate.

Mr. Taney was appointed Chief Justice in 1836, when in his sixtieth year. He presided over the court until his death in October, 1864, a period of twenty-eight years. The Dred Scott decision received no respect after Mr. Lincoln became President, and, without reversal by the court, was utterly disregarded. When Mr. Chase became Chief Justice, colored persons were admitted to practice in the courts of the United States. When President Lincoln, in 1861, authorized the denial of the writ of *habeas corpus* to persons arrested on a charge of treason, Chief Justice Taney delivered an opinion in the case of John Merryman, denying the President's power to suspend the writ, declaring that Congress only was competent to do it. The Executive Department paid no attention to the decision, and Congress, at the ensuing session, added its sanction to the suspension. The Chief Justice, though loyal to the Union, was not in sympathy with the policy or the measures of Mr. Lincoln's administration.

CHAPTER VII.

REVIEW (*continued*). — CONTINUANCE OF THE STRUGGLE FOR KANSAS. — LIST OF GOV-
ERNORS. — ROBERT J. WALKER APPOINTED GOVERNOR BY PRESIDENT BUCHANAN.
— HIS FAILURE. — THE LECOMPTON CONSTITUTION FRAUDULENTLY ADOPTED. — ITS
CHARACTER. — IS TRANSMITTED TO CONGRESS BY PRESIDENT BUCHANAN. — HE
RECOMMENDS THE ADMISSION OF KANSAS UNDER ITS PROVISIONS. — PRONOUNCES
KANSAS A SLAVE STATE. — GIVES FULL SCOPE AND EFFECT TO THE DRED SCOTT
DECISION. — SENATOR DOUGLAS REFUSES TO SUSTAIN THE LECOMPTON INIQUITY. —
HIS POLITICAL EMBARRASSMENT. — BREAKS WITH THE ADMINISTRATION. — VALUE
OF HIS INFLUENCE AGAINST SLAVERY IN KANSAS. — LECOMPTON BILL PASSES THE
SENATE. — COULD NOT BE FORCED THROUGH THE HOUSE. — THE ENGLISH BILL
SUBSTITUTED AND PASSED. — KANSAS SPURNS THE BRIBE. — DOUGLAS REGAINS HIS
POPULARITY WITH NORTHERN DEMOCRATS. — ILLINOIS REPUBLICANS BITTERLY
HOSTILE TO HIM. — ABRAHAM LINCOLN NOMINATED TO CONTEST THE RE-ELECTION
OF DOUGLAS TO THE SENATE. — LINCOLN CHALLENGES DOUGLAS TO A PUBLIC
DISCUSSION. — CHARACTER OF EACH AS A DEBATER. — THEY MEET SEVEN TIMES
IN DEBATE. — DOUGLAS RE-ELECTED. — SOUTHERN SENATORS ARRAIGN DOUGLAS.
— HIS DEFIANT ANSWER. — DANGER OF SECTIONAL DIVISION IN THE DEMOCRATIC
PARTY.

THE Dred Scott decision, in connection with the Democratic
triumph in the national election, had a marked effect upon the
struggle for Kansas. The pro-slavery men felt fresh courage for
the work, as they found themselves assured of support from the
administration, and upheld by the dogmas of the Supreme Court.
The Territory thus far had been one continued scene of disorder
and violence. For obvious reasons, the administration of President
Pierce had selected its governors from the North, and each, in succession, failed to placate the men who were bent on making Kansas
a slave State. Andrew H. Reeder, Wilson Shannon, John W. Geary,
had, each in turn, tried, and each in turn failed. Mr. Buchanan
now selected Robert J. Walker for the difficult task. Mr. Walker
was a Southern man in all his relations, though by birth a Pennsylvanian. He had held high stations, and possessed great ability. It
was believed that he, if any one, could govern the Territory in the
interest of the South, and, at the same time, retain a decent degree
of respect and confidence in the North. As an effective aid to this

policy, Frederick P. Stanton, who had acquired an honorable reputation as representative in Congress from Tennessee, was sent out as secretary of the Territory.

Governor Walker failed. He could do much, but he could not placate an element that was implacable. Contrary to his desires, and against his authority, a convention, called by the fraudulent Legislature, and meeting at Lecompton, submitted a pro-slavery constitution to the people, preparatory to asking the admission of Kansas as a State. The people were not permitted to vote for or against the constitution, but were narrowed to the choice of taking the constitution with slavery or the constitution without slavery. If the decision should be adverse to slavery, there were still some provisions in the constitution, not submitted to popular decision, which would postpone the operation of the free clause. The whole contrivance was fraudulent, wicked, and in retrospect incredible. Naturally the Free-state men refused to have any thing to do with the scandalous device, intended to deceive and betray them. The constitution with slavery was, therefore, adopted by an almost unanimous vote of those who were not citizens of Kansas. Many thousands of votes were returned which were never cast at all, either by citizens of Kansas or marauders from Missouri. It is not possible, without using language that would seem immoderate, to describe the enormity of the whole transaction. The constitution no more represented the will or the wishes of the people of Kansas than of the people of Ohio or Vermont.

Shameful and shameless as was the entire procedure, it was approved by Mr. Buchanan. The Lecompton Constitution was transmitted to Congress, accompanied by a message from the President recommending the prompt admission of the State. He treated the anti-slavery population of Kansas as in rebellion against lawful authority, recognized the invaders from Missouri as rightfully entitled to form a constitution for the State, and declared that "Kansas is at this moment (Feb. 2, 1858) as much a slave State as Georgia or South Carolina." The Dred Scott decision occupied a prominent place in this extraordinary message and received the most liberal interpretation in favor of slavery. The President declared that "it has been solemnly adjudged by the highest judicial tribunal known to our laws that slavery exists in Kansas by virtue of the Constitution of the United States." This was giving the fullest scope to the extreme and revolting doctrine put forward by the advocates of slavery, and, had it been made effective respecting the Territories, there are many reasons for believing that a still more offensive step might have been taken respecting the anti-slavery action of the States.

The attempt to admit Kansas, under the Lecompton Constitution, proved disastrous to the Democratic party. The first decided break was that of Senator Douglas. He refused to sustain the iniquity. He had gone far with the pro-slavery men, but he refused to take this step. He had borne great burdens in their interest, but this was the additional pound that broke the back of his endurance. When the Dred Scott decision was delivered, Mr. Douglas had applauded it, and, as Mr. Lincoln charged, had assented to it before it was pronounced. With his talent for political devices, he had doubtless contrived some argument or fallacy by which he could reconcile that judicial edict with his doctrine of "popular sovereignty," and thus maintain his standing with the Northern Democracy without losing his hold on the South. But events traveled too rapidly for him. The pro-slavery men were so eager for the possession of Kansas that they could not adjust their measures to the needs of Mr. Douglas's political situation. They looked at the question from one point, Mr. Douglas from another. They saw that if Kansas could be forced into the Union with the Lecompton Constitution they would gain a slave State. Mr. Douglas saw that if he should aid in that political crime he would lose Illinois. It was more important to the South to secure Kansas as a slave State than to carry Illinois for Mr. Douglas. It was more important for Mr. Douglas to hold Illinois for himself than to give the control of Kansas to the South. Indeed, his Northern friends had been for some time persuaded that his only escape from the dangerous embarrassments surrounding him was in the admission of Kansas as a free State. If the Missouri Compromise had not been repealed, a free State was assured. If Kansas should become a slave State in consequence of that repeal, it would, in the excited condition of the popular mind, crush Douglas in the North, and bring his political career to a discreditable end.

Mr. Douglas had come, therefore, to the parting of the ways. He realized that he was rushing on political destruction, and that, if he supported the vulgar swindle perpetrated at Lecompton, he would be repudiated by the great State which had exalted him and almost idolized him as a political leader. He determined, therefore, to take a bold stand against the administration on this issue. It was an important event, not only to himself, but to his party; not only to his party, but to the country. Rarely, in our history, has the action of a single person been attended by a public interest so universal; by applause so hearty in the North, by denunciation so bitter in the South. In the debate which followed, Douglas exhibited great power. He had a tortuous record to defend, but he defended it with extraordinary ability and adroitness. From time to time, during the progress of the contest, he was on the point of yielding to some compromise which would have destroyed the heroism and value of his position. But he was sustained by the strong will of others when he himself wavered — appalled, as he often was, by the sacrifice he was making of the Southern support, for which he had labored so long, and endured so much.

Senator Broderick of California imparted largely of his own courage and enthusiasm to Douglas at the critical juncture, and perhaps saved him from a surrender of his proud position. Throughout the entire contest Broderick showed remarkable vigor and determination. Considering the defects of his intellectual training in early life, he displayed unusual power as a political leader and public speaker. He was a native of Washington, born of Irish parents, and was brought up to the trade of a stone-mason. He went to California among the pioneers of 1849, and soon after took part in the fierce political contests of the Pacific coast. Though a Democrat, he instinctively took the Northern side against the arrogant domination of the Southern wing of the party, led by William M. Gwin. Broderick was elected to the United States Senate as Gwin's colleague in 1856, and at once joined Douglas in opposition to the Lecompton policy of the administration. His position aroused fierce hostility on the part of the Democratic leaders of California. The contest grew so bitter in the autumn of 1859, when Broderick was canvassing his State, as to lead to a duel with Judge Terry, a prominent Democrat of Southern birth. Broderick was killed at the first fire. The excitement was greater in the country than ever attended a duel, except when Hamilton fell at the hands of Burr in 1804. The Graves and Cilley duel of 1838, with its fatal ending, affected the whole nation, but not so profoundly as did the death of Broderick. The oration of Senator Baker, delivered in San Francisco at the funeral, so stirred the people that violence was feared. The bloody tragedy influenced political parties, and contributed in no small degree to Lincoln's triumph in California the ensuing year.

In the peculiar position in which Douglas was placed, still maintaining his membership of the Democratic party while opposing the administration on the Lecompton question, he naturally resorted to arguments which were not always of a character to enlist the approval of men conscientiously opposed to slavery. The effect of the arguments, however, was invaluable to those who were resisting the imposition of slavery upon Kansas against the wish of a majority of her people, and Republicans could be content with the end without justifying the means. Douglas frankly avowed that he did not care whether slavery was voted up or voted down, but he demanded that an honest, untrammeled ballot should be secured to the citizens of the Territory. Without the aid of Douglas, the "Crime against Kansas," so eloquently depicted by Mr. Sumner, would have been complete. With his aid, it was prevented.

The Lecompton Bill passed the Senate by a vote of 33 to 25. Besides Broderick, Douglas carried with him only two Democratic senators, — Stuart of Michigan, and Pugh of Ohio. The two remaining members of the old Whig party from the South, who had been wandering as political orphans since the disastrous defeat of 1852, — Bell of Tennessee, and Crittenden of Kentucky, — honored themselves and the ancient Whig traditions by voting against the bill. In view of the events of the preceding four years, it was a significant spectacle in the Senate when Douglas voted steadily with Seward and Sumner and Fessenden and Wade against the political associations of a lifetime. It meant, to the far-seeing, more than a temporary estrangement, and it foretold results in the political field more important than any which had been developed since the formation of the Republican party.

The resistance to the Lecompton Bill in the House was unconquerable. The Administration could not, with all its power and patronage, enforce its passage. Anxious to avert the mortification of an absolute and unqualified defeat, the supporters of the scheme changed their ground, and offered a new measure, moved by Mr. William H. English of Indiana, submitting the entire constitution to a vote of the people If adopted, the constitution carried with it a generous land grant to the new State. If rejected, the alternative was not only the withdrawal of the land grant, but indefinite postponement of the whole question of admission. It was simply a bribe, cunningly and unscrupulously contrived, to induce the people of Kansas to accept a pro-slavery constitution. It was not so outrageous as it would have been to force the constitution upon the people without allowing them to vote upon it at all, and it gave a shadow of excuse to certain Democrats, who did not wish to separate from their party, for returning to the ranks. The bill was at last forced through the House by 112 votes to 103. Twelve Democrats, to their honor be it said, refused to yield. Douglas held all his political associates from Illinois, while the President failed to consolidate the Democrats from Pennsylvania. John Hickman and Henry Chapman honorably and tenaciously held their ground to the last against every phase of the outrage. In New York, John B. Haskin and Horace F. Clarke refused to yield, though great efforts were made to induce them to support the administration. The Senate promptly concurred in the English proposition.

But Kansas would not sell her birthright for a mess of pottage. She had fought too long for freedom to be bribed to the support of slavery. She had at last a free vote, and rejected the Lecompton Constitution, land grant and all, by a majority of more than ten thousand. The struggle was over. The pro-slavery men were defeated. The North was victorious. The repeal of the Missouri Compromise had not brought profit or honor to those who planned it. It had only produced strife, anger, heart-burning, hatred. It had added many drops to the cup of bitterness between North and South, and had filled it to overflowing. It produced evil only, and that continually. The repeal, in the judgment of the North, was a great conspiracy against human freedom. In the Southern States it was viewed as an honest effort to recover rights of which they had been unjustly deprived. Each section held with firmness to its own belief, and the four years of agitation had separated them so widely that a return to fraternal feeling seemed impossible. Confidence, the plant of slowest growth, had been destroyed. Who could restore it to life and strength?

Douglas had, in large degree, redeemed himself in the North from the obloquy to which he had been subjected since the repeal of the Missouri Compromise. The victory for free Kansas was perhaps to an undue extent ascribed to him. The completeness of that victory was everywhere recognized, and the lawless intruders who had worked so hard to inflict slavery on the new Territory gradually withdrew. In the South, Douglas was covered with maledictions. But for his influence, Southern men felt that Kansas would have been admitted with a pro-slavery constitution, and the senatorial equality

of the South firmly re-established.   Northern Republicans, outside of
Illinois, were in a forgiving frame of mind towards Douglas; and
he had undoubtedly regained a very large share of his old popularity.   But Illinois Republicans were less amiable towards him.
They would not forget that he had broken down an anti-slavery
barrier which had been reared with toil and sanctified by time.   He
had not, as they alleged, turned back from any test exacted by the
South, until he had reached the point where another step forward
involved political death to himself.   They would not credit his hostility to the Lecompton Constitution to any nobler motive than the
instinct of self-preservation.   This was a harsh judgment, and yet a
most natural one.   It inspired the Republicans of Illinois, and they
prepared to contest the return of Douglas to the Senate by formally nominating Abraham Lincoln as an opposing candidate.

The contest that ensued was memorable.   Douglas had an her-
culean task before him.   The Republican party was young, strong,
united, conscious of its power, popular, growing.   The Democratic
party was rent with faction, and the Administration was irrevocably
opposed to the return of Douglas to the Senate.   He entered the
field, therefore, with a powerful opponent in front, and with defection and betrayal in the rear.   He was everywhere known as a
debater of singular skill.   His mind was fertile in resources.   He
was master of logic.   No man perceived more quickly than he the
strength or the weakness of an argument, and no one excelled him
in the use of sophistry and fallacy.   Where he could not elucidate
a point to his own advantage, he would fatally becloud it for his
opponent.   In that peculiar style of debate, which, in its intensity,
resembles a physical combat, he had no equal.   He spoke with extraordinary readiness.   There was no halting in his phrase.   He used
good English, terse, vigorous, pointed.   He disregarded the adorn-
ments of rhetoric, — rarely used a simile.   He was utterly destitute
of humor, and had slight appreciation of wit.   He never cited
historical precedents except from the domain of American politics.
Inside that field his knowledge was comprehensive, minute, critical.
Beyond it his learning was limited.   He was not a reader.   His
recreations were not in literature.   In the whole range of his volu-
minous speaking it would be difficult to find either a line of poetry
or a classical allusion.   But he was by nature an orator; and by
long practice a debater.   He could lead a crowd almost irresistibly
to his own conclusions.   He could, if he wished, incite a mob to

desperate deeds. He was, in short, an able, audacious, almost unconquerable opponent in public discussion.

It would have been impossible to find any man of the same type able to meet him before the people of Illinois. Whoever attempted it would probably have been destroyed in the first encounter. But the man who was chosen to meet him, who challenged him to the combat, was radically different in every phase of character. Scarcely could two men be more unlike, in mental and moral constitution, than Abraham Lincoln and Stephen A. Douglas. Mr. Lincoln was calm and philosophic. He loved the truth for the truth's sake. He would not argue from a false premise, or be deceived himself or deceive others by a false conclusion. He had pondered deeply on the issues which aroused him to action. He had given anxious thought to the problems of free government, and to the destiny of the Republic. He had for himself marked out a path of duty, and he walked in it fearlessly. His mental processes were slower but more profound than those of Douglas. He did not seek to say merely the thing which was best for that day's debate, but the thing which would stand the test of time and square itself with eternal justice. He wished nothing to appear white unless it was white. His logic was severe and faultless. He did not resort to fallacy, and could detect it in his opponent, and expose it with merciless directness. He had an abounding sense of humor, and always employed it in illustration of his argument, — never for the mere sake of provoking merriment. In this respect he had the wonderful aptness of Franklin. He often taught a great truth with the felicitous brevity of an Æsop fable. His words did not flow in an impetuous torrent as did those of Douglas, but they were always well chosen, deliberate, and conclusive.

Thus fitted for the contest, these men proceeded to a discussion which at the time was so interesting as to enchain the attention of the nation, — in its immediate effect so striking as to affect the organ-ization of parties, in its subsequent effect so powerful as to change the fate of millions. Mr. Lincoln had opened his own canvass by a carefully prepared speech in which, after quoting the maxim that a house divided against itself cannot stand, he uttered these weighty words: "I believe this government cannot endure permanently half slave, half free. I do not expect the Union to be dissolved; I do not expect the house to fall; but I do expect it will cease to be divided. It will become all one thing or all the other. Either the opponents of slavery will arrest the farther spread of it, and place it where the public mind shall rest in the belief that it is in the course of absolute extinction, or its advocates will push it forward till it shall become alike lawful in all the States, old as well as new, north as well as south."

Mr. Lincoln had been warned by intimate friends to whom he had communicated the contents of his speech, in advance of its delivery, that he was treading on dangerous ground, that he would be misrepresented as a disunionist, and that he might fatally damage the Republican party by making its existence synonymous with a destruction of the government. But he was persistent. It was borne into his mind that he was announcing a great truth, and that he would be wronging his own conscience, and to the extent of his influence injuring his country, by withholding it, or in any degree qualifying its declaration. If there was a disposition to avoid the true significance of the contest with the South, he would not be a party to it. He believed he could discern the scope and read the destiny of the impending sectional controversy. He was sure he could see far beyond the present, and hear the voice of the future. He would not close the book; he would not shut his eyes; he would not stop his ears. He avowed his faith, and stood firmly to his creed.

Mr. Douglas naturally, indeed inevitably, made his first and leading speech against these averments of Mr. Lincoln. He had returned to Illinois, after the adjournment of Congress, with a disturbed and restless mind. He had one great ambition, — to re-instate himself as a leader of the national Democracy, and, as incidental and necessary to that end, to carry Illinois against Mr. Lincoln. The issue embodied in Mr. Lincoln's speech afforded him the occasion which he had coveted. His quick eye discerned an opportunity to exclude from the canvass the disagreeable features in his own political career by arraigning Mr. Lincoln as an enemy of the Union and as an advocate of an internecine conflict in which the free States and the slave States should wrestle in deadly encounter. Douglas presented his indictment artfully and with singular force. The two speeches were in all respects characteristic. Each had made a strong presentation of his case, but the superior candor and directness of Mr. Lincoln had made a deep impression on the popular mind.

In the seven public debates which were held as the result of these preliminary speeches, the questions at issue were elaborately and exhaustively treated. The friends of each naturally claimed the victory for their own champion. The speeches were listened to by tens of thousands of eager auditors; but absorbing, indeed unprecedented, as was the interest, the vast throngs behaved with moderation and decorum. The discussion from beginning to end was an amplification of the position which each had taken at the outset. The arguments were held close to the subject, relating solely to the slavery question, and not even incidentally referring to any other political issue. Protection, free trade, internal improvements, the sub-treasury, all the issues, in short, which had divided parties for a long series of years, and on which both speakers entertained very decided views, were omitted from the discussion. The public mind saw but one issue: every thing else was irrelevant. At the first meeting, Douglas addressed a series of questions to Mr. Lincoln, skillfully prepared and well adapted to entrap him in contradictions, or commit him to such extreme doctrine as would ruin his canvass. Mr. Lincoln's answers at the second meeting, held at Freeport, were both frank and adroit. Douglas had failed to gain a point by his resort to the Socratic mode of argument. He had indeed only given Mr. Lincoln an opportunity to exhibit both his candor and his skill. After he had answered, he assumed the offensive, and addressed a series of questions to Mr. Douglas which were constructed with the design of forcing the latter to an unmistakable declaration of his creed. Douglas had been a party to the duplex construction of the Cincinnati platform of 1856, in which the people of the South had been comforted with the doctrine that slavery was protected in the Territories by the Constitution against the authority of Congress and against the power of the Territorial citizens, until the period should be reached, when, under an enabling act to form a constitution for a State government, the majority might decide the question of slavery. Of this doctrine Mr. Breckinridge was the Southern representative, and he had for that very reason been associated with Mr. Buchanan on the Presidential ticket. On the other hand, the North was consoled, it would not be unfair to say cajoled, with the doctrine of popular sovereignty as defined by Mr. Douglas; and this gave to the people of the Territories the absolute right to settle the question of slavery for themselves at any time. The doctrine had, however, been utterly destroyed by the Dred Scott decision, and, to the confusion of all lines of division and distinction, Mr. Douglas had approved the opinion of the Supreme Court.

Douglas had little trouble in making answer in an *ad captandum* manner to all Mr. Lincoln's questions save one. The crucial test was applied when Mr. Lincoln asked him "if the people of a Territory can, in any lawful way, against the wishes of any citizen of the United States, exclude slavery from their limits prior to the formation of a State constitution?" In the first debate, where Douglas had the opening, he had, in the popular judgment, rather worsted Mr. Lincoln. His greater familiarity with the arts if not the tricks of the stump had given him an advantage. But now Mr. Lincoln had the opening, and he threw Mr. Douglas upon the defensive by the question which reached the very marrow of the controversy. Mr. Lincoln had measured the force of his question, and saw the dilemma in which it would place Douglas. Before the meeting he said, in private, that "Douglas could not answer that question in such way as to be elected both Senator and President. He might so answer it as to carry Illinois, but, in doing so, he would irretrievably injure his standing with the Southern Democracy." Douglas quickly realized his own embarrassment. He could not, in the face of the Supreme-Court decision, declare that the people of the Territory could exclude slavery by direct enactment. To admit, on the other hand, that slavery was fastened upon the Territories, — past all hope of resistance or protest on the part of a majority of the citizens — would be to concede the victory to Mr. Lincoln without further struggle. Between these impossible roads Douglas sought a third. He answered that, regardless of the decision of the Supreme Court, "the people of a Territory have the lawful means to introduce or exclude slavery as they choose, for the reason that slavery cannot exist unless supported by local police regulations. Those police regulations can only be established by the local legislature; and, if the people are opposed to slavery, they will, by unfriendly legislation, effectually prevent its introduction."

This was a lame, illogical, evasive answer; but it was put forth by Douglas with an air of sincerity and urged in a tone of defiant confidence. It gave to his supporters a plausible answer. But Mr. Lincoln's analysis of the position was thorough, his ridicule of it effective. Douglas's invention for destroying a right under the Constitution by a police regulation was admirably exposed, and his new theory that a thing "may be lawfully driven away from a place where it has a lawful right to go" was keenly reviewed by Mr. Lincoln. The debate of that day was the important one of the series. Mr. Lincoln had secured an advantage in the national relations of the contest which he held to the end. At the same time Douglas had escaped a danger which threatened his destruction in the State canvass, and secured his return to the Senate. As to the respective merits of the contestants, it would be idle to expect an agreement among contemporary partisans. But a careful reading of the discussion a quarter of a century after it was held will convince the impartial that in principle, in candor, in the enduring force of logic, Mr. Lincoln had the advantage. It is due to fairness to add that probably not another man in the country, with the disabilities surrounding his position, could have maintained himself so ably, so fearlessly, so effectively, as Douglas.

Douglas was aided in his canvass by the undisguised opposition of the administration. The hostility of President Buchanan and his Southern supporters was the best possible proof to the people of Illinois that Douglas was representing a doctrine which was not relished by the pro-slavery party. The courage with which he fought the administration gave an air of heroism to his canvass and prestige to his position. It secured to him thousands of votes that would otherwise have gone to Mr. Lincoln. For every vote which the administration was able to withhold from Douglas, it added five to his supporters. The result of the contest was, that, while Douglas was enabled to secure a majority of eight in the Legislature in consequence of an apportionment that was favorable to his side, Mr. Lincoln received a plurality of four thousand in the popular vote. In a certain sense, therefore, each had won a victory, and each had incurred defeat. But the victory of Douglas and the means by which it was won proved to be his destruction in the wider field of his ambition. Mr. Lincoln's victory and defeat combined in the end to promote his political fortunes, and to open to him the illustrious career which followed.

This debate was not a mere incident in American politics. It marked an era. Its influence and effect were co-extensive with the Republic. It introduced a new and distinct phase in the controversy that was engrossing all minds. The position of Douglas separated him from the Southern Democracy, and this, of itself, was a fact of great significance. The South saw that the ablest leader of the Northern Democracy had been compelled, in order to save himself at home, to abjure the very doctrine on which the safety of slave institutions depended. The propositions enunciated by Douglas in answer to the questions of Mr. Lincoln, in the Freeport debate, were as distasteful to the Southern mind as the position of Mr. Lincoln himself. Lincoln advocated a positive inhibition of slavery by the General Government. Mr. Douglas proposed to submit Southern rights under the Constitution to the decision of the first mob or rabble that might get possession of a Territorial legislature, and pass a police regulation hostile to slavery. Against this construction of the Constitution the South protested, and the protest carried with it implacable hostility to Douglas.

The separation of the Democratic party into warring factions was, therefore, inevitable. The line of division was the same on which the Republican party had been founded. It was the North against the South, the South against the North. The great mass of Northern Democrats began to consolidate in support of Douglas as determinedly as the mass of Northern Whigs had followed Seward. The Southern Democrats began, at the same time, to organize their States against Douglas. Until his break from the regular ranks in his opposition to the Lecompton Constitution, Douglas had enjoyed boundless popularity with his party in the South. In every slave State, there was still a small number of his old supporters who remained true to him. But the great host had left him. He could not be trusted. He had failed to stand by the extreme faith: he had refused to respond to its last requirement. Even at the risk of permanently dissevering the Democratic party, the Southern leaders resolved to destroy Douglas.

To this end, in the session of Congress following the debate with Mr. Lincoln, the Democratic senators laid down, in a series of resolutions, the true exposition of the creed of their party. Douglas was not personally referred to, but the resolutions were aimed so pointedly at what they regarded his heretical opinions, that his name might as well have been incorporated. The resolutions were adopted during the absence of Douglas from the Senate, on a health-seeking tour, after his laborious canvass. With only the dissenting vote of Mr. Pugh of Ohio among the Democrats, it was declared that "neither Congress nor a territorial legislature, whether by direct legislation, or legislation of an indirect or unfriendly character, possesses the power to impair the right of any citizen of the United States to take his slave property into the common Territories, and there hold and enjoy the same while the territorial condition exists." Not satisfied with this utter destruction of the whole doctrine of popular sovereignty, the Democratic senators gave one more turn to the wrench, by declaring that if "the territorial government should fail or refuse to provide adequate protection to the rights of the slave-holder, it will be the duty of Congress to supply such deficiency." The doctrine thus laid down by the Democratic senators was, in plain terms, that the territorial legislature might protect slavery, but could not prohibit it; and that even the Congress of the United States could only intervene on the side of bondage, and never on the side of freedom.

Anxious as Douglas was to be re-established in full relations with his party, he had not failed to see the obstacles in his way. He now realized that a desperate fight was to be made against him; that he was to be humiliated and driven from the Democratic ranks. The creed laid down by the Southern senators was such as no man could indorse without forfeiting his political life in the free States. Douglas did not propose to rush on self-destruction to oblige the Democracy of the slave States; nor was he of the type of men who, when the right cheek is smitten, will meekly turn the other for a second blow. When his Democratic associates in the Senate proceeded to read him out of the party, they apparently failed to see that they were reading the Northern Democracy out with him. Jefferson Davis and Judah P. Benjamin might construct resolutions adapted to the latitude of the Gulf, and dragoon them through the Senate, with aid and pressure from Buchanan's administration; but Douglas commanded the votes of the Northern Democracy, and to the edict of a pro-slavery caucus he defiantly opposed the solid millions who followed his lead in the free States.

Without wrangling over the resolutions in the Senate, Douglas made answer to the whole series in a public letter of June 22, 1859, in which he said that "if it shall become the policy of the Democratic party to repudiate their time-honored principles, and interpolate such new issues as the revival of the African slave-trade, or the doctrine that the Constitution carries slavery into the Territories beyond the power of the people to legally control it as other property," he would not "accept a nomination for the Presidency if tendered him." The aggressiveness of Southern opinion on the slavery question was thus shown by Douglas in a negative or indirect view. It is a remarkable fact, that, in still another letter, Douglas argued quite elaborately against the revival of the African slave-trade, which he believed to be among the designs of the most advanced class of pro-slavery advocates. So acute a statesman as Douglas could not fail to see, that, at every step of his controversy with Southern Democrats, he was justifying the philosophy of Lincoln when he maintained that the country was to become wholly free, or wholly under the control of the slave power.

The controversy thus precipitated between Douglas and the South threatened the disruption of the Democratic party. That was an event of very serious significance. It would bring the conflict of sections still nearer by sundering a tie which had for so long a period bound together vast numbers from the North and the South in common sympathy and fraternal co-operation. Even those who were most opposed to the Democratic party beheld its peril with a certain feeling of regret not unmixed with apprehension. The Whig party had been destroyed; and its Northern and Southern members, who, but a few years before, had worked harmoniously for Harrison, for Clay, for Taylor, were now enrolled in rival and hostile organizations. A similar dissolution of the Democratic party would sweep away the only common basis of political action still existing for men of the free States and men of the slave States. The separation of the Methodist church into Northern and Southern organizations, a few years before, had been regarded by Mr. Webster as a portent of evil for the Union. The division of the Democratic party would be still more ominous. The possibility of such an event showed how deeply the slavery question had affected all ranks, — social, religious, and political. It showed, too, how the spirit of Calhoun now inspired the party in whose councils the slightest word of Jackson had once been law. This change, beginning with the defeat of Van Buren in 1844, was at first slow; but it had afterwards moved so rapidly and so far, that men in the North, who wished to remain in the ranks of the Democracy, were compelled to trample on the principles, and surrender the prejudices, of a lifetime. Efforts to harmonize proved futile. In Congress the breach was continually widening.

The situation was cause of solicitude, and even grief, with thousands to whom the old party was peculiarly endeared. The traditions of Jefferson, of Madison, of Jackson, were devoutly treasured; and the splendid achievements of the American Democracy were recounted with the pride which attaches to an honorable family inheritance. The fact was recalled that the Republic had grown to its imperial dimensions under Democratic statesmanship. It was remembered that Louisiana had been acquired from France, Florida from Spain, the independent Republic of Texas annexed, and California, with its vast dependencies, and its myriad millions of treasure, ceded by Mexico, all under Democratic administrations, and in spite of the resistance of their opponents. That a party whose history was inwoven with the glory of the Republic should now come to its end in a quarrel over the status of the negro, in a region where his labor was not wanted, was, to many of its members, as incomprehensible as it was sorrowful and exasperating. They protested, but they could not prevent. Anger was aroused, and men refused to listen to reason. They were borne along, they knew not whither or by what force. Time might have restored the party to harmony, but at the very height of the factional contest the representatives of both sections were hurried forward to the National Convention of 1860, with principle subordinated to passion, with judgment displaced by a desire for revenge.

NOTE. — The following are the questions, referred to on p. 147, which were propounded to Mr. Douglas by Mr. Lincoln in their debate at Freeport. The popular interest was centred in the second question.

First, If the people of Kansas shall, by means entirely unobjectionable in all other respects, adopt a State Constitution, and ask admission into the Union under it *before* they have the requisite number of inhabitants, according to the English bill — some ninety-three thousand — will you vote to admit them?

Second, Can the people of a United-States Territory, in any lawful way, against the wish of any citizen of the United States, exclude slavery from its limits prior to the formation of a State Constitution?

Third, If the Supreme Court of the United States shall decide that States cannot exclude slavery from their limits, are you in favor of acquiescing in, adopting, and following such decision as a rule of political action?

Fourth, Are you in favor of acquiring additional territory, in disregard of how such acquisition may affect the nation on the slavery question?

CHAPTER VIII.

THE South was unnaturally and unjustifiably excited. The people of the slave States could not see the situation accurately, but, like a man with disordered nerves, they exaggerated every thing. Their sense of proportion seemed to be destroyed, so that they could no longer perceive the intrinsic relation which one incident had to another. In this condition of mind, when the most ordinary events were misapprehended and mismeasured, they were startled and alarmed by an occurrence of extraordinary and exceptional character. On the quiet morning of October, 1859, with no warning whatever to the inhabitants, the United-States arsenal, at Harper's Ferry, Virginia, was found to be in possession of an invading mob. The town was besieged, many of its citizens made prisoners, telegraph-wires cut, railway-trains stopped by a force which the people, as they were aroused from sleep, had no means of estimating. A resisting body was soon organized, militia came in from the surrounding country, regular troops were hurried up from Washington. By the opening of the second day, a force of fifteen hundred men surrounded

154

the arsenal, and, when the insurgents surrendered, it was found that there had been but twenty-two in all: Four were still alive, including their leader, John Brown.

Brown was a man of singular courage, perseverance, and zeal, but was entirely misguided and misinformed. He had conceived the utterly impracticable scheme of liberating the slaves of the South by calling on them to rise, putting arms in their hands, and aiding them to gain their freedom. He had borne a very conspicuous and courageous part in the Kansas struggles, and had been a terror to the slave-holders on the Missouri border. His bravery was of a rare type. He had no sense of fear. Governor Wise stated that during the fight, while Brown held the arsenal, with one of his sons lying dead beside him, another gasping with a mortal wound, he felt the pulse of the dying boy, used his own musket, and coolly commanded his men, all amid a shower of bullets from the attacking force. While of sound mind on most subjects, Brown had evidently lost his mental balance on the one topic of slavery. His scheme miscarried the moment its execution was attempted, as any one not blinded by fanaticism could have from the first foreseen.

The matter was taken up in hot wrath by the South, with Governor Wise in the lead. The design was not known to or approved by any body of men in the North; but an investigation was moved in the Senate, by Mr. Mason of Virginia, with the evident view of fixing the responsibility on the Northern people, or, at least, upon the Republican party. These men affected to see in John Brown, and his handful of followers, only the advance guard of another irruption of Goths and Vandals from the North, bent on inciting servile insurrection, on plunder, pillage, and devastation. Mr. Mason's committee found no sentiment in the North justifying Brown, but the irritating and offensive course of the Virginia senator called forth a great deal of defiant anti-slavery expression which, in his judgment, was tantamount to treason. Brown was tried and executed. He would not permit the plea of unsound mind to be made on his behalf, and to the end he behaved with that calm courage which always attracts respect and admiration. Much was made of the deliverance of the South, from a great peril, and every thing indicated that the John Brown episode was to be drawn into the political campaign as an indictment against anti-slavery men. It was loudly charged by the South, and by their partisans throughout the North, that such insurrections were the legitimate outgrowth of Republican teaching, and that the national safety demanded the defeat and dissolution of the Republican party. Thus challenged, the Republican party did not stand on the defensive. Many of its members openly expressed their pity for the zealot, whose rashness had led him to indefensible deeds and thence to the scaffold. On the day of his execution, bells were tolled in many Northern towns — not in approval of what Brown had done, but from compassion for the fate of an old man whose mind had become distempered by suffering, and by morbid reflection on the suffering of others; from a feeling that his sentence, in view of this fact, was severe; and lastly, and more markedly, as a Northern rebuke to the attempt on the part of the South to make a political issue from an occurrence which was as unforeseen and exceptional as it was deplorable.

The fear and agitation in the South were not feigned but real. Instead of injuring the Republican party, this very fact increased its strength in the North. The terror of the South at the bare prospect of a negro insurrection led many who had not before studied the slavery question to give serious heed to this phase of it. The least reflection led men to see that a domestic institution must be very undesirable which could keep an entire community of brave men in dread of some indefinable tragedy. Mobs and riots of much greater magnitude than the John Brown uprising had frequently occurred in the free States, and they were put down by the firm authority of law, without the dread hand of a spectre behind which might in a moment light the horizon with the conflagration of homes, and subject wives and daughters to a fate of nameless horror. Instead, therefore, of arresting the spread of Republican principles, the mad scheme of John Brown tended to develop and strengthen them. The conviction grew rapidly that if slavery could produce such alarm and such demoralization in a strong State like Virginia, inhabited by a race of white men whose courage was never surpassed, it was not an institution to be encouraged, but that its growth should be prohibited in the new communities where its weakening and baleful influence was not yet felt

Sentiment of this kind could not be properly comprehended in the South. It was honestly misinterpreted by some, willfully misrepresented by others. All construed it into a belief, on the part of a large proportion of the Northern people, that John Brown was entirely justifiable. His wild invasion of the South, they apprehended, would be repeated as opportunity offered on a larger scale and with more deadly purpose. This opinion was stimulated and developed for political ends by many whose intelligence should have led them to more enlightened views. False charges being constantly repeated and plied with incessant zeal, the most radical misconception became fixed in the Southern mind. It was idle for the Republican party to declare that their aim was only to prevent the extension of slavery to free territory, and that they were pledged not to interfere with its existence in the States. Such distinctions were not accepted by the Southern people. Their leaders had taught them that the one necessarily involved the other, and that a man who was in favor of the Wilmot Proviso was as bitter an enemy to the South as one who incited a servile insurrection. These views were unceasingly pressed upon the South by the Northern Democracy, who, in their zeal to defeat the Republicans at home, did not scruple to misrepresent their aims in the most reckless manner. They were constantly misleading the public opinion of the slave States, until at last the South recognized no difference between the creed of Seward and the creed of Gerrit Smith, and held Lincoln responsible for all the views and expressions of William Lloyd Garrison and Wendell Phillips. The calling of a National Republican Convention was to their disordered imagination a threat of destruction. The success of its candidates would, in their view, be just cause for resistance outside the pale of the Constitution.

It was at the height of this overwrought condition of the Southern mind, that the National Convention of the Democratic party met at Charleston on the 23d of April, 1860. The convention had been assembled in South Carolina, as the most discontented and extreme of Southern States, in order to signify that the Democracy could harmonize on her soil, and speak peace to the nation through the voice which had so often spoken peace before. But the Northern Democrats failed to comprehend their Southern allies. In their anxiety to impress the slave-holders with the depth and malignity of Northern anti-slavery feeling, they had unwittingly implicated themselves as accessories to the crime they charged on others. If they were, in fact, the friends to the South which they so loudly proclaimed themselves to be, now was the time to show their faith by their works. The Southern delegates had come to the convention in a truculent spirit, — as men who felt that they were enduring

wrongs which must then and there be righted. They had a grievance for which they demanded redress, as a preliminary step to further conference. They wanted no evasion, they would accept no
delay. The Northern delegates begged for the nomination of Douglas as the certain method of defeating the Republicans, and asked
that they might not be borne down by a platform which they could
not carry in the North. The Southern delegates demanded a platform which should embody the Constitutional rights of the slave-
holder, and they would not qualify or conceal their requirements.
If the North would sustain those rights, all would be well. If the
North would not sustain them, it was of infinite moment to the
South to be promptly and definitely advised of the fact. The
Southern delegates were not presenting a particular man as candidate. On that point they would be liberal and conciliatory. But
they were fighting for a principle, and would not surrender it or
compromise it.

The supporters of Douglas from the North saw that they would
be utterly destroyed at home if they consented to the extreme Southern demand. Their destruction would be equally sure even with
Douglas as their candidate if the platform should announce principles which he had been controverting ever since his revolt against
the Lecompton bill. For the first time in the history of national
Democratic conventions the Northern delegates refused to submit to
the exactions of the South. Hitherto platforms had been constructed
just as Southern men dictated. Candidates had been taken as their
preference directed. But now the Northern men, pressed by the
rising tide of Republicanism in every free State, demanded some
ground on which they could stand and make a contest at home.

Caleb Cushing of Massachusetts was chosen President of the
Convention. The political career of Mr. Cushing had not been
distinguished for steady adherence to party. He was elected to
Congress in 1834, as representative from the Essex district in Massachusetts. He was at that time a zealous member of the Whig
party, and was active on the Northern or anti-slavery side in the
discussions relating to the "right of petition." He served in the
House for eight years. After the triumph of Harrison in 1840, Mr.
Cushing evidently aspired to be a party leader. In the quarrel
which ensued between President Tyler and Mr. Clay, he saw an
opportunity to gratify his ambition by adhering to the administration. This brought him into very close relations with Mr. Webster,

who remained in Tyler's Cabinet after his colleagues retired, and threw him at the same time into rank antagonism with Mr. Clay, to whose political fortunes he had previously been devoted. In view of the retirement of Mr. Webster from the State Department in 1843, President Tyler nominated Mr. Cushing for Secretary of the Treasury, but the Whig senators, appreciating his power and influence in that important position, procured his rejection. Some Democratic votes from the South were secured against him because of his course in the House of Representatives. The President then nominated him as Commissioner to China, and he was promptly confirmed. Oriental diplomatists never encountered a minister better fitted to meet them with their own weapons.

Upon his return home, Mr. Cushing found that Mr. Webster had resumed his place as the leader of the Northern Whigs. Mr. Clay had meanwhile been defeated for the Presidency, his followers were discouraged, the administration of Mr. Polk was in power. Mr. Cushing at once joined the Democracy, and was made a Brigadier-General in the army raised for the war with Mexico. From that time onward he became a partisan of the extreme State-rights school of the Southern Democracy, and was appropriately selected for Attorney-General by President Pierce in 1853. In conjunction with Jefferson Davis, he was considered to be the guiding and controlling force in the administration. His thorough education, his remarkable attainments, his eminence in the law, his ability as an advocate, rendered his active co-operation of great value to the pro-slavery Democrats of the South. He was naturally selected for the important and difficult duty of presiding over the convention whose deliberations were to affect the interests of the Government, and possibly the fate of the Union.

It was soon evident that the South would have every advantage in the convention which an intelligent and skillful administration of parliamentary law could afford. Without showing unfairness, the presiding officer, especially in a large and boisterous assembly, can impart confidence and strength to the side with which he may sympathize. But, apart from any power to be derived from having the chairman of the convention, the South had a more palpable advantage from the mode in which the standing committees must, according to precedent, be constituted. As one member must be taken from each State, the Southern men obtained the control of all the committees, from the fact that the delegates from California and Oregon steadily voted with them. There were thirty-three States in the Union in 1860, — eighteen free and fifteen slave-holding. California and Oregon, uniting with the South, gave to that section seventeen, and left to the North but sixteen on all the committees. The Democratic delegates from the Pacific States assumed a weighty responsibility in thus giving to the Disunionists of the South preliminary control of the convention, by permitting them to shape authoritatively all the business to be submitted. It left the real majority of the convention in the attitude of a protesting minority. The Southern majority of one on the committees was fatal to Democratic success. In a still more important aspect its influence was in the highest degree prejudicial to the Union of the States.

Constituted in the manner just indicated, the Committee on Resolutions promptly and unanimously agreed on every article of the Democratic creed, except that relating to slavery. Here they divided, stubbornly and irreconcilably. The fifteen slave States, re-enforced by California and Oregon, gave to the Southern interest a majority of one vote on the committee. The other free States, sixteen in all, were hostile to the extreme Southern demands, and reported a resolution, which they were willing to accept. The South required an explicit assertion of the right of citizens to settle in the Territories with their slaves, — a right not "to be destroyed or impaired by Congressional or Territorial legislation." They required the further declaration that it is the duty of the Federal Government, when necessary, to protect slavery "in the Territories, and wherever else its constitutional authority extends." This was in substance, and almost identically in language, the extreme creed put forth by the Southern Democratic senators in the winter of 1858–59, after the "popular sovereignty" campaign of Douglas against Lincoln. It was the most advanced ground ever taken by the statesmen of the South, and its authorship was generally ascribed to Judah P. Benjamin, senator from Louisiana. Its introduction in the Charleston platform was intended apparently as an insult to Douglas. The evident purpose was to lay down doctrines and prescribe tests which Douglas could not accept, and thus to exclude him, not only from candidacy, but from further participation in the councils of the party.

The courage of the Northern Democrats was more conspicuously shown in their resistance to these demands than in the declarations which they desired to substitute. They quietly abandoned all their assertions in regard to popular sovereignty, refrained from any protest against the doctrine that the Constitution carried slavery as far as its jurisdiction extended, and contented themselves with a resolution that " inasmuch as differences of opinion exist in the Democratic party as to the nature and extent of the powers of a Territorial Legislature, and as to the powers and duties of Congress under the Constitution of the United States over the institution of slavery within the Territories, the Democratic party will abide by the decisions of the Supreme Court of the United States upon questions of Constitutional law." . This was perhaps the best device practicable at the time ; and had it been adopted with Douglas as the candidate, and a united Democracy supporting him, it is not improbable that a successful campaign might have been made. But it was a makeshift, uncandid, unfair, cunningly contrived to evade the full responsibility of the situation. It was a temporizing expedient, and did not frankly meet the question which was engaging the thoughts of the people. Had it succeeded, nothing would have been settled. Every thing would have been postponed, and the crisis would have inevitably recurred. So far as the Supreme Court could determine the questions at issue, it had already been done in the Dred Scott decision; and that decision, so far from being final, was a part of the current controversy. There was, therefore, neither logic nor principle in the proposition of the Douglas minority. The Southern delegates keenly realized this fact, and refused to accept the compromise. They could not endure the thought of being placed in a position which was not only evasive, but might be deemed cowardly. They were brave men, and wished to meet the question bravely. They knew that the Republicans in their forthcoming convention would explicitly demand the prohibition of slavery in the Territories. To hesitate or falter in making an equally explicit assertion of their own faith would subject them to fatal assault from their slave-holding constituencies.

The Douglas men would not yield. They were enraged by the domineering course of the Southern Democrats. They could not comprehend why they should higgle about the language of the platform when they could carry the slave States on the one form of expression as well as the other. In the North it was impossible for the Democrats to succeed with the Southern platform, but in the South it was, in their judgment, entirely easy to carry the Douglas platform. From the committee the contest was transferred to the convention, and there the Douglas men were in a majority. They did not hesitate to use their strength, and by a vote of 165 to 138 they substituted the minority platform for that of the majority. It was skillfully accomplished under the lead of Henry B. Payne of Ohio and Benjamin Samuels of Iowa. The total vote of the convention was 303, — the number of Presidential electors; and every vote had been cast on the test question. The South voted solidly in the negative, and was aided by the vote of California and Oregon, and a few scattering delegates from Pennsylvania and New Jersey. The other fourteen States of the North voted unanimously on the side of Douglas, and gave him a majority of twenty-seven.

The Northern victory brought with it a defeat. A large number of the Southern delegates, though fairly and honorably outvoted, refused to abide by the decision. Seven States — Louisiana, Alabama, South Carolina, Mississippi, Florida, Texas, and Arkansas — withdrew from the convention, and organized a separate assemblage, presided over by Senator James A. Bayard of Delaware. By this defection the Douglas men were left in absolute control of the convention. But the friends of Douglas fatally obstructed his progress by consenting to the two-thirds rule, so worded as to require that proportion of a full convention to secure a nomination. The first vote disclosed the full strength of Douglas to be 152. He required 202 to be declared the nominee. After an indefinite number of ballots, it was found impossible to make a nomination; and on the 3d of May the convention adjourned to meet in Baltimore on the 18th of June. In the intervening weeks it was hoped that a more harmonious spirit would return to the party. But the expectation was vain. The differences were more pronounced than ever when the convention re-assembled, and, all efforts to find a common basis of action having failed, the convention divided. The Southern delegates with California and Oregon, and with some scattering members from other States, among whom were Caleb Cushing and Benjamin F. Butler of Massachusetts, nominated John C. Breckinridge of Kentucky for President, and Joseph Lane of Oregon for Vice-President. The Northern convention, with a few scattering votes from the South, nominated Stephen A. Douglas for President, and Herschel V. Johnson of Georgia for Vice-President. Of the seventeen States that made up the Breckinridge convention, it was deemed probable that he could carry all. Of the sixteen that voted for Douglas, it was difficult to name one in which with a divided party he could be sure of victory. United in support of either candidate, the party could have made a formidable contest, stronger in the North with Douglas, stronger in the South with Breckinridge. Had the Democracy presented Douglas and Breckinridge as their National nominees, they would have combined all the elements of strength in their party. But passion and prejudice prevented. The South was implacable towards Douglas, and deliberately resolved to accept defeat rather than secure a victory under his lead.

The disruption of the Democracy was undoubtedly hastened by the political events which had occurred since the adjournment at Charleston. An organization, styling itself the Constitutional-Union Party, representing the successors of the Old Whigs and Americans, had met at Baltimore, and nominated John Bell of Tennessee for President, and Edward Everett of Massachusetts for Vice-President. The strength of the party was in the South. In the slave States it formed the only opposition to the Democratic party, and was as firm in defense of the rights of the slave-holder as its rival. Its members had not been so ready to repeal the Missouri Compromise as the Democrats, and they were unrelenting in their hostility to Douglas, and severe in their exposure of his dogma of popular sovereignty. They had effectively aided in bringing both the doctrine and its author into disrepute in the South, and, if the Democrats had ventured to nominate Douglas, they had their weapons ready for vigorous warfare against him.

With a Southern slave-holder like Mr. Bell at the head of the ticket, and a Northern man of Mr. Everett's well-known conservatism associated with him, the Constitutional-Union Party was in a position to make a strong canvass against Douglas in the South. It was this fact which, on the re-assembling of the Democratic convention at Baltimore, had increased the hostility of the South to Douglas, and made their leaders firm in their resolution not to accept him. Had the Union party nominated a Northern man instead of Mr. Bell for President, the case might have been different for Douglas; but the Southern Democrats feared that their party would be endangered in half the slave States if they should present Douglas as a candidate against a native Southerner and slave-holder of Bell's character and standing. If they were to be beaten in the contest for the Presidency, they were determined to retain, if possible, the control of their States, and not to risk their seats in the Senate and the House in a desperate struggle for Douglas. It would be poor recompense to them to recover certain Northern States from the Republicans, if at the same time, and by co-ordinate causes, an equal number of Southern States should be carried by Bell, and the destiny of the South be committed to a conservative party, which would abandon threats and cultivate harmony. Bell's nomination had, therefore, proved the final argument against the acceptance of Douglas by the Southern Democracy

Meanwhile, between the adjournment of the Democratic convention at Charleston, and its re-assembling in Baltimore, the Republicans had held their national convention at Chicago. It was a representative meeting of the active and able men of both the old parties in the North, who had come together on the one overshadowing issue of the hour. Differing widely on many other questions, inheriting their creeds from antagonistic organizations of the past, they thought alike on the one subject of putting a stop to the extension of slavery. Those who wished to go farther were restrained, and an absolute concord of opinion and action was commanded on this one line. In the entire history of party conventions, not one can be found so characteristic, so earnest, so determined to do the wisest thing, so little governed by personal consideration, so entirely devoted to one absorbing idea. It was made up in great part of young men, though there were gray-haired veterans in sufficient number to temper action with discretion. A large proportion of the delegates were afterwards prominent in public life. At least sixty of them, till then unknown beyond their districts, were sent to Congress. Many became governors of their States, and in other ways received marks of popular favor. It was essentially a convention of the free States — undisguisedly sectional in the political nomenclature of the day. The invitation was general, but, in the larger portion of the South, no one could be found who would risk his life by attending as a delegate. Nevertheless, there were delegates present from the five slave States which bordered on the free States, besides a partial and irregular representation from Texas.

The anti-slavery character of the assemblage was typified by the selection of David Wilmot for temporary chairman, and its conservative side by the choice of an old Webster Whig, in the person of George Ashmun of Massachusetts, for permanent president. This tendency to interweave the radical and conservative elements, and, where practicable, those of Whig with those of Democratic antecedents, was seen in many delegations. John A. Andrew and George S. Boutwell came from Massachusetts, William M. Evarts and Preston King from New York, Thaddeus Stevens and Andrew H. Reeder from Pennsylvania, Thomas Corwin and Joshua R. Giddings from Ohio, David Davis and N. B. Judd from Illinois. Outside of the regular delegations, there were great crowds of earnest men in Chicago, from all the free States. The number in attendance was reckoned by tens of thousands. Considering the restricted facilities for travel at that time, the multitude was surprising and significant. The whole mass was inspired with energy, and believed, without shadow of doubt, that they had come to witness the nomination of the next President of the United States. Confidence of strength is as potential an element in a political canvass as in a military campaign, and never was a more defiant sense of power exhibited than by the Chicago convention of 1860 and by the vast throng which surrounded its meetings. Such a feeling is contagious, and it spread from that centre until it enveloped the free States.

The impression in the country, for a year preceding the convention, was that Mr. Seward would be nominated. As the time drew nigh, however, symptoms of dissent appeared in quarters where it had not been expected. New parties are proverbially free from faction and jealousy. Personal antagonisms, which come with years, had not then been developed in the Republican ranks. It was not primarily a desire to promote the cause of other candidates which led to the questioning of Mr. Seward's availability, nor was there any withholding of generous recognition and appreciation of all that he had done for Republican principles. His high character was gladly acknowledged, his eminent ability conceded, the magnitude and unselfishness of his work were everywhere praised. Without his aid, the party could not have been organized. But for his wise leadership, it would have been wrecked in the first years of its existence. He was wholly devoted to its principles. He had staked every thing upon its success.

Mr. Seward had, however, some weak points as a candidate. A large proportion of the Republicans had been connected with the American organization, and still cherished some of its principles. Mr. Seward had been the determined foe of that party. In battling for the rights of the negro, he deemed it unwise and inconsistent to increase the disabilities of the foreign-born citizen. His influence, more than that of any other man, had broken down the proscriptive creed of the American party, and turned its members into the Republican ranks. But many of them came reluctantly, and in a complaining mood against Mr. Seward. This led political managers to fear that Mr. Seward would lose votes which another candidate might secure. Others thought that the radicalism of Mr. Seward would make him weak, where a more conservative representative of Republican principles might be strong. He had been at the forefront of the battle for twelve years in the Senate, and every extreme thing he had said was remembered to his injury. He had preached the doctrine of an "irrepressible conflict" between the forces of slavery and the forces of freedom, and timid men dreaded such a trial as his nomination would presage. The South had made continuous assault on this speech, and on the particular phrase which distinguished it, and had impressed many Northern men with the belief that Mr. Seward had gone too far. In short, he had been too conspicuous, and too many men had conceived predilections against him.

When the convention assembled, notwithstanding all adverse influences, Mr. Seward was still the leading and most formidable candidate. His case was in strong and skillful hands. Mr. Thurlow Weed, who had been his lifelong confidential friend, presented his claims, before the formal assembling of the convention, with infinite tact. Mr. Weed, though unable to make a public speech, was the most persuasive of men in private conversation. He was quiet, gentle, and deferential in manner. He grasped a subject with a giant's strength, presented its strong points, and marshaled its details with extraordinary power. Whatever Mr. Weed might lack was more than supplied by the eloquent tongue of William M. Evarts. Seldom if ever in the whole field of political oratory have the speeches of Mr. Evarts at Chicago been equaled. Even those who most decidedly differed from him followed him from one delegation to another allured by the charm of his words. He pleaded for the Republic, for the party that could save it, for the great statesman who had founded the party, and knew where and how to lead it. He spoke as one friend for another, and the great career of Mr. Seward was never so illumined as by the brilliant painting of Mr. Evarts.

With all the potential efforts and influences in his behalf, Mr. Seward was confronted with obstacles which were insuperable. He was seriously injured by the open defection of Horace Greeley. Not able, or even desirous, to appear on the New-York delegation, Mr. Greeley sat in the convention as a representative from Oregon.

The old firm of Seward, Weed, and Greeley, according to his own humorous expression, had been dissolved by the withdrawal of the junior partner; and a bitter dissension had in fact existed for six years without public knowledge. With his great influence in the agricultural regions of the country, Mr. Greeley was enabled to turn a strong current of popular feeling against the eminent senator from New York. Mr. Seward sustained further injury by the action of the States which were regarded as politically doubtful. Pennsylvania and Indiana took part against him. Henry S. Lane had just been nominated for governor of Indiana, with Oliver P. Morton — not then known beyond his State — for lieutenant-governor. It was understood that Lane would be sent to the Senate if the Republicans should carry the State, and that Morton, whose strength of character was known and appreciated at home, would become governor. Both candidates, having each a personal stake in the contest, united in declaring that the nomination of Mr. Seward meant a Democratic victory in Indiana. Andrew G. Curtin, who had been nominated for governor of Pennsylvania, gave the same testimony respecting that State; and his judgment was sustained by his faithful friend and adviser, Alexander K. McClure. Delegates from other States, where the contest was close, sympathized with the views of Pennsylvania and Indiana, and there was a rapid and formidable combination against Mr. Seward. The reformer and his creed rarely triumph at the same time, and the fate of Mr. Seward was about to add one more illustration of this truth.

But if not Mr. Seward, who? The Blairs and Horace Greeley answered, "Edward Bates of Missouri," — an old Whig, a lawyer of ability, a gentleman of character. Though still in vigorous life, he had sat in the convention which framed the constitution of Missouri in 1820. He had revered the Compromise of that year, and had joined the Republicans in resentment of its repeal. Ohio, in a half-hearted manner, presented Salmon P. Chase, who, with great ability and spotless fame, lacked the elements of personal popularity. Pennsylvania, with an imposing delegation, named Simon Cameron; New Jersey desired William L. Dayton; Vermont wanted Jacob Collamer; and delegates here and there suggested Judge McLean or Benjamin F. Wade. The popular candidate of 1856, John C. Frémont, had forbidden the use of his name.

Illinois had a candidate. He was held back with sound discretion, and at the opportune moment presented with great enthusiasm. Ever

since the discussion with Douglas, Mr. Lincoln had occupied a prominent place before the public; but there had been little mention of his
name for the Presidency. His friends at home had apparently hoped
to nominate him for Vice-President on the ticket with Mr. Seward.
But as the proofs of hostility to Seward multiplied, speculation was
busy as to the man who could be taken in his stead. At the moment
when doubts of Seward's success were most prevalent, and when
excitement in regard to the nomination was deepest, the Republicans of Illinois met in State convention. It was but a few days
in advance of the assembling of the National convention. By a
spontaneous movement they nominated Mr. Lincoln for President.
It was a surprise to the convention that did it. The man who created
the great outburst for Mr. Lincoln in that Illinois assemblage, who
interpreted the feelings of delegates to themselves, was Richard J.
Oglesby, a speaker of force and eloquence, afterwards honorably
prominent and popular in military and civil life. He was seconded
with unanimity, and with boisterous demonstrations of applause. The
whole State was instantly alive and ablaze for Lincoln. A delegation competent for its work was sent to the convention. David
Davis, O. H. Browning, Burton C. Cook, Gustavus Koerner, and
their associates, met no abler body of men in a convention remarkable for its ability. They succeeded in the difficult task assigned to
them. They did not in their canvass present Mr. Lincoln as a rival
to Mr. Seward, but rather as an admirer and friend. The votes
which were given to Mr. Lincoln on the first ballot were, in large
part, from delegations that could not be induced in any event to
vote for Mr. Seward. The presentation of Mr. Lincoln's name kept
these delegates from going to a candidate less acceptable to the
immediate friends of Mr. Seward. No management could have been
more skillful, no tact more admirable. The result attested the vigor
and wisdom of those who had Mr. Lincoln's fortunes in charge.

Mr. Seward's support, however, after all the assaults made upon
it, was still very formidable. On the first ballot he received 175½
votes, while Mr. Lincoln received but 102. Delegates to the number of 190 divided their votes between Bates, Chase, Cameron, Dayton, McLean, and Collamer. They held the balance of power, and
on the second ballot it was disclosed that the mass of them favored
Mr. Lincoln as against Mr. Seward. The latter gained but nine
votes, carrying his total up to 184½, while Mr. Lincoln received 181.
On the third ballot, Mr. Lincoln was nominated by general consent.

A. Lincoln

PRESIDENT 1861-1865.

It is one of the contradictions not infrequently exhibited in the movement of partisan bodies, that Mr. Seward was defeated because of his radical expressions on the slavery questions, while Mr. Lincoln was chosen in spite of expressions far more radical than those of Mr. Seward. The "irrepressible conflict" announced by Mr. Seward at Rochester did not go so far as Mr. Lincoln's declaration at Springfield, that "the Union could not exist half slave, half free." Neither Mr. Seward nor Mr. Lincoln contemplated the destruction of the government, and yet thousands had been made to believe that Mr. Seward made the existence of the Union depend on the abolition of slavery. Mr. Lincoln had announced the same doctrine in advance of Mr. Seward, with a directness and bluntness which could not be found in the more polished phrase of the New-York senator. Despite these facts, a large number of delegates from doubtful States — delegates who held the control of the convention — supported Mr. Lincoln, on the distinct ground that the anti-slavery sentiment which they represented was not sufficiently radical to support the author of the speech in which had been proclaimed the doctrine of an "irrepressible conflict" between freedom and slavery.

In a final analysis of the causes and forces which nominated Mr. Lincoln, great weight must be given to the influence which came from the place where the convention was held, and from the sympathy and pressure of the surrounding crowd. Illinois Republicans, from Cairo to the Wisconsin line, were present in uncounted thousands. The power of the mob in controlling public opinion is immeasurable. In monarchical governments it has dethroned kings, and in republics it dictates candidates. Had the conditions been changed and the National convention of the Republicans assembled in Albany, it is scarcely to be doubted that Mr. Seward would have been nominated. It is quite certain that Mr. Lincoln would not have been nominated. The great achievement at Chicago was the nomination of Mr. Lincoln without offending the supporters of Seward. This happy result secured victory for the party in the national contest. No wounds were inflicted, no hatreds planted, no harmonies disturbed. The devotion to the cause was so sincere and so dominant, that the personal ambitions of a lifetime were subordinated in an instant upon the demand of the popular tribunal whose decision was final. The discipline of defeat was endured with grace, and self-abnegation was accepted as the supreme duty of the hour.

A wise selection was made for Vice-President. Hannibal Hamlin belonged originally to the school of Democrats who supported Jackson, and who took Silas Wright as their model. After the repeal of the Missouri Compromise he separated himself from his old associates, and proved to be a powerful factor in the formation of the Republican party. His candidacy for Governor of Maine, in 1856, broke down the Democratic party in that State, and gave a great impulse to the Republican campaign throughout the country. In strong common sense, in sagacity and sound judgment, in rugged integrity of character, Mr. Hamlin has had no superior among public men. It is generally fortunate for a political party if the nominee for Vice-President does not prove a source of weakness in the popular canvass. Mr. Hamlin proved a source of strength, and imparted confidence and courage to the great movement against the Democratic party.

In the four Presidential tickets in the field, every shade of political opinion was represented, but only two of the candidates embodied positive policies. Mr. Lincoln was in favor of prohibiting the extension of slavery by law. Mr. Breckinridge was in favor of protecting its extension by law. No issue could have been more pronounced than the one thus presented. Mr. Douglas desired to evade it, and advocated his doctrine of non-intervention which was full of contradictions, and was in any event offensive to the anti-slavery conscience. It permitted what was considered a grievous moral wrong to be upheld, if a majority of white men would vote in favor of upholding it. Mr. Bell desired to avoid the one question that was in the popular mind, and to lead the people away from every issue except the abstract one of preserving the Union. By what means the Union could be preserved against the efforts of Southern secessionists, Mr. Bell's party did not explain. The popular apprehension was that Mr. Bell would concede all they asked, and insure the preservation of the Union by yielding to the demands of the only body of men who threatened to destroy it.

As the canvass grew animated, and the questions at issue were elaborately discussed before the people, the conviction became general that the supporters of Breckinridge contemplated the destruction of the government. This was not simply the belief of the Republicans. It was quite as general among the supporters of Douglas and the supporters of Bell. In an earlier stage of the anti-slavery contest, this fact would have created great alarm in the Northern States, but now the people would not yield to such a fear. They were not only inspired by the principles they upheld, but there was a general desire to test the question thus presented. If a President, constitutionally elected, could not be inaugurated, it was better then and there to ascertain the fact than to postpone the issue by an evasion or a surrender. The Republicans were constantly strengthened by recruits from the Douglas ranks. Many of the friends of Douglas had become enraged by the course of the Southern Democrats, and now joined the Republicans, in order to force the issue upon the men who had been so domineering and offensive in the Charleston and Baltimore conventions. Mr. Lincoln gained steadily and derived great strength from the division of his opponents. But their union could not have defeated him. In New York, New Jersey, and Rhode Island, but one electoral ticket was presented against Mr. Lincoln, his opponents having coalesced in a joint effort to defeat him. In New Jersey, the "Fusion" ticket, as the combination was termed, was made up of three Douglas, two Bell, and two Breckinridge representatives. Owing to the fact that some of the supporters of Douglas refused to vote for the Breckinridge and Bell candidates, Mr. Lincoln received four electoral votes in New Jersey, though, in the aggregate popular vote, the majority was against him. In California and Oregon he received pluralities. In every other free State he had an absolute majority. Breckinridge carried every slave State except four; Virginia, Kentucky, and Maryland voting for Bell, and Missouri voting for Douglas.

The long political struggle was over. A more serious one was about to begin. For the first time in the history of the government, the South was defeated in a Presidential election where an issue affecting the slavery question was involved. There had been grave conflicts before, sometimes followed by compromise, oftener by victory for the South. But the election of 1860 was the culmination of a contest which was inherent in the structure of the government; which was foreshadowed by the Louisiana question of 1812; which became active and angry over the admission of Missouri; which was revived by the annexation of Texas, and still further inflamed by the Mexican war; which was partially allayed by the compromises of 1850; which was precipitated for final settlement by the repeal of the Missouri Compromise, by the consequent struggle for mastery in Kansas, and by the aggressive intervention of the Supreme Court in the case of Dred Scott. These are the events which led, often slowly, but always with directness, to the political revolution of 1860.

The contest was inevitable, and the men whose influence developed and encouraged it may charitably be regarded as the blind agents of fate. But if personal responsibility for prematurely forcing the conflict belongs to any body of men, it attaches to those who, in 1854, broke down the adjustments of 1820 and of 1850. If the compromises of those years could not be maintained, the North believed that all compromise was impossible; and they prepared for the struggle which this fact foreshadowed. They had come to believe that the house divided against itself could not stand; that the Republic half slave, half free, could not endure. They accepted as their leader the man who proclaimed these truths. The peaceful revolution was complete when Abraham Lincoln was chosen President of the United States.

In the closing and more embittered period of the political struggle over the question of Slavery, public opinion in the South grew narrow, intolerant, and cruel. The mass of the Southern people refused to see any thing in the anti-slavery movement except fanaticism; they classed Abolitionists with the worst of malefactors; they endeavored to shut out by the criminal code and by personal violence the enlightened and progressive sentiment of the world. Their success in arousing the prejudice and unifying the action of the people in fifteen States against the surging opinion of Christendom is without parallel. Philanthropic movements elsewhere were regarded with jealousy and distrust. Southern statesmen of the highest rank looked upon British emancipation in the West Indies as designedly hostile to the prosperity and safety of their own section, and as a plot for the ultimate destruction of the Republic. Each year the hatred against the North deepened, and the boundary between the free States and the slave States was becoming as marked as a line of fire. The South would see no way of dealing with Slavery except to strengthen and fortify it at every point. Its extinction they would not contemplate. Even a suggestion for its amelioration was regarded as dangerous to the safety of the State and to the sacredness of the family.

Southern opinion had not always been of this type. It had changed with the increase in the number of slaves, and with the increased profit from their labor. Before the Revolutionary war, Virginia had earnestly petitioned George III. to prohibit the importation of slaves from Africa, and the answer of His Majesty was a peremptory instruction to the Royal Governor at Williamsburg, "not to assent to any law of the Colonial Legislature by which the importation of slaves should in any respect be prohibited or obstructed." Anti-slavery opinion was developed in a far greater degree in the American Colonies than in the mother country. When the Convention of 1787 inserted in the Federal Constitution a clause giving to Congress the power to abolish the slave-trade after the year 1808, they took a step far in advance of European opinion. A society was formed in London, in the year 1787, for the suppression of the slave-trade. Although it was organized under the auspices of the distinguished philanthropists, William Clarkson and Granville Sharp, it had at the time as little influence upon the popular opinion of England as the early efforts of William Lloyd Garrison and the Society for the Abolition of Domestic Slavery had upon the public opinion of the United States. It was not until 1791 that Mr. Wilberforce introduced in Parliament his first bill for the suppression of the slave-trade, and though he had the enlightened sympathy of Mr. Pitt, the eminent premier did not dare to make it a ministerial measure. The bill was rejected by a large vote. It was not until fifteen years later that the conscience of England won a victory over the organized capital engaged in the infamous traffic. It was the young and struggling Republic in America that led the way, and she led the way under the counsel and direction of Southern statesmen. American slave-holders were urging the abolition of the traffic while London merchants were using every effort to continue it, and while Bristol, the very headquarters of the trade, was represented in Parliament by Edmund Burke. Even among the literary men of England, — if Boswell's gossip may be trusted, — Dr. Johnson was peculiar in his hatred of the infamy — a hatred which his obsequious biographer mollifies to an "unfavorable notion," and officiously ascribes to "prejudice and imperfect or false information." The anti-slavery work of England was originally inspired from America, and the action of the British Parliament was really so directed as to make the prohibition of the slave-trade correspond in time with that prescribed in the Federal Constitution. The American wits and critics of that day did not fail to note the significance of the date, and to appreciate the statesmanship and philanthropy which led the British Parliament to terminate the trade at the precise moment when the American Congress closed the market.

The slaves in the United States numbered about seven hundred thousand when Washington's administration was organized. They had increased to four millions when Lincoln was chosen President. Their number in 1860 was less in proportion to the white population than it was in 1789. The immigration of whites had changed the ratio. But the more marked and important change had been in the value of slave labor. In 1789 the slaves produced little or no surplus, and in many States were regarded as a burden. In 1860 they produced a surplus of at least three hundred millions of dollars. The power of agricultural production in the Southern States had apparently no limit. If the institution of Slavery could be rendered secure, the dominant minds of the South saw political power and boundless wealth within their grasp. They saw that they could control the product and regulate the price of a staple in constant demand among every people on the globe. The investment of the South in slaves represented a capital of two thousand millions of dollars, reckoned only upon the salable value of the chattel. Estimated by its capacity to produce wealth, the institution of Slavery represented to the white population of the South a sum vastly in excess of two thousand millions. Without slave-labor, the cotton, rice, and sugar lands were, in the view of Southern men, absolutely valueless. With the labor of the slave, they could produce three hundred millions a year in excess of the food required for the population. Three hundred millions a year represented a remunerative interest on a capital of five thousand millions of dollars. In the history of the world there has perhaps never been so vast an amount of productive capital firmly consolidated under one power, subject to the ultimate control and direction of so small a number of men.

With such extraordinary results attained, the natural desire of slave-holders was to strive for development and expansion. They had in the South more land than could be cultivated by the slaves they then owned, or by their natural increase within any calculable period. So great was the excess of land that, at the time Texas was annexed, Senator Ashley of Arkansas declared that his State alone could, with the requisite labor, produce a larger cotton-crop than had ever been grown in the whole country. In the minds of the extreme men of the South the remedy was to be found in re-opening the African slave-trade. So considerate and withal so conservative a man as Alexander H. Stephens recognized the situation. When he retired from public service, at the close of the Thirty-sixth Congress, in

1859, he delivered an address to his constituents, which was in effect a full review of the Slavery question. He told them plainly that they could not keep up the race with the North in the occupation of new territory "unless they could get more Africans." He did not avowedly advocate the re-opening of the slave-trade, but the logic of his speech plainly pointed to that end.

John Forsythe of Alabama, an aggressive leader of the most radical pro-slavery type, carried the argument beyond the point where the prudence of Mr. Stephens permitted him to go. In recounting the triumphs of the South, he avowed that one stronghold remained to be carried, "the abrogation of the prohibition of the slave-trade." So eminent a man as William L. Yancey formally proposed in a Southern commercial convention, in 1858, that the South should demand the repeal of the laws "declaring the slave-trade to be piracy;" and Governor Adams of South Carolina pronounced those laws to be "a fraud upon the slave-holders of the South." The Governor of Mississippi went still farther, and exhibited a confidence in the scheme which was startling. He believed that "the North would not refuse so just a demand if the South should unitedly ask it." Jefferson Davis did not join in the movement, but expressed a hearty contempt for those "who prate of the inhumanity and sinfulness of the slave-trade."

Quotations of this character might be indefinitely multiplied. The leaders of public opinion in the Cotton States were generally tending in the same direction, and, in the language of Jefferson Davis, were basing their conclusions on "the interest of the South, and not on the interest of the African." Newspapers and literary reviews in the Gulf States were seconding and enforcing the position of their public men, and were gradually but surely leading the mind of the South to a formal demand for the privilege of importing Africans. A speaker in the Democratic National Convention at Charleston, personally engaged in the domestic slave-trade, frankly declared that the traffic in native Africans would be far more humane. The thirty thousand slaves annually taken from the border States to the cotton-belt represented so great an aggregation of misery, that the men engaged in conducting it were, even by the better class of slave-holders, regarded with abhorrence, and spoken of as infamous.

It is worthy of observation that the re-opening of the African slave-trade was not proposed in the South until after the Dred Scott decision. This affords a measure of the importance which pro-slavery statesmen attached to the position of the Supreme Court. In the light of these facts, the repeated protests of Senator Douglas "against such schemes as the re-opening of the African slave-trade" were full of significance; nor could any development of Southern opinion have vindicated more completely the truth proclaimed by Mr. Lincoln, that the country was destined to become wholly anti-slavery or wholly pro-slavery. The financial interest at stake in the fate of the institution was so vast, that Southern men felt impelled to seek every possible safeguard against the innumerable dangers which surrounded it. The revival of the African slave-trade was the last suggestion for its protection, and was the immediate precursor of its destruction.

In reckoning the wealth-producing power of the Southern States, the field of slave labor has been confined to the cotton-belt. In the more northern of the slave-holding States, free labor was more profitable, and hence the interest in Slavery was not so vital or so enduring as in the extreme South. There can be little doubt that the slave States of the border would have abolished the institution at an early period except for the fact that their slaves became a steady and valuable source of labor-supply for the increased demand which came from the constantly expanding area of cotton. But this did not create so palpable or so pressing an interest as was felt in the Gulf States, and the resentment caused by the election of Lincoln was proportionally less. The border States would perhaps have quietly accepted the result, however distasteful, except for the influence brought upon them from the extreme South, where the maintenance of Slavery was deemed vital to prosperity and to safety.

In the passions aroused by the agitation over slavery, Southern men failed to see (what in cooler moments they could readily perceive) that the existence of the Union and the guaranties of the Constitution were the shield and safeguard of the South. The long contest they had been waging with the anti-slavery men of the free States had blinded Southern zealots to the essential strength of their position so long as their States continued to be members of the Federal Union. But for the constant presence of national power, and its constant exercise under the provisions of the Constitution, the South would have no protection against the anti-slavery assaults of the civilized world. Abolitionists from the very beginning of their energetic crusade against slavery had seen the Constitution standing in their way, and with the unsparing severity of their logic had denounced it as "a league with hell and a covenant with death." The men who were directing public opinion in the South were trying to persuade themselves, and had actually persuaded many of their followers, that the election of Lincoln was the overthrow of the Constitution, and that their safety in the Union was at an end. They frightened the people by Lincoln's declaration that the Republic could not exist half slave, half free. They would not hear his own lucid and candid explanation of his meaning, but chose rather to accept the most extreme construction which the pro-slavery literature and the excited harangues of a Presidential canvass had given to Mr. Lincoln's language.

The confidence of Southern men in their power to achieve whatever end they should propose was unbounded. They apparently did not stop to contemplate the effect upon slavery which a reckless course on their part might produce. Having been schooled to the utmost conservatism in affairs of government, they suddenly became rash and adventurous. They were apparently ready to put every thing to hazard, professing to believe that othing could be as fatal as to remain under what they termed the "Government of Lincoln." They believed they could maintain themselves against physical force, but they took no heed of a stronger power which was sure to work against them. They disregarded the enlightened philanthropy and the awakened conscience which had abolished slavery in every other Republic of America, which had thrown the protection of law over the helpless millions of India, which had moved even the Russian Autocracy to consider the enfranchisement of the serf. They would not realize that the contest they were rashly inviting was not alone with the anti-slavery men of the free States, not alone with the spirit of loyalty to the Republic, but that it carried with it a challenge to the progress of civilization, and was a fight against the nineteenth century.

CHAPTER IX.

THE Slavery question was not the only one which developed into a chronic controversy between certain elements of Northern opinion and certain elements of Southern opinion. A review of the sectional struggle would be incomplete if it did not embrace a narrative of those differences on the tariff which at times led to serious disturbance, and, on one memorable occasion, to an actual threat of resistance to the authority of the government. The division upon the tariff was never so accurately defined by geographical lines as was the division upon slavery; but the aggressive elements on each side of both questions finally coalesced in the same States, North and South. Massachusetts and South Carolina marched in the vanguard of both controversies; and the States which respectively followed on the tariff issue were, in large part, the same which followed on the slavery question, on both sides of Mason and Dixon's line.   Anti-slavery zeal and a tariff for protection went hand in hand in New England, while pro-slavery principles became nearly identical with free-trade in the Cotton States.   If the rule had its exception, it was in localities where the strong pressure of special interest was operating, as in the case of the sugar-planter of Louisiana, who was willing to concede generous protection to the cotton-spinner of Lowell if he could thereby secure an equally strong protection, in his own field of enterprise, against the pressing competition of the island of Cuba.

The general rule, after years of experimental legislation, resolved itself into protection in the one section and free-trade in the other.   And this was not an unnatural division.   Zeal against slavery was necessarily accompanied by an appreciation of the dignity of free labor; and free labor was more generously remunerated under the stimulus of protective laws.   The same considerations produced a directly opposite conclusion in the South, where those interested in slave labor could not afford to build up a class of free laborers with high wages and independent opinions.   The question was indeed one of the kind not infrequently occurring in the adjustment of public policies where the same cause is continually producing different and apparently contradictory effects when the field of its operation is changed.

The issues growing out of the subject of the tariff were, however, in many respects entirely distinct from the slavery question. The one involved the highest moral considerations, the other was governed solely by expediency.   Whether one man could hold property in another was a question which took deep hold of the consciences of men, and was either right or wrong in itself.   But whether the rate of duty upon a foreign import should be increased or lowered was a question to be settled solely by business and financial considerations.   Slavery in the United States, as long experience had proved, could be most profitably employed in the cultivation of cotton.   The cost of its production, in the judgment of those engaged in it, was increased by the operation of a tariff, whereas its price, being determined by the markets of the world, derived no benefit from protective duties.   The clothing of the slave, the harness for the horses and mules, the ploughs, the rope, the bagging, the iron ties, were all, they contended, increased in price to the planter without any corresponding advance in the market value of the product.   In the beginning of the controversy it was expected that the manufacture of cotton would grow up side by side with its production, and that thus the community which produced the fibre would share in the profit of the fabric. During this period the representatives from the Cotton States favored high duties; but as time wore on, and it became evident that slave-labor was not adapted to the factory, and that it was undesirable if not impossible to introduce free white labor with remunerative wages side by side with unpaid slave-labor, the leading minds of the South were turned against the manufacturing interest, and desired to legislate solely in aid of the agricultural interest.

It was this change in the South that produced the irritating discussions in Congress,—discussions always resulting in sectional bitterness and sometimes threatening the public safety. The tariff question has in fact been more frequently and more elaborately debated than any other issue since the foundation of the Federal Government. The present generation is more familiar with questions relating to slavery, to war, to reconstruction; but as these disappear by permanent adjustment the tariff returns, and is eagerly seized upon by both sides to the controversy. More than any other issue, it represents the enduring and persistent line of division between the two parties which in a generic sense have always existed in the United States;—the party of strict construction and the party of liberal construction, the party of State Rights and the party of National Supremacy, the party of stinted revenue and restricted expenditure, and the party of generous income with its wise application to public improvement; the party, in short, of Jefferson as against the party of Hamilton, the party of Jackson as against that of Clay, the party of Buchanan and Douglas as against that of Lincoln and Seward. Taxes, whether direct or indirect, always interest the mass of mankind, and the differences of the systems by which they shall be levied and collected will always present an absorbing political issue. Public attention may be temporarily engrossed by some exigent subject of controversy, but the tariff alone steadily and persistently recurs for agitation, and for what is termed settlement. Thus far in our history, settlement has only been the basis of new agitation. and each successive agitation leads again to new settlement.

After the experience of nearly a century on the absorbing question of the best mode of levying duties on imports, the divergence of opinion is as wide and as pronounced as when the subject first engaged the attention of the Federal Government. Theories on the side of high duties and theories on the side of low duties are maintained with just as great vigor as in 1789. In no question of a material or financial character has there been so much interest displayed as in this. On a question of sentiment and of sympathy like that of slavery, feeling is inevitable; but it has been matter of surprise that the adjustment of a scale of duties on importations of foreign merchandise should be accompanied, as it often has been, by displays of excitement often amounting to passion.

The cause is readily apprehended when it is remembered that the tariff question is always presented as one not merely affecting the general prosperity, but as specifically involving the question of bread to the millions who are intrusted with the suffrage. The industrial classes study the question closely; and, in many of the manufacturing establishments of the country, the man who is working for day wages will be found as keenly alive to the effect of a change in the protective duty as the stockholder whose dividends are to be affected. Thus capital and labor coalesce in favor of high duties to protect the manufacturer, and, united, they form a political force which has been engaged in an economic battle from the foundation of the government. Sometimes they have suffered signal defeat, and sometimes they have gained signal victories.

The landmarks which have been left in a century of discussion and of legislative experiment deserve a brief reference for a better understanding of the subject to-day. Our financial experience has been practically as extended as that of the older nations of Europe. When the Republic was organized, Political Economy as understood in the modern sense was in its elementary stage, and indeed could hardly be called a science. Systems of taxation were everywhere crude and ruthless, and were in large degree fashioned after the Oriental practice of mulcting the man who will pay the most and resist the least. Adam Smith had published his "Enquiry into the Nature and Causes of the Wealth of Nations" in the year of the Declaration of Independence. Between that time and the formation of the Federal Government his views had exerted no perceptible influence on the financial system of England. British industries were protected by the most stringent enactments of Parliament, and England was the determined enemy not only of free trade but of fair trade. The emancipated Colonies found therefore in the mother country the most resolute foe to their manufacturing and commercial progress. American statesmen exhibited wisdom, moderation, and foresight in overcoming the obstacles to the material prosperity of the new Republic.

When the administration of Washington was organized in 1789, the government which he represented did not command a single dollar of revenue. They inherited a mountain of debt from the Revolutionary struggle, they had no credit, and the only representative of value which they controlled was the vast body of public land in the North-west Territory. But this was unavailable as a resource for present needs, and called for expenditure in the extensive surveys which were a prerequisite to sale and settlement. In addition therefore to every other form of poverty, the new government was burdened in the manner so expressively described as *land poor*, which implies the ownership of a large extent of real estate constantly calling for heavy outlay, and yielding no revenue. The Federal Government had one crying need, one imperative demand, — money !

An immediate system of taxation was therefore required, and the newly organized Congress lost no time in proceeding to the consideration of ways and means. As soon as a quorum of each branch of Congress was found to be present, the House gave its attention to the pressing demand for money. They did not even wait for the inauguration of President Washington, but began nearly a month before that important event to prepare a revenue bill which might, at the earliest moment, be ready for the Executive approval. Duties on imports obviously afforded the readiest resource, and Congress devoted itself with assiduous industry to the consideration of that form of revenue. With the exception of an essential law directing the form of oath to be taken by the Federal officers, the tariff Act was the first passed by the new government. It was enacted indeed two months in advance of the law creating a Treasury Department, and providing for a Secretary thereof. The need of money was indeed so urgent that provision was made for raising it by duties on imports before the appointment of a single officer of the Cabinet was authorized. Even a Secretary of State, whose first duty it was to announce the organization of the government to foreign nations, was not nominated for a full month after the Act imposing duties had been passed.

All the issues involved in the new Act were elaborately and intelligently debated. The first Congress contained a large proportion of the men who had just before been engaged in framing the Federal Constitution, and who were therefore fresh from the councils which had carefully considered and accurately measured the force of every provision of that great charter of government. It is therefore a fact of lasting importance that the first tariff law enacted under the Federal Government set forth its object in the most succinct and explicit language. It opened, after the excellent fashion of that day, with a stately preamble beginning with the emphatic "whereas," and declaring that "it is necessary for the support of government, for the discharge of the debts of the United States, *and for the encouragement and protection of manufactures*, that duties be laid on imported goods, wares, and merchandise." Among the men who agreed to that declaration were some of the most eminent in our history. James Madison, then young enough to add junior to his name, was the most conspicuous; and associated with him were Richard Henry Lee, Theodorick Bland, Charles Carroll of Carrollton, Rufus King, George Clymer, Oliver Ellsworth, Elias Boudinot, Fisher Ames, Elbridge Gerry, Roger Sherman, Jonathan Trumbull, Lambert Cadwalader, Thomas Fitzsimons, the two Muhlenbergs, Thomas Tudor Tucker, Hugh Williamson, Abraham Baldwin, Jeremiah Van Rensselaer, and many other leading men, both from the North and the South.

It is a circumstance of curious interest that nearly, if not quite, all the arguments used by the supporters and opponents of a protective system were presented at that time and with a directness and ability which have not been surpassed in any subsequent discussion. The "*ad valorem*" system of levying duties was maintained against "specific" rates in almost the same language employed in the discussions of recent years. The "infant manufactures," the need of the "fostering care of the government" for the promotion of "home industry," the advantages derived from "diversified pursuits," the competition of "cheap labor in Europe," were all rehearsed with a familiarity and ease which implied their previous and constant use in the legislative halls of the different States before the power to levy imposts was remitted to the jurisdiction of Congress. A picture of the industrial condition of the country at that day can be inferred from the tariff bill first passed; and the manufactures that were deemed worthy of encouragement are clearly outlined in the debate. Mr. Clymer of Pennsylvania asked for a protective duty on steel, stating that a furnace in Philadelphia "had produced three hundred tons in two years, and with a little encouragement would supply enough for the consumption of the whole Union." The Pennsylvania members at the same time strenuously opposed a duty on coal which they wished to import as cheaply as possible to aid in the development of their iron ores. The manufacture of glass had been started in Maryland, and the members from that State secured a duty on the foreign article after considerable discussion, and with the significant reservation, in deference to popular habits, that "black quart-bottles" should be admitted free.

Mr. Madison opposed a tax on cordage, and "questioned the propriety of raising the price of any article that entered materially into the structure of vessels," making in effect the same argument on that subject which has been repeated without improvement so frequently in later years. Indigo and tobacco, two special products of the South, were protected by prohibitory duties, while the raising of cotton was encouraged by a duty of three cents per pound on the imported article. Mr. Burke of South Carolina said the culture of cotton was contemplated on a large scale in the South, "if good seed could be procured." The manufacture of iron, wool, leather, paper, already in some degree developed, was stimulated by the bill. The fisheries were aided by a bounty on every barrel caught; and the navigation interest received a remarkable encouragement by providing that "a discount of ten per cent on all duties imposed by this Act shall be allowed on such goods, wares, and merchandise as shall be imported in vessels built in the United States, and wholly the property of a citizen or citizens thereof." The bill throughout was an American measure, designed to promote American interests; and as a first step in a wide field of legislation, it was characterized in an eminent degree by wisdom, by moderation, and by a keen insight into the immediate and the distant future of the country. The ability which framed the Constitution was not greater than that displayed by the first generation of American statesmen who were called to legislate under its generous provisions and its wise restrictions.

These great statesmen proceeded in the light of facts which taught them that, though politically separated from the mother country, we were still in many ways dependent upon her, in as large a degree as when we were Colonies, subject to her will and governed for her advantage. The younger Pitt boasted that he had reconquered the Colonies as commercial dependencies, contributing more absolutely and in larger degree to England's prosperity than before

the political connection was severed.   He treated the States, after
the close of the peace of 1783, with a haughty assumption of superiority, if not indeed with contempt — not even condescending to
accredit a diplomatic representative to the country, though John
Adams was in London as Minister Plenipotentiary and Envoy Extraordinary from the United States. English laws of protection
under the Pitt administration were steadily framed against the development of manufactures and navigation in America, and the tendency when the Federal Constitution was adopted had been, in the
planting States especially, towards a species of commercial dependence which was enabling England to absorb our trade.

The first tariff Act was therefore in a certain sense a second
Declaration of Independence; and by a coincidence which could
not have been more striking or more significant, it was approved by
President Washington on the fourth day of July, 1789. Slow as were
the modes of communicating intelligence in those days, this Act of
Congress did, in a suggestive way, arouse the attention of both continents. The words of the preamble were ominous. The duties levied
were exceedingly moderate, scarcely any of them above fifteen per
cent, the majority not higher than ten.   But the beginning was
made ; and the English manufacturers and carriers saw that the
power to levy ten per cent. could at any time levy a hundred per
cent. if the interest of the new government should demand it.   The
separate States had indeed possessed the power to levy imposts, but
they had never exercised it in any comprehensive manner, and had
usually adapted the rate of duty to English trade rather than to the
protection of manufacturing interests at home.   The action of the
Federal Government was a new departure, of portentous magnitude,
and was so recognized at home and abroad.

It was not the percentage which aroused and disturbed England.
It was the power to levy the duty at all.   In his famous speech on
American taxation in the House of Commons fifteen years before,
Mr. Burke asserted that it was "not the weight of the duty, but the
weight of the preamble, which the Americans were unable and unwilling to bear."   The tax actually imposed was not oppressive, but
the preamble implied the power to levy upon the Colonies whatever
tax the British Government might deem expedient, and this led to
resistance and to revolution.   The force of the preamble was now
turned against Great Britain.   She saw that the extent to which the
principle of protective duties might be carried was entirely a matter

of discretion with the young Republic whose people had lately been her subjects and might now become her rivals. The principle of protecting the manufactures and encouraging the navigation of America had been distinctly proclaimed in the first law enacted by the new government, and was thus made in a suggestive and emphatic sense the very corner-stone of the republican edifice which the patriots of the Revolution were aiming to construct.

The opinions of Mr. Madison as thus shown in the first legislation by Congress are the more significant from the fact that he belonged to the Jeffersonian school, believed in the strictest construction of granted power, was a zealous Republican in the partisan divisions of the day, and was always opposed to the more liberal, or, as he would regard them, the more latitudinarian views of the Federal party. In regard to the protection and encouragement of manufactures there seemed to be no radical difference between parties in the early period of the government. On that issue, to quote a phrase used on another occasion, "they were all Federalists and all Republicans." Mr. Hamilton's celebrated report on Manufactures, submitted in answer to a request from the House of Representatives of December, 1790, sustained and elaborated the views on which Congress had already acted, and brought the whole influence of the Executive Department to the support of a Protective Tariff. Up to that period no minister of finance among the oldest and most advanced countries of Europe had so ably discussed the principles on which national prosperity was based. The report has long been familiar to students of political economy, and has had, like all Mr. Hamilton's work, a remarkable value and a singular application in the developments of subsequent years.

Mr. Hamilton sustained the plan of encouraging home manufactures by protective duties, even to the point in some instances of making those "duties equivalent to prohibition." He did not contemplate a prohibitive duty as the means of encouraging a manufacture not already domesticated, but declared it "only fit to be employed when a manufacture has made such a progress, and is in so many hands, as to insure a due competition and an adequate supply on reasonable terms." This argument did not seem to follow the beaten path which leads to the protection of "infant manufactures," but rather aimed to secure the home market for the strong and well-developed enterprises. Mr. Hamilton did not turn back from the consequences which his argument involved. He perceived its logical

conclusions and frankly accepted them.   He considered "the monopoly of the domestic market to its own manufacturers as the reigning
policy of manufacturing nations," and declared that "a similar policy
on the part of the United States in every proper instance was dictated
by the principles of distributive justice, certainly by the duty of
endeavoring to secure to their own citizens a reciprocity of advantages." He avowed his belief that "the internal competition which
takes place, soon does away with every thing like monopoly, and by
degrees reduces the price of the article to the *minimum* of a reasonable profit on the capital employed.   This accords with the reason of
the thing and with experience." He contended that "a reduction
has in several instances immediately succeeded the establishment of
domestic manufacture."   But even if this result should not follow,
he maintained that "in a national view a temporary enhancement
of price must always be well compensated by a permanent reduction
of it."   The doctrine of protection, even with the enlarged experience of subsequent years, has never been more succinctly or more
felicitously stated.

Objections to the enforcement of the "protective" principle
founded on a lack of constitutional power were summarily dismissed
by Mr. Hamilton as "having no good foundation."   He had been a
member of the convention that formed the Constitution, and had
given attention beyond any other member to the clauses relating to
the collection and appropriation of revenue.   He said the "power to
raise money" as embodied in the Constitution "is plenary and indefinite," and "the objects for which it may be appropriated are no less
comprehensive than the payment of the public debts, the providing
for the common defense and the *general welfare*."   He gives the
widest scope to the phrase "general welfare," and declares that "it
is of necessity left to the discretion of the national Legislature to pronounce upon the objects which concern the general welfare, and for
which under that description an appropriation of money is requisite
and proper."   Mr. Hamilton elaborates his argument on this head
with consummate power, and declares that "the only qualification"
to the power of appropriation under the phrase "general welfare" is
that the purpose for which the money is applied shall "be *general*,
and not *local*, its operation extending in fact throughout the Union,
and not being confined to a particular spot."   The limitations and
hypercritical objections to the powers conferred by the Constitution,
both in the raising and appropriating of money, originated in large

part after the authors of that great charter had passed away, and have been uniformly stimulated by class interests which were not developed when the organic law was enacted.

Some details of Mr. Hamilton's report are especially interesting in view of the subsequent development of manufacturing enterprises. "Iron works" he represents as "greatly increasing in the United States," and so great is the demand that "iron furnished before the Revolution at an average of sixty-four dollars per ton" was then sold at "eighty." Nails and spikes, made in large part by boys, needed further "protection," as 1,800,000 pounds had been imported the previous year. Iron was wholly made by "charcoal," but there were several mines of "fossil coal" already "worked in Virginia," and "a copious supply of it would be of great value to the iron industry." Respecting "cotton" Mr. Hamilton attached far more consideration to its manufacture than to its culture. He distrusted the quality of that grown at home because so far from the equator, and he wished the new factories in Rhode Island and Massachusetts to have the best article at the cheapest possible rate. To this end the repeal of the three-cent duty on cotton levied the preceding year was "indispensable." He argued that "not being, like hemp, an universal production of the country, cotton affords less assurance of an adequate internal supply." If the duty levied on glass should not prove sufficient inducement to its manufacture, he would stimulate it "by a direct bounty."

Mr. Hamilton's conceptions of an enlarged plan of "protection" included not only "prohibitive duties," but when necessary a system of "bounties and premiums" in addition. He was earnestly opposed to "a capitation-tax," and declared such levies as an income-tax to be "unavoidably hurtful to industry." Indirect taxes were obviously preferred by him wherever they were practicable. Indeed upon any other system of taxation he believed it would prove impossible for the Republic of 1790 to endure the burden imposed upon the public treasury by the funding of the debt of the Revolution. More promptly than any other financier of that century he saw that ten dollars could be more easily collected by indirect tax than one dollar by direct levy, and that he could thus avoid those burdensome exactions from the people which had proved so onerous in Europe, and which had just aided in precipitating France into bloody revolution.

Important and radical additions to the revenue system promptly followed Mr. Hamilton's recommendations. From that time onward, for a period of more than twenty years, additional tariff laws were passed by each succeeding Congress, modifying and generally increasing the rate of duties first imposed, and adding many new articles to the dutiable list. When the war of 1812 was reached, a great but temporary change was made in the tariff laws by increasing the entire list of duties one hundred per cent. — simply doubling the rate in every case. Not content with this sweeping and wholesale increase of duty, the law provided an additional ten per cent. upon all goods imported in foreign vessels, besides collecting an additional tonnage-tax of one dollar and a half per ton on the vessel. Of course this was war-legislation, and the Act was to expire within one year after a treaty of peace should be concluded with Great Britain. With the experience of recent days before him, the reader does not need to be reminded that, under the stimulus of this extraordinary rate of duties, manufactures rapidly developed throughout the country. Importations from England being absolutely stopped by reason of the war, and in large part excluded from other countries by high duties, the American market was for the first time left substantially, or in large degree, to the American manufacturers.

With all the disadvantages which so sudden and so extreme a policy imposed on the people, the progress for the four years of these extravagant and exceptional duties was very rapid, and undoubtedly exerted a lasting influence on the industrial interests of the United States. But the policy was not one which commanded general support. Other interests came forward in opposition. New England was radically hostile to high duties, for the reason that they seriously interfered with the shipping and commercial interest in which her people were largely engaged. The natural result moreover was a sharp re-action, in which the protective principle suffered. Soon after the Treaty of Ghent was signed, movements were made for a reduction of duties, and the famous tariff of 1816 was the result.

In examining the debates on that important Act, it is worthy of notice that Mr. Clay, from an extreme Western State, was urging a high rate of duties on cotton fabrics, while his chief opponent was Daniel Webster, then a representative from Massachusetts. An additional and still stranger feature of the debate is found when Mr. Calhoun, co-operating with Mr. Clay, replied to Mr. Webster's free-trade speech in an elaborate defense of the doctrine of protection to our manufactures.

Mr. Calhoun spoke with enthusiasm, and gave an interesting *résumé* of the condition of the country as affected by the war with Great Britain. He believed that the vital deficiency in our financial condition was the lack of manufactures, and to supply that deficiency he was willing to extend the protecting arm of the government. "When our manufactures are grown to a certain perfection, as they soon will be under the fostering care of the government, we shall no longer experience these evils. The farmer will find a ready market for his surplus products, and, what is almost of equal consequence, a certain and cheap supply for all his wants. His prosperity will diffuse itself through every class in the community." Not satisfied with this unqualified support of the protective system, Mr. Calhoun supplemented it by declaring that "to give perfection to this state of things, it will be necessary to add as soon as possible a system of internal improvements." Mr. Webster's opposition to protection was based on the fact that it tended to depress commerce and curtail the profits of the carrying-trade.

The tariff of 1816 was termed "moderately protective," but even in that form it encountered the opposition of the commercial interest. It was followed in the country by severe depression in all departments of trade, not because the duties were not in themselves sufficiently high, but from the fact that it followed the war tariff, and the change was so great as to produce not only a re-action but a revolution in the financial condition of the country. All forms of industry languished. Bankruptcy was wide-spread, and the distress between 1817 and 1824 was perhaps deeper and more general than at any other period of our history. There was no immigration of foreigners, and consequently no wealth from that source. There was no market for agricultural products, and the people were therefore unable to indulge in liberal expenditure. Their small savings could be more profitably invested in foreign than in domestic goods, and hence American manufactures received little patronage. The traditions of that period, as given by the generation that lived through it, are sorrowful and depressing. The sacrifice of great landed estates, worth many millions could they have been preserved for the heirs of the next generation, was a common feature in the general distress and desolation. The continuance of this condition of affairs had no small influence on the subsequent division of parties. It naturally led to a change in the financial system, and in 1824 a tariff Act was passed, materially enlarging the scope of the Act of 1816.

The Act of 1824 was avowedly protective in its character and was adopted through the influence of Mr. Clay, then Speaker of the House of Representatives. His most efficient ally on the floor was Mr. Buchanan of Pennsylvania who exerted himself vigorously in aid of the measure. Mr. Webster again appeared in the debate, arguing against the "obsolete and exploded notion of protection," and carrying with him nearly the whole vote of Massachusetts in opposition. Mr. Clay was enabled to carry the entire Kentucky delegation for the high protective tariff, and Mr. Calhoun's views having meanwhile undergone a radical change, South Carolina was found to be unanimous in opposition, and cordially co-operating with Massachusetts in support of free-trade. The effect of that tariff was undoubtedly favorable to the general prosperity, and during the administration of John Quincy Adams every material interest of the country improved. The result was that the supporters of the protective system, congratulating themselves upon the effect of the work of 1824, proceeded in 1828 to levy still higher duties. They applied the doctrine of protection to the raw materials of the country, the wool, the hemp, and all unmanufactured articles which by any possibility could meet with damaging competition from abroad.

It was indeed an era of high duties, of which, strange as it may seem to the modern reader, Silas Wright of New York and James Buchanan of Pennsylvania appeared as the most strenuous defenders, and were personally opposed in debate by John Davis of Massachusetts and Peleg Sprague of Maine. To add to the entanglement of public opinion, Mr. Webster passed over to the side of ultra-protection and voted for the bill, finding himself in company with Martin Van Buren of New York, and Thomas H. Benton of Missouri. It was an extraordinary commingling of political elements, in which it is difficult to find a line of partition logically consistent either with geographical or political divisions. Mr. Webster carried with him not more than two or three votes of the Massachusetts delegation. His colleague in the Senate, Nathaniel Silsbee, voted against him, and in the House such personal adherents as Edward Everett and Isaac C. Bates recorded themselves in the negative. There was a great deal of what in modern phrase would be called "fencing for position" in the votes on this test question of the day. The names of no less than five gentlemen who were afterwards Presidents of the United States were recorded in the yeas and nays on the passage of the bill in the two Houses, — Mr. Van

Buren, General Harrison, John Tyler, in the Senate, and Mr. Polk and Mr. Buchanan in the House.

There was a general feeling that the Act of 1828 marked a crisis in the history of tariff discussion, and that it would in some way lead to important results in the fate of political parties and political leaders. Mr. Calhoun was this year elected Vice-President of the United States, with General Jackson as President, and Mr. Van Buren was transferred from the Senate to the State Department as the head of Jackson's cabinet. When by his address and tact he had turned the mind of the President against Calhoun as his successor, and fully ingratiated himself in executive favor, the quarrel began which is elsewhere detailed at sufficient length. In this controversy, purely personal at the outset, springing from the clashing ambitions of two aspiring men, the tariff of 1828, especially with the vote of Mr. Van Buren in favor of it, was made to play an important part. The quarrel rapidly culminated in Mr. Calhoun's resignation of the Vice-Presidency, his leadership of the Nullification contest in South Carolina, and his re-election to the Senate of the United States some time before the expiration of the Vice-Presidential term for which he had been chosen. The result was a reduction of duties, first by the Act of July, 1832, and secondly by Mr. Clay's famous compromise Act of March 2, 1833, in which it was provided that by a sliding-scale all the duties in excess of twenty per cent. should be abolished within a period of ten years. It was this Act which for the time calmed excitement in the South, brought Mr. Calhoun and Mr. Clay into kindly relations, and somewhat separated Mr. Webster and Mr. Clay, — at least producing one of those periods of estrangement which, throughout their public career, alternated with the cordial friendship they really entertained for each other.

During the operation of this Act, — which was really an abandonment of the protective principle, — the financial crisis of 1837 came upon the country, and a period of distress ensued, almost equal to that which preceded the enactment of the tariff of 1824. Many persons, still in active business, recall with something of horror the hardships and privations which were endured throughout the country from 1837 to 1842. The long-continued depression produced the revolution against the Democratic party which ended in the overthrow of Mr. Van Buren and the election of General Harrison as President of the United States in 1840. The Whig Congress that came into power at the same time, proceeded to enact the law popularly known as the tariff of 1842, which was strongly protective in its character though not so extreme as the Act of 1828. The vote in favor of the bill was not exclusively Whig, as some of the Northern Democrats voted for it and some of the Southern Whigs against it. Conspicuous among the former were Mr. Buchanan of Pennsylvania and Mr. Wright of New York, who maintained a consistency with their vote for the tariff of 1828. Conspicuous among Southern Whigs against it were Berrien of Georgia, Clayton of Delaware, Mangum of North Carolina, Merrick of Maryland, and Rives of Virginia. The two men who above all others deserve honor for successful management of the bill were George Evans, the brilliant and accomplished senator from Maine, and Thomas M. T. McKennan, for many years an able, upright, and popular representative from Pennsylvania. John Quincy Adams, in a public speech delivered in 1843 in the town of Mr. McKennan's residence, ascribed to that gentleman the chief credit of carrying the Protective Tariff Bill through the House of Representatives. The vote showed, as all tariff bills before had, and as all since have shown, that the local interest of the constituency determines in large measure the vote of the representative; that planting sections grow more and more towards free-trade and manufacturing sections more and more towards protection.

The friends of home industry have always referred with satisfaction to the effect of the tariff of 1842 as an explicit and undeniable proof of the value of protection. It raised the country from a slough of despond to happiness, cheerfulness, confidence. It imparted to all sections a degree of prosperity which they had not known since the repeal of the tariff of 1828. The most suggestive proof of its strength and popularity was found in the contest of 1844 between Mr. Polk and Mr. Clay, where the Democrats in the critical Northern States assumed the advocacy of the tariff of 1842 as loudly as the supporters of Mr. Clay. Other issues overshadowed the tariff, which was really considered to be settled, and a President and Congress were chosen without any distinct knowledge on the part of their constituents as to what their action might be upon this question. The popular mind had been engrossed with the annexation of Texas and with the dawn of the free-soil excitement; hence protection and free-trade were in many States scarcely debated from lack of interest, and, in the States where interest prevailed, both parties took substantially the same side.

A deception had however been practiced in the manufacturing States of the North, and when the administration of Mr. Polk was installed, the friends of protection were startled by the appointment of a determined opponent of the tariff of 1842, as Secretary of the Treasury. Robert J. Walker was a senator from Mississippi when the Act was passed, and was bitterly opposed to it. He was a man of great originality, somewhat speculative in his views, and willing to experiment on questions of revenue to the point of rashness. He was not a believer in the doctrine of protection, was persuaded that protective duties bore unjustly and severely upon the planting section with which he was identified; and he came to his office determined to overthrow the tariff Act, which he had been unable to defeat in the Senate. Mr. Walker was excessively ambitious to make his term in the Treasury an era in the history of the country. He had a difficult task before him, — one from which a conservative man would have shrunk. The tariff was undoubtedly producing a valuable revenue; and, as the administration of Mr. Polk was about to engage in war, revenue was what they most needed. Being about to enter upon a war, every dictate of prudence suggested that aggressive issues should not be multiplied in the country. But Mr. Walker was not Secretary of War or Secretary of State, and he was unwilling to sit quietly down and collect the revenue under a tariff imposed by a Whig Congress, against which he had voted, while Buchanan in directing our foreign relations, and Marcy in conducting a successful war, would far outstrip him in public observation and in acquiring the elements of popularity adapted to the ambition which all three alike shared.

Mr. Walker made an elaborate report on the question of revenue, and attacked the tariff of 1842 in a manner which might well be termed savage. He arraigned the manufacturers as enjoying unfair advantages, — advantages held, as he endeavored to demonstrate, at the expense and to the detriment of the agriculturist, the mechanic, the merchant, the ship-owner, the sailor, and indeed of almost every industrial class. In reading Mr. Walker's report a third of a century after it was made, one might imagine that the supporters of the tariff of 1842 were engaged in a conspiracy to commit fraud, and that the manufacturers who profited by its duties were guilty of some crime against the people. But extreme as were his declarations and difficult as were the obstructions in his path, he was able to carry his point. Mr. Buchanan, the head of the Cabinet, had voted for the tariff of 1842, and Mr. Dallas, the Vice-President, had steadily and ably upheld the doctrine of protection when a member of the Senate. It was the position of Buchanan and Dallas on the tariff that won the October election of 1844 for Francis R. Shunk for governor of Pennsylvania, and thus assured the election of Mr. Polk. The administration of·which Buchanan and Dallas were such conspicuous and influential members could not forswear protection and inflict a free-trade tariff on Pennsylvania, without apparent dishonor and the abandonment of that State to the Whigs. It was therefore regarded not only as impracticable but as politically impossible.

It was soon ascertained however that Mr. Polk sympathized with Mr. Walker, and Mr. Buchanan was silenced and overridden. The free-trade tariff of 1846 was passed; and Mr. Dallas, who had been nominated because of his record as a protectionist, was subjected to the humiliation of giving his casting vote as Vice-President in favor of a tariff which was execrated in Pennsylvania, and which was honestly believed to be inimical in the highest degree to the interest of the American manufacturer and the American mechanic. The Act had no small influence in the overthrow of the Polk administration at the elections for the next ensuing Congress, and in the defeat of General Cass for the Presidency in 1848. As senator from Michigan, General Cass had voted for the bill, influenced thereto by his Southern associates, for whom he always did so much, and from whom he always received so little. Pennsylvania was at that time really a Democratic State, but she punished General Cass for his free-trade course by giving her electoral vote to Taylor. If she had given it to Cass he would have been chosen President.

It was in connection with the tariff agitation of 1846 that Simon Cameron originally obtained his strong hold upon the popular sympathy and support of Pennsylvania. He was a Democrat; had long been confidential adviser to Mr. Buchanan, and had supported Mr. Polk. But he was a believer in the doctrine of protection; and as he had aided in carrying Pennsylvania by declaring himself a friend to the tariff of 1842, he maintained his faith. When the Polk administration was organized, a vacancy was created in the Senate by Mr. Buchanan's appointment as Secretary of State. George W. Woodward was the regular nominee of the Democratic party for the place. But Cameron bolted, and with the aid of Whig votes was chosen senator. He resisted the passage of the tariff of 1846, stood firmly and consistently for the industrial interests of his State, cultivated an alliance with the Whigs in the Senate, and by their aid thwarted all the attempts of the Polk administration to interfere with his plans and purposes in Pennsylvania. The President endeavored to heal Judge Woodward's wounds by placing him on the bench of the Supreme Court as the successor of the eminent Henry Baldwin. Cameron induced the Whigs to reject him, and then forced the administration to nominate Robert C. Grier whose appointment was personally acceptable and agreeable to him. In the successful tactics then employed by Cameron may be found the secret of his remarkable career as a party manager in the field in which, for a full half-century, he was an active and indefatigable worker.

The Whig victory of 1848 was not sufficiently decisive to warrant any attempt, even had there been desire, to change the tariff. General Taylor had been elected without subscribing to a platform or pledging himself to a specific measure, and he was therefore in a position to resist and reject appeals of the ordinary partisan character. Moreover the tariff of 1846 was yielding abundant revenue, and the business of the country was in a flourishing condition at the time his administration was organized. Money became very abundant after the year 1849; large enterprises were undertaken, speculation was prevalent, and for a considerable period the prosperity of the country was general and apparently genuine. After 1852 the Democrats had almost undisputed control of the government, and had gradually become a free-trade party. The principles embodied in the tariff of 1846 seemed for the time to be so entirely vindicated and approved that resistance to it ceased, not only among the people but among the protective economists, and even among the manufacturers to a large extent. So general was this acquiescence that in 1856 a protective tariff was not suggested or even hinted by any one of the three parties which presented Presidential candidates.

It was not surprising therefore that with a plethoric condition of the National Treasury for two or three consecutive years, the Democratic Congress, in the closing session of Pierce's administration, enacted what has since been known as the tariff of 1857. By this law the duties were placed lower than they had been at any time since the war of 1812. The Act was well received by the people, and was indeed concurred in by a considerable proportion of the Republican party. The Senate had a large Democratic majority, but in the House three parties divided the responsibility, — no one of them having an absolute majority. The Republicans had a plurality and had chosen Mr. Banks Speaker, but the American party held the balance of power in the House and on several of the leading committees. Some prominent Republicans, however, remaining true to their old Whig traditions, opposed the reduction of duties. Mr. Seward voted against it, but his colleague, Mr. Hamilton Fish, voted for it. Mr. Seward represented the protective tendencies of the country districts of New York, and Mr. Fish the free-trade tendencies of the city. Mr. Sumner and Mr. Wilson both voted for it, as did also Senator Allen of Rhode Island, the direct representative of the manufacturers of that State. Mr. Bell of New Hampshire voted for it, while Senators Collamer and Foote of Vermont voted against it. Mr. Fessenden did not oppose it, but his colleague, Mr. Nourse, voted against it. The Connecticut senators, Foster and Toucey, one of each party, supported the measure.

In the House, the New-England representatives generally voted for the bill, but Mr. Morrill of Vermont opposed it. The Pennsylvania delegation, led by James H. Campbell and John Covode, did all in their power to defeat it. The two Washburns, Colfax, and McKee Dunn headed a formidable opposition from the West. Humphrey Marshall and Samuel F. Swope of Kentucky were the only representatives from slave States who voted in the negative; though in the Senate three old and honored Whigs, John Bell of Tennessee, John B. Thompson of Kentucky, and Henry S. Geyer of Missouri maintained their ancient faith and voted against lowering the duties. It was an extraordinary political combination that brought the senators from Massachusetts and the senators from South Carolina, the representatives from New England and the representatives from the cotton States, to support the same tariff bill, — a combination which had not before occurred since the administration of Monroe. This singular coalition portended one of two results: either an entire and permanent acquiescence in the rule of free-trade, or an entire abrogation of that system, and the revival, with renewed strength, of the doctrine of protection. Which it should be was determined by the unfolding of events not then foreseen, and the force of which it required years to measure.

The one excuse given for urging the passage of the Act of 1857 was that under the tariff of 1846 the revenues had become excessive, and the income of the government must be reduced. But it was soon found to be a most expensive mode of reaching that end. The first and most important result flowing from the new Act was

a large increase in importations and a very heavy drain in consequence upon the reserved specie of the country, to pay the balance
which the reduced shipments of agricultural products failed to meet.
In the autumn of 1857, half a year after the passage of the tariff
Act, a disastrous financial panic swept over the country, prostrat-
ing for the time all departments of business in about the same
degree. The agricultural, commercial, and manufacturing interests
were alike and equally involved. The distress for a time was
severe and wide-spread. The stagnation which ensued was discouraging and long continued, making the years from 1857 to 1860
extremely dull and dispiriting in business circles throughout the
Union. The country was not exhausted and depleted as it was after
the panic of 1837, but the business community had no courage,
energy was paralyzed, and new enterprises were at a stand-still.

It soon became evident that this condition of affairs would carry
the tariff question once more into the political arena, as an active
issue between parties. Thus far, the new Republican organization
had passively acquiesced in existing laws on the subject; but the
general distress caused great bodies of men, as is always the case, to
look to the action of the Government for relief. The Republicans
found therefore a new ground for attacking the Democracy, —
holding them responsible for the financial depression, initiating a
movement for returning to the principle and practice of protection,
and artfully identifying the struggle against slavery with the efforts
of the workingmen throughout the North to be freed from injurious
competition with the cheapened labor of Europe. This phase of the
question was presented with great force in certain States, and the
industrial classes, by a sort of instinct of self-preservation as it
seemed to them, began to consolidate their votes in favor of the
Republican party. They were made to see, by clever and persuasive
speakers, that the slave labor of the South and the ill-paid labor
of Europe were both hostile to the prosperity of the workingman
in the free States of America, and that the Republican party was of
necessity his friend, by its opposition to all the forms of labor which
stood in the way of his better remuneration and advancement.

The convention which nominated Mr. Lincoln met when the feeling against free-trade was growing, and in many States already deep-
rooted. A majority of those who composed that convention had
inherited their political creed from the Whig party, and were profound
believers in the protective teachings of Mr. Clay. But a strong min-

ority came from the radical school of Democrats, and, in joining the Republican party on the anti-slavery issue, had retained their ancient creed on financial and industrial questions. Care was for that reason necessary in the introduction of new issues and the imposition of new tests of party fellowship. The convention therefore avoided the use of the word "protection," and was contented with the moderate declaration that "sound policy requires such an adjustment of imposts as will encourage the development of the industrial interests of the whole country." A more emphatic declaration might have provoked resistance from a minority of the convention, and the friends of protection acted wisely in accepting what was offered with unanimity, rather than continue the struggle for a stronger creed which would have been morally weakened by party division. They saw also that the mere form of expression was not important, so long as the convention was unanimous on what theologians term the "substance of doctrine." It was noted that the vast crowd which attended the convention cheered the tariff resolution as lustily as that which opposed the spread of slavery into free territory. From that hour the Republican party gravitated steadily and rapidly into the position of avowed advocacy of the doctrine of protection. The national ticket which they presented was composed indeed of an original Whig protectionist and an original Democratic free-trader; but the drift of events, as will be seen, carried both alike into the new movement for a protective system.

A review of the tariff legislation in the period between the war of 1812 and the political revolution of 1860 exhibits some sudden and extraordinary changes on the part of prominent political leaders in their relation to the question. The inconsistency involved is however more apparent than real. Perhaps it would be correct to say that the inconsistency was justifiable in the eyes of those who found it necessary to be inconsistent. Mr. Webster was a persistent advocate of free-trade so long as Massachusetts was a commercial State. But when, by the operation of laws against the enactment of which he had in vain protested, Massachusetts became a manufacturing State, Mr. Webster naturally and inevitably became a protectionist. Mr. Calhoun began as a protectionist when he hoped for the diffusion and growth of manufactures throughout all sections alike.

He became a free-trader when he realized that the destiny of the South was to be purely agricultural, devoted to products whose market was not, in his judgment, to be enlarged by the tariff, and whose production was enhanced in cost by its operation. Colonel Benton's change was similar to Mr. Calhoun's, though at a later period, and not so abrupt or so radical. Mr. Van Buren's shifting of position was that of a man eagerly seeking the current of popular opinion, and ready to go with the majority of his party. Of all the great lights, but one burned steadily and clearly. Mr. Clay was always a protectionist, and, unlike Mr. Van Buren, he forced his party to go with him. But as a whole, the record of tariff legislation, from the very origin of the government, is the record of enlightened selfishness; and enlightened selfishness is the basis of much that is wisest in legislation.

It is natural that both sides to the tariff controversy should endeavor to derive support for their principles from the experience of the country. Nor can it be denied that each side can furnish many arguments which apparently sustain its own views and theories. The difficulty in reaching a satisfactory and impartial conclusion arises from the inability or unwillingness of the disputants to agree upon a common basis of fact. If the premises could be candidly stated, there would be no trouble in finding a true conclusion. In the absence of an agreement as to the points established, it is the part of fairness to give a succinct statement of the grounds maintained by the two parties to the prolonged controversy, — grounds which have not essentially changed in a century of legislative and popular contention.

It is maintained by free-traders that under the moderate tariff prevailing from the origin of the government to the war of 1812 the country was prosperous, and manufactures were developing as rapidly as was desirable or healthful. Protectionists on the other hand aver that the duty levied in 1789 was the first of uniform application throughout all the States, and that, regardless of its percentage, its influence and effect were demonstrably protective; that it was the first barrier erected against the absolute commercial supremacy of England, and that it effectually did its work in establishing the foundation of the American system. In the absence of that tariff, they maintain that England, under the influence of actual free-trade, had monopolized our market and controlled our industries. Finally they declare that the free-traders yield the whole case in acknowledging that the first tariff imparted an impetus to manufactures and to commercial independence wholly unknown while the States were under the Articles of Confederation and unable to levy uniform duties on imports.

The free-traders point to the destructive effect of the war tariff of 1812, which unduly stimulated and then inevitably depressed the country. They assume this to be a pregnant illustration of a truth, otherwise logically deduced by them, as to the re-action sure to follow an artificial stimulus given to any department of trade. The protectionists declining to defend the war duties as applicable to a normal condition, find in the too sudden dropping of war rates the mistake which precipitated the country into financial trouble. Depression, they say, would naturally have come; but it was hastened and increased by the inconsiderate manner in which the duties were lowered in 1816. From that time onward the protectionists claim that the experience of the country has favored their theories of revenue and financial administration. The country did not revive, or prosperity re-appear, until the protective tariff of 1824 was enacted. The awakening of all branches of industry by that Act was further promoted by the tariff of 1828, to which the protectionists point as the perfected wisdom of their school. Mr. Clay publicly asserted that the severest depression he had witnessed in the country was during the seven years preceding the tariff of 1824, and that the highest prosperity was during the seven years following that Act.

The free-traders affirm that the excitement in the South and the sectional resistance to the tariff of 1828 show the impossibility of maintaining high duties. The protectionists reply that such an argument is begging the question, and is simply tantamount to admitting that protection is valuable if it can be upheld. The protectionists point to the fact that their system was not abandoned in 1832 upon a fair consideration of its intrinsic merits, but as a peace-offering to those who were threatening the destruction of the government if the duties were not lowered. Many protectionists believe that if Mr. Clay had been willing to give to General Jackson the glory of an absolute victory over the Nullifiers of South Carolina, the revenue system of the country would have been very different. They think however that the temptation to settle the question by compromise instead of permitting Jackson to settle it by force was perhaps too strong to be resisted by one who had so many reasons for opposing and hating the President.

A more reasonable view held by another school of protectionists is that Mr. Clay did the wisest possible thing in withdrawing the tariff question from a controversy where it was complicated with so many other issues, — some of them bitter and personal. He justly feared that the protective principle might be irretrievably injured in the collision thought to be impending. He believed moreover that the best protective lesson would be taught by permitting the free-traders to enforce their theories for a season, trusting for permanent triumph to the popular re-action certain to follow. There was nothing in the legislation to show that Mr. Clay or his followers had in any degree abandoned or changed their faith in protective duties or their confidence in the ultimate decision of the public judgment. The protectionists aver that the evils which flowed from the free-trade tariff of 1833, thus forced on the country by extraneous considerations, were incalculably great, and negatively established the value of the tariff of 1828 which had been so unfairly destroyed. They maintain that it broke down the manufacturing interest, led to excessive importations, threw the balance of trade heavily against us, drained us of our specie, and directly led to the financial disasters of 1837 and the years ensuing. They further declare that this distressing situation was not relieved until the protective tariff of 1842 was passed, and that thenceforward, for the four years in which that Act was allowed to remain in force, the country enjoyed general prosperity, — a prosperity so marked and wide-spread that the opposing party had not dared to make an issue against the tariff in States where there was large investment in manufacturing.

The free-traders consider the tariff of 1846 to be a conclusive proof of the beneficial effect of low duties. They challenge a comparison of the years of its operation, between 1846 and 1857, with any other equal period in the history of the country. Manufacturing, they say, was not forced by a hot-house process to produce high-priced goods for popular consumption, but was gradually encouraged and developed on a healthful and self-sustaining basis, not to be shaken as a reed in the wind by every change in the financial world. Commerce, as they point out, made great advances, and our carrying-trade grew so rapidly that in ten years from the day the tariff of 1846 was passed our tonnage exceeded the tonnage of England. The free-traders refer with especial emphasis to what they term the symmetrical development of all the great interests of the country under this liberal tariff. Manufactures were not stimulated at the expense of the commercial interest. Both were developed in harmony, while agriculture, the indispensable basis of all, was never more flourishing. The farmers and planters at no other period of our history were in receipt of such good prices, steadily paid to them in gold coin, for their surplus product, which they could send to the domestic market over our own railways and to the foreign market in our own ships.

Assertions as to the progress of manufactures in the period under discussion are denied by the protectionists. While admitting the general correctness of the free-trader's statements as to the prosperous condition of the country, they call attention to the fact that directly after the enactment of the tariff of 1846 the great famine occurred in Ireland, followed in the ensuing years by short crops in Europe. The prosperity which came to the American agriculturist was therefore from causes beyond the sea and not at home, —causes which were transient, indeed almost accidental. Moreover an exceptional condition of affairs existed in the United States in consequence of our large acquisition of territory from Mexico at the close of the war and the subsequent and almost immediate discovery of gold in California. A new and extended field of trade was thus opened in which we had the monopoly, and an enormous surplus of money was speedily created from the products of the rich mines on the Pacific coast. At the same time Europe was in convulsion from the revolutions of 1848, and production was materially hindered over a large part of the Continent. This disturbance had scarcely subsided when three leading nations of Europe, England, France, and Russia, engaged in the wasteful and expensive war of the Crimea. This struggle began in 1853 and ended in 1856, and during those years it increased consumption and decreased production abroad, and totally closed the grain-fields of Russia from any competition with the United States.

The protectionists therefore hold that the boasted prosperity of the country under the tariff of 1846 was abnormal in origin and in character. It depended upon a series of events exceptional at home and even more exceptional abroad, — events which by the doctrine of probabilities would not be repeated for centuries. When peace was restored in Europe, when foreign looms and forges were set going with renewed strength, when Russia resumed her export of wheat, and when at home the output of the gold-mines suddenly decreased, the country was thrown into distress, followed by a panic and by long years of depression. The protectionists maintain that from 1846 to 1857 the United States would have enjoyed prosperity under any form of tariff, but that the moment the exceptional conditions in Europe and in America came to an end, the country was plunged headlong into a disaster from which the conservative force of a protective tariff would in large part have saved it. The protectionists claim moreover that in these averments they are not wise after the fact. They show a constant series of arguments and warnings from leading teachers of their economic school, especially from Horace Greeley and Henry C. Carey, accurately foretelling the disastrous results which occurred at the height of what was assumed to be our solid and enduring prosperity as a nation. These able writers were prophets of adversity, and the inheritors of their faith claim that their predictions were startlingly verified.

The free-traders, as an answer to this arraignment of their tariff policy, seek to charge responsibility for the financial disasters to the hasty and inconsiderate changes made in the tariff in 1857, for which both parties were in large degree if not indeed equally answerable. The protectionists will not admit the plea, and insist that the cause was totally inadequate to the effect, considering the few months the new tariff had been in operation. They admit that the low scale of duties in the new tariff perhaps may have added to the distress, by the very rapid increase of importations which it invited; but they declare that its period of operation was entirely too brief to create a result so decided, if all the elements of disaster had not been in existence, and in rapid development, at the time the Act was passed. The tariff of 1846 therefore under which there had been a very high degree of prosperity, was, in the judgment of the protectionists, successfully impeached, and a profound impression in consequence made on the public mind in favor of higher duties.

The question of the tariff was of especial significance and influence in Pennsylvania. Important in that State, it became important everywhere. Pennsylvania had been continuously and tenaciously held by the Democratic party. In the old political divisions she had followed Jefferson and opposed Adams. In the new divisions she had followed Jackson and opposed Clay. She was Republican as against the Federalists, she was Democratic as against the Whigs. From the election of Jackson in 1828 to the year 1860, — a period that measured the lifetime of a generation, — she had, with very few exceptions, sustained the Democratic party. Joseph Ritner was elected governor by the Whigs in 1835, in consequence of Democratic divisions. Harrison, in the political convulsion of 1840, triumphed in the State by the slight majority of three hundred. Taylor received her electoral vote, partly in consequence of dissensions between Cass and Van Buren, and partly in consequence of the free-trade opinions of Cass. In 1854 James Pollock was chosen governor by the sudden uprising and astounding development of the Native-American excitement as organized by the *Know-Nothing* party. The repeal of the Missouri Compromise aided the canvass of Pollock, but that alone would not have loosened the strong moorings of the Pennsylvania Democracy. Mr. Buchanan recovered the State two years afterwards, and would have held it firmly in his grasp but for the financial revulsion and the awakened demand for a protective tariff.

Dissociated from the question of protection, opposition to the extension of slavery was a weak issue in Pennsylvania. This was conclusively shown in the gubernatorial contest of 1857, when David Wilmot, the personal embodiment of Free-soil principles, was the Republican candidate for governor. Besides the general strength of the Territorial issue, Mr. Wilmot had the advantage of all the anti-slavery zeal which was aroused by the announcement of the Dred Scott decision, with the censurable connection therewith of President Buchanan. Thus an angry element was superadded for personal prejudice and effective agitation. Yet Mr. Wilmot was disastrously beaten by the Democratic candidate, Governor Packer, the adverse majority reaching indeed tens of thousands.

The crushing Republican defeat received in the person of Wilmot occurred on the very eve of the financial distress of 1857. The Democratic canvass had been made while there was yet no suspicion of impending panic and revulsion, — made indeed with constant boasts of the general prosperity and with constant ascription of that prosperity to the well-defined and long-continued policy of the Democratic party. From that time the Democratic party became embarrassed in Pennsylvania. With a tariff of their own making, with a President of their own choice, with both branches of Congress and every department of the government under their control, a serious disaster had come upon the country. The promises of Democratic leaders had failed, their predictions had been falsified, and as a consequence their strength was shattered. The Republicans of Pennsylvania, seeing their advantage, pressed it by renewed and urgent demands for a protective tariff. On the other issues of the party they had been hopelessly beaten, but the moment the hostility to slave-labor in the Territories became identified with protected labor in Pennsylvania, the party was inspired with new hopes, received indeed a new life.

It was this condition of public opinion in Pennsylvania which made the recognition of the protective system so essential in the Chicago platform of 1860. It was to that recognition that Mr. Lincoln in the end owed his election. The memorable victory of Andrew G. Curtin, when he was chosen governor by a majority of thirty-two thousand, was largely due to his able and persuasive presentation of the tariff question, and to his effective appeals to the laboring-men in the coal and iron sections of the State. But for this issue there was in fact no reason why Curtin should have been stronger in 1860 than Wilmot was in 1857. Indeed, but for that issue he must have been weaker. The agitation over the repeal of the Missouri Compromise had somewhat subsided with the lapse of years: the free-State victory in Kansas was acknowledged and that angry issue removed; while the Dred Scott decision, failing to arouse popular resentment at the time it was pronounced, could hardly be effective for an aggressive canvass three years later. If Governor Curtin could have presented no other issue to the voters of Pennsylvania, he would undoubtedly have shared the fate which Wilmot met when he had these anti-slavery questions as his only platform. Governor Curtin gave a far greater proportion of his time to the discussion of the tariff and financial issues than to all others combined, and he carried Pennsylvania because a majority of her voters believed that the Democratic party tended to free-trade, and that the Republican party would espouse and maintain the cause of protection.

Had the Republicans failed to carry Pennsylvania, there can be no doubt that Mr. Lincoln would have been defeated. An adverse result in Pennsylvania in October would certainly have involved the loss of Indiana in November, besides California and Oregon and the four votes in New Jersey. The crisis of the national campaign was therefore reached in the triumph of Governor Curtin in the State election which preceded by four weeks the direct choice of President. It would be difficult to compute the possible demoralization in the Republican ranks if Pennsylvania had been lost in October. The division among the Democrats was a fruitful source of encouragement and strength to the Republicans, but would probably have disappeared with the positive assurance of success in the national struggle. Whether in the end Douglas or Breckinridge would have been chosen President is matter of speculation, but it is certain that Mr. Lincoln would have been defeated. The October election of Pennsylvania was for so long a period an unerring index to the result of the contest for the Presidency, that a feeling almost akin to superstition was connected with it. Whichever party carried it was sure, in the popular judgment, to elect the President. It foretold the crushing defeat of John Quincy Adams in 1828; it heralded the disaster to Mr. Clay in 1844; it foredoomed General Cass in 1848. The Republicans, having elected their candidate for governor in 1854 by a large majority, confidently expected to carry the State against Mr. Buchanan in 1856. But the Democratic party prevailed in the October election, and the supporters of Frémont at once recognized the hopelessness of their cause. The triumph of Governor Curtin was the sure precursor of Mr. Lincoln's election, and that very fact added immeasurably to his popular strength in the closing month of the prolonged and exciting struggle.

In reviewing the agencies therefore which precipitated the political revolution of 1860, large consideration must be given to the influence of the movement for Protection. To hundreds of thousands of voters who took part in that memorable contest, the tariff was not even mentioned. Indeed this is probably the fact with respect to the majority of those who cast their suffrages for Mr. Lincoln. It is none the less true that these hundreds of thousands of ballots, cast in aid of free territory and as a general defiance to the aggressions of the pro-slavery leaders of the South, would have been utterly ineffectual if the central and critical contest in Pennsylvania had not resulted in a victory for the Republicans in October. The tariff therefore had a controlling influence not only in deciding the contest for political supremacy but in that more momentous struggle which was to involve the fate of the Union. It had obtained a stronger hold on the Republican party than even the leaders of that organization were aware, and it was destined to a larger influence upon popular opinion than the most sagacious could foresee.

In the foregoing summary of legislation upon the tariff, the terms Free-trade and Protection are used in their ordinary acceptation in this country, — not as accurately defining the difference in revenue theories, but as indicating the rival policies which have so long divided political parties. Strictly speaking, there has never been a proposition by any party in the United States for the adoption of free-trade. To be entirely free, trade must encounter no obstruction in the way of tax, either upon export or import. In that sense no nation has ever enjoyed free-trade. As contradistinguished from the theory of protection, England has realized freedom of trade by taxing only that class of imports which meet no competition in home production, thus excluding all pretense of favor or advantage to any of her domestic industries. England came to this policy after having clogged and embarrassed trade for a long period by the most unreasonable and tyrannical restrictions, ruthlessly enforced, without regard to the interests or even the rights of others. She had more than four hundred Acts of Parliament regulating the tax on imports, under the old designations of "tonnage and poundage," adjusted, as the phrase indicates, to heavy and light commodities. Beyond these, she had a cumbersome system of laws regulating and in many cases prohibiting the exportation of articles which might teach to other nations the skill by which she had herself so marvelously prospered.

When by long experiment and persistent effort England had carried her fabrics to perfection ; when by the large accumulation of wealth and the force of reserved capital she could command facilities which poorer nations could not rival ; when by the talent of her inventors, developed under the stimulus of large reward, she had surpassed all other countries in the magnitude and effectiveness of her machinery, she proclaimed free-trade and persuasively urged it upon all lands with which she had commercial intercourse. Maintaining the most arbitrary and most complicated system of protection so long as her statesmen considered that policy advantageous, she resorted to free-trade only when she felt able to invade the domestic markets of other countries and undersell the fabrics produced by struggling artisans who were sustained by weaker capital and by less advanced skill. So long as there was danger that her own marts might be invaded, and the products of her looms and forges undersold at home, she rigidly excluded the competing fabric and held her own market for her own wares.

England was however neither consistent nor candid in her advocacy and establishment of free-trade. She did not apply it to all departments of her enterprise, but only to those in which she felt confident that she could defy competition. Long after the triumph of free-trade in manufactures, as proclaimed in 1846, England continued to violate every principle of her own creed in the protection she extended to her navigation interests. She had nothing to fear from the United States in the domain of manufactures, and she therefore asked us to give her the unrestricted benefit of our markets in exchange for a similar privilege which she offered to us in her markets. But on the sea we were steadily gaining upon her, and in 1850–55 were nearly equal to her in aggregate tonnage. We could build wooden vessels at less cost than England and our ships excelled hers in speed. When steam began to compete with sail she saw her advantage. She could build engines at less cost than we, and when, soon afterward, her ship-builders began to construct the entire steamer of iron, her advantages became evident to the whole world.

England was not content however with the superiority which these circumstances gave to her. She did not wait for her own theory of Free-trade to work out its legitimate results, but forthwith stimulated the growth of her steam marine by the most enormous bounties ever paid by any nation to any enterprise. To a single line of steamers running alternate weeks from Liverpool to Boston and New York, she paid nine hundred thousand dollars annually, and continued to pay at this extravagant rate for at least twenty years. In all channels of trade where steam could be employed she paid lavish subsidies, and literally destroyed fair competition, and created for herself a practical monopoly in the building of iron steamers, and a superior share in the ocean traffic of the world. But every step she took in the development of her steam marine by the payment of bounty, was in flat contradiction of the creed which she was at the same time advocating in those departments of trade where she could conquer her competitors without bounty.

With her superiority in navigation attained and made secure through the instrumentality of subsidies, England could afford to withdraw them. Her ships no longer needed them. Thereupon, with a promptness which would be amusing if it did not have so serious a side for America, she proceeded to inveigh through all her organs of public opinion against the discarded and condemned policy of granting subsidies to ocean steamers. Her course in effect is an exact repetition of that in regard to protection of manufactures, but as it is exhibited before a new generation, the inconsistency is not so readily apprehended nor so keenly appreciated as it should be on this side of the Atlantic. Even now there is good reason for believing that many lines of English steamers, in their effort to seize the trade to the exclusion of rivals, are paid such extravagant rates for the carrying of letters as practically to amount to a bounty, thus confirming to the present day (1884) the fact that no nation has ever been so persistently and so jealously protective in her policy as England so long as the stimulus of protection is needed to give her the command of trade. What is true of England is true in greater or less degree of all other European nations. They have each in turn regulated the adoption of free-trade by the ratio of their progress towards the point where they could overcome competition. In all those departments of trade where competition could overcome them, they have been quick to interpose protective measures for the benefit of their own people.

The trade policy of the United States at the foundation of the government had features of enlightened liberality which were unknown in any other country of the world. The new government was indeed as far in advance of European nations in the proper conception of liberal commerce as it was on questions relating to the character of the African slave-trade. The colonists had experienced the oppression of the English laws which prohibited export from the mother country of the very articles which might advance their material interest and improve their social condition. They now had the opportunity, as citizens of a free Republic, to show the generous breadth of their statesmanship, and they did so by providing in their Constitution, that Congress should never possess the power to levy "a tax or duty on articles exported from any state."

At the same time trade was left absolutely free between all the States of the Union, no one of them being permitted to levy any tax on exports or imports beyond what might be necessary for its inspection laws. Still further to enforce this needful provision, the power to regulate commerce between the States was given to the General Government. The effect of these provisions was to insure to the United States a freedom of trade beyond that enjoyed by any other nation. Fifty-five millions of American people (in 1884), over an area nearly as large as the entire continent of Europe, carry on their exchanges by ocean, by lake, by river, by rail, without the exactions of the tax-gatherer, without the detention of the custom house, without even the recognition of State lines. In these great channels, the domestic exchanges represent an annual value perhaps twenty-five times as great as the total of exports and imports. It is the enjoyment of free-trade and protection at the same time which has contributed to the unexampled development and marvelous prosperity of the United States.

The essential question which has grown up between political parties in the United States respecting our foreign trade, is whether a duty should be laid upon any import for the direct object of protecting and encouraging the manufacture of the same article at home. The party opposed to this theory does not advocate the admission of the article free, but insists upon such rate of duty as will produce the largest revenue and at the same time afford what is termed "incidental protection." The advocates of actual free-trade according to the policy of England — taxing only those articles which are not produced at home — are few in number, and are principally confined to *doctrinaires*. The instincts of the masses of both parties are against them. But the nominal free-trader finds it very difficult to unite the largest revenue from any article with "incidental protection" to the competing product at home. If the duty be so arranged as to produce the greatest amount of revenue, it must be placed at that point where the foreign article is able to undersell the domestic article and thus command the market to the exclusion of competition. This result goes beyond what the so-called American free-trader intends in practice, but not beyond what he implies in theory.

The American protectionist does not seek to evade the legitimate results of his theory. He starts with the proposition that whatever is manufactured at home gives work and wages to our own people, and that if the duty is even put so high as to prohibit the import of the foreign article, the competition of home producers will, according to the doctrine of Mr. Hamilton, rapidly reduce the price to the consumer. He gives numerous illustrations of articles which under the influence of home competition have fallen in price below the point at which the foreign article was furnished when there was no protection. The free-trader replies that the fall in price has been still greater in the foreign market, and the protectionist rejoins that the reduction was made to compete with the American product, and that the former price would probably have been maintained so long as the importer had the monopoly of our market. Thus our protective tariff reduced the price in both countries. This has notably been the result with respect to steel rails, the production of which in America has reached a magnitude surpassing that of England. Meanwhile rails have largely fallen in price to the consumer, the home manufacture has disbursed countless millions of money among American laborers, and has added largely to our industrial independence and to the wealth of the country.

While many fabrics have fallen to as low a price in the United States as elsewhere, it is not to be denied that articles of clothing and household use, metals and machinery, are on an average higher than in Europe. The difference is due in large degree to the wages paid to labor, and thus the question of reducing the tariff carries with it the very serious problem of a reduction in the pay of the artisan and the operative. This involves so many grave considerations that no party is prepared to advocate it openly. Free-traders do not, and apparently dare not, face the plain truth — which is that the lowest priced fabric means the lowest priced labor. On this point protectionists are more frank than their opponents; they realize that it constitutes indeed the most impregnable defense of their school. Free-traders have at times attempted to deny the truth of the statement; but every impartial investigation thus far has conclusively proved that labor is better paid, and the average condition of the laboring man more comfortable, in the United States than in any European country.

An adjustment of the protective duty to the point which represents the average difference between wages of labor in Europe and in America, will, in the judgment of protectionists, always prove impracticable. The difference cannot be regulated by a scale of averages because it is constantly subject to arbitrary changes. If the duty be adjusted on that basis for any given date, a reduction of wages would at once be enforced abroad, and the American manufacturer would in consequence be driven to the desperate choice of surrendering the home market or reducing the pay of workmen. The theory of protection is not answered, nor can its realization be attained by any such device. Protection, in the perfection of its design as described by Mr. Hamilton, does not invite competition from abroad, but is based on the controlling principle that competition at home will always prevent monopoly on the part of the capitalist, assure good wages to the laborer, and defend the consumer against the evils of extortion.

An argument much relied upon and strongly presented by the advocates of free-trade is the alleged tendency to over-production of protected articles, followed uniformly by seasons of depression and at certain intervals by financial panic and wide-spread distress. These results are unhappily too familiar in the United States, but the protectionists deny that the cause is correctly given. They aver indeed that a glut of manufactured articles is more frequently seen in England than in the United States, thus proving directly the reverse of the conclusion assumed by the free-traders, and establishing the conservative and restraining power of a protective tariff. The protectionists direct attention to the fact that the first three instances in our history in which financial panic and prolonged depression fell upon the country, followed the repeal of protective tariffs and the substitution of mere revenue duties, — the depression of 1819–24, that of 1837–42, and that of 1857–61. They direct further attention to the complementary fact that, in each of these cases, financial prosperity was regained through the agency of a protective tariff, the operation of which was prompt and beneficent.

On the other hand the panic of 1873 and the depression which lasted until 1879 undoubtedly occurred after a protective tariff had been for a long time in operation. Free-traders naturally make much of this circumstance. Protectionists, however, with confidence and with strong array of argument, make answer that the panic of 1873 was due to causes wholly unconnected with revenue systems, — that it was the legitimate and the inevitable outgrowth of an exhausting war, a vitiated and redundant currency, and a long period of reckless speculation directly induced by these conditions. They aver that no system of revenue could have prevented the catastrophe. They maintain however that by the influence of a protective tariff the crisis was long postponed; that under the reign of free-trade it would have promptly followed the return of peace when the country was ill able to endure it. They claim that the influence of protection would have put off the re-action still longer if the rebuilding of Chicago and Boston, after the fires of 1871 and 1872, had not enforced a sudden withdrawal of $250,000,000 of ready money from the ordinary channels of trade to repair the loss which these crushing disasters precipitated.

The assailants of protection apparently overlook the fact that excessive production is due, both in England and in America, to causes beyond the operation of duties either high or low. No cause is more potent than the prodigious capacity of machinery set in motion by the agency of steam. It is asserted by an intelligent economist that, if performed by hand, the work done by machinery in Great Britain would require the labor of seven hundred millions of men, — a far larger number of adults than inhabit the globe. It is not strange that, with this vast enginery, the power to produce has a constant tendency to outrun the power to consume. Protectionists find in this a conclusive argument against surrendering the domestic market of the United States to the control of British capitalists, whose power of production has no apparent limit. When the harmonious adjustment of international trade shall ultimately be established by "the Parliament of man" in "the Federation of the world," the power of production and the power of consumption will properly balance each other; but in traversing the long road and enduring the painful process by which that end shall be reached, the protectionist claims that his theory of revenue preserves the newer nations from being devoured by the older, and offers to human labor a shield against the exactions of capital.

CHAPTER X.

THE winter following the election of Mr. Lincoln was filled with deplorable events. In the whole history of the American people, there is no epoch which recalls so much that is worthy of regret and so little that gratifies pride. The result of the election was unfortunate in the wide divergence between the vote which Mr. Lincoln received in the electoral colleges and the vote which he received at the polls. In the electoral colleges he had an aggregate of 180. His opponents, united, had but 123. Of the popular vote, Lincoln received 1,866,452; Douglas, 1,291,574; Breckinridge, 850,082; Bell, 646,124. Mr. Lincoln's vote was wholly from the free States, except some 26,000 cast for him in the five border slave States. In the other slave States his name was not presented as a candidate. Mr. Douglas received in the South about 163,000 votes. In the North the votes cast distinctively for the Breckinridge electoral

215

ticket were less than 100,000, and distinctively for the Bell electoral ticket about 80,000.

It was thus manifest that the two Northern Presidential candidates, Lincoln and Douglas, had absorbed almost the entire vote in the free States, and the two Southern Presidential candidates, Breckinridge and Bell, had absorbed almost the entire vote in the slave States. The Northern candidates received popular support in the South in about the same degree that the Southern candidates received popular support in the North. In truth as well as in appearance it was a sectional contest in which the North supported Northern candidates, and the South supported Southern candidates. It was the first time in the history of the government in which the President was chosen without electoral votes from both the free and the slave States. This result was undoubtedly a source of weakness to Mr. Lincoln,—weakness made more apparent by his signal failure to obtain a popular majority. He had a large plurality, but the combined vote of his opponents was nearly a million greater than the vote which he received.

The time had now come when the Southern Disunionists were to be put to the test. The event had happened which they had declared in advance to be cause of separation. It was perhaps the belief that their courage and determination were challenged, which forced them to action. Having so often pledged themselves not to endure the election of an anti-slavery President, they were now persuaded that, if they quietly submitted, they would thereby accept an inferior position in the government. This assumed obligation of consistency stimulated them to rash action; for upon every consideration of prudence and wise forecast, they would have quietly accepted a result which they acknowledged to be in strict accordance with the Constitution. The South was enjoying exceptional prosperity. The advance of the slave States in wealth was more rapid than at any other period of their history. Their staple products commanded high prices and were continually growing in amount to meet the demands of a market which represented the wants of the civilized world. In the decade between 1850 and 1860 the wealth of the South had increased three thousand millions of dollars, and this not from an overvaluation of slaves, but from increased cultivation of land, the extension of railways, and all the aids and appliances of vast agricultural enterprises. Georgia alone had increased in wealth over three hundred millions of dollars, no small proportion of which was from commercial and manufacturing ventures that had proved extremely profitable. There never was a community on the face of the globe whose condition so little justified revolution as that of the slave States in the year 1860. Indeed, it was a sense of strength born of exceptional prosperity which led them to their rash adventure of war.

It would however be an injustice to the People of the South to say that in November, 1860, they desired, unanimously, or by a majority, or on the part of any considerable minority, to engage in a scheme of violent resistance to the National authority. The slave-holders were in the main peacefully disposed, and contented with the situation. But slavery as an economical institution and slavery as a political force were quite distinct. Those who viewed it and used it merely as a system of labor, naturally desired peace and dreaded commotion. Those who used it as a political engine for the consolidation of political power had views and ambitions inconsistent with the plans and hopes of law-abiding citizens. It was only by strenuous effort on the part of the latter class that an apparent majority of the Southern people committed themselves to the desperate design of destroying the National Government.

The first effort at secession was made, as might have been expected, by South Carolina. She did not wait for the actual result of the election, but early in October, on the assumption of Lincoln's success, began a correspondence with the other Cotton States. The general tenor of the responses did not indicate a decided wish or purpose to separate from the Union. North Carolina was positively unwilling to take any hasty step. Louisiana, evidently remembering the importance and value of the Mississippi River and of its numerous tributaries to her commercial prosperity, expressed an utter disinclination to separate from the North-West. Georgia was not ready to make resistance, and at most advocated some form of retaliatory legislation. It was evident that even in the Cotton-belt and the Gulf States there was in the minds of sober people the gravest objection to revolutionary measures.

It happened, most unfortunately, that the South-Carolina Legislature assembled early in November for the purpose of choosing Presidential electors, who in that State were never submitted to the popular vote. While it might seem extravagant to ascribe the revolution which convulsed the country to an event so disconnected and apparently so inadequate, it is nevertheless true that the sudden *furor* which seized a large number of the Southern people came directly from that event. Indeed, it is scarcely an exaggeration to say that the great civil war, which shook a continent, was precipitated by the fact that the South-Carolina Legislature assembled at that unpropitious moment. Without taking time for reflection, without a review of the situation, without stopping to count the cost, with a boldness born of passionate resentment against the North, the rash men of South Carolina fired the train. In a single hour they created in their own State a public sentiment which would not brook delay or contradiction or argument. The leaders of it knew that the sober second thought, even in South Carolina, would be dangerous to the scheme of a Southern confederacy. They knew that the feeling of resentment among the Southern people must be kept at white-heat, and that whoever wished to speak a word of caution or moderation must be held as a public enemy, and subjected to the scorn and the vengeance of the people.

In this temper a convention was ordered by the Legislature. The delegates were to be chosen directly by the people, and when assembled were to determine the future relation of South Carolina to the Government of the United States. The election was to be held in four weeks, and the convention was to assemble on the 17th of December. The unnatural and unprecedented haste of this action, by which South Carolina proceeded, as she proclaimed, to throw off her national relations, is more easily comprehended by recalling the difficult mode provided in every State for a change in its constitution. In not a single State of the American Union can the organic law be changed in less than a year, or without ample opportunity for serious consideration by the people. At that very moment the people of South Carolina were inhibited from making the slightest alteration in their own constitution except by slow and conservative processes which gave time for deliberation and reflection. In determining a question momentous beyond all calculation to themselves and to their posterity, they were hurried into the election of delegates, and the delegates were hurried into convention, and the convention was hurried into secession by a terror of public opinion that would not endure resistance and would not listen to reason.

The few who were left in possession of coolness and sound judgment among the public men of South Carolina, desired to stay the rush of events by waiting for co-operation with the other slaveholding States. Their request was denied and their argument answered by the declaration that co-operation had been tried in 1850, and had ended in defeating all measures looking to Disunion. One of the members declared that if South Carolina again waited for co-operation, slavery and State-rights would be abandoned, State-sovereignty and the cause of the South would be lost forever. The action of the convention was still further stimulated by the resignation of Mr. Hammond and Mr. Chestnut, United-States senators from South Carolina, and by the action of Governor Pickens in appointing a cabinet of the same number and of the same division of departments that had been adopted in the National Government.

South Carolina was urged forward in this course by leading Disunionists in other States who needed the force of one bold example of secession to furnish the requisite stimulus to their own communities. The members of the South Carolina convention, recognizing the embarrassment and incongruity of basing their action simply upon the constitutional election of a President, declared that the public opinion of their State "had for a long period been strengthening and ripening for Disunion." Mr. Rhett, eminent in the public service of his State, asserted "that the secession of South Carolina was not produced by Mr. Lincoln's election, or by the non-execution of the Fugitive-slave Law; that it was a matter which had been gathering head for thirty years," and that they were now "determined upon their course at whatever risk."

Among the singular incidents of the South-Carolina secession, followed subsequently by other States, was the solemn import attached to the word *ordinance*. The South gave it a significance which elevated its authority above the Constitution, and above the laws of their own State and of the United States. And yet, neither in legal definition nor in any ordinary use of the word, was there precedent or authority for attaching to it such impressive meaning. An *ordinance* of Parliament was but a temporary Act which the Commons might alter at their pleasure. An *Act* of Parliament could not be changed except by the consent of king, lords, and commons. In this country, aside from the use of the word in declaring the freedom of the North-west Territory in 1787, *ordinance* has uniformly been applied to Acts of inferior bodies, to the councils of cities, to the authorities of towns, to the directors of corporations, — rarely if ever to the Acts of legislative assemblies which represent the power of the State.

It is still more singular that, in passing the ordinance of Secession, the convention worded it so that it should seem to be the repeal of the ordinance of the 23d of May, 1788, whereby the Constitution of the United States was ratified by South Carolina, when, in simple truth, the Act of that State ratifying the Federal Constitution was never called an ordinance. Mirabeau said that words were things; and this word was so used in the proceedings of Secession conventions as to impress the mind of the Southern people with its portentous weight and solemnity. With an amendment to the constitutions of their States they had all been familiar. In the enactment of their laws thousands had participated. But no one of them had ever before seen or heard or dreamed of any thing of such momentous and decisive character as an Ordinance. Even to this day, when disunion, secession, rebellion have all been destroyed by the shock of arms, and new institutions have been built over their common grave, the word "ordinance" has, in the minds of many people both in the North and in the South, a sound which represents the very majesty of popular power.

If the other Southern States had been left to their own counsels, South Carolina would have stood alone, and her Secession of 1860 would have proved as abortive as her Nullification of 1832. The Disunion movement in the remaining States of the South originated in Washington. Finding that the Cotton States, especially those bordering on the Gulf of Mexico, were moving too slowly, the senators from Georgia, Alabama, Louisiana, Arkansas, Texas, Mississippi, and Florida held a meeting in Washington on the 5th of January, 1861. The South had always contended for the right of States to instruct their senators, but now the Southern senators proceeded to instruct their States. In effect they sent out commands to the governing authorities and to the active political leaders, that South Carolina must be sustained; that the Cotton States must stand by her; and that the secession of each and of all of them must be accomplished in season for a general convention to be held at Montgomery, not later than Feb. 15, and, in any event, before the inauguration of Mr. Lincoln. The design was that the new President of the United States should find a Southern Confederacy in actual existence, with the ordinary departments of government in regular operation, with a name and a flag and a great seal, and all the insignia of national sovereignty visible.

It is a suggestive fact that, in carrying out these designs, the political leaders determined, as far as possible, to prevent the submission of the ordinances of Secession to the popular vote. It is not indeed probable that, in the excited condition to which they had by this time brought the Southern mind, Secession would have been defeated; but the withholding of the question from popular decision is at least an indication that there was strong apprehension of such a result, and that care was taken to prevent the divisions and acrimonious contests which such submission might have caused. In the Georgia convention the resolution declaring it to be her right and her duty to secede was adopted only by a vote of 165 to 130. A division of similar proportion in the popular vote would have stripped the secession of Georgia of all moral force, and hence the people were not allowed to pass upon the question.

Georgia was really induced to secede, only upon the delusive suggestion that better terms could be made with the National Government by going out for a season than by remaining steadfastly loyal. The influence of Alexander H. Stephens, while he was still loyal, was almost strong enough to hold the State in the Union; and but for the phantasm of securing better terms outside, the Empire State of the South would have checked and destroyed the Secession movement at the very outset. Mississippi followed Jefferson Davis with a vote amounting almost to unanimity. Florida, Louisiana, and Alabama followed with secession ordained by conventions and no vote allowed to the people. Texas submitted the ordinance, after the other States had seceded, and by the force of their example carried it by a vote of about three to one. These were the original seven States that formed the nucleus of the Confederacy. They had gone through what they deemed the complete process of separation from the Union, without the slightest obstruction from any quarter and without the interposition of any authority from the National Government against their proceedings.

———

Long before the Secession movement had been developed to the extent just detailed, Congress was in session. It assembled one month after the Presidential election, and fifteen days before the Disunionists of South Carolina met in their ill-starred convention. Up to that time there had been excitement, threats of resistance to the authority of the government in many sections of the South, and an earnest attempt in the Cotton States to promote co-operation in the fatal step which so many were bent on taking. But there had been no overt act against the national authority. Federal officers were still exercising their functions in all the States; the customs were still collected in Southern ports; the United-States mails were still carried without molestation from the Potomac to the Rio Grande. But the critical moment had come. The Disunion conspiracy had reached a point where it must go forward with boldness, or retreat before the displayed power and the uplifted flag of the Nation. The administration could adopt no policy so dangerous as to permit the enemies of the Union to proceed in their conspiracy, and the hostile movement to gain perilous headway. At that juncture Mr. Buchanan confronted a graver responsibility than had ever before been imposed on a President of the United States. It devolved on him to arrest the mad outbreak of the South by judicious firmness, or by irresolution and timidity to plunge the Nation into dangers and horrors, the extent of which was mercifully veiled from the vision of those who were to witness and share them.

There could be no doubt in the mind of any one that the destruction of the Union would be deplored by Mr. Buchanan as profoundly as by any living man. His birth and rearing as a Pennsylvanian leave no other presumption possible. In the original Union, Pennsylvania was appropriately denominated the Keystone of the arch, supported by, and in turn supporting, the strength of all. Of the " old thirteen " there were six free States north of her, and six slave States south of her. She was allied as warmly by ties of friendship and of blood with her Maryland and Virginia neighbors on the one side as with those of New Jersey and New York on the other. Her political and social connections on both sides were not more intimate than those of a business and commercial character. As the Union grew in power and increased in membership, Pennsylvania lost nothing of her prestige. She held to the new States as intimate relations as she held to the old. The configuration of the country and the natural channels of communication have bound her closely to all sections. Her northern border touching the great lakes, connected her by sail and steam, before the era of the railway, with the magnificent domain which lies upon the shores of those inland seas. Her western rivers, whose junction marks the site of a great city, form part of the most extensive system of interior water-communication on the globe, affording a commercial highway twenty thousand miles in length through seventeen States not included in the original Union. Patriotic tradition increased Pennsylvania's attachment to the National Government. It was on her soil that the Declaration of Independence was proclaimed. It was in her Legislative halls that the Constitution was formed and the "more perfect Union" of the States ordained. From geographical position therefore, from material interest, from inherited pride, from every association and sympathy, from every aspiration, and from every hope, Pennsylvania was for the Union, inviolable and indissoluble. No threat of its destruction ever came from her councils, and no stress of circumstances could ever seduce her into a calculation of its value, or drive her to the contemplation of its end.

With all his attachment to the Union, Mr. Buchanan had been brought under influences which were hostile to it. In originally constituting his Cabinet, sinister agencies had controlled him, and far-seeing men anticipated trouble when the names were announced. From the South he had selected Howell Cobb of Georgia for the Treasury, John B. Floyd of Virginia for Secretary of War, Jacob Thompson of Mississippi for the Interior, and Aaron V. Brown of Tennessee for Postmaster-General. From the North he had selected Lewis Cass of Michigan for the State Department, Isaac Toucey of Connecticut for the Navy, and Jeremiah S. Black of Pennsylvania for Attorney-General. It seemed extraordinary that out of seven Cabinet officers four should be given to the South, when the North had a vast preponderance of population and wealth. It was hardly less than audacious that the four departments assigned to the South should be those which dealt most intimately and most extensively with the finances, the manufactures, and the commerce of the country. The quiet manner in which the North accepted this inequitable distribution of political power added only another proof of the complete ascendency which the South had acquired in the councils of the Democratic party.

Mr. Buchanan had always looked to the statesmen of the South as a superior class; and after a political life wholly spent in close association and constant service with them, it could not be expected that, even in a crisis threatening destruction to the Union, he would break away from them in a day. They had fast hold of him, and against the influence of the better men in his Cabinet they used him for a time to carry out their own ends. Secessionists and Abolitionists Mr. Buchanan no doubt regarded as equally the enemies of the Union. But the Secessionists all came from the party that elected him President, and the Abolitionists had all voted against him. The Abolitionists, in which phrase Mr. Buchanan included all men of anti-slavery conviction, had no opportunity, even if they had desired, to confer with the President, while the Secessionists, from old and friendly association, were in daily and intimate relations with him.   They undoubtedly persuaded the President by the most plausible arguments that they were not in fault; that the whole responsibility lay at the door of Northern anti-slavery men; and that, if these disturbers of the peace could be suppressed, all would be well.   It was under these influences, artfully insinuated and persistently plied, that Mr. Buchanan was induced to write his mischievous and deplorable message of the first Monday of December, 1860, — a message whose evil effect can never be estimated, and whose evil character can hardly be exaggerated.

The President informed Congress that " the long-continued and intemperate interference of the Northern people with the question of slavery in the Southern States has at last produced its natural effect. . . . The time has arrived so much dreaded by the Father of his Country, when hostile geographical parties have been formed." He declared that he had " long foreseen and often forewarned " his countrymen of " the impending danger."   Apparently arguing the case for the Southern extremists, the President believed that the danger "does not proceed solely from the attempt to exclude slavery from the Territories, nor from the efforts to defeat the execution of the Fugitive-slave Law."   Any or all of these evils, he said, " might have been endured by the South," trusting to time and reflection for a remedy. " The immediate peril," Mr. Buchanan informed the country, " arises from the fact that the long-continued agitation in the free States has at length produced its malign influence on the slaves, and inspired them with vague notions of freedom.   Hence a sense of security no longer exists around the family altar.   The feeling of peace at home has given place to apprehensions of servile insurrections, and many a matron throughout the South retires at night in dread of what may befall herself and her children before morning." The President was fully persuaded that "if this apprehension of domestic danger should extend and intensify itself, disunion will become inevitable."

Having thus stated what he believed to be the grievances of the South, Mr. Buchanan proceeded to give certain reasons why the slave-holders should not break up the government. His defensive plea for the North was worse, if worse were possible, than his aggressive statements on behalf of the South. " The election of any one of our fellow-citizens to the office of President," Mr. Buchanan complacently asserted, " does not of itself afford just cause for dissolving the Union." And then he adds an extraordinary qualification : " This is more especially true if his election has been effected by a mere plurality, and not a majority, of the people, and has resulted from transient and temporary causes, which may probably never again occur." Translated into plainer language, this was an assurance to the Southern Disunionists that they need not break up the government at that time, because Mr. Lincoln was a minority President, and was certain to be beaten at the next election. He reminded the Southern leaders moreover that in the whole history of the Federal Government "no single Act had ever passed Congress, unless the Missouri Compromise be an exception, impairing in the slightest degree the rights of the South to their property in slaves." The Missouri Compromise had been repealed, so that the entire body of national statutes, from the origin of the government to that hour, was, according to President Buchanan, guiltless of transgression against the rights of slave-holders. Coming from such a source, the admission was one of great historic value.

The President found that the chief grievance of the South was in the enactments of the free States known as "personal liberty laws." When the Fugitive-slave Law subjected the liberty of citizens to the decision of a single commissioner, and denied jury trial to a man upon the question of sending him to lifelong and cruel servitude, the issue throughout the free States was made one of self-preservation. Without having the legal right to obstruct the return of a fugitive slave to his servitude, they felt not only that they had the right, but that it was their duty, to protect free citizens in their freedom. Very likely these enactments, inspired by an earnest spirit of liberty, went in many cases too far, and tended to produce conflicts between National and State authority. That was a question to be determined finally and exclusively by the Federal Judiciary. Unfortunately Mr. Buchanan carried his argument beyond that point, coupling it with a declaration and an admission fatal to the perpetuity of the Union. After reciting the statutes which he regarded as objectionable and hostile to the constitutional rights of the South, and after urging their unconditional repeal upon the North, the President said ; " The Southern States, standing on the basis of the Constitution, have a right to demand this act of justice from the States of the North. Should it be refused, then the Constitution, to which all the States are parties, will have been willfully violated by one portion of them in a provision essential to the domestic security and happiness of the remainder. In that event, the injured States, after having used all peaceful and constitutional means to obtain redress, would be justified in revolutionary resistance to the government of the Union."

By this declaration the President justified, and in effect advised, an appeal from the constitutional tribunals of the country to a popular judgment in the aggrieved States, and recognized the right of those States, upon such popular judgment, to destroy the Constitution and the Union. The "constitutional means" of redress were the courts of the country, and to these the President must have referred in the paragraph quoted. After an appeal to the courts, and a decision upon the questions presented, it would have been the plain duty of the parties to accept the decision as authoritative and final. By the advice of the President, the States of the South were to accept the decision obtained by constitutional means, in case it was favorable to them, and to disregard it, and to destroy both the Constitution and the Union, if it should prove to be adverse to the popular opinion in those States.

It is not improbable that the President's language conveyed more than his real meaning. He may have intended to affirm that if the free States should refuse to repeal their obnoxious statutes after a final decision against their constitutionality, then the slave States would be justified in revolutionary resistance. But he had no right to make such an argument or suggest such an hypothesis, for never in the history of the Federal Government had the decision of the Supreme judicial tribunal been disobeyed or disregarded by any State or by any individual. The right of "revolutionary resistance" was not so foreign to the conception of the American citizen as to require suggestion and enforcement from Mr. Buchanan. His argument in support of the right at that crisis was prejudicial to the Union, and afforded a standing-ground for many Southern men who were beginning to feel that the doctrine of Secession was illogical, unsafe, untenable. They now had the argument of a Northern President in justification of "revolutionary resistance." Throughout the South, the right of Secession was abandoned by a large class, and the right of Revolution substituted.

Having made his argument in favor of the right of "Revolution,"

Mr. Buchanan proceeded to argue ably and earnestly against the assumption by any State of an inherent right to secede from the government at its own will and pleasure. But he utterly destroyed the force of his reasoning by declaring that "after much serious reflection" he had arrived at "the conclusion that no power has been delegated to Congress, or to any other department of the Federal Government, to coerce a State into submission which is attempting to withdraw, or has actually withdrawn," from the Union. He emphasized his position by further declaring that, "so far from this power having been delegated to Congress, it was expressly refused by the convention which framed the Constitution." Congress "possesses many means," Mr. Buchanan added, "of preserving the Union by conciliation; but the sword was not placed in their hands to preserve it by force."

The fatal admission was thus evolved from the mind of the President, that any State which thought itself aggrieved and could not secure the concessions demanded, might bring the Government down in ruins. The power to destroy was in the State. The power to preserve was not in the Nation. The President apparently failed to see that if the Nation could not be preserved by force, its legal capacity for existence was dependent upon the concurring and continuing will of all the individual States. The original bond of union was, therefore, for the day only, and the provision of the Constitution which gave to the Supreme Court jurisdiction in controversies between States was binding no further than the States chose to accept the decisions of the Court.

The difference between the President and the Secessionists of the South was a difference of opinion as to the time for action, and as to the name by which that action should be called. In principle there was concurrence. The President insisted that the injured party should appeal to the aggressor, and then to the courts, with the reserved right of revolution always in view and to be exercised if neither the aggressor nor the courts furnished satisfactory redress. The President recognized the reserved right of revolution in the States, and it was a necessary incident of that right that each State might decide when the right should be exercised. He suggested that, as justification of revolution, the Federal Government must be guilty of "a deliberate, palpable, and dangerous exercise" of powers not granted by the Constitution, quoting from the text of the State-rights declaration by Virginia in 1798. But in all his arguments he left the State to be the ultimate judge of the constitutionality of the Acts of the Federal Government. Under these doctrines the Government of the United States was shorn of all power to preserve its own existence, and the Union might crumble and fall while its constituted authorities stood paralyzed and impotent.

This construction was all that the extremists of the South desired. With so much conceded, they had every thing in their own hands. They could march out of the Union at their own will and caprice, without resistance from the National Government, and they could come back upon such conditions as, with the President's aid, they might extort from an alarmed and weakening North. Assured by the language of the President that they could with impunity defy the constitutional authority of the government, the Secessionists were immeasurably encouraged. The Southern men had for three generations been cherishing the belief that they were as a class superior to Northern men, and they were more than ever confirmed in this pleasing illusion when they saw a Northern President, with the power of the nation in his hands, deliberately affirming that he could exercise no authority over or against them.

Men who, under the wholesome restraint of executive power, would have refrained from taking aggressive steps against the National Government, were by Mr. Buchanan's action forced into a position of hostility. Men in the South, who were disposed to avoid extreme measures, were by taunt and reproach driven into the ranks of Secession. They were made to believe, after the President's message, that the South would be ruined if she did not assert a position which the National authority confessed it had no right and no means to contest. The Republicans had been taunting Southern men with the intention of using only bluster and bravado, and if they should now fail to take a decisive step in the direction of Disunion, they felt that it would be a humiliating retraction of all they had said in the long struggle over slavery. It would be an invitation to the Abolitionists and fanatics of the North to deal hereafter with the South, and with the question of slavery, in whatever manner might seem good in their sight. No weapon of logic could have been more forcible; and, wielded as it was by the Southern leaders with skill and courage, they were able to consolidate the public opinion and control the political action of their section.

The evil effects of Mr. Buchanan's message were not confined to the slave States. It did incalculable harm in the free States. It fixed in the minds of tens of thousands of Northern men who were opposed to the Republican party, the belief that the South was justified in taking steps to break up the government, if what they termed a war on Southern institutions should be continued. This feeling had in turn a most injurious influence in the South, and stimulated thousands in that section to a point of rashness which they would never have reached but for the sympathy and support constantly extended to them from the North. Even if a conflict of arms should be the ultimate result of the Secession movement, its authors and its deluded followers were made to believe that, against a South entirely united, there would be opposed a North hopelessly divided. They were confident that the Democratic party in the free States held the views expressed in Mr. Buchanan's message. They had conclusively persuaded themselves that the Democrats, together with a large proportion of the conservative men in the North who had supported Mr. Bell for the Presidency, would oppose an "abolition war," and would prove a distracting and destructive force in the rear of the Union army if it should ever commence its march Southward.

The most alarming feature of the situation to reflecting men in the North was that, so far as known, all the members of Mr. Buchanan's Cabinet approved the destructive doctrines of the message. But as the position of the President was subjected to examination and criticism by the Northern press, uneasiness was manifested in Administration circles. It was seen that if the course foreshadowed by Mr. Buchanan should be followed, the authority of the Union would be compelled to retreat before the usurpations of seceding States, and that a powerful government might be quietly overthrown, without striking one blow of resistance, or uttering one word of protest. General Cass was the first of the Cabinet to feel the pressure of loyalty from the North. The venerable Secretary of State, whose whole life had been one of patriotic devotion to his country, suddenly realized that he was in a false position. When it became known that the President would not insist upon the collection of the national revenue in South Carolina, or upon the strengthening of the United-States forts in the harbor of Charleston, General Cass concluded that justice to his own reputation required him to separate from the Administration. He resigned on the twelfth of December, — nine days after Mr. Buchanan had sent his fatal message to Congress.

Judge Black, who had from the beginning of the Administration been Mr. Buchanan's chief adviser, now became so by rank, as the successor of General Cass in the State Department. He was a man of remarkable character. He was endowed by nature with a strong understanding and a strong will. In the profession of the law he had attained great eminence. His learning had been illustrated by a prolonged service on the bench before the age at which men, even of exceptional success at the bar, usually attract public observation. He had added to his professional studies, which were laborious and conscientious, a wide acquaintance with our literature, and had found in its walks a delight which is yielded to few. In history, biography, criticism, romance, he had absorbed every thing in our language worthy of attention. Shakspeare, Milton, indeed all the English poets, were his familiar companions. There was not a disputed passage or an obscure reading in any one of the great plays upon which he could not off-hand quote the best renderings, and throw original light from his own illumined mind. Upon theology he had apparently bestowed years of investigation and reflection. A sincere Christian, he had been a devout and constant student of the Bible, and could quote its passages and apply its teachings with singular readiness and felicity. To this generous store of knowledge he added fluency of speech, both in public address and private conversation, and a style of writing which was at once unique, powerful, and attractive. He had attained unto every excellence of mental discipline described by Lord Bacon. Reading had made him a full man, talking a ready man, writing an exact man. The judicial literature of the English tongue may be sought in vain for finer models than are found in the opinions of Judge Black when he sat, and was worthy to sit, as the associate of John Bannister Gibson, on the Supreme Bench of Pennsylvania.

In political opinion he was a Democrat, self-inspired and self-taught, for his father was a Whig who had served his State in Congress. He idolized Jefferson and revered Jackson as embodying in their respective characters all the elements of the soundest political philosophy, and all the requisites of the highest political leadership. He believed in the principles of Democracy as he did in a demonstration of Euclid, — all that might be said on the other side was necessarily absurd. He applied to his own political creed the literal teachings of the Bible. If Abraham, Isaac, and Jacob had held slaves without condemnation or rebuke from the Lord of hosts, he believed that Virginia, Carolina, and Georgia might do the same. He found in the case of Onesimus, St. Paul's explicit approval of the Fugitive-slave Law of 1850, and in the cruel case of Passmore Williamson he believed himself to be enforcing the doctrines of the New Testament.   Personally unwilling to hold even a beast of burden in oppressive bondage, nothing could induce him to condemn slave-holding in those whose conscience permitted them to practice it.   In the Abolitionists he found the chief disturbers of the Republic, and he held New England answerable to posterity and to God for all the heresies which afflicted either Church or State.   He had an uncompromising hostility to what are termed New-England ideas, though the tenderest ties of his life were of New-England origin. " The New-Englander individually I greatly affect," he often said, " but, in the mass, I judge them to be stark mad."   "I think, too," he would add, " that if you are going to make much of a New-Englander, he should, like Dr. Johnson's Scotchman, be caught young."

To his native State Judge Black was devotedly attached.   He inherited the blood of two strong elements of its population, — the German and the Scotch-Irish, — and he united the best characteristics of both in his own person.   He had always looked upon Pennsylvania as the guardian of the Federal Union, almost as the guarantor of its safety and its perpetuity.   He spoke of her as the break-water that protected the slave States from the waves of radicalism which were threatening to ingulf Southern institutions.   The success of the Republican party in 1860 he regarded as a portent of direst evil, — indeed, as a present disaster, immeasurably sorrowful.   The excitement in the Southern States over the probability of Mr. Lincoln's election he considered natural, their serious protest altogether justifiable.   He desired the free States to be awakened to the gravity of the situation, to be thoroughly alarmed, and to repent of their sins against the South.   He wished it understood from ocean to ocean that the position of the Republican party was inconsistent with loyalty to the Union, and that its permanent success would lead to the destruction of the government.   It was not unnatural that with these extreme views he should be carried beyond the bounds of prudence, and that, in his headlong desire to rebuke the Republican party as enemies of the Union, he should aid in precipitating a dissolution of the government before the Republicans could enter upon its administration.   He thus became in large degree responsible for the unsound position and the dangerous teachings of Mr. Buchanan.   In truth some of the worst doctrines embodied in the President's evil message came directly from an opinion given by

Judge Black as Attorney-General, and made by Mr. Buchanan still more odious and more dangerous by the quotation of a part and not the whole.

It was soon manifest however to Judge Black, that he was playing with fire, and that, while he was himself desirous only of arousing the country to the dangers of anti-slavery agitation, Mr. Buchanan's administration was every day effectually aiding the Southern conspiracy for the destruction of the Union. This light dawned on Judge Black suddenly and irresistibly. He was personally intimate with General Cass, and when that venerable statesman retired from the Cabinet to preserve his record of loyalty to the Union, Judge Black realized that he was himself confronted by an issue which threatened his political destruction. Could he afford, as Secretary of State, to follow a policy which General Cass believed would destroy his own fame? General Cass was nearly fourscore years of age, with his public career ended, his work done. Judge Black was but fifty, and he had before him possibly the most valuable and most ambitious period of his life. He saw at a glance that if General Cass could not be sustained in the North-West, he could not be sustained in Pennsylvania. He possessed the moral courage to stand firm to the end, in defiance of opposition and regardless of obloquy, if he could be sure he was right. But he had begun to doubt, and doubt led him to review with care the position of Mr. Buchanan, and to examine its inevitable tendencies. He did it with conscience and with courage. He had none of that subserviency to Southern men which had injured so many Northern Democrats. Until he entered the Cabinet in 1857, he had never come into personal association with men from the slave-holding States, and his keen observation could not fail to discern the inferiority to himself of the four Southern members of the Cabinet.

Judge Black entered upon his duties as Secretary of State on the 17th of December, — the day on which the Disunion convention of South Carolina assembled. He found the malign influence of Mr. Buchanan's message fully at work throughout the South. Under its encouragement only three days were required by the convention at Charleston to pass the Ordinance of Secession, and four days later Governor Pickens issued a proclamation declaring "South Carolina a separate, sovereign, free, and independent State, with the right to levy war, conclude peace, and negotiate treaties." From that moment Judge Black's position towards the Southern leaders was radically changed. They were no longer fellow-Democrats. They were the enemies of the Union to which he was devoted : they were conspirators against the government to which he had taken a solemn oath of fidelity and loyalty.

Judge Black's change, however important to his own fame, would prove comparatively fruitless unless he could influence Mr. Buchanan to break with the men who had been artfully using the power of his administration to destroy the Union. The opportunity and the test came promptly. The new "sovereign, free, and independent" government of South Carolina sent commissioners to Washington to negotiate for the surrender of the national forts, and the transfer of the national property within her limits. Mr. Buchanan prepared an answer to their request which was compromising to the honor of the Executive and perilous to the integrity of the Union. Judge Black took a decided and irrevocable stand against the President's position. He advised Mr. Buchanan that upon the basis of that fatal concession to the Disunion leaders he could not remain in his Cabinet. It was a sharp issue, but was soon adjusted. Mr. Buchanan gave way, and permitted Judge Black, and his associates Holt and Stanton, to frame a reply for the administration.

Jefferson Davis, Mr. Toombs, Mr. Benjamin, Mr. Slidell, who had been Mr. Buchanan's intimate and confidential advisers, and who had led him to the brink of ruin, found themselves suddenly supplanted, and a new power installed at the White House. Foiled, and no longer able to use the National Administration as an instrumentality to destroy the National life, the Secession leaders in Congress turned upon the President with angry reproaches. In their rage they lost all sense of the respect due to the Chief Magistrate of the Nation, and assaulted Mr. Buchanan with coarseness as well as violence. Senator Benjamin spoke of him as "a senile Executive under the sinister influence of insane counsels." This exhibition of malignity towards the misguided President afforded to the North the most convincing and satisfactory proof that there had been a change for the better in the plans and purposes of the Administration. They realized that it must be a deep sense of impending danger which could separate Mr. Buchanan from his political associations with the South, and they recognized in his position a significant proof of the desperate determination to which the enemies of the Union had come.

The stand taken by Judge Black and his loyal associates was in the last days of December, 1860.   The re-organization of the Cabinet came as a matter of necessity.   Mr. John B. Floyd resigned from the War Department, making loud proclamation that his action was based on the President's refusal to surrender the national forts in Charleston Harbor to the Secession government of South Carolina.   This manifesto was not necessary to establish Floyd's treasonable intentions towards the government; but, in point of truth, the plea was undoubtedly a pretense, to cover reasons of a more personal character which would at once deprive him of Mr. Buchanan's confidence. There had been irregularities in the War Department tending to compromise Mr. Floyd, for which he was afterwards indicted in the District of Columbia.   Mr. Floyd well knew that the first knowledge of these shortcomings would lead to his dismissal from the Cabinet. Whatever Mr. Buchanan's faults as an Executive may have been, his honor in all transactions, both personal and public, was unquestionable, and he was the last man to tolerate the slightest deviation from the path of rigid integrity.

Mr. Thompson, the Secretary of the Interior, followed Mr. Floyd after a short interval.   Mr. Cobb had left the Treasury a few days before General Cass resigned from the Cabinet, and had gone to Georgia to stimulate her laggard movements in the scheme of destroying the government.   His successor was Philip Francis Thomas of Maryland, who entered the Cabinet as a representative of the principles whose announcement had forced General Cass to resign.   The change of policy to which the President was now fully committed, forced Mr. Thomas to retire, after a month's service.   He frankly stated that he was unable to agree with the President and his other advisers "in reference to the condition of things in South Carolina," and therefore tendered his resignation.   Mr. Thomas adhered to the Union, and always maintained an upright and honorable character; but his course at that crisis deprived him subsequently of a seat in the United-States Senate, though at a later period he served in the House as representative from Maryland.

Mr. Cobb, Mr. Floyd, and Mr. Thompson had all remained in the Cabinet after the Presidential election in November, in full sympathy, and so far as was possible in full co-operation, with the men in the South who were organizing resistance to the authority of the Federal Government.   Neither those gentlemen, nor any friend in their behalf, ever ventured to explain how, as sworn officers of the United States, they could remain at their posts consistently with the laws of honor,—laws obligatory upon them not only as public officials who had taken a solemn oath of fidelity to the Constitution, but also as private gentlemen whose good faith was pledged anew every hour they remained in control of the departments with whose administration they had been intrusted. Their course is unfavorably contrasted with that of many Southern men (of whom General Lee and the two Johnstons were conspicuous examples), who refused to hold official positions under the National Government a single day after they had determined to take part in the scheme of Disunion.

By the re-organization of the Cabinet, the tone of Mr. Buchanan's administration was radically changed. Judge Black had used his influence with the President to secure trustworthy friends of the Union in every department. Edwin M. Stanton, little known at the time to the public, but of high standing in his profession, was appointed Attorney-General soon after Judge Black took charge of the State Department. Judge Black had been associated with Stanton personally and professionally, and was desirous of his aid in the dangerous period through which he was called to serve.

Joseph Holt, who, since the death of Aaron V. Brown in 1859, had been Postmaster-General, was now appointed Secretary of War, and Horatio King of Maine, for many years the upright first assistant, was justly promoted to the head of the Post-office Department. Mr. Holt was the only Southern man left in the Cabinet. He was a native of Kentucky, long a resident of Mississippi, always identified with the Democratic party, and affiliated with its extreme Southern wing. Without a moment's hesitation he now broke all the associations of a lifetime, and stood by the Union without qualification or condition. His learning, his firmness, and his ability, were invaluable to Mr. Buchanan in the closing days of his administration.

General John A. Dix of New York was called to the head of the Treasury. He was a man of excellent ability, of wide experience in affairs, of spotless character, and a most zealous friend of the Union. He found the Treasury bankrupt, the discipline of its officers in the South gone, its orders disregarded in the States which were preparing for secession. He at once imparted spirit and energy into the service,—giving to the administration of this department a policy of pronounced loyalty to the government. No act of his useful and honorable life has been so widely known or will be so long remembered as his dispatch to the Treasury agent at New Orleans to take possession of a revenue cutter whose commander was suspected of disloyalty and of a design to transfer his vessel to the Confederate service. Lord Nelson's memorable order at Trafalgar was not more inspiring to the British navy than was the order of General Dix to the American people, when, in the gloom of that depressing winter, he telegraphed South his peremptory words, "If any man attempts to haul down the American flag, shoot him on the spot."

Thus reconstructed, the Cabinet as a whole was one of recognized power, — marked by high personal character, by intellectual training, by experience in affairs, and by aptitude for the public service. There have been Cabinets perhaps more widely known for the possession of great qualities; but, if the history of successive administrations from the origin of the government be closely studied, it will be found that the re-organized Cabinet of President Buchanan must take rank as one of exceptional ability.

For the remaining two months of Mr. Buchanan's administration the destinies of the country were in the keeping of these constitutional advisers. If in any respect they failed to come to the standard of a loyalty that was quickened by subsequent developments, they no doubt fairly represented the demand of the Northern States at the time. There was everywhere the most earnest desire to avert a conflict, and an unwillingness to recognize the possibility of actual war. The majority of the Republican party in both branches of Congress was not advocating a more decided or more aggressive course with the South, during the months of January and February, than the Cabinet, with Judge Black at its head, was pursuing. The time for executive acts of a more pronounced character was directly after the Presidential election, when the first symptoms of resistance to national authority were visible in the South. If the new Cabinet had been then in power, the history of the civil revolt might have been different. But the force that will arrest the first slow revolution of a wheel cannot stand before it when, by unchecked velocity, it has acquired a destructive momentum. The measures which might have secured repression in November would only have produced explosion in January.

The change of position on the part of Mr. Buchanan was not left to inference, or to the personal assurance of the loyal men who composed his re-organized Cabinet. He announced it himself in a special message to Congress on the 8th of January, 1861. The tone was so different from the message of December, that it did not seem possible that the two could have been written by the same man. It was evident from many passages in the second message that he was trying to reconcile it with the first. This was the natural course suggested by the pride of one who overrated the virtue of consistency. The attempt was useless. The North with unaffected satisfaction, the South with unconcealed indignation, realized that the President had entirely escaped from the influences which dictated the first message. He now asserted that, " as the Chief Executive under the Constitution of the United States," he had no alternative but " to collect the public revenues, and to protect the public property, so far as this might be practicable under existing laws." Remarking that his province " was to execute, and not to make, the laws," he threw upon Congress the duty " of enlarging their provisions to meet exigencies as they may occur." He declared it as his own conviction that " the right and the duty to use military force defensively against those who resist the federal officers in the execution of their legal functions, and against those who assail the property . of the Federal Government, are clear and undeniable." Conceding so much, the mild denial which the President re-asserted, of " the right to make aggressive war upon any State," may be charitably tolerated; for, under the defensive power which he so broadly approved, the whole force of national authority could be used against a State aggressively bent upon Secession.

The President did not fail to fortify his own position at every point with great force. The situation had become so serious, and had " assumed such vast and alarming proportions, as to place the subject entirely above and beyond Executive control." He therefore commended " the question, in all its various bearings, to Congress, as the only tribunal possessing the power to meet the existing exigency." He reminded Congress that " to them belongs exclusively the power to declare war, or to authorize the employment of military force in all cases contemplated by the Constitution." Not abandoning the hope of an amicable adjustment, the President pertinently informed Congress that " they alone possess the power to remove grievances which might lead to war, and to secure peace and union." As a basis of settlement, he recommended a formal compromise by which " the North shall have the exclusive control of the territory above a certain line, and Southern institutions shall have protection below that line." This plan, he believed, " ought to receive universal approbation." He maintained that on Congress, and "on Congress alone, rests the responsibility." As Congress would certainly in a few days be under the control of the Republicans in both branches, — by the withdrawal of senators and representatives from the seceding States, — Mr. Buchanan's argument had a double force. Not only was he vindicating the position of the Executive and throwing the weight of responsibility on the Legislative Department of the government, but he was protecting the position of the Democratic party by saying, in effect, that the President chosen by that party stood ready to approve and to execute any laws for the protection of the government and the safety of the Union which a Republican Congress might enact.

A certain significance attached to the date which the President had selected for communicating his message to Congress. It was the eighth day of January, the anniversary of the Battle of New Orleans, celebrated that year with enthusiastic demonstration in honor of the memory of Andrew Jackson, who had, on a memorable occasion not unlike the present, sworn an emphatic oath that "the Federal Union must and shall be preserved." There was also marked satisfaction throughout the loyal States with Mr. Buchanan's assurance of the peace of the District of Columbia on the ensuing 4th of March, on the occasion of Mr. Lincoln's inauguration. He did not himself "share in the serious apprehensions that were entertained of disturbance" on that occasion, but he made this declaration, which was received in the North with hearty applause: "In any event, it will be my duty to preserve the peace, and this duty shall be performed."

The change of sentiment towards Mr. Buchanan after the delivery of the special message, was as marked in the North as it was in the South, though in the opposite direction. It would not be true to say that any thing like popularity attended the President in his new position; but the change of feeling was so great that the Legislature of Massachusetts, on the 23d of January, 1861, adopted resolutions in which they declared that they regarded "with unmingled satisfaction the determination evinced in the recent firm and patriotic special message of the President of the United States to amply and faithfully discharge his constitutional duty of enforcing the laws, and preserving the integrity of the Union." The Legislature "proffered to the President, through the Governor of the Commonwealth, such aid in men and money as he may require to maintain the authority of the National Government." These resolutions were forwarded to Mr. Buchanan by Governor Andrew. They were only one of many manifestations which the President received of approval of his course.

The Massachusetts Legislature was radically Republican in both branches, and even in making a reference to "men and money" as requisite to maintain the Union, they had gone farther than the public sentiment at that time approved. Coercive measures were generally condemned. A few days after the action of the Legislature, a large meeting of the people of Boston, held in Faneuil Hall, declared that they "depended for the return of the seceding States, and the permanent preservation of the Union, on conciliatory counsels, and a sense of the benefits which the Constitution confers on all the States, and not on military coercion." They declared that they shrunk "with horror from the thought of civil war between the North and the South."

It must always be remembered that the disbelief in ultimate secession was nearly universal throughout the free States. The people of the North could not persuade themselves that the proceedings in the Southern States would lead to any thing more serious than hostile demonstrations, which would end, after coaxing and compromise, in a return to the Union. But with this hope of final security there was, on the part of the great mass of people in the free States, the gravest solicitude throughout the winter of 1860–61, and a restless waiting and watching for a solution of the troubles. Partisan leaders were busy on both sides seeking for an advantage that might survive the pending trials. Northern Democrats in many instances sought to turn the occasion to one of political advantage by pointing out the lamentable condition to which anti-slavery agitation had brought the country. This was naturally answered by Republicans with defiance, and with an affected contempt and carelessness of what the South might do. Much that was written and much that was spoken throughout the North during that winter, both by Democrats and Republicans, would have remained unwritten and unspoken if they had realized the seriousness and magnitude of the impending calamity.

In a final analysis and true estimate of Mr. Buchanan's conduct in the first stages of the revolt, the condition of the popular mind as just described must be taken into account. The same influences and expectations that wrought upon the people were working also upon him. There were indeed two Mr. Buchanans in the closing months of the administration. The first was Mr. Buchanan of November and December, angered by the decision of the Presidential election and more than willing that the North, including his own State, should be disciplined by fright to more conservative views and to a stricter observance of what he considered solemn obligations imposed by the Constitution. If the Southern threat of resistance to the authority of the Union had gone no farther than this, Mr. Buchanan would have been readily reconciled to its temporary violence, and would probably have considered it a national blessing in disguise. — The second was Mr. Buchanan of January and February, appalled by surrounding and increasing perils, grieved by the conduct of Southern men whom he had implicitly trusted, overwhelmed by the realization of the evils which had obviously followed his official declarations, hoping earnestly for the safety of the Union, and yet more disturbed and harrowed in his mind than the mass of loyal people who did not stand so near the danger as he, or so accurately measure its alarming growth. The President of December with Cobb and Floyd and Thompson in his Cabinet, and the President of January with Dix and Stanton and Holt for his councilors, were radically different men. No true estimate of Mr. Buchanan in the crisis of his public career can ever be reached if this vital distinction be overlooked.

It was Mr. Buchanan's misfortune to be called to act in an emergency which demanded will, fortitude, and moral courage. In these qualities he was deficient. He did not possess the executive faculty. His life had been principally devoted to the practice of law in the most peaceful of communities, and to service in legislative bodies where he was borne along by the force of association. He had not been trained to prompt decision, had not been accustomed to exercise command. He was cautious and conservative to the point of timidity. He possessed ability of a high order, and, though he thought slowly, he could master the most difficult subject with comprehensive power. His service of ten years in the House and an equal period in the Senate was marked by a conscientious devotion to duty. He did not rank with the ablest members of either body, but always bore a prominent part in important discussions and maintained himself with credit.

It was said of Mr. Buchanan that he instinctively dreaded to assume responsibility of any kind. His keenest critic remarked that in the tentative period of political issues assumed by his party, Mr. Buchanan could always be found two paces to the rear, but in the hour of triumph he marched proudly in the front rank. He was not gifted with independence or self-assertion. His bearing towards Southern statesmen was derogatory to him as a man of spirit. His tone towards administrations of his own party was so deferential as almost to imply a lack of self-respect. He was not a leader among men. He was always led. He was led by Mason and Soulé into the imprudence of signing the Ostend Manifesto; he was led by the Southern members of his Cabinet into the inexplicable folly and blunder of indorsing the Lecompton iniquity; he was led by Dis- union senators into the deplorable mistake contained in his last annual message. Fortunately for him he was led a month later by Black and Holt and Stanton to a radical change of his compro- mising position.

If Mr. Buchanan had possessed the unconquerable will of Jackson or the stubborn courage of Taylor, he could have changed the history of the revolt against the Union. A great opportunity came to him but he was not equal to it. Always an admirable adviser where prudence and caution were the virtues required, he was fatally want- ing in a situation which demanded prompt action and strong nerve. As representative in Congress, as senator, as minister abroad, as Secretary of State, his career was honorable and successful. His life was singularly free from personal fault or short-coming. He was honest and pure-minded. His fame would have been more enviable if he had never been elevated to the Presidency.

CHAPTER XI.

NO feature of the extraordinary winter of 1860–61 is more singular in retrospect than the formal leave-taking of the Southern senators and representatives in their respective Houses. Members of the House from the seceding States, with few exceptions,
refrained from individual addresses, either of farewell or defiance,
but adopted a less demonstrative and more becoming mode. The
South-Carolina representatives withdrew on the 24th of December
(1860), in a brief card laid before the House by Speaker Penning-
ton. They announced that, as the people of their State had "in their
sovereign capacity resumed the powers delegated by them to the Federal Government of the United States," their "connection with the
House of Representatives was thereby dissolved." They "desired to
take leave of those with whom they had been associated in a common agency, with mutual regard and respect for the rights of each
other." They "cherished the hope" that in future relations they

242

might "better enjoy the peace and harmony essential to the happiness of a free and enlightened people."

Other delegations retired from the House in the order in which their States seceded. The leave-taking, in the main, was not undignified. There was no defiance, no indulgence of bravado. The members from Mississippi "regretted the necessity" which impelled their State to the course adopted, but declared that it met "their unqualified approval." The card was no doubt written by Mr. L. Q. C. Lamar, and accurately described his emotions. He stood firmly by his State in accordance with the political creed in which he had been reared, but looked back with tender regret to the Union whose destiny he had wished to share and under the protection of whose broader nationality he had hoped to live and to die. A few Southern representatives marked their retirement by speeches bitterly reproaching the Federal Government, and bitterly accusing the Republican party; but the large majority confined themselves to the simpler form of the card.

Whether the ease and confidence as to the future which these Southern representatives manifested was really felt or only assumed, can never be known. They were all men of intelligence, some of them conspicuously able; and it seems incredible that they could have persuaded themselves that a great government could be dissolved without shock and without resistance. They took leave with no more formality than that with which a private gentleman, aggrieved by discourteous treatment, withdraws from a company in which he feels that he can no longer find enjoyment. Their confidence was based on the declarations and admissions of Mr. Buchanan's message; but they had, in effect, constructed that document themselves, and the slightest reflection should have warned them that, with the change of administration to occur in a few weeks, there would be a different understanding of Executive duty, and a different appeal to the reason of the South.

The senators from the seceding States were more outspoken than the representatives. They took the opportunity of their retirement to say many things which, even for their own personal fame, should have been left unsaid. A clear analysis of these harangues is impossible. They lacked the unity and directness of the simple notifications with which the seceding representatives had withdrawn from the House. The valedictories in the Senate were a singular compound of defiance and pity, of justification and recrimination.

Some of the speeches have an insincere and mock-heroic tone to the reader twenty years after the event. They appear to be the expressions of men who talked for effect, and who professed themselves ready for a shock of arms which they believed would never come. But the majority of the utterances were by men who meant all they said; who, if they did not anticipate a bloody conflict, were yet prepared for it, and who were too deeply stirred by resentment and passion to give due heed to consequences.

On the 21st of January the senators from Florida, Alabama, and Mississippi formally withdrew from the Senate. Their speeches showed little variety of thought, consisting chiefly of indictments against the free States for placing the government under the control of an anti-slavery administration. Mr. Yulee was the first to speak. He solemnly announced to the Senate that "the State of Florida, through a convention of her people, had decided to recall the powers which she had delegated to the Federal Government, and to assume the full exercise of all her sovereign rights as an independent and separate community." At what particular period in the history of the American continent Florida had enjoyed "sovereign rights," by what process she had ever "delegated powers to the Federal Government," or at what time she had ever been "an independent and separate community," Mr. Yulee evidently preferred not to inform the Senate. His colleague, Mr. Mallory, implored the people of the North not to repeat the fatal folly of the Bourbons by imagining that "the South would submit to the degradation of a constrained existence under a violated Constitution." Mr. Mallory regarded the subjugation of the South by war as impossible. He warned the North that they were dealing with "a nation, and not with a faction."

Mr. Clement C. Clay, Jr., of Alabama, boasted that in the convention which adopted the Ordinance of Secession in his State there was not one friend of the Union; and he resented with indignation what he termed the offensive calumny of the Republicans in denouncing slavery and polygamy as twin relics of barbarism. The action of Alabama, he said, was not from "sudden, spasmodic, and violent passion." It was the conclusion her people had reached "after years of enmity, injustice, and injury at the hands of their Northern brethren." Instead of causing surprise, "it is rather matter of reproach that they have endured so much and so long, and have deferred this act of self-defense until to-day." Mr. Clay's speech was insulting and exasperating to the last degree. His colleague, Mr. Fitzpatrick, a man of better temper, showed reserve and an indisposition to discuss the situation. He contented himself with the expression of a general concurrence in the views of Mr. Clay, adding no word of bitterness himself. He said that he "acknowledged loyalty to no other power than to the sovereign State of Alabama." But for the pressure brought upon him, Mr. Fitzpatrick would have been glad to retain his seat in the Senate and wait the course of events. He was not in his heart a Disunionist, as his colleague was. He would have accepted the nomination for the Vice-Presidency on the ticket with Douglas the preceding year, if the whole political power of the Cotton States had not opposed his wishes and forced him into the support of Breckinridge.

Jefferson Davis expressed his concurrence in the action of the people of Mississippi. He believed that action was necessary and proper, but would "have felt himself equally bound if his belief had been otherwise." He presented an analysis of the difference between the remedies of nullification and secession. Nullification was a remedy inside of the Union; secession a remedy outside. He expressed himself as against the theory of nullification, and explained that, so far from being identical with secession, the two are antagonistic principles. Mr. Calhoun's mistake, according to Mr. Davis, was in trying to "nullify" the laws of the Union while continuing a member of it. He intimated that President Jackson would never have attempted to "execute the laws" in South Carolina as he did against the nullifiers in 1832, if the State had seceded, and that therefore his great example could not be quoted in favor of "coercion." It is not believed that Mr. Davis had the slightest authority for this aspersion upon the memory of Jackson. It seems rather to have been a disingenuous and unwarranted statement of the kind so plentifully used at the time for the purpose of "firing the Southern heart."

There had been an impression in the country that Mr. Davis was among the most reluctant of those who engaged in the secession movement; but in his speech he declared that he had conferred with the people of Mississippi before the step was taken, and counseled them to the course which they had adopted. This declaration was a great surprise to Northern Democrats, among whom Mr. Davis had many friends. For several years he had been growing in favor with a powerful element in the Democracy of the free States, and, but for the exasperating quarrel of 1860, he might have been selected as the

Presidential candidate of his party. No man gave up more than Mr. Davis in joining the revolt against the Union. In his farewell words to the Senate, there was a tone of moderation and dignity not unmixed with regretful and tender emotions. There was also apparent a spirit of confidence and defiance. He evidently had full faith that he was going forth to victory and to power.

Mr. Toombs of Georgia did not take formal leave, but on the 7th of January delivered a speech which, though addressed to the Senate of the United States, was apparently intended to influence public sentiment in Georgia, where there was an uncomfortable halting in the progress of secession. The speech had special interest, not alone from Mr. Toombs's well-known ability, but because it was the only presentation of the conditions on which the scheme of Disunion might be arrested, and the Cotton States held fast in their loyalty to the government, — conditions which, in the language of Mr. Toombs, would "restore fraternity and peace and unity to all of us." It was not believed that Mr. Toombs had the faintest expectation that his propositions would receive favorable consideration in the free States. His point would be fully gained by showing that the free States would not accept conditions which Georgia had the right to exact as the basis of her remaining in the Union. Once firmly persuaded that she was deprived of her constitutional rights, Georgia could the more easily be led or forced into secession.

The first condition prescribed by Mr. Toombs was, that in all territory owned or to be acquired by the United States, slave property should be securely protected until the period of the formation of a State government, when the people could determine the question for themselves. The second condition was, that property in slaves should be entitled to the same protection from the Government of the United States in all its departments everywhere, which is extended to other property, provided that there should be no interference with the liberty of a State to prohibit or establish slavery within its limits. The third condition was, that persons committing crimes against slave property in one State, and fleeing to another, should be delivered up in the same manner as persons committing crimes against other forms of property, and that the laws of the State from which such persons flee should be the test of the criminality of the act. The fourth condition was, that fugitive slaves should be surrendered under the Act of 1850 without being entitled to a writ of *habeas corpus*, or trial by jury, or other obstructions in the States to which they might flee. The fifth and last demand was, that Congress should pass efficient laws for the punishment of all persons in any of the States who should in any manner aid or abet invasion or insurrection in any other State, or commit any other act against the laws of nations tending to disturb the tranquillity of the people or government of any other State. Without the concession of these points Mr. Toombs said the Union could not be maintained. If some satisfactory arrangement should not be made. he was for immediate action. "We are," he said, "as ready to fight now as we shall ever be. I will have equality or war." He denounced Mr. Lincoln as "an enemy to the human race, deserving the execration of all mankind."

Three weeks later the Georgia senators withdrew. Georgia had on the 19th of January, after much dragooning, passed the Ordinance of Secession, and on the 28th, Mr. Alfred Iverson, the colleague of Mr. Toombs, communicated the fact to the Senate in a highly inflammatory speech. He proclaimed that Georgia was the sixth State to secede, that a seventh was about to follow, and that " a confederacy of their own would soon be established." Provision would be made "for the admission of other States," and Mr. Iverson assured the Senate that within a few months "all the slave-holding States of the late confederacy of the United States will be united together in a bond of union far more homogeneous, and therefore more stable, than the one now being dissolved." His boasting was unrestrained, but his conception of the contest which he and his associates were inviting was pitiably inadequate. "Your conquest," said he, addressing the Union senators, "will cost you a hundred thousand lives and a hundred millions of dollars."

The conclusion of Mr. Iverson's harangue disclosed his fear that after all Georgia might prefer the old Union. "For myself," said he, "unless my opinions greatly change, I shall never consent to the reconstruction of the Federal Union. The Rubicon is passed, and with my consent shall never be recrossed." But these bold declarations were materially qualified by Mr. Iverson when he reflected on the powerful minority of Union men in Georgia, and the general feeling in that State against a conflict with the National Government. "In this sentiment," said he, "I may be overruled by the people of my State and of the other Southern States." . . . "Nothing, however, will bring Georgia back except a full and explicit recognition and guaranty of the safety and protection of the institution of domestic slavery." This was the final indication of the original weakness of the secession cause in Georgia, and of the extraordinary means which were taken to impress the people of that State with the belief that secession would lead to reconstruction on a basis of more efficient protection to the South and greater strength to the whole Union.

On the 4th of February Mr. Slidell and Mr. Benjamin delivered their valedictories as senators from Louisiana. Mr. Slidell was aggressively insolent. He informed the Senate that if any steps should be taken to enforce the authority of the Union in the seceded States, they would be resisted. "You may," he said, "under color of enforcing your laws and collecting your revenue, blockade our ports. This will be war, and we shall meet it with different but equally efficient weapons. We will not permit the consumption or introduction of any of your manufactures. Every sea will swarm with our privateers, the volunteer militia of the ocean." He evidently expected foreign aid. "How long," he asked, "will the great naval powers of Europe permit you to impede their free intercourse with their best customers, and to stop the supply of the great staple which is the most important basis of their manufacturing industry?" "You were," said he, adding taunt to argument, "with all the wealth of this once great confederacy, but a fourth or fifth rate naval power. What will you be when emasculated by the withdrawal of fifteen States, and warred upon by them with active and inveterate hostility?"

In a tone of patronizing liberality, Mr. Slidell gave assurances that the new confederacy would recognize the rights of the inhabitants of the valley of the Mississippi and its tributaries to free navigation, and would guarantee to them "a free interchange of agricultural productions without impost, and the free transit from foreign countries of every species of merchandise, subjected only to such regulations as may be necessary for a protection of the revenue system which we may establish." Had Mr. Slidell been less inspired by insolence, and more largely endowed with wisdom, he would have remembered that when the Union contained but six millions of people, they were willing to fight any one of three great European powers for freedom of access to the sea for the inhabitants of the valley of the Mississippi, and that it was from the first a physical impossibility to close it or in any way restrict it against the rights of the North-West. The people of that section, even

STEPHEN A. DOUGLAS.

BENJAMIN F. WADE.

WILLIAM PITT FESSENDEN.

CHARLES SUMNER.

THADDEUS STEVENS.

JOHN C. BRECKENRIDGE.

HENRY WINTER DAVIS.

without the prestige of the national flag, were immeasurably stronger than the people of the South-West, and were, unaided, fully competent to fight their way to the ocean over any obstacles which the powers behind Mr. Slidell could interpose.   In the mere matching of local strength, it was sheer folly for the States of the lower Mississippi to attempt to control the mouth of that river.

Mr. Judah P. Benjamin spoke in a tone of moderation as contrasted with the offensive dictation of Mr. Slidell.   He devoted himself mainly to answering an argument which came instinctively to every man's mind, and which bore with peculiar severity upon the action of Louisiana.   Mr. Benjamin brought his eminent legal ability to the discussion, but failed even to satisfy himself.   The State of Louisiana was formed from territory which had been bought and paid for by the United States out of the common treasury of the whole people.   Whatever specious plea might be made for the independent and separate sovereignty of the old thirteen States, the argument could not apply to Louisiana.   No one could maintain that Louisiana had ever enjoyed a separate sovereignty of any kind, nominal or real.   She had been originally owned by France, had been sold to Spain, had been sold back again to France, and had been bought by the United States.   These sales had been made without protest from any one, and the title conferred at each transfer was undisputed, the sovereignty of the purchasing power undeniable.

Confronting these facts, and realizing the difficulty they presented, Mr. Benjamin was reduced to desperate straits for argument. " Without entering into the details of the negotiation," he said, " the archives of our State Department show the fact to be that although the domain, the public lands and other property of France in the ceded province, were conveyed by absolute title to the United States, the sovereignty was not conveyed *otherwise than in trust*."   This peculiar statement of a sovereignty that was "conveyed in trust" Mr. Benjamin attempted to sustain by quoting the clause in the treaty which gave the right to the people of Louisiana to be incorporated into the Union "on terms of equality with the other States." From this he argued that the sovereignty of the *Territory* of Louisiana held in trust by the Federal Government, and conveyed to the *State* of Louisiana on her admission to the Union, was necessarily greater than the National sovereignty.   Indeed, Mr. Benjamin recognized no "Nation" in the United States and no real sovereignty in the General Government which was but the agent of the sovereign States. It properly and logically followed, according to Mr. Benjamin, that the "sovereignty held in trust," might, when conferred, be immediately and rightfully employed to destroy the life of the trustee. The United States might or might not admit Louisiana to the Union, for the General Government was sole judge as to time and expediency — but when once admitted, the power of the State was greater than the power of the Government which permitted the State to come into existence. Such were the contradictions and absurdities which the creed of the Secessionists inevitably involved, and in which so clever a man as Mr. Benjamin was compelled to blunder and flounder.

Pursuing his argument, Mr. Benjamin wished to know whether those who asserted that Louisiana had been bought by the United States meant that the United States had the right based on that fact to sell Louisiana? He denied in every form that there had ever been such a purchase of Louisiana as carried with it the right of sale. "I deny," said he, "the fact on which the argument is founded. I deny that the Province of Louisiana or the people of Louisiana were ever conveyed to the United States for a price as property that could be bought or sold at will." However learned Mr. Benjamin may have been in the law, he was evidently ill informed as to the history of the transaction of which he spoke so confidently. He should have known that the United States, sixteen years after it bought Louisiana from France, actually sold or exchanged a large part of that province to the King of Spain as part of the consideration in the purchase of the Floridas. He should have known that at the time the Government of the United States disposed of a part of Louisiana, there was not an intelligent man in the world who did not recognize its right and power to dispose of the whole. The theory that the United States acquired a less degree of sovereignty over Louisiana than was held by France when she transferred it, or by Spain when she owned it, was never dreamed of when the negotiation was made. It was an afterthought on the part of the hard-pressed defenders of the right of secession. It was the ingenious but lame device of an able lawyer who undertook to defend what was indefensible.

Mr. Yulee of Florida had endeavored to make the same argument on behalf of his State, feeling the embarrassment as did Mr. Benjamin, and relying, as Mr. Benjamin did, upon the clause in the treaty with Spain entitling Florida to admission to the Union. Mr.

Benjamin and Mr. Yulee should both have known that the guaranty which they quote was nothing more and nothing less than the ordinary condition which every enlightened nation makes in parting with its subjects or citizens, that they shall enter into their new relations without discrimination against them and with no lower degree of civil rights than had already been enjoyed by those who form the nation to which they are about to be annexed. Louisiana, when she was transferred to the United States, received no further guaranty than Napoleon in effect gave to Spain at the treaty of San Ildefonso, or than the Spanish Bourbons had given to the French Bourbons in the treaty of 1763 at the close of the Seven Years' War. In each of the three transfers of the sovereignty of Louisiana, the same condition was perfectly understood as to the rights of the inhabitants. Mr. Benjamin drew the conclusion which was not only diametrically wrong in morals, but diametrically erroneous in logic. Instead of inferring that a State, situated as Louisiana was, should necessarily become greater than the power which purchased it, simply because other States in the Union which she joined had assumed such power, a discriminating mind of Mr. Benjamin's acuteness should have seen that the very position proved the reverse of what he stated, and demonstrated, in the absurdity of Louisiana's secession, the equal absurdity of the secession of South Carolina and Georgia.

It seemed impossible for Mr. Benjamin or for any other leader of Southern opinion to argue the question of State rights fairly or dispassionately. They had been so persistently trained in the heresy that they could give no weight to the conclusive reasoning of the other side. The original thirteen, they averred, were "free, sovereign, and independent States," acknowledged to be such by the King of Great Britain in the Treaty of peace in 1783. The new States, so the argument ran, were all admitted to the Union on terms of equality with the old. Hence all were alike endowed with sovereignty. Even the historical part of this argument was strained and fallacious. Much was made in the South of Mr. Toombs's declaration that "the original thirteen" were as "independent of each other as Australia and Jamaica." So indeed they were as long as they remained British Colonies. Their only connection in that condition was in their common dependence on the Crown. But the first step towards independence of the Crown was to unite. From that day onward they were never separate. Nor did the King of Great Britain acknowledge the "independence and sovereignty" of the thirteen individual and separate States. The Treaty of peace declares that "His Majesty acknowledges the said United States [naming them] to be free, sovereign, and independent States," — not separately and individually, but the "said *United* States." The King then agrees that "the following are and shall be the boundaries of the said United States," — proceeding to give, not the boundaries of each State, but the boundaries of the whole as one unit, one sovereignty, one nationality. Last of all, the commissioners who signed the treaty with the King's commissioner were not acting for the individual States, but for the *United* States. Three of them, John Adams, Benjamin Franklin, and John Jay, were from the North, and Henry Laurens from the South. The separate sovereignties whose existence was so persistently alleged by Mr. Benjamin and Mr. Toombs were not represented when independence was conceded. Mr. Benjamin's conclusion, therefore, was not only illogical, but was completely disproved by plain historical facts.

It seems never to have occurred to Mr. Benjamin, or to Mr. Yulee, or to the Texas senators, or to the Arkansas senators, that the money paid from a common treasury of the nation gave any claim to National sovereignty. Their philosophy seems to have been that the General Government had been paid in full by the privilege of nurturing the new States, of improving their rivers and harbors, of building their fortifications, of protecting them in peace, of defending them in war. The privilege of leading the new communities through the condition of Territorial existence up to the full majesty of States, was, according to secession argument, sufficient compensation, and removed all shadow of the title or the sovereignty of the National Government, the moment the inhabitants thus benefited announced their desire to form new connections. Louisiana had cost fifteen millions of dollars at a time when that was a vast sum of money. It had cost five millions of money and the surrender of a province, to purchase Florida, and nearly a hundred millions more to extinguish the Indian title, and make the State habitable for white men. Texas cost the National Treasury ninety millions of dollars in the war which was precipitated by her annexation, and ten millions more paid to her in 1850, in adjustment of her boundary trouble. All these States apparently regarded the tie that bound them to the National Government as in no degree mutual, as imposing no duty upon them. By some mysterious process still unexplained, the more they gained from connection with the National authority, the less was their obligation thereto, the more perfect their right to disregard and destroy the beneficent government which had created them and fostered them.

In all the speeches delivered by the senators from the seceding States, there was no presentation of the grievances which, in their own minds, justified secession. This fact elicited less notice at the time than it calls forth in retrospect. Those senators held in their hands in the beginning, the fate of the secession movement. If they had advised the Southern States that it was wiser and better to abide in the Union, and at least to wait for some overt act of wrong against the slave States, the whole movement would have collapsed. But they evidently felt that this would be a shrinking and cowardly policy after the numerous manifestoes they had issued. South Carolina had taken the fatal step, and to fail in sustaining her would be to co-operate in crushing her. While these motives and aims are intelligible, it seems utterly incredible that not one of the senators gave a specification of the wrongs which led the South to her rash step. Mr. Toombs recounted the concessions on which the South would agree to remain; but these were new provisions and new conditions, never intended by the framers of the Federal Constitution; and they were abhorrent to the civilization of the nineteenth century.

Mr. Toombs, Mr. Jefferson Davis, and Mr. Benjamin were the three ablest senators who spoke in favor of secession. Not one of them deemed it necessary to justify his conduct by a recital of the grounds on which so momentous a step could bear the test of historic examination. They dealt wholly in generalities as to the past, and apparently based their action on something that was to happen in the future. Mr. John Slidell sought to give a strong reason for the movement, in the statement that, if Lincoln should be inaugurated with Southern assent, the 4th of March would witness, in various quarters, outbreaks among the slaves which, although they would be promptly suppressed, would carry ruin and devastation to many a Southern home. It was from Mr. Slidell that Mr. Buchanan received the information which induced him to dwell at length in his annual message on this painful feature of the situation. But it was probably an invention of Mr. Slidell's fertile brain — imposed upon the President and intended to influence public sentiment in the North.

It was in flat contradiction of the general faith in the personal fealty of their slaves, so constantly boasted by Southern men, — a faith abundantly justified by the subsequent fact that four years of war passed without a single attempt at servile insurrection. At the time of the John Brown disturbance the South resented the imputation of fear, made upon it by the North. If now the danger was especially imminent, Southern leaders were solely to blame. They would not accept the honorable assurance of the Republican party and of the President-elect that no interference with slavery in the States was designed. They insisted in all their public addresses that Mr. Lincoln was determined to uproot slavery everywhere, and they might well fear that these repeated declarations had been heard and might be accepted by their slaves.

The omission by individual senators to present the grievances which justified secession is perhaps less notable than the same omission by the conventions which ordained secession in the several States. South Carolina presented, as a special outrage, the enactment of personal-liberty bills in the free States, and yet, from the foundation of the Federal Government, she had probably never lost a slave in consequence of these enactments. In Georgia the attempt at justification reached the ludicrous when solemn charge was made that a bounty had been paid from the Federal Treasury to New-England fishermen. The tariff was complained of, the navigation laws were sneered at. But these were all public policies which had been in operation with Southern consent and largely with Southern support, throughout the existence of the Republic. When South Carolina attempted, somewhat after the illustrious model of the Declaration of Independence, to present justifying reasons for her course, the very authors of the document must have seen that it amounted only to a parody.

Finding no satisfactory exhibit of grievances, either in the speeches of senators or in the declarations of conventions, one naturally infers that the Confederate Government, when formally organized at Montgomery in February, must have given a full and lucid statement to the world of the reasons for this extraordinary movement. When our fathers were impelled to break their loyalty to the English king, and to establish an independent government, they declared in the very fore-front of the document which contained their reasons, that "when it becomes necessary for one people to dissolve the political bonds which have connected them with another, and to assume among the powers of the earth the separate and equal station to which the laws of Nature and of Nature's God entitle them, a decent respect to the opinions of mankind requires that *they should declare the causes which impel them to the separation.*" They followed this assertion with an exhibit of causes which, in the judgment of the world, has been and ever will be, a complete justification of their revolutionary movement.

The Confederate Government saw fit to do nothing of the kind. Their Congress put forth no declaration or manifesto, and Jefferson Davis in his Inaugural as President utterly failed — did not even attempt — to enumerate the grounds of complaint upon which the destruction of the American Union was based. He said that "the declared compact of the Union from which we have withdrawn was to establish justice, insure domestic tranquillity, provide for the common defense, promote the general welfare, and secure the blessing of liberty to ourselves and our posterity. And when, in the judgment of the sovereign States now composing this confederacy, it has been perverted from the purposes for which it was ordained, and ceases to answer the ends for which it was established, a peaceful appeal to the ballot-box declared, that, so far as they were concerned, the government created by that compact should cease to exist. In this they merely assert the right which the Declaration of Independence of 1776 defined to be inalienable." But in what manner, at what time, by what measure, "justice, domestic tranquillity, common defense, the general welfare," had been destroyed by the government of the Union, Mr. Jefferson Davis did not deign to inform the world to whose opinion he appealed.

Mr. Jefferson, in draughting the Declaration of Independence which Davis quotes as his model, said, "the history of the present King of Great Britain is a history of repeated injuries and usurpations, all having in direct object the establishment of an absolute tyranny over these States." What would have been thought of Mr. Jefferson if he had stopped there and adduced no instance and given no proof of his serious indictment against George III.? But Mr. Jefferson and his fellow-patriots in that great Act proceeded to submit their proof to the judgment of a candid world. They recited twenty-eight distinct charges of oppression and tyranny, depriving them of rights to which they were entitled as subjects of the Crown under the British Constitution. From that hour to this, there has been no disproval of the truth of these charges or of the righteousness of the resistance to which our forefathers resorted. It would have been well for the dignity of the Southern Confederacy in history if one of its many able men had placed on record, in an authentic form, the grounds upon which, and the grievances for which, destruction of the Union could be justified.

In his message to the Confederate Congress, Mr. Davis apparently attempted to cure the defects of his Inaugural address, and to give a list of measures which he declared to have been hostile to Southern interests. But it is to be observed that not one of these measures had been completed. They were merely menaced or foreshadowed. As matter of fact, emphasized by Mr. Buchanan in his message, and known to no one better than to Mr. Davis, not a single measure adverse to the interests of slavery had been passed by the Congress of the United States from the foundation of the government. If the Missouri Compromise of 1820 be alleged as an exception to this sweeping assertion, it must be remembered that that compromise was a Southern and not a Northern measure, and was a triumph of the pro-slavery members of Congress over the anti-slavery members; and that its constitutionality was upheld by the unanimous voice of the Cabinet in which Mr. Crawford of Georgia and Mr. Calhoun of South Carolina were leading members.

On the other hand, the policy of the government had been steadily in favor of slavery; and the measures of Congress which would strengthen it were not only numerous, but momentous in character. They are familiar to every one who knows the simplest elements of our national history. The acquisition of Louisiana, the purchase of Florida, the Mexican war, were all great national movements which resulted in strengthening the slave power. Every demand which the South made for protection had been conceded. More stringent provisions for the return of fugitive slaves were asked, and a law was enacted trampling under foot the very spirit of liberty, and putting in peril the freedom of men who were citizens of Northern States. The Missouri Compromise, passed with the consent and support of the South, was repealed by Southern dictation the moment its operation was found to be hostile to the spread of slavery. The rights of slavery in the Territories required judicial confirmation, and the Supreme Court complied by rendering the famous decision in the case of Dred Scott. Against all these guaranties and concessions for the support of slavery, Mr. Davis could quote, not anti-slavery aggressions which had been made, but only those which might be made in the future.

This position disclosed the real though not the avowed cause of the secession movement. Its authors were not afraid of an immediate invasion of the rights of the slave-holder in the States, but they were conscious that the growth of the country, the progress of civilization, and the expansion of our population, were all hostile to their continued supremacy as the governing element in the Republic. The South was the only section in which there was distinctively a governing class. The slave-holders ruled their States more positively than ever the aristocratic classes ruled England. Besides the distinction of free and slave, or black and white, there was another line of demarcation between white men that was as absolute as the division between patrician and plebeian. The nobles of Poland who dictated the policy of the kingdom were as numerous in proportion to the whole population as the rich class of slave-holders whose decrees governed the policy of their States. It was, in short, an oligarchy which by its combined power ruled the Republic. No President of any party had ever been elected who was opposed to its supremacy. The political revolution of 1860 had given to the Republic an anti-slavery President, and the Southern men refused to accept the result. They had been too long accustomed to power to surrender it to an adverse majority, however lawful or constitutional that majority might be. They had been trained to lead and not to follow. They were not disciplined to submission. They had been so long in command that they had become incapable of obedience. Unwillingness to submit to Constitutional authority was the controlling consideration which drove the Southern States to the desperate design of a revolution, peaceful they hoped it would be, but to a revolution even if it should be one of blood.

CHAPTER XII.

WHILE the Secession leaders were engaged in their schemes
for the disruption of the National Government and the formation of a new confederacy, Congress was employing every effort
to arrest the Disunion tendency by making new concessions, and
offering new guaranties to the offended power of the South. If the
wild precipitation of the Southern leaders must be condemned, the
compromising course of the majority in each branch of Congress
will not escape censure, — censure for misjudgment, not for wrong
intention. The anxiety in both Senate and House to do something
which should allay the excitement in the slave-holding section
served only to develop and increase its exasperation and its resolution. A man is never so aggressively bold as when he finds his
opponent afraid of him; and the efforts, however well meant, of the
National Congress in the winter of 1860–61 undoubtedly impressed

the South with a still further conviction of the timidity of the North, and with a certainty that the new confederacy would be able to organize without resistance, and to dissolve the Union without war.

Congress had no sooner convened in December, 1860, and received the message of Mr. Buchanan, with its elaborate argument that the National Government possessed no power to coerce a State, than in each branch special committees of conciliation were appointed. They were not so termed in the resolutions of the Senate and House, but their mission was solely one of conciliation. They were charged with the duty of giving extraordinary assurances that Slavery was not to be disturbed, and of devising measures which might persuade Southern men against the rashness on which they seemed bent. In the Senate they raised a committee of thirteen, representing the number of the original States of the Union. In the House the committee was composed of thirty-three members, representing the number of States then existing. In the Senate, Mr. Powell of Kentucky was chairman of the committee of thirteen, which was composed of seven Democrats, five Republicans, and the venerable Mr. Crittenden of Kentucky, who belonged to neither party. It contained the most eminent men in the Senate of all shades of political opinion. In the House, Thomas Corwin was made chairman, with a majority of Republicans of the more conservative type, a minority of Democrats, and Mr. Henry Winter Davis of Maryland, who held a position similar to that occupied by Mr. Crittenden in the Senate.

The Senate committee promptly disagreed, and before the close of December reported to the Senate their inability to come to any conclusion. The committee of thirty-three was more fortunate, or perhaps unfortunate, in being able to arrive at a series of conclusions which tended only to lower the tone of Northern opinion without in the least degree appeasing the wrath of the South. The record of that committee is one which cannot be reviewed with pride or satisfaction by any citizen of a State that was loyal to the Union. Every form of compromise which could be suggested, every concession of Northern prejudice and every surrender of Northern pride, was urged upon the committee. The measures proposed to the committee by members of the House were very numerous, and those suggested by the members of the committee themselves seemed designed to meet every complaint made by the most extreme Southern agitators. The propositions submitted would in the aggregate fill a large volume, but a selection from the mass will indicate the spirit which had taken possession of Congress.

Mr. Corwin of Ohio wished a declaration from Congress that it was "highly inexpedient to abolish slavery in the District of Columbia unless with the consent of the States of Maryland and Virginia." Mr. Winter Davis suggested that Congress should request the States to revise their statutes with a view to repeal all personal-liberty bills, and further that the Fugitive-slave Law be so amended as to secure trial by jury to the fugitive slave, not in the free State where he was arrested, but in the slave State to which he might be taken. Mr. Morrill of Vermont offered a resolution declaring that all accessions of foreign territory shall hereafter be made by treaty stipulations, and that no treaty shall be ratified until it has received the legislative assent of two-thirds of all the States of the Union, and that neither Congress nor any Territorial Legislature shall pass any law establishing or prohibiting slavery in any Territory thus acquired until it shall have sufficient population to entitle it to admission to the Union. Mr. Houston of Alabama urged the restitution of the Missouri line of 36° 30′. There was in the judgment of many Southern men a better opportunity to effect an adjustment on this line of partition than upon any other basis that had been suggested. But the plan carried with it a national guaranty and protection of slavery on the southern side of the line, and its effect would inevitably have been in a few years to divide the Republic from ocean to ocean. Mr. Taylor of Louisiana wanted the Constitution so amended that the rights of the slave-holder in the Territories could be guarantied, and further amended so that no person, "unless he was of the Caucasian race and of pure and unmixed blood," should ever be allowed to vote for any officer of the National Government.

Mr. Charles Francis Adams proposed that the Constitution of the United States be so amended that no subsequent amendment thereto, "having for its object any interference with slavery, shall originate with any State that does not recognize that relation within its own limits, or shall be valid without the assent of every one of the States composing the Union." No Southern man, during the long agitation of the slavery question extending from 1820 to 1860, had ever submitted so extreme a proposition as that of Mr. Adams. The most precious muniments of personal liberty never had such deep embedment in the organic law of the Republic as Mr. Adams now proposed for the protection of slavery. The well-grounded jealousy and fear of the smaller States had originally secured a provision that their right to equal representation in the Senate should never be taken from them even by an amendment of the Constitution. Mr. Adams now proposed to give an equal safeguard and protection to the institution of slavery. Yet the proposition was opposed by only three members of the committee of thirty-three, — Mason W. Tappan of New Hampshire, Cadwallader C. Washburn of Wisconsin, and William Kellogg of Illinois.

After a consideration of the whole subject, the majority of the committee made a report embodying nearly every objectionable proposition which had been submitted. The report included a resolution asking the States to repeal all their personal-liberty bills, in order that the recapture and return of fugitive slaves should in no degree be obstructed. It included an amendment to the Constitution as proposed by Mr. Adams. It offered to admit New Mexico, which then embraced Arizona, immediately, with its slave-code as adopted by the Territorial Legislature, — thus confirming and assuring its permanent character as a slave State. It proposed to amend the Fugitive-slave Law by providing that the right to freedom of an alleged fugitive should be tried in the slave State from which he was accused of fleeing, rather than in the free State where he was seized. It proposed, according to the demand of Mr. Toombs, that a law should be enacted in which all offenses against slave property by persons fleeing to other States should be tried where the offense was committed, making the slave-code, in effect, the test of the criminality of the act, — an act which, in its essential character, might frequently be one of charity and good will.

These propositions had the precise effect which, in cooler moments, their authors would have anticipated. They humiliated the North without appeasing or satisfying the South. Five Southern members made a minority report in which still further concessions were demanded. They submitted what was known as the Crittenden Compromise, demanding six amendments to the Constitution for the avowed purpose of placing slavery under the guardianship and protection of the National Government, and, after the example of Mr. Adams's proposed amendment, intrenching the institution where agitation could not disturb it, where legislation could not affect it, where amendments to the Constitution would be powerless to touch it.

— The first amendment proposed that in "all the territory of the

United States south of the old Missouri line, either now held or to be hereafter acquired, the slavery of the African race is recognized as existing, not to be interfered with by Congress, but to be protected as property by all the departments of the Territorial Government during its continuance."

— The second amendment declared that "Congress shall have no power to interfere with slavery even in those places under its exclusive jurisdiction in the slave States."

— The third amendment took away from Congress the exclusive jurisdiction over the District of Columbia, as guarantied in the Constitution, declaring that Congress should "never interfere with slavery in the District, except with the consent of Virginia and Maryland, so long as it exists in the State of Virginia or Maryland, nor without the consent of the inhabitants of the District, nor without just compensation for the slaves. Nor shall Congress prohibit officers of the General Government nor members of Congress from bringing with them their slaves to the District, holding them there during the time their duties may require them to remain, and afterwards taking them from the District."

— The fourth amendment prohibited Congress from interfering with the transportation of slaves from one State to another, or from one State to any Territory south of the Missouri line, whether that transportation be by land, by navigable river, or by the sea.

— The fifth amendment conferred upon Congress the power, and prescribed its duty, to provide for the payment to the owner of a fugitive slave his full value from the National Treasury, in all cases where the marshal was prevented from arresting said fugitive by violence or intimidation, or where the fugitive, after arrest, was rescued by force.

— The sixth amendment provided for a perpetual existence of the five amendments just quoted, by placing them beyond the power of the people to change or revise — declaring that "no future amendment to the Constitution shall ever be passed that shall affect any provision of the five amendments just recited; that the provision in the original Constitution which guaranties the count of three-fifths of the slaves in the basis of representation, shall never be changed by any amendment; that no amendment shall ever be made which alters or impairs the original provision for the recovery of fugitives from service; that no amendment shall be made that shall ever permit Congress to interfere in any way with slavery in the States where it may be permitted."

Before Mr. Corwin submitted his report, Mr. Charles Francis Adams appears to have become disgusted with his own proposition for the amendment of the Constitution. This disgust was caused by the refusal of the Southern members of the committee to agree to the declaration, that "peaceful acquiescence in the election of the Chief Magistrate, accomplished in accordance with every legal and constitutional requirement, is the paramount duty of every good citizen of the United States." The proposition of Mr. Adams to this effect was amended by Mr. Millson of Virginia, who substituted "high and imperative" for "paramount." But even in this modified form, seven Southern members asked to be excused from voting upon it, and Mr. Adams seems wisely to have thought that "if there could not be agreement on a proposition so fundamental and essential as that, it was of no use to seek any remedy for the existence of evils by legislation of Congress." Mr. Adams, therefore, made a report dissenting from the committee, stating that he had changed his course, and now declined to recommend the very measures which he had in good faith offered. This was on the 14th of January.

On the 31st of January Mr. Adams changed his course again, and returned to the unqualified support of the measures proposed by the committee. In his speech of that date, he asked, addressing the South, "How stands the case, then? We offer to settle the question finally in all of the present territory that you claim, by giving you every chance of establishing Slavery that you have any right to require of us. You decline to take the offer because you fear it will do you no good. Slavery will not go there. Why require protection where you will have nothing to protect? . . . All you appear to desire it for is New Mexico. Nothing else is left. Yet you will not accept New Mexico at once, because ten years of experience have proved to you that protection has been of no use thus far." These are somewhat extraordinary words in 1861 from a man who in 1850 had, as a Conscience Whig, declined to support Mr. Webster for making in advance the same statements, and for submitting arguments that were substantially identical.

During the debate, in which Mr. Adams arraigned the Disunionists of the South with considerable power, he was somewhat embarrassed by a Southern member who quoted resolutions which Mr. Adams had introduced in the Massachusetts Legislature in 1844, and which had been passed by that body, respecting the annexation of

Texas. He had declared therein, just as Josiah Quincy had declared with reference to the acquisition of Louisiana, "that the power to unite an independent foreign State with the United States is not among the powers delegated to the General Government by the Constitution of the United States." He declared, further, that "the Commonwealth of Massachusetts, faithful to the compact between the people of the United States, according to the plain meaning and intent in which it was understood and acceded to by them, is sincerely anxious for its preservation; and that it is determined, as it doubts not other States are, to submit to undelegated powers in no body of men on earth; and that the project of the annexation of Texas, unless resisted on the threshold, may tend to drive these States into a dissolution of the Union." This resolution of Mr. Adams was unfortunate in every respect for his position in the debate on that day, since it really included and justified every constitutional heresy entertained by Mr. Calhoun, and claimed for the State of Massachusetts every power of secession or dissolution which was now asserted by the Southern States.

Mr. Webster, in one of his ablest speeches (in reply to Mr. Calhoun in February, 1833), devoted his great powers to demonstrating that the Constitution was not "a compact," and that the people of the States had not "acceded" to it. Mr. Adams had unfortunately used the two words which, according to Mr. Webster, belonged only to the lexicon of disloyalty. "If," said Mr. Webster, "in adopting the Constitution nothing was done but *acceding to a compact*, nothing would seem necessary in order to break it up but to *secede from the same compact*." . . . "Accession," as a word applied to political association, implies coming into a league, treaty, or confederacy. "Secession" implies departing from such league or confederacy. Mr. Adams had further declared that the people of Massachusetts are "faithful to the compact according to the plain meaning and intent in which it was understood by them." But according to Mr. Webster, and in accordance with the principles absolutely essential to maintain a constitutional government, Massachusetts had no part or lot in deciding the question which Mr. Adams's resolution covered. If Massachusetts reserved to herself the right to determine the sense in which she understood her accession to the compact of the Federal Government, she gave full warrant to South Carolina to determine for herself the sense of the compact to which she acceded, and therefore justified the action of the Southern States. Whether Texas was constitutionally or unconstitutionally annexed to the Union was no more to be decided by Massachusetts than the constitutionality of the prohibition of Slavery north of the Missouri line was to be decided by South Carolina. The position of Mr. Adams in 1844 had therefore returned to plague its inventor in 1861, and in a certain sense to weaken the position of the loyal States.

Various reports were submitted by members of the minority, of no special significance, differing often on immaterial points. The members from California and Oregon who represented the Breckinridge party of the North, united in a recommendation for a general convention to be called under the authority of the Constitution, to propose such amendments as would heal all existing differences, and afford sufficient guaranties to the growing interests of the government and people. The only bold words spoken were in the able report by Cadwallader C. Washburn of Wisconsin and Mason W. Tappan of New Hampshire. They made an exhaustive analysis of the situation in plain language. They reviewed ably and conclusively the report made by Mr. Corwin for the majority of the committee, and spoke as became men who represented the justice and the power of a great Republic. They vindicated the conduct of the General Government, and showed that the Union was not to be preserved by compromises nor by sacrifice of principle. They regarded the discontent and hostility in the South as without just cause, and intimated that those States might purchase at a high price some valuable information to be learned only in the school of experience. They embodied their entire recommendations in a single resolution in which they declared that the provisions of the Constitution were ample for the preservation of the Union; that it needed to be obeyed rather than amended; and that "our extrication from present difficulties is to be looked for in efforts to preserve and protect the public property and enforce the laws, rather than in new guaranties for particular interests, or in compromises, or concessions to unreasonable demands."

When the report of the committee of thirty-three came before the House for action, the series of resolutions were first tested by a motion to lay upon the table, which was defeated by a vote of nearly two to one; and after angry debate running through several days, the resolutions, which were only directory in their character, were adopted by a large majority. When the constitutional amendment was reached, Mr. Corwin substituted for that which was originally draughted by Mr. Adams, an amendment declaring that

"no amendment shall be made to the Constitution which will authorize or give to Congress the power to abolish, or interfere, within any
State, with the domestic institutions thereof, including that of persons held to labor or service by the laws of said State." This was
adopted by a vote of 133 to 65. It was numbered as the thirteenth
amendment to the Federal Constitution, and would have made slavery
perpetual in the United States, so far as any influence or power of the
National Government could affect it. It intrenched slavery securely
in the organic law of the land, and elevated the privilege of the slave-
holder beyond that of the owner of any other species of property.
It received the votes of a large number of Republicans who were
then and afterwards prominent in the councils of the party. Among
the most distinguished were Mr. Sherman of Ohio, Mr. Colfax, Mr.
C. F. Adams, Mr. Howard of Michigan, Mr. Windom of Minnesota,
and Messrs. Moorhead and McPherson of Pennsylvania. The sixty-
five negative votes were all Republicans whom the excitement of the
hour did not drag from their moorings, and many of whom have since
done, as they had done before, signal service for their party and their
country. Thaddeus Stevens was at their head, and he was sustained
by the two Washburns, by Bingham of Ohio, by Roscoe Conkling, by
Anson Burlingame, by Owen Lovejoy, by Marston and Tappan of
New Hampshire, by Galusha A. Grow, by Reuben E. Fenton, and
by others who, if less conspicuous, were not less deserving.

When the proposition reached the Senate, it was adopted by a vote
of 24 to 12, precisely the requisite two-thirds. Among those who
aided in carrying it were Hunter of Virginia, Nicholson of Tennessee, Sebastian of Arkansas, and Gwin of California, who soon after
proceeded to join the Rebellion. Eight Republican senators, Anthony of Rhode Island, Baker of Oregon, Dixon and Foster of Connecticut, Grimes and Harlan of Iowa, Morrill of Maine, and Ten Eyck
of New Jersey, voted in the affirmative. Only twelve out of the
twenty-five Republican senators voted in the negative. Mr. Seward,
Mr. Fessenden, Mr. Collamer, and others among the weightiest Republican leaders are not recorded as voting. As pairs were not
announced, it may be presumed that they consented to the passage
of the amendment. Before the resolution could reach the States for
concurrence, either by convention or Legislature, the evidences of
Southern outbreak had so increased that all such efforts at conciliation were seen to be vain, and in the end they proved hurtful. Only
two States, Maryland and Ohio, gave their assent to the amendment.

In the New-England States it was rejected, and in many it was not acted upon. Whoever reads the thirteenth amendment to the Constitution as it now stands, and compares it with the one which was proposed by the Thirty-sixth Congress, will be struck with the rapid revolution of public sentiment, and will not be at a loss to draw some useful lessons as to the course of public opinion and the conduct of public men in times of high excitement.

The propositions of the committee of thirty-three to admit New Mexico as a slave State, and to amend the Fugitive-slave Law, were both passed by the House, but were defeated or not acted upon in the Senate. In that body the efforts of the friends of conciliation were mainly confined to the Crittenden compromise which has already been outlined in the proceedings of the House. But for the eminent respectability and patriotism of the venerable senator from Kentucky, his propositions would have had short consideration. They were of a character not to be entertained by a free people. They dealt wholly in the finding of new guaranties for slavery, without attempting to intimate the possible necessity of new guaranties for freedom. Perhaps the most vicious feature in this whole series of proposed amendments to the Constitution was the guaranty of slavery against the power of Congress in all territory of the United States south of 36° 30'. This offered a premium upon the acquisition of territory, and was an encouragement to schemes of aggression against friendly powers south of the United States, which would always have had the sympathy and support of one-half the Union, and could hardly have been resisted by any moral power of the General Government. It would have opened anew the old struggle for equality between free States and slave States, and would in all probability have led the country to war within three years from its adoption, — war with Mexico for the border States of that Republic, war with Spain for the acquisition of Cuba. This would have followed as matter of policy with Southern leaders, whether they intended to abide in the Union, or whether they intended, at some more advantageous and opportune moment, to secede from it. If they concluded to remain, their political power in the National Government would have been greatly increased from the acquisition of new States. If they desired to secede, they would have acquired a much more formidable strength and vastly larger area by the addition of Southern territory to which the Crittenden propositions would not only have invited but driven them.

While these propositions were under discussion, Mr. Clark of New Hampshire offered as a substitute the resolution with which Messrs. Washburn and Tappan had closed their report in the House, — a resolution of which Mr. Clark was the author, and which he had previously submitted to the consideration of the Senate. The test question in the Senate was whether Mr. Clark's resolution should be substituted for the Crittenden proposition, and this was carried by a vote of 25 to 23. The twenty-five were all Republicans; the twenty-three were all Democrats, except Mr. Crittenden of Kentucky and Mr. Kennedy of Maryland, who had been supporters of Mr. Bell in the Presidential election. It is a fact worthy of note that six senators from the extreme Southern States sat in their seats and refused to vote on the proposition. Had they chosen they could have defeated the action. But they believed, with a certain consistency and wisdom, that no measure could be of value to the South unless it had the concurrence of senators from the North; and with this motive they imposed upon the Republicans of the Senate the responsibility of deciding the Crittenden proposition. It was matter of congratulation with Republicans who did not lose their judgment in that trying season, that the Senate stood firmly against the fatal compromise which was urged by so many strong influences. Much was forgiven for other unwise concessions, so long as this was definitely rejected.

Meanwhile a body of men had assembled in the National Capital upon the invitation of the State of Virginia, for the purpose of making an earnest effort to adjust the unhappy controversy. The Peace Congress, as it was termed, came together in the spirit in which the Constitution was originally formed. Its members professed, and no doubt felt, an earnest desire to afford to the slave-holding States, consistently with the principles of the Constitution, adequate guaranties for the security of their rights. Virginia's proposition was brought to the National Capital by Ex-President John Tyler, deputed by his State to that honorable duty. In response to the invitation twenty-one States, fourteen free and seven slave, had sent delegates, who assembled in Washington on the 4th of February, 1861. After remaining in session some three weeks, the Peace Congress submitted an article of amendment to the Constitution, contained in seven sections, making as many distinct propositions.

— The first section restored the line of the Missouri Compromise as it was before the repeal in 1854.

— The second provided that no further acquisition of territory should be made except by the consent of a majority of all the senators from the slave-holding States and a majority of all the senators from the free States.

— The third declared that no amendment to the Constitution shall be made interfering with Slavery in the States, nor shall Congress prohibit it in the District of Columbia, nor interfere with the inter-State slave-trade, nor place any higher rate of taxation on slaves than upon land. At the same time it abolished the slave-trade in the District of Columbia.

— The fourth provided that no construction of the Constitution shall prevent any of the States aiding, by appropriate legislation, in the arrest and delivery of fugitive slaves.

— The fifth forever prohibited the foreign slave-trade.

— The sixth declared that the amendments to the Constitution herein proposed shall not be abolished or changed without the consent of all the States.

— The seventh provided for the payment from the National Treasury for all fugitive slaves whose recapture is prevented by violence.

These propositions met with little favor in either branch of Congress. Mr. Crittenden, finding that he could not pass his own resolutions, endeavored to substitute these, but could induce only six senators to concur with him. In the House there was no action whatever upon the report. The venerable Ex-President was chosen to preside over the deliberations of the conference, but was understood not to approve the recommendations. Far as they went, they had not gone far enough to satisfy the demands of Virginia, and still less the demands of the States which had already seceded. It is a curious circumstance that one of the delegates from Pennsylvania, who was chosen secretary of the conference, Mr. J. Henry Puleston, was not a citizen of the United States, but a subject of Queen Victoria, and is now (1884), and has been for several years, a member of the British Parliament.

To complete the anomalies and surprises of that session of Congress, it is necessary to recall the fact, that, with a Republican majority in both branches, Acts organizing the Territories of Colorado,

Dakota, and Nevada were passed without containing a word of prohibition on the subject of slavery. From the day that the administration of Mr. Polk began its career of foreign acquisition, the question of slavery in the Territories had been a subject of controversy between political parties. When the Missouri Compromise was repealed, and the Territories of the United States north of the line of 36° 30' were left without slavery inhibition or restriction, the agitation began which ended in the overthrow of the Democratic party and the election of Mr. Lincoln to the Presidency of the United States. It will therefore always remain as one of the singular contradictions in the political history of the country, that, after seven years of almost exclusive agitation on this one question, the Republicans, the first time they had the power as a distinctive political organization to enforce the cardinal article of their political creed, quietly and unanimously abandoned it. And they abandoned it without a word of explanation. Mr. Sumner and Mr. Wade and Mr. Chandler, the most radical men in the Senate on the Republican side, sat still and allowed the bill to be passed precisely as reported by James S. Green of Missouri, who had been the ablest defender of the Breckinridge Democracy in that body. In the House, Mr. Thaddeus Stevens, Mr. Owen Lovejoy, the Washburns, and all the other radical Republicans vouchsafed no word explanatory of this extraordinary change of position.

If it be said in defense of this course that all the Territories lay north of 36° 30', and were therefore in no danger of slavery, it only introduces fresh embarrassment by discrediting the action of the Republican party in regard to Kansas, and discrediting the earnest and persistent action of the anti-slavery Whigs and Free-Soilers, who in 1848 successfully insisted upon embodying the Wilmot Proviso in the Act organizing the Territory of Oregon. Surely, if an anti-slavery restriction were needed for Oregon, it was needed for Dakota which lay in the same latitude. Beyond doubt, if the Territory of Kansas required a prohibition against slavery, the Territory of Colorado and the Territory of Nevada, which lay as far south, needed it also. To allege that they could secure the President's approval of the bills in the form in which they were passed, and that Mr. Buchanan would veto each and every one of them if an anti-slavery proviso were embodied, is to give but a poor excuse, for, five days after the bills received the Executive signature, Mr. Buchanan went out of office, and Abraham Lincoln was installed as President.

If, indeed, it be fairly and frankly admitted, as was the fact, that receding from the anti-slavery position was part of the conciliation policy of the hour, and that the Republicans did it the more readily because they had full faith that slavery never could secure a foot-hold in any of the Territories named, it must be likewise admitted that the Republican party took precisely the same ground held by Mr. Webster in 1850, and acted from precisely the same motives that inspired the 7th of March speech. Mr. Webster maintained for New Mexico only what Mr. Sumner now admitted for Colorado and Nevada. Mr. Webster acted from the same considerations that now influenced and controlled the judgment of Mr. Seward. As matter of historic justice, the Republicans who waived the anti-slavery re-striction should at least have offered and recorded their apology for any animadversions they had made upon the course of Mr. Webster ten years before. Every prominent Republican senator who agreed in 1861 to abandon the principle of the Wilmot Proviso in organ-izing the Territories of Colorado and Nevada, had, in 1850, heaped re-proach upon Mr. Webster for not insisting upon the same principle for the same territory. Between the words of Mr. Seward and Mr. Sum-ner in the one crisis and their votes in the other, there is a discrep-ancy for which it would have been well to leave on record an adequate explanation. The danger to the Union, in which they found a good reason for receding from the anti-slavery restriction on the Territories, had been cruelly denied to Mr. Webster as a justifying motive. They found in him only a guilty recreancy to sacred principle for the same act which in themselves was inspired by devotion to the Union.

It was certainly a day of triumph for Mr. Douglas. He was jus-tified in his boast that, after all the bitter agitation which followed the passage of the Kansas-Nebraska Bill, the Republicans adopted its principle and practically applied its provisions in the first Territory which they had the power to organize. Mr. Douglas had been deprived of his chairmanship of the Committee of Territories by the Southern leaders, and his place had been given to James S. Green of Missouri. His victory therefore was complete when Mr. Seward waived the anti-slavery guaranty on behalf of the Republicans, and when Mr. Green waived the pro-slavery guaranty on behalf of the Breck-inridge Democracy. It was the apotheosis of Popular Sovereignty, and Mr. Douglas was pardonable even for an excessive display of self-gratulation over an event so suggestive and so instructive. Mr. Grow, the chairman of Territories in the House, frankly stated that he had agreed with Mr. Green, chairman of Territories in the Senate, that there should be no reference whatever to the question of slavery in any of the Territorial bills. It cannot be denied that this action of the Republican party was a severe reflection upon their prolonged agitation for prohibition of slavery in the Territories by Congressional enactment. A surrender of the principle with due explanation of the reasons, properly recorded for the instruction of those who should come after, would have left the Republican party in far better position than did the precipitate retreat which they made without a word of apology, without an attempt at justification.

If receding from the anti-slavery creed of the Republican party was intended as a conciliation to the South, the men who made the movement ought to have seen that it would prove ineffectual. The Republicans no more clearly perceived that they risked nothing on the question of slavery in organizing those Territories without restriction, than the Southern leaders perceived that they would gain nothing by it. In vain is the net spread in the sight of any bird. The South had realized their inability to compete with Northern emigration by their experience in attempting to wrest Kansas from the control of free labor. They were not to be deluded now by a nominal equality of rights in Territories where, in a long contest for supremacy, they were sure to be outnumbered, outvoted, and finally excluded by organic enactment. The political agitation and the sentimental feeling on this question were therefore exposed on both sides, — the North frankly confessing that they did not desire a Congressional restriction against slavery, and the South as frankly conceding that the demand they had so loudly made for admission to the Territories was really worth nothing to the institution of slavery. The whole controversy over the Territories, as remarked by a witty representative from the South, related to an imaginary negro in an impossible place.

James Stephens Green, who was so prominent in this legislation, who prepared and reported the bills, and who was followed by a unanimous Senate, terminated his public service on the day Mr. Lincoln was inaugurated. He was then but forty-four years of age, and had served only four years in the Senate. He died soon after. No man among his contemporaries had made so profound an impression in so short a time. He was a very strong debater. He had peers, but no master, in the Senate. Mr. Green on the one side and Mr. Fessenden on the other were the senators whom Douglas most disliked to meet, and who were the best fitted in readiness, in accuracy, in logic, to meet him. Douglas rarely had a debate with either in which he did not lose his temper, and to lose one's temper in debate is generally to lose one's cause. Green had done more than any other man in Missouri to break down the power of Thomas H. Benton as a leader of the Democracy. His arraignment of Benton before the people of Missouri in 1849, when he was but thirty-two years of age, was one of the most aggressive and successful warfares in our political annals. His premature death was a loss. to the country. He was endowed with rare powers which, rightly directed, would have led him to eminence in the public service.

It would be unjust to the senators and representatives in Congress. to leave the impression that their unavailing efforts at conciliating the South were any thing more or less than a compliance with a popular demand which overspread the free States. As soon as the election was decided in favor of Mr. Lincoln, and the secession movement began to develop in the South, tens of thousands of those who had voted for the Republican candidates became affrighted at the result of their work. This was especially true in the Middle States, and to a very considerable extent in New England. Municipal elections throughout the North during the ensuing winter showed a great falling-off in Republican strength. There was, indeed, in every free State what might, in the political nomenclature of the day, be termed an utter demoralization of the Republican party. The Southern States were going farther than the people had believed was possible. The wolf which had been so long used to scare, seemed at last to have come. Disunion, which had been so much threatened and so little executed, seemed now to the vision of the multitude an accomplished fact, — a fact which inspired a large majority of the Northern people with a sentiment of terror, and imparted to their political faith an appearance of weakness and irresolution.

Meetings to save the Union upon the basis of surrender of principle were held throughout the free States, while a word of manly resistance to the aggressive disposition of the South, or in re-affirmation of principles so long contended for, met no popular response. Even in Boston, Wendell Phillips needed the protection of the police in returning to his home after one of his eloquent and defiant harangues, and George William Curtis was advised by the Republican mayor of Philadelphia that his appearance as a lecturer in that city would be extremely unwise. He had been engaged to speak on "The Policy of Honesty." But so great had been the change in popular feeling in a city which Mr. Lincoln had carried by a vast majority, that the owner of the hall in which Mr. Curtis was to appear, warned him that a riot was anticipated if he should speak. Its doors were closed against him. This was less than five weeks after Mr. Lincoln was elected, and the change of sentiment in Philadelphia was but an index to the change elsewhere in the North.

The South, meanwhile, had been encouraged in the work of secession by thousands of Democrats who did not desire or look for the dissolution of the Union, but wished the plot of secession to go far enough, and the danger to the Union to become just imminent enough, to destroy their political opponents. Men who afterwards attested their loyalty to the Union by their lives, took part in this dangerous scheme of encouraging a resistance which they could not measure, and inciting a revolt which they could not repress. They apparently did not comprehend that lighted torches cannot be carried with safety through a magazine of powder; and, though they were innocent of intentional harm, they did much to increase an evil which was rapidly growing beyond all power of control. As already indicated, the position of President Buchanan and the doctrines of his message had aided in the development of this feeling in the North. It was further stimulated by the commercial correspondence between the two sections. The merchants and factors in the South did not as a class desire Disunion, and they were made to believe that the suppression of Abolitionism in the North would restore harmony and good feeling. Abolitionism was but another name for the Republican party, and in business circles in the free States that party had come to represent the source of all our trouble. These men did not yet measure the full scope of the combination against the Union, and persisted in believing that its worst enemies were in the North. The main result of these misconceptions was a steady and rapid growth of strength throughout the slave States in the movement for Secession.

Fruitless and disappointing as were the proceedings of this session of Congress on the subjects which engrossed so large a share of public attention, a most important change was accomplished in the revenue laws, — a change equivalent to a revolution in the economic and financial system of the government. The withdrawal of the Southern senators and representatives left both branches of Congress under the control of the North, and by a considerable majority under the direction of the Republican party. In the preceding session of Congress the House, having a small Republican majority, had passed a bill advancing the rate of duties upon foreign importations. This action was not taken as an avowed movement for protection, but merely as a measure to increase the revenue. During Mr. Buchanan's entire term the receipts of the Treasury had been inadequate to the payment of the annual appropriations by Congress, and as a result the government had been steadily incurring debt at a rate which was afterwards found to affect the public credit at a critical juncture in our history. To check this increasing deficit the House insisted on a scale of duties that would yield a larger revenue, and on the 10th of May, 1860, passed the bill. In the Senate, then under the control of the Democratic party, with the South in the lead, the bill encountered opposition. Senators from the Cotton States thought they saw in it the hated principle of protection, and protection meant in their view, strength and prestige for the manufacturing States of the North. The bill had been prepared in committee and reported in the House by a New-England member, Mr. Morrill of Vermont, which of itself was sufficient in the eyes of many Southern men to determine its character and its fate.

Mr. Robert M. T. Hunter of Virginia was at the time Chairman of the Senate Committee of Finance. He was a man of sturdy common sense, slow in his methods, but strong and honest in his processes of reasoning. He advanced rapidly in public esteem, and in 1839, at thirty years of age, was chosen Speaker of the House of Representatives. He was a sympathizer with the South-Carolina extremists, and coalesced with the Whigs to defeat the regular Democrats who were sustaining the Administration of Mr. Van Buren. In 1847 Mr. Hunter was chosen senator from Virginia, and served continuously till the outbreak of the war. He was a conspicuous example of that class of border State Democrats who were blinded to all interests except those of slavery.

The true wealth of Virginia, in addition to her agriculture and in aid of it, lay in her vast deposits of coal and iron, in her extensive forests, in her unsurpassed water power. Her natural resources were beyond computation, and suggested for her a great career as a commercial and manufacturing State. Her rivers on the eastern slope connected her interior with the largest and finest harbor on the

Atlantic coast of North America, and her jurisdiction extended over an empire beyond the Alleghanies. Her climate was salubrious, and so temperate as to forbid the plea always used in justification of negro slavery in the Cotton States, that the white man could not perform agricultural labor. A recognition of Virginia's true destiny would point to Northern alliances and Northern sympathies. Mr. Hunter's sympathies were by birth and rearing with the South. The alliances he sought looked towards the Gulf and not towards the Lakes. Any measure which was displeasing to South Carolina or Alabama was displeasing to Mr. Hunter, and he gave no heed to what might be the relations of Virginia with the New England, Middle, and Western States. He measured the policy of Virginia by the policy of States whose geographical position, whose soil, climate, products, and capacities were totally different from hers. By Mr. Hunter's policy, Virginia could sell only slaves to the South. A more enlightened view would have enabled Virginia to furnish a large proportion of the fabrics which the Southern States were compelled to purchase in communities far to the north of her. Mr. Hunter was no doubt entirely honest in this course. He was upright in all his personal and political relations, but he could not forget that he was born a Southern man and a slave-holder. He had a full measure of that pride in his State so deeply cherished by Virginians. At the outset of his public career he became associated with Mr. Calhoun, and early imbibed the doctrines of that illustrious senator, who seldom failed to fascinate the young men who fell within the sphere of his personal influence.

Mr. Hunter therefore naturally opposed the new tariff, and under his lead all action upon it was defeated for the session. This conclusion was undoubtedly brought about by considerations outside of the legitimate scope of the real question at issue. The struggle for the Presidency was in progress, and any concession by the slave States on the tariff question would weaken the Democratic party in the section where its chief strength lay, and would correspondingly increase the prestige of Lincoln's supporters in the North and of Mr. Fillmore's followers in the South. Mr. Hunter had himself just received a strong support in the Charleston convention for the Presidency, securing a vote almost equal to that given to Douglas. This was an additional tie binding him to the South, and he responded to the wishes of that section by preventing all action on the tariff bill of the House pending the Presidential struggle of 1860.

But the whole aspect of the question was changed when at the ensuing session of Congress the senators and representatives from the Cotton States withdrew, and betook themselves to the business of establishing a Southern Confederacy. Mr. Hunter's opposition was not relaxed, but his supporters were gone. Opposition was thus rendered powerless, and the first important step towards changing the tariff system from low duties to high duties, from free-trade to protection, was taken by the passage of the Morrill Bill on the second day of March, 1861. Mr. Buchanan was within forty-eight hours of the close of his term and he promptly and cheerfully signed the bill. He had by this time become not only emancipated from Southern thraldom but in some degree embittered against Southern men, and could therefore readily disregard objections from that source. His early instincts and declarations in favor of a protective policy doubtless aided him in a conclusion which a year before he could not have reached without a conflict in his Cabinet that would probably have ended in its disruption.

The passage of the Morrill Tariff was an event which would almost have marked an era in the history of the government if public attention had not been at once absorbed in struggles which were far more engrossing than those of legislative halls. It was however the beginning of a series of enactments which deeply affected the interests of the country, and which exerted no small influence upon the financial ability of the government to endure the heavy expenditure entailed by the war which immediately followed. Theories were put aside in the presence of a great necessity, and the belief became general that in the impending strain on the resources of the country, protection to home industry would be a constant and increasing strength to the government.

On the passage of the bill in the Senate, on the 20th of February, the yeas were 25 and the nays 14. No Democratic senator voted in the affirmative and no Republican senator in the negative. It was not only a sharp division on the party line but almost equally so on the sectional line. Mr. Douglas, Mr. Rice of Minnesota, Mr. Latham of California, and Mr. Lane of Oregon were the only Northern senators who united with the compact South against the bill. Senators from Virginia, North Carolina, Tennessee, and Arkansas were still taking part in the proceedings. Mr. Crittenden of Kentucky and Mr. Kennedy of Maryland were favorable to the policy of protection, but on this bill they withheld their votes. They had not abandoned all hope of an adjustment of the Disunion troubles, and deemed the pending measure too radical a change of policy to be adopted in the absence of the senators and representatives from seven States so deeply interested. Andrew Johnson of Tennessee, sympathizing warmly with the Republicans on all questions relating to the preservation of the Union, was too firmly wedded to the theory of free-trade to appreciate the influence which this measure would exert in aid of the national finances.

The test vote in the House was taken on the 27th of February, on a motion made by Mr. Branch of North Carolina to lay the bill on the table. Only 43 votes were given in favor, while 102 were recorded against this summary destruction of the measure. The sectional line was not so rigidly maintained as it was in the Senate. Of the hostile vote 28 were from the South and 15 from the North. The Virginia delegation, following Mr. Hunter's example, voted solidly in opposition. The Southern men who voted for the bill were in nearly every instance distinguished for their hostility to secession. John A. Gilmer of North Carolina, Thomas A. R. Nelson, and William B. Stokes of Tennessee, William C. Anderson, Francis M. Bristow, Green Adams, and Laban T. Moore of Kentucky, separated from their section, and in their support of a protective tariff openly affiliated with the North.

The Morrill Tariff, as it has since been popularly known, was part of a bill whose title indicates a wider scope than the fixing of duties on imports. It provided also for the payment of outstanding Treasury notes and authorized a loan. These additional features did little to commend it to those who were looking to an alliance with the Secessionists, nor did the obvious necessity of money for the national Treasury induce the ultra disciples of free-trade in the North to waive their opposition to a measure which distinctly looked to the establishment of protection. It was a singular combination of circumstances which on the eve of the Southern revolt led to the inauguration of a policy that gave such industrial and financial strength to the Union in its hour of dire necessity, in the very crisis of its fate.

CHAPTER XIII.

WHEN Southern confidence was at its height, and Northern courage at its lowest point, Mr. Lincoln began his journey from Springfield to Washington to assume the government of a divided and disorganized Republic. His speeches on the way were noticeable for the absence of all declaration of policy or purpose touching the impending troubles. This peculiarity gave rise to unfavorable comments in the public press of the North, and to unfounded apprehensions in the popular mind. There was fear that he was either indifferent to the peril, or that he failed to comprehend it. The people did not understand Mr. Lincoln. The failure to comprehend was on their part, not on his. Had he on that journey gratified the aggressive friends of the Union who had supported him for the Presidency, he would have added immeasurably to the serious troubles which already confronted him. He had the practical faculty of discerning the chief point to be reached, and then bending every energy to reach it. He saw that the one thing needful was his regular, constitutional inauguration as President of the United States. Policies both general and in detail would come after that. He could not afford by imprudent forwardness of speech or premature declaration of measures to increase the embarrassments which already surrounded him. "Let us do one thing at a time and the big things first" was his homely but expressive way of indicating the wisdom of his course.

A man of ordinary courage would have been overwhelmed by the task before him. But Mr. Lincoln possessed a certain calmness, firmness, and faith that enabled him to meet any responsibility, and to stand unappalled in any peril. He reached Washington by a night journey, taken secretly much against his own will and to his subsequent chagrin and mortification, but urged upon him by the advice of those in whose judgment and wisdom he was forced to confide. It is the only instance in Mr. Lincoln's public career in which he did not patiently face danger, and to the end of his life he regretted that he had not, according to his own desire, gone through Baltimore in open day, trusting to the hospitality of the city, to the loyalty of its people, to the rightfulness of his cause and the righteousness of his aims and ends. He came as one appointed to a great duty, not with rashness, not with weakness, not with bravado, not with shrinking, but in the perfect confidence of a just cause and with the stainless conscience of a good man. Threats that he never should be inaugurated had been numerous and serious, and it must be credited to the administration of Mr. Buchanan, that ample provision had been made for the protection of the rightful ruler of the nation.

The active and practical loyalty of Joseph Holt in this crisis deserves honorable mention. When, at the close of December, 1860, he succeeded Mr. Floyd as Secretary of War, no troops were stationed in Washington or its neighborhood. After consultation with General Scott, then in command of the army, and with the full approval of President Buchanan, Secretary Holt thought it wise to take precautions for the safety of the National Capital. Seven companies of artillery and one company of sappers and miners were accordingly brought to Washington. This movement gave offense to the Southern men who still remained in Congress, and Mr. Branch of North Carolina offered a resolution declaring that "the quartering of troops around the capital was impolitic and offensive," and that, "if permitted, it would be destructive of civil liberty, and therefore the troops should be forthwith removed." The House laid the resolution on the table by a vote of 125 to 35. Ex-President Tyler had formally complained to the President from the Peace Congress, that United-States troops were to march in the procession which was to celebrate the 22d of February. When so many of the Southern people were engaged in seizing the forts and other property of the government, it was curious to witness their uneasiness at the least display of power on the part of the National Government.

The tone of Secretary Holt's report to the President in regard to the marshaling of troops in the National Capital was a manifestation of courage in refreshing contrast with the surrounding timidity. He stated in very plain language that "a revolution had been in progress for the preceding three months in several of the Southern States;" that its history was one of "surprises, treacheries, and ruthless spoliations;" that forts of the United States had been captured and garrisoned, and "hostile flags unfurled from the ramparts;" that arsenals had been seized, and the arms which they contained appropriated to the use of the captors; that more than half a million of dollars, found in the mint of New Orleans, had been unscrupulously applied to replenish the treasury of Louisiana; that a conspiracy had been entered into for the armed occupation of Washington as part of the revolutionary programme; and that he could not fail to remember that, if the early admonitions in regard to the designs of lawless men in Charleston Harbor had been acted on, and "adequate re-enforcements sent there before the revolution began, the disastrous political complications which ensued might not have occurred."

The inauguration of Mr. Lincoln was an immense relief to the country. There had been an undefined dread throughout the Northern States, colored and heightened by imagination, that Mr. Lincoln would in some way, by some act of violence or of treachery, be deprived of the Presidency, and the government thrown into anarchy. Mr. Breckinridge was the Vice-President, and there had been a vague fear that the count of the electoral votes, over which he presided, would in some way be obstructed or tampered with, and that the regularity of the succession might be interrupted, and its legitimacy stained. But Mr. Breckinridge had performed his official duty with scrupulous fidelity, and Mr. Lincoln had been declared by him, in the presence of the two Houses of Congress, to be lawfully and constitutionally elected President of the United States. Anarchy and disorder in the North would at that time have proved so advantageous to the leaders of Secession, that the apprehension was firmly fixed in the Northern mind that some attempt would be made to bring it about. The very fact, therefore, that Mr. Lincoln was in possession of the office, that he was quietly living in the Executive mansion, that the Senate of the United States was in session, with a quorum present, ready to act upon his nominations, imparted a new confidence and opened a new prospect to the friends of the Union.

The Inaugural address added to the feeling of hopefulness and security in the North. It effectually removed every trace of unfavorable impression which had been created by Mr. Lincoln's speeches, and gave at once a new view and an exalted estimate of the man. He argued to the South, with persuasive power, that the institution of Slavery in the States was not in danger by his election. He admitted the full obligation under the Constitution for the return of fugitive slaves. He neither affirmed nor denied any position touching Slavery in the Territories. He was fully aware that many worthy, patriotic citizens desired that the National Constitution should be amended; and, while he declined to make any recommendation, he recognized the full authority of the people over the subject, and said he should favor rather than oppose a fair opportunity for them to act upon it. He expressed a preference, if the Constitution was to be amended, for a general convention rather than for action through State Legislatures. He so far departed from his purpose not to speak of particular amendments as to allude to the one submitted by the late Congress, to the effect that the Federal Government shall never interfere with the domestic institutions of States; and he said that, holding such a provision to be now implied in the Constitution, he had no objection to its being made express and irrevocable. He pleaded earnestly, even tenderly, with those who would break up the Union. " In your hands," said he, "my dissatisfied fellow-countrymen, and not in mine, is the momentous issue of civil war. The government will not assail you. You can have no conflict without yourselves being the aggressors. You can have no oath registered in heaven to destroy the government, while I shall have the most solemn one to preserve, protect, and defend it. I am loath to close. We are not enemies, but friends. Though passion may have strained, it must not break, our bonds of affection."

While the effect produced by the Inaugural in the North was so auspicious, no corresponding impression was made in the South. Mr. Lincoln's concise and candid statement of his opinions and purposes in regard to Slavery, his majestic and unanswerable argument against Secession, and his pathetic appeal to the people and States of the South, all alike failed to win back the disaffected communities. The leaders of the Secession movement were only the more enraged by witnessing the favor with which Mr. Lincoln's position was received in the North. The declaration of the President that he should execute the laws in all parts of the country, as required by his oath, and that the jurisdiction of the nation under the Constitution would be asserted everywhere and constantly, inspired the doubting with confidence, and gave to the people of the North a common hope and a common purpose in the approaching struggle. The address left to the seceding States only the choice of retiring from the position they had taken, or of assuming the responsibilities of war. It was clear that the assertion of jurisdiction by two separate governments over the same territory and people must end in bloodshed. In this dilemma was the South placed by the Inaugural address of President Lincoln. Mr. Buchanan had admitted the right of Secession, while denying the wisdom of its exercise; but the right when exercised carried jurisdiction with it. Hence it was impossible for Mr. Buchanan to assert jurisdiction and attempt its exercise over the territory and people of the seceding States. But Mr. Lincoln, by his Inaugural address, set himself free from all logical entanglements. His emphatic words were these: "I therefore consider that, in view of the Constitution and the laws, the Union is unbroken; and to the extent of my ability, I shall take care, as the Constitution itself expressly enjoins upon me, that the laws of the Union be faithfully executed in all the States. . . . I trust this will not be regarded as a menace, but only as a declared purpose of the Union that it will constitutionally defend and maintain itself."

Mr. Lincoln constituted his Cabinet in a manner at least unusual if not unprecedented. It had been the general practice of Presidents, from the first organization of the government, to tender the post of Secretary of State to the man considered to be next in prominence to himself in the party to which both belonged. In the earlier history of the country, the expected successor in the Executive office was selected. This was indeed for a long period so uniform that the appointment to the State Department came to be regarded as a designation to the Presidency. In political phrase, this mode of reaching the coveted place was known as the "easy accession." By its operation Madison succeeded Jefferson, Monroe succeeded Madison, John Quincy Adams succeeded Monroe. After successful application for a quarter of a century the custom fell into disfavor and, by bitter agitation, into disuse. The cause of its overthrow was the appointment of Henry Clay to the State Department, and the baseless scandal of a "bargain and sale" was invented to deprive Mr. Clay of the "easy accession." After a few years, when National Conventions were introduced, it became the habit of the President to tender the State Department to a leading or prominent competitor for the Presidential nomination. Thus General Harrison offered the post to Mr. Clay, who declined; and then to Mr. Webster, who accepted. President Polk appointed Mr. Buchanan. President Pierce appointed Mr. Marcy. President Buchanan appointed General Cass.

Following in the same line, Mr. Lincoln now invited his chief rival, Mr. Seward, to the State Department. But his courtesy did not stop there. He was generous beyond all example to his rivals. He called Salmon P. Chase to the Treasury, appointed Simon Cameron to the War Department, and made Edward Bates of Missouri Attorney-General. These were the three who, next to Mr. Seward, received the largest votes of the minority in the convention which nominated Mr. Lincoln. The Cabinet was completed by the appointment of Gideon Welles of Connecticut Secretary of the Navy, Caleb B. Smith of Indiana Secretary of the Interior, and Montgomery Blair of Maryland Postmaster-General.

The announcement of these names gave fair satisfaction to the party, though the most advanced and radical element of the Republicans regarded its composition with distrust. There had been strong hope on the part of the conservative friends of the Union that some prominent man from the Cotton States would be included in the Cabinet, and overtures were undoubtedly made to that effect directly after the election in November. But the rapidly developing revolt against the Union made such an appointment undesirable if not altogether impracticable. By the time of the inauguration it was found that such an olive-branch from the President would exert no influence over the wild passions which had been aroused in the South. The name most frequently suggested was that of Mr. John A. Gilmer of North Carolina, who was a sincere friend of the Union, and did all in his power to avert a conflict; but his appointment to the Cabinet would have destroyed him at home, without bringing strength at that crisis to the National cause.

The opinions and characteristics of each member of the Cabinet were very closely scanned and criticised. Mr. Seward was known to be fully committed to the policy of conciliation towards the South, and to the adoption of every measure consistent with the honor of the country to avert war and induce the return of the seceding States. Mr. Chase was understood to favor a moderate policy, but did not go so far as Mr. Seward. Mr. Cameron sympathized with Mr. Seward more than with Mr. Chase. Mr. Bates was extremely conservative, but a zealous friend of the Union, and a lifelong disciple of Mr. Clay. Mr. Welles was of Democratic antecedents, a follower of Van Buren and Wright, an associate of John M. Niles, anti-slavery in principle, a strict constructionist, instinctively opposed to Mr. Seward, readily co-operating with Mr. Chase. His appointment was a surprise to New-England Republicans who expected a much more prominent member of the party to be called to the Cabinet. It was understood that the selection was due to the counsel of Vice-President Hamlin, who soon after had such serious differences with Mr. Welles that a state of absolute non-intercourse existed between them during the whole period of his incumbency of the Navy Department. Mr. Caleb B. Smith had been prominent in the House of Representatives when Mr. Lincoln was a member, had been popular as a public speaker in the West, but had no aptitude for so serious a task as the administration of a great department, and did not long retain his position.

Mr. Blair was appointed as a citizen of Maryland. This gave serious offense to many of Mr. Lincoln's most valued supporters, and was especially distasteful to the Union men of Maryland, with Henry Winter Davis at their head. They regarded Mr. Blair as a non-resident, as not in any sense identified with them, and as disposed from the outset to foment disturbance where harmony was especially demanded. Mr. Bates had been appointed from Missouri largely by the influence of Francis P. Blair, Jr.; and the border-State Republicans were dissatisfied that the only two members of the Cabinet from the slave States had been appointed apparently without any general consultation among those who were best fitted to give the President advice on so important a matter. The extreme men in the Republican party, of the type of Benjamin F. Wade and Owen Lovejoy, believed that the Cabinet was so constituted as to insure what they termed "a disgraceful surrender to the South." It was a common saying at the time in Washington, among the radical Republicans, that Mr. Lincoln's Cabinet did not contain three as absolute and strong defenders of the Union as Dix, Holt, and Stanton, who had just retired with Mr. Buchanan.   Thaddeus Stevens, with his accustomed sharpness of speech, said the Cabinet was composed of an assortment of rivals whom the President appointed from courtesy, one stump-speaker from Indiana, and two representatives of the Blair family.

In the seven States which constituted the original Southern Confederacy, the flag of the United States was flying at only three points on the day of Mr. Lincoln's inauguration.   The army of the United States still held Fort Sumter, in the harbor of Charleston; Fort Pickens, opposite the Pensacola Navy Yard; and Key West, the extreme southern point of Florida.   Every other fort, arsenal, dock-yard, mint, custom-house, and court-house had been seized by the Confederacy, and turned to hostile use.   Fort Moultrie, Castle Pinckney, and the United-States arsenal at Charleston had been seized by the troops of South Carolina; Forts Jackson and Pulaski, and the United-States arsenal at Augusta, by the troops of Georgia; the Chattahoochee and St. Augustine arsenals and the Florida forts, by the troops of that State; the arsenal at Baton Rouge, and Forts Jackson and St. Philip, together with the New-Orleans mint and custom-house, by the troops of Louisiana; the Little-Rock arsenal by the troops of Arkansas; Forts Johnson and Caswell by the troops of North Carolina; and General Twiggs had traitorously surrendered to the State of Texas all the military stores in his command, amounting in value to a million and a half of dollars.   By these means the seceding States had come into possession of all the artillery, small arms, ammunition, and supplies of war needed for immediate use, and were well prepared for the opening of the campaign.   On the part of the government there was no such preparation.   Indeed the government did not at that moment have twelve thousand available troops against the most formidable rebellion in history.   Its whole navy could not make one large squadron, and its most effective ships were at points remote from the scene of conflict.   The revenues of the country were not then yielding more than thirty millions per annum, and the credit was so low that one per cent. a month had been paid by the retiring administration for the funds necessary to close its unfortunate career.

In view of all these facts, it cannot be matter of wonder that the Disunion leaders in the South laughed to scorn any efforts on the part of the Government of the United States to arrest their progress, much less to subdue them, and enforce their return to the Union. North Carolina, Virginia, Tennessee, and Arkansas had not yet seceded. The Union sentiment was strong in each one of these States, and the design of Mr. Lincoln was to pursue a policy so mild and conciliatory as to win them to the side of the government. Kentucky, Maryland, and Missouri were excited by strong minorities who desired to aid the South, while no strong element in their population was ready to take decisive measures for the Union. Palliation, conciliation, concession, compromise, were the only words heard, and the almost universal opinion in the South, shared largely by the North, was that to precipitate war would be to abandon the last hope for restoration of the Union.

The extra session of the Senate, called by Mr. Buchanan for the convenience of the new administration, assembled on the 4th of March. All the Southern States were represented in full except those which had members in the Confederate Congress at Montgomery, and from one of those — the State of Texas — both senators, John Hemphill and Louis T. Wigfall, were present. Texas was indeed represented in the Congress of the Confederate States at Montgomery and in the Congress of the United States at Washington at the same time. Some excuse was given for the continuance of the senators by an alleged lack of completeness in the secession proceedings of their State; but to the apprehension of the ordinary mind, a secession that was complete enough to demand representation at Montgomery was complete enough to end it at Washington. The Texas senators, therefore, did not escape the imputation of seizing a mere pretext for remaining in Washington somewhat in the character of spies upon the new administration. John C. Breckinridge of Kentucky and Thomas L. Clingman of North Carolina took the usual oath to support the Constitution — Clingman for his second term, Breckinridge for his first. Salmon P. Chase was sworn in as senator from Ohio, and retired the next day to the Treasury Department. John Sherman was his successor. Among the new senators who entered, and who afterwards became conspicuous, were Howe of Wisconsin and Baker of Oregon. The session was only for Executive purposes, and of course possessed no legislative power; but the debates were of interest and of value to the country.

Mr. Douglas, with the characteristic boldness of a leader and with a patriotism which did him honor, defended the Inaugural address of Mr. Lincoln against the assault of opposition senators. In reply to Wigfall of Texas, who wished to know Douglas's views upon certain points of policy, he said, " I do not choose to proclaim what my policy would be, in view of the fact that the senator does not regard himself as the guardian of the honor and the interests of my country, but is looking to the interests of another which he thinks is in hostility. It would hardly be good policy or wisdom for me to reveal what I think ought to be our policy to one who may so soon be in the councils of the enemy and in the command of his armies." Being pressed by Wigfall to know what he would advise the President to do in the critical condition of Fort Sumter, Douglas sarcastically answered that he "should have no hesitancy in replying to the senator from Texas if that senator held himself bound by his oath to support the Constitution of the United States, and to protect and aid the honor of the country instead of communicating it to the enemy to be used against us." It was a vast gain to the Union that Douglas spoke so boldly in defense of Mr. Lincoln; and it was significant that Wigfall received imputations upon his honor without threats of a duel, and without even using the language of resentment.

Mr. Mason of Virginia came to the aid of Wigfall in the debate, but fared badly at the hands of Douglas. He asked Douglas to define what should be done in this crisis in regard to Fort Sumter. "If the senator from Virginia," said Douglas, "had voted right in the last Presidential election, I should have been, perhaps, in a position to-day to tell him authoritatively what ought to be done. Not occupying that position, I must refer the senator from Virginia to those who have been intrusted by the American people, according to the Constitution, with the decision of that question." The speech of Wigfall had given great offense, and the castigation administered by Douglas was heartily responded to throughout the North. Wigfall had boasted that he owed no allegiance to the government; that he was a foreigner and owed allegiance to another government. On the next day, reciting these words as a preamble, Mr. Foster of Connecticut moved "that Louis T. Wigfall be and hereby is expelled from the Senate." Mr. Clingman of North Carolina moved as a substitute a declaration that "Texas having seceded from the Union, and being no longer one of the United States, is not entitled to be represented in this body." After a brief debate, the resolutions were referred to the Judiciary by the votes of Republican senators, who, not wishing to precipitate any issue prematurely, and persuaded that Wigfall's presence was helping rather than harming the Union cause, concluded to let the matter rest.

A notable debate took place between Breckinridge and Douglas, in which the issues that had led to the disruption of the Democracy in the late Presidential election were, in a certain sense, fought over again. Mr. Breckinridge's speech was carefully prepared, and presented the Southern side in a tone of dignity and confidence; but the reply of Douglas exhibited his superiority as a debater. Breckinridge had declared that whatever settlement be made of other questions, there must be a concession to the South of the right to emigrate into all the Territories, or at least an equitable partition of the National Domain. In reply, Douglas reminded him that the South had, by the action of a Republican Congress, the full right to emigrate into all the territory of the United States; and that, with the consent of the Republican Congress, every inch of the territory of the United States south of the thirty-seventh degree of latitude was at that hour open to slavery. "So far," said he, "as the doctrine of popular sovereignty and non-intervention is concerned, the Colorado Bill and the Nevada Bill and the Dakota Bill are identically the same with the Kansas-Nebraska Bill, and in its precise language." The answer was at once a complete destruction of the argument of Breckinridge, and a severe indictment of the Republican party. Never before in the existence of the Federal Government had its territory been so open, by Congressional enactment and by judicial decision, to the slave-holder as on the day that Abraham Lincoln assumed the office of President of the United States. It is a singular fact that, on the eve of the utter destruction of the institution of Slavery, its legal status was stronger than ever before in the history of the government, and the area over which it might lawfully spread was far larger than at any previous period. Douglas showed in this debate how absolutely groundless was the excuse of slave-holders for basing secession or revolution upon the failure to acquire their rights in the Territories, when never before had their rights in the Territories been so absolutely complete.

Public opinion in March, 1861, was so unsettled, the popular mind so impressible, that a spirit of discontent soon began to spread over the loyal States on the part of those who had hoped for what they termed a vigorous administration. For a few weeks the conduct of the government fell under the animadversion of all classes in the North. To those who wanted an instant settlement, and the return of the seceding States upon their own terms, the administration seemed too radical. To those who demanded that the flag be maintained, and Fort Sumter promptly re-enforced, who would be satisfied with nothing less than the recovery of every piece of public property of which the Confederates had possessed themselves, the administration appeared altogether too conservative. The overwhelming public desire after all was for peace, and the overwhelming public opinion was against the extremists who would, by any possibility, precipitate war. The administration thus began its career with no firm footing beneath it, with an aggressive and defiant enemy in front of it, with a public opinion divided, distrustful, and compromising, behind it.

No more difficult task has ever been presented to any government than that which Mr. Lincoln and his Cabinet assumed in the month of March, 1861. To judge it now by any appearance of irresolution, or by any seeming deficiency of courage, would be trying it by a standard totally inapplicable and unfair. Before and beyond all things, Mr. Lincoln desired to prevent war, and he felt that every day of peace gave fresh hope that bloodshed might be avoided. In his Inaugural address he had taken the strongest ground for the preservation of the Union, and had carefully refrained from every act and every expression which would justify, even in the public opinion of the South, an outbreak of violence on the part of the Confederates. He believed that the Southern revolt had attained its great proportions in consequence of Mr. Buchanan's assertion that he had no power to coerce a seceding State. Mr. Lincoln had announced a different creed, and every week that the South continued peaceful, his hope of amicable adjustment grew stronger. He believed that with the continuance of peace, the Secessionists could be brought to see that Union was better than war for all interests, and that in an especial degree the institution of Slavery would be imperiled by a resort to arms. He had faith in the sober second-thought. If the South would deliberate, the Union would be saved. He feared that the Southern mind was in the condition in which a single untoward circumstance might precipitate a conflict, and he determined that the blood of his brethren should not be on his hands.

Mr. Lincoln saw, moreover, that war between a divided North

and a united South would be a remediless calamity. If, after all efforts at peace, war should be found unavoidable, the Administration had determined so to shape its policy, so to conduct its affairs, that when the shock came it should leave the South entirely in the wrong, and the government of the Union entirely in the right. Consolidated as might be the front which the Rebellion would present, the administration was resolved that it should not be more solid, more immovable, more courageous, than that with which the supporters of the government would meet it. Statesmanship cannot be judged upon theories. It must be decided by results. When that conclusive test is brought to bear, Mr. Lincoln's administration of the government in the weeks immediately following his inauguration deserves the highest praise; and all the more because it was compelled to disregard the clamor and disappoint the expectations of many who had been conspicuously influential in bringing it into power, and who therefore thought themselves entitled to give counsel.

CHAPTER XIV.

THE negotiation which the seceding State of South Carolina had unsuccessfully attempted with President Buchanan, for the surrender of Fort Sumter, was now formally renewed by the Confederate Government with the administration of Mr. Lincoln. The week following the inauguration, John Forsythe of Alabama and Martin J. Crawford of Georgia appeared in Washington in the character of Commissioners from the Confederate States, "with a view," as they defined it, "to a speedy adjustment of all questions growing out of the political separation, upon such terms of amity and good will as the respective interests, geographical contiguity, and future welfare of the two nations, may render necessary." They addressed their communication to the Secretary of State as a matter pertaining to the Foreign Department of the government, and waited with confidence for an answer that would practically recognize the nationality which they assumed to represent. Judge Campbell of the Supreme Court, a citizen of Alabama, had held some conferences with Mr. Seward, the result of which was his personal assurance to the Commissioners that Fort Sumter would be evacuated before the 25th of March; and he urged them not to insist upon too prompt an answer to their demand. At his instance, the reply of Mr. Seward was withheld from official delivery, and, though dated the 15th of March, was really not read by the Commissioners until the 7th or 8th of April.

Mr. Seward's answer threw the Commissioners and the entire South into a rage. He declined to comply with the request of Messrs. Forsythe and Crawford. He saw in them, "not a rightful and accomplished revolution, not an independent nation with an established government, but only the perversion of a temporary and partisan excitement, and an inconsiderate purpose of unjustifiable and unconstitutional aggression upon the rights and the authority vested in the Federal Government." Mr. Seward further advised them that he "looked for the cure of evils which should result from proceedings so unnecessary, so unwise, so unusual, so unnatural, not to irregular negotiations having in view untried relations, but to regular, considerate action of the people of those States through the Congress of the United States, and through such extraordinary conventions, if there be need thereof, as the Federal Constitution contemplates and authorizes to be assembled." Under these circumstances, Mr. Seward informed the Commissioners that his official duties were confined to the conduct of the foreign relations of the country, and did not at all embrace domestic questions, or questions arising between the several States and the Federal Government.

The Secretary of State was unable, therefore, to comply with the request of Messrs. Forsythe and Crawford, and declined to appoint a day on which they might submit the objects of their visit to the President of the United States. He refused to recognize them as diplomatic agents, and would not hold correspondence or further communication with them. Lest the Commissioners might console themselves with the reflection that Mr. Seward was speaking only for himself, and that the President might deal with them less curtly, he informed them that he had cheerfully submitted his answer to Mr. Lincoln, who coincided in the views it expressed, and sanctioned the Secretary's decision declining official intercourse with Messrs. Forsythe and Crawford. The rejoinder of the Confederate Commissioners to Mr. Seward was in a threatening tone, upbraiding him with bad faith, and advising him that "Fort Sumter cannot be provisioned without the effusion of blood;" reminding him also that they had not come to Washington to ask the Government of the United States to recognize the independence of the Confederacy, but for an "adjustment of new relations springing from a manifest and accomplished revolution."

Up to this time there had not been the slightest collision between the forces of the Confederacy and the forces of the Union. The places which had been seized, belonging to the Federal Government, had been taken without resistance; and the authorities at Montgomery appeared to a great many Southern people to be going through blank motions, and to be aping power rather than exercising it. Their defiant attitude had been demoralizing to the public sentiment in the North, but their failure to accomplish any thing in the way of concession from the National Government, and their apparent timidity in refraining from a shock of arms, was weakening the Disunion sentiment in the States which composed the Confederacy. Jefferson Davis had been inaugurated with great pomp and pretension in February, and now April had been reached with practically nothing done but the issuing of manifestoes, and the maintenance of a mere shadow of government, without its substance. The Confederates had as yet no revenue system and no money. They had no armed force except some military companies in the larger cities, organized long before secession was contemplated. They had not the pretense of a navy, or any power apparently to create one. While the administration of Mr. Lincoln, therefore, was disappointing great numbers in the North by its failure to do something decisive towards re-establishing the National authority in the rebellious States, the inhabitants of those States were becoming daily dissatisfied with the fact that the administration of Mr. Davis was doing nothing to consolidate and protect the Confederacy.

Ever since the inauguration of Jefferson Davis, the flag of the United States had been flying over the strongest fortress in the Confederacy, and no forcible effort had been made to displace it. The first flush of joy and congratulation was over, and re-action had begun throughout the revolting States. The Confederate Government was reminded by many of the leading newspapers of the South that unless some decisive step were taken to assert its authority and establish its prestige, it would quietly crumble to pieces. The apparent non-resistance of Mr. Lincoln's administration had, in many minds, the effect of casting contempt upon the whole Southern movement, and the refusal to recognize or receive commissioners of Mr. Davis's appointment was regarded as a direct insult to their government, which, unless met by some decisive step, would subject the leaders to the derision of public opinion throughout the new Confederacy.   Mr. Buchanan had been willing to receive commissioners from seceding States, so far as to confer with them, even when he declared that he had no power to take any action in the premises. Mr. Lincoln had advanced beyond the position of Mr. Buchanan when he refused even to give audience to representatives bearing the commission of the Confederate States.

The situation therefore had become strained.   The point had been reached where it was necessary to go forward or go backward; where the Confederacy must assert itself, or the experiment of secession be abandoned.   From all quarters of the seven States came the demand upon the Montgomery government to do something decisive.   A prominent member of the Alabama Legislature told Jefferson Davis that "unless he sprinkled blood in the face of the Southern people they would be back in the old Union in less than ten days." Public meetings were held to urge the government to action.   At Charleston, in answer to a large crowd who came to pay him honor, Roger A. Pryor (whose attractive eloquence has since been used to better ends) told the people that only one thing was necessary to force Virginia into the Southern Confederacy : "to strike a blow." That done, he promised them that "Virginia would secede in less than an hour by Shrewsbury clock."

The indifference of Mr. Lincoln's administration to the progress of the Southern Confederacy was apparent and not real.   In his Inaugural he had declared that the power confided to him would be used to hold, occupy, and possess the property and places belonging to the government, and to collect the duties and imposts, but, beyond what was necessary for those objects, there would be no invasion, no use of force against or among the people anywhere.   Influential persons connected with Mr. Lincoln's administration may have wavered in regard to the expediency of re-enforcing Major Anderson and holding possession of Fort Sumter, but the President himself wisely concluded that to retreat from that point would be an almost fatal step.   There was not a citizen in the North who had not become interested in the fate of Major Anderson and the brave soldiers under his command. Though many patriotic men of conservative or timid nature advised a quiet withdrawal from Fort Sumter rather than an open conflict for its possession, there was an instinctive undertone in the masses of the people in the Northern States against a concession so humiliating. If prestige were needed for the government at Montgomery, Mr. Lincoln felt that it was needed for the government at Washington, and if he withdrew from Sumter he could not see any point where he could make a stand.

The President determined, therefore, to send supplies to Major Anderson. He wisely saw that if he failed to do this he would be receding from the temperate and conservative position taken in his Inaugural, and that it would give to the Confederates a degree of courage, and to the North a degree of despondency, which would vastly increase the difficulty of restoring the Union. In Mr. Lincoln's own language; "the abandonment of Sumter would be utterly ruinous, under the circumstances." . . . "At home it would discourage the friends of the Union, embolden its adversaries, and go far to insure to the latter a recognition abroad. In fact, it would be our national destruction consummated." Having taken this determination, he communicated it to Governor Pickens of South Carolina just at the time that Mr. Seward delivered to the commissioners of Jefferson Davis the government's refusal to receive them. The answer to the commissioners, and the determination not to permit Anderson to be starved out of Fort Sumter with the hostile guns of the Confederacy pointed at him, brought on the conflict. As soon as the two events were made public, the Confederate Secretary of War instructed General Beauregard that if the information conveyed to Governor Pickens was authentic, he should proceed to reduce the fort. The conflict came on the 12th of April, and after a furious cannonade of thirty-four hours, Major Anderson, being out of provisions, was compelled to surrender. The fleet that was bringing him relief arrived too late, and the flag of the United States was lowered to the Confederacy. Those who had urged Mr. Davis to strike a blow and to sprinkle blood in the faces of the people as a means of consolidating Southern opinion, were undoubtedly successful. Throughout the States of the Confederacy the inhabitants were crazed with success. They had taken from the National Government its strongest fortress on the South-Atlantic coast. They felt suddenly awakened to a sense of power, and became wild with confidence in their ability to defy the authority of the United States.

The Confederate Government, however, had not anticipated the effect of an actual conflict on the people of the North. Until the hour of the assault on Sumter they had every reason for believing that Mr. Lincoln's administration was weak; that it had not a sustaining force of public opinion behind it in the free States; that, in short, Northern people were divided very much on the line of previous party organizations, and that his opponents had been steadily gaining, his supporters as steadily losing, since the day of the Presidential election in November. The Confederates naturally counted much on this condition of Northern sentiment, and took to themselves the comforting assurance that vigorous war could never be made by a divided people. They had treasured all the extreme sayings of Northern Democrats about resisting the march of a Black Republican army towards the South, and offering their dead bodies as obstructions to its progress. They believed, and had good reason for believing, that half the population of the North was opposed to the policy of subjugation, and they accepted the creed of Mr. Buchanan that there was no power in the Constitution to coerce a sovereign State.

Never was popular delusion so suddenly and so completely dispelled. The effect of the assault on Sumter and the lowering of the National flag to the forces of the Confederacy acted upon the North as an inspiration, consolidating public sentiment, dissipating all differences, bringing the whole people to an instant and unanimous determination to avenge the insult and re-establish the authority of the Union. Yesterday there had been doubt and despondency; to-day had come assurance and confidence. Yesterday there had been division; to-day there was unity. The same issue of the morning paper that gave intelligence of the fall of Sumter, brought also a call from the President of the United States for seventy-five thousand men to aid him "in suppressing combinations against the law, too powerful to be suppressed by the ordinary course of judicial proceedings." He notified the people that "the first service assigned to the force hereby called forth will probably be to repossess the forts, places, and property which have been seized from the Union;" and he concluded by convening an extra session of Congress to assemble on the fourth day of the ensuing July. The President stated, in his Proclamation, that the laws of the United States had been "for some time past opposed, and their execution obstructed, in the States of South Carolina, Georgia, Alabama, Florida, Mississippi, Louisiana, and Texas, by combinations too powerful to be suppressed by the ordinary course of judicial procedure, or by the powers vested in the marshals by law." He had therefore "called forth the militia to suppress such combinations, and to cause the laws to be duly executed." He appealed to all loyal citizens "to aid in maintaining the honor, the integrity, and the existence of the National Union, and the perpetuity of popular government." The Proclamation was general. The Call for troops was issued specifically to every State except the seven already in revolt.

The Proclamation was responded to in the loyal States with an unparalleled outburst of enthusiasm. On the day of its issue hundreds of public meetings were held, from the eastern border of Maine to the extreme western frontier. Work was suspended on farm and in factory, and the whole people were roused to patriotic ardor, and to a determination to subdue the Rebellion and restore the Union, whatever might be the expenditure of treasure or the sacrifice of life. Telegrams of congratulation and sympathy fell upon the White House like snow-flakes in a storm; and the President was made to feel, after all the months of gloom and darkness through which he had passed since his election, that light had broken, that day had dawned, and that the open struggle for the Union, however severe and however sanguinary it might prove, was preferable to the slough of despond in which the nation had been cast, and the valley of humiliation through which the government had been groping.

In the history of popular uprisings and of manifestations of National enthusiasm, there is perhaps no equal to that which was seen in the free States of the Union in the weeks immediately following the rash assault on Fort Sumter. While the feeling was too deep to brook resistance, or quietly to endure a word of opposition, it was happily so tempered with discretion as to prevent personal outrages upon the few who did not join in the general chorus for the Union. Suspected men were waited upon and requested to speak for the loyal cause, and newspapers, which before the firing on Sumter had been offensive in tone, were compelled to hoist the National flag over their offices, and open y support the government. But these cases were few and exceptional; and it is due to the Democracy of the North to say, that however strongly they had opposed the election of Mr. Lincoln, and however hostile they had been to the principles which he represented, the mass of the party responded with noble enthusiasm and with patriotic fidelity to the Union. Their great leader, Senator Douglas, set a worthy example by promptly waiting on the President, and expressing his deepest sympathy and his most earnest co-operation in the struggle for the life of the nation.

The patriotic course of Mr. Douglas had been of invaluable service to the government from the hour of Mr. Lincoln's inauguration. The old friendship between the illustrious rivals from Illinois, which had begun when each was in his youth, was now strongly revived. Differing always on political issues, they were at once in accord when the fate of the government was at stake. The position of Douglas during the extra session of the Senate had given marked satisfaction to Mr. Lincoln, and when the deliberations came to a close, on the 28th of March, the President said that a great gain had been made to the cause of the Union, by the direction which the speeches of Douglas would give to the sympathy and action of the Northern Democracy. From the hour of actual danger, Mr. Douglas had spoken no partisan word, had known no partisan divisions, had labored only for the government of the nation, had looked only to its safety and its honor. He had a larger following than any other party leader of his day. Nearly a million and a half of men believed in his principles, were devoted to him personally, trusted him implicitly. The value of his active loyalty to the Union may be measured by the disaster which would have been caused by hesitation on his part. When he returned to his State, after the firing on Sumter, the Republican Legislature of Illinois received him with a display of feeling as profound as that with which they would have welcomed Mr. Lincoln. His address on that memorable occasion was worthy of the loftiest patriot, and was of inestimable value to the cause of the Union. Perhaps no word spoken carried confidence to more hearts, or gave greater strength to the National cause.

Mr. Douglas did not live to return to the Senate. The extra session of March closed his public service. He died in Chicago on the third day of June, 1861, at the early age of forty-eight. His last days were his best days. The hour of his death was the hour of his greatest fame. In his political career he had experienced the extremes of popular odium and of popular approval. His name had at different periods been attended with as great obloquy as ever beset a public man. It was his happy fate to have changed this before his death, and to have secured the enthusiastic approbation of every lover of the Union. His career had been stormy, his partisanship aggressive, his course often violent, his political methods sometimes ruthless. He had sought favor at the South too long to regain mastery in the North, and he had been defeated in the Presidential struggle of 1860,—a struggle in which the ambition of his life had been centred. But with danger to the Union his early affections and the associations of his young life had come back. He remembered that he was a native of New England, that he had been reared in New York, that he had been crowned with honors by the generous and confiding people of Illinois. He believed in the Union of the States, and he stood by his country with a fervor and energy of patriotism which enshrined his name in the history and in the hearts of the American people. His death created the profoundest impression in the country, and the Administration felt that one of the mighty props of the Union had been torn away.

The rank of Mr. Douglas as a statesman is not equal to his rank as a parliamentary leader. As a statesman, he was full of resources, fertile in expedients. But he lacked the truest form of conservatism, and more than once in his career carried partisan contests beyond the point of safety. His participation in the repeal of the Missouri Compromise is an illustration, all the more pertinent and impressive because his own judgment was against the measure, and he allowed himself to be controlled by the fear that another might usurp the place in Southern regard so long held by himself. In parliamentary discussion it is not easy to overstate the power of Mr. Douglas. Indeed, it would be difficult to name his superior. He did not attain the dignity of Webster's stately style. He was not gifted with the fire that burned through Clay's impulsive speech. But as a ready, comprehensive speaker, armed at all points and using his weapons with deadliest effect, he was the equal of either. In the rapidity with which he marshaled the facts favorable to his position, in the consummate skill with which he presented his argument, in the dashing and daring manner by which he overcame an opponent more strongly intrenched than himself, Mr. Douglas is entitled to rank with the most eminent of parliamentary debaters.

The effect of Major Anderson's surrender of Sumter and of the President's call for troops proved prejudicial to the Union sentiment in the slave States which had not yet seceded. It would be more correct, perhaps, to say that Mr. Lincoln's Proclamation was a test of loyalty which revealed the actual character of public sentiment in those States, till then not known in the North. Mr. Lincoln had done every thing in his power to conciliate them, and to hold them fast in their loyalty to the Union. But the sympathy with the South, engendered by the common danger to the institution of Slavery, was too powerful to be resisted. North Carolina, which had always been moderate, conservative, and Union-loving, threw her fortunes with the Confederacy. Tennessee, distracted by the unforeseen defection of such staunch Union men as John Bell and Baillie Peyton, went Southward with the general current. Virginia could not be restrained, although she was warned and ought to have seen, that if she joined the Rebellion she would inevitably become the battle-ground, and would consign her territory to devastation and her property to destruction. The Virginia convention which was in session before the firing on Fort Sumter, and which was animated by a strong friendship for the Union, was carried into the vortex of secession by the surrounding excitement. By a vote of 88 to 55 the State determined to join the Confederacy. The wonder is that in the prevailing excitement and arrogant dictation, there could have been found fifty-five men to resist so powerful a tide of public opinion. The minority was strong enough, however, to command the submission of the ordinance to a vote of the people, — a submission which was in form and not in substance, for in reality no freedom of opinion was conceded.

The ordinance which was passed on the 17th of April, three days after the fall of Sumter, declared that "it should take effect when ratified by a majority of the votes of the people of the State, cast at a poll to be taken thereon on the fourth Thursday in May." The Convention did not submit its work to popular review and decision in a fair and honorable way. Eight days after the act of submission, the Convention passed another ordinance, by which Virginia agreed "to adopt and ratify the Constitution of the Provisional Government of the Confederate States." They provided that this second ordinance should have no effect if the first should be rejected by the people. It is not difficult to see that the action was taken in order to render the rejection of the first ordinance impossible. Under the second ordinance, the Convention at once entered into a formal alliance, offensive and defensive, with the Confederate States. Their

Vice-President, Alexander H. Stephens, appeared in Richmond as commissioner of his government, and the Convention appointed Ex-President John Tyler, William Ballard Preston, James P. Holcombe, and other leading citizens, as commissioners for Virginia. These joint commissioners made a formal compact between Virginia and the Confederate States on the 25th of April, the day after the Convention had adopted the Confederate Constitution. By this compact, Virginia, "looking to a speedy union with the Confederate States," placed "the whole military force of the Commonwealth under the control and direction of the Confederate States, upon the same basis and footing as if said Commonwealth were now a member of said Confederacy."

Without waiting for the decision of the people on the question of secession, the national flag was removed from the public buildings, and the Confederate flag was raised. All the property of the General Government was seized and, by an article in the agreement with the Confederate commissioner, was in due time to be turned over to the Montgomery government. In short, the State Government of Virginia proceeded in its mad career of hostility to the Union, without the slightest regard to the future decision of the people on the important issue which in form had been submitted to them. They evidently intended to make a rejection of the Disunion ordinance impossible. For their own honor, the men who contrived and guided these proceedings would better have adopted the bold precedent of those States which refused altogether to submit the ordinance to popular vote.

It ought not to escape notice that General Robert E. Lee is not entitled to the defense so often made for him, that in joining the Disunion movement he followed the voice of his State. General Lee resigned his commission in the army of the Union and assumed command of Confederate troops, long before Virginia had voted upon the ordinance of secession. He gave the influence of his eminent name to the schemes of those who, by every agency, *fas aut nefas*, were determined to hurl Virginia into secession. The very fact that General Lee had assumed command of the troops in Virginia was a powerful incentive with many to vote against the Union. Jefferson Davis had anticipated and measured the full force of the effect which would be produced upon Virginians by General Lee's identification with the Confederate cause. Whether or not there be ground for making General Lee the subject of exceptional censure, there is surely none for excusing him as one who reluctantly obeyed the voice of his State. If he had remained in the national army until the people of Virginia voted on the ordinance of secession, the strength of the Union cause in his State would have been greater. If he had chosen, as a citizen of Virginia, to stand by the Union until his State decided against him, secession might have been defeated. It is fair that his action should be clearly understood, and that his name should bear its just responsibility.

All pretense of a fair submission of the question to popular vote was finally abandoned, and the abandonment practically proclaimed in a letter of Senator James M. Mason, which was published on the 16th of May, some ten days in advance of the election. "If it be asked," wrote Mr. Mason, "what those shall do who cannot in conscience vote to separate Virginia from the United States, the answer is simple and plain. Honor and duty alike require that they should not vote on the question, and if they retain such opinions they must leave the State." Mr. Mason thus accurately defined what the South understood by the submission of secession ordinances to popular vote. It meant that a man might vote for an ordinance but not against it; if he desired to vote against it, and persisted in the desire, he should leave the State. It is rather a matter of surprise that of 161,000 votes cast in Virginia on the question, 32,000 were registered against secession. These friends of the Government were, it is true, in large part from the western section of the State where slaves were few and the loyal sentiment was strong. It is an interesting fact that along the mountain range through Virginia, North Carolina, Tennessee, and even as far South as Georgia, the inhabitants generally sympathized with the Union. Though often forced to aid the Rebellion, they were at heart loyal to the government of their fathers, and on many important occasions rendered the most valuable service to the National cause. The devotion of large numbers in East Tennessee to the Federal Government seriously embarrassed the new Confederacy. The remaining slave States, Maryland, Kentucky, and Missouri, gave trouble to the administration, but did not succeed in separating themselves from the Union. Large numbers of their people joined the Southern army, but the political power of those States was wielded in favor of the loyal cause. They desired to enact the part of neutrals; but the National Government, from the first, took strong ground against a policy so dishonorable in the States, so injurious to the Union.

The responses made by the Southern governors to the President's call for troops are so characteristic, and afford so true a picture of the times, as to merit notice. Nearly every one returned a scornful and defiant message. Governor Magoffin replied that Kentucky "would furnish no troops for the wicked purpose of subduing her sister States of the South." Governor Letcher declared that "the militia of Virginia would not be furnished to the powers at Washington for any such use or purpose as they had in view, which was the subjugation of the Southern States," and that "the civil war which the powers at Washington had chosen to inaugurate would be met by the South in a spirit as determined." Governor Jackson considered "the call to be illegal, unconstitutional, and revolutionary; its objects to be inhuman and diabolical," and it "would not be complied with by Missouri." Governor Harris said that Tennessee "would not furnish a single man for coercion, but would raise fifty thousand men for the defense of her rights, and those of her Southern brethren." Governor Ellis of North Carolina answered that he "could be no party to the wicked violation of the laws of the country and to the war upon the liberties of a free people." Governor Rector declared that the President's call for troops was only "adding insult to injury, and that the people of Arkansas would defend, to the last extremity, their honor and their property against Northern mendacity and usurpation." Governor Hicks for prudential reasons excused Maryland at the time from responding to the President's call, and when a month afterwards he notified the War Department of his readiness to comply with the request of the Government, he was informed that three-months' men were not needed, and that arrangements had been made for accepting three-years' volunteers from Maryland. Governor Burton of Delaware replied that "there was no organized militia in the State, and no law authorizing such organization." Indisposition to respond to the President was therefore in different degrees manifest in every part of the Union where Slavery had wrought its demoralizing influence. Mr. Lincoln was disappointed at this proof of the sectional character of the contest, and he realized that if American nationality was to be preserved, it must look for help to the abounding resources and the patriotic loyalty of the free States.

It fortunately happened that the governors of the free States were devoted to the Union in as great degree as the Southern governors were devoted to the Confederacy. It may well be doubted whether at any time in the history of the government there had been so large a number of able men occupying the gubernatorial chairs of the Northern States. They were not only eminent in an intellectual point of view, but they had a special fitness for the arduous and patriotic duties so unexpectedly devolved upon them. They became popularly known as the "War Governors," and they exercised a beneficent and decisive influence upon the fortunes of the Union.

The Governor of Massachusetts, John A. Andrew, added fervor to the patriotism of the whole people, and nobly led his State in her generous outpouring of aid and comfort to the loyal cause. The vigor which Massachusetts had imparted to the Revolution against the Crown was surpassed by the ardor with which she now threw herself into the contest for the Union. She had been often reproached for urging forward the anti-slavery agitation, which was the excuse of the South for rebelling against the National authority. A somewhat similar accusation had been lodged against her by the Royal Governors and by the Tories a century before. But the men who found this fault with Massachusetts — a fault wholly on virtue's side — will not deny that when the hour of trial came, when convictions of conscience were to be maintained by the strength of the right arm, and faith in principle was to be attested by a costly sacrifice of blood, her sons added imperishable honor to their ancestral record of heroism in the cause of human Liberty and Constitutional Government.

The other New-England States were not less ardent than Massachusetts. Israel Washburn, the Governor of Maine, impulsive, energetic, devoted to the cause of the Union, was sustained by the people of the State without regard to party and with the noblest enthusiasm. William A. Buckingham of Connecticut, of mature years and stainless life, was a young man once more when his country demanded his best energies. The young Governor of Rhode Island, William Sprague, laid aside the civilian's dress for the uniform of a soldier, and led the troops of his State to the National Capital. Ichabod Goodwin of New Hampshire and Erastus Fairbanks of Vermont, two of their most honored and useful men, filled out the list of New England's worthy Executives. Throughout the six States there was but one anxiety, one resolve, — anxiety for the safety of the government, resolve to subdue the revolt against it.

New England is not mentioned first except in a geographical

sense. More important even than her patriotic action was the course of the great Central and Western States. New York and Pennsylvania of themselves constituted no mean power, with a population of seven millions, with their boundless wealth, and their ability to produce the material of war. Edwin D. Morgan was the Executive of New York. He was a successful merchant of high character, of the sturdiest common sense and soundest judgment. A man of wealth himself, he possessed the entire confidence of the bankers and capitalists of the metropolis. His influence in aid of the finances of the government in its early period of depression was given without stint and was of incalculable value. In the neighboring State of New Jersey, Governor Charles Olden was ready for hearty co-operation, and seconded with patriotic zeal every movement in aid of the loyal cause.

Of a different type from Governor Morgan, but equally valuable and more enthusiastic, was the Governor of Pennsylvania, Andrew G. Curtin. Circumstances had thrown him into close and confidential relations with Mr. Lincoln,—relations which had their origin at the time of the Chicago Convention, and which had grown more intimate after Mr. Lincoln was inaugurated. Before the firing on Sumter, but when the States of the Confederacy were evidently preparing for war, Mr. Lincoln earnestly desired a counter signal of readiness on the part of the North. Such a movement in New England would have been regarded in the South merely as a fresh ebullition of radicalism. In New York the tone was too conservative and Governor Morgan too cautious to permit the demonstration to be made there. Governor Curtin undertook to do it in Pennsylvania at the President's special request. On the eleventh day of April, one day before the South precipitated the conflict, the Legislature of Pennsylvania passed an Act for the better organization of the militia, and appropriated five hundred thousand dollars to carry out the details of the measure. The manifest reference to the impending trouble was in the words prescribing the duty of the Adjutant-General of the State in case the President should call out the militia. It was the first official step in the loyal States to defend the Union, and the generous appropriation, made in advance of any blow struck by the Confederacy, enabled Governor Curtin to rally the forces of the great Commonwealth to the defense of the Union with marvelous promptness. His administration was vigorous, and his support of the Union cause was in the highest degree efficient, patriotic, and successful. He attained an exceptional popularity with the soldiers, and against the most bitter attacks never lost his hold on the confidence and personal regard of Mr. Lincoln.

In the West the commanding figure among a number of distinguished Executives was Oliver P. Morton of Indiana. He was of stalwart frame, full health, and the highest physical vigor. His energy was untiring, his will unconquerable. In the closely balanced condition of parties in his State, he had been trained to the most aggressive and exacting form of leadership, so that he entered upon his gubernatorial duties with a certain experience in the control of men which was of marked value. He possessed a mind of extraordinary strength; and in frequent contests at the bar and upon the stump, he had thoroughly disciplined his faculties. In debate he was formidable. It cannot be said that he exhibited striking originality of thought, or that he possessed in large degree the creative power. But in the art of presenting with force and clearness a subject which he had studied, of analyzing it and simplifying it to the comprehension of the common mind, of clothing it in language as plain and forcible as the diction of John Bunyan, he has had few equals among the public men of America.

The Governor of Iowa was Samuel J. Kirkwood, a man of truth, courage, and devoted love of country. Distinguished for comprehensive intelligence, for clear foresight, for persuasive speech, for spotless integrity, for thorough acquaintance with the people, he was a model of executive efficiency. Alexander Ramsey, the first governor of the Territory of Minnesota, was now governor of the State. As strong in character as he was in popularity, as able as he was patriotic, he broadened by his executive career a personal fame already enviable. Austin Blair of Michigan was a worthy compeer of these eminent officials, and administered his high trust with honor to himself and with advantage to his country. Richard Yates of Illinois had been chosen governor the day Mr. Lincoln was elected President, and enjoyed an exceptional popularity with the people of his State. William Dennison had succeeded Salmon P. Chase in the gubernatorial chair of Ohio, and was unremitting in his labor for the Union. Alexander W. Randall of Wisconsin had contributed in no small degree by public and attractive speech to the triumph of Mr. Lincoln, and was now intrusted with an important duty, to which he gave himself with genuine zeal.

In these sixteen States — all the non-slaveholding Commonwealths east of the Rocky Mountains — the governors were members of the Republican party. They were in political accord, and in complete personal sympathy with the administration. This was regarded by Mr. Lincoln as not in all respects a fortunate circumstance. It was his belief, as it was the belief of many others, that if loyal Democrats had been in the executive chairs of some of the largest States, the effect would have been more impressive. It would have suggested a more absolute unity of the Northern people in support of the government. It would in some degree have relieved the struggle for national life from the opprobrium contained in the reproach which subsequently became too common, that after all it was " a Republican war," waged merely for the abolition of slavery.

The two States on the Pacific coast had Democratic governors, and, by reason of the strong influence which the Southern Democracy had exercised in both under the influence of William M. Gwin and Joseph Lane, there was deep solicitude as to the course of events in that important outpost of the Union. The loyal adherence of those States to the National Government was a profound disappointment to the Confederacy. Jefferson Davis had expected, with a confidence amounting to certainty, and based, it is believed, on personal pledges, that the Pacific Coast, if it did not actually join the South, would be disloyal to the Union, and would, from its remoteness and its superlative importance, require a large contingent of the national forces to hold it in subjection. It was expected by the South that California and Oregon would give at least as much trouble as Kentucky and Missouri, and would thus indirectly but powerfully aid the Southern cause. The enthusiastic devotion which these distant States showed to the Union was therefore a surprise to the South and a most welcome relief to the National Government. The loyalty of the Pacific Coast was in the hearts of its people, but it was made more promptly manifest and effective by the patriotic conduct of Governor Downey and Governor Whittaker, and by the fervid and persuasive eloquence of Thomas Starr King.

The war wrought a great change in the relative position of parties in California. In the autumn of 1861 the Republican candidate, Leland Stanford, was chosen Governor of the State. He received 56,036 votes, while John Conness, a war Democrat, received 30,944, and McConnell who was the representative of the Gwin Democracy, which had so long controlled the State, received 32,750. The men who supported Conness, if driven to the choice, would have supported Stanford as against McConnell, thus showing the overwhelming sentiment of California in favor of the Union. Two years before, in the election of 1859, Mr. Stanford, as the Republican candidate, received but 10,110 votes, while Milton S. Latham, representing the Buchanan administration, received 62,255, and Curry, the Douglas candidate, 31,298. The majority of the Douglas men, if forced to choose, would have voted for Latham as against Stanford. In the Presidential election of 1860 California gave Mr. Lincoln 38,734 votes, Mr. Douglas 38,120, Mr. Breckinridge 33,975, Mr. Bell 9,136. The vote which Governor Stanford received in September, 1861, shows how rapid, radical and complete was the political revolution caused in California by the Southern Rebellion.

In the eager desire of the loyal people to hasten all measures of preparation for the defense of the Union, fault was found with Mr. Lincoln for so long postponing the session of Congress. Between the date of his proclamation and the date of the assembling of Congress, eighty days were to elapse. Zealous and impatient supporters of the loyal cause feared that the Confederacy would be enabled to consolidate its power, and to gather its forces for a more serious conflict than they could make if more promptly confronted with the power of the Union. But Mr. Lincoln judged wisely that time was needed for the growth and consolidation of Northern opinion, and that senators and representatives, after the full development of patriotic feeling in the free States, would meet in a frame of mind better suited to the discharge of the weighty duties devolving upon them. An additional and conclusive reason with the President was, that Kentucky had not yet elected her representatives to the Thirty-seventh Congress, and would not do so, under her constitution and laws, until the ensuing August. Mr. Lincoln desired to give ample time for canvassing Kentucky for the special election, which was immediately ordered by the governor of the State for the twentieth of June. From the first, Mr. Lincoln had peculiar interest in the course and conduct of Kentucky. It was his native State, and Mr. Clay had been his political exemplar and ideal. He believed also that in the action of her people would be found the best index and the best test of the popular opinion of the Border slave States. He did every thing therefore that he could properly do, to aid Kentucky in reaching a conclusion favorable to the Union. He was rewarded with a great victory. Of the ten representatives chosen, nine were decided friends of the Union, with the venerable Crittenden at their head, ably seconded by Robert Mallory and William H. Wadsworth. Only one member, Henry C. Burnett, was disloyal to the government, and he, after a few months' tarry in the Union councils, went South and joined the Rebellion. The popular vote showed 92,365 for the Union candidates, and 36,995 for the Secession candidates, giving a Union majority of more than 55,000. Mr. Lincoln regarded the result in Kentucky as in the highest degree auspicious, and as amply vindicating the wisdom of delaying the extra session of Congress. The effect was to stimulate a rapidly developing loyalty in the western part of Virginia, to discourage rebellious movements in Missouri, and to arrest Disunion tendencies in Maryland.

Under the protection of the administration, and inspired by the confidence of its support, the Union men of Kentucky had done for that State what her Union men might have done for Tennessee if John Bell and his Whig associates had been as bold and as true to their old principles as John J. Crittenden and Garrett Davis had proved in Kentucky. The conduct of Mr. Bell was a sad surprise to his Northern friends, and a keen mortification to those Southern Whigs who had remained firm in their attachment to the Union. The vote which he had received in the South at the Presidential election was very nearly as large as that given to Breckinridge. The vote of Bell and Douglas united, exceeded that given to Breckinridge in the slave States by more than a hundred thousand. The popular judgment in the North had been that the Disunion element in the South was massed in support of Breckinridge, and that all who preferred the candidacy of Bell or of Douglas might be relied upon in the supreme crisis as friends of the Union. Two Southern States, Kentucky and Tennessee, had given popular majorities for Mr. Bell, and there was no reason for supposing that the Union sentiment of Tennessee was any less pronounced than that of Kentucky. Indeed, Tennessee had the advantage of Mr. Bell's citizenship and long identification with her public service, while Kentucky encountered the personal influence and wide-spread popularity of Mr. Breckinridge, who took part against the Union.

If Mr. Bell had taken firm ground for the Union, the Secession movement would have been to a very great extent paralyzed in the

South. Mr. Badger of North Carolina, of identically similar principles with Crittenden, could have given direction to the old Whig sentiment of his State, and could have held it as steadily as Kentucky was held to the Union. The Bell and Everett campaign had been conducted upon the single and simple platform of the Union and the Constitution, — devotion to the Union, obedience to the Constitution. Mr. Everett, whose public life of grace, eloquence, and purity had not been especially distinguished for courage, pronounced with zeal and determination in favor of Mr. Lincoln's administration, and lent his efforts on the stump to the cause of the Union with wonderful effect throughout the Northern States. If Mr. Bell had stood beside him with equal courage and equal determination, Tennessee would never have seceded, and the Rebellion would have been confined to the seven original States. The eagerness of Virginia Democrats never could have swept their State into the whirlpool of Secession if the supporters of Mr. Bell in Tennessee and North Carolina had thrown themselves between the Old Dominion and the Confederacy. With that aid, the former Whigs of Virginia, led by Stuart and Botts and Wickham and Baldwin, and united with the loyal Democrats of the mountain and the valley, could have held the State firmly to the support of the Union, and could have effectively nullified the secret understanding between Mr. Mason and the Montgomery government, that Virginia should secede as soon as her open co-operation was needed for the success of the Southern revolt.

A large share of the responsibility for the dangerous development of the Rebellion must therefore be attributed to John Bell and his half million Southern supporters, who were all of the old Whig party. At the critical moment they signally failed to vindicate the principles upon which they had appealed in the preceding canvass for popular support. They are not justly chargeable with original Disunion proclivities. Sentiments of that kind had been consolidated in the Breckinridge party. But they are responsible for permitting a party whose rank and file did not outnumber their own to lead captive the public opinion of the South, and for permitting themselves to be pressed into a disavowal of their political principles, and to the adoption of the extreme views against which they had always warred. The precipitate manner in which the Southern men of the ancient Whig faith yielded their position as friends of the Union was an instructive illustration of the power which a compact and desperate minority can wield in a popular struggle. In a secret ballot, where every man could have voted according to his own convictions and desires, the Secession scheme would have been defeated in Virginia, North Carolina, Georgia, Tennessee, and Arkansas. But the men who led the Disunion movement, understood the practical lesson taught by the French revolutionist, that "audacity" can overcome numbers. In such a contest conservatism always goes down, and radicalism always triumphs. The conservative wishes to temporize and to debate. The radical wishes to act, and is ready to shoot. By reckless daring a minority of Southern men raised a storm of sectional passion to which the friends of the Union bowed their heads and surrendered.

It would be incorrect to speak of a Whig party in the South at the outbreak of the civil war. There were many Whigs, but their organization was gone. It was the destruction of that party which had prepared the way for a triumph of the Democratic Disunionists. In the day of their strength the Whigs could not have been overborne in the South by the Secessionists, nor would the experiment have been tried. No party in the United States ever presented a more brilliant array of talent than the Whigs. In the South, though always resting under the imputation of not being so devoted to the support of Slavery as their opponents, they yet maintained themselves, by the power of intellect and by the prestige of chivalric leadership, in some extraordinary political battles. Many of their eminent men have a permanent place in our history. Others, with less national renown, were recognized at home as possessing equal power. In their training, in their habits of mind, in their pride and independence, in their lack of discipline and submission, they were perhaps specially fitted for opposition, and not so well adapted as men of less power, to the responsibility and detail of administration. But an impartial history of American statesmanship will give some of its most brilliant chapters to the Whig party from 1830 to 1850. If their work cannot be traced in the National statute-books as prominently as that of their opponents, they will be credited by the discriminating reader of our political annals as the English of to-day credit Charles James Fox and his Whig associates — for the many evils which they prevented.

CHAPTER XV.

THE Thirty-seventh Congress assembled according to the President's proclamation, on the fourth day of July, 1861. There had been no ebb in the tide of patriotic enthusiasm which overspread the loyal States after the fall of Sumter. Mr. Lincoln's sagacity in fixing the session so late had apparently been well approved. The temper of the senators and representatives as they came together could not have been better for the great work before them. Startling events, following each other thick and fast, had kept the country in a state of absorbing excitement, and Congress saw around it on every side the indications of a sanguinary struggle to come. Even after the firing on Sumter, anxious and thoughtful men had not given up all hope of an adjustment. The very shock of arms in the harbor of Charleston, it was believed by many, might upon sober second thought induce Southern men to pause and consider and negotiate before taking the fatal plunge. Such expectations were vain. The South felt that their victory was pre-ordained. Jefferson Davis answered Mr. Lincoln's call for seventy-five thousand men by a proclamation ordering the enlistment of one hundred thousand. The Confederacy was growing in strength daily. State after State was joining it, and energy and confidence prevailed throughout all its borders. The situation grew every day more embarrassing and more critical. Without waiting for the action of Congress, Mr. Lincoln had called for forty-two thousand additional volunteers, and added eleven new regiments, numbering some twenty-two thousand men, to the regular army. A blockade of the Southern ports had been ordered on the 19th of April, and eighteen thousand men had been added to the navy.

No battle of magnitude or decisive character had been fought when Congress assembled; but there had been activity on the skirmish line of the gathering and advancing forces and, at many points, bloody collision. In Baltimore, on the historic 19th of April, the mob had endeavored to stop the march of Massachusetts troops hurrying to the protection of the National Capital. In Missouri General Nathaniel Lyon had put to flight the disloyal governor, and established the supremacy of National authority. In Western Virginia General McClellan had met with success in some minor engagements, and on the upper Potomac the forces under General Robert Patterson had gained some advantages. A reverse of no very serious character had been experienced at Big Bethel, near Hampton Roads, by the troops under General Benjamin F. Butler. General Robert C. Schenck, in command of a small force, had met with a repulse a few miles from Washington, near Vienna in the State of Virginia. These incidents were not in themselves of special importance, but they indicated an aggressive energy on the part of the Confederates, and foreshadowed the desperate character which the contest was destined to assume. Congress found itself legislating in a fortified city, with patrols of soldiers on the streets and with a military administration which had practically superseded the civil police in the duty of maintaining order and protecting life. The situation was startling and serious, and for the first time people began to realize that we were to have a war with bloody fighting and much suffering, with limitless destruction of property, with costly sacrifice of life.

The spirit in both branches of Congress was a fair reflection of that which prevailed in the North. Andrew Johnson of Tennessee was the only senator who appeared from the eleven seceding States. John C. Breckinridge was present from Kentucky, somewhat mortified by the decisive rebuke which he had received in the vote of his State. The first important act of the Senate was the seating of James H. Lane and Samuel C. Pomeroy as senators from the new State of Kansas, which had been admitted at the last session of Congress as a free State, — in a bill which, with historic justice, Mr. Buchanan was called upon to approve, after he had announced to Congress, during the first year of his administration, that Kansas was as much a slave State as South Carolina. The first question of moment growing out of the Rebellion was the presentation of credentials by Messrs. Willey and Carlile, who claimed seats as senators from Virginia, the right to which was certified by the seal of the State with the signature of Francis H. Pierpont as governor. The credentials indicated that Mr. Willey was to take the seat vacated by Mr. Mason, and Mr. Carlile that vacated by Mr. Hunter. The loyal men of Virginia, especially from the western counties, finding that the regularly organized government of the State had joined the Rebellion, extemporized a government composed of the Union men of the Legislature which had been in session the preceding winter in Richmond. This body had met in Wheeling, and elected two men as senators who had stood firmly for the Union in the convention which had forced Virginia into secession. Their admission to the Senate was resisted by Mr. James A. Bayard, then senator from Delaware, and by the few other Democratic senators who still held seats. But after discussion, Mr. Willey and Mr. Carlile were sworn in, and thus the first step was taken which led soon after to the partition of the Old Dominion and the creation of the new State of West Virginia. The free States had a unanimous representation of Republican senators, with the exception of John R. Thompson from New Jersey, Jesse D. Bright from Indiana, James W. Nesmith from Oregon, and the two senators from California, Milton S. Latham and James A. McDougall, the latter of whom was sworn in as the successor of William M. Gwin.

The Senate, though deprived by secession of many able men from the South, presented an imposing array of talent, statesmanship, and character. William Pitt Fessenden had already served one term with distinction, and was now in the third year of his second term. He possessed a combination of qualities which gave him just eminence in his public career. He was brilliant from his youth upward; had led the Maine Legislature when but a few years beyond his majority; and, at a time when members of the legal profession are struggling for a first foot-hold, he had stepped to the front rank in the bar of Maine. He was elected a representative in Congress in 1840 at thirty-four years of age. He never enjoyed popularity in the sense in which that word is ordinarily used, but he had the absolute confidence and admiration of his constituents. He possessed that peculiar strength with the people — the most valuable and most enduring a public man can have — which comes from a sense of pride in the ability and character of the representative. Somewhat reserved and distant in manner to the world at large, he was genial and delightful to the intimate circle whom he called friends.

As a debater Mr. Fessenden was exceptionally able. He spoke without apparent effort, in a quiet, impressive manner, with a complete mastery of pure English. He preserved the *lucidus ordo* in his argument, was never confused, never hurried, never involved in style. A friend once said to him that the only criticism to be made of his speeches in the Senate was that he illustrated his point too copiously, throwing light upon it after it was made plain to the comprehension of all his hearers. "That fault," said he, "I acquired in addressing juries, where I always tried to adapt my argument to the understanding of the dullest man of the twelve." It was a fault which Mr. Fessenden overcame, and in his later years his speeches may be taken as models for clearness of statement, accuracy of reasoning, felicity of expression, moderation of tone. There

---

NOTE. — The following is a complete list of the Senators who served in the Thirty-seventh Congress. Republicans in Roman, Democrats in Italic, American or Old-Line Whigs in small capitals.

CALIFORNIA. — *Milton S. Latham; James A. McDougall.*

CONNECTICUT. — James Dixon; Lafayette S. Foster.

DELAWARE. — *James A. Bayard; Willard Saulsbury.*

ILLINOIS. — *Stephen A. Douglas*, died June 3, 1861; Lyman Trumbull; Orville H. Browning, appointed in place of Douglas; *William A. Richardson*, elected in place of Douglas.

INDIANA. — *Jesse D. Bright*, expelled Feb. 5, 1862; Henry S. Lane; Joseph A. Wright, appointed in place of Bright; *David Turpie*, elected in place of Bright.

IOWA. — James W. Grimes; James Harlan.

KANSAS. — James H. Lane; Samuel C. Pomeroy.

KENTUCKY. — *Lazarus W. Powell; John C. Breckinridge*, expelled Dec. 4, 1861; GARRETT DAVIS, elected in place of Breckinridge.

MAINE. — Lot M. Morrill; William Pitt Fessenden.

MARYLAND. — ANTHONY KENNEDY; JAMES A. PEARCE, died Dec. 20, 1862; Thomas H. Hicks, elected in place of Pearce.

MASSACHUSETTS. — Charles Sumner; Henry Wilson.

MICHIGAN. — Zachariah Chandler; Kinsley S. Bingham, died Oct. 5, 1861; Jacob M. Howard, elected in place of Bingham.

have been members of the Senate who achieved greater distinction than Mr. Fessenden, but it may well be doubted whether in the qualities named he ever had a superior in that body. His personal character was beyond reproach. He maintained the highest standard of purity and honor. His patriotism was ardent and devoted. The general character of his mind was conservative, and he had the heartiest contempt of every thing that savored of the demagogue in the conduct of public affairs. He was never swayed from his conclusions by the passion of the hour, and he met the gravest responsibilities with even mind. He had a lofty disregard of personal danger, possessing both moral and physical courage in a high degree. He was constant in his devotion to duty, and no doubt shortened his life by his public labors.

Mr. Sumner, though five years the junior, was senior in senatorial service to Mr. Fessenden, and had attained wider celebrity. Mr. Sumner's labor was given almost exclusively to questions involving our foreign relations, and to issues growing out of the slavery agitation. To the latter he devoted himself, not merely with unswerving fidelity but with all the power and ardor of his nature. Upon general questions of business in the Senate he was not an authority, and rarely participated in the debates which settled them; but he did more than any other man to promote the anti-slavery cause, and to uprear its standard in the Republican party. He had earned, in an unexampled degree, the hatred of the South, and this fact had

---

MINNESOTA. — Morton S. Wilkinson; *Henry M. Rice.*

MISSOURI. — *Trusten Polk,* expelled Jan. 10, 1862; John B. Henderson, appointed in place of Polk; *Waldo P. Johnson,* expelled Jan. 10, 1862; *Robert Wilson,* appointed in place of Johnson.

NEW HAMPSHIRE. — John P. Hale; Daniel Clark.

NEW JERSEY. — *John R. Thomson,* died Sept. 12, 1862; John C. Ten Eyck; Richard S. Field, appointed in place of Thomson; *James W. Wall,* elected in place of Thomson.

NEW YORK. — Preston King; Ira Harris.

OHIO. — Benjamin F. Wade; Salmon P. Chase, resigned March 5, 1861, to become Secretary of Treasury; John Sherman, elected in place of Chase.

OREGON. — *James W. Nesmith;* Edward D. Baker, died Oct. 21, 1861; *Benjamin Stark,* appointed in place of Baker; *Benjamin F. Harding,* elected in place of Baker.

PENNSYLVANIA. — David Wilmot, elected in place of Cameron; Edgar Cowan; Simon Cameron, resigned March 5, 1861.

RHODE ISLAND. — James F. Simmons, resigned December, 1862; Henry B. Anthony; Samuel G. Arnold, elected in place of Simmons.

TENNESSEE. — Andrew Johnson, resigned March 4, 1862, to be military governor of Tennessee.

VERMONT. — Solomon Foot; Jacob Collamer.

VIRGINIA. — Waitman T. Willey; John S. Carlile.

WISCONSIN. — James R. Doolittle; Timothy O. Howe.

increased the zeal for him among anti-slavery men throughout the North. The assault, made upon him by Preston S. Brooks, a South-Carolina representative, for his famous speech on Kansas, had strengthened his hold upon his constituency, which was not merely the State of Massachusetts but the radical and progressive Republicans of the entire country.

Mr. Sumner was studious, learned, and ambitious. He prepared his discussions of public questions with care, but was not ready as a debater. He presented his arguments with power, but they were laborious essays. He had no faculty for extempore speech. Like Addison, he could draw his draft for a thousand pounds, but might not have a shilling of change. This did not hinder his progress or lessen his prestige in the Senate. His written arguments were the anti-slavery classics of the day, and they were read more eagerly than speeches which produced greater effect on the hearer. Colonel Benton said that the eminent William Pinkney of Maryland was always thinking of the few hundred who came to hear him in the Senate Chamber, apparently forgetting the million who might read him outside. Mr. Sumner never made that mistake. His arguments went to the million. They produced a wide-spread and prodigious effect on public opinion and left an indelible impression on the history of the country.

Jacob Collamer of Vermont was a senator of eminent worth and ability. He had earned honorable fame as a member of the House of Representatives, and as a member of the Cabinet in the administration of General Taylor. He had entered the Senate at a ripe age, and with every qualification for distinguished service. To describe him in a single word, he was a wise man. Conservative in his nature, he was sure to advise against rashness. Sturdy in his principles, he always counseled firmness. In the periods of excitement through which the party was about to pass, his judgment was sure to prove of highest value — influenced, as it always was, by patriotism, and guided by conscience. Without power as an orator, he was listened to in the Senate with profound attention, as one who never offered counsel that was not needed. He carried into the Senate the gravity, the dignity, the weight of character, which enabled him to control more ardent natures; and he brought to a later generation the wisdom and experience acquired in a long life devoted to the service of his state and of his country.

Zachariah Chandler had been the recognized leader of the Republican party in Michigan from its formation.   He had superseded General Cass with a people in whose affections the latter had been strongly intrenched before Chandler was born.   He had been four years in the Senate when the war broke out, and he was well established in reputation and influence.   He was educated in the common schools of his native State of New Hampshire, but had not enjoyed the advantage of collegiate training.   He was not eloquent according to the canons of oratory; but he was widely intelligent, had given careful attention to public questions, and spoke with force and clearness. He was a natural leader.   He had abounding confidence in himself, possessed moral courage of a high order, and did not know the sensation of physical fear.   He was zealous in the performance of public duty, radical in his convictions, patriotic in every thought, an unrelenting foe to all forms of corruption.   He distinguished between a friend and an enemy.   He was always ready to help the one, and, though not lacking in magnanimity, he seldom neglected an opportunity to cripple the other.

Lyman Trumbull had entered the Senate six years before, when Illinois revolted against the course of Douglas in destroying the Missouri Compromise.   Mr. Lincoln had earnestly desired the place, but waived his claims.   The election of Trumbull was considered desirable for the consolidation of the new party, and the Republicans of Whig antecedents were taught a lesson of self-sacrifice by the promptness with which Mr. Lincoln abandoned the contest.   Judge Trumbull had acquired a good reputation at the bar of his State, and at once took high rank in the Senate.   His mind was trained to logical discussion, and as a debater he was able and incisive.   His political affiliations prior to 1854 were with the Democracy, and aside from the issue in regard to the extension of slavery, he did not fully sympathize with the principles and tendencies of the Republican party.   He differed from Mr. Lincoln just as Preston King, senator from New York, differed from Mr. Seward.   Lincoln and Seward believed in Henry Clay and all the issues which he represented, while Trumbull and King were devoted to the policies and measures which characterized the administration of Jackson.   The two classes of men composing the Republican party were equally zealous in support of the principles that led to the political revolution of 1860, but it was not easy to see what would be the result of other issues which time and necessity might develop.

Benjamin F. Wade of Ohio had been ten years in the Senate

when the war broke out. He entered in March, 1851 — the immediate successor of Thomas Ewing who had been transferred to the Senate from the Cabinet of Taylor, to take the place of Thomas Corwin who left the Senate to enter the Cabinet of Fillmore. Mr. Wade was elected as a Whig — the last senator chosen by that party in Ohio. His triumph was a rebuke to Mr. Corwin for his abandonment of the advanced position which he had taken against the aggressions of the slave power. It was rendered all the more significant by the defeat of Mr. Ewing, who with his strong hold upon the confidence and regard of the people of Ohio, was too conservative to embody the popular resentment against the odious features of the Compromise of 1850. Mr. Wade entered the Senate with Mr. Sumner. Their joint coming imparted confidence and strength to the contest for free soil, and was a powerful re-enforcement to Mr. Seward, Mr. Chase, and Mr. Hale, who represented the distinctively anti-slavery sentiment in the Senate. The fidelity, the courage, the ability of Mr. Wade gave him prominence in the North, and were a constant surprise to the South. He brought to the Senate the radicalism which Mr. Giddings had so long upheld in the House, and was protected in his audacious freedom of speech by his steadiness of nerve and his known readiness to fight.

Henry B. Anthony entered the Senate on the 4th of March, 1859, at forty-four years of age. He had been Governor of Rhode Island ten years before. He received a liberal education at Brown University, and was for a long period editor of the *Providence Journal*, a position in which he established an enviable fame as a writer and secured an enduring hold upon the esteem and confidence of his State. In the Senate he soon acquired the rank to which his thorough training and intelligence, his graceful speech, his ardent patriotism, his stainless life entitled him. No man has ever enjoyed, among his associates of all parties, a more profound confidence, a more cordial respect, a warmer degree of affection.

John P. Hale of New Hampshire was still pursuing the career which he had begun as an early advocate of the anti-slavery cause, and in which he had twice overthrown the power of the Democratic party in New Hampshire. — Henry Wilson was the colleague of Mr. Sumner, and was a man of strong parts, self-made, earnest, ardent, and true. — Lot M. Morrill was the worthy associate of Mr. Fessenden, prominent in his profession, and strong in the regard and confidence of the people of his State. — The author of the Wilmot Proviso came from Pennsylvania as the successor of Simon Cameron, and as the colleague of Edgar Cowan, whose ability was far greater than his ambition or his industry. — James W. Grimes, a native of New Hampshire, who had gone to Iowa at the time of its organization as a Territory and had been conspicuously influential in the affairs of the State, entered the Senate in March, 1859. He possessed an iron will and sound judgment. He was specially distinguished for independence of party restraint in his modes of thought and action. He and Judge Collamer of Vermont were the most intimate associates of Mr. Fessenden, and the three were not often separated on public questions. — The colleague of Mr. Grimes was James Harlan, one of Mr. Lincoln's most valued and most confidential friends, and subsequently a member of his Cabinet. — James R. Doolittle came from Wisconsin, a far more radical Republican than his colleague, Timothy O. Howe, and both were men of marked influence in the councils of their party. — John Sherman filled the vacancy occasioned by the appointment of Mr. Chase to the Treasury. Mr. Chase had been chosen as the successor of George E. Pugh, and remained in the Senate but a single day. Mr. Sherman had been six years in the House, and had risen rapidly in public esteem. He had been the candidate of his party for Speaker, and had served as chairman of Ways and Means in the Congress preceding the war. — From the far-off Pacific came Edward Dickinson Baker, a senator from Oregon, a man of extraordinary gifts of eloquence; lawyer, soldier, frontiersman, leader of popular assemblies, tribune of the people. In personal appearance he was commanding, in manner most attractive, in speech irresistibly charming. Perhaps in the history of the Senate no man ever left so brilliant a reputation from so short a service. He was born in England, and the earliest recollection of his life was the splendid pageant attending the funeral of Lord Nelson. He came with his family to the United States when a child, lived for a time in Philadelphia, and removed to Illinois, where he grew to manhood and early attained distinction. He served his State with great brilliancy in Congress, and commanded with conspicuous success one of her regiments in the war with Mexico. The Whigs of the North-West presented Colonel Baker for a seat in the Cabinet of President Taylor. His failure to receive the appointment was a sore mortification to him. He thought his political career in Illinois was broken; and in 1852, after the close of his service in Congress, he joined the throng who were seeking fortune and fame on the Pacific slope. When leaving Washington he said to a friend that he should never look on the Capitol again unless he could come bearing his credentials as a senator of the United States. He returned in eight years.

Among the opposition senators, some fourteen in number, the most prominent was John C. Breckinridge of Kentucky, who had stepped from the Vice-President's chair to the floor of the Senate as the successor of Mr. Crittenden. Mr. Breckinridge at that time was forty years of age, attractive in personal appearance, graceful and cordial in manner, by inheritance and by cultivation a gentleman. He came from a section where family rank gave power and influence. He united in his person the best blood of the South and the North, — preserving and combining the most winning traits of each. His lineage in Kentucky naturally brought to him the sympathy and support of the State. He was born to success and authority among his people. Originally he had anti-slavery convictions, as had all the members of his eminent family. So strongly was this tendency developed in his mind that, when he came to the bar, he removed to the Territory of Iowa, intending to identify himself with the growth of the free North-West. Circumstances overcame this determination, and carried him back to Kentucky, where he was welcomed at the hearth-stones and in the hearts of her people.

At twenty-five years of age Mr. Breckinridge was appointed major in one of the Kentucky regiments, which served in the Mexican war. After his return he entered upon the practice of his profession in Lexington, and against all the traditions of his family identified himself with the Democratic party. An apparently slight incident had an important bearing upon his earlier political career. He was selected to deliver the address of welcome to Mr. Clay on his return to Kentucky in the autumn of 1850, from the field of his senatorial triumph in securing the adoption of the celebrated compromise of that year. Mr. Breckinridge's speech was graceful and effective. He eulogized Mr. Clay's work with discrimination, and paid the highest tribute to the illustrious statesman. Mr. Clay was visibly touched by the whole scene. His old opponents were present by the thousand to do him honor. The enmities and antagonisms of earlier years were buried. He had none but friends and supporters in Kentucky. He responded with earnestness, and even with emotion : "My welcome," he said, "has been made all the more grateful from being pronounced by my eloquent young friend, the son of an eloquent father, the grandson of a still more eloquent grandfather, both of whom were in days long gone my cherished companions, my earnest supporters." Mr. Clay's words were so warm, his manner was so cordial, that it seemed as if he intended to confer upon Breckinridge the leadership in Kentucky, which, after a half century's domination, he was about to surrender. Undoubtedly the events of that day aided Breckinridge the next year in carrying the Ashland District for Congress, and drew to him thereafter the support of many influential Whigs. He entered Congress when the slavery discussion was absorbing public attention, and by the irresistible drift of events he was carried into an association with extreme Southern men. It was by their friendly influence that he was promoted to the Vice-Presidency as soon as he became eligible under the Constitution. During the four stormy years of Buchanan's administration, when the sectional contest approached its crisis, Mr. Breckinridge became more and more the representative of Southern opinion, and, though unequal to Douglas in the arena of debate, he became the leader of those who opposed the "popular sovereignty" dogma of the Illinois senator. He was thence drawn by influences which he could not have controlled if he had desired, into the prolonged and exciting controversy which disrupted the Democratic party. Intellectually Mr. Breckinridge was not the equal of many Southern men who deferred to him as a leader. His precedence was due to his personal character, to his strong connections, to his well-tempered judgment, and especially to a certain attractiveness of manner which was felt by all who came in contact with him.

The prominence of New England in the Senate was exceptional. So many positions of influence were assigned to her that it created no small degree of jealousy and ill-feeling in other sections. The places were allotted according to the somewhat rigid rules of precedence which obtain in that body, but this fact did not induce senators from the Middle and Western States to acquiesce with grace. The chairmanship of the Committee on Foreign Relations was given to Mr. Sumner; Mr. Fessenden was placed at the head of the Finance Committee, which then included Appropriations; Mr. Wilson was made chairman of Military Affairs; Mr. John P. Hale, chairman of Naval Affairs; Mr. Collamer, chairman of Post-office and Post-roads; Mr. Foster of Connecticut, chairman of Pensions; Mr. Clark of New Hampshire, chairman of Claims; Mr. Simmons of Rhode Island, chairman of Patents; Mr. Foot of Vermont, chairman of Public Buildings and Grounds; Mr. Anthony, chairman of Printing; Mr. Dixon of

Connecticut, chairman of Contingent Expenses. Mr. Lot M. Morrill, who had just entered the public service from Maine, was the only New-England senator left without a chairmanship. There were in all twenty-two committees in the Senate. Eleven were given to New England. But even this ratio does not exhibit the case in its full strength. The Committees on Foreign Relations, Finance, Military Affairs, and Naval Affairs shaped almost the entire legislation in time of war, and thus New England occupied a most commanding position. The retirement of Mr. Seward, Mr. Chase, and Mr. Cameron from the Senate to enter the Cabinet undoubtedly increased the number of important positions assigned to New England. Twenty-two States were represented in the Senate, and it was impossible to make sixteen of them, including the four leading States of the Union, recognize the justice of placing the control of National legislation in the hands of six States in the far North-East. It was not a fortunate arrangement for New England, since it provoked prejudices which proved injurious in many ways, and lasted for many years.

The House of Representatives was promptly organized by the election of Galusha A. Grow of Pennsylvania as Speaker. Mr. Grow came from the Wilmot district, on the northern border of the State, where the anti-slavery sentiment had taken earliest and deepest root. As Connecticut had in the Colonial period claimed a large part of the area of North Pennsylvania, her emigration tended in that direction, and this fact had given a distinct and more radical type to the population. Mr. Grow was himself a native of Connecticut. He was chosen Speaker because of his activity in the anti-slavery struggles of the House, and because of his aptitude for the duties of the chair. Francis P. Blair, Jr., of Missouri was a rival candidate, and was supported by strong influences. It was not considered expedient to hold a party caucus, and the Democratic minority declined to present a candidate. On the roll call, Mr. Grow received 71 votes, Mr. Blair 40, while 48 votes, principally of Democratic representatives, were cast for different gentlemen who were in no sense candidates. Accepting Mr. Grow's plurality as the best form of nomination to the office, a large number of the friends of Mr. Blair changed their votes before the result was authoritatively declared, and Mr. Grow was announced as receiving 99 votes, — a majority of all the members.

Two members appeared from Virginia. The other Confederate States were without representation. Emerson Etheridge of Tennessee was chosen Clerk, in compliment to his fidelity and courage as a Union man.

The House was filled with able men, many of whom had parliamentary experience. The natural leader, who assumed his place by common consent, was Thaddeus Stevens, a man of strong peculiarities of character, able, trained, and fearless. Born in Vermont and educated at Dartmouth, he had passed all his adult years in Pennsylvania, and was thoroughly identified with the State which he had served with distinction both in her own Legislature and in Congress. He had the reputation of being somewhat unscrupulous as to political methods, somewhat careless in personal conduct, somewhat lax in personal morals; but to the one great object of his life, the destruction of slavery and the elevation of the slave, he was supremely devoted. From the pursuit of that object nothing could deflect him. Upon no phase of it would he listen to compromise. Any man who was truly anti-slavery was his friend. Whoever espoused the cause and proved faithless in never so small a degree, became his enemy, inevitably and irreconcilably. Towards his own race he seemed often to be misanthropic. He was learned in the law, and for a third of a century had held high rank at the bar of a State distinguished for great lawyers. He was disposed to be taciturn. A brilliant talker, he did not relish idle and aimless conversation. He was much given to reading, study, and reflection, and to the retirement which enabled him to gratify his tastes. As was said of Mr. Emerson, Mr. Stevens loved solitude and understood its uses.

Upon all political questions Mr. Stevens was an authority. He spoke with ease and readiness, using a style somewhat resembling the crisp, clear sententiousness of Dean Swift. Seldom, even in the most careless moment, did a sentence escape his lips, that would not bear the test of grammatical and rhetorical criticism. He possessed the keenest wit, and was unmerciful in its use towards those whom he did not like. He illustrated in concrete form the difference between wit and humor. He did not indulge in the latter. He did not enjoy a laugh. When his sharp sallies would set the entire House in uproar, he was as impassive, his visage as solemn, as if he were pronouncing a funeral oration. His memory of facts, dates, and figures was exact, and in argument he knew the book and chapter and page for reference. He was fond of young men, invited their society, encouraged and generously aided them. He was easily moved by the distress of others. He was kind, charitable, lavish of his money in the relief of poverty. He had characteristics which seemed contradictory, but which combined to make one of the memorable figures in the Parliamentary history of the United States, — a man who had the courage to meet any opponent, and who was never overmatched in intellectual conflict.

Mr. Stevens had efficient colleagues from Pennsylvania. The most distinguished was John Hickman, who had been a Democrat until 1860, and who in debate was skillful and acute. William D. Kelley entered the House at this session for the first time, and

---

Note. — The following is a list of Representatives in the Thirty-seventh Congress. Republicans are given in Roman, Democrats in Italic, American or Old-Line Whigs in small capitals.

CALIFORNIA. — Aaron A. Sargent; Frederick F. Low; Timothy G. Phelps.

CONNECTICUT. — Dwight Loomis ; *James E. English ; George C. Woodruff ;* Alfred A. Burnham.

DELAWARE. — George P. Fisher.

ILLINOIS. — Elihu B. Washburne; Isaac N. Arnold; Owen Lovejoy; William Kellogg; *William A. Richardson,* elected Senator; *John A. McClernand,* resigned 1861 to enter the army; *James C. Robinson ; Philip B. Fouke ; John A. Logan,* resigned 1861 to enter the army; *William J. Allen,* elected in place of Logan; *Anthony L. Knapp,* elected in place of McClernand.

INDIANA. — *John Law ; James A. Cravens ; William S. Holman ;* George W. Julian; Albert G. Porter; *Daniel W. Voorhees;* Albert S. White; Schuyler Colfax; William Mitchell; John P. C. Shanks; W. McKee Dunn.

IOWA. — Samuel R. Curtis, resigned Aug. 4, 1861, to enter the army; William Vandever; James F. Wilson, elected in place of Curtis.

KANSAS. — Martin F. Conway.

KENTUCKY. — *Henry C. Burnett,* expelled Dec. 3, 1861; JAMES S. JACKSON, died in 1862; HENRY GRIDER; *Aaron Harding ; Charles A. Wickliffe ;* GEORGE W. DUNLAP; ROBERT MALLORY; *John W. Menzies ;* SAMUEL L. CASEY, elected in place of Burnett; WILLIAM H. WADSWORTH; JOHN J. CRITTENDEN; GEORGE H. YEAMAN, elected in place of Jackson.

LOUISIANA. — BENJAMIN F. FLANDERS, seated in February, 1863; MICHAEL HAHN, seated in February, 1863.

MAINE. — John N. Goodwin; Charles W. Walton, resigned May 26, 1862; Samuel C. Fessenden; Anson P. Morrill; John H. Rice; Frederick A. Pike; Thomas A. D. Fessenden, elected in place of Walton.

MARYLAND. — JOHN W. CRISFIELD; EDWIN H. WEBSTER; *Cornelius L. L. Leary ;* FRANCIS THOMAS; CHARLES B. CALVERT; *Henry May.*

MASSACHUSETTS. — Thomas D. Eliot; James Buffinton; Benjamin F. Thomas; Alexander H. Rice; William Appleton, resigned in 1861; John B. Alley; Daniel W. Gooch; Charles R. Train; Goldsmith F. Bailey, died May 8, 1862; Charles Delano; Henry L. Dawes; Samuel Hooper, elected in place of Appleton; Amasa Walker, elected in place of Bailey.

MICHIGAN. — Bradley F. Granger; Fernando C. Beaman; Francis W. Kellogg; Rowland E. Trowbridge.

MINNESOTA. — Cyrus Aldrich; William Windom.

was destined to serve his State for a long series of years, with ability, fidelity, and usefulness. James K. Moorhead, John Covode, Edward McPherson, and John W. Killinger were active and influential members.

New York sent Reuben E. Fenton, already prominent, popular, and strong in the public service; Elbridge G. Spaulding, who became useful and even eminent as an adviser in financial legislation; William A. Wheeler, afterwards Vice-President of the United States; Theodore Pomeroy, the neighbor and confidential friend of Mr. Seward; Charles B. Sedgwick, of pronounced ability in the law;

MISSOURI. — Francis P. Blair, Jr., resigned in 1862; JAMES S. ROLLINS; *Elijah H. Norton; John W. Reid*, expelled Dec. 2, 1861; *John W. Noell; John S. Phelps; William A. Hall; Thomas L. Price*, elected in place of Reid.

NEW HAMPSHIRE. — Gilman Marston; Edward H. Rollins; Thomas M. Edwards.

NEW JERSEY. — John T. Nixon; John L. N. Stratton; *William G. Steele; George T. Cobb; Nehemiah Perry.*

NEW YORK. — E. Henry Smith; MOSES F. ODELL; *Benjamin Wood;* William Wall; Frederick A. Conkling; *Elijah Ward; Edward Haight;* Charles H. Van Wyck;, *John B. Steele;* Stephen Baker; Abraham B. Olin; James B. McKean; William A. Wheeler; Socrates N. Sherman; *Chauncey Vibbard;* Richard Franchot; Roscoe Conkling; R. Holland Duell; William E. Lansing; Ambrose W. Clark; Charles B. Sedgwick; Theodore M. Pomeroy; John P. Chamberlain; Alexander S. Diven; Robert B. Van Valkenburgh; Alfred Ely; Augustus Frank; Burt Van Horn; Elbridge G. Spaulding; Reuben E. Fenton; *Erastus Corning; James E. Kerrigan;* Isaac C. Delaplaine.

OHIO. — *George H. Pendleton;* John A. Gurley; *Clement L. Vallandigham; William Allen;* James M. Ashley; *Chilton A. White;* Richard A. Harrison; Samuel Shellabarger; *Warren P. Noble;* Carey A. Trimble; Valentine B. Horton; *Samuel S. Cox;* Samuel T. Worcester; Harrison G. Blake; William P. Cutler; *James R. Morris;* Sidney Edgerton; Albert G. Riddle; John Hutchins; John A. Bingham; *R. H. Nugen.*

OREGON. — *George K. Shiel.*

PENNSYLVANIA. — *William E. Lehman;* John P. Verree; William D. Kelley; William M. Davis; John Hickman; *Thomas B. Cooper,* died April 4, 1862; *John D. Stiles,* elected in place of Cooper, deceased; *Sydenham E. Ancona;* Thaddeus Stevens; John W. Killinger; James H. Campbell; *Hendrick B. Wright;* Philip Johnson; Galusha A. Grow, Speaker; James T. Hale; *Joseph Bailey;* Edward McPherson; Samuel S. Blair; John Covode; *Jesse Lazear;* James K. Moorhead; Robert McKnight; John W. Wallace; John Patton; Elijah Babbitt; *Charles J. Biddle.*

RHODE ISLAND. — William P. Sheffield; George H. Browne.

TENNESSEE. — GEORGE W. BRIDGES; ANDREW J. CLEMENTS; HORACE MAYNARD.

VERMONT. — Portus Baxter; Justin S. Morrill; Ezekiel P. Walton.

VIRGINIA. — Jacob B. Blair, elected in place of Carlile; William G. Brown; John S. Carlile, elected Senator July, 1861; Joseph E. Segar; Charles H. Upton; Killian V. Whaley.

WISCONSIN. — Luther Hanchett, died Nov. 24, 1862; Walter D. McIndoe, elected in place of Hanchett; John F. Potter; A. Scott Sloan.

Territorial Delegates. — Colorado, Hiram P. Bennett; Dakota, John B. S. Todd; Nebraska, Samuel G. Daily; Nevada, John Cradlebaugh; New-Mexico, John S. Watts; Utah, John M. Bernhisel; Washington, William H. Wallace.

Charles H. Van Wyck, who afterwards sought distinction in the West; and Abraham Olin, subsequently well known in judicial life. The ablest and most brilliant man of the delegation was Roscoe Conkling. He had been elected to the preceding Congress when but twenty-nine years of age, and had exhibited a readiness and eloquence in debate that placed him at once in the front rank. His command of language was remarkable. In affluent and exuberant diction Mr. Conkling was never surpassed in either branch of Congress, unless, perhaps, by Rufus Choate.

The Ohio delegation was especially strong. John A. Bingham, the oldest in service on the Republican side, was an effective debater, well informed, ready, and versatile. A man of high principle, of strong faith, of zeal, enthusiasm, and eloquence, he could always command the attention of the House. His colleague, Samuel Shellabarger, was distinguished for the logical and analytical character of his mind. Without the gift of oratory, paying little heed to the graces of speech, Mr. Shellabarger conquered by the intrinsic strength of his argument, which generally amounted to demonstration. His mind possessed many of the qualities which distinguished Mr. Lincoln. In fairness, lucidness, fullness of statement, the two had a striking resemblance. Valentine B. Horton was a valuable member on all questions of finance and business; and on the issues touching slavery James M. Ashley followed the radical example of Mr. Giddings. Among the Democrats, George H. Pendleton, Clement L. Vallandigham, and Samuel S. Cox were especially conspicuous. Mr. Pendleton was regarded as the leader of the Democratic side of the House by a large section of his party, and his assignment to the Committee of Ways and Means by the Speaker was intended as a recognition of that fact. Mr. Cox gave much attention to foreign affairs, to which his mind had been drawn by a brief but fruitful participation in the diplomatic service of the country. Mr. Vallandigham possessed ability, and a certain form of dogged courage, combined with a love of notoriety, which allured him to the assumption of extreme positions and the advocacy of unpopular measures. No other State was in the aggregate so ably represented as Ohio.

Indiana was influential in the House. Schuyler Colfax was at the height of his successful career on the floor and destined to eminent promotion in the public service. Among his Republican colleagues were George W. Julian, long and creditably identified with the anti-slavery cause, and especially esteemed for the conscientious

ROBERT C. SCHENCK.

WILLIAM D. KELLEY.

SAMUEL SHELLABARGER.

ELIHU B. WASHBURNE.

JUSTIN S. MORRILL.

GEORGE S. BOUTWELL.

REUBEN E. FENTON.

ENGRAVED BY W. WELLSTOOD & CO. N.Y.

attention he had given to all questions relating to the public lands; Albert G. Porter, in his second Congress, well trained for debate, with ability and high character, rapidly winning public favor, but cut off from his legislative career by a Democratic majority in his district, although his strength with the people has since been strikingly attested; William McKee Dunn, a man of sound judgment, to be known and appreciated afterwards in other fields of honorable duty. On the Democratic side, William S. Holman already ranked as an old member. His efforts were steadily and persistently directed to the enforcement of public economy; and though he may have sometimes been unreasonable, and though he was often accused of acting the part of a demagogue, the country owes him a debt of gratitude for the integrity, intelligence, and simplicity with which he has illustrated a most honorable career as representative of the people. Daniel W. Voorhees, by nature a fierce partisan, yet always filled with generous impulses, was in his second Congress. His character was significantly illustrated by his willingness to lend his attractive eloquence in the Virginia courts in defense of one of John Brown's associates in the Harper's Ferry tragedy, — a magnanimous act in view of the risk to his position among the pro-slavery Democracy, with whom he was strongly identified in party organization.

Illinois sent Elihu B. Washburne, already eight years a representative in Congress, a man of courage, energy, and principle, devoted to the Republican party, constant in attendance upon the sessions of the House, expert in its rules, its most watchful and most careful member, an economist by nature, a foe to every form of corruption. Owen Lovejoy, though a native of Maine, springing from Puritan ancestry, and educated to the Christian ministry in the faith taught by Calvin, had the fiery eloquence of a French Revolutionist. Not even the exasperating wit of Thaddeus Stevens, or the studied taunts of John Quincy Adams, ever threw the Southern men into such rage as the speeches of Lovejoy. He was recklessly bold. His brother had been killed by a mob for preaching the doctrine of the Abolitionists, and he seemed almost to court the same fate. He was daring enough to say to the Southern Democrats, at a time of great excitement in the House, in a speech delivered long before the war, that the negroes were destined to walk to emancipation, as the children of Israel had journeyed to the promised land, "through the *Red Sea*." Among the Democrats the most conspicuous was William A. Richardson, who had been a devoted adherent of Douglas, and had co-operated with him in the repeal of the Missouri Compromise. A younger adherent of Douglas was John A. Logan, serving in his second term. He remained however but a short time in the Thirty-seventh Congress. His ardent patriotism and ambitious temperament carried him into the war, where his brilliant career is known and read of all men.

The most distinguished accession to the House was John J. Crittenden of Kentucky. He had never before served in that branch, but he had been chosen to the Senate six times by the Legislature of his State, — for five full terms and for the remainder of Mr. Clay's term when he retired in 1842. Only one other man, William R. King of Alabama, has ever been so many times elected to the Senate. Mr. Crittenden, like Mr. Clay, entered the Senate at thirty years of age. His service began the day that Madison left the Presidency, and ended the day of Lincoln's inauguration. But in this long period he had served only two full terms, and his total service in the Senate was little more than twenty years. He resigned in 1819 "to get bread for his family," as he expressed it; the compensation of a senator for the session of Congress not averaging at that time more than nine hundred dollars per annum. He resigned in 1841 to become Attorney-General in the Cabinet of Harrison. He resigned in 1848 to run for Governor of Kentucky in aid of General Taylor's candidacy, and he left the governorship in 1850, after the death of Taylor, to accept his old position in the Cabinet. He was appointed to the Supreme Bench by John Quincy Adams in the last year of his administration; but the Senate, already under the influence of the Jackson men, refused to confirm him. Mr. Clay wrote to Mr. Crittenden in anticipation of his failure, bidding him "cultivate calmness of mind and prepare for the worst event."

Mr. Crittenden's ability was of a high order. He stood at the head of that class of statesmen who were next to the highest grade. Like so many other eminent Whigs, he was excluded from the full recognition of his power by the overshadowing prestige of Mr. Clay and Mr. Webster. The appearance of Mr. Crittenden in the House in his seventy-fourth year was his patriotic response to the roll-call of duty. He loved his country and his whole country, and every effort of his waning strength was put forth in behalf of the Union. It was his influence, more than that of any other man, which saved his State from the vortex of Rebellion. But for his strong hold upon the sympathy and pride of Kentucky, the malign influence of

Breckinridge might have forced the State into the Confederacy. Mr. Lincoln considered Mr. Crittenden's course entitled to the admiration and gratitude of every man who was loyal to the Union.

Another Kentuckian gave noble aid to the National cause. Charles A. Wickliffe was a contemporary of Mr. Crittenden, and had for many years belonged to the same party. In the Whig dissensions which followed the accession of Mr. Tyler to the Presidency, Mr. Wickliffe supported the Administration. As an effective blow to Mr. Clay, the President called Mr. Wickliffe to his Cabinet. He served as Postmaster-General through Mr. Tyler's term, and with his chief went over to the Democratic party, supporting Mr. Polk in 1844. There was much anger over his course, on the part of the Kentucky Whigs, resulting in personal estrangements. He was a man of ability, of commanding appearance, of high character. His return to Congress, where he had originally entered nearly forty years before, brought a valuable support to the cause of the Union.

Associated with Crittenden and Wickliffe were three men of mark. Robert Mallory, William H. Wadsworth, and James S. Jackson were younger but not less devoted friends of the Union. Their example was especially valuable in holding thousands of young Kentuckians from following Breckinridge into the Confederate army. Jackson gave his life to his country on one of the battle-fields of the war.

— Missouri sent Francis P. Blair, Jr., and James S. Rollins, who had already been in the smoke and fire of civil conflict, and whose loyalty to the Union, under every form of peril, entitled them to the respect and confidence of patriotic men.

— Massachusetts sent Benjamin F. Thomas of rare eloquence; Alexander H. Rice, afterwards the governor of his State; Thomas D. Elliott, John B. Alley, the venerable William Appleton; and Henry L. Dawes, whose long service attests his character, his ability, and the confidence of his constituents.

— From New Hampshire came Gilman Marston, who soon after gained credit in the field; from Vermont, Justin S. Morrill, one of the most useful, industrious, and honorable members of the House; from Maine, its distinguished ex-governor, Anson P. Morrill; and Frederick A. Pike, of strong mind, keen and incisive in debate, but lacking the ambition necessary to give him his proper rank in the House. Samuel C. Fessenden and Thomas A. D. Fessenden, brothers of the distinguished senator, were members of this House,

— the only instance in which three brothers were ever in Congress at the same time from the same State.   Three Washburns had served in the preceding Congress, but they represented three States.

— The far North-West was well represented by young men.   William Windom came from Minnesota, and from Iowa James F. Wilson, a man of positive strength, destined to take very prominent part in legislative proceedings.   Fernando C. Beaman came from Michigan, and John F. Potter and A. Scott Sloan from Wisconsin.   Martin F. Conway came from the youngest State of the Union, fresh from the contests which had made Kansas almost a field of war.

The organization of the House was so promptly effected that the President's message was received on the same day.   Throughout the country there was an eagerness to hear Mr. Lincoln's views on the painful situation.   The people had read with deep sympathy the tender plea to the South contained in his Inaugural address.   The next occasion on which they had heard from him officially was his proclamation for troops after the fall of Sumter.   Public opinion in the North would undoubtedly be much influenced by what the President should now say.   Mr. Lincoln was keenly alive to the importance of his message, and he weighed every word he wrote.   He maintained, as he always did, calmness of tone, moderation in expression.   He appealed to reason, not to prejudice.   He spoke as one who knew that he would be judged by the public opinion of the world.   It was his fortune to put his name to many state papers of extraordinary weight, but never to one of graver import than his first message to Congress.

The President informed Congress that he would not call their attention "to any ordinary subject of legislation."   In fact there were but two things for Congress to do in the national exigency — provide for the enlistment of an army, and for the raising of money necessary to the conduct of a great war.   The President vividly narrated the progressive steps in the South which had brought about the existing status of affairs.   He depicted in strong colors the condition in which he found the government when he assumed office; how "the forts, arsenals, dock-yards, and custom-houses" of the National Government had been seized; how "the accumulations of national revenue" had been appropriated; how "a disproportionate share of Federal muskets and rifles" had found their way into the Southern States, and had been seized to be used against the government; how the navy had been "scattered in distant seas, leaving but a small part of it within immediate reach of the government;" how seven States had seceded from the Union, and formed "a separate government, which is already invoking recognition, aid, and intervention from foreign powers." With this critical situation he was compelled to deal at once, and the policy which he had chosen when he entered upon his office looked to the exhaustion of all peaceful measures before a resort to stronger ones.

In pursuing this policy of peace, the President had "sought only to hold the public places and property not already wrested from the government, and to collect the revenue — relying for the rest on time, discussion, and the ballot-box." He had even gone so far as "to promise a continuance of the mails at government expense to the very people who were resisting the government;" and he had given "repeated pledges" that every thing should be "forborne without which it was believed possible to keep the government on foot;" that there should be no "disturbances to any of the people, or to any of their rights." He had gone in the direction of conciliation as far as it was possible to go without consenting to a disruption of the government.

The President gave in detail the events which led to the assault on Sumter. He declared that the reduction of the fort "was in no sense a matter of self-defense on the part of the assailants." They well knew "that the garrison in the fort could by no possibility commit an aggression upon them;" they were expressly notified that "the giving of bread to the few brave and hungry men of the garrison was all which would be attempted, unless themselves, by resisting so much, should provoke more." They knew that the National Government desired to keep the garrison in the fort, "not to assail them, but merely to maintain visible possession, and thus to preserve the Union from actual and immediate dissolution." The Confederate Government had "assailed and reduced the fort for precisely the reverse object — to drive out the visible authority of the Federal Union, and thus force it to immediate dissolution."

"In this act," said Mr. Lincoln, "discarding all else, they have forced upon the country the distinct issue — immediate dissolution or blood; and this issue embraces more than the fate of these United States. It presents to the whole family of man the question, whether a Constitutional Republic, a government of the people by the same people, can or cannot maintain its territorial integrity against its own domestic foes." The President presented this point with elaboration. The question really involved, was "whether discontented individuals, too few in number to control the administration according to the organic law, can always, upon the pretenses made in this case, or any other pretenses, or arbitrarily without pretenses, break up the government, and thus practically put an end to free government upon the earth. It forces us to ask, *Is there in all Republics this inherent and fatal weakness?* Must a government of necessity be too strong for the liberties of its own people, or too weak to maintain its own existence?"

The President was severe upon Virginia and Virginians. He had made earnest effort to save the State from joining the Rebellion. He had held conferences with her leading men, and had gone so far on the 13th of April as to address a communication, for public use in Virginia, to the State convention then in session at Richmond, in answer to a resolution of the convention asking him to define the policy he intended to pursue in regard to the Confederate States. In this he re-asserted the position assumed in his Inaugural, and added that "if, as now appears to be true, an unprovoked assault has been made on Fort Sumter, I shall hold myself at liberty to repossess it if I can, and the like places which had been seized before the government was devolved upon me. I shall, to the best of my ability, repel force by force." This letter was used to inflame public sentiment in Virginia, and to hurl the State into Secession through the agency of a Convention elected to maintain the Union. Mr. Lincoln afterwards believed that the letter had been obtained from him under disingenuous pretenses and for the express purpose of using it, as it was used, against the Union and in favor of the Confederacy.

The President's resentment towards those who had thus, as he thought, broken faith with him is visible in his message. Referring to the Virginia convention, he observed that, "the people had chosen a large majority of professed Union men" as delegates. "After the fall of Sumter, many members of that majority went over to the original Disunion minority, and with them adopted an ordinance withdrawing the State from the Union." In his own peculiar style, Mr. Lincoln made the stinging comment, "Whether this change was wrought by their great approval of the assault upon Sumter, or by their great resentment at the government's resistance to that assault, is not definitely known." Though the Virginia convention had submitted the ordinance of Secession to a vote of the people, to be taken on a day nearly a month in the future, the President informed Congress that "they immediately commenced acting as if the State was already out of the Union." They seized the arsenal at Harper's Ferry, and the navy-yard at Norfolk, and "received, perhaps invited, large bodies of troops from the so-called seceding States." They "sent members to their Congress at Montgomery, and finally permitted the insurrectionary government to be transferred to their Capitol at Richmond." Mr. Lincoln concluded with an ominous sentence which might well have inspired Virginians with a sense of impending peril; "The people of Virginia have thus allowed this giant insurrection to make its nest within her borders, and this government has no choice left but to deal with it where it finds it." In that moment of passion these words, with all their terrible significance, were heard by Southern men only to be jeered at.

When the President came to specific recommendations he was brief and pointed. He asked that Congress would place "at the control of the government at least four hundred thousand men, and four hundred millions of money." He said this number was about one-tenth of those of proper age within the regions where all were apparently willing to engage, and the sum was "less than a twenty-third part of the money value owned by men who seem ready to devote the whole." He argued that "a debt of six hundred millions of dollars is now a less sum per head than the debt of the Revolution when we came out of that struggle, and the money value in the country bears even a greater proportion to what it was then than does the population." "Surely," he added, "each man has as strong a motive now to *preserve* our liberties as each had then to *establish* them."

After arguing at length as to the utter fallacy of the right of Secession, and showing how the public "mind of the South had been drugged and insidiously debauched with the doctrine for thirty years," the President closed his message "with the deepest regret that he found the duty of employing the war power of the government forced upon him;" but he "must perform this duty, or surrender the existence of the government." Compromise had been urged upon the President from every quarter. He answered all such requests frankly: "No compromise by public servants could in this case be a cure; not that compromises are not often proper, but that no popular government can long survive a marked precedent that those who carry an election can only save the government from immediate destruction by giving up the main point upon which the people gave the election. The people themselves, and not their servants, can safely reverse their own deliberate decisions."

Mr. Lincoln thus saw his duty clearly and met it boldly. In his own person was centred, as he profoundly realized, the fate of Republican government. He had been elected President of the United States in strict accordance with all the requirements of the Constitution. He had been chosen without bribe, without violence, without undue pressure, by a majority of the electoral votes. If there had been outrage upon the freedom of the ballot it was not among his supporters; if there had been a terror of public opinion, overawing the right of private judgment, it was not in the States which had voted for him, but in those Southern communities where, by threats of violence, the opportunity to cast a ballot was denied to electors favorable to his cause. If he should now yield, the evil results would be immeasurable and irremediable. "As a private citizen," he said, "the Executive could not have consented that Republican institutions shall perish; much less could he in betrayal of so vast and so sacred a trust as these free people have confided to him." He avowed that, in full view of his great responsibility, he had so far done what he had deemed his duty. His words seem almost to foreshadow the great tragedy of after years when declaring that *he felt he had no moral right to shrink, or even to count the chances of his own life in what might follow.* In conclusion he said to Congress, "having thus chosen our own course without guile, and with pure purpose, let us renew our trust in God, and go forward without fear, and with manly hearts."

The effect of this message upon the public opinion of the North was very great. If there had been hesitation by any party or any class upon the subsidence of the first glow of patriotism which had animated the country after the assault on Sumter, Mr. Lincoln's words arrested it, and restored enthusiasm and ardor to all hearts. Indeed, men of thought and discretion everywhere saw that the course of the President was fixed, and even if they differed from his conclusions, they were persuaded that safety could be secured only by following his counsels, and upholding his measures. Mr. Lincoln had been throughout his life much given to reading, to argument, to induction, to speculation, to reflection. He was now before the world as a man of whom decision and action were required, with the lives and fortunes of unborn millions depending upon his wisdom, with the fate of Republican liberty and Constitutional government at stake upon his success. The history of the world shows no example of a man upon whom extraordinary public duties and perilous responsibilities were so suddenly thrust. No antecedent training had apparently fitted him for his work; no experience in affairs had given assurance that he could master a situation which demanded an unprecedented expenditure of treasure, which involved the control of armies larger than the fabled host of Xerxes, which developed questions of state-craft more delicate and more difficult than those which had baffled the best minds in Europe.

Under the inspiration of the message, and in strict accordance with its recommendations, Congress proceeded to its work. No legislation was attempted, none was even seriously suggested, except measures relating to the war. In no other session of Congress was so much accomplished in so brief a time. Convening on the fourth day of July, both Houses adjourned finally on the 6th of August. There were in all but twenty-nine working-days, and every moment was faithfully and energetically employed. Seventy-six public Acts were passed. With the exception of four inconsiderable bills, the entire number related to the war, — to the various modes of strengthening the military and naval forces of the Union, to the wisest methods of securing money for the public service, to the effectual building up of the National credit. Many of these bills were long and complex. The military establishment was re-organized, the navy enlarged, the tariff revised, direct taxes were levied, and loan-bills perfected. Two hundred and seven millions of dollars were appropriated for the army, and fifty-six millions for the navy. Some details of these measures are elsewhere presented under appropriate heads. They are referred to here only to illustrate the patriotic spirit which pervaded Congress, and the magnitude of the work accomplished under the pressure of necessity.

Seventeen days after the extra session began, and fifteen days before it closed, the country was startled and profoundly moved by a decisive defeat of the Union army at Bull Run in Virginia. The National troops were commanded by General Irvin McDowell, and the Confederates by General Beauregard. The battle is remarkable for the large number of division and brigade commanders who afterwards became widely known. Serving under General McDowell were General William T. Sherman, General Hunter, General Burnside, General Miles, General Heintzelman, General Fitz-John Porter, and General Howard. Serving under General Beauregard were Stonewall Jackson, General Longstreet, General Ewell, General J. E. B. Stuart. General Joseph E. Johnston re-enforced Beauregard with another army during the fight, and became the ranking-officer on the field. The defeat of the Union army was complete; it was a *rout*, and on the retreat became a panic. When the troops reached the protection of the fortifications around Washington, a thorough demoralization pervaded their ranks. The holiday illusion had been rudely dispelled, and the young men who had enlisted for a summer excursion, suddenly found that they were engaged in a bloody war in which comrades and friends had been slain by their side, and in which they saw nothing before them but privation, peril, loss of health, and possibly loss of life. The North had been taught a lesson. The doubting were at last convinced that the Confederates were equipped for a desperate fight, and intended to make it. If the Union was to be saved, it must be saved by the united loyalty and the unflinching resolution of the people.

The special and immediate danger was an outbreak in the Border slave States. Their people were seriously divided; but the Union men, aided by the entire moral influence and in no small degree by the military force of the Nation, had thus far triumphed. The repulse of the National arms, with the consequent loss of prestige, necessarily emboldened the enemies of the Union, who, by playing upon the prejudices and fears of the slave-holders, might succeed in seducing them from their allegiance. To prevent the success of such appeals Mr. Crittenden, whose wise counsels were devoted with sleepless patriotism to the preservation of loyalty in the Border States, offered in the House a resolution defining the objects of the National struggle. The resolution set forth that "the deplorable civil war has been forced upon the country by the Disunionists of the Southern States now in arms against the Constitutional Government;" that "in this National emergency, Congress, banishing all feelings of mere passion or resentment, will recollect only its duty to the whole country;" that "the war is not waged in any spirit of oppression, or for any purpose of conquest or subjugation, or the overthrowing or interfering with the rights or established institutions of those States, but to defend and maintain the supremacy of the Constitution, and to preserve the Union with all the dignity, equality, and rights of the several States unimpaired;" and that, "as soon as these objects are accomplished, the war ought to cease." The resolution was adopted by the House without debate, and with only two negative votes.

The same resolution was offered in the Senate by Andrew Johnson of Tennessee two days after its adoption in the House. It led to a somewhat acrimonious debate. Mr. Polk of Missouri desired an amendment declaring that the war had been "forced upon the country by the Disunionists of the Southern and Northern States." He was asked by Mr. Collamer of Vermont, whether he had ever "heard of any Northern Disunionists being in revolt against the government." He replied by asserting his belief that there were Disunionists North as well as South. He had "read Fourth of July speeches, in which the country was congratulated that there was now to be a dissolution of the Union." The amendment was rejected, receiving only four votes.

— Mr. Collamer spoke ably for the resolution. He was not however afraid of the word "subjugation." Its literal, classical meaning was, to pass under the yoke, but in the popular acceptation it meant that "all the people of the United States should submit to the Constitution and laws."

— Mr. Harris of New York expressed his approval of the resolution "precisely as it was offered. Every expression in it was apt and appropriate." If slavery should be abolished as a result of the war, he would not "shed a tear over that result; but yet it is not the purpose of the government in prosecuting the war to overthrow slavery."

— Mr. Fessenden of Maine agreed with Mr. Collamer as to the word "subjugation." It expressed the idea clearly, and he was "satisfied with it. The talk about subjugation is mere clap-trap."

— Mr. Doolittle of Wisconsin said the use of the word "subjugation" in the resolution did not imply that it was not "the purpose of the government to compel the Disunionists to submit to the Constitution and the laws."

— Mr. Willey of Virginia said that there was great sensitiveness in his section; that there was a fear among many that the object of the war was subjugation; that "its design was to reduce the Old Dominion to a province, and to make the people (in the language of the senator from Vermont) pass under the yoke."

— Mr. Hale of New Hampshire favored the resolution. He said the most radical abolitionists had "always disclaimed the idea or the power of interfering with slavery in the States."

— Mr. Clark, the colleague of Mr. Hale, would support the resolution, and would oppose any amendment offered to it, not because he liked its phraseology, but because "it was drawn by the senator from Tennessee and suited him and the region from which he came." — Mr. Breckinridge of Kentucky could not vote for the resolution, because he did not "agree with the statement of facts contained in it." He would not go into the antecedents of the unhappy difficulties. He did not consider that "the rupture in the harbor of Charleston, the firing on the *Star of the West*, and the collision at Fort Sumter, justified those proceedings on the part of the President which have made one blaze of war from the Atlantic to the western borders of the Republic." He did not believe that "the President had a right to take that step which produced the war, and to call (under Presidential authority alone) the largest army into the field ever assembled on the American continent, and the largest fleet ever collected in American harbors." He believed that "the responsibility for the war is to be charged, first, to the majority in the two Houses last winter in rejecting amendments to the Constitution; and, secondly, to the President, for calling out an armed force."

— Mr. Sherman of Ohio replied with great spirit to Mr. Breckinridge. He said Ohio and Kentucky stood side by side, and had always been friends; but if the senator who had just spoken, spoke the voice of his State, then he feared that Kentucky and Ohio would soon be enemies. He felt confident however that "the views expressed do not represent the sentiments of Kentucky's patriotic citizens." The senator had charged the President with bringing on the war. On the contrary, no person with the authority of President Lincoln "ever forbore so patiently." The people of the loyal States had "forborne with the Disunionists of the Southern States too much and too long." There was not a line, not a syllable, not a provision, in the Constitution which the people of the loyal States did not religiously obey. "The South has no right to demand any other compromise. The Constitution was the bond of union; and it was the South that sought to change it by amendments, or to subvert it by force. The Disunionists of the Southern States are traitors to their country, and must be, and will be, subdued."

— Mr. Breckinridge, replying to Mr. Sherman, believed that he truly represented the sentiment of Kentucky, and would submit the matter to the people of his State. "If they should decide that the prosperity and peace of the country would be best promoted by an unnatural and horrible fraternal war, and should throw their own energies into the struggle," he would "acquiesce in sadness and tears, but would no longer be the representative of Kentucky in the American Senate." He characterized personal allusions which had been made to himself as ungenerous and unjust, and declared that he had "never uttered a word or cherished a thought that was false to the Constitution and Union."

— Mr. Browning of Illinois, the successor of Stephen A. Douglas in the Senate, closed the debate. He spoke of "the indulgence shown to Mr. Breckinridge," and of his having used it to "assail the President vehemently, almost vindictively, while he had not a single word of condemnation for the atrocious conduct of the rebellious States." Was the senator from Kentucky here to vindicate them, and to hurl unceasing denunciations at the President, "who was never surpassed by any ruler in patriotism, honor, integrity, and devotion to the great cause of human rights"?

The resolution was adopted with only five dissenting votes, — Breckinridge and Powell of Kentucky, Johnson and Polk of Missouri, and Trumbull of Illinois. Mr. Trumbull voted in the negative, because he did not like the form of expression.

The Crittenden Resolution, as it has always been termed, was thus adopted respectively, not jointly, by the two Houses of Congress. Its declarations, contained in the concluding clauses, though made somewhat under the pressure of national adversity, were nevertheless a fair reflection of the popular sentiment throughout the North. The public mind had been absorbed with the one thought of restoring the Union promptly and completely, and had not even contemplated interference with slavery as an instrumentality to that end. Many wise and far-seeing men were convinced from the first that the Rebellion would result in the destruction of slavery, but for various reasons deemed it inexpedient to make a premature declaration of their belief. Indeed, the wisest of them saw that a premature declaration would probably prove a hinderance and not a help to the conclusion they most desired. In the Senate it was noted that Mr. Sumner withheld his vote, as did Thaddeus Stevens and Owen Lovejoy in the House. But almost the entire Republican vote, including such men as Fessenden, Hale, Chandler, and Grimes, sustained the resolution. It was the voice of the Republican party, with no one openly opposing it in either branch of Congress.

It was soon discovered however that if the National Government did not interfere with slavery, slavery would seriously interfere with the National Government. In other words, it was made apparent that the slaves if undisturbed were to be a source of strength to the Rebellion. Mr. Crittenden's resolution had hardly passed the House when it was learned from the participants in the battle of Bull Run that slaves by the thousand had been employed on the Confederate side in the construction of earthworks, in driving teams, in cooking, in the general work of the Quartermaster and Commissary Departments, and in all forms of camp drudgery. To permit this was simply adding four millions to the population from which the Confederates could draw their quotas of men for military service. It was no answer to say that they never intended to put arms in the hands of negroes. Their use in the various forms of work to which they were allotted, and for which they were admirably qualified, released the same number of white men, who could at once be mustered into the ranks. The slaves were therefore an effective addition to the military strength of the Confederacy from the very beginning of the war, and had seriously increased the available force of fighting men at the first engagement between the two armies.

As soon as this fact became well established, Congress proceeded to enact the first law since the organization of the Federal Government by which a slave could acquire his freedom. The "Act to confiscate property used for insurrectionary purposes" was on the calendar of the Senate when the disaster at Bull Run occurred, and had been under consideration the day preceding the battle. As originally framed, it only confiscated "any property used or employed in aiding, abetting, or promoting insurrection, or resistance to the laws." The word "property" would not include slaves, who, in the contemplation of the Federal law, were always "persons." A new section was now added, declaring that "whenever hereafter during the present insurrection against the Government of the United States, any person held to labor or service under the law of any State shall be required or permitted by the person to whom such labor or service is due to take up arms against the United States, or to work in or upon any fort, dock, navy-yard, armory, intrenchment, or in any military or naval service whatever against the Government of the United States, the person to whom such service or labor is due shall forfeit his claim thereto." The law further provided in effect that "whenever any person shall seek to enforce his claim to a slave, it shall be a sufficient answer to such claim, that the slave had been employed in the military or naval service against the United States contrary to the provisions of this Act."

The virtue of this law consisted mainly in the fact that it exhibited a willingness on the part of Congress to strike very hard blows and to trample the institution of slavery under foot whenever or wherever it should be deemed advantageous to the cause of the Union to do so. From that time onward the disposition to assail slavery was rapidly developed, and the grounds on which the assurance contained in the Crittenden Resolution was given, had so changed in consequence of the use of slaves by the Confederate Government that every Republican member of both Senate and House felt himself absolved from any implied pledge therein to the slave-holders of the Border States. Humiliating as was the Bull Run disaster to the National arms, it carried with it many compensating considerations, and taught many useful lessons. The nation had learned that war must be conducted according to strict principles of military science, and cannot be successfully carried on with banners and toasts and stump speeches, or by the mere ardor of patriotism, or by boundless confidence in a just cause. The Government learned that it is lawful to strike at whatever gives strength to the enemy, and that an insurgent against the National authority must, by the law of common sense, be treated as beyond the protection of the National Constitution, both as to himself and his possessions.

Though the Act thus conditionally confiscating slave property was signed by Mr. Lincoln, it did not meet his entire approval. He had no objection to the principle involved, but thought it ill-timed and premature, — more likely to produce harm than good. He believed that it would prove *brutum fulmen* in the rebellious states, and a source of injury to the Union cause in the Border slave states. From the outbreak of hostilities, Mr. Lincoln regarded the position of those states as the key to the situation, and every thing which tended to weaken their loyalty as a blow struck directly and with fearful power against the Union. He could not however veto the bill, because that would be equivalent to declaring that the Confederate army might have the full benefit of the slave population as a military force. What he desired was that Congress should wait on his recommendations in regard to the question of Slavery. He felt assured that he could see the whole field more clearly; that, above all, he knew the time and the method for that form of intervention which would smite the States in rebellion and not alienate the slave States which still adhered to the Union.

The rapidity with which business was dispatched at this session gave little opportunity for any form of debate except that which was absolutely necessary in the explanation of measures. Active interest in the House centred around the obstructive and disloyal course of Mr. Vallandigham of Ohio and Mr. Burnett of Kentucky. Still greater interest attached to the course of Mr. Breckinridge in the Senate. He had returned to Washington under a cloud of suspicion. He was thoroughly distrusted by the Union men of Kentucky, who had in the popular election won a noble victory over the foes of the National Government, of whom Mr. Breckinridge had been reckoned chief. No overt act of treason could be charged against him, but the prevalent belief was that his sympathies were wholly with the government at Richmond. He opposed every act designed to strengthen the Union, and continually found fault with the attitude and with the intentions of the National Government. He was considered by many to be in Washington only that he might the more efficiently aid the cause of the Confederacy. During the consideration of " a bill to suppress insurrection and sedition," a debate arose between Mr. Breckinridge and Mr. Baker, the new senator from Oregon, which fixed the attention of the country upon the former, and subjected him to general condemnation in the Loyal States.

The Oregon senator, with his ardent nature, and his impulse to take part in every conflict, had raised a regiment of volunteers principally composed of men from the Pacific coast. It was known as the California Regiment, and was encamped near Washington. On the 1st of August, while performing the double and somewhat anomalous duty of commanding his regiment and representing Oregon in the Senate, Mr. Baker entered the chamber in the full uniform of a Colonel of the United-States army. He laid his sword upon his desk and sat for some time listening to the debate. He was evidently impressed by the scene of which he was himself a conspicuous feature. Breckinridge took the floor shortly after Baker appeared, and made a speech, of which it is fair criticism to say that it reflected in all respects the views held by the members of the Confederate Congress then in session at Richmond. Colonel Baker evidently grew restive under the words of Mr. Breckinridge. His face was aglow with excitement, and he sprang to the floor when the senator from Kentucky took his seat. His reply, abounding in denunciation and invective, was not lacking in the more solid and convincing argument. He rapidly reviewed the situation, depicted the character of the Rebellion, described the position of Breckinridge, and passionately asked "What would have been thought, if, in another Capitol, in a yet more martial age, a senator, with the Roman purple flowing from his shoulders, had risen in his place, surrounded by all the illustrations of Roman glory, and declared that advancing Hannibal was just, and that Carthage should be dealt with on terms of peace? What would have been thought, if, after the battle of Cannæ, a senator had denounced every levy of the Roman people, every expenditure of its treasure, every appeal to the old recollections and the old glories?"

Mr. Fessenden, who sat near Baker, responded in an undertone "He would have been hurled from the Tarpeian Rock." Baker, with his aptness and readiness, turned the interruption to still further indictment of Breckinridge: "Are not the speeches of the senator from Kentucky," he asked, "intended for disorganization? are they not intended to destroy our zeal? are they not intended to animate our enemies? Sir, are they not words of brilliant, polished *treason*, even in the very Capitol of the Republic?"

It is impossible to realize the effect of the words so eloquently pronounced by the Oregon senator. In the history of the Senate, no more thrilling speech was ever delivered. The striking appearance of the speaker in the uniform of a soldier, his superb voice, his graceful manner, all united to give to the occasion an extraordinary interest and attraction.

The reply of Mr. Breckinridge was tame and ineffective. He did not repel the fierce characterizations with which Colonel Baker had overwhelmed him. He did not stop to resent them, though he was a man of unquestioned courage. One incident of his speech was grotesquely amusing. He was under the impression that the suggestion in regard to the Tarpeian Rock had been made by Mr. Sumner, and he proceeded to denounce the senator from Massachusetts with bitter indignation. Mr. Sumner looked surprised, but having become accustomed · to abuse from the South, said nothing. When next day it was shown by the *Globe* that Mr. Fessenden was the offender, Mr. Breckinridge neither apologized to Mr. Sumner, nor attacked the senator from Maine. The first was manifestly his duty. From the second he excused himself for obvious reasons. After his experience with Baker, Breckinridge evidently did not court a conflict with Fessenden.

The course of Mr. Breckinridge was in direct hostility to the prevailing opinion of his State. The Legislature of Kentucky passed a resolution asking that he and his colleague, Lazarus W. Powell, should resign their seats, and, in the event of refusal, that the Senate would investigate their conduct, and, if it were found to be disloyal, expel them. Mr. Breckinridge did not wait for such an investigation. In the autumn of 1861 he joined the Rebellion, and was welcomed by the leaders and the people of the Confederacy with extravagant enthusiasm. His espousal of their cause was considered by them to be as great an acquisition as if a fresh army corps had been mustered into their service. His act called forth the most bitter denunciations throughout the North, and among the loyal people of Kentucky. He had not the excuse pleaded by so many men of the South, that he must abide by the fortunes of his State, and the worst interpretation was placed upon his presence at the July session of Congress.

Among the earliest acts at the next session was the expulsion of Mr. Breckinridge from the Senate. It was done in a manner which marked the full strength of the popular disapprobation of his course. The senators from the rebellious States had all been expelled at the July session, but without the application of an opprobrious epithet. There had also been a debate as to whether expulsion of the persons, or a mere declaration that the seats were vacant, were the proper course to be pursued by the Senate. Andrew Johnson maintained the latter, and all the Democratic senators, except McDougall of California, voted with him. But in the case of Mr. Breckinridge there was not a negative vote — his own colleague Powell remaining silent in his seat while five Democratic senators joined in the vote for his expulsion. The resolution, draughted by Mr. Trumbull, was made as offensive as possible, curtly declaring that "John C. Breckinridge, the traitor, be and is hereby expelled from the Senate."

The mutation of public opinion is striking. Mr. Breckinridge lived to become a popular idol in Kentucky. Long before his death (which occurred in 1875 in his fifty-fourth year) he could have had any position in the gift of his State. If his political disabilities could have been removed, he would undoubtedly have returned to the Senate. His support did not come solely from those who had sympathized with the South, but included thousands who had been loyally devoted to the Union. He possessed a strange, fascinating power over the people of Kentucky, — as great as that which had been wielded by Mr. Clay, though he was far below Mr. Clay in intellectual endowment. No man gave up more than he when he united his fortunes with the seceding States. If he had remained loyal, no prize would have been beyond his grasp. It was his sense of personal fidelity to the Southern men who had been faithful to him, that blinded him to the higher obligation of fidelity to country, and to the higher appreciation of self-interest which is inseparably bound up with duty. He wrecked a great career. He embittered and shortened a life originally devoted to noble aims, and in its darkest shadows filled with generous impulses.

The original aim of Kentucky to preserve a position of neutrality in the impending contest was found to be impracticable. The Confederates were the first to violate it, by occupying that section of the State bordering on the Mississippi River with a considerable force under the command of General Polk, the Episcopal Bishop of Louisiana. This was on the 4th of September. Two days later the Colonel of the Twenty-first Illinois Volunteers, who was in command at Cairo, took possession of Paducah. It was the first important step in a military career which fills the most brilliant pages in the military annals of our country. The name of the Illinois Colonel was Ulysses S. Grant.

The Confederate victory at Bull Run produced great effect throughout the South. The fall of Sumter had been a signal encouragement to those who had joined the revolt against the Union, but as no blood had been spilled, and as the garrison had been starved out rather than shelled out, there was a limit to enthusiasm over the result. But now a pitched battle had been fought within cannon sound of the National Capital, and the forces of the Union had been put to flight. Jefferson Davis had come from Richmond during the battle, and telegraphed to the Confederate Congress that the night had "closed upon a hard-fought field," but that the enemy were routed, and had "precipitately fled, abandoning a large amount of arms, knapsacks, and baggage;" that "too high praise cannot be bestowed upon the skill of the Confederate officers or the gallantry of all their troops;" that "the Confederate force was fifteen thousand, and the Union army was thirty-five thousand." He evidently knew the effect which these figures would have upon the pride of the South, and he did not at the moment stop to verify his statements. The actual force under McDowell was much less, that under Beauregard much greater, than Mr. Davis stated. McDowell was certainly outnumbered after General Johnston's army arrived on the field. If General Patterson, who was in command in the Shenandoah Valley, had been able to engage or detain Johnston, the fate of the day might have been different. But Johnston outgeneraled Patterson, and achieved what military genius always does, — he had his force in the right place at the right time.

The effect of the Rebel victory at Bull Run was at once visible in the rigorous policy adopted by the Confederate Government. The people of the Confederacy knew that their numbers were less than those of the Union, but Jefferson Davis had in effect told them that fifteen Southern men might be relied upon to put to flight thirty-five Northern men, and on this ratio they felt equal to the contest. The Congress at Richmond went to every extreme in their legislation. A fortnight after the battle they passed " an Act respecting alien enemies," " warning and requiring every male citizen of the United States, fourteen years old and upwards, to depart from the Confederate States within forty days from the date of the President's Proclamation," which was issued on the 14th of August. Those only could remain who intended to become citizens of the Confederacy. With the obvious design of avoiding every thing which could chill the sympathy with the Confederacy so largely prevailing in the Border States, the Proclamation excepted from its operation the States of Delaware, Maryland, Kentucky, Missouri, the District of Columbia, the Territories of New Mexico, Arizona, and the Indian Territory. This was a manifest declaration of what they expected to include in the Confederacy when the National Government should finally surrender. Wherever a slave was held, the Confederate leaders adjudged the people to be their friends and their future allies.

This warning to alien enemies could not however be regarded as a measure of special harshness, or one beyond the fair exercise of the war power. But the next step was of a different nature. A law was enacted sequestrating " the estates, property, and effects of alien enemies." Mr. Judah P. Benjamin, who was at the time Attorney-General of the Confederate Government, proceeded to enforce the Act with the utmost rigidity. The exception of Border States and Territories, already noted, was also made under this law, but towards the citizens of States of unquestioned loyalty no mercy was shown. A close search was instituted by Mr. Benjamin, in which agents, former partners, attorneys, trustees, and all who might have the slightest knowledge of a piece of property within the limits of the Confederacy, belonging to a loyal citizen of the United States, were compelled to give information under penalty of a fine which might be as high as five thousand dollars, and imprisonment which might last for six months. They were forced to tell of any lands, chattels, rights, interests, an alien enemy might have, and also of any debts which might be due to an alien enemy. Mr. Benjamin's letter of instruction included among alien enemies all "subjects of Great Britain, France, or other neutral nations, who have a domicile or are carrying on business or traffic within the States at war with the Confederacy." It was a scheme of wholesale, cruel confiscation of the property of innocent persons, and the most ingenious lawyer of the Confederacy was selected to enforce it by inquisitorial processes which disregarded the confidence of friendship, the ties of blood, and the loyalty of affection.

The National legislation had given no precedent or warrant for proceedings so harsh. At the extra session there had been no attempt at the confiscation of any property except that directly used in aid of the insurrection. Slaves were added to this class only after it was learned that they were thus employed by the Confederates. Not only therefore did the Confederacy introduce slaves as a component element of the military force, but it resorted to confiscation of a cruel and rigorous type as one of the sources of financial strength. If the Confederate authorities had not thus set the example, it would have been difficult, perhaps impracticable, to induce Congress to entertain such a line of policy. Many were in favor of it from the first, but so many were against it that its adoption could have been secured only with discord and harm to the loyal cause. A fair judgment of the case must decide that the precedent thus established by the Confederacy was not only an irresistible temptation but a justifying cause for lines of National policy which were afterwards complained of as unusual and oppressive.

CHAPTER XVI.

THE first session of the Thirty-seventh Congress came to an end amid the deep gloom caused by the disastrous defeat at Bull Run. The second session opened in December, 1861, under the shadow of a grave disaster at Ball's Bluff, in which the eloquent senator from Oregon, Edward D. Baker, lost his life. Despite these reverses the patriotic spirit of the country had constantly risen, and had increased the Union forces until the army was six hundred thousand strong. Winfield Scott had gone upon the retired list at the ripe age of seventy-five, and George B. McClellan had succeeded him in command of the army. The military achievements thus far had been scarcely more than defensive. The National Capital had been fortified; Maryland, West Virginia, Kentucky, and Missouri had been wrenched from rebel domination; while on our Southern coast two landings had been effected by the Union troops, — the first at Hatteras in North Carolina, the second at Port Royal in South

Carolina. There was serious danger of a division of popular sentiment in the North growing out of the Slavery question; there was
grave apprehension of foreign intervention from the arrest of Mason
and Slidell. The war was in its eighth month; and, strong and
energetic as the Northern people felt, it cannot be denied that a
confidence in ultimate triumph had become dangerously developed
throughout the South.

The message of Mr. Lincoln dealt with the situation in perfect
candor. He did not attempt to withhold any thing or to color any
thing. He frankly acknowledged that "our intercourse with foreign
nations has been attended with profound solicitude." He recognized
that "a nation which endures factious domestic division is exposed
to disrespect abroad; and one party, if not both, is sure, sooner or
later, to invoke foreign intervention." With his peculiar power of
condensing a severe expression, he said that "the disloyal citizens
of the United States have offered the ruin of our country in return
for the aid and comfort which they have invoked abroad." This offer
was made on the presumption that some commercial or substantial
gain would accrue to other nations from the destruction of the
Republic; but Mr. Lincoln believed with confidence that "foreign
governments would not in the end fail to perceive that one strong
nation promises more durable peace, and a more extensive, valuable,
and reliable commerce, than can the same nation broken into hostile
fragments," and for this reason he believed that the rebel leaders had
received from abroad "less patronage and encouragement than they
probably expected."

The President dwelt with satisfaction upon the condition of the
Border States, concerning whose course he had constantly exhibited
the profoundest solicitude. He now informed Congress that "noble
little Delaware led off right, from the first," and that Maryland,
which had been "made to seem against the Union," had given
"seven regiments to the loyal cause, and none to the enemy, and
her people, at a regular election, have sustained the Union by a
larger majority and a larger aggregate vote than they ever before
gave to any candidate on any question." Kentucky, concerning
which his anxiety had been deepest, was now decidedly, and, as he
thought, "unchangeably, ranged on the side of the Union." Missouri he announced as comparatively quiet, and he did not believe
she could be again overrun by the insurrectionists. These Border
slave States, none of which "would promise a single soldier at first,

have now an aggregate of not less than forty thousand in the field for the Union; while of their citizens certainly not more than a third of that number, and they of doubtful whereabouts and doubtful existence, are in arms against it." Beyond these results the President had some "general accounts of popular movements in behalf of the Union in North Carolina and Tennessee," and he expressed his belief that "the cause of the Union is advancing steadily and certainly Southward."

The one marked change in the popular opinion of the free States, now reflected in Congress, was in respect to the mode of dealing with Slavery. Mr. Lincoln was conservative, and always desired to keep somewhat in the rear rather than too far in advance of the public judgment. In his message he avoided all direct expression upon the Slavery question, but with the peculiar shrewdness which characterized his political discussions he announced a series of general truths respecting labor and capital which, in effect, were deadly hostile to the institution. He directed attention to the fact that "the insurrection is largely if not exclusively a war upon the first principle of popular government — the rights of the people." Conclusive evidence of this appeared in "the maturely considered public documents as well as in the general tone of the insurgents." He discerned a disposition to abridge the right of suffrage and to deny to the people the "right to participate in the selection of public officers except those of the Legislature." He found indeed that "monarchy itself is sometimes hinted at as a possible refuge from the power of the people." While he did not think it fitting to make "a general argument in favor of popular institutions," he felt that he should scarcely be justified were he "to omit raising a warning voice against this approach of returning despotism." It was, he said, "the effort to place capital on an equal footing with, if not above, labor in the structure of government," and it assumed "that labor is available only in connection with capital; that nobody labors unless somebody else, owning capital, somehow by the use of it induces him to labor."

Mr. Lincoln found that the next step in this line of argument raised the question, "whether it is best that capital shall hire laborers, and thus induce them to work by their own consent, or buy them, and drive them to it without their consent?" thus leading to the conclusion that "all laborers are either hired laborers or what we call slaves," and that "whoever is once a hired laborer is fixed in that condition for life." From all these theories Mr. Lincoln radically dissented, and maintained that "labor is the superior of capital, and deserves much the higher consideration." "No men living," said he, "are more worthy to be trusted than those who toil up from poverty — none less inclined to take or touch aught which they have not honestly earned. Let them beware of surrendering a political power which they already possess, and which, if surrendered, will surely be used to close the door of advancement, and to fix new disabilities and burdens upon them till all of liberty shall be lost." If Mr. Lincoln had directly attempted at that early stage of the contest to persuade the laboring men of the North that it was best for them to aid in abolishing Slavery, he would have seriously abridged the popularity of his administration. He pursued the wiser course of showing that the spirit of the Southern insurrection was hostile to all free labor, and that in its triumph not merely the independence of the laborer but his right of self-defense, as conferred by suffrage, would be imperiled if not destroyed. Until the discussion reached the higher plane on which Mr. Lincoln placed it, the free laborer in the North was disposed to regard a general emancipation of the slaves as tending to reduce his own wages, and as subjecting him to the disadvantage of an odious contest for precedence of race. The masses in the North had united with the Republican party in excluding Slavery from the Territories because the larger the area in which free labor was demanded the better and more certain was the remuneration. But against a general emancipation Mr. Lincoln was quick to see that white laborers might be readily prejudiced by superficial reasoning, and hence he adduced the broader argument which appealed at once to their humanity, to their sense of manly independence, and to their instinct of self-preservation against the mastery and the oppression of capital.

The agitation of the Slavery question, while unavoidable, was nevertheless attended with serious embarrassments to the Union cause. The great outburst of patriotism which followed the fall of Sumter contemplated a rally of the entire North for the defense of the Flag and the preservation of the Union. Neither political party was to take advantage of the situation, but all alike were to share in the responsibility and in the credit of maintaining the government inviolate. Every month however had demonstrated more and more that to preserve the government without interfering with Slavery would be impossible; and as this fact became clearly evident to the

Republican vision, a large section of the Democratic party obdurately refused to acknowledge it or to consent to the measures which it suggested. It was apparent therefore within the first six months of the struggle that a division would come in the North, which would be of incalculable advantage to the insurrectionists, and that if the division should go far enough it would insure victory to the Confederate cause. If the Democratic party as a whole had in the autumn of the year 1861 taken the ground which a considerable section of it assumed, it would have been impossible to conduct the war for the Union successfully. Great credit therefore was due and was cordially given to the large element in that party which was ready to brave all the opprobrium of their fellow-partisans and to accept the full responsibility of co-operating with the Republicans in war measures.

Congress had hardly come together when the change of opinion and action upon the Slavery question became apparent. Mr. Holman of Indiana, reciting the Crittenden resolution which had been passed the preceding session with only two adverse votes, offered a resolution that its principles "be solemnly re-affirmed by this House." Objection was made by several members. Mr. Thaddeus Stevens moved to lay the resolution on the table, and the motion prevailed on a yea and nay vote by 71 to 65. The majority were all Republicans. The minority was principally made up of Democrats, but Republicans as conspicuous as Mr. Dawes of Massachusetts and Mr. Shellabarger of Ohio voted in the negative. The wide divergence between this action on the part of the Republicans on the third day of December, 1861, and that which they had taken on the preceding 22d of July, was recognized and appreciated by the country, and thus began the open division on the Slavery question which continually widened, which consolidated the Republican party in support of the most radical measures, and which steadily tended to weaken the Democratic party in the loyal States.

At the height of the excitement in Congress over the engagement at Ball's Bluff there was a change in the head of the War Department. The disasters in the field and the general impatience for more decisive movements on the part of our armies led to the resignation of Secretary Cameron. He was in his sixty-third year, and though of unusual vigor for his age, was not adapted by education or habit to the persistent and patient toil, to the wearisome detail of organization, to the oppressive increase of responsibility, necessarily incident to military operations of such vast proportions as were entailed by the progress of the war. He was nominated as Minister to Russia, and on the eleventh day of January, 1862, was succeeded in the War Department by Edwin M. Stanton.

Mr. Stanton signalized his entrance upon duty by extraordinary vigor in war measures, and had the good fortune to gain credit for many successes which were the result of arrangements in progress and nearly perfected under his predecessor. A week after he was sworn in, an important victory was won at Mill Springs, Kentucky, by General George H. Thomas. The Confederate commander, General Zollicoffer, was killed, and a very decisive check was put to a new development of Secession sympathy which was foreshadowed in Kentucky. A few days later, on the 27th of January, under the inspiration of Mr. Stanton, the President issued a somewhat remarkable order commanding "a general movement of the land and naval forces of the United States against the insurgent forces on the 22d of February." He especially directed that the army at and about Fortress Monroe, the Army of the Potomac, the Army of Western Virginia, the army near Munfordsville, Kentucky, the army and flotilla at Cairo, and the naval force in the Gulf of Mexico be ready for a movement on that day. The order did not mean what was stated on its face. It was evidently intended to mislead somebody.

The Illinois colonel who had taken possession of Paducah in the preceding September was now known as Brigadier-General Grant. He had been made prominent by a daring fight at Belmont, Missouri, on the 7th of November (1861) against a largely superior force under the command of the Confederate General Pillow. For the numbers engaged it was one of the most sanguinary conflicts of the war. The quarter-master of the expedition intimated to General Grant that in case of a reverse he had but two small steamers for transportation to the Illinois shore. The General's only reply was that in the event of his defeat "the steamers would hold all that would be left." He was now in command at Cairo, and co-operating with him was a flotilla of hastily constructed gunboats under the command of Flag-officer A. H. Foote of the navy. General Grant evidently interpreted Mr. Lincoln's order to mean that he need not wait until the 22d, and he began his movement on the first day of February.

By the 16th he had captured Fort Henry and Fort Donelson. The flotilla had been more active than the troops, against Fort Henry, which was speedily evacuated, but Fort Donelson did not surrender until after a hard-fought land battle in which the characteristic tenacity, skill, and bravery of General Grant were for the first time fully shown to the country. "The victory achieved," he announced in his congratulatory order to the troops, "is not only great in the effect it will have in breaking down the rebellion, but has secured the greatest number of prisoners of war ever taken in a single battle on this continent." The number of prisoners exceeded ten thousand; forty pieces of cannon and extensive magazines of ordnance with military stores of all kinds were captured. The Confederate commander was General S. B. Buckner, who had joined the rebellion under circumstances which gained him much ill will in the Loyal States. Under a flag of truce he asked General Grant on the morning of the 16th for an armistice to "settle the terms of capitulation." General Grant's answer was, "No terms except unconditional surrender can be accepted. I propose to move immediately on your works." General Buckner felt himself "compelled to accept the ungenerous and unchivalrous terms" which General Grant proposed. It is due to General Buckner to say that he had been left in a humiliating position. The two generals who ranked him, Gideon J. Pillow and John B. Floyd, seeing the inevitable, had escaped from the fort the preceding night with five thousand men, leaving to Buckner the mortification of surrender. In view of this fact the use of the term "unchivalrous" by the Confederate commander can be justly appreciated.

The effect of the victory upon the country was electric. The public joy was unbounded. General Grant had become in a day the hero of the war. His fame was on every tongue. The initials of his name were seized upon by the people for rallying-cries of patriotism, and were woven into songs for the street and for the camp. He was "Unconditional Surrender," he was "United States," he was "Uncle Sam." Not himself only but his State was glorified. It was an Illinois victory. No less than thirty regiments from that State were in General Grant's command, and they had all won great credit. This fact was especially pleasing to Mr. Lincoln. Indiana, Iowa, Missouri, and Kentucky were all gallantly represented on the field, but the prestige of the day belonged to Illinois. Many of her public men, prominent in political life before and since the war, were in command of regiments. The moral force of the victory was increased by the fact that so large a proportion of these prominent officers had been, like General Grant, connected with the Democratic party, — thus adding demonstration to assurance that it was an uprising of a people in defense of their government, and not merely the work of a political party seeking to extirpate slavery. John A. Logan, Richard J. Oglesby, William R. Morrison, and William Pitt Kellogg were among the Illinois officers who shared in the renown of the victory. General Lewis Wallace commanded a division made up of Indiana and Kentucky troops, and was honorably prominent. The total force under General Grant was nearly fifty regiments, furnishing about twenty-eight thousand men for duty. They had captured the strongest Confederate intrenchment in the West, manned by nearly seventeen thousand men. The defeat was a great mortification to Jefferson Davis. He communicated intelligence of the disaster to the Confederate Congress in a curt message in which he described the official reports of the battle as "incomplete and unsatisfactory," and stated that he had relieved Generals Floyd and Pillow from command.

Two important results followed the victory. The strong fortifications erected at Columbus, Kentucky, to control the passage of the Mississippi, were abandoned by the Confederates; and Nashville, the capital of Tennessee, was surrendered to the Union army without resistance. The Confederate force at the latter point was under command of General Albert Sidney Johnston, who, unable to offer battle, sullenly retreated southward. If the Confederate troops had been withdrawn from Fort Donelson in season to effect a junction with Johnston at Nashville, that able general might have delivered battle there on terms possibly advantageous to his side. It was this feature of the case which rendered the loss of Donelson so serious and so exasperating to the Confederate Government, as shown in the message of Jefferson Davis.

Another victory for the Union was gained on the coast of North Carolina under the joint efforts of the army and the navy. General Burnside was in command of the former and Commodore Gouldsborough of the latter. The battle of Roanoke Island was fought the day after the capture of Fort Henry, and the Union victory led to a lodgment of the national forces on the soil of North Carolina, which was held firmly to the end. Events beyond the Mississippi were also favorable to the National Government. General Sterling

Price had been the cause of much trouble in Missouri, where he was personally popular. He had led many young men into rebellion, and his efforts to carry the State into the Confederacy were energetic and unremitting. He had been dominating a large section of Missouri and creating grave apprehensions for its safety. On the 18th of February General Halleck, who had succeeded General Frémont in the command of the Western Department, telegraphed the Secretary of War: "General Curtis has driven Price from Missouri, and is several miles across the Arkansas line, cutting up Price's rear and hourly capturing prisoners and stores. The Army of the South-West is doing its duty nobly. The flag of the Union is floating in Arkansas."

These victories coming almost simultaneously produced a profound impression throughout the Loyal States. Men rushed to the conclusion that the war would be closed and the Union restored before the end of the year. The most sedate communities become mercurial and impressible in time of deep excitement. The rejoicing was universal. Congress ordered the illumination of the Capitol and other public buildings in Washington on the 22d of February "in honor of the recent victories of our army and navy;" and "as a mark of respect to the memory of those who had been killed and in sympathy with those who have been wounded" the House of Representatives on the 19th of February, on the motion of Mr. Washburne of Illinois, adjourned without transacting business. The flags taken in the recent victories were to be publicly exhibited, and a day of general congratulation was to be associated with the memory of Washington and "the triumph of the government which his valor and wisdom had done so much to establish." In the midst of the arrangements for this celebration, the members of the Cabinet jointly communicated to Congress on the 21st of February the intelligence that "the President of the United States is plunged into affliction by the death of a beloved child." Congress immediately ordered that the illumination of the public buildings be omitted, and, "entertaining the deepest sentiments of sympathy and condolence with the President and his family," adjourned. The reading of Washington's Farewell Address on the 22d, before the two Houses, was the only part accomplished of the brilliant celebration that had been designed.

A fortnight later, on the 8th of March (1862), came the remarkable engagement in Hampton Roads between the *Monitor* and the

Merrimac. The former vessel arrived at Fortress Monroe after the *Merrimac* had destroyed the United-States sloop-of-war *Cumberland* and the frigate *Congress*, and had driven the steam-frigate *Minnesota* aground just as darkness put an end to the fight. On Sunday morning, March 9, the *Merrimac* renewed her attack upon the *Minnesota*, and was completely surprised by the appearance of a small vessel which, in the expressive description of the day, resembled a cheese-box on a raft. She had arrived from New York at the close of the first day's fight. From her turret began a furious cannonade which not only diverted the attack from the *Minnesota* but after a ferocious contest of many hours practically destroyed the *Merrimac*, which was compelled to seek the shelter of Confederate batteries at Sewell's Point, and never re-appeared in service. The relief to the North by this victory was incalculable. Not only had the *Merrimac* been stopped in her expected bombardment of Northern cities, but the success of the *Monitor* assured to the government a class of armor-plated vessels that could be of great value in the coast service to which our naval operations were principally confined. Against land batteries they would prove especially formidable. Ericsson who constructed the *Monitor* and Lieutenant Worden who commanded her, divided the honors, and were everywhere recognized as having rendered an invaluable service to the country. The modesty and heroism of Worden secured him an unbounded share of popular admiration and respect.

In the ensuing month of April the navy performed another great service by the capture of New Orleans. The fleet was in command of Captain Farragut, and successfully passed the fortifications which had been erected by the National Government to prevent a foreign foe from entering the Mississippi. New Orleans made no resistance to the approach of the fleet, and General B. F. Butler, in command of the Department of the Gulf, established his headquarters in the city. The importance of this conquest to the Union cause could hardly be estimated. It enabled the government to embarrass the trans-Mississippi States in their support of the rebel army, and thus inflicted a heavy blow upon the fortunes of the Confederacy. New Orleans in the control of the National Government was easy to defend, and it afforded a base for offensive operations in so many directions that no amount of vigilance could anticipate the attacks that might be made by the Union forces.

Viewed in connection with the effective work of Flag-officer

Foote in supporting General Grant in the Henry and Donelson campaign, and of Gouldsborough in supporting Burnside on the coast of North Carolina, these later and greater achievements of the navy served to raise that branch of the service in popular esteem. Besides the intrinsic merit which attached to the victories, they had all the advantage of a genuine surprise to the public. Little had been expected from the navy in a contest where the field of operation seemed so restricted. But now the people saw that the most important post thus far wrenched from the Confederacy had been taken by the navy, and that it was effectively sustaining and strengthening the army at all points. It was no longer regarded as a mere blockading force, but was menacing the coast of the Confederate States, penetrating their rivers, and neutralizing the strength of thousands of Rebel soldiers who were withdrawn from armies in the field to man the fortifications rendered necessary by this unexpected form of attack. These facts made a deep impression on Congress. Since the close of the second war with Great Britain the navy had enjoyed no opportunity for distinction. The war with Mexico was wholly a contest on land, and for a period of forty-five years the navy of the United States had not measured its strength with any foe. Meanwhile however it had made great advance in the education and training of its officers and in the general tone of the service. Under the secretaryship of George Bancroft, the eminent historian, (in the Cabinet of Mr. Polk,) an academy had been established at Annapolis for the scientific training of naval officers. By this enlightened policy, inaugurated if not originally conceived by Mr. Bancroft, naval officers had for the first time been placed on an equal footing with the officers of the army who had long enjoyed the advantages of the well-organized and efficient school at West Point. The academy had borne fruit, and at the outbreak of the war, the navy was filled with young officers carefully trained in the duties of their profession, intelligent in affairs, and with an *esprit de corps* not surpassed in the service of any other country. Their efficiency was supplemented by that of volunteer officers in large numbers who came from the American merchant marine, and who in all the duties of seamanship, in courage, capacity, and patriotism, were the peers of any men that ever trod a deck.

Congress now realized that a re-organization of the naval service was necessary, that the stimulus of promotion should be more liberally used, the pride of rank more generously indulged. An Act was therefore passed on the 16th of July greatly enlarging the scope of the naval organization and advancing the rank of its officers. Farragut had won his magnificent triumph at New Orleans while holding the rank of captain, — the highest then known to our service, — and Worden had achieved his great fame at Hampton Roads with the commission of a lieutenant. David D. Porter, with no higher rank, had been exercising commands which in any European government would have been assigned to an admiral. Perhaps no navy in the world had at that time abler officers than ours, while the rank and emolument, except for the lowest grades, were shamefully inadequate. The old navy had only the grades of passed-midshipman, lieutenant, commander, and captain. The new law gave nine grades, — midshipman, ensign, master, lieutenant, lieutenant-commander, commander, captain, commodore, and rear-admiral. The effect of the increased rank was undoubtedly stimulating to the service and valuable to the government. Two higher grades of vice-admiral and admiral were subsequently added, and were filled by Farragut and Porter to whom in the judgment of the Department special and emphatic honor was due. The navy had conquered its own place in the public regard, and had performed an inestimable service in the contest against the rebellion.

The brilliant success in the early spring, both of the army and navy, was unfortunately not continued in the subsequent months. General Grant, after the fall of Nashville, marched southward to confront the army of General A. S. Johnston, and on the 6th and 7th of April a terrible battle was fought at Pittsburg Landing on the Tennessee River. The battle was originally called by that name in the annals of the Union, but the title of "Shiloh" given to it by the Confederate authorities, is the one more generally recognized in history. In the first day's engagement the Union army narrowly escaped a crushing defeat; but before the renewal of the contest on the following morning General Buell had effected a junction with the forces of General Grant, and the two, united, recovered all the lost ground of the day before and gained a substantial victory for the Union, though at great cost of life. The Union army lost some eighteen hundred men killed and nearly eight thousand wounded. The Confederate loss was not less. There is no doubt that General Grant was largely outnumbered on the first day, but after the junction of Buell he probably outnumbered the Confederates. Sixty thousand was perhaps the maximum of the Union forces on the second day, while the Confederate army, as nearly as can be ascertained, numbered fifty thousand. One great event of the battle was the death of Albert Sidney Johnston, a soldier of marked skill, a man of the highest personal character. Jefferson Davis made his death the occasion of a special message to the Confederate Congress, in which he said that, "without doing injustice to the living, our loss is irreparable." The personal affliction to Mr. Davis was sore. The two had been at West Point together, and had been close friends through life. William Preston Johnston, son of the fallen General, a young man of singular excellence of character and of most attractive personal traits, was at the time private secretary to Mr. Davis. He has since been widely known in the South in connection with its educational progress.

Deep anxiety had preceded the battle throughout the North, and the relief which followed was grateful. It was made the occasion by the President for a proclamation in which the people were asked "to assemble in their places of public worship and especially acknowledge and render thanks to our Heavenly Father for the successes which have attended the Army of the Union." But after the first flush of victory, the battle became the subject of controversy in the newspapers. Criticism of officers was unsparing, the slaughter of our soldiers was exaggerated, crimination and recrimination were indulged in respecting the conduct of troops from certain States. General Grant was accused of having been surprised and of having thereby incurred a danger which narrowly escaped being a defeat. The subject was brought into Congress and warmly debated. Senator Sherman of Ohio introduced a resolution calling for all the reports from the officers in command, and made a speech defending the conduct of the Ohio troops, upon which some reflections had been inconsiderately and most unjustly cast. Mr. Elihu Washburne made an elaborate speech in the House on the 2d of May, in which he gave a full account of the battle, and defended General Grant with much warmth against all possible charges which, either through ignorance or malice, had been preferred against him for his conduct of the battle. This speech, which was of great value to General Grant, both with the Administration and the country, laid the foundation of that intimate friendship which so long subsisted between him and Mr. Washburne. Mr. Richardson of Illinois followed his colleague, and expressed his disgust with even the introduction of the subject in Congress. He felt that our armies would gain more renown and secure greater victories if the "Riot Act" could be read, and both Houses of Congress dispersed to their homes at the very earliest moment.

General Halleck, who had command of the Western Department, became anxious for reputation on the field, and was thought by many to be jealous of the daily increasing fame of General Grant. After the battle of Shiloh he took command in person of the army which Grant had already rendered illustrious, leaving Grant to command its right wing. Uniting the Western forces into one large army General Halleck marched southward in pursuit of the Confederate column now under the command of Beauregard, and strongly intrenched at Corinth. As the army approached, Corinth was evacuated, and the campaign of General Halleck, leading to no important engagement, did not add to his military fame. Meanwhile there had been increasing dissatisfaction in Congress and among the people with the supersedure of General Grant, and to relieve the situation General Halleck was called to Washington in the early part of July to take command of the army which had been relinquished by McClellan in March, when he set forth upon the Peninsular campaign. In the intervening months there had been no General-in-Chief of the army, the duties being performed by the Secretary of War.

The Western victories, important as they were, did not remove the pressure in the East. The popular interest was more largely concentrated in the success of the Army of the Potomac, which would secure the safety of the National Capital, and possibly the possession of the capital of the Confederacy. High hopes had been staked upon the issue. Elaborate preparations had been made and the utmost care had been taken in the organization and discipline of the army.

General George B. McClellan was intrusted with the command. He was a native of Pennsylvania, a distinguished graduate of West Point, a man of high personal character. His military skill was vouched for by older officers whose opinions would have weight with the President. But he had been six months in command of the Army of the Potomac and had done nothing in the field. The autumn had passed in inaction, the winter had worn away, and the spring had come without finding him ready to move. Whatever might be the justification for delay, it was his misfortune to become the subject of controversy. There was a McClellan party and an anti-McClellan party, in the press, among the people, in Congress, and in the army. How far this may have impaired the efficiency of his command cannot be known, but it no doubt seriously undermined him in the confidence of the War Department. Before he had fired a gun in the Peninsular campaign he was in a disputation with both the President and Secretary Stanton. On the 9th of April (1862) Mr. Lincoln wrote him, " Your dispatches complaining that you are not properly sustained, while they do not offend me, do pain me very much." General McClellan had complained that the President had detained McDowell's corps, and thus weakened the strength of his army, and the President was defending the policy as one necessary to the safety of Washington. McClellan protested that he had but eighty-five thousand men at Yorktown. The President insisted that he had a hundred and eight thousand. "And once more," said the President, " in conclusion, let me tell you it is indispensable to you that you strike a blow. I am powerless to help this. You will do me the justice to remember that I always insisted that going down the bay in search of a field, instead of fighting at or near Manassas, was only shifting and not surmounting the difficulty; that we would find the same enemy and the same or equal intrenchments at either place. The country will not fail to note (is now noting) that the present hesitation to move upon the intrenched enemy is but the story of Manassas repeated. I beg to assure you that I have never written you or spoken to you in greater kindness of feeling than now, nor with a fuller purpose of sustaining you so far as in my most anxious judgment I consistently can."

This condition of affairs with the indication of increasing discord between the Commander-in-Chief and General McClellan boded no good to the Union cause, and the entire Peninsular campaign was but a succession of " hopes deferred " that made the heart sick ; of disappointment, of great sacrifice of life and treasure, and in the end of positive disaster and humiliating retreat.

As General McClellan neared Richmond and needed re-enforcements for a decisive battle with General Lee's army, the Confederates used the most admirable tactics for the purpose of alarming the authorities at Washington and compelling them to withhold help from the Army of the Potomac. Stonewall Jackson came thundering down the Shenandoah Valley with a force which the exaggeration of the day placed far beyond his real numbers. He brushed aside the army of General Banks at Winchester by what might well be termed a military cyclone, and created such consternation that our troops in the Potomac Valley were at once thrown upon the defensive. McDowell with his corps was at Fredericksburg, hurrying to Hanover Court-House for the purpose of aiding McClellan. With our forces thus remote from Washington, and the fortifications around the city imperfectly manned, something akin to panic seized upon the Government. General McDowell, by direct order of the President, was turned from his march on Richmond, to follow or intercept Jackson. On the 25th of May the Secretary of War telegraphed to the governors of the Loyal States: "Intelligence from various quarters leaves no doubt that the enemy in great force are marching on Washington. You will please organize and forward immediately all the militia and volunteer forces in your State." The governors in turn issued alarming proclamations, some of which were eminently calculated to spread the contagion of fear prevailing at Washington. Governor Andrew, with evident apprehension of the worst, informed the people of Massachusetts that "The wily and barbarous horde of traitors to the people, to the Government, to our country, and to liberty, menace again the National Capital: they have attacked and routed Major-General Banks, are advancing on Harper's Ferry, and are marching on Washington. The President calls on Massachusetts to rise at once for its rescue and defense." Throughout the entire North there was for several days a genuine belief that the National Capital might soon be in possession of the Confederate army, and the senators and representatives in Congress be seized as prisoners of war.

Meanwhile Stonewall Jackson having marched to the very banks of the Potomac and shelled Harper's Ferry, and having succeeded beyond his most sanguine expectation in the object which he had in view, deliberately began his retreat. He was followed up the Shenandoah Valley by the commands of four Major-Generals and one Brigadier-General of the Union army. He drew these united forces after him precisely as he desired, for the benefit of Lee's army at Richmond. He did not fly from them as if dreading a battle, for that would have been to dismiss the large Union force to the aid of General McClellan. Occasionally detailing a fraction of his command to engage in a skirmish with his pursuers, who far outnumbered his whole force, he managed to keep his main body at a safe distance, and to reserve it for a more important work ahead. After thus drawing our troops so far up the valley that it was impossible for them to retrace their steps in season for concentration on Richmond, he rapidly transported the main body of his own troops by rail from Staunton, and rejoined General Lee in time to take part in the final and memorable series of engagements which, by the close of June, had compelled General McClellan to take refuge on the banks of the James, where he could have the co-operation of the gunboats which lay at Harrison's Landing.

General Halleck took command as General-in-Chief of the army directly after the Army of the Potomac had closed its campaign against Richmond. He visited Harrison's Landing on the 24th of July to make personal inquiry into the situation, and the result was an order for the transfer of the army to Acquia Creek. General McClellan protested earnestly and, in the judgment of many of the most skilled in military science, wisely, against this movement. The Army of the Potomac, he said, was "within twenty-five miles of Richmond, and with the aid of the gunboats we can supply the army by water during its advance to within twelve miles of Richmond. At Acquia Creek we would be seventy miles from Richmond, with land transportation all the way." He thought the government had ample troops to protect Washington and guard the line of the Potomac, and he could not see the wisdom of transporting the Army of the Potomac two hundred miles at enormous cost, only to place it three times as far from Richmond as it then was. General Halleck's position was sustained by the President and the Secretary of War, and the argument of General McClellan, convincing and conclusive as it seems, was overruled by the peremptory mandate of his military superiors.

The failure of the Peninsular campaign will always be a subject of controversy. At the time it was one of prolonged and angry dispute. Where military critics so widely differ, civilians gain the right to a personal judgment. The weakness of that great military movement was the lack of cordiality and confidence between the commander and the Administration at Washington. The seeds of distrust had been sown and a bountiful crop of disaster was the natural growth. The withdrawal of McDowell's corps was a fatal blow to McClellan. Before a military court which was inquiring into the transaction, General McClellan stated under oath that he had "no doubt that the Army of the Potomac would have taken Richmond had not the corps of General McDowell been separated from it; and that, had the command of General McDowell in the month of May joined the Army of the Potomac by way of Hanover Court-House, we would have had Richmond a week after the junction." He added, with evident reference to Mr. Lincoln and Mr. Stanton, "I do not hold General McDowell responsible for a failure to join me on that occasion."

When General McDowell was turned back from Fredericksburg to take part in the fruitless chase after Stonewall Jackson in the Shenandoah Valley, he was doing precisely what the President of the Confederate States would have ordered, had he been able to issue the orders of the President of the United States. McDowell saw the blunder, but his directions were peremptory and nothing was left but to obey. He telegraphed to the Secretary of War, "The President's order is a crushing blow to us." Mr. Lincoln personally and immediately replied to General McDowell, "The change is as painful to me as it can possibly be to you or to any one." McDowell then ventured to argue the case with the President. He distinctly told Mr. Lincoln that he could effect nothing in trying to cut off Stonewall Jackson in the Shenandoah Valley. "I shall," he continued, "gain nothing for you there, and I shall lose much for you here. It is therefore not only on personal grounds that I have a heavy heart in this matter, but I feel that it throws us all back, and from Richmond north we shall have all our large mass paralyzed, and shall have to repeat what we have just accomplished." Mr. Lincoln's order and the whole of this correspondence were by telegraph on the twenty-fourth day of May. Conclusive as the reasoning of General McDowell seems, it did not move Mr. Lincoln from his purpose; and the heavy re-enforcement which was then within three days of the point where it could most effectively aid McClellan, was diverted to a hopeless and useless pursuit. Had McDowell been allowed to proceed as he desired and as General McClellan confidently expected, he would have re-enforced the Army of the Potomac for an attack on Lee while Stonewall Jackson's corps was in the Shenandoah Valley. By the unfortunate diversion ordered by Mr. Lincoln, precisely the reverse occurred. Stonewall Jackson's corps arrived before Richmond in season to aid in defeating McClellan, while McDowell with his splendid contingent was aimlessly loitering in a distant part of Virginia.

The President was led into this course by the urgent advice of the Secretary of War. When McClellan went to the field, Mr. Stanton undertook personally to perform the duties of General-in-Chief in Washington. This was evidently an egregious blunder. Neither by education, temper, temperament, nor by any other trait of his character, was Mr. Stanton fitted for this duty. He was very positively and in a high degree unfitted for it. With three Major-generals — McDowell, Banks, and Frémont — exercising independent commands in the Potomac Valley, with their movements exerting a direct and important influence upon the fortunes of the main army under McClellan, there was especial need of a cool-headed, experienced, able general at the Capital. Had one of the three great soldiers who have been at the head of the army since the close of the war, then been in chief command at Washington, there is little hazard in saying that the brilliant and dashing tactics of Stonewall Jackson would not have been successful, and that if General McClellan had failed before Richmond, it would not have been for lack of timely and adequate re-enforcement.

Before these military disasters occurred, Congress had made progress in its legislation against the institution of Slavery. At the beginning of the war there had been an ill-defined policy, or rather an absence of all policy, in relation to the most important of pending questions. The winter preceding the outbreak of the rebellion had been so assiduously devoted by Congress to efforts of compromise and conciliation, that it was difficult to turn the public mind promptly to the other side, and to induce the people to accept the logical consequences of the war. There was no uniform policy among our generals. Each commander was treating the question very much according to his own personal predilection, and that was generally found to be in accordance with his previous political relations. The most conspicuous exception to this rule was General Benjamin F. Butler, who had been identified with the extreme pro-slavery wing of the Democratic party. He was in command in May, 1861, at Fortress Monroe, and he found that when fugitive slaves sought the protection of his camp they were pursued under flags of truce, and their return was requested as a right under the Constitution of the United States by the men who were in arms against the Constitution. The anomaly of this situation was seen by General Butler, and he met it promptly by refusing to permit the slaves to be returned, declaring them to be contraband of war. As they were useful to the enemy in military operations, they were to be classed with arms and ammunition. This opinion was at first received jocularly by the country, and the word "contraband" became the synonym of fugitive slave. But General Butler's judgment is justified by the rules of modern warfare, and its application solved a question of policy which otherwise might have been fraught with serious difficulty. In the presence of arms the Fugitive-slave Law became null and void, and the Dred Scott decision was trampled under the iron hoof of war.

The first exercise of legislative power hostile to the institution of slavery, already detailed, was promptly followed by one still more decisive. Congress provided for the abolition of the institution in the District of Columbia. A bill for this purpose was introduced in the Senate on the 16th of December, 1861, and two months later Mr. Morrill of Maine, from the Committee on the District, reported it to the Senate with a favorable recommendation. Garrett Davis of Kentucky spoke in support of an amendment requiring the colonization, beyond the limits of the United States, of all persons who might be liberated by the Act. He was firmly persuaded that the liberation of slaves with their continued residence among the whites would result in a war of races. Mr. Hale of New Hampshire combated his opinion by arguments and facts drawn from the history of emancipation in Jamaica. Mr. Wilson of Massachusetts gave an interesting history of the circumstances which led to the selection of the site for the National Capital upon slave territory.

Mr. Sumner dealt with the subject at great length, enforcing his views by numerous authorities drawn from history, from the decisions of courts, and from the opinions of publicists and statesmen of modern times. The opponents of the measure did not conceal their apprehension that the abolition of slavery in the District of Columbia portended its overthrow in the States. Mr. Sumner and his associates hailed the movement as the inauguration of a policy destined to produce that result. "The future," said the Massachusetts senator, "cannot be doubtful. At the National Capital slavery will give way to freedom. But the good work will not stop here: it must proceed. What God and Nature decree, Rebellion cannot arrest." Mr. Sherman of Ohio maintained that it was not a measure for the preservation of the government, but a municipal regulation, and that the time had come when it was evidently wise to exercise the powers granted by the Constitution. Mr. Willey of Virginia deprecated the existence of slavery in the capital of the country, but he opposed the emancipation bill as the first of a series of measures that would end in the abolition of slavery in all the States by act of Congress. The bill passed the Senate the third day of April by a vote of 29 to 14.

When the measure reached the House and was read for information it was at once challenged by Mr. Vallandigham of Ohio; and upon the parliamentary question "Shall the bill be rejected?" the yeas were 45 and the nays were 93. The debate which immediately followed was in good temper, with a notable absence of the exasperation which it was feared the subject would call forth. Mr. Crittenden of Kentucky stated the objections of the minority, and especially of the Border slave States, fairly and temperately. The time seemed to him unpropitious inasmuch as the moving cause of the secession of the States was the apprehension on their part that Congress was likely to take measures for the abolition of slavery. The passage of the bill necessarily rendered futile every attempt at reconciliation. Secondly, there was an implied agreement with Virginia and Maryland at the time of the cession of the District that "the system of slavery shall not be disturbed." And finally, the bill, although it provided for compensation to lawful owners, was in effect a measure of confiscation. It passed the House by a vote of 92 to 38. The President accompanied his approval with a special message in which, while not doubting the constitutionality of the measure, he intimated that there were "matters within and about the Act which might have taken a course or shape more satisfactory to his judgment." He especially commended the provision made for compensation to the owners of slaves, and referred with satisfaction to the appropriation made to aid any colored person of the District who might desire to emigrate "to Liberia, Hayti, or any country beyond the limits of the United States which the President may determine." The sum of one hundred thousand dollars was appropriated for this purpose by the Act — one hundred dollars being allowed to each emigrant. The experiment came to nothing. The colored persons who had resided in the United States as slaves were obviously desirous of trying their fortunes as freemen among the people whom they knew, and in the homes to which they were attached.

Mr. Lincoln had always been a firm believer in the scheme of African colonization; and in his message of December, 1861, he recommended a provision for colonizing the slaves set free by the influence of war. From the slave States which had remained loyal to the Union he was willing to accept slaves in lieu of the direct tax, according to some mode of valuation that might be agreed upon, and he was anxious that adequate provision should be made for their settlement in some place or places with a climate congenial to them. But the experiment with the manumitted negroes of the District, which was made in compliance with this recommendation of the President and in deference to his personal wishes, frequently and earnestly expressed, demonstrated the impracticability of the plan. Colonization could be effected only by the forcible removal of the colored people, and this would have been a more cruel violation of their natural rights than a continuance of the slavery in which they were born. If free choice between the two conditions had been offered, nine-tenths, perhaps even a larger proportion of the slaves, would have preferred to remain in their old homes. In an economic point of view the scheme was indefensible. We were at the time the only country with undeveloped agricultural resources in warm latitudes, that was not engaged in seeking labor from all quarters of the world. The Colonization scheme deliberately proposed to strip the United States of patient, faithful laborers, acclimated to the cotton and sugar fields of the South, and capable of adding great wealth to the nation. Colonization would deprive us of this much needed labor, would entail vast expense in the deportation of the negroes, and would devolve upon this country, by a moral responsibility which it could not avoid, the protection and maintenance of the feeble government which would be planted on the shores of Africa. The Liberian experiment, honorable as it was to the colored race, and successful as it had proved in establishing civilization in Africa, had not attained such material prosperity as would justify the United States in the removal of millions of its population to a remote country where there was no demand for labor.

Mr. Lincoln's course on the Slavery question at that period of his Administration was steadily and studiously conservative. He had checked the Secretary of War (Mr. Cameron) in the issuing of an anti-slavery order which was considered premature and unwise; he had countermanded and annulled the proclamations of General Hunter and General Frémont declaring the slaves to be free within the districts of their respective commands. He now recommended a measure in the line of his conservative policy, to which he attached great weight, and from which he anticipated important consequences. On the 6th of March, 1862, the President sent a message to Congress recommending the adoption of a joint resolution declaring that "the United States ought to co-operate with any State which may adopt gradual abolishment of slavery, giving to such State pecuniary aid to be used in its discretion to compensate for the inconveniences, public and private, produced by such change of system." Mr. Lincoln believed that if the leaders of the existing Rebellion could conquer their independence, the Border slave states would necessarily join them from sympathy with their institutions. By the initiation of emancipation all possible desire or tendency in that direction would be removed, and thus a severe blow be given to the Rebellion. He believed in compensation to the slave-holder, and expressed his opinion that "gradual and not sudden emancipation is better for all." He asked Congress to consider "how very soon the current expenses of the war would purchase at a fair valuation all the slaves in any named State."

When the message reached the House it was referred to the Committee of the Whole on the State of the Union. Four days later Mr. Roscoe Conkling moved to suspend the rules in order to bring the resolution before the House "in the exact form in which the President had recommended it." The motion prevailed by 86 to 35. Francis P. Blair of Missouri and the representatives from West Virginia were the only Border State men who voted to suspend the rules. Mr. Conkling thought an immediate vote might be taken because he presumed "every member had made up his mind on the question involved." But the Kentucky delegation desired time for consultation. They concluded to oppose the resolution. Mr. Crittenden, speaking the sentiments of all, asked, "Why do you exact of Kentucky more than she has already done to show her loyalty? Has she not parted with all her former allies, with all her natural kindred in other States? Why should it be asked that she should now surrender up her domestic institutions?" Against the protest of Kentucky the resolution was passed, such radical abolitionists as Owen Lovejoy warmly supporting the proposition to pay for slaves out of the Treasury of the United States. Mr. Henderson of Missouri and Mr. Willey of West Virginia were the only Border State senators who saw the vast advantage to be secured to their own constituents by the passage of the measure. They supported it ably and heartily. It was earnestly opposed by the senators from Kentucky, Maryland, and Delaware. Mr. Carlile of West Virginia was the only senator in nominal sympathy with the Administration who voted against it. The hostility to the President's policy by senators from the Border slave states was so fixed as to prevent even a free discussion of the measure, and it was therefore remanded to a future day for consideration.

A still more aggressive movement against slavery was made by Congress before the close of this eventful session. On the day that Congress convened, in the preceding December, Mr. Trumbull gave notice of his intention to introduce a bill "for the confiscation of the property of rebels, and giving freedom to the persons they hold in slavery." Three days later he formally introduced the bill, and made a lucid explanation of its provisions and its objects. He "disdained to press it upon the ground of a mere military power superior to the civil in time of war." "Necessity," said he, "is the plea of tyrants; and if our Constitution ceases to operate, the moment a person charged with its observance thinks there is a necessity to violate it, it is of little value." So far from admitting the superiority of the military over the civil power in time of war, Mr. Trumbull held that "under our Constitution the military is as much the subject of control by the civil power in war as in peace." He was for suppressing the rebellion "according to law, and in no other way;" and he warned his countrymen who stood "ready to tolerate almost any act done in good faith for the suppression of the rebellion, not to sanction usurpations of power which may hereafter become precedents for the destruction of constitutional liberty." Though the bill was introduced on the second day of December, 1861, it did not become a law until the 17th of July in the next year.

In the months intervening, it was elaborately debated, almost every senator taking part in the discussion. Garrett Davis of Kentucky, who had succeeded Mr. Breckinridge in the Senate, made a long speech against the bill, contending that Congress had no power to free any slaves. He wanted a bill of great severity against the rebel leaders: "to those that would repent" he would give "immunity, peace, and protection; to the impenitent and incorrigible he would give the gallows, or exile and the forfeiture of their whole estate." Such a law as that, he said, his "own State of Kentucky desired. As Hamilcar brought his infant son Hannibal to the family altar, and made him swear eternal enmity to the Roman power, so I have sworn and will ever maintain eternal enmity to the principle of secession and all its adherents." It was seen throughout the debate that the bill under consideration was in large part provoked by the confiscation measures of the Confederate Congress, and Mr. Davis declared that "the debts due to the North, estimated at $200,000,000, seized, confiscated, and appropriated by the rebel government, shall be remunerated fully."

Mr. John B. Henderson of Missouri who, as a Union man of prominence and ability, had succeeded Trusten Polk in the Senate, opposed the bill because it would "cement the Southern mind against us and drive new armies of excited and deluded men from the Border States to espouse the cause of rebellion." He urged that "the Union sentiment of the South should be cultivated, and radical measures tending to destroy that sentiment should be dropped." Mr. Fessenden was conservative on this as on other questions, and insisted upon the reference of Mr. Trumbull's bill to a committee; which was the occasion of some little passages between himself and Mr. Trumbull, not without temper. Mr. Trumbull suggested that "the senator from Maine would not be likely to get any light from the deliberations of five men unless he were himself one of them." Retorting in the same spirit, but, as he said, good-naturedly, Mr. Fessenden said he should not "hope that *any* deliberation of anybody would enlighten the senator from Illinois."

Sustaining the extreme power of confiscation, Mr. Sumner desired "the Act to be especially leveled at the institution of Slavery." He recalled the saying of Charles XII. of Sweden, that the cannoneers were perfectly right in directing their shots at him, for the war would be at an instant end if they could kill him; whereas they would reap little from killing his principal officers. "There is," said the senator, "no shot in this war so effective as one against Slavery, which is king above all officers; nor is there better augury of complete success than the willingness at last to fire upon this wicked king." By this means, Mr. Sumner believed that we should "take from the rebellion its mainspring of activity and strength, stop its chief stores of provisions and supplies, remove a motive and temptation to prolonged resistance, and destroy forever the disturbing influence which, so long as it exists, will keep this land a volcano, ever ready to break forth anew." Mr. Sumner, Mr. Wade, and Mr. Chandler, the senators who were regarded as most radical, desired more stringent provisions than they could secure. The really able lawyers of the Senate, Mr. Fessenden and Judge Collamer, repressed the extreme measures which but for their interposition would have been enacted. As the bill was finally perfected, Mr. Chandler and his colleague Mr. Howard voted against it, as did also Mr. Browning of Illinois and the Border-State Senators Davis of Kentucky, Henderson of Missouri, and Carlile of Virginia. To the Michigan senators the bill was too weak; to the others it was too strong. Mr. Willey of Virginia was the only senator from a slave-holding State who voted on the radical side. With the exceptions noted, Republican senators all voted for the bill.

A series of measures in the House relating to confiscation were under discussion while the Senate was considering the same subject. The House passed a more stringent bill than the Senate would accept, and the subject was finally sent to a committee of conference, which from the points of disagreement framed the measure that ultimately became a law. As in the Senate, the Border-State men opposed the measure, but were overborne by the popular opinion which nearly consolidated the Republican vote of the North in favor of it. It was however an undoubted weakness, morally and politically, that such men as Crittenden and Mallory of Kentucky, James S. Rollins of Missouri, and Francis Thomas and Edward Webster of Maryland were recorded against it. The bill was passed in the House by a vote of 82 to 42. The conference report having somewhat strengthened the original measure passed by the Senate, Messrs. Howard and Chandler of Michigan gave it their support, but for the same reason Mr. Cowan of Pennsylvania and Mr. Willey of Virginia opposed it. The final vote was 27 in favor to 12 against it.

The Act, as finally passed, affixed to the crime of treason the punishment of death, or, at the discretion of the court, imprisonment for not less than five years and a fine of not less than ten thousand dollars, — all the slaves, if any, to be declared free. "To insure the speedy termination of the present rebellion" it was made the duty of the President to cause the seizure of the estate and property, money, stocks, credits, and effects of the following classes of persons: first, all those hereafter acting as officers of the army or the navy of the rebels in arms against the government of the United States; second, of any person acting as President, Vice-President, member of Congress, judge of any court, cabinet officer, foreign minister, commissioner, or consul of the so-called Confederate States; third, of any person acting as governor of a State, member of a convention or Legislature, or judge of any court of any of the so-called Confederate States of America; fourth, of any person who having held an office of honor, trust, or profit in the United States shall hereafter hold an office in the so-called Confederate States; fifth, of any person hereafter holding any office or agency under the so-called Confederate States or under any of the several States of said Confederacy; sixth, of any person who owning property in any loyal State or Territory of the United States, or in the District of Columbia, shall hereafter assist and give aid and comfort to the rebellion. "And all sales, transfers, or conveyances of any such property shall be null and void; and it shall be a sufficient bar to any suit brought by such persons for the possession or use of such property, or any of it, to allege and prove that he is one of the persons described in this section."

In the provisions of the Act directly affecting slavery it was declared that "All slaves of persons who shall hereafter be engaged in rebellion against the Government of the United States or who shall in any way give aid or comfort thereto, escaping from such persons and taking refuge within the lines of the army, and all slaves captured from such persons, or deserted by them and coming under the control of the Government of the United States, and all slaves of such persons found or being within any place occupied by rebel forces and afterwards occupied by the forces of the United States, shall be deemed captives, shall be forever free of their servitude, and not again held as slaves." This provision had a very sweeping application. Even if the war had ended without a formal and effective system of emancipation, it is believed that this statute would have so operated as to render the slave system practically valueless. When the war closed it is probable that not less than one-half of all the slaves of the rebel States had come within the scope of this statute, and had therefore been declared legally free by the legislative power of the United States.

Mr. Lincoln signed the Confiscation Act with reluctance. Indeed he had prepared a veto, but a joint resolution had been passed in order to remove the objections which in the President's view were absolutely fatal to the original bill, either as regarded its justice or its constitutionality. He had insisted to certain senators that the Confiscation Law must in terms exclude the possibility of its being applied to any act done by a rebel prior to its passage, and that no punishment or proceeding under it should be so construed as to work a forfeiture of the real estate of the offender beyond his natural life. These, with some minor defects, being corrected, the President affixed his signature and made public proclamation of the intended enforcement of the Act as qualified by the joint resolution approved on the same day. But there is good reason for believing that Mr. Lincoln would have been glad to confine its application to slave property, and he felt moreover that he could deal with that subject without the co-operation of Congress. The military situation was so discouraging that in the President's view it would have been wiser for Congress to refrain from enacting laws which, without success in the field, would be null and void, and which, with success in the field, would be rendered unnecessary. Congress adjourned on the same day that Mr. Lincoln approved the bill, and on returning home the senators and representatives found their constituents depressed, anxious, and alarmed for the country.

It cannot be said that the results flowing from this measure, either in restraining the action of Southern men or in securing to the National Treasury money derived from confiscated property, were at all in proportion to the importance ascribed to it in the discussions of both branches of Congress. Indeed the effect both morally and materially was far short of expectation. It is highly probable that if the stringent measure of the Confederate Congress and its stringent enforcement under the vigorous administration of Attorney-General Benjamin had not been attempted, the Congress of the United States could not have been induced to enter upon a course of legislation concerning which there existed much doubt and division of opinion among Republicans. It is at least certain that but for the causes named, the scope of the Confiscation Act would have been confined within those limits which would have directly influenced the institution of Slavery, and would not have interfered with any other species of property. Whatever distress therefore came to Southern men, from the provisions in the Confiscation Act outside of those relating to Slavery, may fairly and properly be traced to the spirit of retaliation (always an effective weapon in time of war) which naturally followed the causeless and cruel procedure of the Confederate Government.

CHAPTER XVII.

ON the day that Congress convened, (December 2, 1861,) Mr. Roscoe Conkling offered a resolution which was unanimously agreed to by the House, requesting "the Secretary of War, if not incompatible with the public service, to report to the House whether any, and if any, what, measures have been taken to ascertain who is responsible for the disastrous movement of our troops at Ball's Bluff." A few days later Mr. Chandler of Michigan offered a resolution in the Senate, directing an inquiry by a committee of three "into the disasters at Bull Run and Ball's Bluff." Mr. Grimes of Iowa offered a substitute which, after various modifications, directed the appointment of a "joint committee of three members of the Senate, and four members of the House of Representatives, to inquire into the conduct of the present war, with power to send for persons and papers, and with leave to sit during the sessions of either branch of Congress." The resolutions led to some debate. Mr. Chandler maintained that "it is the duty of the Senate to ascertain who is responsible for sending eighteen hundred men across the Potomac, in two old scows, without any means of retreat." Mr. McDougall thought a discussion of the question at that time was impolitic. Mr. Wilson of Massachusetts, chairman of the Committee on Military Affairs, while admitting that many mistakes had been made, asserted that "the greatest error in the conduct of the war has been the series of irresponsible proclamations issued by generals on the field." The joint resolution was adopted by the Senate with only three dissenting votes (Messrs. Latham, Carlile, and Rice) and by the House unanimously. Mr. Wade of Ohio, Mr. Chandler of Michigan, and Mr. Andrew Johnson of Tennessee on the part of the Senate, with Mr. Gooch of Massachusetts, Mr. Covode of Pennsylvania, Mr. Julian of Indiana, and Mr. Odell of New York on the part of the House, constituted the committee.

The Secretary of War, in answer to Mr. Conkling's resolution touching the disaster at Ball's Bluff, stated that Major-General McClellan, commanding the army, "is of opinion that an inquiry on the subject of the resolution would at this time be injurious to the public service." The answer did not satisfy Mr. Conkling. He immediately moved another resolution declaring that the communication from the Secretary of War was "not responsive nor satisfactory to the House, and that the secretary be directed to return a further answer." A spirited debate followed, taking a somewhat extended range. Mr. Conkling said that his resolution related to "the most atrocious military murder ever committed in our history as a people. It relates to a lost field; to a disastrous and humiliating battle; to a blunder so gross that all men can see it, — a blunder which cost us confessedly nine hundred and thirty men, the very pride and flower of the States from which they came." . . . "The Bluff is a mile in length up and down the river, and the landing and ascent were made in the middle of it. Behind this was a six-acre lot skirted by woods on three sides. Into this burial-ground, one by one, as the boat brought them over, went up the devoted seventeen hundred. . . . Behind them rolled a deep river which could never be repassed. Before them and surrounding them on every side was a tree-sheltered and skulking foe, three or four times their number. . . . In an hour, in less than an hour, the field was a hell of fire raging from every side. The battle was lost before it was begun. It was from the outset a mere sacrifice, a sheer immolation, without a promise of success or a hope of escape." . . . "On the same side of the river with Leesburg," said Mr. Conkling, "within a day's march of that place, lay General McCall commanding a division containing fifteen regiments which marched fully eleven thousand men. If Leesburg were to be attacked, or if a reconnoissance in force were to be made in that direction, one of the first wonders in this case is, that the work should have been assigned to General Stone's division, divided as it was from the scene of action by a great river, when the division of General McCall was within a day's march of the spot, with neither river, mountain, nor barrier to be traversed."

— Mr. Richardson of Illinois thought Mr. Conkling's resolution was calculated "to raise an issue between the House of Representatives and the army, and divide the country." He thought this would injure the cause of the Union. In military matters he would "rather trust the commanding general of the army than a committee of the House."

— Mr. Crittenden of Kentucky protested against "the House interfering in the conduct of the war and the management of the army by investigating transactions which are in their nature purely military." He maintained that "such a policy takes control out of the hands of men supposed to be competent and puts it in the hands of men supposed not to be competent." "If," continued Mr. Crittenden, "we are to find fault with every movement, why not appoint a committee of the House to attend the Commander-in-chief? Why not send them with your army so that the power of Congress may be felt in battle as well as in the halls of legislation?"

— Mr. Lovejoy of Illinois gave a characteristic turn to the debate. "I believe before God," said he, — "and if it be fanaticism now it will not be when history traces the events of the day, — that the reason why we have had Bull Run and Ball's Bluff and other defeats and disasters is that God, in his providence, designs to arraign us before this great question of human freedom, and make us take the right position." Slavery, according to Mr. Lovejoy, was the Jonah on board the National ship, and the ship would founder unless Jonah were thrown overboard. "When Jonah was cast forth into the sea, the sea ceased from raging." . . . Our battles, in Mr. Lovejoy's belief, "should be fought so as to hurt slavery," and enable the President to decree its destruction. "To be President, to be king, to be victor, has happened to many: to be embalmed in the hearts of mankind through all generations as liberator and emancipator has been vouchsafed to few."

— Mr. Wickliffe of Kentucky believed we should "preserve the

Union and slavery under it." He wished to "throw the Abolitionists overboard."

— Mr. Mallory of Kentucky, while not believing slavery to be
incompatible with our liberty under the Constitution, declared that
so far as he understood the feeling of the people of Kentucky, "if
they ever come to regard slavery as standing in the way of the
Union, they will not hesitate to wipe out the institution." Loud
applause followed this remark.

— Mr. McKee Dunn of Indiana, while believing that "if slavery
stands in the way of the Union it must be destroyed," was not yet
"willing to accept Mr. Lovejoy as prophet, priest, or king." He
thought "the gentleman from Illinois was not authorized to interpret
God's providence" in the affairs of men.

— Mr. Thaddeus Stevens, in recalling the debate to the immediate
question before the House, took occasion to protest against the doctrine of non-interference laid down by Mr. Crittenden. "Has it
come to this," said Mr. Stevens, "that Congress is a mere automaton,
to register the decrees of another power, and that we have nothing
to do but to find men and money? . . . This is the doctrine of despotism, better becoming that empire which they are attempting to
establish in the South."

The resolution offered by Mr. Conkling was adopted by a vote of
79 to 54, on a call of the yeas and nays. The affirmative vote was
wholly Republican. A few Republicans voted with the Democrats
in the negative. The reply of Secretary Cameron was no more satisfactory than to the first resolution. He informed the House that
"measures have been taken to ascertain who is responsible for the
disastrous movement of our troops at Ball's Bluff, but it is not
deemed compatible with the public interest to make known these
measures at the present time." The difference between this answer
and the first, was that the Administration assumed the responsibility
of withholding the information, and did not rest it upon the judgment of the general in command of the army.

Brigadier-General Charles P. Stone was a graduate of West
Point Military Academy, from Massachusetts. His family belonged
to the old Puritan stock of that commonwealth, and had been honorably represented in every war in which the American people had
engaged. General Stone served as a lieutenant in the Mexican war
with high credit, and in 1855 resigned his commission and became
a resident of California. It happened that he was in Washington

at the breaking out of the civil war, and in response to the request of his old commander, General Scott, took a prominent part in the defense of the capital, considered to be in danger after the rising of the Baltimore mob. His conduct was so admirable that when the President, a few weeks later, directed the organization of eleven new regiments in the Regular Army, he appointed General Stone to the Colonelcy of the 14th United-States Infantry. After the battle of Bull Run, when General McClellan was promoted to the command of the Army of the Potomac, General Stone was selected to command a division which was directed to occupy the valley of the Potomac above Washington, as a corps of observation. The Union troops, engaged in the disastrous battle of Ball's Bluff, belonged to his corps, but were under the immediate command of Colonel E. D. Baker. The repulse and slaughter on that melancholy field were followed by excitement and indignation throughout the country quite as deep as that shown in Congress. The details of the disaster were greatly exaggerated. The official summary of losses, made up with care, showed that the total number killed, including both officers and men, was 49; wounded, 158; missing, 714, of whom a few were drowned, and the great mass taken prisoners. The popular admiration for Colonel Baker was unbounded, and the suspicion that his life had been needlessly destroyed created such a feeling as demanded a victim. General Stone was selected for the sacrifice, and popular wrath was turned upon him with burning intensity. Rumors and exaggerations filled the newspapers; and the public, in that state of credulity which is an incident to the victim-hunting mania, accepted every thing as true. It was widely believed that Colonel Baker said mournfully, as he marched to the battle-field, "I will obey General Stone's order, but it is my death-warrant."

Goaded by these injurious and unfounded rumors, General Stone, in a letter to the Adjutant-General of the army, written a fortnight after the battle, deemed it his "duty to answer the persistent attacks made through the press by the friends of the lamented Colonel Baker." He called attention to the "distinct violations by Colonel Baker of his orders and instructions," and declared that he was left "to use his own discretion about crossing his force, or retiring that already over." He found it "painful to censure the acts of one who gallantly died.on the field of battle," but justice to himself required "that the full truth should be made to appear." Colonel Baker did not receive the order "as a death-warrant," for it was delivered to him "at his own request." That "Colonel Baker was determined to fight a battle" was made evident by the fact that "he never crossed to examine the field, never gave an order to the troops in advance, and never sent forward to ascertain their position, until he had ordered over his force, and passed over a considerable portion of it." On the 5th of January, 1862, General Stone appeared before the Committee on the Conduct of the War, and was examined under oath as to every detail of the Ball's-Bluff disaster which could in any way, directly or remotely, involve his responsibility as a commander. His answers were frank, withholding nothing, and were evidently intended to communicate every pertinent fact. So far as may be inferred from the questions and comments, the evidence was entirely satisfactory to the committee.

After the examination of General Stone, many officers of his command appeared before the committee. The captains and lieutenants, fresh from private life, whose names he probably did not know, and with whom he perhaps never exchanged a word, were summoned in large number. They had remarkable stories to tell about General Stone's disloyalty; about his holding secret correspondence with the enemy; about his permitting letters and packages to be taken across the line without examination; about his allowing rebels to go freely back and forth; and finally about his passing within the rebel lines to hold confidential interviews with the officers commanding the force opposed to him. It is singular that men of the acuteness and high character of those composing the committee did not carefully sift the testimony and subject it to the test of a rigorous cross-examination. The stories told by many of these swift witnesses were on the surface absurd, and should have been exposed. Publicity alone would have largely counteracted the evil effect of their narratives, but the examination was secret, and the witnesses evidently felt that the strongest bias against General Stone was the proper turn to give their testimony. The atmosphere was, as it often is in such cases, unfavorable to the suspected man; and his reputation was mercilessly assailed where he could not reply, and was not even allowed to hear. When officers of the higher grades, who came near to General Stone, who shared his confidence and assisted in his councils, were examined, the weight of the testimony was markedly different. General F. W. Lander regarded General Stone as "a very efficient, orderly, and excellent officer." Colonel Isaac J. Wistar, who succeeded Colonel Baker in the command of

the California regiment, gave the highest testimony to General
Stone's loyalty, and to the "full confidence" reposed in him by men
of every rank in the brigade with which he was serving.   Colonel
Charles Devens who, with his regiment, the Fifteenth Massachusetts
Infantry, had borne an honorable part on the bloody field, testified
that he and the officers of the Fifteenth "had confidence in General
Stone."   Colonel James H. Van Allen, commanding a regiment of
cavalry in General Stone's division, gave the most cordial testimony
to his loyalty and high character.

After the larger part of the evidence adverse to General Stone
had been heard, he received an intimation through General McClellan that it might be well for him to appear again before the Committee on the Conduct of the War.   He obtained leave of absence
from his command, repaired to Washington, and presented himself
before the committee on the 31st of January, twenty-six days after
his first testimony had been given.   For some reason which the
committee did not deem it necessary to explain, General Stone was
not furnished with the names of the witnesses who had testified
against him in the dark; their testimony was not submitted to him;
it was not even read in his hearing.   He was simply informed by the
chairman — Senator Wade of Ohio — that "in the course of our
investigations there has come out in evidence matters which may be
said to impeach you.   I do not know that I can enumerate all the
points, but I think I can.   In the first place is your conduct in the
Ball's-Bluff affair — your ordering your forces over without sufficient
means of transportation, and in that way endangering your army, in
case of a check, by not being able to re-enforce them. . . . Another
point is that the evidence tends to show that you have had undue
communication with the enemy by letters that have passed back and
forth, by intercourse with officers from the other side, and by permitting packages to go over unexamined, to known Secessionists.
. . . The next and only other point that now occurs to me is that
you have suffered the enemy to erect formidable fortifications or
batteries on the opposite side of the river, within the reach of your
guns, and which you could easily have prevented."   General Stone's
answer was as lucid, frank, and full as could be made to charges of
so sweeping a character.   His explanations were unreserved, and
his justification apparently complete and unanswerable against every
form of accusation which the chairman submitted.   To the charge
of disloyalty General Stone replied with much feeling, "That is

one humiliation I had hoped I should never be subjected to. I thought there was one calumny that could not be brought against me. Any other calumny I should expect after what I have received, but that one I should have supposed that you personally, Mr. Chairman, would have rejected at once. *You* remember last spring when the Government had so few friends here, when the enemy had this city I might almost say in his power, I raised all the volunteer troops that were here during the seven dark days. I disciplined and posted those troops. I commanded them, and they were the first to invade the soil of Virginia, and I led them." Mr. Wade here interrupted, and said, "I was not so unjust as not to mention that circumstance to the committee." General Stone resumed, "I could have surrendered Washington. And now I will swear that this government has not a more faithful soldier, of poor capacity it may be, but not a more faithful soldier from the day I was called into service to this minute."

Subsequent developments proved that three days before this second examination General McClellan had in his possession an order from Edwin M. Stanton, Secretary of War, directing him "to relieve General Stone from his command of a division of the Army of the Potomac, and that he be placed in arrest and kept in close custody until further orders." It is evident therefore that so far as the War Department was involved, the case had been prejudged, or judged at least without giving the accused man an opportunity to be heard in his own defense. It is difficult to understand why his testimony did not have the effect to recall or suspend the order of arrest, but despite the candor and evident honesty of his explanations, the blow fell upon him. Early on Saturday the eighth day of February General McClellan directed the provost marshal of the district, General Andrew Porter, "to arrest Brigadier-General Charles P. Stone at once, and to send him under close custody by first train to Fort Lafayette, where he will be placed in charge of the commanding officer, and have no communication with any one from the time of his arrest." Brigadier-General Sykes, commanding the City Guard, executed the order, taking General Stone from his bed at midnight in the hotel where he was stopping, and making him a close prisoner. Shortly after daylight the following morning General Stone addressed a note to General Seth Williams, Adjutant-General on the staff of General McClellan, informing him of his arrest, and adding, "Conscious of having been at all times a faithful soldier of the United

States, I most respectfully request that I may be furnished at as early a moment as practicable with a copy of whatever charges may have been preferred against me, with the opportunity of promptly meeting them."

To this respectful communication no answer was made, and General Stone was hurried off to Fort Lafayette, under strict guard, with an order from General McClellan for his imprisonment. At the fort the money which he had in his pockets was taken from him, and he was placed in solitary confinement in a room ordinarily used for quarters of enlisted men. No letter was allowed to leave him or reach him without the most rigid inspection. Under this close *surveillance*, with an armed sentinel pacing before the door of his room, without opportunity for outdoor air or exercise, he was kept for forty-nine days. He applied at different times to the military authorities in Washington for a statement of the charges against him, for a speedy trial, for access to the records of his own office and his own headquarters, for change of the place of his confinement. To none of these applications was answer of any kind returned. After he had been nearly two months in prison he asked that his wife might be allowed to visit him. She was in the deepest anguish, and her society in his imprisonment could have subjected the government to no danger, because she would have been under the same restraint and espionage as her husband. This natural and reasonable request, made only after his confinement promised to be indefinite, was peremptorily and curtly refused by the War Department.

On the fiftieth day the place of his imprisonment was changed from Fort Lafayette to Fort Hamilton near by, and the opportunity for open-air exercise within the fort was accorded him, though always under the eye of a sentinel. Here he renewed his request for the charges against him, without eliciting answer. He applied to the officer in command of the fort to learn of what possible crime he was accused, and the officer replied that he knew nothing of it; he was absolutely ignorant of any ground for General Stone's imprisonment. After striving for more than sixty days to ascertain the nature of his offense, and secure an opportunity to vindicate himself, the prisoner adopted another course. He applied for suspension of arrest with liberty to join the army just setting forth under General McClellan for the Peninsular campaign. No reply was made to his request. A few weeks later, when the Union forces under General Banks were defeated in the valley of the Shenandoah, he again asked the privilege of active duty, and again was treated with contemptuous silence. On the 4th of July he telegraphed directly to President Lincoln, recalling the honorable service in which he had been engaged just one year before. Reminding the President of the pressing need which the country then had "of the services of every willing soldier," he begged to be sent to the field. With manly dignity he declared, "I am utterly unconscious of any act, word, or design which should make me less eligible to an honorable place among the soldiers of the Republic than upon any day of my past life."

Meanwhile the subject had forced itself upon the attention of Congress. On the 24th of March, Senators Latham and McDougall of California, the first a supporter of Breckinridge in 1860, the other a supporter of Douglas, with Aaron A. Sargent, representative from the same State and a most radical Republican, united in an energetic memorial to Secretary Stanton, on behalf of General Stone as a citizen of California. They stated that "the long arrest of General Stone without military trial or inquiry has led to complaints from many quarters. . . . Having known General Stone for years, and never having had cause to doubt his loyalty, we feel it our duty to inquire of the government through you for some explanation of a proceeding which seems to us most extraordinary." To this memorial no reply was made, and after waiting nearly three weeks Mr. McDougall introduced in the Senate a very searching resolution of inquiry, requesting the Secretary of War to state upon whose authority the arrest was made, and upon whose complaint; why General Stone had been denied his rights under the articles of war; why no charges and specifications of his offense had been made; whether General Stone had not frequently asked to be informed of the charges against him; and finally upon what pretense he was still kept in prison. Mr. McDougall spoke in the Senate on the 15th of April in support of his resolution, making some interesting personal statements. General Stone was arrested on the night of Saturday the 8th of February. "On the Wednesday evening before that," said Mr. McDougall, "I met General Stone, dressed as became a person of his rank, at the house of the President, where no one went on that evening except by special invitation. He was there mingling with his friends, receiving as much attention and as much consideration from all about him as any man there present. . . . Only two evenings after that, if I remember aright, he was the guest under similar circumstances of the senior general in command of our army [McClellan], and there again receiving the hospitalities of the men first in office and first in the consideration of the country. On, I think, the very day of his arrest he was in the War Department, and was received by the head of that department as a man who had the entire confidence of the government, and of himself as one of the government's representatives. On that evening he was seized, taken from his home and family at midnight, carried off to Fort Lafayette and imprisoned, as are men convicted and adjudged guilty of the highest offense known to the law. . . . I undertake to say upon good authority that almost presently before his arrest he said to the present Secretary of War [Stanton], 'Sir, I hear complaints about my conduct as an officer at Ball's Bluff. I wish you to inquire into it and have the matter determined.' He was assured that there were no charges against him, and the secretary advised him in substance in these words: 'There is no occasion for your inquiry; go back to your command.' That was the day of the night on which he was arrested." Mr. McDougall's statement, the accuracy of which was not challenged by any one, disclosed the fact that while General Stone was a guest at the White House and at the residence of General McClellan, the latter had in his possession the order for arrest, and had held it for several days.

The resolution of Mr. McDougall was debated at some length in the Senate, Mr. Wade making a fiery speech in defense of the course pursued by the Committee on the Conduct of the War, and Mr. Browning of Illinois defending the President, upon whom there had been no imputation of any kind. Mr. Doolittle suggested that the resolution be referred to a committee. Mr. Wilson of Massachusetts submitted a substitute, simply requesting "the President of the United States to communicate to the Senate any information touching the arrest and imprisonment of General Stone, not deemed incompatible with the public interest." Mr. Sumner had "no opinion to express in the case, for he knew nothing about it;" but "it seemed clear" to him "that General Stone ought to be confronted with his accusers at an early day, unless there be some reason of an overbearing military character which would render such a trial improper." Mr. Sumner had "seen in various newspapers a most persistent attempt" to connect him "with the credit or discredit of the arrest." He declared that from the beginning he "had been an absolute stranger to it." The arrest was made, he repeated, without his "suggestion or hint, direct or indirect." He declared that he "was as free from all connection with it" as "the intimate friends and family relatives of the prisoner." At the close of the debate Mr. McDougall accepted Mr. Wilson's resolution as a substitute for his, and on the 21st of April the latter was adopted by general consent.

The unfounded assumption of Mr. Sumner's connection with the arrest sprang perhaps from some censorious remarks in the Senate made by him in December touching General Stone's alleged course in sending back fugitive slaves. Subsequent intelligence indicated that Mr. Sumner had been misinformed on this matter, and that the facts did not inculpate General Stone. But instead of writing to Mr. Sumner to correct the statements made in his speech, General Stone, most unwisely and most reprehensibly, addressed to the senator on the 23d of December an ill-tempered and abusive letter. Mr. Henry Melville Parker of Massachusetts investigated all the facts and incidents of the case, and came to the conclusion that Mr. Sumner, as an act of revenge for the insolent letter, had caused General Stone's arrest. But the facts do not warrant Mr. Parker's conclusion. Aside from Mr. Sumner's public denial on the floor of the Senate — which of itself closed the issue — he was never known to be guilty of an act of revenge. That passion belongs to meaner natures. The dates, moreover, remove the imputation of Mr. Parker. General Stone's hasty and ill-considered letter was placed in Mr. Sumner's hands on Christmas Day, 1861. The arrest was made on the 8th of February, 1862 — forty-six days later. The intervening circumstances nowhere involve Mr. Sumner in the remotest degree.

In answer to the call upon the President for information, Mr. Lincoln sent a message to the Senate on the 1st of May, saying, "General Stone was arrested and imprisoned under my general authority, and upon evidence which, whether he be guilty or innocent, required, as appears to me, such proceedings to be had against him for the public safety." The President deemed it "incompatible with the public interest, and perhaps unjust to General Stone, to make a more particular statement of the evidence." After saying that General Stone had not been tried because the officers to constitute a court-martial could not be withdrawn from duty without serious injury to the service, the President gave this public assurance: "He will be allowed a trial without unnecessary delay: the charges and specifications will be furnished him in due season, and every facility for his defense will be afforded him by the War Department." This message on its face bears evidence that it was prepared at the War Department, and that Mr. Lincoln acted upon assurances furnished by Mr. Stanton. The arrest was made upon his "general" authority, and clearly not from any specific information he possessed. But the effect of the message was to preclude any further attempt at intervention by Congress. Indeed the assurance that General Stone should be tried "without unnecessary delay" was all that could be asked. But the promise made to the ear was broken to the hope, and General Stone was left to languish without a word of intelligence as to his alleged offense, and without the slightest opportunity to meet the accusers who in the dark had convicted him without trial, subjected him to cruel punishment, and exposed him to the judgment of the world as a degraded criminal.

Release from imprisonment came at last by the action of Congress, coercing the Executive Department to the trial or discharge of General Stone. In the Act of July 17, 1862, "defining the pay and emolument of certain officers," a section was inserted declaring that "whenever an officer shall be put under arrest, except at remote military posts, it shall be the duty of the officer by whose orders he is arrested to see that a copy of the charges shall be served upon him within eight days thereafter, and that he shall be brought to trial within ten days thereafter unless the necessities of the service prevent such trial; and then he shall be brought to trial within thirty days after the expiration of said ten days, or the arrest shall cease." The Act reserved the right to try the officer at any time within twelve months after his discharge from arrest, and by a *proviso* it was made to apply "to all persons now under arrest and waiting trial." The bill had been pending several months, having been originally reported by Senator Wilson before General Stone's arrest.

The provision of the Act applicable to the case of General Stone was only a full enforcement by law of the seventy-ninth article of war, which declared that "no officer or soldier who shall be put in arrest shall continue in confinement more than eight days, or until such time as a court-martial can be assembled." It was a direct violation of the spirit of this article, and a cruel straining of its letter, to consign General Stone to endless or indefinite imprisonment. Any man of average intelligence in the law — and Secretary Stanton was eminent in his profession — would at once say that the time beyond the eight days allowed for assembling a court-martial must be a reasonable period, and that an officer was entitled to prompt trial, or release from arrest. The law now passed was imperative. Within eight days the arrested officer must be notified of the charges against him, within ten days he must be tried, and "if the necessities of the service prevent a trial" within thirty days after the ten, the officer is entitled to an absolute discharge. General Stone's case fell within the justice and the mercy of the law. The eight days within which he should be notified of the charges against him had been long passed; the ten days had certainly expired; but by the construction of the War Department the victim was still in the power that wronged him for thirty days more. From the 17th of July, thirty days were slowly told off until the 16th of August was at last reached, and General Stone was once more a free man. He had been one hundred and eighty-nine days in prison, and was at last discharged by the limitation of the statute without a word of exculpation or explanation. The routine order simply recited that "the necessities of the service not permitting the trial, within the time required by law, of Brigadier-General Charles P. Stone, now confined in Fort Lafayette, the Secretary of War directs that he be released from arrest."

The order simply turned him adrift. He was a Colonel in the Regular Army and a Brigadier-General in the volunteer service; and the Secretary, according to the rule of the War Department, should have given him some instruction, — either assigning him to duty or directing him to report at some place and await orders. Thinking it might be an omission, General Stone telegraphed the War Department that he had the honor "to report for duty." He waited five days in New York for an answer, and receiving none repaired to Washington. Reporting promptly at the office of the Adjutant-General, he was told they had no orders for him, and knew nothing about his arrest. He then applied to General McClellan, on the eve of the Antietam campaign, for permission to serve with the army. General McClellan on the 7th of September wrote to Secretary Stanton that he would be glad to avail himself of General Stone's services, and that he had "no doubt as to his loyalty and devotion." No answer was returned by the War Department. On the 25th of September General Stone, still eager to confront his accusers, applied to General-in-Chief Halleck for a copy of any charges or allegations against him, and the opportunity of promptly meeting them. He reminded the general that two hundred and twenty-eight days had elapsed since his arrest, and that if he were to be tried for any offense those who had served under him must be the witnesses of his conduct, and that from battle and disease these witnesses were falling by hundreds and thousands; the casualties were so great indeed that his command was already reduced one-half. General Halleck replied that he had no official information of the cause of General Stone's arrest, and that so far as he could ascertain no charges or specifications were on file against him.

Several weeks later, on the 1st of December, 1862, General Stone applied to General McClellan, calling his attention to the Act of July 17, under which an officer arrested had the right to "a copy of the charges against him within eight days." He therefore respectfully requested General McClellan, as the officer who ordered the arrest, to furnish him a copy of the charges. General McClellan replied on the 5th of December that the order for arrest had been given him by the Secretary of War, who told him it was at the solicitation of the Committee on the Conduct of the War, and based on testimony taken by them. He further informed General Stone that he had the order, in the handwriting of Secretary Stanton, several days before it was carried into effect, and added the following somewhat remarkable statement: " On the evening when you were arrested I submitted to the Secretary of War the written result of the examination of a refugee from Leesburg. This information to a certain extent agreed with the evidence stated to have been taken by the Committee, and upon its being imparted to the Secretary he again instructed me to cause you to be arrested, which I at once did." This discloses the fact that General McClellan was cognizant of the character of the testimony submitted against General Stone, and so rigidly withheld from the knowledge of the person most interested. On receipt of General McClellan's note, General Stone immediately asked him for the name of the Leesburg refugee and for a copy of his statement. A member of General McClellan's staff answered the inquiry, stating that the general "does not recollect the name of the refugee, and the last time he recollects seeing the statement was at the War Department immediately previous to your arrest." General Stone, victim of the perversity which had uniformly attended the case, was again baffled. He was never able to see the statement of the "refugee" or even to get his name, though, according to General McClellan, the testimony of the refugee was the proximate and apparently decisive cause of General Stone's arrest.

General Stone applied directly to the President, asking "if he could inform me why I was sent to Fort Lafayette." The President replied that "if he told me all he knew about it he should not tell me much." He stated that while it was done under his general authority, he did not do it. The President referred General Stone to General Halleck who stated that the arrest was made on the recommendation of General McClellan. This was a surprise to General Stone, for General McClellan had but recently written him that he had full confidence in his devotion and loyalty. General Halleck replied that he knew of that letter, and that "the Secretary of War had expressed great surprise at it because he said that General McClellan himself had recommended the arrest, and now seemed to be pushing the whole thing on his [the secretary's] shoulders." The search for the agency that would frankly admit responsibility was rendered still more difficult by the denial of the Committee on the Conduct of the War that the arrest had ever been recommended by them, either collectively or individually. They had simply forwarded to the Secretary of War such evidence as was submitted to them.

General Stone appeared before the Committee on the Conduct of the War on the 27th of February, 1863 — nearly five months after his release from imprisonment. He was allowed to see the testimony which had hitherto been withheld from him, and answered all the accusations in detail with convincing candor and clearness. As he proceeded in his triumphant responses to all the accusations against him, the committee said, "Why did you not give us these explanations when you were here before?" — "Because," replied General Stone, "if the chairman will remember, the committee did not state to me the particular cases. . . . I gave general answers to general allegations." General Stone stated further to the committee that he ought himself to have asked for a Court of Inquiry after the reverse at Ball's Bluff. "The reason why I did not," he continued, "was this: while General McClellan was at Edward's Ferry, he showed me a telegram which he had written to the President to the effect that he had examined into the affair at Ball's Bluff and that General Stone was entirely without blame." "After the expression of that opinion," said General Stone, "it would not have been respectful to ask for a Court of Inquiry. It was given by the highest authority and sent to the highest authority, and as a soldier I had no right to ask for justification except of my superiors." Subsequently, on the occasion of Mr. Conkling's speech "severely criticising" General Stone's conduct in connection with the affair at Ball's Bluff, the General applied to the aide-de-camp of General McClellan, as likely to be informed of the Commander's wishes, to know if he "should ask for a Court of Inquiry," and the reply was "No." He then asked if he should make a statement correcting the mistakes in Mr. Conkling's speech. The reply was "Write nothing; say nothing; keep quiet." The committee asked General Stone, as a military man, "Who had the power to bring you to trial?" He answered "When I was arrested, the General-in-Chief, General McClellan, had that power. I know I should claim that power if any man under my command were arrested."

The responsibility for the arrest and imprisonment of General Stone must, according to the official record of the case, rest on Secretary Stanton, Major-General McClellan, and the Committee on the Conduct of the War. It is very clear that Mr. Lincoln, pressed by a thousand calls and placing implicit confidence in these three agencies, took it for granted that ample proof existed to justify the extraordinary treatment to which General Stone was subjected. General Stone is not to be classed in that long list of private citizens temporarily confined without the benefit of *habeas corpus*, on the charge of sympathizing with the Rebellion. The situation of those persons more nearly assimilates with that of prisoners of war. It differs totally from the arrest of General Stone in that the cause of detention was well known and very often proudly avowed by the person detained. The key of their prison was generally in the hands of those who were thus confined, — an honest avowal of loyalty and an oath of allegiance to the National Government securing their release. If they could not take the oath they were justifiably held, and were no more injured in reputation than the millions with whose daring rebellion they sympathized. But to General Stone the government permitted the gravest crime to be imputed. A soldier who will betray his command belongs by the code of all nations to the most infamous class — his death but feebly atoning for the injury he has inflicted upon his country. It was under the implied accusation of this great guilt that General Stone was left in duress for more than six weary months, deprived of all power of self-defense, denied the inherited rights of the humblest citizen of the Republic. In the end, not gracefully but tardily, and as it seemed grudgingly, the government was compelled to confess its own wrong and to do partial justice to the injured man by restoring him to honorable service under the flag of the Nation. No reparation was made to him for the protracted defamation of his character, no order was published acknowledging that he was found guiltless, no communication was ever made to him by National authority giving even a hint of the grounds on which for half a year he was pilloried before the nation as a malefactor. The wound which General Stone received was deep. From some motive, the source of which will probably remain a mystery, his persecution continued in many petty and offensive ways, until he was finally driven, towards the close of the war, when he saw that he could be no longer useful to his country, to tender his resignation. It was promptly accepted. He found abroad the respect and consideration which had been denied him at home, and for many years he was Chief of the General Staff to the Khedive of Egypt.

It is not conceivable that the flagrant wrong suffered by General Stone was ever designed by any one of the eminent persons who share the responsibility for its infliction. They were influenced by and largely partook of the popular mania which demanded a victim to atone for a catastrophe. The instances in which this disposition of the public mind works cruel injury are innumerable, and only time, and not always time, seems able to render justice. Too often tne object of popular vengeance is hurried to his fate, and placed beyond the pale of that reparation which returning reason is eager to extend. Fortunately the chief penalty of General Stone was the anguish of mind, the wounding of a proud spirit. His case will stand as a warning against future violations of the liberty which is the birthright of every American, and against the danger of appeasing popular clamor by the sacrifice of an innocent man. Throughout the ordeal, General Stone's bearing was soldierly. He faced accusation with equanimity and endured suffering with fortitude. He felt confident of ultimate justice, for he knew that it is not the manner of his countrymen "to deliver any man to die before that he which is accused have the accusers face to face, and have license to answer for himself concerning the crime laid against him."

CHAPTER XVIII.

WHEN the civil war began, the Government of the United
States owed a less sum than it owed under the administration
of Washington after the funding of the debt of the Revolution. The
population in 1861 was nine times as large, the wealth thirty times
as great as in 1791. The burden therefore was absolutely inconsiderable when contrasted with our ability to pay. But there had
been such gross mismanagement of the Treasury, either from incom-
petency or design, under the administration of Howell Cobb, that
the credit of the government was injured. There was embarrassment when there should have been security; there was scarcity
when the most ordinary prudence would have insured plenty. So
much depended at that moment on the ability of the government
to raise money by pledging its faith, that Mr. Cobb perhaps thought
he was dealing the deadliest blow at the nation by depriving it of
the good name it had so long held in the money markets of the
world. With unblemished credit at the opening of the war, the
government could have used its military power with greater confidence, and consequently with greater effectiveness.

At the beginning of the year 1861 it was necessary for the government to raise about $10,000,000 to meet Treasury notes outstanding and the interest accrued upon them. Congress had passed, on the 17th of December, 1860, a law authorizing the issue of new Treasury notes for this amount, bearing interest at the rate of six per cent., and redeemable after one year; but the Secretary of the Treasury was authorized to issue them, upon public notice, at the best rates of interest offered by responsible bidders. Before the close of the month negotiations were completed, after unusual effort, and it was found that the notes were issued at various rates, only $70,200 at six per cent., $5,000 at seven per cent., $24,500 at eight per cent., $355,000 at rates between eight per cent. and below ten per cent., $3,283,500 at ten per cent. and fractions below eleven per cent., $1,432,700 at eleven per cent., and by far the larger share, $4,840,000, at twelve per cent. The average for the whole negotiation made the rate of interest ten and five-eighths per cent.

The Treasury was empty, for the nominal balance was only $2,233,220 on the 1st of January. Obligations were accruing to such an extent that General John A. Dix, as Secretary of the Treasury, informed the Committee on Ways and Means of the House of Representatives, that the revenue exhibited, on the 1st of February, a deficit of $21,677,524. The committee estimated that the sum needed to carry on current operations was at least $5,000,000 in addition. A loan of $25,000,000 was proposed, to meet these demands. Secretary Dix, who felt the pulse of the financial centres, recommended in a letter to the Ways and Means Committee that the several States be asked to pledge the United-States "deposit funds" in their hands for the security of the loan. His immediate predecessor, Philip F. Thomas, had, in his annual report in the preceding December, urged that the "public lands be unconditionally pledged for the ultimate redemption of all the Treasury notes which it may become necessary to issue."

Such suggestions seem strange to the ears of those who were afterwards accustomed to the unbounded credit of the Republic. But these secretaries were called to hear from capitalists the declaration that the national debt had increased from $28,460,958 on the 1st of July, 1857, to $64,640,838 on the 1st of July, 1860, and that the figures were still mounting upward. In the mean time the revenues were falling off, the sales of public lands were checked, and the estimates of customs for the current year were practically overthrown by the secession of the Southern States and the denial of the authority of the Union.

The task of Congress might well strike some thoughtful legislators as that of making bricks without straw. As the Rebellion took form and organization, it became clear that the ability and willingness of the people to raise large sums of money were vital factors in the problem of the maintenance of the Union. It was well that no one knew just how great were the burdens which the loyal people must bear. It is no disparagement to the leading statesmen of that era, that they did not at first propose measures adequate to the emergency, because no standards existed by which the magnitude of that emergency could be estimated. If Congress had understood on the 1st of July, 1861, that the ordinary expenditures of the government would be, within the fiscal years 1863 and 1864, more than the entire expenditures of the National Government from the foundation of the nation to that day, paralysis would have fallen upon the courage of the bravest. If the necessity had been proclaimed of raising by loans before the 1st of July, 1865, two thousand millions of dollars more than the National Treasury had ever received from loans and revenue combined, the audacity of the demand would have fo' _aen serious consideration. If the Ways and Means Committee had been notified that before the end of 1865, the annual charge for interest on the national debt, for which provision must be made, would reach $150,977,697, much more than twice the total expenditure of the preceding year, skill and energy would have undergone the crucial _est. But the surprise of legislators would have been equally great if they could then have unrolled the future records of the Treasury, and have seen that in the year in which the Rebellion would be suppressed, the receipts from customs would attain the vast sum of $179,046,651, while from internal revenue, a source not yet drawn upon, the enormous aggregate of $309,226,813 would be contributed to maintain the public credit.

We are so familiar with the vast sums which the war against the Rebellion caused the National Government to disburse, that it is difficult to appreciate the spirit with which the legislators of 1861 approached the impending burdens. They knew that their task was great. They were in imminent peril, not only from open hostility, but from doubt and fear. The resources of the Republic had not been measured, the uprising of popular patriotism had not yet astonished foreign foes and even the most sanguine of domestic participants. With the information which was then before the world, it may be questioned whether a complete scheme for providing the money necessary for the struggle could have been passed through Congress, or rendered effective with capitalists. The needs of each crisis were supplied as each arose. Congress did not try to look far into the future. It exerted itself to give daily bread to the armies of the Union, to provide munitions of war, to build and equip the navy.

The first receipts into the Treasury in 1861, other than from the ordinary revenues under preceding statutes, came from the loan of February 5, which authorized the issue of bonds bearing six per cent. interest, payable within not less than ten, or more than twenty years. The amount authorized was $25,000,000, and the secretary was able to negotiate $18,415,000 at the average rate of eighty-nine and three one-hundredths (89.03) per cent.

The Congress which closed its sessions on the 4th of March, 1861, among its final acts provided for a loan of $10,000,000 in bonds, or the issue of a like sum in Treasury notes; and the President was also empowered to issue Treasury notes for any part of loans previously authorized. Under this statute, notes were issued to the amount of $12,896,350, payable sixty days after date, and $22,468,100 payable in two years. This measure indicates the disposition to provide for pressing exigencies by devices which covered only the present hour, and left heavier responsibilities to the future. An incident of this period was the settlement of the debt incurred in the war in Oregon against the Indians, by giving to the claimants or their representatives six per cent. bonds redeemable in twenty years. The bonds were taken to the amount of $1,090,850, showing that such securities were welcome to claimants even at par.

The chief dependence of the United States for revenue had always been upon customs. But no real test had ever been made of the sum that might be collected from this source. The aim had been to see with how small an amount the National Government could be supported, not how large an amount might be collected. The time was now upon us when this critical experiment was to be tried, and the initial step in that direction was the Morrill Tariff which went into effect on the first day of April. It radically changed the policy of our customs duties from the legislation of 1846 and 1857, and put the nation in the attitude of self-support in manufactures. Although introduced before secession attained its threatening proportions, it was well adapted to the condition in which the country was placed at the time of its enactment. It was a measure carefully elaborated, and based upon principles which were applied with studious accuracy to all its parts. Under it the imposts which had averaged about nineteen per cent. on dutiable articles, and fifteen per cent. on the total importations, mounted to thirty-six per cent. on dutiable articles, and to twenty-eight per cent. on the total importations. Thus, although the goods brought into the country fell off unavoidably by reason of the war, and especially of the difficulties encountered by our vessels from the rebel privateers, the customs duties rather increased than diminished, and something was thus secured in the way of a basis of credit for the immense loans which became necessary. The measure, Mr. Sherman of Ohio stated, would in ordinary times produce an income of $65,000,000 a year to the Treasury.

The Morrill Tariff was found to meet the exigencies of the situation to such a degree that when Congress came together in response to the call of President Lincoln, Mr. Thaddeus Stevens, as head of the committee charged with the subject, informed the House that it had been determined not to enter upon a general revision. He reported a measure to extend the schedule of dutiable articles with the view of adding immediately to the revenue about $22,250,000 annually. After disagreement with the Senate his bill with slight alteration was enacted and became the tariff of Aug. 5, 1861. In Dec. 24, 1861, the duties on tea, coffee, and sugar were increased directly as a war measure. During the consideration of this bill, Mr. Morrill presented estimates showing that the revenue would be increased by about $7,000,000, and Mr. Vallandigham of Ohio took occasion to dwell on the falling off of importations, asking, "How are you to have revenue from imports when nothing is imported? Your expenditures are $500,000,000, your income but $50,000,000." He was much nearer the actual figures than political rhetoric is apt to be. Mr. Morrill's response was only to hope that the gentleman from Ohio had some proposition to offer more acceptable than the pending bill. That bill was indeed a reasonable and, so far as it went, an effective measure, and Mr. Vallandigham had no substitute to offer.

In his annual report as Secretary of the Treasury, Howell Cobb had, on the 4th of December, 1860, estimated that the receipts of the Treasury for the fiscal year ending with June, 1862, would amount to $64,495,891, while he reckoned that the expenditures would be $68,363,726. With the prospect of peace and national unity he predicted a deficiency of $3,867,834 for that year. His figures were so preposterously incorrect as to justify the suspicion of intentional misstatement. The deficiency for the four years of Mr. Buchanan's administration had been, according to a statement by Mr. Sherman of Ohio in the House of Representatives, almost exactly $20,000,000 a year. This deficiency had been met by continual borrowing. On the 11th of February Secretary Dix reported to the Committee of Ways and Means that provision must be made before the 4th of March for a final deficiency of $9,901,118. This necessity was provided for by a clause in the Morrill Tariff Act; and the authority to issue Treasury notes to the full amount of loans previously permitted, gave to the administration of President Lincoln the means to start upon its difficult career.

With a revenue which no one estimated beyond $5,000,000 a month, with a credit at the low ebb which the sales of its bonds had already exhibited, the nation was to prepare for a war of untold magnitude. Mr. Chase, as Secretary of the Treasury, began to try the fruitfulness of the loan laws under which he must proceed. April 2, 1861, he offered $8,000,000, but the prices were not satisfactory to him, and he sold only $3,099,000 at the rate of 94.01. Nine days later he received bids for $1,000,000 of Treasury notes bearing six per cent. interest, and with considerable exertion he secured the increase of this sum to $5,000,000 at par. A committee of the New-York Chamber of Commerce led in a movement, representing the banks of some of the chief cities, to assist the Treasury in borrowing the means required for its pressing exigencies. By this co-operation Mr. Chase raised in May $7,310,000 on bonds at rates from eighty-five to ninety-three per cent. and $1,684,000 by Treasury notes at par.

When Congress met in special session under the call of Mr. Lincoln July 4, Secretary Chase found it necessary to declare that while the laws still permitted loans amounting to $21,393,450, the authority was unavailable because of the limitation that the securities, whether bonds or Treasury notes, should be issued only at par, on the basis of six per cent. interest. Practically therefore no power existed to borrow money. While, on the first of the month then current, there was a nominal balance in the Treasury of $2,355,635, charges by reason of appropriations for account of the preceding fiscal year were outstanding to the extent of $20,121,880. The short loans already made, constituted also an immediate claim, and these amounted to $12,639,861. All these burdens were to be borne in addition to the demands of the year, which, as already demonstrated, would be one of extended military operations and of costly preparations and movements at sea. The total for which the secretary asked that Congress might provide resources, reached according to his estimates the sum of $318,519,581 for the fiscal year. Far-seeing men believed that even this enormous aggregate would fall short of the actual demand.

Mr. Chase proposed that $80,000,000 be raised by taxation, and $240,000,000 by loans. The suggestion was already urged that even a larger proportion of the money needed, should be raised by taxation. But unwillingness to create friction and opposition doubtless entered into the considerations which determined the recommendations of the secretary. He proposed to rely upon the tariff for a large share of the basis of credit, and, while adding to its provisions, to impose a direct tax, and to levy duties upon stills and distilled liquors, on ale and beer, on tobacco, spring-carriages, bank-notes, silver ware, jewellery, and legacies.

Congress made haste to consider and substantially to carry out the recommendations of Secretary Chase. The legislators were not inclined to go farther than the head of the Treasury suggested. No practical proposition was made for a broader scheme of taxation. The tariff, as has been indicated, was enlarged. A bill was passed, levying a direct tax of $20,000,000, to be apportioned among all the States, of which the sum of $12,000,000 was apportioned among the States which had not seceded from the Union. Instead of the scheme of internal taxes which Mr. Chase had proposed, an income tax was substituted, to be collected on the results of the year ending April 1, 1862, and assessed at three per cent. on all incomes in excess of $800; but before any collections were made under it, the broader internal-revenue system went into effect. Direct taxes had been tried in 1800 and again in 1814, but the receipts had always been disappointing. The results under Secretary Chase's proposition were altogether unsatisfactory; and on the 1st of July, 1862, an Act was passed limiting the tax to one levy previous to April 1, 1865, when the law should have full force. The estimates of collections were set at $12,000,000 annually, or very near that sum. For four years, 1862–1865 inclusive, the receipts were only $4,956,657: in 1867 they became $4,200,233, and then dribbled away.

Inadequate as is now seen to be the legislation of 1861 with reference to actual revenue, the receipts fell far below the calculations of experts. For the fiscal year 1862 the customs amounted to only $49,056,397, and the direct tax to $1,795,331; and the total receipts, excluding loans, were only $51,919,261 instead of $80,000,000, as expected under the estimates of the Treasury. The plea may perhaps be pressed in defense of Congress, that financial legislation, laggard as it was, ran before popular readiness to raise money by taxes. There was a wide-spread opposition among the strongest advocates of the war, to all measures which would, at an early stage, render the contest pecuniarily oppressive, and hence make it unpopular.

President Lincoln in his message at the opening of the special session had called upon Congress for $400,000,000 in money, and 400,000 men. Mr. Chase's figures were $320,000,000. He doubtless deemed it wise to ask for no more than Congress would promptly grant. As the struggle proceeded, it was demonstrated that those calculated most justly who relied most completely on the popular purpose to make every sacrifice to maintain the national integrity. This was however the period of depression after the first battle of Bull Run, of hesitation before casting every thing into the scale for patriotism.

The eloquent fact about the Loan Bill is that Congress made haste to enact it. It was introduced into the House of Representatives on the 9th of July. On the next day Mr. Stevens, chairman of the Ways and Means Committee, called up the bill, and, upon going into committee of the whole, induced the House to limit general debate to one hour. In the committee the entire time was occupied by Mr. Vallandigham of Ohio, in a criticism on the President's message and on the general questions involved in the prosecution of the war. Mr. Holman of Indiana addressed to the gentleman from Ohio two inquiries bearing on the purpose of the latter to aid in maintaining the Union. No response was made to the speech of Mr. Vallandigham. The committee rose, and the bill was passed by a vote of 105 to 5. In the Senate no discussion took place, certain amendments looking to the perfection of the measure were adopted, and the bill was passed without division. The House at once concurred in the Senate amendments, and the act was consummated by which the first of the great war loans was authorized.

This Act became law on the 17th of July. Its provisions created a system by which the Secretary of the Treasury might offer bonds not exceeding $250,000,000 in the aggregate at seven per cent. interest, redeemable after twenty years; or he might issue Treasury notes payable three years after date, and bearing seven and three-tenths per cent. interest, — the notes not to be of less denomination than fifty dollars. A separate section permitted the secretary to offer not more than $100,000,000 abroad, payable in the United States or in Europe. The same Act authorized for a part of the sum not exceeding $50,000,000, the exchange for coin or the use in payment of salaries or other dues, of notes of less denomination than fifty dollars but not less than ten dollars, and bearing interest at the rate of three and sixty-five one-hundredths per cent. payable in one year; or these might be payable on demand and without interest. This loan might therefore be in bonds for sale in this country or in a different form for sale abroad; or, second, it might be in Treasury notes of not less than fifty dollars each, bearing seven and three-tenths per cent. interest; or, third, a part of the loan not exceeding $50,000,-000 might be in notes of even as low denomination as ten dollars at three and sixty-five one-hundredths per cent.; and, finally, this latter part might be in notes without interest payable on demand. The bonds were to run at least twenty years; the seven-thirties three years; and the three-sixty-fives were payable in one year, and exchangeable into seven-thirties at the pleasure of the holder. A supplementary Act was passed Aug. 5, 1861, which permitted the secretary to issue six per cent. bonds, payable at the pleasure of the United States after twenty years, and the holders of seven-thirty notes were allowed to exchange their notes for such bonds. The minimum of the denominations of Treasury notes was reduced to five dollars, and all the demand notes of less denomination than fifty dollars were receivable for payment of public dues. By Act of Feb. 12, 1862, the limit of demand notes was raised to $60,000,000. In this modified form the statute directed the movements of the Treasury during the autumn of the first year of the Rebellion.

In his report, dated December 9, 1861, the Secretary of the Treasury related the steps which he had taken to raise money under these laws. Mr. Chase informed Congress that "his reflections led him to the conclusion that the safest, surest, and most beneficial plan would be to engage the banking institutions of the three chief commercial cities of the seaboard to advance the amounts needed for disbursement in the form of loans for three years' seven-thirty bonds, to be reimbursed, as far as practicable, from the proceeds of similar bonds, subscribed for by the people through the agencies of the national loan; using, meanwhile, himself, to a limited extent, in aid of these advances, the power to issue notes of smaller denominations than fifty dollars, payable on demand." Representatives of the banks of New York, Boston, and Philadelphia united to give moneyed support to the government. The secretary opened books of subscription throughout the country. The banks subscribed promptly for $50,000,000, paying $5,000,000 at once in coin, and agreeing to pay the balance, also in coin, as needed by the government. For this loan the banks received seven-thirty notes, and the proceeds of the popular loan were transferred to them. The sales to the public amounted to little more than half that sum; but the banks, when called upon, made a second advance of $50,000,000. By these and other agencies, Mr. Chase was able to present an encouraging summary of the Treasury operations.

He stated that "there were paid to creditors, or exchanged for coin at par, at different dates, in July and August, six per cent. two years' notes, to the amount of $14,019,034.66; there was borrowed at par, in the same months, upon sixty days' six per cent. notes, the sum of $12,877,750; there were borrowed at par, on the 19th of August, under three years' seven-thirty bonds, issued for the most part to subscribers to the national loan, $50,000,000; there were borrowed on the 1st of October, upon like securities, $50,000,000; there were borrowed at par for seven per cent., on the 10th of November, upon twenty years' six per cent. bonds, reduced to the equivalent of sevens, including interest, $45,795,478.48; there have been issued, and were in circulation and on deposit with the treasurer on the 30th of November, of United-States notes payable on demand, $24,550,325,— making an aggregate realized from loans in various forms of $197,-242,588.14." The loan operations had therefore been fairly successful, for they were still in progress; and President Lincoln was justified in stating in his message that "the expenditures made necessary by the Rebellion are not beyond the resources of the loyal people, and the same patriotism which has thus far sustained the government will continue to sustain it, till peace and union shall yet bless the land."

But the shadows were growing thick, and the situation was very serious. Mr. Chase was compelled to report that his estimates of revenue must be reduced below the figures which he gave in July by $25,447,334: at the same time the expenditures must be reckoned at an increase of $213,904,427. Predictions as to the speedy close of the war had ceased. Provision must be made, not only for the deficiencies presented, but for the ensuing year, during which the secretary estimated that the expenditures would be $475,331,245. He proposed to amend the direct tax law, so as to collect under it $20,000,000; to establish a system of internal revenue as he had suggested in July, and to increase some of the customs duties. From these sources, united with the receipts from the public lands, the revenue would be $95,800,000. With this basis, reliance must be placed on loans for the enormous sum of $654,980,920, and under existing laws he could borrow only $75,449,675.

The sale of public lands had furnished some part of the resources of the nation from an early day. The annual product had not been large as a rule. In 1834 and 1835 the sales had been abnormal, amounting in the latter year to $24,877,179, and only about $10,000,000 less in the preceding year. They were $11,497,-049 in 1855, but they had fallen until they were less than $2,000,000 in 1859. It was natural to consider whether any help could be derived from this quarter in the hour of national necessity. A forced sale of lands was impossible to any such extent as to affect the receipts of the Treasury in the ratio of its demands. The pledge of the domain as security for loans was suggested only to be rejected. As was natural, purchases of the public domain ceased almost entirely while the young men of the country were summoned to the national defense, and the better strength of immigrants went into the field of battle. From the public lands therefore the Treasury could hope for little, and very little was in fact received from them during the Rebellion. Secretary Chase had estimated in July that $3,000,000 might be annually derived from this source; but the receipts from the sales of lands never reached even $1,000,000 a year until two years after the Rebellion had been suppressed. Practically the public lands passed out of consideration as a source of revenue. Unfortunately also the attempt to levy a direct tax was received by the people with grave manifestations of disapproval. Its enforcement was likely to prove mischievous. The close of the year 1861 was therefore heavy with discouragement to the government. The military reverses at Bull Run and Ball's Bluff had outweighed in the popular mind the advantages we had gained elsewhere; the surrender of Slidell and Mason, though on every consideration expedient, had wounded the national pride; and now the report of the Secretary of the Treasury tended to damp the ardor of those who had with sanguine temperament looked forward to an easy victory over the Rebellion.

It was felt by all that the National credit, which had been partially restored under Mr. Chase's administration of the Treasury, could not be maintained except from the pockets of the people, and that every man must expect to contribute of his substance to the support of the government in the great task it had assumed. Happily all considerate and reflecting men saw that, desperate as the struggle might be, it must be accepted with all its cost and all its woe. They could at least measure it and therefore could face it. On the side of defeat they could not look. That was a calamity so great as to be immeasurable, and it left to the loyal millions no choice. If the struggle then in progress had been with a foreign power, popular opinion would have overthrown any administration that would not at once make peace. But peace on the basis of a dissevered Union, a disintegrated people, a dishonored nationality, could not be accepted and would not be endured.

The discouragement in financial circles produced by the Treasury report of Mr. Chase, hastened if it did not cause the suspension of specie payment by the banks of New-York City. Many country banks had ceased to pay specie some time before; indeed, many had been only on a nominal basis of coin since the financial crisis of 1857. So long however as the specie standard was upheld by the New-York banks, the business of the country was securely maintained on the basis of coin. It was therefore a matter of serious moment and still more serious portent that the financial pressure became so strong in the last days of the year 1861 as to force the banks of the metropolis to confess that they could no longer maintain a specie standard. It had been many years since the government had paid any thing but coin over its counters, but Treasury notes had just been issued payable on demand, and many millions were already in circulation. They would now be presented for redemption, and if promptly met, the Treasury would be rapidly drained of its specie. There were twenty-five millions less of gold coin in the government vaults than Secretary Chase had expected. This fact had of itself enforced a larger issue of demand notes than would otherwise have been called for, and had thus doubly complicated the financial situation. The Treasury had disbursed a larger amount of demand notes and received a smaller amount of gold coin than the well considered estimates of the secretary had anticipated.

The presumption was in favor of our being much stronger in coin than we were found to be. The discovery of gold in California had resulted in an enormous product, — surpassing any thing known in the history of mining. But we had been encouraging the importation of goods from Europe which were confessedly somewhat cheaper than our own fabrics, and in amount largely in excess of our export of cotton and cereals. We were therefore constantly paying the difference in coin. The political economists who had been in control of our finances insisted upon treating our gold as an ordinary product, to be exported in the same manner that we exported wheat and pork. The consequence was that during the decade preceding the war our exports of specie and bullion exceeded our imports of the same by the enormous aggregate of four hundred and fifty millions of dollars. For that whole period there had been a steady shipment of our precious metals to Europe at a rate which averaged nearly four millions of dollars per month.

Advocates of protection had found the drain of our specie the proximate cause of the financial panic of 1857. They now believed that the same cause had produced a suspension of coin payment at a much earlier date than the war pressure alone would have brought it about. They did not lose the opportunity of demonstrating that a system of protection which would have manufactured more and imported less, and which would thus have retained many millions of our specie at home, would have enabled us to meet the trials of the war with greater strength and confidence. If the Morrill Tariff had been enacted four years before, it would have been impossible for Secretary Cobb to stab the national credit. He would have been dealing constantly with a surplus instead of a deficit, and could not have put the nation to shame by forcing it to hawk its paper in the money markets at the usurious rate of one per cent. per month. One of the wisest financiers in the United States has expressed the belief that two hundred millions of coin, which might easily have been saved to the country by a protective tariff between 1850 and 1860, would have kept the National debt a thousand millions below the point which it reached. Of all the arguments with which protectionists have arraigned free-traders, perhaps the mos' difficult to answer is that which holds them responsible for the weak financial condition of 1860–61 in that they had deliberately driven our specie from the country for the ten preceding years.

CHAPTER XIX.

AT the opening of the year 1862, from causes narrated in the
preceding chapter, the government finances were in an embarrassed and critical situation. In Europe the general opinion —
founded in many influential quarters on the wish — was that the
Union would be dissolved; that with the success of the South,
there would be still further division between the East and the
West; and that the only compact power would be the Confederacy
founded on slavery, with the world's great staples as the basis of
its wealth and its assured development. We had but recently and
narrowly escaped war with England on account of the Trent affair,
and in the crafty and adventurous Emperor of France we had a
secret enemy who saw in our downfall the possible extension of his
power and the strengthening of his throne. Confederate bonds were
more popular in England than the bonds of the United States.
The world's treasures were closed against us. The bankers of
Europe, with the Rothschilds in the lead, would not touch our

securities. Their united clientage included the investors of Great Britain and the Continent, and a popular loan could not be effected without their aid and co-operation. We were engaged therefore in a threefold contest, — a military one with the Confederacy, a diplomatic and moral one with the governments of England and France, a financial one with the money power of Europe.

These causes threw us upon our own resources. The problem to be solved was the utilization of our wealth without the aid which comes from the power to borrow foreign money. Congress had obviously failed at the extra session of July to use the taxing power to the extent which financial wisdom demanded, and though it was now willing to correct the error, there was not time to wait the slow process of enactment, assessment, and collection. Our need was instant and pressing. The banks of the country, many of them in reckless, speculative hands, were freed by the suspension of specie payment from their just responsibility, and might flood the country with worthless paper which would entail great distress upon the people. The Treasury notes not being paid in coin on demand, as promised on their face, became discredited to such a degree that the banks of the leading commercial cities would receive them only as a special deposit, and not as money of account. So entirely were these notes distrusted in the opening month of 1862 that in more than one instance State banks exchanged their own bills for them as an act of patriotism, in order that the bounty due to soldiers just recruited might be paid before they left their State rendezvous to join the armies in the field. Troops already in the service had seen more than one pay-day go by without sight of the paymaster, and tens of millions were overdue to them. Discontent in all the camps was the natural result.

With no power to exchange our bonds for coin except at such rates as would destroy national credit, with only a hundred millions of coin in all our banks when the war began, and a hundred and fifty millions hoarded among the people, with the lavish products of our mines transferred to Europe to pay for articles which it would have been wiser to manufacture at home, our situation was not merely one of anxiety but of peril. Never in the history of national progress through trials and crises, were wise statesmanship and financial sagacity more imperatively demanded. The Rebels might fight without money, for they had no national credit to protect; but to the Union, bankruptcy meant final and hopeless ruin.

The first thing to be secured was a currency. That was demanded to pay the debt of honor due to the soldiers; to remove stagnation in business; to put the people in heart and hope. It had been demonstrated that Treasury notes, without punctual and regular redemption, would not circulate. When A paid them to B in satisfaction of a debt, B had no assurance that he might in turn cancel an obligation by paying them to C. It would perhaps occur to C, that for a lawful debt he had the right to demand gold or silver; for the law told him in explicit terms that nothing else constituted a legal-tender. It was obviously impossible to conduct the business of the country and to carry on the war, in coin payments, with the small amount of coin at command. Few would insist upon coin, but as the power to insist upon it was a legal right, it was a continuing menace to the confidence of trade.

In the opinion of the majority, the one imperative duty was that the government should take control of the currency, issue its own paper as a circulating medium, and make it equal and alike to all, by declaring it to be a legal-tender in the payment of debts. It was the most momentous financial step ever taken by Congress, — as it is the one concerning which the most pronounced and even exasperating difference of opinion was manifested at the time, has since continued, and will probably never entirely subside so long as the government keeps one legal-tender note in circulation. It was admitted to be a doubtful if not dangerous exercise of power; but the law of necessity overrides all other laws, and asserts its right to govern. All doubts were decided in favor of the nation, in the belief that dangers which were remote and contingent could be more easily dealt with than those which were certain and imminent.

Relief came promptly. On the 22d of January, 1862, Mr. E. G. Spaulding of New York reported the legal-tender bill to the House. It had been maturely considered by the Committee of Ways and Means, — a committee made up of very able men. Mr. Spaulding is entitled to rank as the author of the measure. It is difficult to assign absolute originality in any case where so many minds are at work in the same field of investigation, and where, with an approximate identity of date, there is a general similarity of conclusion. But the formal proposition and the public advocacy belong to Mr. Spaulding. He had been all his life engaged in financial affairs, was a banker of recognized ability in the city of Buffalo, and enjoyed a high reputation throughout the State of New York for intelligence and probity.

He had not waited for advice or even for consultation, but on the thirtieth day of December, 1861, — the day on which the banks of New York suspended specie payment, — he introduced the original legal-tender bill in the House of Representatives.

The first provision of the bill now reported, was for the issue of $150,000,000 of Treasury notes, differing from those previously authorized by being declared a legal-tender for all obligations, public and private, except duties on imports and interest on the public debt. The notes were also to be exchangeable into six per cent. bonds, redeemable at the pleasure of the United States after five years. In reporting the bill, Mr. Spaulding called it "a war measure, a measure of necessity not of choice, to meet the most pressing demands upon the Treasury, to sustain the army and navy until they can make a vigorous advance upon the traitors and crush out the Rebellion." He argued, "These notes will find their way into all the channels of trade among the people; and as they accumulate in the hands of capitalists, they will exchange them for the six per cent. twenty years' bonds:" the notes will "be equally as good, and in many cases better, than the present irredeemable circulation issued by the banks." Mr. Spaulding argued that the Constitution justified such legislation in the emergency, and he declared that by this plan "the government will be able to get along with its immediate and pressing necessities without being obliged to force its bonds on the market at ruinous rates of discount: the people under heavy taxation will be shielded against high rates of interest, and capitalists will be afforded fair compensation for the use of their money during the pending struggle for national existence."

Mr. Spaulding admitted that "a suspension of specie payment is greatly to be deplored," but he contended that "it is not a fatal step in an exigency like the present. The British Government and the Bank of England remained under suspension from 1797 to 1821–22, a period of twenty-five years. During this time England successfully resisted the power of the Emperor Napoleon, and preserved her own imperiled existence. As a measure of necessity, she made the Bank of England notes virtually a legal-tender by suspending the specie restriction. Throughout this period the people of Great Britain advanced in wealth, population, and resources." Mr. Spaulding maintained that "gold is not as valuable as the productions of the farmer and the mechanic, for it is not as indispensable as are food and raiment. Our army and navy must have what is far more valuable to them than gold and silver. They must have food, clothing, and the material of war. Treasury notes, issued by the government on the faith of the whole people, will purchase these indispensable articles."

When the bill was taken up for consideration on the 29th of January, the objections which had been raised in the public press were elaborated in the Committee of the Whole. Mr. Pendleton of Ohio was the first in opposition. In beginning a long argument, he insisted that "the feature of this bill which first strikes every thinking man, even in these days of novelties, is the proposition that these notes shall be made a legal-tender in discharge of all pecuniary obligations, as well those which have accrued in virtue of contracts already made as those which are yet to accrue in pursuance of contracts which shall hereafter be made. Do gentlemen appreciate the full import and meaning of that clause? Do they realize the full extent to which it will carry them? Every contract for the payment of money is in legal contemplation a contract for the payment of gold and silver coin. Every promissory note, every bill of exchange, every lease reserving rent, every loan of money reserving interest, every bond issued by this government, is a contract to which the faith of the obligor is pledged, that the amount, whether rent, interest, or principal, shall be paid in the gold and silver coin of the country." Mr. Pendleton deemed it a very serious matter that "the provisions of this bill contemplate impairing the obligation of every contract of that kind, and disturbing the basis upon which every judgment and decree and verdict has been entered." He concluded by referring to the depreciated paper of the French Revolution, to the long suspension of specie currency in England, and the throes attending return to it in 1822. Quoting Daniel Webster's words that "gold and silver currency is the law of the land at home, the law of the world abroad: there can, in the present condition of the world, be no other currency," Mr. Pendleton made an earnest appeal to the House "to heed this lesson of wisdom."

Repeated declarations were made during the debate that the Secretary of the Treasury had not given his approval of the pending measure. This impression was seriously impeding the progress of the bill, and, if it had been confirmed, would probably have defeated it. A belief was prevalent that Mr. Chase would be glad to have the advantage of the measure in the management of the Treasury without assuming the responsibility of its recommendation. But it was soon evident that he could not remain in a passive and receptive position without defeating the bill. Its real opponents took advantage of the rumors; and its supporters, annoyed if not angered, by the suggestion of hostility on the part of the Treasury, were determined that Secretary Chase should take open ground. The embarrassment was relieved by a letter from the Secretary to the Committee of Ways and Means, dated Jan. 29, and read in the House on the 4th of February by Mr. Spaulding. The letter had great influence on Congress. Without it, the measure would probably have been defeated.

Mr. Chase, assuming that "the provision making United-States notes a legal-tender has doubtless been well considered by the committee," deemed it his duty to say that "in respect to the provision, his reflections had conducted him to the same conclusions the committee had reached." He did not wish to conceal that he felt "a great aversion to making any thing but coin a legal-tender in payment of debts." He had been anxious "to avoid the necessity of such legislation." He found it however "impossible, in consequence of the large expenditures entailed by the war and the suspension of the banks, to procure sufficient coin for disbursements." He declared therefore that it "had become indispensably necessary that we should resort to the issue of United-States notes. Making them a legal-tender might however still be avoided, if the willingness manifested by the people generally, by railroad companies, and by many of the banking institutions, to receive and pay them as money in all transactions were absolutely or practically universal; but unfortunately there are some persons and some institutions that refuse to receive and pay them, and their action tends, not merely to the unnecessary depreciation of the notes, but to establish discriminations in business against those, who, in this matter, give a cordial support to the government, and in favor of those who do not. Such discrimination should if possible be prevented; and the provision making the notes a legal-tender, in a great measure at least, prevents it by putting all citizens in this respect on the same level, both of rights and duties." In addition to this official communication, Mr. Spaulding felt justified in reading a personal note from Mr. Chase, in which he said that he "came with reluctance to the conclusion that the legal-tender clause is a necessity," but that he "came to it decidedly and supported it earnestly."

Thaddeus Stevens threw the whole weight of his influence in

favor of the measure. To alternative propositions which had been submitted, he made strenuous objection. Certain bankers of New York had suggested that the immediate wants of the government might be supplied by pledging seven and three-tenths per cent. bonds with a liberal margin, payable in one year, to the banks, which would advance a portion in gold and the rest in currency. Mr. Stevens argued that "the effect of this would be that the government would pay out to its creditors the depreciated notes of non-specie-paying banks. And as there is no probability that the pledges would be redeemed when due, they would be thrown into the market and sold for whatever the banks might choose to pay for them. The folly of this scheme needs no illustration." Another proposition, pressed very earnestly, was to strike out the legal-tender clause, and make the notes receivable for all taxes and public dues, but not to make any provision for redeeming them in coin on demand. Mr. Stevens did not "believe that such notes would circulate anywhere except at a ruinous discount. Notes not redeemable on demand, and not made a legal-tender, have never been kept at par." Even those who could use them for taxes and duties would, in Mr. Stevens's opinion, "discredit them that they might get them low." He was convinced that "if soldiers, mechanics, contractors, and farmers were compelled to take them from the government, they must submit to a heavy shave before they could use them. The knowledge that they were provided for by taxation, and would surely be paid twenty years hence, would not sustain them."

To two prominent amendments which had been submitted, Mr. Stevens manifested earnest opposition. He said "the one moved by the gentleman from Ohio (Mr. Vallandigham) proposes the same issue of notes, but objects to legal-tender, and does not provide for their redemption in coin. He fears our notes would depreciate. Let him who is sharp enough, instruct the House how notes that every man must take can be less valuable than the same notes that no man need take and few would, since they are irredeemable on demand." As to the constitutionality of the bill, he thought that whoever "admits our power to emit bills of credit, nowhere expressly authorized by the Constitution, is an unreasonable doubter when he denies the power to make them a legal-tender." "The proposition of the gentleman from New York" (Mr. Roscoe Conkling), continued Mr. Stevens, "authorizes the issuing of seven per cent. bonds, payable in thirty-one years, to be sold ($250,000,000 of it) or exchanged for the currency of the banks of Boston, New York, and Philadelphia. This suggestion seems to lack every element of wise legislation. Make a loan payable in irredeemable currency, and pay that in its depreciated condition to our contractors, soldiers, and creditors generally! The banks would issue unlimited amounts of what would become trash, and buy good hard-money bonds of the nation. Was there ever such a temptation to swindle? The gentleman from New York further proposes to issue $200,000,000 United-States notes, redeemable in coin in one year. Does he not know that such notes must be dishonored, and the plighted faith of the government be broken? If we are to use suspended notes to pay our expenses, why not use our own?"

The minority of the Ways and Means Committee, through Mr. V. B. Horton of Ohio, had submitted a plan, as Mr. Stevens characterized it, "to issue United-States notes, not a legal-tender, bearing an interest of three and sixty-five hundredths per cent., and fundable in seven and three-tenths per cent. bonds, not payable on demand, but at the pleasure of the United States. This gives one and three-tenths per cent. higher interest than our loan, and, not being redeemable on demand, would share the fate of all non specie-paying notes not a legal-tender." Mr. Stevens believed that the government was reduced to a narrow choice. It must either throw bonds at six or seven per cent. on the market within a few months in amount sufficient to raise at least $600,000,000 in money, — $557,000,000 being already appropriated, — or it must issue United-States notes, not redeemable in coin, but fundable in specie-paying bonds at twenty years; such notes either to be made a legal-tender, or to take their chance of circulation by the voluntary act of the people. The sturdy chairman of Ways and Means maintained that "the highest rate at which we could sell our bonds would be seventy-five per cent., payable in currency, itself at a discount, entailing a loss which no nation or individual doing a large business could stand for a single year." He contended that "such issue, without being made legal-tender, must immediately depreciate, and would go on from bad to worse. If made a legal-tender, and not issued in excess of the legitimate demand, the notes will remain at par, and pass in all transactions, great and small, at the full value of their face; we shall have one currency for all sections of the country, and for every class of people, the poor as well as the rich."

Mr. Owen Lovejoy of Illinois on the other hand marked out a

very different plan. He advocated as the first step, "adequate taxation, if need be to the extent of $200,000,000." In the next place, he would so legislate as to " compel all banking institutions to do business on a specie basis. Every piece of paper that claimed to be money but was not, he would chase back to the man or corporation that forged it, and visit upon the criminal the penalties of the law. He would not allow a bank note to circulate that was not constantly, conveniently, and certainly convertible into specie." In the third place, he would issue interest-paying bonds of the United States, and "go into the market and borrow money and pay the obligations of the government. This would be honest, business-like, and in the end economical. This could be done. Other channels of investment are blocked up, and capital would seek the bonds as investment." As contrasted with the measure proposed by the Ways and Means Committee, Mr. Lovejoy intimated that his represented " the health and vigor of the athlete ; " the other, " the bloated flesh of the beer-guzzler."

Mr. Roscoe Conkling of New York expressed hearty agreement with Mr. Lovejoy. He agreed "with some other gentleman who said that this bill was a legislative declaration of national bankruptcy." He agreed " with still another gentleman who said that we were following at an humble and a disgraceful distance the Confederate Government, as it is called, which has set up the example of making paper a legal-tender, and punishing with death those who deny the propriety of the proposition." Mr. Conkling declared that "insolvency is ruin and dissolution;" and he believed that " in passing this bill, as was said by the gentleman from Massachusetts [Mr. Thomas], we are to realize the French proposition about virtue,— that it is the first step that costs. Another and another and another $100,000,000 of this issue will follow. We are plunging into an abyss from which there are to be no resuscitation and no resurrection." Mr. Conkling thought "it right to learn of an enemy," and already " the *London Times* hails this $150,000,000 legal-tender bill as the dawn of American bankruptcy, the downfall of American credit." The public debt by the first of the ensuing July, within less than a year from the first battle of the war, was already estimated at $806,000,000. " Who can credit these figures," said Mr. Conkling, " when he remembers that the world's greatest tragedian closed his bloody drama at St. Helena leaving the public debt of France less than seventy million of pounds?" He believed that

" all the money needed can be provided by means of unquestionable legality and safety." He believed the substitute he had offered would effect that result.

Mr. Hooper of Massachusetts, a man of large experience in financial and commercial affairs, spoke ably in support of the legal-tender clause. "No one," said he, "supposes for one moment that government notes will be sold for coined money, or that coined money will be borrowed on them. It is fair to suppose that the opponents of the administration well understand that this would be the effect of accepting the amendment to strike out the legal-tender clause from the bill; and that their object, while they talk about coined money to deceive some of our friends, is to oblige the government to give up the sub-treasury, and to use for its payment the depreciated bills of the suspended banks; thereby flooding the whole country with these irredeemable notes, and producing, in time, a state of financial confusion and distress that would ruin any administration. The proposed issue of government notes guards against this effect of inflating the currency by the provision to convert them into government bonds, the principal and interest of which, as before stated, are payable in specie."

Mr. Morrill of Vermont supported the bill proposed by the minority of the Ways and Means Committee. He described the legal-tender feature as "not blessed by one sound precedent, but damned by all." As a war measure he thought "it was not waged against the enemy, but might well make him grin with delight." He would as soon provide " Chinese wooden guns for the army as paper money alone for the Treasury." Mr. Morrill declared that there never was a greater fallacy than to pretend that as "the whole United States are holden for the redemption of these notes, they will, if made a legal-tender, pass at par." He contended that, as currency, "no more of them can be used than enough to fill the demands of commerce." He directed attention to the fact that of the Treasury notes already issued, payable in specie on demand, "the government succeeded in circulating but $27,000,000 of the $50,000,000 authorized, and of these the banks had held $7,000,000." The sanguine feeling in regard to the length of the war was disclosed by Mr. Morrill. Speaking on the 4th of February, 1862, he ridiculed the suggestion that "the war would be prolonged until July 1, 1863." He declared that "we could close the war by the thirtieth day of July next, as well as in thirty years." This opinion was the one commonly accepted at the time in Congressional circles, though discountenanced by the wisest among those holding important commands in the army.

Mr. Bingham of Ohio spoke earnestly in favor of the bill. He could not "keep silent" when he saw "efforts made to lay the power of the American people to control their currency, a power essential to their interests, at the feet of brokers and of city bankers who have not a tittle of authority save by the assent or forbearance of the people to deal in their paper issues as money." Mr. Bingham argued that as there "is not a line or word or syllable in the Constitution which makes any thing a legal-tender, — gold or silver or any thing else, — it follows that Congress, having 'the power to regulate commerce,' may determine what shall be a lawful tender in the discharge of obligations payable in money only." The "limitation of the power to impair the obligation of contracts," as Mr. Bingham pointed out, was "a limitation upon the States only, and did not restrain the action of Congress."

Mr. Sheffield of Rhode Island argued earnestly against the bill, and predicted the same fate for it, if enacted, that overcame a similar attempt in his State during the Revolutionary war "to make paper a legal-tender." The people would not submit to it, and "the courts set it aside as an unlawful exercise of legislative power."

Mr. Frederick A. Pike of Maine made one of the clearest and ablest speeches delivered in the House in favor of the bill. He regarded it as an experiment forced upon the country by necessity. "We issue $150,000,000," said Mr. Pike, "on a venture." We measure it "with population and wealth and existing currency. We compare it with the action of the past." The issue of Continental notes had reached $20,000,000 by the month of April, 1777, besides a large amount of currency by the States. "And yet," said Mr. Pike, "no marked signs of depreciation had appeared." The whole property of the country did not at that time in his judgment "exceed five hundred millions." From these facts he deduced our ability to stand the proposed issue of paper. Mr. Pike had little faith in the infallibility of any one's judgment as to the ultimate result of financial experiments. He recalled the circumstance that Sir Robert Peel's famous bank bill was introduced in Parliament in 1844 with the confident declaration by Her Majesty's Government that "inquiry had been exhausted." But in the "first mercantile pinch" the measure which was "the embodiment of financial wisdom" did not work favorably, and "the government was compelled to interpose on behalf of the bank and of the business community." "Tax, fight, and emancipate," Mr. Pike declared to be "the Trinity of our salvation."

Mr. Valentine B. Horton of Ohio was opposed to giving the legal-tender quality to government paper. He said "the country was never so wealthy as to-day; never was so little due to foreign countries; never were the people so free from embarrassment. The one drawback is that the Treasury wants money to an immense amount." He believed that an appeal to the capitalists would call forth "gold in the utmost abundance." To pass the legal-tender bill would, in his judgment, be "a legislative declaration that the administration is not equal to the occasion for which it was elected." He thought "the time for oracular utterances about a great movement," by which bankers had been inspired with undue hope, had passed by, and that something practical and actual would soon be accomplished.

Mr. John B. Alley supported the bill by arguments which came from his own wide experience in business. The choice, he said, was between notes of the government and "an irredeemable bank currency, a great deal of which will be found, as it was after the war of 1812, utterly worthless."

Mr. Charles W. Walton of Maine spoke briefly but ably on the constitutional power of Congress to pass the bill. He contended that the authority to declare a legal-tender "was an implied and not a direct power;" that, admitting it to belong to the Government, it exists "without limitation." The question before the House, therefore, is "one of expediency only," and on that ground he earnestly supported the measure.

Mr. Shellabarger of Ohio answered the "charges of bad faith and injustice" which had been brought against the bill by its opponents. The cry of ruin to the country he compared with similar fears for England on the part of her economists, and showed how, in every case, they had been disproved by the rising power and growing wealth of that kingdom. He said the legal-tender notes would be "borne up by all the faith and all the property of the people, and they will have all the value which that faith untarnished and that property inestimable can give them."

Mr. John Hickman of Pennsylvania, having no doubt as to the power of Congress to pass the bill, supported it as a governmental necessity.

The debate in the House was able and spirited throughout. Judging by the tone and number of the Republicans who spoke against the bill, a serious party division seemed to be impending. The measure came to a vote on the 6th of February, the interest in the discussion continuing to the last. Mr. Owen Lovejoy sought occasion to give the measure a parting malediction, declaring that " there is no precipice, no chasm, no yawning bottomless gulf before this nation, so terrible, so appalling, so ruinous, as the bill before the House," and Mr. Roscoe Conkling sought the floor to say that he concurred " in every word " Mr. Lovejoy had spoken. Mr. Conkling said the debate had been allowed to close " without pretext of solid argument by any member in favor of the constitutionality of the one feature of the bill."

The essential difference between the plan of the minority and that of the committee had reference to the legal-tender clause. In fact the other details of the Loan Bill could have been agreed upon in a single day's discussion, and the delay was occasioned solely by the one feature of legal-tender. On substituting the measure of the minority the vote was 55 yeas to 95 nays. The bill was then passed by a vote of 93 to 59. The yeas were all Republicans. Among the nays — principally Democrats — were found some of the ablest and most influential members of the Republican party. Valentine B. Horton of Ohio, Justin S. Morrill of Vermont, Roscoe Conkling, F. A. Conkling, and Theodore M. Pomeroy of New York, Albert G. Porter of Indiana, Owen Lovejoy of Illinois, William H. Wadsworth of Kentucky, Benjamin F. Thomas of Massachusetts, and Edward H. Rollins of New Hampshire, were conspicuous for their hostility to the legal-tender clause.

The Senate received the bill on the next day, and on the 10th it was reported from the Finance Committee for immediate action. Mr. Fessenden explained the amendments which the committee had embodied in the House Bill. In the first section they provided that the interest on the national debt should be paid in coin. Upon this point Mr. Fessenden considered that the public credit, in large degree, depended. As to the legal-tender feature of the notes, he could not make up his mind to support it. " Will your legal-tender clause," he inquired, " make your notes any better? Do you imagine that because you force people to take these notes they are to be worth the money, and that no injury is to follow? What is the consequence? Does not property rise? You say you are injuring the soldier if you compel him to take a note without its being a legal-tender; but will not the sutler put as much more on his goods? And if the soldier sends the notes to his wife to be passed at a country store for necessaries for his family, what will be the result? The goods that are sold are purchased in New York; the price is put on in New York; a profit is added in the country; and thus the soldier loses just as much. You are not saving any thing for any body."

Mr. Fessenden then inquired, "What do we offer without this legal-tender clause? We are offering notes, with the interest secured beyond a question if the amendments proposed by the Committee on Finance of the Senate are adopted, based on the national faith, and with the power to deposit and receive five per cent. interest in any sub-treasury, and the power of the government to sell its stock at any price, to meet whatever it may be necessary to meet. Will notes of this kind stand better when going out, if you put the confession upon their face, that they are discarded by you, and that you know they ought not to be received, and would not be, unless their reception is compelled by legal enactment?"

The argument against this view, according to Mr. Fessenden, "is simply that the banks will not take the notes unless they are made a legal-tender, and therefore they will be discredited. It was thus reduced to a contest between the government and the banks; and the question is whether the banks have the will and the power to discredit the notes of the United-States Treasury." With all his objections to the legal-tender feature,—and they were very grave, — Mr. Fessenden intimated his willingness to vote for it if it were demonstrated to be a necessity. On the constitutional question involved he did not touch. He preferred, he said, "to have his own mind uninstructed" upon that aspect of the case.

In illustration of the doubt and diversity of opinion prevailing, Mr. Fessenden stated that on a certain day he was advised very strongly by a leading financial man that he must at all events oppose the legal-tender clause, which he described as utterly destructive. On the same day he received a note from another friend, assuring him that the legal-tender bill was an absolute necessity to the government and the people. The next day the first gentleman telegraphed that he had changed his mind, and now thought the legal-tender bill peremptorily demanded by public exigency. On the ensuing day the second gentleman wrote that he had changed his mind, and now saw clearly that the legal-tender bill would ruin the country. There can be no harm in stating that the authors of these grotesque contradictions were Mr. James Gallatin and Mr. Morris Ketchum of New York.

Mr. Collamer of Vermont followed Mr. Fessenden in an exhaustive argument against the bill as a violation of the Constitution. He believed "in the power of the government to sustain itself in the strife physically and pecuniarily." He was not willing to say to a man, " Here is my note : if I do not pay it, you must steal the amount from the first man you come to, and give him this note in payment." He would not be governed in this matter, as Mr. Fessenden intimated he might be, " by necessity." He had taken an oath to support the Constitution, and he believed this bill violated it. He "would not overthrow the Constitution in the Senate Chamber while the rebels are endeavoring to overthrow it by war."

Senator Wilson looked upon the contest as one "between the men who speculate in stocks, and the productive, toiling men of the country." He believed "the sentiment of the nation approaches unanimity in favor of this legal-tender clause." He had received letters from large commercial houses in Massachusetts, representing millions of capital, and "they declare that they do not know a merchant in the city of Boston engaged in active business who is not for the legal-tender bill."

Senator Sherman of Ohio urged the adoption of the measure, because "all the organs of financial opinion in this country agree that there is a majority" for it; and he cited the New-York Chamber of Commerce, the Committee on Public Safety in New York, and the Chambers of Commerce of Boston and Philadelphia, as taking that ground. He proceeded "to show the necessity of it from reason." He stated that the government must "raise and pay out of the Treasury of the United States before the first day of July next, according to the estimate of the Committee of Ways and Means, the sum of $343,235,000. Of this sum $100,000,000 is now due and payable to soldiers, contractors, to the men who have furnished provisions and clothing for the army; to officers, judges, and civil magistrates." Mr. Sherman argued that "a question of hard necessity presses upon the government. This money cannot be obtained from the banks. With a patriotic feeling not usually attributed to money corporations, the banks have already exhausted their means. The aggregate capital of the banks of the three principal cities of the United States is but $105,000,000, and they have taken more than their capital in the bonds of the United States." It was, therefore, idle to look to the banks for relief. "They have," continued the senator, "already tied up their whole capital in the public securities. They ask this currency to enable them to assist further in carrying on the government. Among others, the cashier of the Bank of Commerce, the largest bank corporation in the United States and one that has done much to sustain the government, appeared before the Committee on Finance, and stated explicitly that his bank, as well as other banks of New York, could not further aid the government, unless its currency was stamped by, and invested with, the legal form and authority of lawful money, which they could pay to others as well as receive themselves."

Senator James A. Bayard of Delaware argued that the proposed measure violated the Constitution. "No one," said he, "can deny the fact that in the contracts between man and man, and in government contracts to pay money, the obligation is to pay intrinsic value. If you violate that by this bill, which you certainly do, how can you expect that the faith of the community will be given to the law which you now pass, in which you say that you will pay hereafter the interest on your debt in coin? Why should they give credit to that declaration? If you can violate the Constitution of the United States, in the face of your oaths, in the face of its palpable provision, what security do you offer to the lender of money?"

Senator Sumner did not join his colleague in enthusiastic support of the bill. He was indeed much troubled by its provisions. "Is it necessary," he inquired, "to incur all the unquestionable evils of inconvertible paper, forced into circulation by Act of Congress, to suffer the stain upon our national faith, to bear the stigma of a seeming repudiation, to lose for the present that credit which in itself is a treasury, and to teach debtors everywhere that contracts may be varied at the will of the stronger? Surely there is much in these inquiries which may make us pause. If our country were poor or feeble, without population and without resources; if it were already drained by a long war; if the enemy had succeeded in depriving us of the means of livelihood,— then we should not even pause. But our country is rich and powerful, with a numerous population, busy, honest, and determined, and with unparalleled resources of all kinds, agricultural, mineral, industrial, and commercial. It is yet undrained by the war in which we are engaged, nor has the enemy succeeded in depriving us of any of the means of livelihood." But he concluded, "whatever may be the national resources, they are not now within reach except by summary process." He consented "reluctantly, painfully, that the process should issue." He could not however "give such a vote without warning the government against the danger of such an experiment. The medicine of the Constitution must not become its daily bread."

The bill came to a vote in the Senate on the 13th of February. The government exigency was so pressing that the Senate discussion was limited to four days. On the motion of Mr. Collamer to strike out the legal-tender clause, the vote stood 17 yeas to 23 nays. Anthony of Rhode Island, Collamer and Foot of Vermont, Fessenden of Maine, King of New York, Cowan of Pennsylvania, Foster of Connecticut, and Willey of Virginia, among the Republicans, voted to strike out. The vote to retain the legal-tender feature was Republican, with the exception of Garrett Davis of Kentucky, McDougall of California, Rice of Minnesota, and Wilson of Missouri. This question being settled, the bill, with the legal-tender clause embodied, passed by a vote of 30 to 7. Mr. Anthony of Rhode Island stated that, having voted against the legal-tender provision, he "could not take the responsibility of voting against the only measure which is proposed by the government, and which has already passed the House of Representatives." Three Republicans, Collamer, Cowan, and King, and four Democrats, Kennedy, Pearce, Powell, and Saulsbury, were the senators who voted against the bill on its final passage.

The bill was returned to the House of Representatives the next day. The Senate amendments were taken up on the 19th. Mr. Spaulding objected to them generally, and especially to the provisions for selling the bonds at the market price and for paying the interest in coin. Mr. Pomeroy of New York advocated concurrence in the amendments of the Senate, as did Mr. Morrill of Vermont. Upon the amendment to pay interest in coin, the House divided, with 88 ayes to 56 noes. Upon the clause allowing the secretary to sell bonds at the market value, there were 72 ayes to 66 noes. A conference on the points of difference between the two Houses was managed by Senators Fessenden, Sherman, and Carlile, and Representatives Stevens, Horton, and Sedgwick. The report of the Conferees was agreed to in both Houses, and the Act was approved and became a law on the 25th of February. Its leading provisions were for the issue of legal-tender notes, on which the debate chiefly turned, and of coupon or registered bonds not to exceed

$500,000,000 in the aggregate, bearing six per cent. interest, redeemable at the pleasure of the United States after five years, and payable twenty years after date. The bonds were to be sold at their market value for coin or Treasury notes, and the notes to be exchangeable into them in sums of fifty dollars, or any multiple of fifty. These securities became widely known and popular as the five-twenties of 1862. The fourth section allowed deposits of United-States notes with designated depositaries to draw interest at five per cent., and to be paid after ten days' notice, but the total of such deposits was not to exceed $25,000,000 at any time. By the fifth section, duties on imported goods were required to be paid in coin, and the proceeds were pledged, first, to the payment in coin of the interest on the bonds of the United States; and second, to a sinking-fund of one per cent. of the entire debt for its ultimate payment.

Certificates of indebtedness were authorized by Act of Congress passed without debate and approved on the first day of March. These could be granted to any creditor whose claim had been audited, and they drew six per cent. interest, payable at first in coin, but by Act of March 3, 1863, lawful money was substituted for interest. By Act of March 17, 1862, these certificates could be given in discharge of checks drawn by disbursing officers, if the holders of the latter chose to accept them. The secretary was clothed with power by the Act of March 17, 1862, to buy coin with any bonds or notes on such terms as he might deem advantageous. The same Act gave legal-tender value to the demand notes previously authorized. The limitation upon temporary deposits was also raised to $50,000,000.

Mr. Chase, by a communication of June 7 (1862), asked for a further issue of legal-tender notes to the amount of $150,000,000, and he urged that the limit of five dollars be removed, and denominations as low as a single dollar be permitted. He declared that it was impossible to obtain coin necessary to pay the soldiers, and that the plan proposed would remove from disbursing officers the temptation to exchange coin for small bank notes. A reserve of one-third of the temporary deposits would take $34,000,000, and the replacement of the demand notes $56,500,000 more, so that for immediate use the Treasury would get only $59,500,000 of the sum asked for. Mr. Spaulding of New York on the 17th of June presented the measure as reported from the Ways and Means Committee. He argued that this form of loan was "so popular with the people and so advantageous to the government, that it should be extended so far as it could be done safely." Objections such as were offered to the original policy were presented to the additional notes. It was already suggested to authorize notes for fractions of a dollar, but the majority decided against it. The bill passed the House of Representatives on the 24th of June. In the Senate, Mr. Sherman of Ohio attempted to add a clause for the taxation of the circulation of banks, but it was not received with favor. With certain amendments the bill passed the Senate on the 2d of July. On a disagreement which ensued, the conferees were Senators Fessenden, Sherman, and Wright, and Representatives Stevens, Spaulding, and Phelps of Missouri. By their action the volume of notes of denominations less than five dollars was restricted to $35,000,000, and the reserve for meeting deposits was fixed at $75,000,000. While exchangeable into six per cent. bonds, the notes might also be paid in coin under the direction of the Secretary of the Treasury. The report was accepted by the Senate on the 7th of July, and by the House on the 8th. It became a law by the President's approval on the 11th of July.

On the 14th of July, Secretary Chase called the attention of Congress to the great evils arising from the issue by non specie-paying banks and unauthorized persons of depreciated currency, and the consequent disappearance of small coin. As a remedy an Act was passed, and approved July 17, for the use of postage and other stamps in payment of fractional parts of a dollar. These stamps were made exchangeable by assistant treasurers for United-States notes in sums not less than five dollars. Banks and persons were forbidden, from the first day of the ensuing August, to make or issue any note or token for a less sum than one dollar, intended to be used as money, under the penalty of a fine not exceeding $500, or imprisonment not exceeding six months, or both. "Shinplasters" had become almost like the frogs of Egypt for multitude. They were in every man's hands and were of all degrees of value. They were sometimes issued for purposes of fraud. Silver had become lost to view, and business houses resorted to the use of their own notes as a convenience. The government stamps were not well adapted to circulate as currency, and they soon gave way to notes of handsome design which came into universal use as the "small change" of the country.

The proper order of the leading measures of finance has always been a subject of contention. Grave differences of opinion exist, even to this day, concerning the necessity and expediency of the legal-tender provision. The judgment of many whose financial sagacity is entitled to respect is, that if the internal tax had been first levied, and the policy adopted of drawing directly upon the banks from the Treasury for the amounts of any loans in their hands, the resort by the government to irredeemable paper might at least have been postponed and possibly prevented. The premium on gold became the measure of the depreciation of the government credit, and practically such premiums were the charge made for every loan negotiated. In his report of December, 1862, Secretary Chase justified the legal-tender policy. He explained that by the suspension of specie payments the banks had rendered their currency undesirable for government operations, and consequently no course other than that adopted was open. Mr. Chase declared that the measures of general legislation had worked well. "For the fiscal year ending with June," he said, "every audited and settled claim on the government and every quartermaster's check for supplies furnished, which had reached the Treasury, had been met." For the subsequent months, the secretary "was enabled to provide, if not fully, yet almost fully, for the constantly increasing disbursements."

The political effects of the legal-tender bill were of large consequence to the Administration and to the successful conduct of the war. If it had been practicable to adhere rigidly to the specie standard, the national expenditure might have been materially reduced; but the exactions of the war would have been all the time grating on the nerves of the people and oppressing them with remorseless taxation. Added to the discouragement caused by our military reverses, a heavy financial burden might have proved disastrous. The Administration narrowly escaped a damaging defeat in 1862, and but for the relief to business which came from the circulation of legal-tender notes, the political struggle might have been hopeless. But as trade revived under the stimulus of an expanding circulation, as the market for every species of product was constantly enlarging and prices were steadily rising, the support of the war policy became a far more cheerful duty to the mass of our people.

This condition of affairs doubtless carried with it many elements of demoralization, but the engagement of the people in schemes of money-making proved a great support to the war policy of the government. We saw the reproduction among us of the same causes and the same effects which prevailed in England during her prolonged contest with Napoleon. Money was superabundant, speculation was rife, the government was a lavish buyer, a prodigal consumer.   Every man who could work was employed at high wages; every man who had commodities to sell was sure of high prices. The whole community came to regard the prevalent prosperity as the outgrowth of the war.   The ranks of the army could be filled by paying extravagant bounty after the ardor of volunteering was past, and the hardship of the struggle was thus in large measure concealed if not abated.   Considerate men knew that a day of reckoning would come, but they believed it would be postponed until after the war was ended and the Union victorious.

The policy of the legal-tender measure cannot therefore be properly determined if we exclude from view that which may well be termed its political and moral influence upon the mass of our people. It was this which subsequently gave to that form of currency a strong hold upon the minds of many who fancied that its stimulating effect upon business and trade could be reproduced under utterly different circumstances.   Argument and experience have demonstrated the fallacy of this conception, and averted the evils which might have flowed from it.   But in the judgment of a large and intelligent majority of those who were contemporary with the war and gave careful study to its progress, the legal-tender bill was a most effective and powerful auxiliary in its successful prosecution.

Grateful as was the relief to the people from legal-tender notes, it was apparent to Congress that a government cannot, any more than an individual, maintain a state of solvency by the continuous issuing of irredeemable paper.   Money must not merely be promised, it must be paid.   The Government therefore required a strong, efficient system of taxation — one that would promptly return large sums to the Treasury.   From customs, an increasing revenue was already enriching the Government vaults, but the amount derivable from that source was limited by the ability of the people to consume foreign goods, and wise economists did not desire an enlarged revenue the collection of which was at war with so many domestic interests. The country therefore turned by common instinct to a system of internal duties, — fo incomes, to excise, to stamps.   In the extra session of the preceding year, Congress had, by the Act of August 5, 1861, laid the foundation for a system of internal revenue by providing for a direct tax of twenty millions of dollars on the real estate of the country, and for an income tax of three per cent. on all incomes in excess of eight hundred dollars per annum. But the appointment of assessors and collectors under the bill had been postponed "until after the second Tuesday of February, 1862," which was practically remanding the whole subject to the further consideration of Congress before any man should be asked to pay a dollar of tax under the law. The intervening months had not decreased but had on the contrary largely developed the necessities of the National Treasury, and enhanced the necessity of a stable revenue system. The exigency had become so great that Congress was compelled for the first time in our history, to resort to the issue of government notes as a legal-tender currency. Promptness and decision were essential to the preservation of the National credit. The sources, the extent, the limitations of the taxing power were closly examined by Secretary Chase in his report and the subject was remanded to Congress for determination.

The Constitution gives to Congress the power to levy imposts, and prohibits it to the States. It gives also to Congress the power to levy internal taxes and excises, leaving to the States the right to do the same. It is one of the traditions of the Convention which met in Philadelphia in 1787 to frame the Federal Constitution, that Mr. Hamilton remarked in a conference of its leading members that if the power to levy impost and excise should be given to the new government, it would prove strong and successful. If the power were not to be given he did not desire to waste his time in repeating the failure of the old Confederation, and should return at once to New York. It was undoubtedly his influence which secured the wide and absolute field of taxation to the General Government. He well knew that direct taxes are onerous, and as the majority insisted on levying them in proportion to population, as in the old Confederation, their use as a resource to the General Government was practically nullified. Such a system involved the absurdity that men taken *per capita* average the same in respect to wealth, and that one hundred thousand people in New York should pay no more tax than the same number in Arkansas. Statesmen and financiers saw from the first that the direct tax clause in the Constitution would be valuable only in forcing the use of the excise. But for the dread of this, the States would not have yielded all the sources of indirect taxation to the National Government.

When appointed Secretary of the Treasury, Mr. Hamilton insisted upon the prompt levy of excises. He induced the first Congress to lay a tax on all distilled spirits. If made from molasses or sugar or other foreign substance, the tax should be from eleven to thirty cents per gallon according to the percentage above or below proof. If made from domestic products, the tax should be from nine to twenty-five cents per gallon. The first was practically a tax on rum, the second on whiskey. This excise was followed in subsequent years by duties on carriages, on snuff, on property sold at auction, on refined sugar, and by the sale of stamps. Other articles were in after years added to the list, and to aid the Treasury during the period of the second war with Great Britain, a heavy imposition of internal duties was resorted to as the most prompt and efficient mode of replenishing the hard pressed Treasury.

The excise was from the first unpopular. The men who insisted that "black quart-bottles" should be admitted free of duty when the first tariff bill was passed, did not relish the levying of a heavy tax on the whiskey that was to fill them. The exciseman was to their view precisely what Dr. Johnson had defined him in his dictionary: "an odious wretch, employed to collect an unjust tax." Revolutionary proceedings had been inaugurated by resistance to a tax on tea. But tea at that day was looked upon as a luxury in which only a few could indulge, while whiskey was regarded as a necessity, of universal consumption. Resistance went so far as to organize an insurrection in Western Pennsylvania against the official authority which attempted to collect the tax. The outbreak was promptly suppressed by the power of the General Government but the result of the agitation was a deep-seated prejudice against the Federal party. Pennsylvania sympathized with the more liberal views of Jefferson, and in the Presidential election of 1796 gave him fourteen of her fifteen electoral votes. John Adams received the other vote, and as he was chosen by a majority of one, his Pennsylvania support, small as it was, proved timely and valuable.

Resistance to internal duties was tried by legal methods. A heavy duty had been laid on carriages — two dollars per year for those of simplest form and fifteen dollars for the most costly. The tax applied to all carriages for the conveyance of persons, whether kept for private use or for public hire. One Daniel Lawrence Hylton of Virginia resisted the payment of the tax and the case was ultimately heard before the Supreme Court in the February term of 1796. Mr. Hamilton who had resigned from the Treasury Department the preceding year, argued the case for the Government in conjunction with the Attorney-General, Charles Lee. Mr. Campbell, Attorney for the Virginia District and Mr. Ingersoll, the Attorney-General of Pennsylvania appeared for the plaintiff. The case turned wholly upon the point whether the tax, on carriages kept for private use was a direct tax. If not a direct tax, it was admitted to be properly levied according to that clause in the Constitution which declares that "all duties, imposts and excises shall be uniform throughout the United States." If a direct tax it was wrongfully levied because the Constitution declares that "no capitation or other direct tax shall be laid unless in proportion to the census or enumeration of the inhabitants of the United States.

The well-known decision of the court, delivered by Judge Samuel Chase, pronounced the tax to be constitutional. Justice James Wilson who concurred in the decision had taken a very prominent part as a delegate from Pennsylvania in the convention which framed the Constitution, and ranked at the time as one of the ablest lawyers in the Union. The opinion of the judges seemed to be, though no formal decision was rendered to that effect, that a tax on land, and a capitation or poll tax, are the only levies which within the terms of the Constitution are to be considered *direct* taxes. The decision was one of extraordinary interest to the Government, as, had it been the other way, one great resource for the raising of money, indeed the greatest resource, would have been taken from the Federal Government. The appearance of Mr. Hamilton was an indication of the dignity and importance which were attached to the case by Washington's Administration.

A singular feature of the proceedings was the allegation by Mr. Hylton that he "owned, possessed and kept one hundred and twenty-five chariots for the conveyance of persons — exclusively for his own separate use and not to let out to hire, or for the conveyance of persons for hire." What particular necessity a Virginia gentleman of the last century had for that number of chariots "for his own separate use" is nowhere explained. It may have been the mere filling of the blanks in a legal declaration in which the declarant was permitted a free use of figures, but as it stands in the reports of Supreme Court decisions, it seems to be one of the odd incidents which make up the humor of the Law.

The system of internal duties and excises continued in various forms for thirty years, practically disappearing at last in 1821. But for the financial demands precipitated by the war of 1812 and the period of depression which ensued, the system would have been abolished at an earlier date. During the period of their existence, from 1790 to 1820, the internal taxes had yielded to the Government the gross sum of $22,000,000, an average of a little more than $700,000 per annum. It thus proved a very valuable resource to the Republic in the period of its early financial trials.

Congress now determined under the recommendation of Secretary Chase to use this great source of revenue to the fullest practicable extent. Immediately after the passage of the Legaltender Act the subject of internal revenue was taken up, elaborately investigated by committees, exhaustively discussed in both Senate and House. The final result was the enactment of a bill "to provide internal revenue to support the Government and to pay interest on the public debt," which received the President's approval on the first day of July (1862). It was one of the most searching, thorough, comprehensive systems of taxation ever devised by any Government. Spirituous and malt liquors and tobacco were relied upon for a very large share of revenue; a considerable sum was expected from stamps; and three per cent. was exacted from all annual incomes over six hundred dollars and less than ten thousand, and five per cent. — afterwards increased to ten per cent. — on all incomes exceeding ten thousand dollars. Manufactures of cotton, wool, flax, hemp, iron, steel, wood, stone, earth, and every other material were taxed three per cent. Banks, insurance and railroad companies, telegraph companies, and all other corporations were made to pay tribute. The butcher paid thirty cents for every beef slaughtered, ten cents for every hog, five cents for every sheep. Carriages, billiard-tables, yachts, gold and silver plate, and all other articles of luxury were levied upon heavily. Every profession and every calling, except the ministry of religion, was included within the far-reaching provisions of the law and subjected to tax for license. Bankers and pawnbrokers, lawyers and horse-dealers, physicians and confectioners, commercial brokers and peddlers, proprietors of theatres and jugglers on the street, were indiscriminately summoned to aid the National Treasury. The law was so extended and so minute that it required thirty printed pages of royal octavo and more than twenty thousand words to express its provisions.

Sydney Smith's striking summary of English taxation was originally included in a warning to the United States after the war of 1812 against indulging a martial spirit or being inflamed with a desire for naval renown. "Taxes," said the witty essayist in the *Edinburgh Review*, "are the inevitable consequences of being too fond of glory." He bade us beware of Essex, Porter, and Stephen Decatur. Even in the second year of the civil war in which we were struggling for life rather than glory, we had come to realize every exaction ascribed to the British system. We were levying "taxes upon every article which enters into the mouth or covers the back or is placed under the foot; taxes on every thing which it is pleasant to see, hear, feel, smell, or taste; taxes upon warmth, light, and locomotion; taxes on every thing on earth and the waters under the earth; taxes on every thing that comes from abroad or is grown at home; on the sauce which pampers man's appetite and on the drug that restores him to health; on the ermine which decorates the judge and the rope which hangs the criminal; on the poor man's salt and the rich man's spice; on the brass nails of the coffin and the ribbons of the bride."

The system of internal revenue of which the foregoing is no exaggeration proved in all respects effective. Congress rendered the taxes more palatable and less oppressive to the producers by largely increasing the duties on imports by the Tariff Act of July 14, 1862, thus shutting out still more conclusively all competition from foreign fabrics. The increased cost was charged to the consumer, and taxes of fabulous amount were paid promptly and with apparent cheerfulness by the people. The internal revenue was bounteous from the first, and in a short period increased to a million of dollars per day for every secular day of the year. The amount paid on incomes for a single year reached seventy-three millions of dollars, the leading merchant of New York paying in one check a tax of four hundred thousand dollars on an income of four millions. Mr. Webster said that "Hamilton smote the rock of the National resources and abundant streams of revenue gushed forth." But Hamilton's Funding Bill was not more powerful in establishing the credit of the young Republic after the Revolution than was the Internal-revenue Act in imparting strength to the finances of the matured Nation in the throes and agonies of civil war. It was the crowning glory of Secretary Chase's policy, and its scope and boldness entitle him to rank with the great financiers of the world.

CHAPTER XX.

POPULAR interest in the summer of 1862 was divided between events in the field and the election of Representatives to the Thirty-eighth Congress. A year before, the line of partisan division had been practically obliterated in the Loyal States — the whole people uniting in support of the war. The progress of events had to a large extent changed this auspicious unanimity, and the Administration was now subjected to a fight for its life while it was fighting for the life of the Nation.

The conservatism which Mr. Lincoln had maintained on the Slavery question had undoubtedly been the means of bringing to the support of the war policy of his Administration many whom a more radical course at the outset would have driven into hostility. As he advanced however towards a more aggressive position, political divisions became at each step more pronounced. The vote on the question of abolishing slavery in the District of Columbia had been

435

strictly on the line of party, and the same is true of the proposition for compensated emancipation in the Border States, and of the Act confiscating the property of Rebels. Not a single Democrat in the Senate or House sustained one of these measures. They were all passed by Republican votes alone, the Democratic minority protesting each time with increasing earnestness and warmth.

The second session of the Thirty-seventh Congress adjourned on the 17th of July, 1862, but long before that date the excitement prevailing in Congress had extended to the people, and political divisions were every day growing more earnest, partisan leaders every day more active, their followers every day more excited. The Slavery question was the source of the agitation, and by a common instinct throughout the free States, the Democrats joined in the cry against an Abolition war. They were as ready, they declared, as on the day after the firing on Sumter, to uphold all measures necessary for the defense of the Government and the maintenance of the Union, and they demanded that the Republicans should restrict the war to its legitimate ends — as defined by the supporters of the Administration in July, 1861, by the unanimous adoption of the Crittenden Resolution. They would not listen to any change of action based on change of circumstances, and they prepared to enforce at the ballot-box their opinions touching the new departure of Congress and the President.

The Democratic State Conventions in Pennsylvania and Ohio, both held on the 4th of July, reflected the feeling which so largely pervaded the ranks of the party throughout the North. In Pennsylvania the Convention unanimously declared that "the party of fanaticism or crime, whichever it may be called, that seeks to turn loose the slaves of the Southern States to overrun the North and to enter into competition with the white laboring masses, thus degrading their manhood by placing them on an equality with negroes, is insulting to our race and merits our most emphatic and unqualified condemnation." They further declared that "this is a government of white men and was established exclusively for the white race"; that "the negroes are not entitled to and ought not to be admitted to political or social equality with the white race."

The Democratic Convention of Ohio made an equally open appeal to race prejudice. They avowed their belief that the Emancipation policy of the Republican party if successful "would throw upon the Border free States an immense number of negroes to compete with and under-work the white laborers and to constitute in various ways an unbearable nuisance"; and that "it would be unjust to our gallant soldiers to compel them to free the negroes of the South and thereby fill Ohio with a degraded population to compete with these same soldiers upon their return to the peaceful avocations of life." It was not by mere chance that the Democratic party of these two great States held their conventions on the National Anniversary. It had been carefully pre-arranged with the view of creating a serious impression against the Administration.

The Democrats of Indiana went beyond their brethren of Ohio and Pennsylvania in the vigor with which they denounced the anti-slavery policy of the President. Their convention was held a month later, and unanimously demanded that "the public authorities of Indiana should see that the constitution and laws of the State are enforced against the entrance of free negroes and mulattoes," declaring that "when the people of Indiana adopted the negro exclusion clause in their constitution by a majority of ninety-four thousand votes they meant that the honest laboring white man should have no competitor in the black race; that the soil of Indiana should belong to the white man, and that he alone was suited to the form of her institutions." In Illinois the Democratic party adopted substantially the same platform as that proclaimed in Indiana. They made the distinct and unmistakable issue that a war for the abolition of slavery could not have their support; that the Government of the United States was made for white men, and that negroes could not be admitted to terms of equality in civil rights.

The most important election of the year was that to be held in New York, not merely because of the prestige and power of the State, but on account of the peculiar elements that entered into the contest. The Democratic party proceeded in the selection of candidates and in the definition of issues with great circumspection. They avoided the rancorous expressions used in Pennsylvania and Ohio, declared that they would continue to render the government their sincere and united support in the use of all legitimate means to suppress the rebellion, and cited the Crittenden Resolution, unanimously passed by Congress in July, 1861, as embodying the principles upon which they appealed for popular support. They expressed their "willingness to withhold their views upon all questions not rendered imperative by the imperiled condition of the country." They had not one word to say on the subject of slavery, and they avowed their readiness to act in the coming election with any class of loyal citizens who agreed with them in the principles embodied in their platform. This last clause related to a third party, the remnant of those who had supported Mr. Bell in 1860 and who had just held a convention at Troy. They had comprised their entire platform in "the Constitution, the Union and the enforcement of the laws," and had nominated Horatio Seymour for governor.

It was not difficult to see that politically the case was well managed, and that the most partisan of partisans in the person of Mr. Seymour, was enabled to appear before the voters of New York in the attitude of one who could graciously correct the errors of the Administration, and direct the course of the war in channels of patriotism that would harmonize the entire people. The nomination of Mr. Seymour was made with great enthusiasm by the Democracy, and the policy of the National Administration was thus challenged in the leading State of the Union. Mr. Lincoln looked upon the situation as one of exceeding gravity. The loss to the Administration, of the House of Representatives in the Thirty-eighth Congress, would place the control of the war in the hands of its opponents, and, as the President believed, would imperil the fate of the National struggle. The power of the purse controls the power of the sword. The armies in the field required a vast and constant expenditure, and to secure the money a rigorous system of taxation must be enforced. A House of Representatives controlling the power to tax and the power to appropriate could, if hostile to the war, neutralize and destroy all the efforts of the Executive.

The President measured the extent of the danger and prepared to meet it. He clearly read the signs of the times. He saw that the anti-slavery policy of Congress had gone far enough to arouse the bitter hostility of all Democrats who were not thoroughly committed to the war, and yet not far enough to deal an effective blow against the institution. He saw that as the Administration was committed to the partial policy which involved all the danger of a re-action and a retreat, it would be wise to commit it to the bold, far-reaching, radical and aggressive policy from which it would be impossible to turn without deliberately resolving to sacrifice our nationality. He determined therefore to lay before the people a choice between the Union and Slavery. He would persuade them that both could not be saved and that they must choose the one which they regarded as the more worthy of preservation. Slavery was not only the inciting cause of the rebellion but was its chief strength and support in the South and at the same time a weakening element to the Union cause in the Loyal States. No man had looked at the question in all its bearings so closely as Mr. Lincoln. He had studied the consequences of every step and had proceeded with the utmost caution.

The President kept his own counsels so closely, and relied so confidently upon his own conclusions, that it is not possible to say when he first seriously entertained the thought of general emancipation as a war measure. Mr. George S. Boutwell of Massachusetts who enjoyed Mr. Lincoln's confidence and who at this period of the contest was appointed Commissioner of Internal Revenue, is authority for some interesting statements. About the time that the anti-slavery legislation now under discussion was in progress Mr. Lincoln received a letter written by a loyal citizen of Louisiana, containing a strong argument against emancipation. He depicted in vivid colors the bad results to flow from it and appealed earnestly to the President not to take so dangerous a step. Without combating in detail the arguments of his correspondent who personally enjoyed his confidence, Mr. Lincoln said, "You must not expect me to give up this government without playing my last card."

During an interview with Mr. Lincoln after the adjournment of Congress in July, and when military disasters were falling thick and fast upon us, Mr. Boutwell suggested to the President that we could not hope to succeed until the slaves were emancipated. To which Mr. Lincoln answered, "You would not have it done now, would you? Had we not better wait for something like a victory?" The statement, widely made in the autumn of 1862 that Mr. Lincoln had been frightened or driven into the issuing of the proclamation by the meeting of the governors of the Loyal States at Altoona, had no foundation in fact. When the President's attention was called to it, he said, "The truth is, I never thought of the meeting of the governors at all. When Lee came over the Potomac I made a resolve that if McClellan drove him back I would send the proclamation after him. The battle of Antietam was fought Wednesday, but I could not find out until Saturday whether we had won a victory or lost a battle. It was then too late to issue it that day, and on Sunday I fixed it up a little, and on Monday I let them have it." This colloquial style was characteristic of Mr. Lincoln, and the frankness with which it was spoken disposes utterly of the claims made in behalf of Mr.

Chase and Mr. Sumner that they contributed to the text of the Monitory Proclamation of 1862.

Two months before issuing the Proclamation Mr. Lincoln had urgently requested the senators and representatives of the Border States to give their effective co-operation in aid of compensated emancipation. In his letter of July 12 he said, "Before leaving the Capitol, consider and discuss this subject among yourselves. You are patriots and statesmen, and as such I pray you to consider this proposition and at least commend it to the consideration of your States and people. As you would perpetuate popular government, I beseech you that you do in no wise omit this. Our common country is in great peril, demanding the loftiest views and boldest action to bring a speedy relief. Once relieved, its form of government is saved to the world, its beloved history and cherished memories are vindicated, its happy future assured and rendered inconceivably grand. To you more than to any others the privilege is given to assure that happiness, to swell that grandeur, to link your own names therewith forever."

The majority of the senators and representatives from the Border States did not concur with Mr. Lincoln's views and did not respond favorably to his earnest appeal. The Maryland delegation in Congress, the Kentucky delegation with one exception, and the Missouri delegation with one exception, entered into a long argument dissenting from the conclusions of the President. The West Virginia men (with the exception of Mr. Carlile), Mr. Casey of Kentucky, Mr. John W. Noell of Missouri, Mr. George P. Fisher of Delaware, together with Mr. Horace Maynard and Mr. A. J. Clements from Tennessee (not a Border State), expressed their readiness to co-operate with Mr. Lincoln. Mr. Maynard wrote a separate letter distinguished by breadth of view and strength of expression. It is impossible to comprehend the determination of the Border State men at that crisis. Having resisted in vain the aggressive legislation of Congress already accomplished, they could hardly fail to see that the institution of slavery was threatened with utter destruction. It seems absolutely incredible that, standing on the edge of the crater, they made no effort to escape from the upheaval of the volcano, already visible to those who stood afar off.

The Monitory Proclamation of Emancipation was issued on the 22d of September. It gave public notice that on the first day of January, 1863 — just one hundred days distant — "all persons held as slaves within any State or designated part of a State, the people whereof shall be in rebellion against the United States, shall be then thenceforward and forever free." It was a final notice to those engaged in rebellion that every agency, every instrumentality would be employed by the government in its struggle for self-preservation. It brought — as Mr. Lincoln intended it should bring — the seriousness of the contest to the hearts and consciences of the people in the Loyal States. He plainly warned them that every thing was at stake and that if they were unwilling to meet the trial with the courage and the sacrifice demanded, they were foredoomed to disaster, to defeat, to dishonor. He knew that the policy would at first encounter the disapproval of many who had supported him for the Presidency, and that it would be violently opposed by the great mass of the Democratic party. But his faith was strong. He believed that the destruction of slavery was essential to the safety of the Union, and he trusted with composure to the discerning judgment and ultimate decision of the people. If the Administration was to be defeated, he was determined that defeat should come upon an issue which involved the whole controversy. If the purse of the Nation was to be handed over to the control of those who were not ready to use the last dollar in the war for the preservation of the Union, the President was resolved that every voter in the Loyal States should be made to comprehend the deadly significance of such a decision.

The effect of the policy was for a time apparently disastrous to the Administration. The most sagacious among political leaders trembled for the result. Only the radical anti-slavery men of the type of Sumner and Stevens and Lovejoy were strong and unyielding in faith. They could not doubt, they would not doubt the result. For many weeks the elections in the North promised nothing but adversity. Maine voted a few days before the Proclamation was issued. Ever since the repeal of the Missouri Compromise the majorities against the Democracy in that State had varied from ten to nineteen thousand. Under the pressure of military reverses and the cry of an abolition war, the majority for Abner Coburn, the Republican candidate for governor, was a little over four thousand; and for the first time in ten years one of the districts returned a Democratic representative to Congress in the person of L. D. M. Sweat. Vermont, contrary to the tide of opinion elsewhere, increased her majority for the Administration — an event due in large part to the loyal position taken by Paul Dillingham who had been the leader of the Democratic party in the State.

The October elections were utterly discouraging. In Ohio the Democrats prevailed in fourteen of the Congressional districts, leaving the Republicans but five, — registering at the same time a popular majority of some seven thousand against the Administration. The extent of this reverse may be measured by the fact that in the preceding Congressional election Republican representatives had been chosen in thirteen districts. In Indiana the result was overwhelming against the President. The Republicans had held their convention early in the summer and had re-affirmed the Crittenden Resolution as embodying their platform of principles. They were not in position therefore to withstand the furious onslaught made by the Democrats on the Slavery question. Of the eleven Congressional districts the Republicans secured but three, and the Democrats had a large majority on the popular vote. — In Pennsylvania whose election was usually accepted as the index to the average public opinion of the country, the Democrats secured a majority of four thousand, and elected one-half the delegation to Congress. In November, 1860, Mr. Lincoln had received a majority of sixty thousand in Pennsylvania, and this change marked the ebb of popular favor created by the anti-slavery policy of the Administration.

Against the candidacy of Mr. Seymour for the governorship of New York, the Republicans nominated James S. Wadsworth, formerly a partisan of Mr. Van Buren and Silas Wright. He was a gentleman of the highest character, of large landed estate which he had inherited, and of wide personal popularity. He had volunteered for the war and was then in the service, with the rank of Brigadier-General. The convention which nominated him assembled after Mr. Lincoln's decisive action. They hailed "with the profoundest satisfaction the recent proclamation of the President declaring his intention to emancipate the slaves of all rebels who did not return to their allegiance by the 1st of January, 1863," and they urged upon the National Government "to use all the means that the God of battles had placed in its power against a revolt so malignant and so pernicious." Lyman Tremaine, a distinguished citizen who had been theretofore connected with the Democratic party, was nominated for Lieutenant-Governor.

The contest was extremely animated, enlisting the interest of the entire country. The result was a victory for Mr. Seymour.

His majority over General Wadsworth was nearly ten thousand. His vote almost equaled the total of all the Democratic factions in the Presidential election of 1860, while Mr. Wadsworth fell nearly seventy thousand behind the vote given to Mr. Lincoln. The discrepancy could be well accounted for by the greater number of Republicans who had gone to the war, and for whose voting outside the State no provision had been made. No result could have been more distasteful to the Administration than the triumph of Mr. Seymour, and the experience of after years did not diminish the regret with which they had seen him elevated to a position of power at a time when the utmost harmony was needed between the National and State Governments.

To the President the most mortifying event of the year was the overwhelming defeat in Illinois. Great efforts were made by the Republican party to save the State. Personal pride entered into the contest almost as much as political principle, but against all that could be done the Democrats secured a popular majority of seventeen thousand, and out of the fourteen representatives in Congress they left but three to the Republicans. They chose a Democratic Legislature, which returned William A. Richardson to the Senate for the unexpired term of Mr. Douglas, — filled since his death by O. H. Browning who had been appointed by the Governor. The crushing defeat of Mr. Lincoln in his own State had a depressing effect upon the party elsewhere, and but for the assurance in which the Administration found comfort and cheer, that the Democrats were at home to vote while the Republicans were in the field to fight, the result would have proved seriously discouraging to the country and utterly destructive of the policy of emancipation as proclaimed by the President.

In the five leading free States, the Administration had thus met with a decisive defeat. The Democratic representatives chosen to Congress numbered in the aggregate fifty-nine, while those favorable to the Administration were only forty. In some other States the results were nearly as depressing. New Jersey, which had given half of its electoral vote to Mr. Lincoln two years before, now elected a Democratic governor by nearly fifteen thousand majority, and of her five representatives in Congress only one was friendly to the policy of the Administration. Michigan, which had been Republican by twenty thousand in 1860, now gave the Administration but six thousand majority, though Senator Chandler made almost superhuman efforts to bring out the full vote of the party. Wisconsin, which had given Mr. Lincoln a large popular majority, now gave a majority of two thousand for the Democrats, dividing the Congressional delegation equally between the two parties.

If this ratio had been maintained in all the States, the defeat of the war party and of the anti-slavery policy would have been complete. But relief came and the Administration was saved. The New-England States which voted in November stood firmly by their principles, though with diminished majorities. The contest in Massachusetts resulted in the decisive victory of Governor Andrew over General Charles Devens, who ran as a Coalition candidate of the Democrats and Independents against the emancipation policy of the Administration. New Hampshire which voted the ensuing spring had the benefit of a Loyal re-action and sustained the Administration. In the West, Iowa, Kansas and Minnesota cheered the Administration with unanimous Republican delegations to Congress, and on the Pacific coast California and Oregon stood firmly by the President.

The result in the Border slave States amply vindicated the sagacity and wisdom of the President in so constantly and carefully nurturing their loyalty and defending them against the inroads of the Confederates. They responded nobly, and in great part repaired the injury inflicted by States which were presumptively more loyal to the Administration, and which had a far larger stake in the struggle for the Union. Delaware's one representative was Republican, Missouri elected a decisive majority of friends to the Administration, and in the ensuing year Kentucky, West Virginia, and Maryland materially increased the strength of the government. The Administration was finally assured that it would be able to command a majority of about twenty in the House. But for the aid of the Border slave States the anti-slavery position of Mr. Lincoln might have been overthrown by a hostile House of Representatives. It is true therefore in a very striking sense that the five slave States which Mr. Lincoln's policy had held to their loyalty, were most effectively used by him in overpowering the eleven slave States which had revolted against the Union.

The third and last session of the Thirty-seventh Congress assembled four weeks after the close of the exciting contest for the control of the next House of Representatives. The message of Mr. Lincoln made no reference whatever to the political contest in the country, and unlike his previous communications to Congress gave no special summary of the achievements by our forces either upon the land or the sea. He contented himself with stating that he transmitted the reports of the Secretaries of War and of the Navy, and referred Congress to them for full information. He dwelt at length upon the total inadequacy of Disunion as a remedy for the differences between the people of the two sections, and quoted with evident satisfaction the declarations he had made in his Inaugural address upon that point. In his judgment "there is no line, straight or crooked, suitable for a National boundary upon which to divide. Trace it through from east to west upon the line between the free and the slave country, and we shall find a little more than one-third of its length are rivers easy to be crossed; and populated, or soon to be populated, thickly on both sides, while nearly all its remaining length are merely surveyor's lines over which people may walk back and forth without any consciousness of their presence. No part of this line can be made any more difficult to pass by writing it down on paper or parchment as a National boundary." In the President's view "a nation may be said to consist of its territory, its people, and its laws. The territory is the only part which is of certain durability. That portion of the earth's surface which is inhabited by the people of the United States is well adapted for the home of one National family, but it is not well adapted for two or more."

Mr. Lincoln was still anxious that the Loyal slave States should secure the advantage of compensated emancipation which he had already urged, and he recommended an amendment to the Constitution whereby a certain amount should be paid by the United States to each State that would abolish slavery before the first day of January, A.D. 1900. The amount was to be paid in bonds of the United States on which interest was to begin from the time of actual delivery to the States. The amendment was further to declare that "all slaves who enjoyed actual freedom by the chances of the war at any time before the end of the rebellion shall be forever free," but the individual owners, if loyal, shall be compensated at the same rate that may be paid to those in States abolishing slavery. The amendment also proposed to give to "Congress the right to appropriate money for the colonization of the emancipated slaves, with their own consent, at any place outside of the United States."

Congress had scarcely time to consider this grave proposition when the President issued on the first day of the new year (1863) his formal Proclamation abolishing slavery in all the States in rebellion against the Government, with the exception of Tennessee, and of certain parishes in Louisiana and certain counties in Virginia whose population was considered loyal to the Government. Tennessee was excepted from the operation of the Proclamation at the urgent request of Andrew Johnson who, after the fall of Nashville in the preceding spring, had resigned from the Senate to accept the appointment of military governor of his State. His service in the Senate, with his State in flagrant rebellion, was felt to be somewhat anomalous and he was glad to accept a position in which he could be more directly helpful to the loyal cause. He possessed the unbounded confidence of Mr. Lincoln who yielded to his views respecting the best mode of restoring Tennessee to the Union, and her inhabitants to their duty to the National Government. There is good reason for believing that both Mr. Lincoln and Mr. Johnson afterwards regarded the omission of Tennessee from the Proclamation of Emancipation as a mistake, honestly made in the first place by Governor Johnson and too readily acceded to by the President.

The recommendation of Mr. Lincoln for a system of compensated emancipation was taken up promptly and cordially by the Republican members of both branches of Congress. The House appointed a special committee on the subject. With but little delay a bill was passed appropriating to Missouri, the first State considered, ten millions of dollars with the restriction that the money should be paid only to the loyal slave-holders. The Senate increased the amount to fifteen millions of dollars and returned it to the House for concurrence in the amendment. The measure had been thus passed in both branches but with stubborn opposition on the part of some prominent Democratic leaders from Missouri. John B. Henderson in the Senate and John W. Noell in the House labored earnestly to secure the compensation for their State, but the bill was finally defeated in the House. By factious resistance, by dilatory motions and hostile points of order, the Democratic members from Missouri were able to force the bill from its position of parliamentary advantage, and to prevent its consideration within the period in which a majority of the House could control its fate. The just responsibility for depriving Missouri of the fifteen millions of dollars must be charged in an especial degree to Thomas L. Price, Elijah H. Norton, and William A. Hall, representatives from that State, who on the 25th of February,

1863, by the use of objectionable tactics deprived the House of the opportunity even to consider a bill of such value and consequence to their constituents. A large majority stood ready to pass it, but the determined hostility of the Democratic members from Missouri defeated the kindly and generous intentions of Congress towards their own State. At a later period in the session the attempt was made to pass the bill by a suspension of the Rules, but this motion though it received the support of a majority was defeated for lack of two-thirds of the votes as required. The Democratic members of Missouri were again active in resisting the boon which was offered to their State and so earnestly pressed by the Republicans of the House.

The course of the Missouri representatives was sustained by the solid vote of the Democratic members from the free States, and received the co-operation of a majority of representatives from the Border slave States. If the bill for Missouri had passed, a similar relief would have been offered to Kentucky, West Virginia, Maryland and Delaware. Mr. Crittenden whose influence with the representatives from these States was deservedly great could not be persuaded to adopt the President's policy. The consideration which influenced him and other Border State men to the course which subsequent events proved to be unwise, was their distrust of the success of the Union arms. The prospect had grown steadily discouraging ever since the adjournment of Congress in the preceding July, and with the exception of General McClellan's success at Antietam there had been nothing to lighten the gloom which deeply beclouded the military situation. The daily expenditures of the nation were enormous, and the Secretary of the Treasury had at the opening of the session estimated that the National debt at the close of the current fiscal year would exceed seventeen hundred millions of dollars. The Border State men chose therefore to maintain possession of their four hundred thousand slaves, even with the title somewhat shaken by war, rather than to part with them for the bonds of a Government whose ability to pay they considered extremely doubtful.

They could readily have secured, indeed they were urged to accept, fifty millions of dollars, the equivalent of gold coin, in securities which became in a few years the favorite investment of the wisest capitalists in the world. Such opportunities are never repeated. The magnanimous policy of the President and the wise liberality of the Republican party were precisely adapted, if the

Border State men could have seen it, to the critical situation of the hour. Subsequent events prevented the repetition of the offer, and the slave-holders were left to thank themselves and their representatives for the loss of the munificent compensation proffered by the Government. They could not believe Mr. Lincoln when at the pressing moment he pleaded with them so earnestly to accept the terms, and flavored his appeal with the humorous remark to Mr. Crittenden: " You Southern men will soon reach the point where bonds will be a more valuable possession than bondsmen. Nothing is more uncertain now than two-legged property."

After the unfortunate issue of the Peninsular campaign and in the fear that Lee might turn directly upon Washington, a new army was organized on the 27th of June, 1862, and placed under the command of Major-General John Pope. It included the forces which had been serving under Frémont, Banks and McDowell, and was divided into three corps with these officers respectively in command. General Frémont considering the designation below his rank asked to be relieved from the service, and his corps was assigned to General Rufus King, and soon after to General Sigel. General Pope took the field on the 14th of July with a formidable force. General McClellan was still within twenty-five miles of Richmond, and with Pope in front of Washington, the Confederate authorities were at a standstill and could not tell which way to advance with hope of success or even with safety.

If the army of Lee should move towards Washington he might be compelled to fight General Pope protected by the extensive fortifications on the south side of the Potomac, leaving Richmond at the same time uncovered, with the possibility that McClellan, re-enforced by Burnside's corps which lay at Fortress Monroe, would renew his attack with an army of ninety thousand men. But as soon as the Confederates ascertained that McClellan was ordered back to the Potomac, they saw their opportunity and made haste to attack Pope. Fault was found with the slowness of McClellan's movements. His judgment as a military man was decidedly against the transfer of his army from the point it occupied near Richmond, and it cannot be said that he obeyed the distasteful order with the alacrity with which he would have responded to one that agreed with his own judgment.

ZACHARIAH CHANDLER

JOHN P. HALE

HENRY B. ANTHONY

OLIVER P. MORTON

JAMES W. GRIMES

THOMAS A. HENDRICKS

SIMON CAMERON

ENGRAVED BY W. WELLSTOOD & CO. N.Y.

No reason can be assigned why if the Army of the Potomac was to be brought back in front of Washington it should not have been transferred in season to re-enforce General Pope and give a crushing blow to Lee.   General McClellan was directed on the third day of August to withdraw his entire army to Acquia Creek, and as General Halleck declares, "in order to make the movement as rapidly as possible General McClellan was authorized to assume control of all the vessels in the James River and Chesapeake Bay, of which there was then a vast fleet." General McClellan did not begin the evacuation of Harrison's Landing until the 14th of August — eleven days after it was ordered.   General Burnside's corps was ordered on the 1st of August to move from Newport News to Acquia Creek, and an estimate of the transportation facilities at command of General McClellan, may be formed from the fact that Burnside's whole corps reached their destination in forty-eight hours.   General Lee knew at once by this movement that it was not the design to attack Richmond, and he made haste to throw his army on Pope before the slow moving army from Harrison's Landing could re-enforce him.   General McClellan did not himself reach Acquia Creek until the 24th of August.   The disasters sustained by General Pope in the month of August could not have occurred if the forces of the Union, readily at command, had been brought seasonably to his aid.   It was at this crisis that unfortunate movements were made, the full responsibility for which, perhaps the exact character of which, may never be determined, but the sorrowful result of which was that the Union forces, much larger in the aggregate than Lee's, were divided and continually outnumbered on the field of battle.

Flushed with success the Confederate authorities pushed their fortunes with great boldness.   General Bragg invaded Kentucky with a large army and General Lee prepared to invade Pennsylvania. The cruel defeat of General Pope disabled him for the time as a commander, and the Administration, fearing for the safety of Washington, and yielding somewhat to the obvious wishes of the soldiers, ordered General McClellan on September 2 to assume command of all the troops for the defense of the Capital.   General Lee avoiding the fortifications of Washington, passed over to Maryland, and prepared to invade Pennsylvania with a force formidable in numbers and with the added strength of a supreme confidence in its invincibility. General McClellan moved promptly westward to cut off Lee's progress northward.   After preliminary engagements the main battle of

Antietam was fought on the 17th of September, resulting in a Union victory. Lee was severely repulsed and retreated across the Potomac.

General McClellan fought the battle of Antietam under extraordinary embarrassment caused by the surrender of Harper's Ferry to the Confederates on the 13th, with a loss to the Union army of more than twelve thousand men. Could he have had the advantage of this force on the battle-field, under a competent commander, at the critical moment, his victory over Lee might have been still more decisive. His success however was of overwhelming importance to the National Government and put a stop to an invasion of Pennsylvania which might have been disastrous in the extreme. He was blamed severely, perhaps unjustly, for not following Lee on his retreat and reaping the fruits of his victory. He had the misfortune to fall into a controversy once more with the authorities at Washington. After a correspondence with the War Department he was peremptorily ordered by the General-in-Chief Halleck on the 6th of October in these words: "The President directs that you cross the Potomac and give battle to the enemy or drive him south. Your army must move now while the roads are good. . . . I am directed to add that the Secretary of War and the General-in-Chief fully concur with the President in these instructions." The order was not promptly obeyed. The Army of the Potomac — as those who spoke for General McClellan maintained — had been for six months engaged in a laborious campaign in which they had fought many battles and experienced much hardship. They needed rest, recruitment, clothes, shoes, and a general supply of war material before setting out on what would prove a winter march. The authorities at Washington asserted, and apparently proved on the testimony of Quartermaster-General Meigs, a most accomplished, able, and honorable officer, that the Army of the Potomac, when it received its first orders to move in October, was thoroughly and completely equipped. General McClellan thought however that if intrusted with the command of the army he should be allowed to direct its movements. He crossed the Potomac near Harper's Ferry in the last week of October, and began an advance through Virginia which effectually covered Washington. He had reached Warrenton, and, before the plan of his campaign was developed, received at midnight, of the 7th of November, a direct order from President Lincoln to "surrender the command of the army to General Burnside, and to report himself immediately at Trenton, the capital of New Jersey."

The reasons for this sudden and peremptory order were not given, and if expressed would probably have been only an assertion of the utter impossibility that the War Department and General McClellan should harmoniously co-operate in the great military movements which devolved upon the Army of the Potomac. But the time of removal was not opportunely selected by the Administration. After General McClellan's failure on the Peninsula, a large proportion of the Northern people clamored for his deposition from command, and it would have been quietly acquiesced in by all. At the end of those disastrous days when he was falling back on the line of the James River, General McClellan had telegraphed the Secretary of War "If I save this army now, I tell you plainly that I owe no thanks to you or to any persons in Washington. You have done your best to sacrifice this army." Perhaps no such dispatch was ever before sent by a military officer to the Commander-in-Chief of the army — to the ruler of the nation. In any other country it would have been followed with instant cashiering. Mr. Lincoln, with his great magnanimity, had however condoned the offense, and after the defeat of Pope the Administration had enlarged the command of McClellan and trusted the fortunes of the country to his generalship. The trust had not been in vain. He had rolled back the tide of invasion by a great battle in which for the first time the army of Lee had been beaten. He was now marching forward with his army strengthened for another conflict, and without explanation to the country or to himself was deprived of his command. A large part of the people and of the public press and an overwhelming majority in the army were dissatisfied with the act, and believed that it would entail evil consequences.

This ended the military career of General McClellan which throughout its whole period had been a subject of constant discussion — a discussion which has not yet closed. The opinion of a majority of intelligent observers, both civil and military, is that he was a man of high professional training, admirably skilled in the science of war, capable of commanding a large army with success, but at the same time not original in plan, not fertile in resource, and lacking the energy, the alertness, the daring, the readiness to take great risks for great ends, which distinguish the military leaders of the world. For a commander of armies, in an offensive campaign, his caution was too largely developed. He possessed in too great a degree what the French term the *defensive instinct of the engineer*, and was apparently incapable of doing from his own volition what he did so well on the bloody field of Antietam, when under the pressure of an overwhelming necessity.

General Burnside assumed the command with diffidence. After a consultation with General Halleck he moved down the Rappahannock opposite Fredericksburg where he confronted General Lee's army on the 16th of December, and made an attack upon it under great disadvantages and with the legitimate result of a great defeat. The total loss of killed and wounded of the Union army exceeded ten thousand men. The public mind was deeply affected throughout the North by this untoward event. All the prestige which Lee had lost at Antietam had been regained, all the advantage we had secured on that field was sacrificed by the disaster on the still bloodier field of Fredericksburg. It added immeasurably to the gloom of a gloomy winter, and in the rank and file of the army it caused a dissatisfaction somewhat akin to mutiny. So pronounced did this feeling become and so plainly was it manifested that the subject attracted the attention of Congress and led to some results which, despite the seriousness of the situation, were irresistibly amusing.

On the 23d of January Mr. Wilson of Massachusetts offered a somewhat extraordinary resolution, — instructing the Committee on the Conduct of the War to "inquire whether Major-General Burnside has since the battle of Fredericksburg formed any plans for the movement of the Army of the Potomac or any portion of the same, and if so whether any subordinate generals of said army have written to or visited Washington, to oppose or interfere with the execution of such movements, and whether such proposed movements have been arrested or interfered with, and if so by what authority." The consideration of the resolution was postponed under the rule, and three days later it was called up by Mr. Anthony of Rhode Island and its adoption urged " with the view of finding out whether officers were coming up here from the Army of the Potomac to interfere with the plans of General Burnside." There was indeed no doubt that some of the general officers connected with the army had been in Washington, and confidentially informed the President of the dispirited and depressed condition of the whole force.

General Burnside's character was one of great frankness, truth, and fidelity. He was full of courage and of manliness, and he conceived from circumstances within his knowledge, that certain officers in his command were gradually undermining and destroying him in the confidence of the army and of the public. He had not desired the position to which the President called him as the successor of General McClellan. He did not feel himself indeed quite competent to the task of commanding an army of one hundred thousand men. But there as in every other position in life he would try to do his best. He failed and failed decisively. It would probably have been wise for him to resign his command immediately after the defeat at Fredericksburg. On January 23, the Friday before the Senate resolution was adopted, General Burnside, highly incensed by the injury which he thought had been done him, wrote an order peremptorily "dismissing, subject to the approval of the President, Major-General Joseph E. Hooker from the Army of the United States, for having been guilty of unjust and unnecessary criticism of his superior officers, and for having by the general tone of his conversation endeavored to create distrust in the minds of officers who have associated with him, and for having habitually spoken in disparaging terms of other officers." The order declared that General Hooker was dismissed "as a man unfit to hold an important commission during a crisis like the present when so much patience, charity, confidence, consideration, and patriotism is due from every person in the field." The same order dismissed Brigadier-General John Newton and Brigadier-General John Cochrane for going to the President with criticisms on the plans of the commanding officer, and relieved Major-General William B. Franklin, Major-General W. F. Smith, Brigadier-General Sturgis and several others from further service in the Army of the Potomac.

The outcome of this extraordinary proceeding was very singular. General Burnside took the order, before its publication, to the President who instead of approving it, very good-naturedly found a command for the General in the West, and on the very day that the Senate passed the resolution of inquiry, two orders were read at the headquarters of the Army of the Potomac, — one from General Burnside announcing that Major-General Joseph E. Hooker was assigned to the command of the Army of the Potomac and asking the army to "give to the brave and skillful General, who is now to command you, your full and cordial support and co-operation;" the other from General Hooker assuming command of the Army of the Potomac by direction of the President and conveying to the late commander, General Burnside, "the most cordial good wishes of the whole army."

In the South-West where General Grant, General Sherman, and General Rosecrans were stubbornly contesting the ground, no decisive results were attained. The army went into winter quarters, with a general feeling of discouragement pervading the country. A substantial advantage was gained by General Buell's army in driving Bragg out of Kentucky, and a very signal and helpful encouragement came to the Government from the fact that the public manifestations in Kentucky were decisively adverse to the Confederates, and that Lee's army in Maryland met no welcome from any portion of the population. General McClellan's army was cheered everywhere in Maryland as it marched to the field of Antietam; and as Bragg retreated through the mountain sections of Kentucky his stragglers were fired upon by the people, and the women along the route upbraided the officers with bitter maledictions. Perhaps the feature of the two invasions most discouraging to the Confederates was the condition of the popular mind which they found in the Border States. They had expected to arouse fresh revolt, but they met a people tired of conflict and longing for repose under the flag of the Nation.

Congress felt that the situation was one of uncertainty if not of positive adversity. They did not however abate one jot or tittle of earnest effort in providing for a renewal of the contest in the ensuing spring. They appropriated some seven hundred and forty millions of dollars for the army and some seventy-five millions for the navy, and they took the very decisive step of authorizing "the President to enroll, arm, equip, and receive into the land and naval service of the United States such number of volunteers of African descent as he may deem useful to suppress the present Rebellion for such term of service as he may prescribe, not exceeding five years." The enactment of this bill was angrily resisted by the Democratic party and by the Union men of the Border States. But the Republicans were able to consolidate their ranks in support of it. In the popular opinion it was a radical measure, and therein lay its chief merit. Aside from the substantial strength which the accession of these colored men to the ranks would give to the Union army, was the moral effect which would be produced on the minds of Southern men by the open demonstration that the President did not regard the Proclamation of Emancipation as *brutum fulmen*, but intended to enforce it by turning the strong arm of the slave against the person of the master. It was a policy that required great moral courage, and it was abundantly rewarded by successful results. It signalized to the whole world the depth of the earnestness with which the Administration was defending the Union, and the desperate extent to which the contest would be carried before American nationality should be surrendered. The measure had long been demanded by the aggressive sentiment of the North, and its enactment was hailed by the mass of people in the Loyal States as a great step forward.

A subject of striking interest at this session of Congress was the passage of the "Act relating to *habeas corpus*, and regulating judicial proceedings in certain cases." The President had ordered for the public safety, and as an act necessary to the successful prosecution of the war, the arrest and confinement of certain persons charged with disloyal practices. No punishment was attempted or designed except that of confinement in a military fortress of the United States. It became a matter of argument not only in Congress but throughout the country, whether the President was authorized by the Constitution to suspend the writ of *habeas corpus*. In order to set the question at rest it was now proposed to pass an Act of indemnity for past Acts to all officers engaged in making arrests, and also to confirm to the President by law the right which he had of his own power been exercising. The bill declared that "during the present Rebellion the President of the United States, whenever in his judgment the public safety may require it, is authorized to suspend the privilege of the writ of *habeas corpus* in any case throughout the United States or any part thereof; and wherever the said writ shall be suspended no military or other officer shall be compelled, in answer to any writ of *habeas corpus*, to return the body of any person or persons detained by him by authority of the President."

The bill was stubbornly resisted by the Democratic party, and after its passage by the House thirty-six Democratic representatives asked leave to enter upon the Journal a solemn protest against its enactment. They recited at length their grounds of objection, the principal of which was "the giving to the President the right to suspend the writ of *habeas corpus* throughout the limits of the United States, whereas by the Constitution the power to suspend the privilege of that writ is confided to the discretion of Congress alone and is limited to the place threatened by the dangers of invasion or insurrection," and also because "the bill purports to confirm and make valid by act of Congress arrests and imprisonments which were not only not warranted by the Constitution of the United States but were in palpable violation of its express prohibitions." Mr. Thaddeus Stevens peremptorily moved to lay the request on the table, and on a call of the ayes and noes the motion prevailed by a vote of 75 to 41. The division in the House by this time amounted to a strict line, on one side of which was the war party and on the other side the anti-war party.

The crowning achievement of the session in aid of the Union was the passage of an "Act for enrolling and calling out the National forces and for other purposes." By its terms all able-bodied citizens of the United States between the ages of twenty and forty-five years, with a few exemptions which were explicitly stated, were declared to "constitute the National forces and shall be employed to perform military duty in the service of the United States when called on by the President for that purpose." Volunteering was not to be relied upon as the sole means of recruiting the army, but the entire population within the arms-bearing age was now to be devoted to the contest. Taken in connection with other legislation already adverted to — the enormous appropriations for the forthcoming campaign, the organization of African regiments, the suspension of the writ of *habeas corpus* at the President's discretion — this last measure was the conclusive proof of the serious determination with which Congress and the people would continue the contest. The spirit with which the President and Congress proceeded in that depressing and depressed period proved invaluable to the country. The situation had so many elements of a discouraging character that the slightest hesitation or faltering among those controlling the administration of the Government would have been followed by distrust and dismay among the people.

CHAPTER XXI.

The President's Border-State Policy. — Loyal Government erected in Virginia. — Recognized by Congress and Senators admitted. — Desire for a New State. — The Long Dissatisfaction of the People of Western Virginia. — The Character of the People and of their Section. — Their Opportunity had come. — Organization of the Pierpont Government. — State Convention and Constitution. — Application to Congress for Admission. — Anti-slavery Amendment. — Senate Debate: Sumner, Wade, Powell, Willey, and Others. — House Debate: Stevens, Conway, Bingham, Segar. — Passage of Bill in Both Branches. — Heavy Blow to the Old State. — Her Claims deserve Consideration. — Should be treated as generously at least as Mexico.

THE great importance attached by Mr. Lincoln to the preservation of Loyalty in the line of slave States which bordered upon the free States was everywhere recognized. As Delaware, Maryland, Kentucky, and Missouri had been promptly placed under the control of governments friendly to the Union, there remained of the States in rebellion only Virginia with territory adjacent to the Loyal States. Virginia bordered on the Ohio River for two hundred and fifty miles; she was adjacent to Pennsylvania for a distance of one hundred and twenty miles, half on the southern, half on the western line of that State. Her extreme point stretched to the northward of Pittsburg, and was within twenty-five miles of the parallel of latitude that marks the southern boundary of New England. The continued exercise of even a nominal jurisdiction so far North, by the State which contained the capital of the Rebel Confederacy, would be a serious impeachment of the power of the National Government, and would detract from its respect at home and its prestige abroad. But the National Government was of itself capable only of enforcing military occupation and proclaiming the jurisdiction of the sword. What the President desired was the establishment of civil government by a loyal people, with the reign of law and order everywhere recognized. Happily the disposition of the inhabitants was in harmony with the wishes of the Administration and the necessities of the Union.

457

After the adoption of the Secession Ordinance by the Virginia Convention on the 17th of April, the loyal people of the Western section of the State were prompt to act. As early as the 13th of May — a fortnight before the day appointed for the popular vote on the Secession Ordinance in Virginia — five hundred staunch Union men came together in a Convention at Wheeling, denounced the Ordinance of Secession and pledged their loyalty to the National Government and their obedience to its laws. If the Ordinance should be approved by the popular vote of Virginia, this preliminary conference requested the people in all the counties represented, to appoint delegates on the fourth day of June to a General Convention to assemble in Wheeling on the 11th of the same month. These Union-loving men were energetic and zealous. They realized that with the secession of Virginia, completed and proclaimed, they must do one of two things — either proceed at once to organize a State government which would be faithful to the National Constitution, or drift helplessly into anarchy and thus contribute to the success of the rebellion. Their prompt and intelligent action is a remarkable illustration of the trained and disciplined ability of Americans for the duties of self-government.

The members of the Convention which was organized on the 11th of June were even more determined than those who had assembled the preceding month. Without delay they declared the State offices of Virginia vacant because of the treason and disloyalty of those who had been elected to hold them, and they proceeded to fill them and to form a regular State organization of which Francis H. Pierpont was appointed the executive head. They did not assume to represent a mere section of the State, but in the belief that the loyal people were entitled to speak for the whole State they declared that their government was the Government of Virginia. This Western movement was subsequently strengthened by the accession of delegates from Alexandria and Fairfax Counties in Middle Virginia and from Accomac and Northampton Counties on the Eastern Shore. Thus organized, the Government of the State was acknowledged by Congress as the Government of Virginia and her senators and representatives were admitted to seats.

Notwithstanding the compliance with all the outward forms and requirements, notwithstanding the recognition by Congress of the new government, it was seen to be essentially and really the Government of West Virginia. It was only nominally and by construction the Government of the State of Virginia. It did not represent the political power or the majority of the people of the entire State. That power was wielded in aid of the rebellion. The senators and representatives of Virginia were in the Confederate Congress. The strength of her people was in the Confederate Army, of which a distinguished Virginian was the commander. The situation was anomalous, though the friends of the Union justified the irregularity of recognizing the framework of government in the hands of loyal men as the actual civil administration of the State of Virginia.

The people of the Western section of Virginia realized that the position was unnatural, — one which they could not sustain by popular power within the limits of the State they assumed to govern, except for the protection afforded by the military power of the National Government. Between the two sections of the State there had long been serious antagonism. Indeed from the very origin of the settlement of West Virginia, which had made but little progress when the Federal Constitution was adopted, its citizens were in large degree alienated from the Eastern and older section of the State. The men of the West were hardy frontiersmen, a majority of them soldiers of the Revolution and their immediate descendants, without estates, with little but the honorable record of patriotic service and their own strong arms, for their fortunes. They had few slaves. They had their land patents, which were certificates of patriotic service in the Revolutionary war, and they depended upon their own labor for a new home in the wilderness. A population thus originating, a community thus founded, were naturally uncongenial to the aristocratic element of the Old Dominion. They had no trade relations, no social intercourse, with the tide-water section of the State. Formidable mountain ranges separated the two sections, and the inhabitants saw little of each other. The business interests of the Western region led the people to the Valley of the Ohio and not to the shores of the Chesapeake. The waters of the Monongahela connected them with Pennsylvania and carried them to Pittsburg. All the rivers of the western slope flowed into the Ohio and gave to the people the markets of Cincinnati and Louisville. Their commercial intercourse depended on the navigation of Western waters, and a far larger number had visited St. Louis and New Orleans than had ever seen Richmond or Norfolk. The West-Virginians were aware of the splendid resources of their section and were constantly irritated by the neglect of the parent State to aid in their development. They enjoyed a climate as genial as that of the Italians who dwell on the slopes of the Apennines; they had forests more valuable than those that skirt the upper Rhine; they had mineral wealth as great as that which has given England her precedence in the manufacturing progress of the world. They were anxious for self-government. Their trustworthy senator, Waitman T. Willey, declared that the people west of the Alleghany range had for sixty years "desired separation." The two sections, he said, had been time and again on the eve of an outbreak and the Western people could with difficulty be held back from insurrection. Criminations and recriminations had been exchanged at every session of the Legislature for forty years and threats of violence had been hurled by one section at the other.

The opportunity for a new State had now come. Its organization and admission to the Union would complete the chain of loyal Commonwealths on the south side of Mason and Dixon's line, and would drive back the jurisdiction of rebellious Virginia beyond the chain of mountains and interpose that barrier to the progress of the insurrectionary forces Westward and Northward. The provision in the Federal Constitution that no new State shall be formed within the jurisdiction of any other State without the consent of the Legislature of the State as well as of Congress, had always been the stumbling-block in the way of West Virginia's independence. Despite the hostilities and antagonisms of the two populations, Virginia would insist on retaining this valuable section of country within her own jurisdiction. But now, by the chances of war, the same men who desired to create the new State were wielding the entire political power of Virginia, and they would naturally grant permission to themselves to erect a State that would be entirely free from the objectionable jurisdiction which for the time they represented. They were not slow to avail themselves of their opportunity.

The Pierpont Government, as it was now popularly termed, adopted an Ordinance on the 20th of August, 1861, providing "for the formation of a new State out of a portion of the territory of this State." The Ordinance was approved by a vote of the people on the fourth Thursday of October, and on the 26th of November the Convention assembled in Wheeling to frame a constitution for the new government. The work was satisfactorily performed, and on the first Thursday of April, 1862, the people approved the constitution by a vote of 18,862 in favor of it with only 514 against it.

The work of the representatives of the projected new State being thus ratified, the Governor called the Legislature of Virginia together on the sixth day of May, and on the 13th of the same month that body gave its consent, with due regularity, to "the formation of a new State within the jurisdiction of the said State of Virginia." A fortnight later, on the 28th of May, Senator Willey introduced the subject in Congress by presenting a memorial from the Legislature of Virginia together with a certified copy of the proceedings of the Constitutional Convention and the vote of the people.

The constitution was referred to the Committee on Territories and a bill favorable to admission was promptly reported by Senator Wade of Ohio. The measure was discussed at different periods, largely with reference to the effect it would have upon the institution of slavery, and Congress insisted upon inserting a provision that "the children of slaves, born in the State after the fourth day of July, 1863, shall be free; all slaves within the said State who shall at that time be under the age of ten years shall be free when they arrive at the age of twenty-one years; all slaves over ten and under twenty-one shall be free at the age of twenty-five years; and no slave shall be permitted to come into the State for permanent residence therein." This condition was to be ratified by the Convention which framed the constitution, and by the people at an election held for the purpose, and, upon due certification of the approval of the condition to the President of the United States, he was authorized to issue his proclamation declaring West Virginia to be a State of the Union.

Mr. Sumner was not satisfied with a condition which left West Virginia with any form of slavery whatever. He said there were "twelve thousand human beings now held in bondage in that State, and all who are over a certain age are to be kept so for their natural lives." He desired to strike out the provision which permitted this and to insert one in lieu thereof, declaring that "within the limits of the said State there shall be neither slavery nor involuntary servitude otherwise than in the punishment of crime whereof the party shall have been duly convicted." Mr. Sumner's amendment was opposed by some of the most radical anti-slavery men in the Senate, notably by Collamer and Foot of Vermont, by Wade of Ohio, and by Howe of Wisconsin. They believed that the convictions of the people of West Virginia had developed to the point embodied in the bill, and that to attempt the immediate extirpation of slavery might lead to re-action and possibly to the rejection of the constitution. Mr. Sumner's amendment was therefore defeated by 24 votes against 11. Of the 24 votes 17 were given by Republican senators.

Mr. Powell of Kentucky vigorously opposed the bill in all its parts. He contended that "if the cities of New York and Brooklyn, with the counties in which they are located, were to get up a little bogus Legislature and say they were the State of New York, and ask to be admitted and cut off from the rest of the State, I would just as soon vote for their admission as to vote for the pending bill." No senator, he said, could pretend to claim that "even a third part of the people of Virginia have ever had any thing to do with rendering their assent to the making of this new State within the territorial limits of that ancient Commonwealth." He declared this to be "a dangerous precedent which overthrows the Constitution and may be fraught with direful consequences." " Out of the one hundred and sixty counties that compose the State of Virginia," he continued, "less than one-fourth have assumed to act for the entire State; and even within the boundaries of the new State more than half the voters have declined to take part in the elections."

Mr. Willey argued that the Legislature represented the almost unanimous will of the loyal people of West Virginia. He said that "besides the 19,000 votes cast, there were 10,000 men absent in the Union army, and that, the conclusion being foregone, the people had not been careful to come out to vote, knowing that the constitution would be overwhelmingly adopted." On the 14th of July, three days before Congress adjourned, the bill passed the Senate by a vote of 23 to 17. Mr. Rice of Minnesota was the only Democrat who favored the admission of the new State. The other Democratic senators voted against it. Mr. Chandler and Mr. Howard of Michigan voted in the negative because the State had voluntarily done nothing towards providing for the emancipation of slaves; Mr. Sumner and Mr. Wilson, because the Senate had rejected the anti-slavery amendment; Mr. Trumbull and Mr. Cowan, because of the irregularity of the whole proceeding.

The bill was not considered in the House until the next session. It was taken up on the 9th of December and was vigorously attacked by Mr. Conway of Kansas. He questioned the validity of the Pierpont Government and asked whether the law which gave him his warrant of authority had come from "a mob or from a mass-meeting." He said he had "serious reason to believe that it is the intention of the President to encourage the formation of State organizations in all the seceded States, and that a few individuals are to assume State powers wherever a military encampment can be effected in any of the rebellious districts." Mr. Conway denounced this scheme as "utterly and flagrantly unconstitutional, as radically revolutionary in character and deserving the reprobation of every loyal citizen." It aimed, he said, at "an utter subversion of our constitutional system and will consolidate all power in the hands of the Executive." He was answered with spirit by Mr. Colfax of Indiana, who reviewed the successive steps by which the legality of the Virginia government had been recognized by the President and by all the departments of the executive government. He argued that West Virginia had taken every step regularly and complied with every requirement of the Constitution.

Mr. Crittenden of Kentucky said the Wheeling government could be regarded as the government of the whole State of Virginia "only by a mere fiction. We *know* the fact to be otherwise." He said it was the party applying for admission that consented to the admission, and that was the whole of it. When the war should cease and the National authority should be re-established he wanted the Union as it was. This would be "a new-made Union — the old majestic body cut and slashed by passion, by war, coming to form another government, another Union. The Constitution gives us no power to do what we are asked to do." Mr. Maynard said there were "two governors and two Legislatures assuming authority over Virginia simultaneously. The question here is, which shall the Government of the United States recognize as the true and lawful Legislature of Virginia?" He contended that it had already been settled, by the admission of members of both branches of Congress under the Pierpont Government. Mr. Dawes affirmed that "nobody has given his consent to the division of the State of Virginia and the erection of a new State who does not reside within the new State itself." He contended therefore that "this bill does not comply with the spirit of the Constitution. If the remaining portions of Virginia are under duress while this consent is given, it is a mere mockery of the Constitution." Mr. Brown of Virginia, from that part which was to be included in the new State, corrected Mr. Dawes, but the latter maintained that while a member of the Legislature " was picked up in Fairfax and two or three gentlemen in other parts of the State, they protested themselves that they did not pretend to represent the counties from which they hailed."

Mr. Thaddeus Stevens said he did not desire to be understood as "sharing the delusion that we are admitting West Virginia in pursuance of any provision of the Constitution." He could "find no provision justifying it, and the argument in favor of it originates with those who either honestly entertain an erroneous opinion, or who desire to justify by a forced construction an act which they have predetermined to do." He maintained that it was "but mockery to say that the Legislature of Virginia has ever consented to the division. Only two hundred thousand out of a million and a quarter of people have participated in the proceedings." He contended that "the State of Virginia has a regular organization, and by a large majority of the people it has changed its relations to the Federal Government." He knew that this was treason in the individuals who participated in it; but so far as the State was concerned, it was a valid act. Our government, he argued, "does not act upon a State. The State, as a separate distinct body, is the State of a majority of the people of Virginia, whether rebel or loyal, whether convict or free men. The majority of the people of Virginia is the State of Virginia, although individuals have committed treason." "Governor Pierpont," continued Mr. Stevens, "is an excellent man, and I wish he were the Governor elected by the people of Virginia. But according to my principles operating at the present time I can vote for the admission of West Virginia without any compunctions of conscience — only with some doubt about the policy of it. None of the States now in rebellion are entitled to the protection of the Constitution. These proceedings are in virtue of the laws of war. We may admit West Virginia as a new State, not by virtue of any provision of the Constitution but under our absolute power which the laws of war give us in the circumstances in which we are placed. I shall vote for this bill upon that theory, and upon that alone. I will not stultify myself by supposing that we have any warrant in the Constitution for this proceeding."

Mr. Bingham of Ohio made an able argument principally devoted to rebutting the somewhat mischievous ground assumed by Mr. Stevens. He affirmed that "the minority of the people of the State cannot be deprived of their rights because the majority have committed treason." He argued that, the majority of the people of Virginia having become rebels, the State was in the hands of the

loyal minority, who in that event had a right to administer the
laws, maintain the authority of the State government, and elect a
State Legislature and a Governor, through whom they might call
upon the Federal Government for protection against domestic violence, according to the express guaranty of the Constitution. " To
deny this proposition," continued Mr. Bingham, "is to say that
when the majority in any State revolt against the laws, the State
government can never be re-organized nor the rights of the minority
protected so long as the majority are in revolt."   He contended that
the doctrine he advocated was not a new one, that it was as old as
the Constitution, and he called attention to the remarkable letter of
"The Federalist," addressed by Mr. Madison to the American people
in which " he who is called the author of the Constitution " asked :
"Why may not illicit combinations for purposes of violence be
formed as well by a majority of a State as by a majority of a county
or a district of the same State?   And if the authority of the State
ought in the latter case to protect the local magistracy, ought
not the Federal authority in the former case to support the State
authority ? "

Mr. Segar, who represented the district including Fortress Monroe,
pleaded very earnestly against the dismemberment of his State and
he argued, as Mr. Powell had argued in the Senate, that there was
no evidence that a majority of the people within the counties which
were to compose the new State had ever given their assent to its
formation.   The ordinary vote of those counties he said was 48,000
while on the new State question the entire vote cast was only 19,000.
He named ten counties included in the new State organization in
which not a single vote had been cast on either side of the question
at the special election.   Though loyal to the Union and grieving
over the rebellious course of Virginia he begged that this humiliation might be spared her.   " Let there not be two Virginias ; let us
remain one and united.   Do not break up the rich cluster of glorious
memories and associations which gather over the name and the
history of this ancient and once glorious Commonwealth."

On the passage of the bill the ayes were 96 and the noes were
55.   The ayes were wholly from the Republican party, though several
prominent Republicans opposed the measure.   Almost the entire
Massachusetts delegation voted in the negative, as did also Mr. Roscoe Conkling, Mr. Conway of Kansas and Mr. Francis Thomas of
Maryland.   The wide difference of opinion concerning this act was

not unnatural. But the cause of the Union was aided by the addition of another loyal commonwealth, and substantial justice was done to the brave people of the new State who by their loyalty had earned the right to be freed from the domination which had fretted them and from the association which was uncongenial to them.

To the old State of Virginia the blow was a heavy one. In the years following the war it added seriously to her financial embarrassment, and it has in many ways obstructed her prosperity. As a punitive measure, for the chastening of Virginia, it cannot be defended. Assuredly there was no ground for distressing Virginia by penal enactments that did not apply equally to every other State of the Confederacy. Common justice revolts at the selection of one man for punishment from eleven who have all been guilty of the same offense. If punishment had been designed there was equal reason for stripping Texas of her vast domain and for withdrawing the numerous land grants which had been generously made by the National Government to many of the States in rebellion. But Texas was allowed to emerge from the contest without the forfeiture of an acre, and Congress, so far from withdrawing the land grants by which other Southern States were to be enriched, took pains to renew them in the years succeeding the war. The autonomy of Virginia alone was disturbed. Upon Virginia alone fell the penalty, which if due to any was due to all.

Another consideration is of great weight. An innocent third party was involved. Virginia owed a large debt, held in great part by loyal citizens of the North and by subjects of foreign countries. The burden was already as heavy as she could bear in her entirety, and dismemberment so crippled her that she could not meet her obligations. The United States might well have relieved Virginia and have done justice to her creditors by making some allowance for the division of her territory. Regarding her only as entitled to the rights of a public enemy so long as she warred upon the Union, we may confidently maintain that she is entitled at least to as just and magnanimous treatment as the National Government extends to a foreign foe. In our war with Mexico it became our interest to acquire a large part of the territory owned by that republic. We had conquered her armies and were in possession of her capital. She was helpless in our hands. But the high sense of justice which has always distinguished the United States in her public policies would not permit the despoilment of Mexico. We negotiated therefore for the territory needed, and paid for it a larger price than would have been given by any other nation in the world. The American Government went still farther. Many of our citizens held large claims against Mexico, and the failure to pay them had been one of the causes that precipitated hostilities. Our government in addition to the money consideration of fifteen millions of dollars which we paid for territory, agreed to exonerate Mexico from all demands of our citizens, and to pay them from our own Treasury. This supplementary agreement cost the National Treasury nearly four million dollars.

If the United States were willing to place Virginia on the basis on which they magnanimously placed Mexico after the conquest of that Republic, a sufficient allowance would be made to her to compensate at least for that part of her public debt which might presumptively be represented by the territory taken from her. If it be said in answer to such a suggestion that it would be fairer for West Virginia to assume the proportional obligation thus indicated, the prompt rejoinder is that in equity her people are not held to such obligation. The public improvements for which the debt was in large part incurred had not been so far completed as to benefit West Virginia when the civil war began, — their advantages being mainly confined to the Tide-water and Piedmont sections of the State. There is indeed neither moral nor legal responsibility resting upon West Virginia for any part of the debt of the old State.

In determining the relative obligations of the National Government and of the government of West Virginia, concerning the debt, it is of the first importance to remember that the new State was not primarily organized and admitted to the Union for the benefit of her own people, but in far larger degree for the benefit of the people of the whole Union. The organic law would not have been strained, legal fictions would not have been invented, contradictory theories would not have been indulged, if a great national interest had not demanded the creation of West Virginia. If it had not been apparent that the organization of West Virginia was an advantage to the loyal cause; if the border-State policy of Mr. Lincoln, so rigidly adhered to throughout the contest, had not required this link for the completion of its chain, — the wishes of the people most directly involved would never have had the slightest attention from the Congress of the United States. Strong and equitable as was the case of West Virginia, irritating and undesirable as her relations to the older State might be, advantageous to the people as the new government might prove, these considerations would not of themselves have offered sufficient inducement to engage the attention of Congress for an hour at that critical period. They would have been brushed aside and disregarded with that cool indifference by which all great legislative bodies prove how easy it is to endure the misery of other people. West Virginia indeed got only what was equitably due, and what she was entitled to claim by the natural right of self-government. The war brought good fortune to her as conspicuously as it brought ill fortune to the older State from which she was wrenched. West Virginia is to be congratulated, and her creditable career and untiring enterprise since she assumed the responsibilities of self-government show how well she deserved the boon. But the wounds inflicted on the mother State by her separation will never be healed until Virginia is relieved from the odium of having been specially selected from the eleven seceding States for the punishment that struck at once against her prosperity and against her pride of empire.

Nor should it be forgotten that the State of Virginia before the war might well be regarded as the creditor and not the debtor of the National Government. One of her earliest acts of patriotism as an independent State was the cession to the General Government of her superb domain on the north side of the Ohio River, from the sale of which more than one hundred millions of dollars have been paid into the National Treasury. A suggestive contrast is presented to-day between the condition of Virginia and the condition of Texas and Florida. It was the aggressive disunionism of the two latter States which aided powerfully in dragging Virginia into rebellion. But for the urgency of the seven original Confederate States, in which Texas and Florida were numbered, Virginia Loyalists would have been able to hold their State firm in her National allegiance. Since the war Texas has traveled the highway to wealth and power, founded on the ownership of her public lands, of which the National Government could have deprived her with as little difficulty as was found in dividing Virginia. Florida has likewise enjoyed general prosperity, and secured rapid development from the resources of land which the National Government had generously given her before the war and of which she was not deprived for her acts of rebellion.

True-hearted Americans rejoice in the prosperity of these States which adorn the southern border of the Republic; but they cannot help seeing, and seeing with regret, how differently the ancient Commonwealth of Virginia has fared at the hands of the National Government.

If the hurt to Virginia were of a general character, which could not be specified or defined, her case might be passed over with the plea of *damnum absque injuriâ.* But, unfortunately, — or it may be fortunately, — the detriment to her public credit can be stated with substantial precision, and can be traced directly to her despoilment. That took from her the power to pay her debt. If the harm resulting therefrom were confined to the State and to the holders of her securities, the National Government might the more easily disregard the equities of the case. But Virginia's embarrassment is of widespread concern, and injuriously affects the public credit of other States. Nor can it be said that the precedent of aiding Virginia could be quoted for aid to every State that might get into financial trouble. It could be quoted only for the case — which will perhaps never again occur — where the National Government shall strip the State of a large and valuable part of her territory, and thus take from her the ability to meet her obligations. The precedent might then be quoted, and should be unhesitatingly followed.

In the formal and necessarily austere administration of public affairs there is little room for the interposition of sentiment. Yet sentiment 'has its place. We stimulate the ardor of patriotism by the mere display of a flag which has no material force, but which is emblematic of all material force, and typifies the glory of the Nation. We stir the ambition of the living by rearing costly monuments to the heroic dead. It may surely be pardoned if Americans shall feel a deep personal interest in the good name and good fortune of a State so closely identified with the early renown of the Republic, — a State with whose soil is mingled the dust of those to whom all States and all generations are debtors, — the Father of his Country, the author of the Declaration of Independence, the chief projector of the National Constitution.

CHAPTER XXII.

NATIONAL CURRENCY AND STATE BANK CURRENCY. — IN COMPETITION. — LEGAL-TENDER
BILL TENDED TO EXPAND STATE BANK CIRCULATION. — SECRETARY CHASE'S REC-
OMMENDATION. — FAVORABLY RECEIVED. — STATE BANK CIRCULATION, $150,000,000.
— PRELIMINARY BILL TO ESTABLISH NATIONAL BANKS. — FESSENDEN. — SHERMAN.
— HOOPER. — NATIONAL BANK SYSTEM IN 1862. — DISCUSSED AMONG THE PEOPLE. —
RECOMMENDED BY THE PRESIDENT. — MR. CHASE URGES IT. — BILL INTRODUCED
AND DISCUSSED IN SENATE. — DISCUSSION IN THE HOUSE. — BILL PASSED. — HUGH
MCCULLOCH OF INDIANA APPOINTED COMPTROLLER OF THE CURRENCY. — AMENDED
BANK ACT. — TO REMEDY DEFECTS, CIRCULATION LIMITED TO $300,000,000. — NA-
TIONAL POWER. — STATE RIGHTS. — TAXATION. — RENEWED DEBATE IN SENATE AND
HOUSE. — BILL PASSED. — MERITS OF THE SYSTEM. — FORMER SYSTEMS. — FIRST
BANK IN THE UNITED STATES. — CHARTERS OF UNITED-STATES BANKS, 1791-1816.
— NATIONAL BANKS COMPARED WITH UNITED-STATES BANKS. — ONE DEFECTIVE
ELEMENT. — FOUNDED ON NATIONAL DEBT.

THE Secretary of the Treasury had not failed to see that a constant conflict and damaging competition must ensue between
the currency of the Nation and the currency of the State banks.
It was the course of the banks more than any other agency that
had discredited the "demand notes" and demonstrated to the Treasury Department and to Congress the absolute necessity of imparting
the legal-tender quality to the paper issued by the government.
As this paper took the place of gold and silver in the payment of
every obligation, both corporate and individual, — except duties on
imports and interest on the National debt, — it was made easy for the
State banks to extend their circulation. It was quite practicable for
them to keep a sufficient amount of legal-tender paper in their
vaults to meet all the probable requirements of redemption, and
they were thus tempted to expand their loans and issue their own
bills to a dangerous extent. It was indeed hardly necessary to provide legal-tender notes to redeem their own bills. One kind of
paper money, to a large proportion of the public, was practically as
good as another. Coin redemption being abandoned, the banks in a
certain sense lost all moral and legal restraint. The enactment of

the Legal-tender Bill had not therefore given the control of the currency to the government. It had only increased the dangers of inflation by the stimulus it imparted and the protection it afforded to the circulation of State bank notes.

Secretary Chase had grasped the situation earlier than the experienced financiers who assumed to be his special advisers, and while he was, in the opinion of unjust critics, completely in the hands of the State banks, he surprised the country by recommending in his report of December, 1861, the establishment of a National system that should give the General Government complete control of the currency. The State bank circulation in the loyal States he estimated at $150,000,000. "The whole of it" he regarded as "a loan without interest from the people to the banks." The secretary thought "it deserves consideration whether sound policy does not require that the advantages of this loan be transferred from the banks, representing the interest of stockholders, to the government representing the aggregate interest of the whole people." Attention was called to the fact that "the existing circulation depends on the laws of thirty-four States and the character of some sixteen hundred private corporations." It was somewhat startling to learn that "the circulation is usually furnished in greatest proportion by institutions of least actual capital and is commonly in the inverse ratio of solvency."

The bold and comprehensive recommendation of Mr. Chase was favorably received by many of the leading men in Congress and by many of the ablest financiers of the country. The committees of both Senate and House were well disposed, but preferred time for consultation and deliberation. The Secretary of the Treasury, with the aid of Mr. E. G. Spaulding, Mr. Sherman, and Mr. Samuel Hooper, engaged in the preparation of a bank bill which in due time was submitted to the Committee of Ways and Means. The committee was at the moment engaged on the Internal-revenue Bill, the important character of which absorbed the attention of Congress. The adjustment of the tariff duties to the excise taxes was also a serious labor which left no adequate time to mature a bank bill in season for its consideration at that session. Indeed the committee was not able to report the bill to the House until the 12th of July, 1862, when five thousand extra copies were printed for distribution among the financial institutions of the country. It was deemed wise to give the people time to consider so important a measure, and with that end in view all further action was postponed to the next session.

Meanwhile the bill was published in the leading papers of the loyal States and elicited the most diverse opinions. It was however received with favor by the public. Those interested in the State banks were at first exceedingly hostile to it. The proposition to tax their circulation two per cent. in addition to the three per cent. imposed upon incomes by the new law was considered harsh and unjust. The object was to compel the retirement of the State bank circulation. In no other way could a national system be at once generally introduced. The courts had repeatedly held the authority of the States to charter banks with power to issue and circulate notes as money, to be constitutional. Congress could not abridge this right in any way by direct legislation. Its power to tax was however undoubted. The friends of the State bank system claimed that the indirect method of destroying the institution by taxing its notes out of existence was an arbitrary exercise of questionable power.

The advocates of a uniform and stable system of banking to cure the manifold evils then prevailing, admitted that the prerogative of the States could not be questioned, but urged that the exercise of it had invariably increased and often produced the financial troubles which had afflicted the country in the past. If the States would not surrender their prerogative, the National Government would be compelled to exercise its larger prerogative embodied in the power to tax. The right of the nation to do this had been asserted by the head of the Treasury under a Democratic administration some years before. Recognizing as he did the necessity of a reform in the system of banking, Secretary Guthrie in his report to Congress in 1855 declared that " if the States shall continue the charter and multiplication of banks with authority to issue and circulate notes as money, and fail to apply any adequate remedy to the increasing evil, and also fail to invest Congress with the necessary power to prohibit the same, Congress may be justified in the exercise of the power to levy an excise upon them, and thus render the authority to issue and circulate them valueless."

During the autumn of 1862 the bank question was subjected to a thorough discussion among the people. The legal-tender notes had already become popular, and were evidently preferred by the public to the notes of local banks. The depression naturally inci-

dent to continued reverses in the field led to the defeat of the Administration in many of the State elections, but despite the operation
of all adverse causes the general trade of the country was good.
The crops had been abundant and prices were remunerative. All
that had been claimed for the legal-tender bill by its most sanguine
advocates had been realized in the business of the country. The one
disappointment was their failure to keep at par with gold; but even
this, in the general prosperity among the people, did not create discouragement. The Internal-revenue system had but just gone into
operation, and the only feature embarrassing to the people was the
requirement that the taxes should be paid in the legal-tender paper
of the government. No provision of law could have operated so
powerfully for a system of National banks. The people were subjected to annoyance and often to expense in exchanging the notes
of their local banks for the government medium. The internal
fiscal machinery of the government evidently required places of
deposit. The tax-collectors could not intrust the funds in their
hands to State banks except at their own risk. The money of the
government was thus liable to loss from the absence of responsible
agencies under the control of National power. The fact that the
bills of State banks were not receivable for taxes tended constantly
to bring them into disrepute. The refusal of the government to
trust its funds in the keeping of the State banks was nothing less
than the requirement of the Sub-treasury Act, but to the popular
apprehension it was a manifestation of distrust which did the banks
great harm. The total revenue of the National Government had
before the war been collected at a few custom-houses on the coast,
and the public had not been generally familiar with the mode of its
safe-keeping. The system of internal taxes now reached the interior,
and the people were made daily witnesses of the fact that the government would not trust a dollar of its money in the vaults of a
State bank.

Under the influences thus at work, the friends of the State banks
plainly saw that the National system was growing in favor, and they
began to admit that its creation might facilitate the financial operations of the country. Many of them were willing to give it a
fair trial. The advocates of the National system constantly pressed
their cause among the people. The five-twenty six per cent. bonds,
into which the legal tenders were convertible, offered, as they explained, an excellent basis for banking. Their absorption for that

purpose would create not only a market for that class of securities but inevitably cause them to appreciate in value. The government would thus be largely benefited, and its cause would be strengthened by the silent influence of self-interest which would certainly be developed by the general distribution of its bonds as the basis of a national currency. It was also urged that the existing banks could with great facility and without sacrifice re-organize under the proposed national law.

The popular mind having been thus favorably turned towards the system of national banks, the President specifically approved it in his message to Congress in December, 1862. Expressing his doubts "whether a circulation of United-States notes, payable in coin, and sufficiently large for the wants of the people, can be permanently, usefully, and safely maintained," Mr. Lincoln asked if there was "any other mode by which necessary provision for the public wants can be made, and the great advantage of a safe and uniform currency secured?" He declared that he knew of none "which promises so certain results, and is at the same time so unobjectionable, as the organization of banking associations under a general law of Congress well guarded in its provisions." Mr. Chase elaborated his recommendation of the preceding year to the same effect. He asked that "a tax might be imposed on the notes of existing banks such as would practically exclude them from circulation." In their stead the legal-tender notes would be used, but he preferred "a circulation furnished by the government but issued by banking associations organized under a general Act of Congress."

Mr. Chase said "the central idea of the proposed measure is the establishment of one uniform circulation, of equal value throughout the country, upon the foundation of national credit combined with private capital." He suggested that "these associations be entirely voluntary. Any persons desirous of employing real capital in sufficient amounts, can, if the plan be adopted, unite together under proper articles, and having contributed the requisite capital can invest such part of it, not less than a fixed minimum, in United-States bonds, and having deposited these bonds with the proper officer of the United States can receive United-States notes in such denominations as may be desired, and employ them as money in discounts and exchanges." As a further inducement, the secretary said "the stockholders of any existing banks can in like manner organize under the Act, and transfer, by such degrees as may be found convenient, the capital of the old to the use of the new associations. The notes thus put into circulation will be payable until resumption in United-States notes, and after resumption in specie, by the association which issues them, on demand, and if not so paid will be redeemable at the Treasury of the United States from the proceeds of the bonds pledged in security." The secretary thought it would be "difficult to conceive of a note circulation which will combine higher local and general credit than this. After a few years no other circulation would be used, nor could the issues of the national circulation be easily increased beyond the legitimate demands of business. Every dollar of circulation would represent real capital actually invested in national stocks, and the total amount issued could at all times be easily and quickly ascertained from the books of the Treasury."

The bill to carry out these suggestions was introduced in the Senate on the 26th of January, 1863, by Mr. Sherman, and was reported from the Finance Committee on the 2d of February. On the 9th the Senate took it up for consideration. Mr. Sherman advocated the proposed system in an elaborate argument on several distinct grounds: " The banks would furnish a market for United-States bonds; they would absorb the circulation of the State banks gradually and without harsh measures; they would create a community of interest between the stockholders of the banks, the people, and the government, where now there existed a great contrariety of opinion and a great diversity of interests; adequate safeguards would be established against counterfeiting; the currency proposed would be uniform and would take the place of the notes of sixteen hundred banks, differing in style, and so easily imitated and altered that while notes of one-sixth of the existing banks had been counterfeited, 1,861 kinds of imitations were afloat, and 3,039 alterations, in addition to 1,685 spurious notes, in which hardly any care had been taken to show any resemblance tc the genuine." The national banks would be depositories of public moneys and their notes would be receivable for taxes. He concluded by declaring that "we cannot maintain our nationality unless we establish a sound and stable financial system, and as the basis of it we must have a uniform national currency." Accordingly he deemed the passage of the pending bill "more important than any other measure now pending either in Senate or House."

— Mr. Henderson of Missouri sought to limit the system to banks with a capital not less than $300,000, and thought "it would be infinitely better that all the banks should be established in New York, Philadelphia, Boston, Cincinnati, St. Louis, and such cities as those." He said "they had had some experience in the West with banking laws which permitted the organization of banks in out-of-the-way places, obscure villages, and unknown cross-roads."

— Mr. Powell of Kentucky, who was most persistent in his advocacy of a currency based on gold and silver coin, moved to "strike from the bill the words which prevented the acceptance of the National bank notes for duties on imports." These duties were payable in coin in order to secure gold with which to pay the interest on the public debt. In supporting his amendment, Senator Powell said that if the bill became a law the fact that they could not be received for customs would tend to depreciate the notes, and he wanted the credit of the paper money kept up if the country was to have no other. His motion was defeated.

— Mr. Ira Harris of New York secured the adoption of three sections, to be added at the end of the bill, which would enable State banks to accept its provisions and become National institutions more readily and more easily. He said that he was not opposed to a fair trial of the new system, but he doubted very much whether the banks of New York could be induced to abandon their State charters. "The banking system of New York was the best in the world. The banks enjoyed privileges which they could not be induced to surrender and the people would be reluctant to trust any others."

— Mr. John Carlile of West Virginia voted against all amendments because he wanted the bill to kill itself, which would happen if it were not improved. He voted against Senator Henderson's amendment to limit charters to banks with $300,000 capital. If the bill passed as it came from the Finance Committee there "will be banks established at every cross-road in the country. The State banks will be destroyed, and widows and orphans whose all is invested in the stock of these institutions will be impoverished."

— Mr. Clark of New Hampshire thought the proposed system might be improved by providing "that there shall be a visitation on the part of the States." He thought it would give confidence to the banks if the States "had the right to know how they stood."

— Mr. Pomeroy of Kansas thought the right to organize with a capital as low as $50,000 was a good provision and would "tend to popularize and extend the National banks throughout the country."

— Mr. Howard of Michigan opposed the bill because he thought its effect would be to "wage a very unnecessary and dangerous war upon the State institutions," and also because he deplored "the contest which will probably arise out of it in our local politics."

— Mr. Garrett Davis, avowing himself an advocate of the old United-States Bank which President Jackson destroyed, was opposed to the pending bill because "it does not provide for the convertibility of its paper into coin." The "system is based on government bonds, and they sold in New York yesterday at a discount of fifty-three per cent."

— Mr. Chandler of Michigan corrected Mr. Davis. "Gold sold at fifty-three per cent. premium, but that did not mean a discount of fifty-three per cent. on the bonds."

— Mr. Davis maintained that if he "had to pay $153 in greenbacks for $100 in gold, as a plain cornfield proposition, there was fifty-three per cent. difference."

— Mr. Wilson of Massachusetts pertinently asked Mr. Davis "if the credit of the government is not good enough, where is there left in the country any thing good enough to bank on? If the government goes down, there is not a considerable bank in America that does not go down with it."

— Mr. Doolittle of Wisconsin regarded it as "a necessity that the government should take control of the paper currency of the country. In some way we must restrain the issues of State banks. If we permit those banks to flood the channels of circulation, we destroy ourselves."

— Mr. Collamer of Vermont denied the right to tax the State banks out of existence, and to establish corporations in the States and Territories. Independently of the power of visitation by those States and Territories, he objected to making the government responsible for the ultimate redemption of the bills by the securities deposited. He inquired in what respect the promises of the National banks would be better than the notes of the government, and why should they be substituted for them?

— Mr. Chandler of Michigan claimed that when the whole system was in operation the government would borrow $300,000,000 at four per cent. per annum, because, while the bonds deposited with the banks would draw six per cent., the tax would bring back two per cent. He did not know how far the bill would go, but "all that is in it is good."

The bill came to a vote in the Senate on the 12th of February, and narrowly escaped defeat. The yeas were twenty-three, the nays twenty-one. The senators from Oregon, Nesmith and Harding, were the only Democrats who voted in the affirmative. Nine Republican senators voted against it.

The House of Representatives received the bill on the 19th. Mr. Spaulding of New York advocated it very earnestly. He stated that its principle was based on the free banking law of New York, which had been in successful operation since 1838. He dwelt upon the national character of the proposed notes, on their use in payment of taxes, and on the advantage to accrue from the exemption of the banking associations from State and United-States taxation. —Mr. Fenton of New York expressed the belief that the measure would aid in extricating the government from the financial difficulties in which it was involved, and pronounced it " one of the most potent means by which the representatives could strengthen the government and the people in the struggle to put down the enemies of the country, and give hope and courage to the hearts of those brave men who have gone forth to battle." Considerable opposition was offered, chiefly on details and by amendments. But the House sustained the measure as it came from the Senate, and passed it on the 20th of February, by the close vote of 78 to 64, on the call of the ayes and noes. It was approved by the President on the 25th.

The Currency Bureau of the Treasury Department provided for in the National Banking Act was organized by the appointment of Hugh McCulloch, who was then at the head of one of the largest State banking institutions in Indiana. He was recognized as possessing executive capacity and large experience in financial affairs. He had originally been opposed, as were many others interested in State banks, to the National Banking Act, but, as he says, the more he examined "the system" the more it "grew into favor with him day by day." This appears to have been the result with all who gave the question a fair and candid consideration, even when biased by personal interests or political prejudice. The law was defective in many particulars and some of its provisions made it difficult for existing State banks to accept charters under it. The first annual report of the comptroller of the currency shows that by Nov. 28, 1863, 134 banks had been organized under the Act. Fourteen of these were in the New-England States, sixteen in New York, twenty in Pennsylvania, twenty in Indiana, thirty-eight in Ohio;

New Jersey, the District of Columbia, and Kentucky each had one; Illinois seven, Iowa six, Michigan and Wisconsin four each, and Missouri two. Their total capital was $7,184,715. The bonds deposited with the Treasurer of the United States were $3,925,275, their deposits $7,467,059, and their loans and discounts $5,413,963.

In his report Mr. McCulloch pointed out defects of the law which had become apparent by the test of experience, and made many suggestions for its improvement. The whole subject was taken into consideration by the Ways and Means Committee of the House at the first session of the Thirty-eighth Congress. An amended bill, which repealed the Act of February 25, 1863, and supplied its place, was reported from the committee March 14, 1864. It was carefully considered in the committee of the whole, section by section, and against the protest of its advocates an amendment was ingrafted upon it giving to the States the right to impose taxes on the bank shares for State and municipal purposes to the same degree that taxes were imposed upon the property of other moneyed corporations. The bill was reported to the House from the committee of the whole on the 16th of April, when Mr. Stevens moved a substitute in which the tax amendment was left out. The substitute was defeated, and thereupon the immediate friends of the bill united with its opponents and laid the whole subject on the table. Mr. Stevens was totally opposed to the exercise of any power whatever by the States over banks established by National authority.

In the height of the war excitement, when men's minds were inflamed by a just resentment toward the Southern theory of States' rights, there was a tendency to go to extremes in the other direction. Some of the Republican leaders, notably Mr. Stevens, were very radical in their views in this respect, and would scarcely have hesitated at the abolition of all the checks upon Federal power which the Constitution wisely gives to the States. But apart from considerations of this character it was believed by many of the friends of the national banking system that the imposition of State taxes, in addition to those to be imposed by the General Government, would defeat the object of the bill. Others in their anxiety to strengthen the National Government were anxious to reserve to it exclusively the largest possible scope of taxation. It soon became apparent however that some concession must be made to those of both political parties who believed that the States could not constitutionally be deprived of the right to levy uniform taxes on property within their jurisdiction. To meet the views of these gentlemen the Ways and Means Committee reported a bill with a provision intended to reconcile all differences of opinion. This gave to the States the power to tax the capital stock, circulation, dividends, or business of national banks at no higher rate than was imposed upon the same amount of moneyed capital in the hands of individual citizens of the State, provided no tax was imposed upon that part of the capital invested in United-States bonds. This was adopted by a vote of 70 to 60 on the 18th of April, 1864.

The opposition to the bill in all other respects save this question of taxation was confined mainly to the Democratic members of the House. The measure was by this time regarded favorably by all Republicans. It was considered to be a part of the Administration policy, and one that would contribute largely to strengthen the government in its struggle. Its success thus far had demonstrated that under a perfected law it would soon become the general and popular banking system of the country. It was daily growing in favor with business men, and there was no longer doubt that a large proportion of the surplus capital of the nation would be invested in United-States bonds and in the stock of National banks. In the debate in the House which was prolonged, two speeches of particular interest were elicited. Mr. James Brooks of New York, as the leader of the Democratic minority on the question, ably summarized the objections of his party. He was a man of education and great intelligence. He had traveled extensively and was a close observer. He had been a writer for the metropolitan press for many years, and was familiar with the political and financial history of the country from an early period. He was an effective speaker. On this occasion he was in large part supplied with facts by Mr. James Gallatin, who as president of one of the principal banks of New-York City had unsuccessfully attempted to dictate the financial policy of the government in 1861. Mr. Gallatin had conceived an intense hostility to Mr. Chase, and inspired Mr. Brooks to make in the course of the debate on the bank bill some unfounded charges against the Secretary. The speech of Mr. Brooks was a general attack upon the financial policy of the administration directed principally against the Legal-tender Act, and at the same time a qualified defense of the State bank system. He asserted that the government could have successfully carried on the war upon a specie basis, but his authority for this claim was Mr. Gallatin. Mr. Samuel

Hooper at the close of the debate defended the financial policy of the Administration and disposed of the argument of Mr. Brooks. He asserted that Mr. Gallatin had induced the banks of New-York City on December 30, 1861, to suspend specie payments, and briefly related his presumptuous attempt to dictate to the Secretary of the Treasury the financial policy of the Nation. He declared that the issue of legal-tender notes was the only resource left to the government, and "was wise as well as necessary." In his review of the financial history of the country he dealt unsparingly with the old State-bank system, and exposed in a masterly manner its inherent defects even in those States where the greatest care had been exercised by Legislative power to hedge it about with limitations.

In the Senate the debate on the House bill was chiefly confined to amendments proposed by the Finance Committee. The provision incorporated by the House in regard to taxation was amplified so as to make it more specific and definite. Considerable opposition was shown to this action, but Mr. Fessenden, chairman of Finance, defended the recommendation of his committee and successfully replied to the arguments against it. An effort was made by Senators Doolittle, Henderson, and Trumbull on the Republican side to prevent the establishment of any more banks under the law than were in existence in May, 1864, unless they redeemed their notes in coin. The banks then organized, possessed an aggregate capital of about $36,000,000, with bonds deposited to secure circulation to the extent of a little more than $33,000,000. The argument was that this addition to the legal-tender notes already in circulation supplied an ample currency for the business of the country. The issue of the whole $300,000,000 of National bank notes authorized by the bill, these senators claimed, would be such an expansion of the currency as would sink its value to almost nothing. They proposed also to compel the State banks to retire their circulation, but permitted them to organize on the specie basis as National banks. Mr. John P. Hale of New Hampshire thought that "it would be much simpler to incorporate in the bill a provision abolishing all such instruments as had previously been known as State constitutions." Senator Collamer proposed to require the banks to retain in their vaults one-fourth of all the gold they received as interest on their bonds deposited to secure circulation until the resumption of specie payments.

These amendments were voted down, and the bill finally passed the Senate on the 10th of May by a vote of 30 to 9, ten senators being absent or not voting. A conference committee of the two Houses agreed upon the points of difference. The report was adopted and the bill was approved by the President on the 3d of June, 1864. By the end of November 584 National banks had been organized, with an aggregate capital of $108,964,597.28, holding $81,961,450 of the bonds of the United States to secure a circulation of $65,864,650. These banks at once became agencies for the sale of the government's securities, and their officers being usually the men of most experience in financial affairs in their respective communities, gave encouragement and confidence to their neighbors who had money to invest. The sale of government bonds was in this way largely increased. The National banks thus became at once an effective aid to the government. By the close of the fiscal year 1864 $367,602,-529 of bonds were disposed of by the banks. During the fiscal year 1865 bonds to the amount of $335,266,617 were sold over their counters. On the 1st of October, 1865, there were in existence 1,513 National banks, with an aggregate capital of $395,729,597.83, with $276,219,950 of bonds deposited with the Treasurer of the United States to secure circulation.

Experience has justified the authors and promoters of the national banking system. Originally the circulation was limited to a total volume of $300,000,000, apportioned, one-half according to representative population, and the remainder by the Secretary of the Treasury among associations with "due regard to the existing banking capital, resources, and business of the respective States, Districts, and Territories." Complaint arose that by such limitation and apportionment injustice was done and monopolies created. After the war this restriction was removed and banking under the national system became entirely free. The advantages of uniform circulation on a basis of undoubted strength and availability have won almost universal favor among business men and prudent thinkers. The restoration of the multiform State system, with notes of varying value and banks of doubtful solvency, would receive no support among the people.

The National bank system with all its merits has not escaped serious opposition. The Bank of the United States, as twice established, incurred the hostility of the Democratic party, — their two greatest leaders, Jefferson and Jackson, regarding the creation of such an institution as not warranted by the Constitution. A persistent attempt has been made by certain partisans to persuade the people that the national banks of to-day are as objectionable as those which encountered serious hostility at earlier periods in our history. An examination into the constitution of the banks formerly organized by direct authority of the General Government will show how wide is the difference between them and the present system of national banks. It will show that the feature of the earlier banks which evoked such serious opposition and ultimately destroyed them is not to be found in the present system and could not be incorporated in it. It was from the first inapplicable and practically impossible.

The most important financial institution established in the United States before the adoption of the Constitution was the Bank of North America, still doing business in Philadelphia, with unbroken career through all the mutations of the eventful century which has passed since it was called into existence. It had its origin in 1780, when certain patriotic citizens of Pennsylvania resolved to "open a security subscription of three hundred thousand pounds *in real money*," the object being to procure supplies for the army, "then on the point of mutiny for lack of the common necessaries of life." The enterprising men who had the matter in hand addressed themselves to the task of providing three million rations and three hundred hogsheads of rum for the famished troops. The Continental Congress recognized their patriotic conduct and pledged "the faith of the government for the effectual reimbursement of the amount advanced." It fell to Robert Morris, Superintendent of Finance for the government, to organize the bank which owed its origin to these circumstances. While engaged in this arduous task he received two letters of advice from an anonymous source, ably written, and displaying considerable knowledge of the science of banking, then almost unknown in America. Indeed the methods of banking—it might be proper to say its secrets—were jealously guarded by the capitalists who monopolized it in the financial centres of Europe. Mr. Morris was struck by the ability and originality of his unknown correspondent, and was amazed to find that Alexander Hamilton, then but twenty-three years of age, was the author of the letters. It was the first exhibition of that mastery of finance which gave Mr. Hamilton his enduring fame.

When Mr. Hamilton assumed control of the Treasury Department under the Presidency of Washington he found that the Bank of North America had accepted a State charter from Pennsylvania and was not therefore in a position to fulfil the functions of a National

bank which he desired to establish as an aid to the financial operations of the government. After his funding of the Revolutionary
debt he applied to Congress for the charter of a National bank, with
a capital of $10,000,000, twenty-five per cent. of which must be paid
in coin and the remainder in the bonds of the United States. The
government was to own $2,000,000 of the stock of the bank and
was obviously to become its largest borrower. The measure encountered the determined opposition of the Secretary of State, Jefferson,
and the Attorney-General, Edmund Randolph, and it finally became
an almost distinctly sectional issue — the Northern members of Congress with few exceptions sustaining it; the Southern members under
the lead of Mr. Madison almost wholly opposing it. It became a law
on the 25th of February, 1791.

When the charter of the bank — which was granted for twenty
years — expired in 1811 the administration of Mr. Madison favored
its renewal. The eminent financier, Albert Gallatin, then Secretary
of the Treasury, informed Congress that the bank had been "wisely
and skillfully managed." The hostility to it originated in political
considerations. It was regarded as an aristocratic institution, was
violently opposed by the State banks which by this time had become
numerous, and notwithstanding the change of Mr. Madison in its
favor, the bill to re-charter was defeated. The contest however was
severe. In the House the opponents of the bill had but one majority, and there being a tie in the Senate the re-charter was defeated
by the casting vote of George Clinton the Vice-President. By this
course Congress gave to the State banks a monopoly of the circulating medium. The war of 1812 followed, and in the sweep of its
disastrous influences a large majority of these banks were destroyed,
their notes never redeemed, and great distress consequently inflicted
upon the people.

It was this result which disposed Congress, as soon as the war was
over, to establish for the second time a Bank of the United States.
The charter was drawn by Alexander J. Dallas who had succeeded
Mr. Gallatin in the Treasury. In the main it followed the provisions
of the first bank, but owing to the growth of the country the capital
stock was enlarged to twenty-five millions, of which the government
subscribed for one-fifth, payable wholly in its own bonds. Individual
subscribers were required to pay one-fourth in coin and three-fourths
in government bonds. The charter was again limited to twenty years.
It was this bank which encountered the bitter opposition of Presi-

dent Jackson, and which was seriously injured by his order to the Secretary of the Treasury, Roger B. Taney, in 1834, to withhold the deposit of government funds from its vaults. The act of President Jackson is usually referred to as "a removal of the deposits." This is incorrect. The government deposits were not removed from the United-States Bank, except in the ordinary course of business for the needs of the Treasury. But the order of the President prevented further deposits of government money being made, and thus destroyed one of the principal resources upon which the bank had been organized. A short time before the charter of the United-States Bank expired, a State charter was obtained from the Legislature of Pennsylvania, under which the bank continued business until 1841, when its affairs were wound up with heavy loss to the stockholders.

These brief outlines of the charters of the United-States banks of 1791 and 1816 show how entirely dissimilar they were in many essentials from the system of national banks established under the Acts of 1863 and 1864. In the first the government was a large stockholder and the officers of the Treasury practically directed all the operations and all the details of the bank. In the system now prevailing the government cannot be a stockholder, and takes no part in the management of banks except to see that the laws are complied with and that the safeguards for the public are rigidly maintained. An especially odious feature in the United-States Bank was the favoritism shown in its loans, by which it constantly tended to debauch the public service. Political friends of the institution were too often accommodated on easy terms, and legitimate banking was thus rendered impossible. No such abuse is practicable under the present system. Indeed there is such an entire absence of it that the opponents of the National banks have not even brought the accusation.

There was special care taken to place the Currency Bureau entirely beyond partisan influence. The misfortunes which had come upon the United-States Bank from its connection with party interests were fully appreciated by the wise legislators who drafted the National Bank Act. They determined to guard against the recurrence of the calamities which destroyed the former system. The original Act of 1863, organizing the National system, provided that the Comptroller of the Currency should be appointed by the President upon the nomination of the Secretary of the Treasury, and, unlike any other Federal officer at that time, his term was fixed at five years. This period of service was established in order that it should not come to an end with the Presidential term. It was also specifically provided, long in advance of the tenure-of-office Act, that the President could not remove the Comptroller unless with the advice and consent of the Senate. The Comptroller was thus excepted by statute from that long list of officers who were for many years subjected to change upon the incoming of each Administration. From the organization of the National Banking system to this time (1884) there have been four Comptrollers, — three of whom voluntarily resigned. The present incumbent of the office, Mr. John Jay Knox, has discharged his important duties with great satisfaction for twelve years, and with his predecessors has conclusively established in practice the non-partisan character which is indispensable to the successful Administration of the Bureau.

The division and distribution of bank capital under the National system do not merely carry its advantages to every community, but they afford the most complete guaranty against every abuse which may spring from a large aggregation of capital. The Bank of the United States in 1816 had a capital of thirty-five millions of dollars. If a similar institution were established to-day, bearing a like proportion to the wealth of the country, it would require a capital of at least six hundred millions of dollars — many fold larger than the combined wealth of the Bank of England and the Bank of France. It is hardly conceivable that such a power as this could ever be intrusted to the management of a Secretary of the Treasury or to a single board of directors, with the temptations which would beset them. It is the contemplation of such an enormous power placed in the hands of any body of men that gives a more correct appreciation of the conduct and motives of General Jackson in his determined contest with the United-States Bank. His instincts were correct. He saw that such an institution increasing with the growth of the country would surely tend to corruption, and by its unlimited power would interfere with the independence of Congress and with the just liberty of the people.

The single feature of resemblance between the Bank of the United States and the system of National banks is found in the fact that Government bonds constitute the foundation of each. But the use to which the bonds are devoted in the new system is entirely different from that of the old. The United-States Bank retained its bonds in its own vaults, liable to all the defalcation and mismanagement which might affect the other assets. In the present system the National Bank deposits its bonds with the Treasury Department, where they are held as special security for the redemption of the bills which the bank puts in circulation. The United-States Bank circulated its bills according to its own discretion, and there was no assurance to the holder against an over-issue and no certainty of ultimate redemption. The National Bank can issue no bills except those furnished by the Treasury Department in exchange for the bonds deposited to assure prompt redemption. In the former case there was no protection to the people who trusted the bank by taking its bills. In the case of the National Bank, the government holds the security in its own hands and protects the public from the possibility of loss.

The one defective element in the National bank system is that it requires the permanence of National debt as the basis of its existence. In a Republican government the people naturally oppose a perpetual debt, and could with difficulty be persuaded to consent to it for any incidental purpose however desirable. But so long as a National debt exists no use has been found for it more conducive to the general prosperity than making it the basis of a banking system in which flexibility and safety are combined to a degree never before enjoyed in this country and never excelled in any other. In no other system of banking have the bills had such wide circulation and such absolute credit. They are not limited to the United States. They are current in almost every part of the American continent, and are readily exchangeable for coin in all the marts of Europe.

CHAPTER XXIII.

AT no time during the war was the depression among the people
of the North so great as in the spring of 1863. When the
Thirty-seventh Congress came to its close on the 3d of March,
partisan feeling was so bitter that a contest of most dangerous
character was foreshadowed in the Loyal States. The anti-slavery
policy of the President was to be attacked as tending to a fatal
division among the people; the conduct of the war was to be
arraigned as impotent, and leading only to disaster. Circumstances
favored an assault upon the Administration. The project of free-
ing the slaves had encountered many bitter prejudices among the
masses in the Loyal States, and reverses in the field had created
a dread of impending conscriptions which would send additional
thousands to be wasted in fruitless assaults upon impregnable

fortifications. General Hooker had succeeded to the command of the Army of the Potomac, still sore under the cruel sacrifice of its brave men in the previous December. General Grant was besieging Vicksburg, which had been fortified with all the strength that military science could impart, and was defended by a very strong force under the command of J. C. Pemberton, a graduate of West Point, and a lieutenant-general in the Confederate army.

The opponents of the Administration intended to press the attack, to destroy the prestige of Mr. Lincoln, to bring hostilities in the field to an end, to force a compromise which should give humiliating guaranties for the protection of Slavery, to bring the South back in triumph, and to re-instate the Democratic party in the Presidential election of the ensuing year for a long and peaceful rule over a Union in which radicalism had been stamped out and Abolitionists placed under the ban. Such was the flattering prospect which opened to the view of the party that had so determinedly resisted and so completely defeated the Administration in the great States of the Union the preceding year. The new crusade against the President was begun by Mr. Vallandigham, who if not the ablest was the frankest and boldest member of his party. He took the stump soon after the adjournment of the Thirty-seventh Congress. It was an unusual time of the year to begin a political contest; but the ends sought were extraordinary, and the means adopted might well be of the same character. On the first day of May Mr. Vallandigham made a peculiarly offensive, mischievous, disloyal speech at Mount Vernon, Ohio, which was published throughout the State and widely copied elsewhere. It was perfectly apparent that the bold agitator was to have many followers and imitators, and that in the rapidly developing sentiment which he represented, the Administration would have as bitter an enemy in the rear as it was encountering at the front. The case was therefore critical. Mr. Lincoln saw plainly that the Administration was not equal to the task of subduing two rebellions. While confronting the power of a solid South he must continue to wield the power of a solid North.

After General Burnside had been relieved from the command of the Army of the Potomac he was sent to command the Department of Ohio. He established his headquarters in Cincinnati in April (1863). He undoubtedly had confidential instructions in regard to the mode of dealing with the rising tide of disloyalty which, beginning in Ohio, was sweeping over the West. The Mount-Vernon speech of Mr. Vallandigham would inevitably lead to similar demonstrations elsewhere, and General Burnside determined to deal with its author. On Monday evening the 4th of May he sent a detachment of soldiers to Mr. Vallandigham's residence in Dayton, arrested him, carried him to Cincinnati, and tried him by a military commission of which a distinguished officer, General Robert B. Potter, was president. Mr. Vallandigham resisted the whole proceeding as a violation of his rights as a citizen of the United States, and entered a protest declaring that he was arrested without due process of law and without warrant from any judicial officer, that he was not in either the land or naval forces of the United States nor in the militia in actual service, and therefore was not triable by a court-martial or military commission, but was subject only, by the express terms of the Constitution, to be tried on an indictment or presentment of a grand jury. Of the offense charged against him there was no doubt, and scarcely a denial; and the commission, brushing aside his pleas, convicted him, and sentenced him to be placed in close confinement, during the continuance of the war, in some fortress of the United States — the fortress to be designated by the commanding officer of the department. General Burnside approved the proceeding, and designated Fort Warren in the harbor of Boston as the place of Mr. Vallandigham's detention.

The President, with that sagacity which was intuitive and unfailing in all matters of moment, disapproved the sentence, and commuted it to one sending Mr. Vallandigham beyond our military lines to his friends of the Southern Confederacy. The estimable and venerable Judge Leavett of the United-States District Court was applied to for a writ of *habeas corpus*, but he refused to issue it. The judge declared that the power of the President undoubtedly implies the right to arrest persons who by their mischievous acts of disloyalty impede or hinder the military operations of the government. The Democratic party throughout the United States took up the case with intemperate and ill-tempered zeal. Meetings were held in various places to denounce it, and to demand the right of Vallandigham to return from the rebel lines within which he had been sent. Governor Seymour of New York in a public letter denounced the arrest as "an act which has brought dishonor upon our country, and is full of danger to our persons and our homes. If this proceeding is approved by the government and sanctioned by the people it is not merely a step toward revolution, it is revolution; it will not only lead to military despotism, it establishes military despotism. In this respect it must be accepted, or in this respect it must be rejected. If it is upheld our liberties are overthrown." Waxing still bolder Governor Seymour said "the people of this country now wait with the deepest anxiety the decision of the Administration upon these acts. Having given it a generous support in the conduct of the war, we now pause to see what kind of government it is for which we are asked to pour out our blood and our treasure. The action of the Administration will determine, in the minds of more than one-half of the people of the Loyal States, whether this war is waged to put down rebellion in the South or to destroy free institutions at the North."

The evil effect upon the public opinion of the North of such language from a man of Governor Seymour's high personal character and commanding influence with his party can hardly be exaggerated. It came at a time when the Administration was sorely pressed and when it could not stand an exasperating division in the North. The governor's letter was publicly read at a large meeting of the Democratic party in Albany, presided over by Erastus Corning, and called to consider the act of the Administration. A long series of resolutions denouncing Vallandigham's arrest were adopted and forwarded to the President. But Mr. Lincoln rose to the occasion as if inspired, and his letter of June 12 to the Albany Committee turned the popular tide powerfully in favor of the Administration. One of the points presented made a deep impression upon the understanding and profoundly stirred the hearts of the people. "Mr. Vallandigham was not arrested," said the President, "because he was damaging the political prospects of the Administration or the personal interests of the commanding general, but because he was damaging the army, upon the existence and vigor of which the life of this Nation depends. . . . If Mr. Vallandigham was not damaging the military power of the country, then his arrest was made on mistake of facts, which I would be glad to correct on reasonable, satisfactory evidence. I understand the meeting whose resolutions I am considering, to be in favor of suppressing the Rebellion by military force — by armies. Long experience has shown that armies cannot be maintained unless desertion shall be punished by the severe penalty of death. The case requires, and the law and the Constitution sanction, this punishment. Must I shoot a simple-minded soldier-boy who deserts, while I must not touch a hair of the wily agitator who induces him to desert? This is none the less injurious when effected by getting father or brother or friend into a public meeting, and there working upon his feelings until he is persuaded to write the soldier-boy that he is fighting in a bad cause, for a wicked Administration of a contemptible government, too weak to arrest and punish him if he shall desert. I think that in such a case to silence the agitator and to save the boy is not only constitutional, but is withal a great mercy." No other man in our history has so fully possessed the power of presenting an argument in concrete form, overthrowing all the logic of assailants, and touching the chords of public feeling with a tenderness which becomes an irresistible force.

The Democrats of Ohio took up the arrest of Vallandigham with especial earnestness, and were guilty of the unspeakable folly of nominating him as their candidate for governor. They appointed an imposing committee — one from each Congressional district of the State — to communicate with the President in regard to the sentence of banishment. They arrived in Washington about the last of June, and addressed a long communication to Mr. Lincoln, demanding the release and return of Mr. Vallandigham. They argued the case with ability. No less than eleven of the committee were or had been members of Congress, with George H. Pendleton at their head. Mr. Lincoln's reply under date of June 29 to their communication was as felicitous, as conclusive, as his reply to the Albany Committee. He expressed his willingness in answer to their request, to release Mr. Vallandigham without asking pledge, promise, or retraction from him, and with only one simple condition. That condition was that " the gentlemen of the committee themselves, representing as they do the character and power of the Ohio Democracy, will subscribe to three propositions: *First*, That there is now a rebellion in the United States, the object and tendency of which are to destroy the National Union, and that in your opinion an army and navy are constitutional means for suppressing that rebellion. *Second*, That no one of you will do any thing which in his own judgment will tend to hinder the increase or favor the decrease or lessen the efficiency of the army and navy while engaged in the effort to suppress that rebellion. And *Third*, That each of you will in his sphere do all he can to have the officers, soldiers, and seamen of the army and navy, while engaged in the effort to suppress the Rebellion, paid, fed, clad, and otherwise well provided for and supported."

Mr. Lincoln sent duplicates of these three conditions to the committee, one of which was to be returned to him indorsed with their names as evidence of their agreement thereto, the publication of which indorsement should be of itself a revocation of the order in relation to Mr. Vallandigham. If the Ohio gentlemen subscribed to these conditions as essential and obligatory, they thereby justified the arrest of Vallandigham for resisting each and every one of them. If they would not subscribe to them they placed themselves before the people of Ohio in an attitude of hostility to the vigorous and successful conduct of the war, on which the fate of the Union depended. The committee made a very lame rejoinder to the President. He had in truth placed them in a dilemma, from which they could not extricate themselves, and they naturally fell under popular condemnation. Mr. Lincoln's hit had indeed been so palpable that its victims were laughed at by the public, and their party was foredoomed by their course to political annihilation in the coming election.

While these interesting events were in progress the military exigency was engaging the attention of the people with an interest almost painfully intense. There was an urgent demand for an early movement by the Army of the Potomac. Mr. Lincoln realized that prompt success was imperatively required. The repetition of the disasters of 1862 might fatally affect our financial credit, and end with the humiliation of an intervention by European Powers. General Hooker was impressed by Mr. Lincoln with the absolute necessity of an early and energetic movement of the Army of the Potomac. On the 2d and 3d of May he fought the battle of Chancellorsville. He had as large a force as the Union army mustered on a single battle-field during the war, — not less perhaps than one hundred and twenty thousand men. He made a lamentable failure. Without bringing more than one-third of his troops into action he allowed himself to be driven across the Rappahannock by Lee, who, on the 7th of May, issued a highly congratulatory and boastful order detailing his victory.

In the issuing of orders General Hooker was one day in advance of Lee. He tendered to the soldiers his " congratulations on the achievements of the past seven days," and assured them that " if all has not been accomplished that was expected, the reasons are well known to the army." He further declared that " in withdrawing from the south bank of the Rappahannock before delivering a general battle to our adversaries, the army has given renewed evidence of its confidence in itself and of its fidelity to the principles it represents. Profoundly loyal and conscious of its strength," the General continued, " the Army of the Potomac will give or decline battle whenever its interest or its honor may demand." The General thought "the events of the past week may swell with pride the heart of every officer and soldier in the army. By your celerity and secrecy of movement our advance was undisputed; and on our withdrawal, not a rebel ventured to follow." The questionable character of these compliments exposed General Hooker to ridicule, and increased the public sense of his unfitness for high command, though he was a gallant and brave soldier and admirably fitted for a division or a corps. The Union loss was serious. The killed and wounded exceeded eleven thousand. The year thus opened very inauspiciously. The gloom of 1862 was not dispelled. The shadows had not lifted. The weightiest anxiety oppressed both the government and the people. The Confederacy had sustained a heavy loss in the death of Stonewall Jackson. He had a genius for war, and in a purely military point of view it would perhaps have been better for the Confederates to lose the battle than to lose the most aggressive officer in their Army.

The spirit of the Confederates rose high. They believed they would be able to hold the line of the Mississippi against the army of Grant, and in the defeat and demoralization of the army of the Potomac they saw their way clear to an invasion of Pennsylvania, for which General Lee began his preparations with leisure and completed them with thoroughness. After General Hooker's failure at Chancellorsville, and his remarkable order which followed it, he evidently lost the confidence of the President. Some of the hasty notes and telegrams sent to General Hooker after his defeat are in Mr. Lincoln's most characteristic vein. June 5 the President wrote, "If you find Lee coming to the north of the Rappahannock, I would by no means cross to the south of it. . . . In one word, I would not take any risk of being entangled up on the *river like an ox jumped half over a fence, liable to be torn by dogs, front and rear, without a fair chance to gore one way or kick the other.*" Later, on June 10, the President wrote, "Lee's Army and not Richmond is your true objective point. If he comes towards the upper Potomac, follow on his flank on the inside track, shortening your lines while he lengthens his. Fight him when opportunity offers. If he stays where he is *fret him and fret him.*"[1]   Lee was, by the date of this note, well on his way towards the North, and the military situation grew every hour more critical.

The indispensable requisite to Union success was a commander for the Army of the Potomac in whose competency the Administration, the people, and most of all the soldiers would have confidence. In the judgment of military men it was idle to intrust another battle to the generalship of Hooker; and as the army moved across Maryland to meet Lee on the soil of Pennsylvania, General Hooker was relieved and the command of the army assigned to General George G. Meade.   This change of commanders was made by order of the President on the 28th of June, only two days before the opening engagement of the great battle of Gettysburg.   By the middle of June the advance guard of Lee's army had reached the upper Potomac, and on its way had literally destroyed the division of the Union army commanded by General Milroy and stationed at Winchester.   The agitation throughout the country was profound.   On the 15th of June as the magnitude of Lee's movement became more apparent, the President issued a proclamation stating that "Maryland, West Virginia, Pennsylvania and Ohio were threatened with invasion and required an immediate addition to the military forces."   He called therefore for one hundred thousand militia from those four States to serve for six months ; ten thousand each from Maryland and West Virginia, thirty thousand from Ohio, and fifty thousand from Pennsylvania.   All the surrounding States were aroused.   Governor Seymour sent fifteen thousand extra men from New York.   Governor Parker sent a valuable contingent from New Jersey.   Western Maryland was occupied at various points as early as the 20th of June, and during the last week of that month rebel detachments were in the southern counties of Pennsylvania committing depredations and exacting tribute, — in York, Cumberland, Franklin, Fulton and Adams.

The two armies finally converged at Gettysburg, and on the 1st, 2d, and 3d of July the battle was fought which in many of its aspects was the most critical and important of the war.   The Confederates began with the self-assurance of victory ; and with victory they confidently counted upon the occupation of Philadelphia by Lee's army, upon the surrender of Baltimore, upon the flight of the Presi-

---

[1] The Italicized words were underscored in the original letters of the President.

dent and his Cabinet from Washington. It was within the extravagant and poetic dreams of the expectant conquerors to proclaim the
success of the Confederacy from the steps of Independence Hall,
and to make a treaty with the fugitive Government of the United
States for half the territory of the Republic. But it was not so
fated. The army under Meade proved unconquerable. In conflicts
on Virginia soil the army of Lee had been victorious. Its invasion
of the North the preceding year had been checked by McClellan
before it reached the border of the free States. It was now fighting
on ground where the spirit which had nerved it in Virginia was
transferred to the soldiers of the Union. With men of the North the
struggle was now for home first, for conquest afterwards, and the
tenacity and courage with which they held their ground for those
three bloody days attest the magnificent impulse which the defense
of the fireside imparts to the heart and to the arm of the soldier.

General Meade had not been widely known before the battle, but
he was at once elevated to the highest rank in the esteem and love
of the people. The tide of invasion had been rolled back after the
bloodiest and most stubbornly contested field of the war. The numbers on each side differed but little from the numbers engaged at
Waterloo, and the tenacity with which the soldiers of the British
Isles stood that day against the hosts of Napoleon, was rivaled on
the field of Gettysburg by men of the same blood, fighting in the
ranks of both armies.

The relief which the victory brought to the North is indescrib-
able. On the morning of the Fourth of July a brief Executive order
was telegraphed from the Executive mansion to all the free States,
announcing the triumph, for which " the President especially desires
that on this day, He whose will, not ours, should ever be done, be
everywhere remembered and reverenced with the profoundest gratitude." By one of those coincidences that have more than once
happened in our history, the Fourth of July of this year was made
especially memorable. Rejoicings over the result at Gettysburg had
scarcely begun when word came from General Grant that the Confederate forces at Vicksburg had surrendered, and that at ten o'clock
of the Fourth, the very hour when Mr. Lincoln issued the bulletin
proclaiming the victory of Gettysburg, General Pemberton's forces
marched out and stacked arms in front of their works, prisoners of
war to General Grant. The city of Vicksburg was immediately
occupied by the Union troops, the first division of which was com-

manded by General John A. Logan. Jackson, the Capital of Mississippi, defended by General Joseph E. Johnston, capitulated a few days later to General Sherman, and the Confederate forces at Port Hudson surrendered to the army of General Banks. This was the last obstruction to the navigation of the Mississippi, and the great river flowed unvexed to the sea.

The entire situation was changed by these important victories. Heart and spirit were given to the people, hope grew into confidence, the strength of the Government was vastly increased, the prestige of the Administration was greatly heightened. Could the election for the Thirty-eighth Congress have taken place in the autumn of 1863, and not in the autumn of 1862, instead of being a close struggle it would have been an overwhelming triumph for the war policy which had wrought out such splendid results. The popular re-action was attested in every State where an election gave opportunity. Governor Curtin was re-chosen by a large majority in Pennsylvania over Judge George W. Woodward, who had pronounced a judicial decision against the constitutionality of the proscription law; the course of Governor Seymour was rebuked in New York by the thirty thousand majority given to the Republican State ticket, which was headed by the brilliant Chauncy M. Depew, then but twenty-nine years of age; while in Ohio the Democratic party was overwhelmed by an avalanche of popular indignation which responded to the nomination of Vallandigham with a majority of a hundred and one thousand for the Administration.

The Thirty-eighth Congress met on the first Monday of December, 1863. The House was promptly organized by the election of Schuyler Colfax to the Speakership. He received 101 votes; all other candidates 81. Mr. Samuel S. Cox received 42 votes, the highest given to any candidate of the opposition. The vote for Mr. Colfax was the distinctive Republican strength in the House. On issues directly relating to the war the Administration was stronger than these figures indicate, being always able to command the support of Mr. Stebbins, Mr. Odell, and Mr. Griswold of New York, and of several members from the Border States.

Schuyler Colfax was especially fitted for the duties of the Chair. He had been a member of the House for eight years, having been

chosen directly after the repeal of the Missouri Compromise. He
came from good Revolutionary stock in New Jersey, but had been
reared in the West; had learned the trade of a printer, and had
edited a successful journal at South Bend. He was a paragon of
industry, with keen, quick, bright intellect. He mingled freely and
creditably in the debates. With a wisdom in which many able
members seem deficient, he had given studious attention to the Rules
of the House, and was master of their complexities. Kindly and
cordial by nature it was easy for him to cultivate the art of popularity, which he did with tact and constancy. He came to the Chair
with absolute good will from both sides of the House, and as a
presiding officer proved himself able, prompt, fair-minded, and just
in all his rulings.

The political re-action of 1862 had seriously affected the membership of the House. Many of those most conspicuous and influential
in the preceding Congress had either been defeated or had prudently
declined a renomination. E. G. Spaulding, Charles B. Sedgwick,
Roscoe Conkling, and A. B. Olin did not return from New York;
John A. Bingham and Samuel Shellabarger were defeated in Ohio;
Galusha A. Grow was not re-elected in Pennsylvania, and lost in
consequence a second term as Speaker; Albert G. Porter and McKee
Dunn gave way to Democratic successors in Indiana. In the delegations of all the large States radical changes were visible, and the
narrow escape of the Administration from total defeat in the preceding year was demonstrated afresh by the roll-call of the House.

But the loss of prominent members was counterbalanced by
the character and ability of some of the new accessions. Henry
Winter Davis took his seat as representative from one of the districts of the city of Baltimore. He had been originally elected
to the House as a member of the American party in 1854, and had
been re-elected in 1856 and 1858. He had been defeated for the
Thirty-seventh Congress. He had not co-operated with the Republican party before the war, and had supported Mr. Bell for the Presidency in 1860. He was always opposed to the Democratic party,
and was under all circumstances a devoted friend of the Union, an
arch-enemy of the Secessionists. Born a Southern man, he spoke for
the South, — for its duty to the Federal Government, for its best and
highest destiny. To him before and above all other men is due the
maintenance of loyalty in Maryland. His course was censured by
the Democratic Legislature of his State in the winter preceding the

Rebellion. He replied through an address "to the voters of Maryland," which for eloquence of expression, force, and conclusiveness of reasoning is entitled to rank in the political classics of America as the Address to the Electors of Bristol ranks in the political classics of England. As a debater in the House Mr. Davis may well be cited as an exemplar. He had no boastful reliance upon intuition or inspiration or the spur of the moment, though no man excelled him in extempore speech. He made elaborate preparation by the study of all public questions, and spoke from a full mind with complete command of premise and conclusion. In all that pertained to the graces of oratory he was unrivaled. He died at forty-eight. Had he been blessed with length of days, the friends who best knew his ability and his ambition believed that he would have left the most brilliant name in the Parliamentary annals of America.

Robert C. Schenck was an invaluable addition to the House. He had been serving in the field since the outbreak of the war, but had been induced to contest the return of Vallandigham to Congress. His canvass was so able and spirited that though in other parts of the State the Democrats captured eight Republican districts, he defeated Vallandigham in a Democratic district. Mr. Schenck had originally entered Congress in 1843 at thirty-four years of age, and after a distinguished service of eight years was sent by President Fillmore as Minister-Plenipotentiary to Brazil. After his return he had taken no part in political affairs until now. His re-appearance in Congress was therefore significant. He was at once placed at the head of the Committee on Military Affairs, then of superlative importance, and subsequently was made chairman of Ways and Means, succeeding Mr. Stevens in the undoubted leadership of the House. He was admirably fitted for the arduous and difficult duty. His perceptions were keen, his analysis was extraordinarily rapid, his power of expression remarkable. On his feet, as the phrase went, he had no equal in the House. In the five-minute discussion in Committee of the Whole he was an intellectual marvel. The compactness and clearness of his statement, the facts and arguments which he could marshal in that brief time, were a constant surprise and delight to his hearers. No man in Congress during the present generation has rivaled his singular power in this respect. He was able in every form of discussion, but his peculiar gift was in leading and controlling the Committee of the Whole.

Several new members entered the Thirty-eighth Congress who

were destined to long service and to varying degrees of prominence. James A. Garfield came from Ohio with a valuable reputation acquired in the Legislature of his State and with a good military

---

THIRTY-EIGHTH CONGRESS.

REPUBLICANS IN ROMAN; DEMOCRATS IN ITALIC.

The Senate was composed of same members as in Thirty-seventh Congress (given on pp. ——), with the following exceptions: —

ILLINOIS. — *William A. Richardson* succeeded O. H. Browning.

INDIANA. — *Thomas A. Hendricks* succeeded *David Turpie.*

MAINE. — Nathan A. Farwell succeeded William Pitt Fessenden.

MARYLAND. — *Reverdy Johnson* succeeded *James Alfred Pearce.*

MINNESOTA. — Alexander Ramsey succeeded *Henry M. Rice.*

MISSOURI. — B. Gratz Brown succeeded *Robert Vilson.*

NEW JERSEY. — *William Wight* succeeded *James W. Wall.*

NEW YORK. — Edwin D. Morgan succeeded Preston King.

PENNSYLVANIA. — *Charles R. Buckalew* succeeded David Wilmot.

RHODE ISLAND. — William Sprague succeeded Samuel G. Arnold.

☞ Waitman T. Willey and Peter G. Van Winkle were admitted as the first senators from West Virginia. Lemuel J. Bowden took Mr. Willey's place as senator from Virginia, and colleague of John Carlile. The political power of West Virginia was thus actually represented at one time by four senators.

☞ James W. Nye and William M. Stewart took their seats Feb. 1, 1865, as senators from the new State of Nevada.

☞ Ten States were unrepresented.

HOUSE OF REPRESENTATIVES.

CALIFORNIA. — Cornelius Cole, William Higby, Thomas B. Shannon.

CONNECTICUT. — Augustus Brandegee, Henry C. Deming, *James E. English,* John H. Hubbard.

DELAWARE. — Nathaniel B. Smithers.

ILLINOIS. — *James C. Allen; William J. Allen;* Isaac N. Arnold; *John R. Eden;* John F. Farnsworth; *Charles M. Harris;* Ebon C. Ingersoll, elected in place of Owen Lovejoy, deceased; *Anthony L. Knapp;* Owen Lovejoy, died March 25, 1864; *William R. Morrison; Jesse O. Norton; James C. Robinson; Lewis W. Ross; John T. Stuart;* Elihu B. Washburne.

INDIANA. — Schuyler Colfax, *James A. Cravens,* Ebenezer Dumont, *Joseph K. Edgerton, Henry W. Harrington, William S. Holman,* George W. Julian, *John Law, James F. McDowell,* Godlove S. Orth, *Daniel W. Voorhees.*

IOWA. — William B. Allison, Joseph B. Grinnell, Asahel W. Hubbard, John A. Kasson, Hiram Price, James F. Wilson.

KANSAS. — A. Carter Wilder.

KENTUCKY. — Lucien Anderson, Brutus J. Clay, Henry Grider, Aaron Harding, Robert Mallory, William H. Randall, Green Clay Smith, *William H. Wadsworth,* George H. Yeaman.

MAINE. — James G. Blaine, Sidney Perham, Frederick A. Pike, John H. Rice, Lorenzo D. M. Sweat.

MARYLAND. — John A. J. Creswell, Henry Winter Davis, *Benjamin G. Harris,* Francis Thomas, Edwin H. Webster.

MASSACHUSETTS. — John B. Alley, Oakes Ames, John D. Baldwin, George S. Boutwell, Henry L. Dawes, Thomas D. Eliot, Daniel W. Gooch, Samuel Hooper, Alexander H. Rice, William B. Washburn.

record, established in the war and recognized by the conferment of a Major-General's commission which he had won on the field. William B. Allison, John A. Kasson and Hiram Price of Iowa,

MICHIGAN. — Augustus C. Baldwin, Fernando C. Beaman, John F. Driggs, Francis W. Kellogg, John W. Longyear, Charles Upson.

MINNESOTA. — Ignatius Donnelly, William Windom.

MISSOURI. — Francis P. Blair, Jr., seat successfully contested by Samuel Knox; Henry T. Blow; Sempronius H. Boyd; *William A. Hall; Austin A. King;* Samuel Knox, seated in place of Mr. Blair, June 15, 1864; Benjamin Loan; Joseph W. McClurg; James S. Rollins; *John G. Scott.*

NEVADA. — Henry G. Worthington, seated Dec. 21, 1864.

NEW HAMPSHIRE. — *Daniel Marcy*, James W. Patterson, Edward H. Rollins.

NEW JERSEY. — *George Middleton, Nehemiah Perry, Andrew J. Rogers,* John F. Starr, *William G. Steele.*

NEW YORK. — *James Brooks; John W. Chanler;* Ambrose W. Clark; Freeman Clarke; Thomas T. Davis; Reuben E. Fenton, resigned Dec. 10, 1864; Augustus Frank; *John Ganson;* John A. Griswold; *Anson Herrick;* Giles W. Hotchkiss; Calvin T. Hulburd; *Martin Kalbfleisch;* Orlando Kellogg; *Francis Kernan;* DeWitt C. Littlejohn; James M. Marvin; Samuel F. Miller; Daniel Morris; *Homer A. Nelson; Moses F. Odell;* Theodore M. Pomeroy; *John V. L. Pruyn; William Radford;* Henry G. Stebbins, resigned 1864; *John B. Steele; Dwight Townsend*, elected in place of Mr. Stebbins; Robert B. Van Valkenburgh; *Elijah Ward; Charles H. Winfield; Benjamin Wood; Fernando Wood.*

OHIO. — James M. Ashley, *George Bliss, Samuel S. Cox,* Ephraim R. Eckley, *William E. Finck*, James A. Garfield, *Wells A. Hutchins, William Johnson, Francis C. LeBlond, Alexander Long, John F. McKinney, James R. Morris, Warren P. Noble, John O'Neill, George H. Pendleton,* Robert C. Schenck, Rufus P. Spalding, *Chilton A. White, Joseph W. White.*

OREGON. — John R. McBride.

PENNSYLVANIA. — *Sydenham E. Ancona, Joseph Baily,* John M. Broomall, *Alexander H. Coffroth, John L. Dawson, Charles Denison, James T. Hale, Philip Johnson,* William D. Kelley, *Jesse Lazear, Archibald McAllister, William H. Miller,* James K. Moorhead, Amos Myers, Leonard Myers, Charles O'Neill, *Samuel J. Randall,* Glenni W. Scofield, Thaddeus Stevens, *John D. Stiles, Myer Strouse,* M. Russell Thayer, Henry W. Tracy, Thomas Williams.

RHODE ISLAND. — Nathan F. Dixon, Thomas A. Jenckes.

VERMONT. — Portus Baxter, Justin S. Morrill, Fred. E. Woodbridge.

WEST VIRGINIA. — Jacob B. Blair, William G. Brown, Killian V. Whaley.

WISCONSIN. — *James T. Brown,* Amasa Cobb, *Charles A. Eldridge,* Walter D. McIndoe, Ithamar C. Sloan, *Ezra Wheeler.*

TERRITORIAL DELEGATES.

ARIZONA. — Charles D. Poston.

COLORADO. — Hiram P. Bennett.

DAKOTA. — William Jayne, *John B. S. Todd.*

IDAHO. — William H. Wallace.

MONTANA. — *Samuel McLean*, seated June 6, 1865.

NEBRASKA. — Samuel G. Daily.

NEVADA. — Gordon N. Mott.

NEW MEXICO. — Francisco Perea.

UTAH. — John F. Kenney.

WASHINGTON. — *George E. Cole.*

John A. J. Creswell of Maryland, Glenni W. Scofield of Pennsylvania, all earned honorable distinction in after years. George S. Boutwell entered from Massachusetts at forty-five years of age. Twelve years before, as a radical Democrat and Free-Soiler, he had been chosen governor of his State. James G. Blaine entered from Maine at thirty-three years of age. Among the new members on the Democratic side of the House were Samuel J. Randall, with the reputation of conspicuous service in the Pennsylvania Legislature, and William R. Morrison, fresh from his duty in the field as colonel of an Illinois regiment, and, though still young, old enough to have served with credit in the Mexican war. Fernando Wood, who had been elected a member of the House in 1840, and had served one term, now entered again. Francis Kernan appeared in public life for the first time, having defeated Roscoe Conkling in the Utica district. Charles A. Eldridge of Wisconsin became one of the ablest parliamentarians of the House.

In the Senate some important changes were made. Governor Morgan entered from New York as the successor of Preston King; Governor Sprague came from Rhode Island, and Governor Ramsey from Minnesota. These elections were all made in direct recognition of the valuable service which these Republican War-Governors had rendered the country. John Conness, a follower of Douglas, who had done much for the cause of the Union on the Pacific coast, now bore the credentials of California. B. Gratz Brown came from Missouri as pledge of the radical regeneration of that State.

To the Democratic side of the chamber three able men were added. Reverdy Johnson of Maryland succeeded to the seat made vacant the preceding autumn by the death of James Alfred Pearce. Mr. Johnson had long been eminent at the Bar of the Supreme Court. He was a warm supporter of Mr. Clay, and was chosen to the Senate as a Whig in 1845. He was attorney-general in the Cabinet of President Taylor, and after the defeat of the Whigs in 1852 had co-operated with the Democrats. He had stood firmly by the Union, and his re-appearance in the Senate added largely to the ability and learning of that body. Thomas A. Hendricks entered from Indiana as the successor of Jesse D. Bright, who had been expelled upon a charge of disloyalty. Mr. Hendricks had served in the House of Representatives from 1851 to 1855. He was but thirty-one years of age when first chosen and his record in the House had not prepared the public to expect the strength and ability which he displayed as senator. He was in the full maturity of his powers when he took his seat, and he proved able, watchful, and acute in the discharge of his public duties. He was always at his post, was well prepared on all questions, debated with ability, and rapidly gained respect and consideration in the Senate. Charles R. Buckalew of Pennsylvania succeeded David Wilmot. Both he and Mr. Hendricks were fruits of the violent re-action against the Administration the preceding year. Mr. Buckalew came with high reputation, but did not gain so prominent a position in the Senate as his friends had anticipated. He did not seem ambitious, was not in firm health, and though his ability was recognized, his service did not strengthen his party either in the Senate or in his State. A Democrat from Pennsylvania is somewhat out of harmony with the members of his party elsewhere, on account of the advocacy of the Protective system to which he is forced by the prevailing opinion among his constituents.

Congress assembled in December, 1863, in very different spirit from that which prevailed either at the opening or the adjournment of the preceding session. The President in his annual message recognized the great change for which " our renewed and profoundest gratitude to God is due." Referring to the depressing period of the year before, he said, "The tone of public feeling at home and abroad was not satisfactory. With other signs the popular elections then just passed indicated uneasiness among ourselves, while amid much that was cold and menacing, the kindest words coming from Europe were uttered in accents of pity, that we were too blind to surrender a hopeless cause. Our commerce was suffering greatly by a few armed vessels built upon and furnished from foreign shores, and we were threatened with such additions from the same quarter as would sweep our trade from the sea and raise our blockade. We had failed to elicit from European governments any thing hopeful on this subject. . . .

" We are now permitted to take another view. The rebel borders are pressed still farther back, and by the complete opening of the Mississippi the country, dominated by the Rebellion, is divided into distinct parts with no practical communication between them. Tennessee and Arkansas have been substantially cleared of insurgent control, and influential citizens in each, — owners of slaves and advocates of slavery at the beginning of the Rebellion, — now declare openly for emancipation in their respective States. Of those States not included in the Emancipation Proclamation, Maryland and Missouri, neither of which three years ago would tolerate any restraint upon the extension of slavery into new territories, only now dispute as to the best mode of removing it within their own limits." The President dwelt with much satisfaction upon the good behavior of the slave population. "Full one hundred thousand of them are now in the United-States military service, about one-half of which number actually bear arms in the ranks, thus giving the double advantage, — of taking so much labor from the insurgents' cause, and supplying the places which otherwise might be filled with so many white men. So far as tested it is difficult to say that they are not as good soldiers as any. No servile insurrection or tendency to cruelty has marked the measures of emancipation and the arming of the blacks. . . . Thus we have the new reckoning. The crisis which threatened to divide the friends of the Union is past."

The Thirty-seventh Congress was distinguished for its effective legislation on all subjects relating to the finances and to the recruitment of a great army. It was reserved to the Thirty-eighth Congress to take steps for the final abolition of slavery by the submission to the States of a Thirteenth Amendment to the Constitution. The course of events had prepared the public mind for the most radical measures. In the short space of three years, by the operation of war, under the dread of national destruction, a great change had been wrought in the opinions of the people of the Loyal States. When the war began not one-tenth of the citizens of those States were in favor of immediate and unconditional emancipation. It is very doubtful whether in September, 1862, the proclamation of the President would have been sustained by the majority of the Northern people. In every instance the measures of Congress were in advance of public opinion, but not so far in advance as to invite a calamity through re-action. The President was throughout more conservative than Congress. He had surprised every one with the Emancipation Proclamation, but he was so anxious for some arrangement to be made for compensating the Border States for their loss of slaves, that he did not at once recommend the utter destruction of the institution by an amendment to the Fundamental Law of the Republic. He left Congress to take the lead.

Mr. James M. Ashley of Ohio is entitled to the credit of having made the first proposition in Congress to amend the Constitution so as to prohibit slavery throughout the United States. During the entire contest Mr. Ashley devoted himself with unswerving fidelity and untiring zeal to the accomplishment of this object. He submitted his proposition on the fourteenth day of December. Mr. Holman of Indiana objected to the second reading of the bill, but the speaker overruled the objection and the bill was referred to the Committee on the Judiciary. Mr. Wilson of Iowa, chairman of the Judiciary Committee, and Mr. Arnold of Illinois subsequently introduced joint resolutions proposing a like amendment to the Constitution. Mr. Holman moved to lay the resolution of Mr. Arnold on the table. The motion failed by a vote of 79 nays to 58 yeas. The vote thus disclosed was so far from the two-thirds necessary to carry the constitutional amendment as to be discouraging to the supporters of the measure.

On the thirteenth day of January, 1864, Mr. Henderson of Missouri introduced in the Senate a joint resolution proposing a complete abolition of slavery by an amendment to the Constitution, and on the tenth day of February Mr. Trumbull, chairman of the Judiciary Committee, reported the proposition to the Senate in these words: "Neither slavery nor involuntary servitude except as a punishment for crime, whereof the party shall have been duly convicted, shall exist in the United States or any place subject to their jurisdiction." Mr. Garrett Davis of Kentucky proposed to amend the resolution so as to exclude the descendants of negroes on the maternal side from all places of office and trust under the government of the United States. Mr. Davis betrayed by this motion his apprehension that freedom to the negro would be followed by the enjoyment of civil rights and the exercise of political power. Mr. Davis proposed at the same time to amend the Constitution so as to consolidate New England into two States to be called East New England and West New England, the evident attempt being to avenge the overthrow of the slave system by the degradation of that section of the country in which the anti-slavery sentiment had originated and received its chief support.

— It fell to Mr. Trumbull, as the senator who had reported the resolution, to open the debate. He charged the war and all its manifold horrors upon the system of slavery. He stated with clearness the views of the opposition in regard to the legal effect of the proclamation of emancipation, and with eloquent force of logic he portrayed the necessity of universal freedom as the chief means of ending not only the controversy on the battle-field, but the controversy of opinion. — Mr. Willard Saulsbury of Delaware on the 31st of March replied to Mr. Trumbull, and discussed the subject of slavery historically, citing the authority of the old and the new dispensations in its support. — Mr. Hendricks of Indiana objected to a proposition to amend the Constitution while eleven States of the Union were unable to take part in the proceedings. He wished a constitution for Louisiana as well as for Indiana, for Florida as well as for New Hampshire. — Mr. Clark of New Hampshire criticised the Constitution, and traced the woes which the country was then enduring to the recognition of slavery in that instrument. From the twenty-eighth day of March until the eighth day of April, when the final vote was taken, the attention of the Senate was given to the debate, with only unimportant interruptions. Upon the passage of the resolution, the yeas were 38, and the nays 6. The nays were Messrs. Garrett Davis, Hendricks, McDougall, Powell, Riddle, and Saulsbury. Upon the announcement of the vote, Mr. Saulsbury said, "I bid farewell to all hope for the reconstruction of the American Union."

When the joint resolution, passed by the Senate, was read in the House, Mr. Holman objected to the second reading, and on the question, "Shall the joint resolution be rejected?" the yeas were 55, and the nays 76, an even more discouraging vote than the first. With 55 members opposed to the amendment, it would require 110 to carry it, or 34 more than the roll-call had disclosed. The debate was opened by Mr. Morris of New York who treated the abolition of slavery as a necessary preliminary to the reconstruction of the Union. — Mr. Fernando Wood denounced the movement as "unjust in itself, a breach of good faith utterly irreconcilable with expediency."

— Mr. Eben C. Ingersoll of Illinois made a strong and eloquent appeal for the passage of the amendment and the liberation of the slave, With the accomplishment of that grand end, said he, "our voices will ascend to Heaven over a country re-united, over a people disinthralled, and God will bless us."

— Mr. Samuel J. Randall of Pennsylvania argued earnestly against the amendment. He regarded it as the beginning of radical changes in our Constitution, and the forerunner of usurpations. The policy pursued was uniting the South and dividing the North.

— Mr. Arnold of Illinois said, "in view of the long catalogue of wrongs which it has inflicted upon the country, I demand to-day the death of African slavery."

— Mr. Mallory of Kentucky maintained that Mr. Lincoln had been forced to issue the Proclamation of Emancipation by the governors who met at Altoona. He was answered by Mr. Boutwell of Massachusetts, who most effectively disproved the charge.

— Mr. Pendleton of Ohio maintained that three-fourths of the States possessed neither the power to establish nor to abolish slavery in all the States. He contended that the power to amend did not carry with it the power to revolutionize and subvert the form and spirit of the government.

The vote on the passage of the amendment was taken on the fifteenth day of June. The yeas were 93, the nays were 65. The yeas were 27 short of the necessary two-thirds. Mr. Ashley of Ohio, who had by common consent assumed parliamentary charge of the measure, voted in the negative, and in the exercise of his right under the rules, entered upon the journal a motion to reconsider the vote. This ended the contest in the first session of the Thirty-eighth Congress. Mr. Ashley gave notice that the question would go to the country, and that upon the re-assembling of Congress in December he should press the motion to reconsider, and he expected that the amendment would be adopted. This result forced the question into the Presidential canvass of 1864, and upon the decision of that election depended the question of abolishing slavery. The issue thus had the advantage of a direct submission to the votes of the people before it should go to the State Legislatures for ultimate decision.

In the previous Congress an Act had been passed which was approved by the President on the first day of July, 1862, to aid in the construction of a railroad and telegraph line from the Missouri River to the Pacific Ocean, and to secure to the government the use of the same for postal, military, and other purposes. The company authorized to build it was to receive a grant of public land amounting to five alternate sections per mile on each side of the road. In addition to the lands the Government granted the direct aid of $16,000 per mile in its own bonds, payable upon the completion of each forty miles of the road. The bill was passed by a vote which in the main but not absolutely was divided on the line of party. The necessity of communication with our Pacific possessions was so generally recognized that Congress was willing to extend generous aid to any company which was ready to complete the enterprise. The association of gentlemen who had organized under the provisions of the Act, were unable, as they reported, to construct the road upon the conditions prescribed and the aid tendered. It was impossible to realize money from the lands under the grant, as they were too remote for settlement, and $16,000 per mile was declared insufficient to secure the means requisite for the construction of the road across trackless plains, and through rugged passes of the Rocky Mountains.

The corporators had accordingly returned to Congress in 1864 for further help, and such was the anxiety in the public mind to promote the connection with the Pacific that enlarged and most generous provision was made for the completion of the road. The land-grant was doubled in amount; the Government for certain difficult portions of the road allowed $32,000 per mile, and for certain mountainous sections $48,000 per mile. The whole of this munificent grant was then subordinated as a second mortgage upon the road and its franchise, and the company was empowered to issue a first mortgage for the same amount for each mile — for $16,000, $32,000 and $48,000, according to the character of the country through which the road was to pass. Mr. Washburne of Illinois and Mr. Holman of Indiana made an earnest fight against the provisions of the bill as needlessly extravagant, and as especially censurable in time of war when our resources were needed in the struggle for our national life. Mr. Washburne had sustained the original bill granting the aid of lands and of bonds. He alleged, and produced a tabular statement in support of the assertion, that the Government was granting $95,000,000 to the enterprise, besides half of the land in a strip twenty miles wide from the Missouri River to the Pacific Ocean.

So earnest however was the desire of the Government to secure the construction of the road that the opponents of the bill were unable to make any impression upon the House. On an amendment by Mr. Holman declaring that "the roads constructed under the Act shall be public highways and shall transport the property and the troops of the United States, when transportation thereof shall be required, free of toll or other charge," there could be secured but 39 votes in the affirmative. On an amendment by Mr. Washburne to strike out the section which subordinated the government mortgage to that of the railroad company on the lands and the road, but 38 voted in the affirmative and the bill passed without a call of the yeas and nays. In the Senate there were only five votes against the bill.   Mr. Ten Eyck of New Jersey was the only Republican senator who voted in the negative.   Whatever may have subsequently occurred to suggest that the grant was larger than was needed for the construction of the highway to the Pacific, there can be no doubt that an overwhelming sentiment, not only in Congress but among the people, was in favor of the bountiful aid which was granted.   The terrible struggle to retain the Southern States in the Union had persuaded the Administration and the Government that no pains should be spared and no expenditure stinted to insure the connection which might quicken the sympathy and more directly combine the interests of the Atlantic and Pacific coasts of the United States.   A more careful circumspection might perhaps have secured the same work with less expenditure ; but even with this munificent aid a full year passed before construction began from the eastern end of the road, and for a considerable period it was felt that the men who embarked their money in the enterprise were taking a very hazardous task on their hands.   Many capitalists who afterwards indulged in denunciations of Congress for the extravagance of the grants, were urged at the time to take a share in the scheme, but declined because of the great risk involved.

Two organizations, composed of powerful men, were formed to prosecute the work.   The California Company, with Governor Leland Stanford and the indomitable C. P. Huntington at the head, constructed the thousand miles stretching from the Bay of San Francisco to Salt Lake, and a company headed by Oakes Ames and Oliver Ames, two Massachusetts men noted for strong business capacity, industry, and integrity, constructed the thousand miles from the Missouri River to the point of junction.   In the history of great enterprises, no parallel can be found to the ability and energy displayed in the completion of this great work.   With all the aids and adjuncts of surrounding civilization, there had never been two thousand miles of rail laid so rapidly as this was across trackless plains, over five rugged ranges of mountain, through a country without inhabitants, or inhabited only by wild Indians who offered obstruction and not help.

On the first day of the session, December 7, 1863, Mr. Elihu B. Washburne of Illinois introduced a bill to empower the President to appoint a Lieutenant-General for all our forces. It was avowedly intended for General Grant who had already been appointed a Major-General in the Regular Army. Some opposition was shown to the measure, when it was formally reported from the Military Committee by Mr. Farnsworth of Illinois who ably supported it. Mr. Thaddeus Stevens indicated his intention to oppose it and was followed by Mr. Garfield who thought the action premature. Mr. Schenck also intimated that it might be difficult at that moment to say who would in the end command precedence among our generals. Eighteen months before, McClellan would have been chosen; after Gettysburg Meade would have been selected; at one time in the midst of his successes in the South-West Rosecrans might have been appointed. As a matter of course Grant would now be selected. Mr. Schenck however announced his intention to support the measure.

Mr. Washburne closed the debate with an impressive plea for the bill. He avowed that it meant General Grant who had been "successful in every fight from Belmont to Lookout Mountain. The people of this country want a fighting general to lead their armies, and General Grant is the man upon whom we must depend to fight out this rebellion to the end." Mr. Washburne gave a unique description of General Grant in the critical campaign below Vicksburg: "General Grant did not take with him the trappings and paraphernalia so common to many military men. As all depended on celerity of movement it was important to be encumbered with as little baggage as possible. General Grant took with him neither a horse nor an orderly nor a servant nor a camp-chest nor an overcoat nor a blanket nor even a clean shirt. His entire baggage for six days — I was with him at that time — was a tooth-brush. He fared like the commonest soldier in his command, partaking of his rations and sleeping upon the ground with no covering except the canopy of heaven." The speech of Mr. Washburne was very earnest and very effective, and, the vote coming at its conclusion, the House passed the bill by 96 yeas to 41 nays. It was not strictly a party vote. Randall of Pennsylvania, Morrison of Illinois, Eldridge of Wisconsin, Voorhees of Indiana and several other Democratic partisans supported the measure, while Thaddeus Stevens, Winter Davis, Garfield, Broomall of Pennsylvania and others among the Republicans opposed it.

The bill was desired by the President who approved it on the 29th of February, 1864, and immediately nominated Ulysses S.

Grant to be Lieutenant-General. Mr. Lincoln saw the obvious advantage of placing a man of General Grant's ability in command of all the armies. The General was ordered to Washington at once, and arrived at the capital on the eighth day of March. Mr. Lincoln had never before seen him, though both were citizens of Illinois and General Grant had been distinguished in the field for more than two years. A new era opened in our military operations and abundant vigor was anticipated and realized. General Sherman was left in command of the great army in the West. He had up to this time been serving with General Grant but was now to assume command of an enormous force and to engage in one of the most arduous, heroic, and successful campaigns in the military history of the country. The march from Vicksburg to Chattanooga, thence to Atlanta, to Savannah and Northward to the Potomac, is one of the longest ever made by an army. From Vicksburg to Chattanooga the army was under command of General Grant, but the entire march of the same body of troops must have exceeded two thousand miles through the very heart of the insurrectionary country. But the great operations of both Grant and Sherman were incomplete when Congress adjourned on the Fourth of July. Its members returned home to engage in a canvass of extraordinary interest and critical importance.

————————

The character and ability of General Sherman were not fully appreciated until the second year of the war. He had not aimed to startle the country at the outset of his military career with any of the brilliant performances attempted by many officers who were heard of for a day and never afterwards. With the true instinct and discipline of a soldier, he faithfully and skillfully did the work assigned to him, and he gained steadily, rapidly, and enduringly on the confidence and admiration of the people. He shared in the successful campaigns of General Grant in the South-West, and earned his way to the great command with which he was now intrusted, — a command which in one sense involved the prompt success of all the military operations of the Government. Disaster to his army did not of course mean the triumph of the Rebellion, but it meant fresh levies of troops, the prolongation of the struggle, and a serious increase to the heavy task that General Grant had assumed in Virginia.

General Sherman was a graduate of West Point, and while still a young man had served with marked credit for some twelve years in the army. But he had more than a military education. Through a checkered career in civil life, he had enlarged his knowledge of the country, his acquaintance with men, his experience in affairs. He had been a banker in California, a lawyer in Kansas, President of a college in Louisiana, and, when the war began, he was about to take charge of a railroad in Missouri. It would be difficult, if not impossible to find a man who has so thorough, so minute a knowledge of every State and Territory of the Union. He has made a special study of the geography and products of the country. Some one has said of him, that if we should suddenly lose all the maps of the United States, we need not wait for fresh surveys to make new ones, because General Sherman could reproduce a perfect map in twenty-four hours. That this is a pardonable exaggeration would be admitted by any one who had conversed with General Sherman in regard to the topography and resources of the country from Maine to Arizona.

General Sherman's appearance is strongly indicative of his descent. Born in the West, he is altogether of Puritan stock, his father and mother having emigrated from Connecticut where his family resided for nearly two centuries. All the characteristics of that remarkable class of men re-appear in General Sherman. In grim, determined visage, in commanding courage, in mental grasp, in sternness of principle, he is an Ironside Officer of the Army of Cromwell, modified by the impulsive mercurial temperament which eight generations of American descent, with Western birth and rearing, have impressed upon his character.

tention over the important Treasury offices in New York, in which Mr. Chase appeared on the one side and the rival influences in the Administration on the other, and this contest was interpreted as a part of the political and Presidential struggle.   Mr. Chase having consented to the use of his name as a candidate, his friends began active work on his behalf.   Early in the winter of 1863-64 what was known as the "Pomeroy circular" was sent out, ostensibly as a confidential paper, but promptly finding its way into print.   It derived its name from the Kansas senator who was prominent in the advocacy of Mr. Chase's nomination.   The circular represented that Mr. Lincoln's re-election was impossible; that his "manifest tendency toward compromises and temporary expedients of policy" rendered it undesirable; that Mr. Chase united more of the qualities needed in a President for the next four years than were combined in any other available candidate; and that steps should be taken at once to effect a general organization to promote his nomination.

But the effort met with small response.   It aroused no popular sympathy.   Its chief effect indeed was to call forth the always constant if sometimes latent attachment of the people to Mr. Lincoln, and to develop an irresistible desire for his re-election.   A few days after the issue of the "Pomeroy circular" the Republican members of the Ohio Legislature passed a resolution in favor of Mr. Lincoln's renomination, and Mr. Chase availed himself of this unmistakable action in his own State to withdraw his name as a candidate.   The signal failure of the movement however did not entirely arrest the effort to prevent Mr. Lincoln's renomination.   Restless spirits still persisted in an opposition as destitute of valid reason as it was abortive in result.   With the view of promptly settling the disturbing question of candidates and presenting an undivided front to the common foe, the Republican National Convention had been called to meet on the 7th of June.   The selection of this early date, though inspired by the most patriotic motives, was made an additional pretext for factious warfare.   An address was issued inviting the "radical men of the nation" to meet at Cleveland on the 31st of May, with the undisguised design of menacing and constraining the Republican Convention.   This call passionately denounced Mr. Lincoln by implication as prostituting his position to perpetuate his own power; it virulently assailed the Baltimore Convention, though not yet held, as resting wholly on patronage; it challenged the rightful title of that authoritative tribunal of the party, and declared for the principle of one term. There had been no election of delegates to this Cleveland assemblage, and it possessed no representative character. It was simply a mass convention, and numbered about a hundred and fifty persons claiming to come from fifteen different States.

The platform adopted by the Convention was brief, and in some directions extreme. It demanded that the rebellion be suppressed without compromise, and that the right of *habeas corpus* and the privilege of asylum be held inviolate; declared for the Monroe doctrine and for constitutional amendments prohibiting the re-establishment of Slavery and providing for the election of President for one term only and by direct vote of the people; and finally advocated the confiscation of the lands of rebels and their distribution among the soldiers and actual settlers. General Frémont was selected as the candidate for President, and General John Cochrane of New York for Vice-President. General Frémont hurried forward his letter of acceptance, which was dated only four days after his nomination and three days before the Baltimore Convention. It repudiated the proposed confiscation, but approved the remainder of the platform. It was chiefly devoted to a vehement attack upon Mr. Lincoln's Administration, which was charged with incapacity and with infidelity to the principles it was pledged to maintain. General Frémont further hinted that if the Baltimore Convention would select some candidate other than Mr. Lincoln he would retire from the contest, but plainly declared that if the President were renominated there would be no alternative but to organize every element of opposition against him.

Three days before the Baltimore Convention, a mass meeting was held in New York to give public voice to the gratitude of the country to General Grant and his command, for their patriotic and successful services. While this was the avowed object of the demonstration, there was a suspicion that it had a political design and that its real purpose was to present General Grant as a Presidential candidate. If such were the intent, it was effectually frustrated both by the emphatic refusal of General Grant to countenance the use of his name, and by the admirable and impressive letter of Mr. Lincoln. Paying a warm tribute to the heroic commander of the army, the President said appealingly, "He and his brave soldiers are now in the midst of their great trial, and I trust that at your meeting you will so shape your good words that they may turn to men and guns, moving to his and their support." This patriotic singleness of thought for the country's safety defeated and scattered all mere political plans, and the hearts of the people turned more and more to Mr. Lincoln. He had been steadily growing in the esteem of his countrymen. The patience, wisdom, and fidelity with which he had guided the government during its unprecedented trials and dangers had won the profound respect and affection of the people. Besides this deepening sentiment of personal devotion and confidence, there was a wide conviction that, in his own expressive phrase, "it is not wise to swap horses while crossing the stream."

Under these circumstances the Union-Republican National Convention met in Baltimore. The feeling with which it convened was one of patriotic and exultant confidence. The doubts prevailing a few months before had been dissipated. The accession of General Grant to the command of all our armies, and the forward movement both in the East and in the West, inspired faith in the speedy and complete triumph of the Union cause. Many eminent men were included in the roll of delegates to the Convention. Not less than five of the leading War Governors were chosen to participate in its councils. Vermont sent Solomon Foot who had stood faithful in the Senate during the struggles before the war. Massachusetts had commissioned her eloquent Governor John A. Andrew; the delegation from New York embraced Henry J. Raymond; Daniel S. Dickinson, who was to be prominently named for Vice-President; and Lyman Tremain who, like Dickinson, was one of the able war Democrats that had joined the Republican party. New Jersey and Ohio each sent two ex-governors — Marcus L. Ward and William A. Newell from the former, and William Dennison and David Tod from the latter. Simon Cameron, Thaddeus Stevens, and Ex-Speaker Grow of Pennsylvania; Governor Blair and Omer D. Conger of Michigan; Angus Cameron of Wisconsin and George W. McCrary of Iowa were among the other delegates who have since been identified with public affairs and have occupied positions of responsibility.

In calling the Convention to order Governor Morgan of New York made a brief speech advocating a constitutional amendment abolishing slavery. Dr. Robert J. Breckinridge of Kentucky was chosen temporary chairman. The appearance on the platform of this venerable and venerated divine was in itself an event of great interest. By birth and association he was connected with the aristocratic class which furnished the pillars of the Confederacy; he belonged to a family conspicuously identified with the rebellion; yet among his own order he was the strongest and sturdiest champion of the Union cause south of the Ohio. His pointed eloquence was equaled by his indomitable courage. The aggressive qualities of his staunch Scotch ancestry shone in his own resolute and unyielding character, and he was distinguished both in Church and in State as an able and uncompromising controversialist. His years and his history inspired a general feeling of reverence; and as he was conducted to the chair of the Convention, his tall figure, strong face, and patriarchal beard imparted to him something of personal majesty. His speech well illustrated his rugged attributes of character. It was sharp, sinewy, and defiant. At the beginning he hurled out the declaration that "the nation shall not be destroyed;" and referring to the plea which treated the Constitution as the sacred shield of the system that was waging war on the Union and which insisted that it must remain untouched, he proclaimed that "we shall change the Constitution if it suits us to do so." He solemnly affirmed "that the only enduring, the only imperishable cement of all free institutions has been the blood of traitors." He alluded to the fact that he had lived amid the surroundings of slavery, and had been among those who sustained and upheld the system; but, recognizing that it was this institution which had lifted the sword against the Union, he aroused the enthusiasm of his vast audience by his unhesitating declaration that we must "use all power to exterminate and extinguish it." Next to the official platform itself, the speech of Dr. Breckinridge was the most inspiring utterance of the Convention.

When the question of calling the roll of the Southern States and of receiving their delegates was reached, Thaddeus Stevens objected on the ground that such an act might be regarded as recognizing the right of States in rebellion to participate in the Electoral College. The Convention decided however to call the roll of all the States, and to refer the question of admitting their delegates to the Committee on Credentials. Ex-Governor Dennison of Ohio was elected permanent president. Preston King of New York from the Committee on Credentials reported in favor of admitting the Radical Union delegation from Missouri, and excluding the Conservative Union or Blair delegation. It was proposed to amend by admitting both delegations to seats; but the recognition of the Radical Union delegation was urged on the ground not only that they were regularly elected, but that it was the duty of the Convention to strengthen the advanced Union sentiment of the South, and that their admission would be the practical adhesion of the national party to the broad anti-slavery policy which was essential to the salvation of the country. This view prevailed by a vote of 440 to 4. The admission of the delegations from Tennessee, Arkansas, and Louisiana was a question of no less interest. It involved the effect of the rebellion upon the relation of rebelling States to the Union. Could they have a voice in public affairs without specific measures of restoration, or were the acts of secession a nullity without influence upon their legal status? The committee reported in favor of admitting the delegations from these States, without the right to vote. The chairman, Mr. King, was the only member who dissented, and he moved to amend by admitting them on the same footing as all other delegates. The question was first taken on Tennessee, and the amendment was carried by a vote of 310 to 153 — a decision which had an important bearing on the subsequent nomination for Vice-President. The delegates from Arkansas and Louisiana were given the right to vote by 307 to 167. The Territories of Colorado, Nebraska, and Nevada were soon to enter the Union as States, and their delegates were allowed to vote. The remaining Territories and the States of Virginia and Florida were admitted without the right to vote.

With the completion of the organization the Committee on Resolutions made their report through Mr. Henry J. Raymond. The platform upon which it had unanimously agreed was a trenchant and powerful declaration of policy. Its tone was elevated, its expression was direct and unequivocal. It pledged every effort to aid the Government in quelling by force of arms the rebellion against its authority; it approved "the determination of the government not to compromise with rebels nor to offer them any terms of peace except such as may be based upon an unconditional surrender of their hostility and a return to their just allegiance to the Constitution and the laws of the United States;" and it called upon the government to prosecute the war with the utmost possible vigor to the complete suppression of the Rebellion. It resolved that "as slavery was the cause and now constitutes the strength of this Rebellion, and as it must be always and everywhere hostile to the principles of Republican government, justice and the national safety demand its utter and complete extirpation from the soil of the Republic;" and it declared for "such an amendment to the Constitution as shall terminate and forever prohibit the existence of

slavery within the limits or the jurisdiction of the United States."
The heroism of the soldiers and sailors of the Republic was grate-
fully acknowledged. The wisdom, patriotism, and fidelity of President Lincoln, and his measures for the defense of the nation were
approved. A general expression that harmony should prevail in the
national councils was interpreted as contemplating a possible reconstruction of the Cabinet. Declarations for the encouragement of
foreign immigration by a liberal policy, for the speedy construction
of a Pacific railroad, for the inviolability of the National faith, and
for the re-assertion of the Monroe doctrine, completed a platform
which in all its parts was pervaded by the most vigorous spirit. Its
commanding feature was its explicit demand for the abolition of
slavery. The President's Proclamation of Emancipation had been
issued more than a year before, but this was the first National
assemblage with power to make it the fixed policy of a party. The
Baltimore platform, which was adopted by acclamation, made this
the paramount issue, and from that hour Freedom and the Union
were inseparably associated.

The nomination for President being in order, there was a strife
for the honor of naming Mr. Lincoln. General Simon Cameron
offered a resolution declaring Abraham Lincoln the choice of the
Union party for President, and Hannibal Hamlin its candidate for
Vice-President. To this proposition the immediate objection was
made that it might be open to the misconstruction of not permitting
a free vote, and that it complicated the selection for the first place
with the contest over the second. After some discussion General
Cameron withdrew his resolution, and on a general demand, in order
to remove all ground for the charge that the nomination was forced,
the roll of the Convention was called. Abraham Lincoln was named
by 497 delegates, — all of the Convention except the 22 from Missouri, who under instructions voted for General Grant. Amid great
enthusiasm Mr. Lincoln's nomination was then declared to be unanimous.

The Vice-Presidency had excited an animated contest. While
many felt that the old ticket should remain unbroken, and that Mr.
Hamlin should continue to be associated with Mr. Lincoln, there was
a wide sentiment in favor of recognizing the war Democrats, who
had acted with the Union party, by selecting one of their number
for the second place. Two prominent representatives of this class
were suggested, — Daniel S. Dickinson of New York and Andrew

Johnson of Tennessee. One was identified with the patriotic Democrats of the North, and the other with the sturdy and intrepid Unionists of the South. Mr. Dickinson, by reason both of his earnest loyalty and of his coming from the important State of New York, was regarded in many quarters with special favor. The Massachusetts delegation early declared their preference, and sent a message to the New-York delegation announcing their purpose to vote for him if New York would present him as a candidate. Had New York given him a united support his nomination would not have been doubtful. But the very reasons which commended him in other sections excited jealousy in his own State, and prompted an opposition which led to his defeat.

Mr. Dickinson's career had been long and honorable. He had been chosen to the State Senate in 1837, and quickly attained a leading place. After serving as lieutenant-governor, he was in 1844 appointed United-States senator by Governor Bouck to fill a vacancy, and was subsequently elected by the Legislature for a full term. Appearing in the Senate at the important juncture when the annexation of Texas and the Mexican war were agitating the country, he soon took an active part in the discussions. He was particularly distinguished for his aptness in repartee, and for his keen and incisive humor. Politically he belonged to the conservative or *Hunker* wing of the Democracy. Entering the Senate just as Silas Wright was leaving it to assume the Governor's chair, he joined Secretary Marcy and the influences that moulded Polk's Administration, against the able and powerful statesman who had so long held sway over the Democratic party in New York. Mr. Dickinson's talent made him the leader of the Hunkers, and in 1852 he was one of their candidates for President. When the war came, he declared himself unreservedly on the side of the Government, and rendered valuable service to the Union party. He was especially effective on the stump. His sharp wit, his rich fund of anecdote, his sparkling humor, his singular facility and aptness of biblical illustration, which had earned for him the popular name of "Scripture Dick," served to give him wonderful command over an audience, and the effect was heightened by his personal appearance, which his long, flowing silvery locks made strikingly impressive.

The suggestion of Mr. Dickinson's name for Vice-President was cordially received by many delegates. But some of the controlling influences among the New-York Republicans were not well disposed towards the advancement of those who came from the Democratic ranks. They feared, besides, that if the candidate for Vice-President were taken from New York, it might prejudice her claims for the Cabinet, and might endanger Mr. Seward's position as Secretary of State. For these reasons their influence was thrown against Mr. Dickinson's nomination. On a test-vote in the New-York delegation, Dickinson received 28, Johnson 32, and Hamlin 6. This result was fatal to Mr. Dickinson's chances, and brought Mr. Johnson prominently forward. His record and character had much to attract the patriotic respect of the country. The vigor and boldness with which, though a Southern senator, he had denounced secession at the beginning of the outbreak, had taken strong hold of the popular heart. The firmness and unyielding loyalty he had displayed as Military Governor of Tennessee greatly deepened the favorable impression. The delegates from his own and other Southern States had been admitted to the Convention as an evidence that the Republican party honored the tried and faithful loyalists of the South, and many felt that the nomination of Mr. Johnson would emphasize this sentiment, and free the party from the imputation of sectional passion and purpose. The ballot for Vice-President gave Johnson 200; Dickinson 113; Hamlin 145; General B. F. Butler 26; General L. H. Rousseau 21; with a few scattering votes. Before the final announcement, several delegations changed to Johnson, until as declared the ballot stood, Johnson 492; Dickinson 17; Hamlin 9. Mr. Johnson was then unanimously nominated. The Convention had completed its work, and the results were hailed with satisfaction throughout the country.

The Republicans had been compelled in 1856 and 1860 to nominate their candidates both for President and Vice-President from the North. This was contrary to the patriotic traditions of the country which with a single exception had in all parties divided the candidates between the two great sections of the country. Strangely enough both parties violated the practice in the exciting canvass of 1828, when Jackson and Calhoun were the candidates of the Democratic party and Adams and Rush were the candidates of the National Republican party. The nomination now of Andrew Johnson from the South tended, in the phrase of the day, to *nationalize* the Republican party, and this consideration gave it popularity throughout the North. It was nevertheless felt by many of Mr. Hamlin's friends to be an injustice to him. But it did him no injury. He accepted the result in a cordial manner and worked earnestly for the success of the nominees. The whole country saw that the grounds upon which Mr. Hamlin was superseded were not in derogation of the honorable record he had made in his long and faithful public career.

The Democratic National Convention was held nearly three months after the Republican Convention had renominated Mr. Lincoln, and only two months prior to the election. It had originally been called to meet in Chicago on the 4th of July; but as the time approached, the brighter military prospects and the rekindled national hopes left a darker Democratic outlook, and the assembling of the Convention had been delayed to the 29th of August. Several reasons had combined to secure the selection of this unusually late day. It gave longer opportunity to observe the course of the military campaign, and to take advantage of any unfavorable exigencies; it allowed more time to compose Democratic dissensions; and it furnished more scope for the party, whose chances rested solely upon the degree of popular discontent, to seize upon any disturbed state of the public mind, and turn it to account.

The delay of nearly two months had been accompanied by a marked change in the situation. The advance of the Union cause which had depressed Democratic expectations in the spring, had been succeeded by inactivity and doubts which revived Democratic hopes in August. The postponement which had been ordered that they might avail themselves of any unfavorable course of affairs, thus deluded them into a bold abandonment of all reserve. Changes in the military situation were sometimes sudden and swift. Had the Convention been postponed another week, its tone and action might have been essentially different; for its tumultuous session had scarcely closed before the clouds that hung over the country during the summer were scattered, and our armies entered upon the most brilliant movements and triumphs of the war — triumphs which did not cease until the surrender at Appomattox.

But the Convention assembled at a time of uncertainty if not of gloom and depression. The issue of the great struggle was not yet clear. General Grant, with his unquailing resolution " to fight it out on this line," had cut his way through the Wilderness over the bloody field of Spottsylvania, and against the deadly lines of Cold Harbor. He had fastened his iron grip upon Petersburg, and there the opposing armies were still halting in their trenches. In the Shenandoah Valley, Early was defiant and aggressive. In the West, the delay at Kenesaw, the fall of the heroic McPherson, and other reverses had marked a campaign of slow advances. The assaults upon Mr. Lincoln's Administration had been renewed with increased venom and persistence. Mistaken and abortive peace negotiations with pretended rebel commissioners at Niagara Falls had provoked much criticism and given rise to unfounded charges. The loyal spirit and purpose of the people were unshaken; but there was some degree of popular impatience with the lack of progress, and it was the expectation of the Democratic managers that this restive feeling might be turned into the channel of opposition to the Administration.

The Convention included among its delegates many of the most distinguished leaders of the Democratic party. Massachusetts sent Josiah G. Abbott and George Lunt. The credentials of Connecticut were borne by the positive and aggressive William W. Eaton. Among the representatives of New York were the accomplished Governor Seymour; the acute Dean Richmond; Samuel J. Tilden, who had not yet achieved his national distinction; Sanford E. Church, who afterwards became chief judge of the Court of Appeals; and Ex-Governor Washington Hunt, whose Silver-Gray conservatism had carried him into the Democratic party. Ohio counted on the roll of her delegates William Allen, who had been the contemporary of Webster and Clay in the Senate; George H. Pendleton and Allen G. Thurman, who were yet to take high rank in that body; and Clement L. Vallandigham, just then more prominent with a doubtful celebrity than any one of his abler colleagues. Pennsylvania contributed Ex-Governor Bigler, and William A. Wallace already showing the political talent which afterwards gave him a leading position. The Indiana delegation was led by Joseph E. McDonald, and the Kentucky delegation by Governor Powell, James Guthrie and by Ex-Governor Wickliffe who had been driven by Mr. Lincoln's anti-slavery policy into the ranks of his most bitter opponents. In ability and leadership the Convention fairly represented the great party whose principles and policy it had met to declare. Besides the accredited delegates, it brought together a large number of the active and ruling members of the Democratic organization. The opposition to the war was stronger in the West than in the East, and the presence of the Convention in the heart of the region where disloyal societies were rife, gathered about it a large and positive representation of the Peace party, which manifested itself in public meetings and in inflammatory utterances.

The representatives inside and outside of the Convention were united in opposing the War and in demanding Peace. But there were different shades of the Peace sentiment. One portion of the Convention, led chiefly by the adroit New-York managers, arraigned the whole conduct and policy of the Administration, and insisted upon a cessation of hostilities, but at the same time modified the force and effect of this attitude by urging the nomination of General McClellan for President. They concurred in the demand for an armistice, but made a reservation in favor of continuing the war in case the rebels refused to accept it. Another portion sought to make the declaration against the war so broad and emphatic that neither General McClellan nor any man who had been identified with the struggle for the Union could become the candidate. Both divisions agreed in denouncing the war measures of the Administration, in resisting emancipation, in calling for immediate cessation of military movements, and in opposing the requirement of any conditions from the Southern States. They differed only in the degree of their hostility to the war. The faction peculiarly distinguished as the Peace party was led by Mr. Vallandigham of Ohio, who was the central figure of the Convention. He had been conspicuous in Congress as the most vehement and violent opponent of every measure for the prosecution of the war. Subsequent events had increased his notoriety, and given explicit significance to his participation in the National Convention of his party.

The Convention, meeting in the same city where Abraham Lincoln had first been nominated four years before, struck its keynote in opposition to his Administration. Mr. August Belmont, Chairman of the National Committee, opened the proceedings with a violent speech. "Four years of misrule," he said, "by a sectional, fanatical, and corrupt party have brought our country to the very verge of ruin. . . . The past and present are sufficient warnings of the disastrous consequences which would befall us if Mr. Lincoln's re-election should be made possible by our want of patriotism and unity." In still more explicit terms he went on to picture the direful effects of that catastrophe. "The inevitable results of such a calamity," he said, "must be the utter disintegration of our whole political and social system amid bloodshed and anarchy, with the great problems of liberal progress and self-government jeopardized for generations to come."

Ex-Governor Bigler of Pennsylvania was made temporary chairman, and followed in a speech which expressed similar sentiments in more discreet and temperate language than Mr. Belmont had used. He contented himself with general utterances, and was not betrayed into personal reflections or prophecies of ruin. The organization was promptly completed, and the character of the platform was foreshadowed when it was known that Mr. Vallandigham was a ruling spirit in the Committee on Resolutions. It was a suggestive incident that Ex-Governor Wickliffe of Kentucky presented letters from two delegates chosen to represent that State, explaining their absence by the fact that they were imprisoned by the Union Government, without cause, as they alleged, but presumably for disloyal conduct. Various individual propositions were then brought forward. The temper and purpose of the Convention may be judged from the offer of a resolution by so conservative and moderate a man as Ex-Governor Hunt of New York, declaring in favor of an armistice and of a convention of States "to review and amend the Constitution so as to insure to each State the enjoyment of all its rights and the constitutional control of its domestic concerns," — meaning in plainer words the perpetuation and protection of slavery. This policy aimed to stop the Rebellion by conceding what the rebels fought for. Then came a characteristic proposition from Alexander Long of Ohio. Mr. Long was a member of Congress, and next to Mr. Vallandigham had been most active in resisting war measures. For a speech which was treasonable in tone he had been publicly censured by the House. His proposition provided for the appointment of a committee to proceed at once to Washington, and urge President Lincoln to stop the draft until the people could decide the question of peace or war. These various propositions, following the usual course, were referred to the Committee on Resolutions.

Governor Horatio Seymour of New York was chosen permanent president, and on taking the chair made the most elaborate and important address of the Convention. He was exceedingly popular with his party, and was justly recognized as among the ablest defenders of its views. By virtue both of his official position and of his personal strength he was looked to more than any other leader for the exposition of Democratic policy. Singularly prepossessing in manner, endowed with a rare gift of polished and persuasive speech, he put in more plausible form the extreme and virulént utterances of intemperate partisans. He was skilled in dialectics, and his rhetorical dexterity had more than once served him and his friends in good stead. He was well-nigh the idol of his party, and no other man could so effectively rally its strength or direct its policy. His address as presiding officer was intended to be free from the menacing tone which marked most of the speeches of the Convention, but it veiled the same sentiment in more subtle and specious phrase. He charged both the cause and the continuance of the war upon the Republican party. "Four years ago," he said, "a convention met in this city when our country was peaceful, prosperous, and united. Its delegates did not mean to destroy our government, to overwhelm us with debt, or to drench our land with blood; but they were animated by intolerance and fanaticism, and blinded by an ignorance of the spirit of our institutions, the character of our people, and the condition of our land. They thought they might safely indulge their passions, and they concluded to do so. Their passions have wrought out their natural results." Governor Seymour had no criticism for those who had drawn the sword against the government; he did not impute to them any responsibility for the war; but he charged the wrong upon those who were defending the Union. In advocating an armistice which would involve a practical surrender of the contest he said: "The Administration will not let the shedding of blood cease, even for a little time, to see if Christian charity or the wisdom of statesmanship may not work out a method to save our country. Nay, more, they will not listen to a proposal for peace which does not offer that which this government has no right to ask." It was the abolition of slavery which "the government has no right to ask." As he advanced towards his conclusion Governor Seymour grew more pronounced and less discreet. "But as for us," he said, "we are resolved that the party which has made the history of our country since its advent to power seem like some unnatural and terrible dream, shall be overthrown. We have forborne much because those who are now charged with the conduct of public affairs know but little about the principles of our government." The entire speech was able, adroit, and mischievous.

In the preparation of the platform the champions of the peace policy had their own way. The friends of General McClellan were so anxious to secure his nomination and to conciliate the opposition that they studiously avoided provoking any conflict with the predominant peace sentiment. The substance and vital spirit of the platform were contained in the second resolution as follows: "That this Convention does explicitly declare as the sense of the American people, that after four years of failure to restore the Union by the experiment of war, during which under the pretense of a military necessity of a war power higher than the Constitution, the Constitution itself has been disregarded in every part, and public liberty and private right alike trodden down, and the material prosperity of the country essentially impaired, justice, humanity, liberty, and the public welfare demand that immediate efforts be made for a cessation of hostilities with a view to an ultimate convention of all the States, or other peaceable means, to the end that at the earliest practicable moment peace may be restored on the basis of the Federal Union of the States." The few remaining resolutions pledged fidelity to the Union, condemned the alleged interference of the military authority with certain State elections, denounced what were recited as arbitrary acts of Administrative usurpation, reprobated "the shameful disregard of the Administration of its duty in respect to our fellow-citizens who now are and long have been prisoners of war," and declared the sympathy of the Democratic party with the soldiers of the Republic.

The extreme Peace party having carried the platform, the less radical section of the Convention secured the candidate for President. But General McClellan was not nominated without a vehement protest. The presentation of his name was the signal for a stormy debate. Mr. Harris of Maryland passionately declared that one man named as a candidate "was a tyrant." "He it was," continued the speaker, "who first initiated the policy by which our rights and liberties were stricken down. That man is George B. McClellan. Maryland which has suffered so much at the hands of that man will not submit in silence to his nomination." This attack produced great confusion, and to justify his course Mr. Harris read General McClellan's order for the arrest of the Maryland Legislature. He proceeded "All the charges of usurpation and tyranny that can be brought against Lincoln and Butler can be made and substantiated against McClellan. He is the assassin of State rights, the usurper of liberty, and if nominated will be beaten everywhere, as he was at Antietam."

General Morgan of Ohio warmly defended McClellan. He declared that there was a treasonable conspiracy in Maryland to pass an ordinance of secession, and that McClellan had thwarted it. Mr. Long espoused the other side. "You have arraigned Lincoln," he said, "as being guilty of interfering with the freedom of speech, the freedom of elections, and of arbitrary arrests, and yet you propose to nominate a man who has gone even farther than Lincoln has gone in the perpetration of similar tyrannical measures. McClellan is guilty of the arrest of the Legislature of a sovereign State. He has suspended the writ of *habeas corpus*, and helped to enforce the odious Emancipation Proclamation of Lincoln, the willing instrument of a corrupt and tyrannical administration. He has aided while possessing military power all its efforts to strip American freemen of their liberties."

The heated debate lasted till darkness forced an adjournment, and on re-assembling in the morning a ballot was immediately taken. General McClellan received 162 votes, and 64 votes were divided among Horatio Seymour, Thomas H. Seymour of Connecticut and others; but before the result was announced several changes were made, and the vote as finally declared was 202½ for McClellan and 23½ for Thomas H. Seymour. For Vice-President two ballots were taken. On the first, James Guthrie of Kentucky had 65½ votes; George H. Pendleton of Ohio, 54½; Governor Powell of Kentucky, 32½; George W. Cass of Pennsylvania, 26. Mr. Guthrie had been identified with the war party; Mr. Pendleton as a member of Congress had opposed the war and was the favorite of the Peace party; and on the second ballot Mr. Guthrie's name was withdrawn and Mr. Pendleton unanimously nominated. This act completed the work of the Convention.

The response of the country to the action of the Democratic representatives was an immediate outburst of indignant rebuke. There were thousands of patriotic Democrats who deeply resented the hostility of the Convention to the loyal sentiment of the people, and who felt that it was as fatal as it was offensive. The general expression of condemnation, and the manifestations on all sides foreshadowed the doom of the Chicago ticket. General McClellan and his friends felt the necessity of doing something to placate the aroused sentiment which they could not resist, and he vainly sought to make his letter of acceptance neutralize the baneful effect of the Democratic platform.

In truth General McClellan practically disavowed the platform. He ignored the demand for a cessation of hostilities and the declaration that the war was a failure. "The re-establishment of the Union," he said, "in all its integrity is and must continue to be the indispensable condition in any settlement. So soon as it is clear, or even probable, that our present adversaries are ready for peace upon the basis of the Union, we should exhaust all the resources of statesmanship practiced by civilized nations and taught by the traditions of the American people, consistent with the honor and interests of the country, to secure such peace, re-establish the Union, and guarantee for the future the constitutional rights of every State. The Union is the one condition of peace. We ask no more." While thus proposing to "exhaust the resources of statesmanship" to secure peace, he indicated that if such efforts were unavailing the responsibility for consequences would fall upon those who remained in arms against the Union. But the letter failed to attain its object. Its dissent from the dangerous and obnoxious propositions of the platform was too guarded and reserved to be satisfactory. The people felt moreover that the deliberate declarations of the Convention and not the individual expressions of the candidate defined the policy of the party.

One of the first results of the Democratic position was the withdrawal of General Frémont from the canvass. As a loyal man he could not fail to see that his position was entirely untenable. Either Mr. Lincoln or General McClellan would be the next President and his duty was made so plain that he could not hesitate. The argument for Mr. Lincoln's re-election addressed itself with irresistible force to the patriotic sentiment and sober judgment of the country. Apart from every consideration growing out of the disloyal attitude of the Democratic Convention, it was felt that the rejection of Mr. Lincoln would be regarded by the rebels as the condemnation of the war policy and would encourage them to renewed, prolonged, and more desperate resistance. This conviction appealed to patriotic men of all parties. Mere political feeling largely subsided, and the people were actuated by a higher sense of public duty. Especially was every effort made to remove all grounds of difference which had divided members of the Union party. The Baltimore platform had indicated some dissatisfaction with the Cabinet, and, acting upon this suggestion, the President requested and received the resignation of Postmaster-General Blair. It is but just to Mr. Blair to say that he gave to Mr. Lincoln his earnest and faithful support in the election.

From the hour of the Chicago Convention the whole course of events steadily strengthened the canvass for Mr. Lincoln. The turn of the political tide came with sudden and overpowering force. The news of the capture of Fort Morgan burst upon the Democratic Convention while it was declaring the war a failure, and the day after its adjournment brought the still more inspiring intelligence that Sherman had taken Atlanta. The swift successes of Farragut in Mobile Bay, following this fall of the rebel stronghold in the South, filled the country with joy. Within two days from the hour when the Chicago delegates separated with the demand for a practical surrender to the rebellion, President Lincoln was able to issue a proclamation for thanksgiving in all the churches for the great Union triumphs; and this was followed by national salutes from every navy-yard and arsenal and from all military headquarters. The political effect of the victories was instantaneous and overwhelming. As Secretary Seward expressed it in a public speech, "Sherman and Farragut have knocked the planks out of the Chicago platform."

The tide of victory swept on. While Grant was holding Lee as in a vise at Petersburg, and Sherman was breaking the shell of the Confederacy at Atlanta, Sheridan was dashing through the Shenandoah Valley. Three striking victories crowned his bold and brilliant progress. The battles of Winchester and Fisher's Hill came within three weeks of Atlanta and within three days of each other. The third exploit at Cedar Creek was still more dramatic and thrilling. The succession of matchless triumphs was the theme of every journal and of every orator, and the North was aflame with the enthusiasm it kindled. In the light of the answer flashed back from a score of battle-fields, the Chicago declaration that the war was a failure was not only seen to be unpatriotic and mischievous but was made contemptible by universal ridicule and obloquy.

The political effect of these victories was precisely what Mr. Lincoln had foreseen and foretold. Speaking of the issue to a friend, he said, "With reverses in the field the case is doubtful at the polls. With victory in the field the election will take care of itself." And so it was. Vermont and Maine in September, Pennsylvania, Ohio, and Indiana in October, registered in advance the edict of the people in regard to the Presidency. The result in November was an overwhelming triumph for Mr. Lincoln. Of the twenty-two States participating in the election, General McClellan received the electoral votes of but three. It is perhaps a still stronger statement to say that of the eighteen free States he received the vote of but one. New Jersey gave him her electors, and Kentucky and Delaware, angered by the impending destruction of Slavery, turned against the Administration and against the prosecution of the war. Maryland had escaped from all influences connected with Slavery by its abolition the preceding October, and now cast her vote for Mr. Lincoln. Missouri and West Virginia, the only other slave States loyal to the Union, stood firmly by the President. Mr. Lincoln received two hundred and twelve electoral votes, and General McClellan received twenty-one.

The chief interest of the whole country for the last month of the campaign had centred in New York. As nearly as Mr. Lincoln was willing to regard a political contest as personal to himself, he had so regarded the contest between Mr. Seymour and Mr. Fenton. Governor Seymour's speech in the Chicago Convention had been an indictment of a most malignant type against the Administration. The President felt that he was himself wholly wrong or Governor Seymour was wholly wrong, and the people of New York were to decide which. They rendered their verdict in the election of Reuben E. Fenton to the Governorship by a majority of thousands over Mr. Seymour. Without that result Mr. Lincoln's triumph would have been incomplete. For its accomplishment great credit was awarded to the Republican candidate for the admirable thoroughness of his canvass and for the judicious direction of public thought to the necessity of vindicating the President against the aspersions of Mr. Seymour. The victory in the Nation was the most complete ever achieved in an election that was seriously contested.

CHAPTER XXV.

SUSTAINED by so emphatic a vote of popular confidence, President Lincoln greeted Congress on the first Monday of December, 1864, with a hopeful and cheerful message. He reported that our armies, holding all the lines and positions gained, "have steadily advanced, thus liberating the regions left in the rear." The President regarded "General Sherman's march of three hundred miles directly through an insurgent country" as the "most remarkable feature in the military operations of the year." It was in progress when the President delivered his message, and "the result not yet being known, conjecture in regard to it cannot be here indulged." The President reported that the actual disbursements in money from the Treasury for the past fiscal year were $865,234,087.86.

Mr. Lincoln had finally abandoned the project of compensating the Border States for their loss of property in slaves. The people of those States had, through their representatives, blindly and willfully rejected the offer when it was urged upon them by the Administration, and had defeated the bill embodying the proposition on the eve of its passage in the House when it had already passed the Senate. The situation was now entirely changed. Maryland, without waiting for National action and regardless of compensation, had in the preceding October taken the matter under her own control and deliberately abolished slavery. Mr. Lincoln now announced the State as "secure to liberty and union for all the future. The genius of rebellion will no longer claim Maryland. Like another foul spirit being driven out, it may seek to tear her, but it will woo her no more." There was no reason why the other Border States should not follow her example — and there was the strongest argument against compensating another State for doing what Maryland had done of her own free will and from an instinct of patriotism, as the one act which would conclusively separate her from all possibility of sympathy with the rebellion.

Freed thus from what he may have regarded as the obligations of his Border-State policy and upheld by the great popular majority which he had received in the election, the President warmly recommended to Congress the adoption of the Thirteenth Amendment to the Constitution. He called attention to the fact that it had already received the sanction of the Senate, but failed in the House for lack of the requisite two-thirds vote. There was no doubt that the large Republican majority, already elected to the Thirty-ninth Congress, would adopt the Amendment, but such adoption implied postponement for a whole year, with loss of the moral influence which would be gained by prompter action. It implied also that the Amendment would depend solely upon Republican votes, and the President was especially anxious that it should receive Democratic support. Still another reason wrought upon the President's mind. He believed the rebellion to be near its end, and no man could tell how soon a proposition might come for surrender of the Confederate Armies and the return of the Rebel States to their National allegiance. If such a proposition should be made, Mr. Lincoln knew that there would be a wild desire among the loyal people to accept it, and that in the forgiving joy of re-union they would not insist upon the conditions which he believed essential to the future safety and strength of the National Government. Slavery had been abolished in the District of Columbia by a law of Congress, and in Maryland by her own action. It still existed in the other Border States and in Tennessee, and its abolition in the remaining States of the Confederacy depended upon the validity of the President's Proclamation of Emancipation.

Without discussing the validity of the Proclamation Mr. Lincoln incidentally assumed it, with an emphatic assertion of his own position, which came nearer the language of threat than his habitual prudence and moderation had ever permitted him to indulge. " In presenting the abandonment of armed resistance on the part of the insurgents as the only indispensable condition to ending the war," said the President, " I retract nothing heretofore said as to slavery. . . . While I remain in my present position I shall not attempt to retract or modify the Emancipation Proclamation. Nor shall I return to slavery any person who is free by the terms of that Proclamation or by any of the Acts of Congress. *If the people should, by whatever mode or means, make it an Executive duty to re-enslave such persons, another, and not I, must be their instrument to perform it.*" This was fair notice by Mr. Lincoln to all the world that so long as he was President the absolute validity of the Proclamation would be maintained at all hazards.

This position enabled the President to plead effectively with Congress for the adoption of the Thirteenth Amendment and the consequent avoidance of all possible conflicts between different departments of the Government touching the legal character of the Proclamation. Recognizing the fact that he was addressing the same House of Representatives which had already rejected the anti-slavery amendment, he made a special appeal, though without using partisan names, to the Democratic members. " Without questioning the wisdom or patriotism of those who stood in opposition," said the President, " I venture to recommend the reconsideration and passage of the measure at the present session. Of course the abstract question is not changed, but an intervening election shows almost certainly that the next Congress will pass the measure if this Congress does not. Hence there is only a question of time as to when the proposed amendment will go to the States for their action, and as it is to go at all events, may we not agree that the sooner the better?" He urged the argument still more closely upon the Democratic members. " In a great national crisis like ours, unanimity of action among those seeking a common end is very desirable, almost indispensable, and yet no approach to such unanimity is attainable unless some deference shall be paid to the will of the majority." Mr. Lincoln found much encouragement in the fact that in the national election " no candidate for any office whatever, high or low, ventured to seek votes on the avowal that he was in favor of giving up the Union. . . . In the distinct issue of Union or no Union the politicians have shown their instinctive knowledge that there is no diversity among the people."

The proposed Constitutional amendment was brought before the House on the 6th of January by Mr. Ashley of Ohio, upon whose motion to reconsider the adverse vote of the preceding session, the question continued to have a parliamentary status. He made a forcible speech in support of the amendment, but the chief value of his work did not consist in speaking, but in his watchful care of the measure, in the quick and intuitive judgment with which he discerned every man on the Democratic side of the House who felt anxious as to the vote he should give on the momentous question, and in the pressure which he brought to bear upon him from the best and most influential of his constituents. The issue presented was one that might well make thoughtful men pause and consider. The instant restoration to four millions of human beings of the God-given right of freedom so long denied them, depended upon the vote of the House of Representatives. It addressed itself to the enlightened judgment and to the Christian philanthropy of every member. Each one had to decide for himself whether so far as lay in the power of his own vote he would give liberty to the slave, or forge his fetters anew. The constitutional duty of not interfering with slavery in the States could not be pleaded at the bar of conscience for an adverse vote. There was no doubt that under the terms of the Constitution such interference was unwarranted. But this was a question of changing the Constitution itself so as to confer upon Congress the express power to enlarge the field of personal liberty and make the Republic free indeed. It came therefore as an original and a distinct question whether millions of people with their descendants for all time should be doomed to slavery or gifted with freedom.

It was a singular opportunity for the Democratic party. Its members had always professed to be endued with a broader spirit of liberty than their opponents who under various organizations had confronted them in the political contests of the preceding half-century. In their evangelization of Liberty the Democrats had halted at the color-line, but, as they alleged, only because the solemn obligations of the Constitution forbade a step beyond. Here by the converging exigencies of war it became of vast interest to the white race that slavery should be smitten and destroyed. Its destruction was indeed the deadliest blow that could be given to the Rebellion which was threatening destruction to the Republic. It was not unfair to say, as was said by many during the crisis, that it was brought to every man's conscience to decide whether he would continue to imperil the fate of the Union by refusing to enfranchise the slave.

It fell to Mr. George H. Pendleton to play an important part in this crisis. His leadership on the Democratic side of the House had been confirmed by the popular voice of his party in the nomination for the Vice-Presidency, and though he had been defeated in the election he returned to the House with increased prestige among his own political associates. The argument he had made the preceding session was now repeated with earnest spirit and in plausible form. He maintained that "three-fourths of the States do not possess the constitutional power to pass this amendment." A colleague from Ohio (Mr. S. S. Cox) had made a radical argument in the other direction, asserting that "three-fourths of the States have the right to amend the Constitution in every particular except the two specified in the instrument; they have the right to do any thing, even to erect a monarchy!" Without carrying the argument so far, Mr. Cox might well have reminded his colleague that four years before, in the winter of compromise preceding the war, the one point sought to be gained by all who asked additional guaranties for slavery was that the power to abolish the institution by constitutional amendment should be taken from the States. It would have been a precious consolation at that time to Mr. Pendleton's Southern friends, to hear from him the argument that no such power existed and that slavery was in no danger from its attempted exercise. Such action by the Federal Government was the one thing which the South had especially dreaded and which all the amendments to the Constitution proposed by the Peace Congress of 1861 aimed to prevent. Mr. Pendleton omitted his argument therefore at the most pertinent time for its submission, but he made it now with freshness and vigor and with evident effect upon his political associates.

Mr. Pendleton was very effectively answered by many members on the Republican side of the House; by General Garfield elaborately, by Mr. Boutwell briefly but most pointedly. The debate was prolonged and able. At least one-third of the entire House took part in it. The ground was somewhat beaten, but many of the arguments were of permanent historic interest. Among the most valuable were the speeches of Mr. Glenni W. Scofield of Pennsylvania, Mr. John A. Kasson of Iowa, and Mr. James S. Rollins of Missouri. As the representative of a slave-holding constituency the **argument** and vote of Mr. Rollins were of special weight. The tone and temper of the speeches exhibited assurance on one side and failing confidence on the other. The moral pressure was steadily for the Amendment and its strength grew rapidly both in Congress and the country. It had been borne into the minds of the people that slavery had produced the war, and it seemed a righteous retribution that slavery should end with the war. It had drawn the sword ; let it perish by the sword.

When the hour arrived for the final struggle, on Tuesday, January 31, 1865, the galleries of the House were filled in every part, largely no doubt by friends of the measure. There were eight absentees, without pairs. They were all Democrats. It may be assumed that they assented to the amendment, but that they were not prepared to give it positive support. This list comprised Jesse Lazear of Pennsylvania, John F. McKinney and Francis C. Le Blond of Ohio, Daniel W. Voorhees and James F. McDowell of Indiana, George Middleton and A. J. Rogers of New Jersey, and Daniel Marcy of New Hampshire. The members of the Democratic party who gave their votes for the amendment, and thus secured its passage by the Thirty-eighth Congress, were James E. English of Connecticut, Anson Herrick, William Radford, Homer A. Nelson, John B. Steele and John Ganson of New York, A. H. Coffroth and Archibald McAllister of Pennsylvania, Wells A. Hutchins of Ohio, and Augustus C. Baldwin of Michigan. Mr. Nelson had not voted at the first session, but all the others are recorded against the proposition. With the aid of these eleven, the vote was 119 yeas to 56 nays — more than the constitutional two-thirds. When the announcement was made, the Speaker became powerless to preserve order. The members upon the Republican side sprang upon their seats cheering, shouting, and waving hands, hats, and canes, while the spectators upon the floor and in the galleries joined heartily in the demonstrations. Upon the restoration of order Mr. Ingersoll of Illinois rose and said, " Mr. Speaker, in honor of this immortal and sublime event, I move that this House do now adjourn." The Speaker declared the motion carried, but Mr. Harris of Maryland demanded the ayes and noes, and the House adjourned by a vote of 121 to 24.

The great act of Liberation, so far as Congress could control it, was complete. The amendment was at once submitted to the States, and by official proclamation of December 18, 1865, — less than eleven months after Congress had spoken, — the Secretary of State announced that it had been ratified by the Legislatures of twenty-seven States and was a part of the Constitution. The result was attained by the united action of one party and the aid of a minority of the other party. The co-operation of the Democratic members had gained for the cause of emancipation a whole year. The action was of transcendent importance — lofty in conception, masterful in execution. Slavery in the United States was dead. To succeeding and not distant generations its existence in a Republic, for three-quarters of a century, will be an increasing marvel.

The language of the Thirteenth Amendment is so comprehensive and absolute that vital questions of law are not likely at any time to arise under it. The Article is in two parts. *First*, " Neither slavery nor involuntary servitude, except as a punishment for crime whereof the party shall have been duly convicted, shall exist within the United States, or any place subject to their jurisdiction. *Second*, Congress shall have power to enforce this Article by appropriate legislation." By this Amendment the relation between the National and State Governments, respecting the question of Human Liberty, was radically changed. Before its adoption slavery could be established or abolished in any State at the will of the majority. The National prohibition now extended everywhere that the flag floated; freedom of the person became thenceforth a matter of National concern. The power of the State was subordinated to the continuing and supreme authority of the Nation.

The Supreme Court has had occasion in a few cases only to deal with the Thirteenth Amendment, and in those cases the questions raised did not touch the validity or scope of the Article. In the case of *White* v. *Hart*, reported in 13 *Wallace*, the Court held that a note given for slaves at a time prior to emancipation was a valid contract and could be enforced. This judgment was rendered in the face of the fact that the Reconstructed Constitution of the State of Georgia, where the contract was made, contained a provision that no Court should have or take " jurisdiction in any case of debt the consideration of which was a slave or the hire thereof." The Court held that the provision in the Georgia Constitution was invalid as to all agreements made prior to its adoption, upon the ground that it was a violation of the Constitution of the United States which provides that no State shall make any law "impairing the obligation of contracts." In the case of *Osborne* v. *Nicholson*, 13 *Wallace*, where

the cause of action was a note given for a slave in Arkansas, March
20, 1861, the Court held that the Thirteenth Amendment did not
constitute a bar to the claim.   These cases serve to show the narrow
and restricted character of the issues made under the Article —
issues long since passed by the limitation of time.

One point in the adoption of the Amendment caused much
speculation at the time, not unaccompanied with anxiety. The whole
number of States was thirty-six.   The assent of three-fourths of that
number was required to amend the Constitution.   Twenty-seven
States voted through their Legislatures in favor of the Amendment,
— precisely the requisite number.   But of these, nine had been in
rebellion and had not at the time been restored to the enjoyment
of their rights as States in the Union.   They had not been re-
admitted to representation either in the House or the Senate.   The
majority of these States were not considered to be entitled to representation in Congress for three years after they had given their
formal assent to the Thirteenth Amendment.   The question as to
whether they could give valid assent to an amendment to the Constitution was one which might possibly be raised.   If they were not
in condition to enjoy representation in Congress, it might be asked
how they could be in condition to perform a much higher function.
If they could not participate in the enactment of Statute Law, how
could they participate in the far weightier duty of framing the
Organic Law of the Republic?

If the same judges who pronounced the Dred Scott decision had
been still on the Bench, serious trouble might have arisen.   But
there had been a radical change in the Judicial Department, not
simply in the *personnel* of the judges but in the views they entertained touching the functions, powers, and duties of the Federal
Government.   It fell to Mr. Lincoln's lot to appoint a majority of
the judges and thus practically to constitute a new Court.   Washington, the elder Adams, and Jackson were the only Presidents
before him who had appointed a Chief Justice, and when he nominated Mr. Chase, there had been only one other chief justice named
for sixty-three years.   He appointed as associate justices Noah
Swayne of Ohio, Samuel F. Miller of Iowa, David Davis of Illinois,
all in 1862, and Stephen J. Field of California the year following.
Mr. Lincoln's sound judgment was apparent in this as in other great
duties.   There are single judges in our history who, in point of
learning, rank higher in the estimation of the legal profession, but

perhaps never a majority of the court who were superior in all the qualities which adorn the Judicial character.

Considering that the tenure is for life, it seemed as if an extraordinary number of Judicial appointments fell to one President. But as the eminence which fits a man for the high station is not attained until past the middle period of life, the changes are necessarily somewhat rapid. Washington in his Presidency of eight years nominated, for a Court of six members, eleven judges who served, besides one who declined and one who was rejected. Down to this period in our history (1884) it has fallen to the lot of each of our twenty-one Presidents except Harrison, Taylor, and Johnson, to nominate at least one associate justice. Under Jackson and Van Buren the entire Court was revolutionized. A Chief Justice and six associates were appointed, selected exclusively from their political supporters. From that time onward until the Administration of Mr. Lincoln, every judge was selected from the Democratic party, with the exception of Benjamin R. Curtis who was appointed by President Fillmore. When Mr. Lincoln entered upon his official duties, the Judicial Department of the Government differenced in every conceivable way from his construction of the Constitution in so far as the question of slavery was involved. But one judge could be expected to look with favor upon the course he would pursue. The venerable John McLean, though placed on the Bench by Jackson, had changed his political views and relations, and he alone of all the justices sympathized with Mr. Lincoln.

The Southern States prior to 1860 had secured a large majority of appointments on the Supreme Bench. In originally constituting the Court Washington had equally divided the judges between the slave States and the free States. After his Administration and until the incoming of President Lincoln, the Court uniformly contained a majority of Southern men. From the beginning of the Government until the election of Mr. Lincoln, there had been eighteen associate justices appointed from the slave States, and but fifteen from the free States. The average term of service of the judges from the South had been about fourteen years; from the North about twelve years. From 1789 to 1860, the Chief Justice had been from the South during the whole period with the exception of twelve years. It is a fact worth noting that neither the elder nor the younger Adams appointed a Northern man to the Bench. They appointed three from the South. It is not among the least of the honors belonging to the elder Adams that he gave to the country the illustrious Chief Justice Marshall.

Directly after the adoption of the Thirteenth Amendment came a wide-spread rumor that negotiations for peace were in progress which might interfere with the anti-slavery action of Congress. On the 8th of February Mr. Thaddeus Stevens moved and the House unanimously adopted a resolution requesting "the President to communicate to the House such information as he may deem not incompatible with the public interest relative to the recent conference between himself and the Secretary of State and Messrs. Alexander H. Stephens, Robert M. T. Hunter, and John A. Campbell in Hampton Roads." Mr. Lincoln replied at once, giving in detail every step which had led to the conference, and all that was accomplished by it. It was brought about by the elder Francis P. Blair, who under a flag of truce had visited Richmond early in January. Mr. Lincoln had steadily insisted on three preliminary conditions: first, the absolute restoration of the national authority in all the States; second, no receding from the positions taken on the slavery question; third, no cessation of military operations on the part of the Government till the hostile forces surrendered and disbanded. On these conditions the Confederate agents could not treat, and the conference came to no agreement. In his message Mr. Lincoln made one significant remark. "By the other party it was not said that in any event or on any condition they would ever consent to re-union; and yet they equally omitted to declare that they would not so consent." The proceedings left no special interest, except one characteristic anecdote of Mr. Lincoln. The Confederate agents desired the recognition of the power of "President" Davis to make a treaty. Mr. Lincoln would not consent to this, would not in any event or in any way recognize another "President" within the territory of the United States. Mr. Hunter cited the example of Charles I. treating with rebels in his own kingdom. Mr. Lincoln replied that his only distinct recollection of that matter was that Charles lost his head!

Soon after the Chicago Convention Mr. Chase resigned his position as Secretary of the Treasury. The relations between himself and the President had become personally somewhat unpleasant, but that there had been no loss of confidence or respect was proven by the President's nomination of Mr. Chase to be Chief Justice of the United States as the successor of the venerable Roger B. Taney, who died on the 12th of October (1864). William Pitt Fessenden succeeded Mr. Chase in the Treasury, and entered upon his duties on the fifth day of July. He was admirably fitted by every mental and moral quality for the position, but he did not possess the physical strength necessary for the arduous labor which it imposed. He consented in response to the very earnest request of Mr. Lincoln to accept the trust for a brief period. It was of great importance to the country, to the Administration, and to Mr. Lincoln personally that Mr. Chase should be succeeded by a man of no less eminent character.

In his report of December 6, 1864, Mr. Fessenden discussed the financial situation with comprehensive ability. He urged additional taxation, some plan for making the public lands available as a source of revenue, and arrangements for carrying out the laws for a sinking-fund. He opposed the suggestion of resorting to foreign loans for any part of the money needed. He said, " This nation has been able thus far to conduct a domestic war of unparalleled magnitude and cost without appealing for aid to any foreign people. It has chosen to demonstrate its power to put down insurrection by its own strength, and furnish no pretense for doubt of its entire ability to do so, either to domestic or foreign foes. The people of the United States have felt a just pride in this position before the world. In the judgment of the secretary it may well be doubted whether the national credit abroad has not been strengthened and sustained by the fact that foreign investments in our securities have not been sought by us, and whether we have not found a pecuniary advantage in self-reliance." Reciting the steps which he had taken for placing loans, he declared : " These negotiations have afforded satisfactory evidence not only of the ability of the people to furnish at a short notice such sums as may be required but of the entire confidence felt in the national securities. After nearly four years of a most expensive and wasting war, the means to continue it seem apparently undiminished, while the determination to prosecute it with vigor to the end is unabated."

Liberal response was made by Congress to Mr. Fessenden's request for enlarged power to borrow money. The internal revenue was made more stringent, the tariff was amended and made still more protective, and to facilitate the raising of troops the Conscription Act was made more severe and exacting. Congress proceeded as if the war were still to continue for years. Nothing was neglected, nothing relaxed. But every one could see that the Confederacy was tottering to its fall. Sherman's magnificent march across Georgia, to which the President referred as in progress when he sent his message to Congress, had been completed with entire success, with an *éclat* indeed which startled Europe as well as America. He had captured Savannah, and was marching North driving the army of General Joseph E. Johnston before him. General Grant meanwhile was tightening his hold on Richmond and on the army of General Lee. From his camp on the James he was directing military operations over an area of vast extent. The great victory which General Thomas had won over Hood's army in the preceding December at Nashville had effectually destroyed the military power of the Confederacy in the South-West, and when Congress adjourned on the day of Mr. Lincoln's second inauguration there was in the mind of the people everywhere a conviction that the end was near.

The President himself spoke guardedly in his Inaugural address. He simply said that "the progress of our armies is reasonably satisfactory and encouraging. With high hope for the future, no prediction in regard to it is ventured." The tone of the address, so far from being jubilant as the mass of his hearers felt, was ineffably sad. It seemed to bear the wail of an oppressed spirit. The thought and the language were as majestic as those of the ancient prophets. As if in agony of soul the President cried out: "Fondly do we hope, fervently do we pray that this mighty scourge of war may speedily pass away. Yet if God wills that it continue until all the wealth piled by the bondsman's two hundred and fifty years of unrequited toil shall be sunk, and until every drop of blood drawn with the lash shall be paid with another drawn with the sword, as was said three thousand years ago, so still it must be said that the judgments of the Lord are true and righteous altogether."

The fall of the military power of the rebellion was in the end more rapid and more complete than the most sanguine had dared to expect. The month of March was one of great activity with our military forces. Three weeks after his inauguration the President went to City Point, Virginia, partly to escape the pressure of duty at Washington and partly to be near the scene of final triumph to settle any important questions that might arise, if an offer of surrender should be made by the Confederate commander. On the day

WILLIAM WINDOM

JOHN A. LOGAN

JOHN B. HENDERSON

JOHN SHERMAN

CARL SCHURZ

JOHN J. INGALLS

FREDERICK T. FRELINGHUYSEN

before his inauguration he had directed the Secretary of War to say to General Grant that he wished him to "have no conference with General Lee unless for the capitulation of his army or for some purely military matter." The President did "not wish General Grant to decide, discuss or confer upon any political question." He would not submit such questions "to military conferences or conventions." He returned to Washington on the 8th of April and on the succeeding day the Army of Lee surrendered to General Grant.

The rejoicing throughout the Loyal States cannot be pictured. Congratulation was universal. The end had come. Sympathy with the South in her exhausted and impoverished condition mingled largely with the exultant joy over a restored Union, a triumphant flag, an assured future of National progress. Admiration was not withheld from the soldiers of the Confederacy, who had borne their banner so bravely against every discouragement on a hundred fields of battle. The bearing of General Grant and General Lee at the final surrender was marked by a spirit of chivalric dignity which was an instructive lesson to all their countrymen — alike to the victor and to the vanquished.

General Grant's active service in the field closed with the surrender of Lee. All the commanders of Confederate forces followed the example of their General-in-Chief, and before the end of the month the armed enemies of the Union had practically ceased to exist. The fame of General Grant was full. He had entered the service with no factitious advantage, and his promotion, from the first to the last, had been based on merit alone, — without the aid of political influence, without the interposition of personal friends. Criticism of military skill is but idle chatter in the face of an unbroken career of victory. General Grant's campaigns were varied in their requirements and, but for the fertility of his resources and his unbending will, might often have ended in disaster. Courage is as contagious as fear, and General Grant possessed in the highest degree that faculty which is essential to all great commanders, — the faculty of imparting throughout the rank and file of his army the same determination to win with which he was himself always inspired.

One peculiarity of General Grant's military career was his constant readiness to fight. He wished for no long periods of preparation, lost no opportunity which promptness could turn to advantage. He always accepted, without cavil or question, the position to which he might be assigned. He never troubled the War Department with requests or complaints, and when injustice was inflicted upon him, he submitted silently, and did a soldier's duty. Few men in any service would have acquiesced so quietly as did General Grant, when at the close of the remarkable campaign beginning at Fort Henry and ending at Shiloh, he found himself superseded by General Halleck, and assigned to a subordinate command in an army whose glory was inseparably associated with his own name. Self-control is the first requisite for him who aims to control others. In that indispensable form of mental discipline General Grant exhibited perfection.

When he was appointed Lieutenant-General, and placed in command of all the armies of the Union, he exercised military control over a greater number of men than has any general since the invention of fire-arms. In the campaigns of 1864 and 1865, the armies of the Union contained in the aggregate not less than a million of men. The movements of all the vast forces were kept in harmony by his comprehensive mind, and in the grand consummation which insured Union and Liberty, his name became inseparably associated with the true glory of his country.

Six days after the surrender of Lee the Nation was thrown into the deepest grief by the assassination of the President. The gloom which enshrouded the country was as thick darkness. The people had come, through many alternations of fear and hope, to repose the most absolute trust in Mr. Lincoln. They realized that he had seen clearly where they were blind, that he had known fully where they were ignorant. He had been patient, faithful, and far-seeing. Religious people regarded him as one divinely appointed, like the prophets of old, to a great work, and they found comfort in the parallel which they saw in his death with that of the leader of Israel. He too had reached the mountain's top, and had seen the land redeemed unto the utmost sea, and had then died.

Mr. Lincoln had been some time in the Presidency before the public estimate of him was correct or appreciative. The people did not at first understand him. In the glamour of the Presidential canvass they had idealized him, — attributing to him some traits above and many below his essential qualities. After his election and before his inauguration there was a general disposition to depreciate him. He became associated in the popular mind with an impending calamity, and tens of thousands who had voted for him, heartily repented the act and inwardly execrated the day that committed the destinies of the Union to his keeping. The first strong test brought upon Mr. Lincoln was this depressing re-action among so many of his supporters. A man with less resolute purpose would have been cast down by it, but Mr. Lincoln preserved the *mens æqua in arduis*. Through the gloom of the weeks preceding his inauguration he held his even way. Perhaps in the more terrible crises through which he was afterwards called to pass, a firmer nerve was required, but not so rare a combination of qualities as he had shown in the dismal months with which the year 1861 opened.

Mr. Lincoln united firmness and gentleness in a singular degree. He rarely spoke a harsh word. Ready to hear argument and always open to conviction, he adhered tenaciously to the conclusions which he had finally reached. Altogether modest, he had confidence in himself, trusted to the reasoning of his own mind, believed in the correctness of his own judgment. Many of the popular conceptions concerning him are erroneous. No man was farther than he from the easy, familiar, jocose character in which he is often painted. While he paid little attention to form or ceremony he was not a man with whom liberties could be taken. There was but one person in Illinois outside of his own household who ventured to address him by his first name. There was no one in Washington who ever attempted it. Appreciating wit and humor, he relished a good story, especially if it illustrated a truth or strengthened an argument, and he had a vast fund of illustrative anecdote which he used with the happiest effect. But the long list of vulgar, salacious stories attributed to him, were retailed only by those who never enjoyed the privilege of exchanging a word with him. His life was altogether a serious one — inspired by the noblest spirit, devoted to the highest aims. Humor was but an incident with him, a partial relief to the melancholy which tinged all his years.

He presented an extraordinary combination of mental and moral qualities. As a statesman he had the loftiest ideal, and it fell to his lot to inaugurate measures which changed the fate of millions of living men, of tens of millions yet to be born. As a manager of political issues and master of the art of presenting them, he has had no rival in this country unless one be found in Jefferson. The complete discomfiture of his most formidable assailants in 1863, especially of those who sought to prejudice him before the people on account of the arrest of Vallandigham, cannot easily be paralleled

for shrewdness of treatment and for keen appreciation of the re-
actionary influences which are certain to control public opinion.
Mr. Van Buren stands without rival in the use of partisan tactics.
He operated altogether on men, and believed in self-interest as the
mainspring of human action.   Mr. Lincoln's ability was of a far
higher and broader character.   There was never the slightest lack of
candor or fairness in his methods.   He sought to control men through
their reason and their conscience.   The only art he employed was
that of presenting his views so convincingly as to force conviction
on the minds of his hearers and his readers.

The Executive talent of Mr. Lincoln was remarkable.   He was
emphatically the head of his own Administration, ultimate judge
at all points and on all occasions where questions of weight were
to be decided.   An unwise eulogist of Mr. Seward attributes to
him the origination and enforcement of the great policies which
distinguished the Administration.   So far is this from the truth that
in more than one instance the most momentous steps were taken
against the judgment and contrary to the advice of the Secretary
of State.   The position of control and command so firmly held by
Mr. Lincoln was strikingly shown when the Peace Conference was
about to assemble at Fortress Monroe.   He dispatched Mr. Seward
to the place of meeting in advance of his own departure from Washington, giving him the most explicit instructions as to his mode of
action, — prescribing carefully the limitations he should observe, and
concluding with these words: " *You will hear all they may choose to
say, and report it to me.   You will not assume to definitely consummate
any thing.*"   Assuredly this is not the language of deference.   It
does not stop short of being the language of command.   It is indeed
the expression of one who realized that he was clothed with all the
power belonging to his great office.   No one had a more sincere
admiration of Mr. Seward's large qualities than the President; no
one more thoroughly appreciated his matchless powers.   But Mr.
Lincoln had not only full trust in his own capacity, but a deep
sense of his own responsibility — a responsibility which could not
be transferred and for which he felt answerable to his conscience
and to God.

There has been discussion as to Mr. Lincoln's religious belief.
He was silent as to his own preference among creeds.   Prejudice
against any particular denomination he did not entertain.   Allied all
his life with Protestant Christianity, he thankfully availed himself of

the services of an eminent Catholic prelate — Archbishop Hughes of New York — in a personal mission to England, of great importance, at a crisis when the relations between the two countries were disturbed and threatening. Throughout the whole period of the war he constantly directed the attention of the nation to dependence on God. It may indeed be doubted whether he omitted this in a single state paper. In every message to Congress, in every proclamation to the people, he made it prominent. In July, 1863, after the battle of Gettysburg he called upon the people to give thanks because "it has pleased Almighty God to hearken to the supplications and prayers of an afflicted people and to vouchsafe signal and effective victories to the Army and Navy of the United States," and he asked the people "to render homage to the Divine Majesty and to invoke the influence of His Holy Spirit to subdue the anger which has produced and so long sustained a needless and cruel rebellion." On another occasion, recounting the blessings which had come to the Union, he said, "No human counsel hath devised, nor hath any mortal hand worked out, these great things. They are the gracious gifts of the Most High God who, while dealing with us in anger for our sins, hath nevertheless remembered mercy." Throughout his entire official career, — attended at all times with exacting duty and painful responsibility, — he never forgot his own dependence, or the dependence of the people, upon a Higher Power. In his last public address, delivered to an immense crowd assembled at the White House on the 11th of April, to congratulate him on the victories of the Union, the President, standing as he unconsciously was in the very shadow of death, said reverently to his hearers "In the midst of your joyous expression, He from whom all blessings flow must first be remembered"!

Not only in life but in treasure the cost of the war was enormous. In addition to the large revenues of the Government which had been currently absorbed, the public debt at the close of the struggle was $2,808,549,437.55. The incidental losses were innumerable in kind, incalculable in amount. Mention is made here only of the actual expenditure of money — estimated by the standard of gold. The outlay was indeed principally made in paper, but the faith of the United States was given for redemption in coin — a faith which has never been tarnished, and which in this instance has been signally vindicated by the steady determination of the people. Never, in the same space of time, has there been a National expenditure so great.

Other nations have made costly sacrifices in struggles affecting their existence or their master passions. In the memorable campaigns of the French in 1794, when the Republic was putting forth its most gigantic energies, the expenses rose to 200,000,000 francs a month, or about $450,000,000 a year. For the three years of the rebellion, after the first year, our War Department alone expended $603,314,-411.82, $690,391,048.66, and $1,030,690,400 respectively. The French Directory broke down under its expenditures by its lavish issue of *assignats* and the French Republic became bankrupt. Our Government was saved by its rigorous system of taxation imposed upon the people by themselves. Under Napoleon, in addition to the impositions on conquered countries, the budgets hardly exceeded in francs the charges of the United States for the rebellion, in dollars. Thus in 1805 the French budget exhibited total expenditures of 666,155,139 francs, including 69,140,000 francs for interest on the debt. In the same year the minister stated to the Chambers that income was derived from Italy of 30,000,000 francs, and from Germany and Holland 100,000,000, leaving 588,998,705 to be collected from France. In 1813 the French expenditures had risen to 953,-658,772 francs, and the total receipts from French revenue were 780,959,847 francs. The French national debt has been measured since 1797 by the interest paid, fixed at that time at five per cent. From 1800 to 1814, the period of the Consulate and the Empire, this interest was increased by 23,091,635 francs, indicating an addition of twenty times that sum to the principal of the debt. The Government of the Restoration added in 1815, 101,260,635 francs to the annual interest. Thus the cost of the Napoleonic wars to France may be stated at about $487,000,000 added to the principal of the debt, or less than one-fifth of the increment of our national obligations on account of the rebellion. The French burdens were extended over the whole period from 1800 to 1814. Our own were concentrated into the space of four years.

The total expenditures of Great Britain during the French Revolution and the career of Napoleon were £1,490,000,888, or nearly five times that sum in dollars. The largest expenditures in any single year were in 1815, £130,305,958, or in dollars, $631,976,894.

After 1862 our expenditures were not so low as that in any year, and they were more than double that sum in the closing year of the war when the great armies were mustered out of service and final payment was made to all.

The British expenditures in the war against the French during the period of the Revolution were a little more than £490,000,000, and against Napoleon a little less than £1,000,000,000; or $4,850,-000,000 in the aggregate, for twenty-three years. The total outlay was therefore larger than our payments on account of the rebellion. But there was no period of ten years in her wars with the French, in which Great Britain expended so much as the United States expended in four years. The loss of Great Britain by discounts in raising money or by the use of depreciated paper was greater than that incurred by the United States. A leading English authority says that of the vast burden up to 1816, the "artificial enhancements due to discounts in raising money were so great that for every £100 received into the treasury a national debt of £173 was created."

No other wars than those of England and France can be compared with ours in point of expenditure. For the war between France and Germany in 1870 the indemnity demanded by the conqueror was 5,000,000,000 francs, equivalent in American money to $930,000,000. This sum was much in excess of the outlay of Germany. The expenses of France on her own account in that contest were 1,873,238,000 francs, or $348,432,068, and this is only from one-half to one-third of the annual outlay of the United States during the rebellion. France added to the interest charge at this time 349,637,116 francs, indicating that the whole sum of the indemnity and other war expenditures has passed into the principal of the permanent debt of the country.

The one grand feature of this lavish expenditure of wealth by the Government of the United States is that it was directed and enforced by the people themselves. No imperial power commanded it, no kingly prerogative controlled it. It was the free, unbiased, unchangeable will of the Sovereign People. They declared at the ballot-box, by untrammeled popular suffrage, that the war must go on. "The American people,"— said Henry Winter Davis in the House of Representatives at one of the most exciting periods of the struggle,— "the American people, rising to the height of the occasion, dedicate this generation to the sword, and, pouring out the blood of their children, demand that there be no compromise; that ruin to the Republic or ruin to the Rebel Confederacy are the only alternatives; that no peace shall be made except under the banner of Victory. Standing on this great resolve to accept nothing but victory or ruin, Victory is ours!"

At the outbreak of hostilities the Government discovered that it had no Navy at command. The Secretary, Mr. Welles, found upon entering his office but a single ship in a Northern port fitted to engage in aggressive operations. In the beginning of the great contest which was at once to be waged upon the seas, wherein the Government proposed to close Southern ports, and the South to destroy Northern commerce, the advantage was clearly with the South. From Cape Henry to the Rio Grande the Navy of the United States was called upon to create an effective blockade against all ingress and egress. The conformation of the coast, which along great distances prevented the entrance and exit of ocean-going vessels, materially aided in the task, but it was still such an one as had never before been attempted in the naval history of the world. The line to be subjected to blockade was as long as the line from the Bay of Biscay to the Golden Horn and in many respects it was far more difficult to control.

This blockade was an absolute necessity imposed on the United States. The South relied with implicit faith upon its ability to secure by the sale of cotton the means of carrying on the war. The Confederate Government did not believe that the United States would hazard a conflict with the manufacturing nations of Europe, by attempting a blockade that would prevent the export of the staple; or if they did believe it, they looked upon it as the fatuous step on the part of the National Government that would promptly induce intervention by the combined power of England and France. This reliance was explicitly stated in advance by Mr. Hammond of South Carolina, who three years before the inauguration of Mr. Lincoln, on the fourth day of March, 1858, made this declaration in the United-States Senate: —

"Without firing a gun, without drawing a sword, should the North make war on us, we could bring the whole world to our feet. What would happen if no cotton was furnished for three years? I will not stop to depict what every one can imagine, but this is certain, England would topple headlong and carry the whole civilized world with her. No, you dare not make war on cotton. No Power on earth dares to make war upon cotton. *Cotton is King*."

Boastful and impotent as the declaration of Mr. Hammond now seems, it had a better basis of fact to stand upon than many of the fiery predictions in which Southern statesmen were wont to indulge. The importance of cotton to the civilized world could hardly be exaggerated, and yet it was this very importance that forced the United States to the course which was pursued. The National Government could not permit the export of cotton without constantly aggrandizing the power of the rebellion, and it could not prevent its export without tempting the manufacturing nations of Europe to raise the blockade. The Administration wisely prepared to enforce the blockade and to meet all the consequences.

To accomplish its undertaking, the energy of the Nation was devoted to the creation of a navy. By the end of the year 1863 the government had six hundred vessels of war which were increased to seven hundred before the rebellion was subdued. Of the total number at least seventy-five were ironclad. It may be instanced with laudable pride that one enterprising man, honorably distinguished as a scientific engineer, constructed in less than a hundred days an armored squadron of eight ships, in the aggregate of five thousand tons burden, capable of steaming nine knots per hour and destined for effective service upon the rivers of the South-West. When the contractor, Mr. James B. Eads of St. Louis, agreed to furnish these steamers to the Government, the timber from which they were to be built was still standing in the forest and the machinery with which the armor was to be rolled was not constructed.

A year after the first battle was fought the naval force of the United States had practically interdicted all legitimate commerce with the Southern States. No more effective method of warfare could have been devised. At the outbreak of the war the States in rebellion were able to manufacture but few of the articles indispensable to the ordinary life of a people. Their wealth was purely agricultural. Cotton and tobacco were their only exports. For a supply of manufactures the South had depended wholly upon its trade with the North and with Europe. The natural effect of the war was greatly to lessen production, and the blockade made it impossible to find a market for any large portion of the diminished

product of cotton. As a striking evidence of the prosperity in the
South at the time it complained of oppression, the largest cotton crop
which had ever been grown was that of 1860. It numbered more
than five million two hundred thousand bales, nearly four and a half
millions of which had found a ready market in Europe and the
North before the outbreak of the war. The crop of 1861 was little
more than one-half that of the preceding year. Of the three and a
half millions which remained available for export at the end of 1861
it was estimated that up to August, 1862, not more than fifty
thousand bales had been carried to England, the principal foreign
consumer.

The demand for food created by the Southern army caused a
majority of the plantations to raise corn, and the cotton crop of
1862 did not amount to more than one million bales, very little
of which found a foreign market; and the supply and exportation
diminished from this time onward. Cotton which sold in December,
1861, in Liverpool for $11\frac{3}{4}d$. per pound had risen in December, 1862,
to $24\frac{1}{2}d$. per pound, and as a result, half a million persons in England, dependent for their daily bread upon this manufacturing industry, were thrown out of employment and reduced to beggary.
So great was the distress that by April, 1863, nearly two million
pounds sterling had been expended for their relief, and this sum
does not include the vast amounts expended in local volunteer
charities. English manufacturers saw that the supply of the raw
product from America could no longer be depended upon, and
efforts were made to introduce the manufacture of the inferior
staple from India, but the experiment proved in the main unsatisfactory and unprofitable.

The stringency of the blockade which prevented the exportation
of cotton, prevented also the importation of manufactured articles.
While compelled to acknowledge this fact, the Confederate Secretary of State, Mr. Benjamin, attempted very cleverly to turn it to
account by showing the advantages which would accrue to the
commercial and manufacturing classes of England by the speedy
triumph of the rebellion. Writing to Mr. Mason, who represented
the Confederacy in England, Mr. Benjamin said, "The almost
total cessation of external commerce for the last two years has
produced the complete exhaustion of all articles of foreign growth
and manufacture, and it is but a moderate computation to estimate the imports into the Confederacy at three hundred millions

of dollars for the first six months which will ensue after the treaty of peace." The unexpressed part of the proposition which this statement covered was the most interesting. The merchants and ship-owners of England were to understand that the sale and transportation of this vast amount of fabrics would fall into the hands of England if the Confederacy should succeed, and that if it should fail, the domestic trade of the United States would absorb the whole of it. It was a shrewd appeal to a nation whose foreign policy has always been largely influenced by considerations of trade.

The economic condition of the South at this time may be compared to that of a man with full purse, lost in a desert. Southern cotton would easily sell in the markets of New York or of Liverpool for four times its price in Charleston, while the manufactures of Manchester or of Lowell were worth in Charleston four times the price in Liverpool or New York. Exchange was rendered by the blockade practically impossible. When the profits of a successful voyage from Liverpool to Charleston and return, would more than repay the expense of the construction of the best steamer and of the voyage, the temptation to evade the blockade was altogether too strong to be resisted by the merchants and manufacturers of England. Blockade-running became a regular business with them, and the extent to which it was carried may be inferred from the fact that during the war the American fleet captured or sunk more than seven hundred vessels bound from British ports to ports of the Confederacy. How many vessels escaped our navy and safely ran the blockade may never be known, but for three years it was a steady contest between the navy of the United States and the blockade-runners of England. The persistent course of the latter was stimulated both by cupidity and by ill will to this country. They were anxious to make pecuniary gains for themselves and to aid the Confederacy at the same time. They were checked only by the extra-hazardous character imparted to the trade by the alertness and superior vigilance of our cruisers which sent many millions of English ventures to less profitable markets and many millions to the adjudication of our own Prize-courts.

The establishment and maintenance of a blockade is not accounted by naval officers as the most brilliant service to which in the line of their profession they may be deputed, but it was a service of inestimable value to the cause of the Union, and it was performed with a skill and thoroughness never surpassed. The blockade required an enormous force of men. In addition to the marines, to the large body of soldiers transferred from time to time to the navy, and to the rebel prisoners that joined in the service, there were 121,807 men specially enlisted in the navy during the war. But for the aid thus rendered by the navy, the hard fight would have been longer and more sanguinary. Had not the South been thus deprived of the munitions of war, of clothing and of all manner of supplies which England and France were eager to furnish her, we should not have seen the end of the civil war in 1865, and we should have been sub-jected to all the hazards implied by the indefinite continuance of the struggle.

The census of 1860 shows that the thirty-three States and seven Territories, which at that time composed the United States, con-tained a population of 31,443,790. Fifteen of these States with 12,140,296 inhabitants were slave-holding, more than four millions of the population being slaves; eighteen with an aggregate popula-tion of 19,303,494 were classed as free. Four of the fifteen slave States, Delaware, Maryland, Missouri, and Kentucky, whose people numbered three and one-half millions, constituted what were known as the Border slave States — West Virginia being added to the list in 1862. Though a considerable proportion of the inhabitants of these States, from association and interest, sympathized with the South, they contributed to the Union cause an army equal to two hundred thousand men enlisted for three years, and throughout the war they were loyal to the National Government. Many of the in-habitants of these States fought in the Confederate Army, but this loss was more than compensated by the effective aid rendered by the loyal men who joined the Union Army from the rebellious States. Tennessee furnished more than thirty thousand men to the armies of the Union, and from almost every State which formed a portion of the Confederacy men enlisted in the loyal forces. It may with reasonable precision be affirmed that the encouragement which the Confederacy received from the slave States that remained true to the Union, was more than offset by the effective aid rendered by loyal men residing within the limits of the rebellious States.

As the source of supply for an army the Southern Confederacy had eleven States with an aggregate population of nine millions. It is difficult to estimate with accuracy the numerical strength of the army which they organized at the beginning of the war. In a semi-official publication it was asserted that the army numbered more than five hundred thousand men, but as twenty thousand of this army were credited to Maryland and thirty-five thousand to Missouri, the number given was evidently a gross exaggeration. The statement was probably made for effect upon the North rather than in the interest of truth. A member of the Confederate Congress from North Carolina stated in debate in 1864 that the Confederate muster-roll numbered more than four hundred thousand men, "of whom probably one-half were not there." During the entire period of the war it is probable that eleven hundred thousand men were embodied in the Confederate Army, though its effective strength did not at any time consist of more than one-half that number. But this force was obtained by the South at great sacrifice. The necessity of a stringent conscription was felt as early as April 16, 1862, at which time the first Enrolment Act was passed by the Confederate Congress. Under this Act, which was amended on the 27th of September of the same year, Mr. Davis issued on the 15th of July, 1863, his first conscription proclamation which called into the service of the Confederacy all white men between the ages of eighteen and forty-five who were not legally exempted from military service. The date of the proclamation shows that it was forced upon the Confederate by Lee's abortive invasion of Pennsylvania, and was intended to fill the ranks of the army which had been shattered and beaten on the field of Gettysburg. Further legislation by the Confederate Congress in February, 1864, extended the enrolment so as to include all white male residents of the Confederate States between the ages of seventeen and fifty. In February, 1865, Mr. Davis estimated that more than one hundred and fifty thousand men were added to the Confederate armies by this forced conscription.

Comparing the strength of the Confederate Army with the population from which it was recruited, and taking into account the absolute lack of provision made for the comfort of the Southern soldier, the insufficient provision made for his sustenance and clothing, and the consequent desertion which made it imperative to repair diminished strength, it is evident that the conscriptive legislation bore with fearful severity upon the people of the South. Comprehensive as was the Enrolment Act, which rendered liable to military duty the entire male population between the ages of seventeen and fifty, the South was compelled to overstep its self-imposed limit. The forces which Lee and Johnston surrendered contained so many boys unfitted by youth and so many men unfitted by age for military service, that a Northern General epigrammatically remarked that for its armies the Confederacy had been compelled in the end to rob alike the cradle and the grave.

Grave misstatements however have been made in regard to the diminished forces of the Confederacy at the cessation of the war. The astounding assertion has crept into statements intended to be historical that Lee surrendered an army of only ten thousand men, and Johnston an army of most insignificant numbers in comparison with that of Sherman. An accurate count made of the forces surrendered by the Confederacy and paroled by the North at the conclusion of the war, shows that the following numbers were embodied in the various Southern armies and were rendering active service in the field : —

The army of Virginia under General Robert E. Lee	28,356
The army of Tennessee under General Joseph E. Johnston . . .	37,047
The army of Florida under Major-General Samuel Jones . . .	2,113
The army of Alabama under Lieutenant-General Richard Taylor . .	12,723
The Trans-Mississippi army of General E. Kirby Smith	10,167
The Arkansas army of Brigadier-General M. Jeff Thompson . . .	5,048
Total	95,454

These figures are given as the result of actual count made of the paroles signed, and have been verified by officers both of the Union Army and of the Confederate Army. They represent the actual force engaged in the field, and upon the basis of calculation adopted in the North would indicate a Confederate Army of nearly three hundred thousand men at the close of the struggle. When the frequent desertions from the Southern Army are remembered, and the losses in prisoners and those disabled in the fearful fights of the months which preceded the surrender of Lee, it will not be exaggeration to say that the South had at the opening of General Grant's campaign in Virginia the preceding summer more than five hundred thousand men borne upon the rolls of its armies. The waste of the Confederate forces during the sixty days immediately preceding the final surrender was very great. The knowledge of the situation had penetrated the ranks, and the men lost spirit and hope. The result which followed was precisely that which has always happened with armies so circumstanced. The ranks melted away, and there was neither resource nor discipline to fill them again.

It would be but poor compliment to the soldiers of the Union to withhold just recognition of the brave opponents who met them on so many hard-fought fields. Nor is there any disposition among loyal men to stint the praise which is always due to courage. Never perhaps was an army organized with fighting qualities superior to those of the army put into the field by the Confederacy. They fought with an absolute conviction, however erroneous, that their cause was just; and their arms were nerved by the feeling which their leaders had instilled deeply into their minds, that they were contending against an intolerable tyranny and protecting the sacredness of home. In a war purely defensive, as was that of the Confederacy, an army such as they raised and maintained can baffle the efforts of vastly superior numbers. The Confederates found from their own experience how changed was the task when they assumed the offensive and ventured to leave their own territory, with their perfect knowledge of its topography and with a surrounding population of sympathizers and helpers. In their first attempt at invasion they did not get beyond cannon-sound of the Potomac, and in the second they were turned back by the result of the first battle. These facts do not impeach the prowess of the Confederate soldiery, but they illustrate the task imposed on the Army of the Union and they suggest the vast difference in the responsibilities which the invading and the defensive forces were called upon to meet.

For so large an army as the Government of the Union was compelled to raise, volunteering could not be relied upon as a steady resource for recruitment. Great as was the ardor among the loyal people at the beginning of the struggle, it was soon found, as it has always been found in other nations, that unaided patriotism could not supply the heavy demands constantly made to repair the waste from the casualties of war and from the ravages of disease. The Act of Congress of March 3, 1863, provided for the enrolment of all able-bodied male citizens between the ages of twenty and forty-five years, while the Act of February 24, 1864, granted freedom to all male slaves between the ages of twenty and forty-five who might enlist in the Northern armies. Reward was made to go with duty, and by the Act of July 4, 1864, Congress ameliorated the rigors of the conscription by paying to each drafted man a bounty for one year's service, at the same time doubling and trebling the amount for two and three years' service respectively. The Secretary of War was by the same law directed to discharge from service at the request of parents all persons under the age of eighteen years who might have enlisted in the army, and it was made an offense punishable with loss of commission for any officer knowingly to enlist a person less than sixteen years of age. Conscription laws have been unpopular in all countries, and though resisted among us on one occasion with riot, they were upheld with strong courage by the mass of the loyal people. Representatives in Congress who had voted for the enactments were returned by large majorities, and Mr. Lincoln was re-elected with an overwhelming expression of popular favor at the very time when he was directing the enforcement of the draft. The vote of 1864 was perhaps the most significant exhibition of patriotism made during the war, and had an extraordinary influence in discouraging those who were directing the fortunes of the Confederacy.

In the Loyal States the Government called for more than 2,750,-000 men at various times throughout the war. In the South nearly every white person capable of bearing arms rendered at one time or another service in the army. A leading military authority of England, speaking of the strength of the armies of the United States and of the Confederacy, says, "The total number of men called under arms by the Government of the United States between April, 1861, and April, 1865, amounted to 2,759,049, of whom 2,656,053 were actually embodied in the armies. If to these be added the 1,100,000 men embodied by the Southern States during the same time, the total armed forces reach the enormous amount of nearly 4,000,000, drawn from a population of only 32,000,000 of all ages. Before this vast aggregate, the celebrated uprising of the French nation in 1793, or the recent efforts of France and Germany in the war of 1870–71, sink into insignificance. And within three years the whole of these vast forces were peaceably disbanded and the army had shrunk to a normal strength of only 30,000 men."

Germany with a population of 41,000,000 can in time of war furnish an army of 1,250,000 men. France with a population of 36,000,000 claims that she can set more than 1,500,000 men afield. With a population of less than 25,000,000 from which to levy troops, the Government of the United States had when the war closed more than 1,000,000 men upon the muster-rolls of the army to be paid off and discharged. Of this vast force probably not more than forty per cent. were available for operations on the field. The wounded, the sick, those upon furlough, upon detail in other service, upon military service elsewhere than in the field, together with those in military parlance absent or "not accounted for," would, it is estimated, be equal to sixty per cent. of the entire army.

The area over which the armies of the Union were called to operate was 800,000 square miles in extent, — as large as the German Empire, France, Spain, Portugal, Belgium, and Holland combined. Those who led in the secession movement relied confidently upon the impossibility of overcoming a population inhabiting so great an expanse of territory. Their judgment was confirmed by that of the best military critics of Europe who looked pityingly upon the folly of the United States for undertaking a task which after years of suffering and great loss of life could end only in defeat, with hopeless bankruptcy for the surviving remnant of the Republic. Could the Government have had the advantage of a small area for its military operations, its power to overcome the rebellion would have been greatly enhanced, and an army not exceeding half of that which was raised could have vindicated the authority of the flag and maintained the integrity of the Union. The National expenditures would have been decreased in even greater ratio, for aside from reducing the number of troops, the enormous cost involved in transportation would have been lessened by hundreds of millions of dollars in the four years of the war.

Another cause of increased expenditure was the haste necessarily attendant upon all the military preparations of the Government. Armies were to be created from the basis of an organization hardly greater than would serve as a police force for the Republic. When Fort Sumter was fired upon, the Army of the United States, rank and file, scarcely exceeded sixteen thousand men. The Government was compelled to equip its vast forces from stores of which hardly a nucleus existed. Arms, ammunition, military supplies, were all to be instantly gathered. The growth of the great host, its equipment, its marshaling, its prodigious strength, are among the marvels and the glories of our history. To admit that mistakes were made is only to say that the work was in human hands. Criticism may well be drowned in the acclaim of success. No National emergency has ever been met with greater courage, promptness, or skill.

The loss to the country and the expenditures from its Treasury could not be estimated when the war closed. We knew that a half-million citizens of the Republic had laid down their lives — three hundred thousand in defending the Union, two hundred thousand in attempting to destroy it. We knew the enormous amounts which had been paid in supporting our armies. But we were not wholly prepared for the millions that must be paid in satisfaction of claims which there had been no mode of reckoning. Nor had there been any standard by which an estimate could be made of the sums required by the pensions which the gratitude and the justice of the Government would be called upon to grant. It was soon apparent that the need of relief was proportional to the magnitude of the struggle, and the Government prepared to respond with a munificence never paralleled.

Nine months after the outbreak of hostilities the organization and equipment of the National forces were placed under the direction of Edwin M. Stanton as Secretary of War. Outside of his professional reputation, which was high, Mr. Stanton had been known to the public by his service in the Cabinet of Mr. Buchanan during the last three months of his Administration. In that position he had undoubtedly exhibited zeal and fidelity in the cause of the Union. He was a member of the Democratic party, a thorough believer in its principles, and a hearty opponent of Mr. Lincoln in the contest of 1860. In speech and in writing he referred to Mr. Lincoln's supporters in the extreme partisan phrase of the day, — as "Black Republicans." He had no sympathy with Mr. Lincoln's views on the subject of slavery, and was openly hostile to any revival of the doctrine of Protection. If Mr. Buchanan had been governed by the views of Mr. Stanton he would undoubtedly have vetoed the Morrill Tariff bill, and thus an unintended injury would have been inflicted upon the reviving credit of the nation. A citizen of the District of Columbia, Mr. Stanton was not called upon to make a personal record in the Presidential election of 1860, but his sympathies were well understood to be with the supporters of Breckinridge.

With these political principles and affiliations, Mr. Stanton was not even considered in connection with the original organization of Mr. Lincoln's Cabinet. But the fact of his being a Democrat was now in his favor, for Mr. Lincoln was anxious to signify by some decisive expression, his appreciation of the patriotism which had induced so large a proportion of the Democratic party to lay aside prejudice and unite in support of his Administration. He had a high estimate of Mr. Stanton's capacity, derived from personal intercourse in a professional engagement some three years before. He had learned something of his powers of endurance, of his trained habits of thought, of his systematic method of labor, and he had confidence that at forty-seven years of age, with vigorous health and a robust constitution, Mr. Stanton could endure the strain which the increasing labor of the War Department would impose. His nomination was confirmed without delay, and the whole country received his appointment with profound satisfaction.

No Cabinet minister in our history has been so intemperately denounced, so extravagantly eulogized. The crowning fact in his favor is that through all the mutations of his stormy career he was trusted and loved by Mr. Lincoln to the end of his days. He was at all times and under all circumstances absolutely free from corruption, and was savagely hostile to every man in the military service who was even suspected of irregularity or wrong. He possessed the executive faculty in the highest degree. He was prompt, punctual, methodical, rapid, clear, explicit in all his work. He imparted energy to every branch of the service, and his vigorous determination was felt on the most distant field of the war as a present and inspiring force.

Mr. Stanton had faults. He was subject to unaccountable and violent prejudice, and under its sway he was capable of harsh injustice. Many officers of merit and of spotless fame fell under his displeasure and were deeply wronged by him. General Stone was perhaps the most conspicuous example of the extremity of outrage to which the Secretary's temper could carry him. He was lacking in magnanimity. Even when intellectually convinced of an error, he was reluctant to acknowledge it. He had none of that grace which turns an enemy to a friend by healing the wounds which have been unjustly inflicted. While oppressing many who were under his control, he had the keenest appreciation of power, and to men who were wielding great influence he exhibited the most deferential consideration. He had a quick insight into character, and at a glance could tell a man who would resist and resent from one who would silently submit. He was ambitious to the point of uncontrollable greed for fame, and by this quality was subject to its counterpart of jealousy, and to an envy of the increasing reputation of others. It was a sore trial to him that after his able and persistent organization of all the elements of victory, the share of credit which justly belonged to him, was lost sight of in the glory which surrounded the hero of a successful battle.

But his weaknesses did not obscure the loftiness of his character. The capricious malignity and brutal injustice of the Great Frederick might as well be cited against the acknowledged grandeur of his career, as an indictment be brought against Stanton's fame on his personal defects, glaring and even exasperating as they were. To the Nation's trust he was sublimely true. To him was committed, in a larger degree than to any other man except the President alone, the successful prosecution of the war and the consequent preservation of the Union. Against those qualities which made him so many enemies, against those insulting displays of temper which wounded so many proud spirits helplessly subject to him for the time, against those acts of rank injustice which, in the judgment of his most partial eulogist, will always mar his fame, must be remembered his absolute consecration of all that he was and of all he could hope to be, to the cause of his country. For more than three years, of unceasing and immeasurable responsibility, he stood at his post, by day and by night, never flagging in zeal, never doubting in faith. Even his burly frame and rugged strength were overborne by the weight of his cares and by the strain upon his nerves, but not until his work was finished, not until the great salvation had come. Persecution and obloquy have followed him into the grave, but an impartial verdict must be that he was inspired with the devotion of a martyr, and that he wore out his life in a service of priceless value to all the generations of his countrymen.

CHAPTER XXVI.

AT the close of the year 1860 the long series of irritating and dangerous questions which had disturbed the relations of the United States and Great Britain, from the time of the Declaration of Independence, had reached final and friendly solution. The fact gave unalloyed satisfaction to the American people and to their Government. Mr. Buchanan was able to say in his message of December, in language which Lord Lyons truly described as "the most cordial which has appeared in any President's message "since the foundation of the Republic," —

" Our relations with Great Britain are of the most friendly char-"acter. Since the commencement of my administration the two "dangerous questions arising from the Clayton-Bulwer Treaty and "from the right of search claimed by the British Government have "been amicably and honorably adjusted. The discordant construc-"tions of the Clayton-Bulwer Treaty, which at different periods of "the discussion bore a threatening aspect, have resulted in a final "settlement entirely satisfactory to this government. The only "question of any importance which still remains open is the dis-"puted title between the two governments to the Island of San

"Juan in the vicinity of Washington Territory." It was obvious that neither government looked forward to any trouble from this source.

To give manifestation of the cordiality with which our friendship was reciprocated, Her Majesty had selected this auspicious year for a visit of her son, the Prince of Wales, to this country. His Royal Highness was received everywhere by the government and the people with genuine and even enthusiastic hospitality, and at the termination of his visit Lord Lyons was instructed to express the thanks of Her Majesty.

"One of the main objects," His Lordship wrote to Secretary Cass on the 8th of December, 1860, "which Her Majesty had in view in "sanctioning the visit of His Royal Highness was to prove to the "President and citizens of the United States the sincerity of those "sentiments of esteem and regard which Her Majesty and all classes "of her subjects entertain for the kindred race which occupies so "distinguished a position in the community of nations. Her Majesty "has seen with the greatest satisfaction that her feelings and those "of her people in this respect have been met with the warmest sym- "pathy in the great American Union; and Her Majesty trusts that "the feelings of confidence and affection, of which late events have "proved beyond all question the existence, will long continue to "prevail between the two countries to their mutual advantage "and to the general interests of civilization and humanity. I am "commanded to state to the President that the Queen would be "gratified by his making known generally to the citizens of the "United States her grateful sense of the kindness with which they "received her son, who has returned to England deeply impressed "with all he saw during his progress through the States, and more "especially so with the friendly and cordial good will manifested "towards him on every occasion by all classes of the community."

Mr. William Henry Trescott, then Assistant Secretary of State, replied to Lord Lyons's note without delay, writing on the 11th of December: "I am instructed by the President to express the gratifi- "cation with which he has learned how correctly Her Majesty has "appreciated the spirit in which His Royal Highness was received "throughout the Republic, and the cordial manifestation of that "spirit by the people of the United States which accompanied him "in every step of his progress. Her Majesty has justly recognized "that the visit of her son aroused the kind and generous sympathies "of our citizens, and, if I may so speak, has created an almost per-

"sonal interest in the fortunes of the Royalty which he so well
"represents. The President trusts that this sympathy and interest
"towards the future representative of the Sovereignty of Great Brit-
"ain are at once an evidence and a guaranty of that consciousness
"of common interest and mutual regard which have bound in the
"past, and will in the future bind together more strongly than
"treaties, the feelings and the fortunes of the two nations which rep-
"resent the enterprise, the civilization, and the constitutional liberty
"of the same great race. I have also been instructed to make this
"correspondence public, that the citizens of the United States may
"have the satisfaction of knowing how strongly and properly Her
"Majesty has appreciated the cordial warmth of their welcome to
"His Royal Highness."

Time was soon to test "the sincerity of those sentiments of es-
"teem and regard which Her Majesty and all classes of her subjects
"entertain for the kindred race which occupies so distinguished a
"position in the community of nations." Within a few days after
the exchange of this correspondence it became the duty of Lord
Lyons to announce to his government that the domestic differences
"in the great American Union" were deepening into so fierce a feud
that from different motives both General Cass the Secretary of State,
to whom his letter had been addressed, and Mr. Trescott the Assistant Secretary of State, by whom it had been answered, had resigned,
and that the United States, one "of the two great nations which
"represent the enterprise, the civilization, and the constitutional lib-
"erty of the same great race," was about to confront the gravest
danger that can threaten national existence.

The State of South Carolina passed its Ordinance of Secession
December 17, 1860. From that date until the surrender of Fort
Sumter, April 14, 1861, many of the most patriotic and able statesmen of the country and a large majority of the people of the North
hoped that some reasonable and peaceful adjustment of the difficulties would be found. The new Administration had every right to
expect that foreign powers would maintain the utmost reserve, both
in opinion and in action, until it could have a fair opportunity to
decide upon a policy. The great need of the new President was
time. Both he and his advisers felt that every day's delay was a
substantial gain, and that the maintenance of the *status quo*, with no
fresh outbreak at home and no unfriendly expression abroad, was of
incalculable advantage to the cause of the Union.

Amid the varying and contradictory impressions of the hour, Lord Lyons had reported events as they occurred, with singular fairness and accuracy. Just one month before Mr. Lincoln was inaugurated, on the 4th of February, 1861, His Lordship wrote to Lord John Russell, at that time Her Majesty's Minister of Foreign Affairs: "Mr. Seward's real view of the state of the country appears to be "that if bloodshed can be avoided until the new government is "installed, the seceding States will in no long time return to the "Confederation. He seems to think that in a few months the evils " and hardships produced by secession will become intolerably griev- "ous to the Southern States, that they will be completely re-assured " as to the intentions of the Administration, and that the conservative "element which is now kept under the surface by the violent press- "ure of the Secessionists will emerge with irresistible force. From "all these causes he confidently.expects that when elections for the " State Legislatures are held in the Southern States in November "next, the Union party will have a clear majority and will bring the "seceding States back into the Confederation. He then hopes to "place himself at the head of a strong Union party having extensive "ramifications both in the North and in the South, and to make "' Union ' or ' Disunion,' not ' Freedom ' or ' Slavery,' the watchwords "of political parties." It can scarcely escape notice how significant, even at this early period, is the use in this dispatch of the word "confederation" as applied to the United States, — a use never before made of it in diplomatic communication since the establishment of the Constitution, and indicating, only too clearly, the view to be taken by the British Government of the relation of the States to the Union.

Whatever may have been the estimate at home of the policy attributed to Mr. Seward, it was certainly one which would commend itself to the sympathy of a friendly nation, and one, to the success of which no neutral power would hesitate to contribute all the aid it could rightfully render. The dispatch of Lord Lyons was received in London on the 18th of February, and on the 20th Lord John Russell replied as follows: "The success or failure of Mr. Seward's "plans to prevent the disruption of the North-American Union is a "matter of deep interest to Her Majesty's Government, but they " can only expect and hope. They are not called upon nor would " they be acting prudently were they to obtrude their advice on the "dissentient parties in the United States. Supposing however that

"Mr. Lincoln, acting under bad advice, should endeavor to provide "excitement for the public mind by raising questions with Great "Britain, Her Majesty's Government feel no hesitation as to the "policy they would pursue. They would in the first place be very "forbearing. They would show by their acts how highly they value "the relations of peace and amity with the United States. But they "would take care to let the government which multiplied provoca- "tions and sought for quarrels understand that their forbearance "sprung from the consciousness of strength and not from the timid- "ity of weakness. They would warn a government which was "making political capital out of blustering demonstrations that our "patience might be tried too far."

It is impossible to mistake the spirit or the temper of this dis- patch. It is difficult to account for the manifest irritation of its tone except upon the ground that Lord John Russell saw in a possible reconciliation, between North and South, something that threatened the interest or jarred upon the sympathy of the British Government. It was at least sufficient and ominous warning of what the United States might expect from "the confidence and affection" which had only a few weeks before been outpoured so lavishly by Her Majesty's Government. The fact is worthy of emphasis that since the cordial interchange of notes touching the visit of the Prince of Wales there had not been a single word of unkindness in the correspondence of the two governments. But our embarrassments had been steadily deepening, and according to many precedents in the career of that illustrious statesman, Lord John seems to have considered the period of our distress a fitting time to assert that "British forbearance "springs from the consciousness of strength and not from the tim- "idity of weakness."

On the 4th of March, 1861, the administration of Mr. Lincoln assumed the responsibility of government. At that date the organi- zation of the Southern Confederacy had not been perfected. Four States which ultimately joined it had not yet seceded from the Union. There had been no overt act of violence. The Administration still believed in the possibility of a peaceful settlement. But on the 12th of April Fort Sumter was attacked. On the 14th it was surrendered. On the 15th the President issued his Proclamation calling out seventy- five thousand militia and summoning Congress to meet on the 4th of

July. On the 17th the President of the Confederacy authorized the issue of letters of marque. On the 19th the President of the United States proclaimed a blockade of the Southern ports and declared that privateers with letters of marque from the Southern Confederacy would be treated as pirates.

This condition of affairs rendered the relation of foreign powers to the Union and to the Confederacy at once urgent and critical. It is true that Fort Sumter had surrendered to a warlike demonstration, but fortunately no blood had been shed. It is true that letters of marque had been authorized, but none had been actually issued. It is true that a blockade had been proclaimed, but some time must elapse before it could be practically enforced. All that can be said is that the rebellion had organized itself with promptness and courage for a conflict. There was still a pause. Neither party thoroughly realized the horror of the work before them, though every day made it more clearly apparent. Until then the United States was the only organized government on our soil known to England, and with it she had for three-quarters of a century maintained commercial and political relations which had grown closer and more friendly every year. The vital element of that government was Union. Whatever might be the complicated relations of their domestic law, to the world and to themselves the United States of America was one indivisible government. This instinct of union had gathered them together as colonies, had formed them into an imperfect confederation, had matured them under a National Constitution. It gave them their vigor at home, their power and influence abroad. To destroy their union was to resolve them into worse than colonial disintegration.

But the separation of the States was more than the dissolution of the Union. For, treating with all due respect the conviction of the Southern States as to the violation of their constitutional rights, no fair-minded man can deny that the central idea of the secession movement was the establishment of a great slave-holding empire around the Gulf of Mexico. It was a bold and imperial conception. With an abounding soil, with millions of trained and patient laborers, with a proud and martial people, with leaders used to power and skilled in government, controlling some of the greatest and most necessary of the commercial staples of the world, the haughty oligarchy of the South would have founded a slave republic which, in its successful development, would have changed the future of this continent and of the world. When English statesmen were called upon to deal with such a crisis, the United States had a right to expect, if not active sympathy, at least that neutrality which would confine itself within the strict limit of international obligation, and would not withhold friendly wishes for the preservation of the Union.

England had tested slowly but surely the worth of the American Union. As the United States had extended in territory, had developed in wealth, had increased in population, richer and richer had become the returns to England's merchants and manufacturers; question after question of angry controversy had been amicably settled by the conviction of mutual, growing, and peaceful interests. And while it had become a rhetorical truism with English historians and statesmen, that relations with the independent Republic were stronger, safer, and more valuable than those of the old colonial connection, her own principles of constitutional liberty were re-invigorated by the skill and the breadth with which they were applied and administered by her own children in a new country. England could not but know that all this was due to the Union, — the Union which had concentrated the weakness of scattered States into a government that protected the citizen and welcomed the immigrant, which carried law and liberty to the pioneer on the remotest border, which had made of provincial villages centres of wealth and civilization that would not have discredited the capitals of older nations, and which above all had created a Federal representative government whose successful working might teach England herself how to hold together the ample colonies that still formed the outposts of her Empire.

More than all, a Cabinet, every member of which by personal relation or traditional connection belonged to the great liberal party that felt the achievement of Emancipation to be a part of its historic glory, should have realized that no diminution of a rival, no monopoly of commerce, could bring to England any compensation for the establishment of a slave-holding empire upon the central waters of the world.

With this natural expectation the Government in less than sixty days after Mr. Lincoln's inauguration, sent its minister to London, confident that he would at least be allowed to present to the British Government for friendly consideration, the condition and policy of the Republic before any positive action should disturb the apparently amicable relations of the two countries. Mr. Charles Francis

Adams, who was selected for this important duty, was instructed to explain to the British Government that the peculiar relation of the States to the Federal Government, and the reticence and reservations consequent upon a change of administration, had hitherto restrained the action of the President in the formation and declaration of his policy; that without foreign interference the condition of affairs still afforded reasonable hope of a satisfactory solution; and especially that it was necessary, if there existed a sincere desire to avoid wrong and injury to the United States, for foreign powers to abstain from any act of pretended neutrality which would give material advantage or moral encouragement to the organized forces of the rebellion.

Before Mr. Adams could cross the Atlantic the British Government, although aware of his mission and its object, decided upon its own course, in concerted action with France, and without reference to the views or wishes or interest of the United States. On the day before Mr. Adams's arrival in England, as if to give him offensive warning how little his representations would be regarded, Her Majesty's Government issued a proclamation recognizing the confederated Southern States as belligerents. It is entirely unnecessary to discuss the question of the right to recognize belligerency. The great powers of Europe had the same right to recognize the Southern Confederacy as belligerent that they had to recognize it as an established nationality, and with the same consequences, — all dependent upon whether the fact so recognized were indeed a fact. But the recognition of belligerency or independence may be the means to achieve a result, and not simply an impartial acquiescence in a result already achieved. The question therefore was not whether foreign powers had a right to recognize, but whether the time and method of such recognition were not distinctly hostile, — whether they were not the efficient and coldly calculated means to strengthen the hands of the Rebellion.

Events proved that if the English Government had postponed this action until the Government of the United States had been allowed a frank discussion of its policy, no possible injury to English interests could have resulted. It was but a very short time before the rebellion assumed proportions that led to the recognition of the Confederacy as a belligerent by the civil, judicial, and military authorities of the Union; a recognition by foreign powers would then have been simply an act of impartial neutrality. But, declared with such precipitancy, recognition could be regarded only as an act of unfriendliness to the United States. The proof of this is inherent in the case : —

1. The purpose of the secession, openly avowed from the beginning, was the dissolution of the Union and the establishment of an independent slave-empire ; and the joint recognition was a declaration that such a result, fraught with ruin to us, was not antagonistic to the feelings or to the supposed interests of Europe, and that both the commercial ambition of England and the military aspirations of France in Mexico hoped to find profit in the event.

2. This recognition of belligerency in defiance of the known wishes and interests of the United States, accompanied by the discourteous refusal to allow a few hours' delay for the reception of the American minister, was a significant warning to the seceded States that no respect due to the old Union would long delay the establishment of new relations, and that they should put forth all their energies before the embarrassed Administration could concentrate its efforts in defense of the National life.

3. The recognition of the belligerent flag of the Southern Confederacy, with the equal right to supplies and hospitality, guarantied by such recognition, gave to the insurgents facilities and opportunities which were energetically used, and led to consequences which belong to a later period of this history, but the injury and error of which were emphatically rebuked by a judgment of the most important tribunal that has ever been assembled to interpret and administer International law.

The demand which naturally followed for a rigid enforcement of the blockade, imposed a heavy burden upon the Government of the United States just at the time when it was least prepared to assume such a burden. Apologists for the unfriendly course of England interpose the plea that the declaration of blockade by the United States was in fact a prior recognition of Southern belligerency. But it must be remembered that when the United States proposed to avoid this technical argument by closing the insurgent ports instead of blockading them, Mr. Seward was informed by Lord Lyons, acting in concert with the French minister, that Her Majesty's Government " would consider a decree closing the ports of the South actually in "possession of the insurgent or Confederate States, as null and "void, and that they would not submit to measures on the high seas "in pursuance of such decree." Bitterly might Mr. Seward announce

the fact which has sunk deep into the American heart: "It is in
"deed manifest in the tone of the speeches, as well as in the general
"tenor of popular discussion, that neither the responsible ministers
"nor the House of Commons nor the active portion of the people of
"Great Britain sympathize with this government, and hope, or even
"wish, for its success in suppressing the insurrection; and that on
"the contrary the whole British nation, speaking practically, desire
"and expect the dismemberment of the Republic."

This very decided step towards a hostile policy was soon followed
by another even more significant. On the 9th of May, 1861, only
a few days before the Proclamation of Her Britannic Majesty, recognizing the belligerency of the Southern Confederacy and thus
developing itself as a part of a concerted and systematic policy, Lord
Cowley, the British Ambassador at Paris, wrote to Lord John Russell:
"I called this afternoon on M. Thouvenel, Minister of Foreign
"Affairs, for the purpose of obtaining his answer to the proposals
"contained in your Lordship's dispatch of the 6th inst. relative to
"the measures which should be pursued by the Maritime Powers of
"Europe for the protection of neutral property in presence of the
"events which are passing in the American States. M. Thouvenel
"said the Imperial Government concurred entirely in the views of
"Her Majesty's Government in endeavoring to *obtain of the belliger-*
"*ents* a *formal* recognition of the second, third, and fourth articles of
"the Declaration of Paris. Count de Flahault (French Ambassador
"in London) would receive instructions to make this known offi-
"cially to your Lordship. With regard to the manner in which this
"endeavor should be made, M. Thouvenel said that he thought a
"communication should be addressed to both parties *in as nearly as
"possible the same language*, the consuls being made the organs of
"communication with the Southern States."

Communicating this intelligence to Lord Lyons in a dispatch
dated May 18, 1861, Lord John Russell added these instructions:
"Your Lordship may therefore be prepared to find your French
"colleague ready to take the same line with yourself in his commu-
"nications with the Government of the United States. I need not
"tell your Lordship that Her Majesty's Government would very
"gladly see a practice which is calculated to lead to great irregu-
"larities and to increase the calamities of war renounced by *both* the
"contending parties in America as it has been renounced by almost
"*every other nation* of the world. . . . You will take such means as

"you shall judge most expedient to transmit to Her Majesty's consul "at Charleston or New Orleans a copy of my previous dispatch to "you of this day's date, to be communicated at Montgomery to the "President of the so-styled Confederate States."

The identity of the address and the equality upon which both the belligerents were invited to do what had been done by "almost "every other *nation* of the world" need not be emphasized.

On July 5, 1861, Lord Lyons instructed Mr. Bunch, the British Consul at Charleston, South Carolina: —

"The course of events having invested the States assuming the "title of the Confederate States of America with the character of "belligerents, it has become necessary for Her Majesty's Government "to obtain from the existing government in those States securities "concerning the proper treatment of neutrals. I am authorized by "Lord John Russell to confide the negotiation on this matter to you, "and I have great satisfaction in doing so. In order to make you "acquainted with the views of Her Majesty's Government, I trans- "mit to you a duplicate of a dispatch to me in which they are fully "stated." His Lordship then proceeded to instruct the consul as to the manner in which it might be best to conduct the negotiation, the object being to avoid as far as possible a direct official communi- cation with the authorities of the Confederate States. Instructions to the same purport were addressed by the French Government to their consul at Charleston.

What then was the point of the negotiation committed to these consuls? It will be found in the dispatch from Lord John Russell, communicated by his order to Mr. Bunch. It was the accession of the United States and of the Confederate States to the Declaration of Paris of April 16, 1856. That Declaration was signed by the Ministers of Austria, France, Great Britain, Prussia, Russia, Sar- dinia, and Turkey. It adopted as articles of Maritime Law the fol- lowing points: —

"1. Privateering is and remains abolished.

"2. The neutral flag covers enemy's goods with the exception of "contraband of war.

"3. Neutral goods, with the exception of contraband of war, are not "liable to capture under the enemy's flag.

"4. Blockades in order to be binding must be effective, — that is to "say, maintained by a force sufficient really to prevent access to the "coast of the enemy."

The Powers signing the Declaration engaged to bring it to the knowledge of those Powers which had not taken part in the Congress of Paris, and to invite them to accede to it; and they agreed that "the present Declaration is not and shall not be binding except "between those Powers which have acceded or shall accede to it." It was accepted by all the European and South American Powers. The United States, Mexico, and the Oriental Powers did not join in the general acceptance.

The English and French consuls in Charleston, having received these instructions, sought and found an intermediary whose position and diplomatic experience would satisfy their requirements. This agent accepted the trust on two conditions, — one, that he should be furnished with the instructions as proof to the Confederate Government of the genuineness of the negotiation, the other, that the answer of the Confederate Government should be received in whatever shape that government should think proper to frame it. The negotiations in Richmond which had by this time become the seat of the Insurgent Government were speedily concluded, and on the 13th of August, 1861, the Confederate Government passed the following resolution : —

"WHEREAS the Plenipotentiaries of Great Britain, Austria, "France, Prussia, Russia, Sardinia, and Turkey, in a conference held "at Paris on the 16th of April, 1856, made certain declarations con- "cerning Maritime Law, to serve as uniform rules for their guidance "in all cases arising out of the principles thus proclaimed ;

"AND WHEREAS it being desirable not only to attain certainty "and uniformity as far as may be practicable in maritime law, but "also to maintain whatever is just and proper in the established "usages of nations, the Confederate States of America deem it im- "portant to declare the principles by which they will be governed "in their intercourse with the rest of mankind: Now therefore "be it

"*Resolved*, by the Congress of the Confederate States of America, "1st, That we maintain the right of privateering as it has been long "established by the practice and recognized by the law of nations.

"2d, That the neutral flag covers enemy's goods with the exception "of contraband of war.

"3d, That neutral goods, with the exception of contraband of war, "are not liable to capture under the enemy's flag.

"4th, Blockades in order to be binding must be effective; that is to

"say, maintained by a force sufficient really to prevent access to the
"coast of the enemy.

"These resolutions," says Mr. Bunch to Lord Lyons on Aug. 16,
1861, "were passed on the 13th inst., approved on the same day by
"the President, and I have the honor to enclose herewith to your
"Lordship the copy of them which has been sent to Mr. —— by the
"Secretary of State to be delivered to M. de Belligny and myself."
On Aug. 30, 1861, Lord Lyons wrote to Lord John Russell: "I have
"received, just in time to have the enclosed copy made for your Lord-
"ship, a dispatch from Mr. Consul Bunch reporting the proceedings
"taken by him in conjunction with his French colleague M. de Bel-
"ligny to obtain the adherence of the so-called Confederate States
"to the last three articles of the Declaration of Paris;" and a few
days later he says, "I am confirmed in the opinion that the negotia-
"tion, which was difficult and delicate, was managed with great tact
"and judgment by the two consuls."

Upon the discovery of this "difficult and delicate negotiation,"
Mr. Seward demanded the removal of Mr. Bunch. Lord John
Russell replied to Mr. Adams Sept. 9, 1861, "The undersigned will
"without hesitation state to Mr. Adams that in pursuance of an
"agreement between the British and French Governments, Mr.
"Bunch was instructed to communicate to the persons exercising
"authority in the so-called Confederate States the desire of those
"governments that the second, third, and fourth articles of the
"Declaration of Paris should be observed by those States in the
"prosecution of the hostilities in which they were engaged. Mr.
"Adams will observe that the commerce of Great Britain and
"France is deeply interested in the maintenance of the articles pro
"viding that the flag covers the goods, and that the goods of a
"neutral taken on board a belligerent ship are not liable to confisca-
"tion. Mr. Bunch therefore, in what he has done in this matter,
"has acted in obedience to the instructions of his government,
"who accept the responsibility of his proceedings so far as they are
"known to the Foreign Department, and who cannot remove him
"from his office for having obeyed instructions."

Here then was a complete official negotiation with the Confederate States. Mr. Montagu Bernard, in his ingenious and learned
work, *The Neutrality of Great Britain during the American War*,
conceals the true character of the work in which the British Government had been engaged: "The history of an unofficial application

"made to the Confederate States on the same subject is told in the
"two following dispatches. It will be seen that the channel of com-
"munication was a private person instructed by the British and
"French consuls, who had been themselves instructed by the minis-
"ters of their respective governments at Washington." The presence
of a private intermediary at one point cannot break the chain of official communication if the communications are themselves official.
For certain purposes the governments of England and France con-
sulted and determined upon a specific line of policy. That policy
was communicated in regular official instructions to their ministers
in Washington. The Ministers were to select the instruments to
carry it out, and the persons selected were the official consular representatives of France and England, who although residing at the
South held their *exequaturs* from the United-States Government.
They were instructed to make a political application to the government of the Confederacy, and Lord John Russell could not disguise
that government under the mask of "the persons exercising authority
"in the so-called Confederate States." Their application was received by the Confederate Government through their agent just as it
would have been received through the mail addressed to the Secretary of State. Their application was officially acted upon by the
Confederate Congress, and the result contained in an official document was transmitted to them, and forwarded by them to their
immediate official superiors in Washington, who recognized it as a
successful result of "a difficult and delicate negotiation." It was
then sent to the Foreign Secretaries of the two countries, and the
responsibility of the act was fully and finally assumed by those
ministers.

Nor can it be justified as an application to a belligerent, informing
him that in the exercise of belligerent rights England and France
would expect a strict conformity to International Law. The four
articles of the Treaty of Paris were not provisions of International
Law. They were explicit modifications of that law as it had long
existed, and the Declaration itself stated that it was not to bind any
of the Powers which had not agreed expressly to accept it. It was
therefore an invitation, not to a belligerent but to the Southern
Confederacy, to accept and thus become a party to an international
compact to which in the very nature of things there could be no
parties save those whose acceptance constituted an international
obligation. It has never yet been claimed that a mere insurgent

belligerent, however strong, occupied such position. If instead of declaring by resolution that the second, third, and fourth articles of the Declaration of Paris were principles which by their own voluntary action they would adopt as rules for their own government, the Confederate States had, with an astute policy which the invitation itself seems intended to suggest, demanded that they should be allowed to accept the Declaration in the same method in which it had been accepted " by every other nation," it is difficult to see how their demand could have been refused; and if it had been admitted, what would have been wanting to perfect the recognition of the independence of the Southern Confederacy?

The motive of England and France in this extraordinary negotiation with the Confederacy is plain. The right of privateering was not left untouched except with deep design. By securing the assent of the Confederacy to the other three articles of the Paris Convention, safety was assured to British and French cargoes under the American flag, while every American cargo was at risk unless protected by a Foreign flag — generally the flag of England. It would have been impossible to invent a process more gainful to British commerce, more harmful to American commerce. While the British and French consuls were conducting this negotiation with the Confederate States, the British and French ministers were conducting another to the same purport with the United States. Finally Mr. Seward offered to waive the point made by Secretary Marcy many years before at the date of the Declaration, and to accept the four articles of the Paris Convention, pure and simple. But this could not be done, because the Confederate States had not accepted the first article abolishing privateering and her privateers must therefore be recognized. England and France used this fact as a pretext for absolutely declining to permit the accession of the United States, one of the great maritime powers of the world, to a treaty which was proclaimed to be a wise and humane improvement of the old and harsh law of nations, and to which in former years the United States had been most earnestly invited to give her assent. This course throws a flood of light on the clandestine correspondence with the Confederacy, and plainly exposes the reasons why it was desired that the right of privateering should be left open to the Confederates. Through that instrumentality great harm could be inflicted on the United States and at the same time England could be guarded against a cotton famine. To accomplish these ends she negotiated what was little less than a hostile treaty with an Insurgent Government. This action was initiated before a single battle was fought, and was evidently intended as encouragement and inspiration to the Confederates to persist in their revolutionary proceedings against the Government of the United States. Any reasonable man, looking at the condition of affairs, could not doubt that the public recognition of the independence of the Confederacy by England and France, was a foregone and rapidly approaching conclusion.

With this condition of affairs leading necessarily to a more pronounced unfriendliness, an incident occurred towards the close of the year which seriously threatened a final breach of amicable relations. On the 9th of November, 1861, Captain Wilkes of the United-States steamer *San Jacinto*, seized the persons of James M. Mason and John Slidell, ministers from the Southern Confederacy, and their secretaries, on board the British mail-steamer *Trent* on her way from Havana to Kingston. Messrs. Mason and Slidell were accredited by the Executive of the Southern Confederacy to the Governments of England and France. Their avowed object was to obtain the recognition by those governments of the independence of the new Southern Republic, and their success would have been a most dangerous if not a fatal blow to the cause of the Union. But they were not by any recognized principle of international law contraband of war, and they were proceeding from a neutral port to a neutral port in a neutral vessel. The action of the officer who seized them was not authorized by any instructions, and the seizure was itself in violation of those principles of maritime law for which the United States had steadily and consistently contended from the establishment of its national life. The difficulty of adjustment lay not in the temper or conviction of either government, but in the passionate and very natural excitement of popular feeling in both countries. In the United States there was universal and enthusiastic approval of the act of Captain Wilkes. In England there was an equally vehement demand for immediate and signal reparation.

Lord John Russell, after reciting the facts, instructed Lord Lyons in a dispatch of Nov. 30, 1861: "Her Majesty's Government there- "fore trust that when this matter shall have been brought under the "consideration of the Government of the United States, that govern-

" ment will of its own accord offer to the British Government such
" redress as alone would satisfy the British nation; namely, the lib-
" eration of the four gentlemen and their delivery to your Lordship
" in order that they may again be placed under British protection,
" and a suitable apology for the aggression which has been committed.
" Should these terms not be offered by Mr. Seward you will propose
" them to him." In a dispatch of the same date Lord John Russell
says to Lord Lyons: " In my previous dispatch of this date I have
" instructed you by command of Her Majesty to make certain de-
" mands of the Government of the United States. Should Mr.
" Seward ask for delay in order that this grave and painful matter
" should be deliberately considered, you will consent to a delay not
" exceeding seven days. If at the end of that time no answer is
" given, or if any other answer is given except that of compliance
" with the demands of Her Majesty's Government, your Lordship is
" instructed to leave Washington with all the members of your Lega-
" tion, bringing with you the archives of the Legation, and to repair
" immediately to London. If however you should be of opinion that
" the requirements of Her Majesty's Government are substantially
" complied with you may report the facts to Her Majesty's Govern-
" ment for their consideration, and remain at your post until you
" receive further orders." The communication of this peremptory
limitation of time for a reply would have been an offensive threat;
but it was a private instruction to guide the discretion of the minister, not to be used if the condition of things upon its arrival
promised an amicable solution. It must also in justice be remembered that excited feeling had been shown by different departments
of our own Government as well as by the press and the people. The
House of Representatives had unanimously adopted a resolution
thanking Captain Wilkes " for his brave, adroit, and patriotic con-
" duct;" and the Secretary of the Navy, Mr. Gideon Welles, had
publicly and officially approved his action.

The spirit in which Lord Lyons would receive his instructions
was indicated in advance by his own dispatch to Lord John Russell
of Nov. 19, 1861: " I have accordingly deemed it right to maintain
" the most complete reserve on the subject. To conceal the distress
" which I feel would be impossible, nor would it if possible be desir-
" able; but I have expressed no opinion on the questions of inter-
" national law involved; I have hazarded no conjecture as to the
" course which will be taken by Her Majesty's Government. On

"the one hand I dare not run the risk of compromising the honor
"and inviolability of the British flag by asking for a measure of repa-
"ration which may prove to be inadequate. On the other hand I am
"scarcely less unwilling to incur the danger of rendering a satisfac-
"tory settlement of the question more difficult by making a demand
"which may turn out to be unnecessarily great. In the present im-
"perfect state of my information I feel that the only proper and
"prudent course is to wait for the orders which your Lordship will
"give, with a complete knowledge of the whole case. I am unwill-
"ing moreover to deprive any explanation or reparation which the
"United-States Government may think it right to offer, of the grace
"of being made spontaneously. I know too that a demand from me
"would very much increase the main difficulty which the govern-
"ment would feel in yielding to any disposition which they may have
"to make amends to Great Britain. The American people would
"more easily tolerate a spontaneous offer of reparation made by its
"government from a sense of justice than a compliance with a
"demand for satisfaction from a foreign minister."

In accordance with the sentiments thus expressed, Lord Lyons,
interpreting his discretion liberally and even generously, called upon
Mr. Seward on the 19th of December, 1861, and the following is his
official account of the interview : "The Messenger Seymour delivered
"to me at half-past eleven o'clock last night your Lordship's dispatch
"of the 30th ultimo, specifying the reparation required by Her
"Majesty's Government for the seizure of Mr. Mason and Mr. Slidell
"and their secretaries on board the royal mail-steamer *Trent*. I
"waited on Mr. Seward this afternoon at the State Department,
"and acquainted him in general terms with the tenor of that dis-
"patch. I stated in particular, as nearly as possible in your Lord-
"ship's words, that the only redress which could satisfy Her Majesty's
"Government and Her Majesty's people would be the immediate
"delivery of the prisoners to me in order that they might be placed
"under British protection, and moreover a suitable apology for the
"aggression which had been committed. I added that Her Majesty's
"Government hoped that the Government of the United States
"would of its own accord offer this reparation; that it was in order
"to facilitate such an arrangement that I had come to him without
"any written demand, or even any written paper at all, in my hand;
"that if there was a prospect of attaining this object I was willing
"to be guided by him as to the conduct on my part which would

"render its attainment most easy. Mr. Seward received my com-
"munication seriously and with dignity, but without any manifes-
"tation of dissatisfaction. Some further conversation ensued in
"consequence of questions put by him with a view to ascertain the
"exact character of the dispatch. At the conclusion he asked me
"to give him to-morrow to consider the question and to communi-
"cate with the President. On the day after he should, he said, be
"ready to express an opinion with respect to the communication I
"had made. In the mean time he begged me to be assured that he
"was very sensible of the friendly and conciliatory manner in which
"I had made it."

On the 26th of December Mr. Seward transmitted to Lord Lyons
the reply of the United States to the demand of the British Government. In forwarding it to his Government Lord Lyons said : " Be-
"fore transmitting to me the note of which a copy is enclosed in my
"immediately preceding dispatch of to-day's date, Mr. Seward sent
"for me to the State Department, and said with some emotion that
"he thought that it was due to the great kindness and consideration
"which I had manifested throughout in dealing with the affair of the
"*Trent*, that he should tell me with his own lips that he had been
"able to effect a satisfactory settlement of it. He had now how-
"ever been authorized to address to me a note which would be sat-
"isfactory to Her Majesty's Government. In answer to inquiries
"from me Mr. Seward said that of course he understood Her Majesty's
"Government to leave it open to the Government of Washington to
"present the case in the form which would be most acceptable to the
"American people, but that the note was intended to be and was a
"compliance with the terms proposed by Her Majesty's Government.
"He would add that the friendly spirit and discretion which I had
"manifested in the whole matter from the day on which the intelli-
"gence of the seizure reached Washington up to the present moment
"had more than any thing else contributed to the satisfactory settle-
"ment of the question."

In his reply Mr. Seward took the ground that we had the right
to detain the British vessel and to search for contraband persons
and dispatches, and moreover that the persons named and their
dispatches were contraband. But he found good reason for surrendering the Confederate envoys in the fact that Captain Wilkes
had neglected to bring the *Trent* into a Prize Court and to submit
the whole transaction to Judicial examination. Mr. Seward cer-

tainly strained the argument of Mr. Madison as Secretary of State in 1804 to a most extraordinary degree when he apparently made it cover the ground that we would quietly have submitted to British right of search if the "Floating Judgment-seat" could have been substituted by a British Prize Court. The seizure of the *Trent* would not have been made more acceptable to the English Government by transferring her to the jurisdiction of an American Prize Court, unless indeed that Court should have decided, as it most probably would have decided, that the seizure was illegal. Measuring the English demand not by the peremptory words of Lord John Russell but by the kindly phrase in which Lord Lyons in a personal interview verbally communicated them, Mr. Seward felt justified in saying that "the claim of the British Government is not made in a "discourteous manner." Mr. Seward did not know that at the very moment he was writing these conciliatory words, British troops were on their way to the Dominion of Canada to menace the United States, and that British cannon were shotted for our destruction.

Lord John Russell, however much he might differ from Mr. Seward's argument, found ample satisfaction to the British Government in his conclusion. He said in reply : " Her Majesty's Government "having carefully taken into their consideration the liberation of the "prisoners, the delivery of them into your hands, and the explana-"tions to which I have just referred, have arrived at the conclusion "that they constitute the reparation which Her Majesty and the "British nation had a right to expect." And thus, by the delivery of the prisoners in the form and at the place least calculated to excite or wound the susceptibilities of the American people, this dangerous question was settled. It is only to be regretted that the spirit and discretion exhibited by the eminent diplomatist who represented England here with such wisdom and good temper, had not been adopted at an earlier date and more steadily maintained by the British Government. It would have prevented much angry controversy, much bitter feeling; it would have averted events and consequences which still shadow with distrust a national friendship that ought to be cordial and constant.

The painful event impressed upon the Government of the United States a profound sense of its isolation from the sympathy of Europe. The principle of maritime law, which was so promptly and rigorously applied, was one for which the United States had contended in its weakness against the usages of the world and against the arms of

Great Britain. There was apparent now an eager resolution to enforce it, when that enforcement was sure to embarrass us and to provoke a spirit of derisive triumph in our foes. It was clear that no effort would be spared to restrict our belligerent rights within the narrowest possible limits. Not content with leaving us to settle this question with England, France and Prussia and Austria hastened to inform us in language professedly friendly, that England would be supported in her demand for reparation, cost what it might to us in prestige, and in power to deal with the Rebellion at home. At this time there was but one among the great nations of the world which adhered to an active and avowed friendship for us. " We " desire above all things the maintenance of the American Union as "one indivisible nation," was the kindly and always to be remembered greeting that came to us from the Emperor of Russia.

The profound ability exhibited by Mr. Seward as Secretary of State has long been acknowledged and emphasized by the admiration and gratitude of the country. In the *Trent* affair he acted under a pressure of circumstances more harassing and perplexing than had ever tested the skill of American diplomacy. It is with no disposition to detract from the great service rendered by him that a dissent is expressed from the ground upon which he placed the surrender of Mason and Slidell. It is not believed that the doctrine announced by Mr. Seward can be maintained on sound principles of International Law, while it is certainly in conflict with the practice which the United States had sought to establish from the foundation of the Government. The restoration of the envoys on any such apparently insufficient basis did not avoid the mortification of the surrender; it only deprived us of the fuller credit and advantage which we might have secured from the act. It is to be regretted that we did not place the restoration of the prisoners upon franker and truer ground, viz., that their seizure was in violation of the principles which we had steadily and resolutely maintained — principles which we would not abandon either for a temporary advantage or to save the wounding of our National pride.

The luminous speech of Mr. Sumner, when the papers in the *Trent* case were submitted to Congress, stated the ground for which the United States had always contended with admirable precision. We could not have refused to surrender Mason and Slidell without trampling upon our own principles and disregarding the many precedents we had sought to establish. But it must not be forgotten that the sword of precedent cut both ways. It was as absolutely against the peremptory demand of England for the surrender of the prisoners as it was against the United States for the seizure of them. Whatever wrong was inflicted on the British Flag by the action of Captain Wilkes, had been time and again inflicted on the American Flag by officers of the English Navy, — without cause, without redress, without apology. Hundreds and thousands of American citizens had in time of peace been taken by British cruisers from the decks of American vessels and violently impressed into the naval service of that country.

Lord Castlereagh practically confessed in Parliament that this offense against the liberty of American citizens had been repeated thirty-five hundred times. According to the records of our own department of State as Mr. Sumner alleges "the quarter-deck of a "British man-of-war had been made a floating judgment-seat six thou-"sand times and upwards, and each time some citizen or other person "was taken from the protection of our national flag without any form "of trial whatever." So insolent and oppressive had British aggression become before the war of 1812, that Mr. Jefferson in his somewhat celebrated letter to Madame de Staël-Holstein of May 24, 1813, said, "No American could safely cross the ocean or venture "to pass by sea from one to another of our own ports. *It is not long* "*since they impressed at sea two nephews of General Washington* "*returning from Europe, and put them, as common seamen, under the* "*ordinary discipline of their ships of war.*"

After the war of 1812 these unendurable insults to our flag were not repeated by Great Britain, but her Government steadily refused to make any formal renunciation of her right to repeat them, so that our immunity from like insults did not rest upon any better foundation than that which might be dictated by considerations of interest and prudence on the part of the offending Power. The wrong which Captain Wilkes committed against the British flag was surely not so great as if he had seized the persons of British subjects — subjects, if you please, who were of kindred blood to one who stands as high in the affection of the British people as Washington stands in the affection of the American people, — if indeed there be such a one in English tradition.

The offense of Captain Wilkes was surely far below that in the essential quality of outrage. He had not touched the hair of a British subject's head. He had only removed from the hospitality and shelter of a British ship four men who were bent on an errand of destruction to the American Union. His act cannot be justified by the canons of International Law as our own Government has interpreted and enforced them. But in view of the past and of the long series of graver outrages with which Great Britain had so wantonly insulted the American flag, she might have refrained from invoking the judgment of the civilized world against us, and especially might she have refrained from making in the hour of our sore trial and our deep distress, a demand which no British Minister would address to this Government in the day of its strength and its power.

It would be ungracious to withhold an expression of the lasting appreciation entertained in this country of the course pursued by Her Majesty, the Queen of England, throughout this most painful ordeal. She was wiser than her Ministers, and there can be little doubt that but for her considerate interposition, softening the rigor of the British demand, the two nations would have been forced into war. On all the subsequent occasions for bitterness towards England, by reason of the treatment we experienced during the war, there was an instinctive feeling among Americans that the Queen desired peace and good will, and did not sympathize with the insidious efforts at our destruction, which had their origin in her dominions. It was fortunate that the disposition of the Queen, and not of her Ministry, was represented in Washington by Lord Lyons. The good sense and good temper of His Lordship were of inestimable value to both countries, in making the task of Mr. Seward practicable, without increasing the resentment of our people.

———————

It was well that the Government and people of the United States were so early taught that their value to the world of foreign principles, foreign feeling, and foreign interests was only what they could themselves establish; that in this contest they must depend upon themselves; and that the dissolution of their National Unity and the destruction of their free, popular Government from the lack of courage and wisdom in those whose duty it was to maintain them, would not be unwelcome to the Principalities and Powers that " were "willing to wound, but yet afraid to strike." This is not the time to describe the vacillating and hesitating development of this hostile policy; but as the purpose of the United-States Government grew more steady, more resolute, and more self-reliant, a sickening doubt seemed to becloud the ill-concealed hope of our ruin. It was not long until the brave and deluded rebels of the South learned that there was no confidence to be placed in the cruel and selfish calculation which encouraged their desperate resistance with the show of sympathy, but would not avow an open support or make a manly sacrifice in their behalf.

This initial policy of foreign powers had developed its natural consequences. It not only excited but it warranted in the Southern Confederacy the hope of early recognition. It seemed impossible that, with this recognized equality between the belligerents, there would not occur somewhere just such incidents as the seizure of the *Trent* or the capture of the *Florida* which would render it very difficult to maintain peaceful relations between foreign Powers and the United States. The neutrality laws were complicated. Men-of-war commanded by ambitious, ardent, and patriotic officers would sometimes in the excitement of honorable feeling, sometimes in mistaken sense of duty, vindicate their country's flag; while it was the interest of the officers of the Confederate cruisers, as bold and ingenious men as ever commanded ship, to create, wherever they could, difficulties which would embarrass the interests of neutrals and intensify between the United States and foreign Powers the growing feeling of distrust. Thus from month to month the Government of the United States could never feel secure that there would not arise questions which the indignation of its own people and the pride and latent hostility of foreign governments would place beyond the power of friendly adjustment. Such questions did arise with England, France, Brazil, Spain, and even with Mexico, which the common disinclination to actual war succeeded in postponing rather than settling. But as the civil war went on, three classes of questions took continuous and precise shape. Their scope and result can be fairly and fully considered. These were —

1. The building and equipping of Confederate cruisers and their treatment as legitimate national vessels of war in the home and colonial ports of foreign powers.

2. The establishment at such ports as Nassau, in the immediate vicinity of the blockaded ports of the Southern States, of depots of supplies, which afforded to the Confederates enormous advantages in the attempt to break the blockade.

3. The distinct defiance of the traditional policy of the United States by the invasion of the neighboring Republic of Mexico for the avowed purpose of establishing there a foreign and monarchical dynasty.

No sooner had Her Britannic Majesty's proclamation, recognizing the belligerent rights of the Southern Confederacy, been issued, than a naval officer of remarkable ability and energy was sent from Montgomery to Liverpool. In his very interesting history of the services rendered by him, that officer says: " The chief object of this narrative " is to demonstrate by a plain statement of facts that the Confederate " Government, through their agents, did nothing more than all other " belligerents have heretofore done in time of need; namely, tried to " obtain from every possible source the means necessary to carry on " the war in which they were engaged, and that in so doing they took "particular pains to understand the municipal law of those countries " in which they sought to supply their wants, and were especially " careful to keep within the statutes.

.   .   .   .

" The object of the Confederate Government was not merely to build " a single ship, but it was to maintain a permanent representative of " the Navy Department abroad, and to get ships and naval supplies " without hindrance as long as the war lasted. To effect this purpose " it was manifestly necessary to act with prudence and caution and " to do nothing in violation of the municipal law, because a single " conviction would both expose the object and defeat the aim." His solicitor " therefore drew up a case for counsel's opinion and sub- " mitted it to two eminent barristers, both of whom have since filled " the highest judicial positions. The case was submitted; was a " general and not a specific proposition. It was not intimated for " what purpose or on whose behalf the opinion was asked, and the " reply was therefore wholly without bias, and embraced a full ex- " position of the Act in its bearing upon the question of building and " equipping ships in Her Majesty's dominions.

" The inferences drawn from the investigation of the Act by " counsel were put in the following form by my solicitor: —

" ' 1. It is no offense (under the Act) for British subjects to equip, " ' etc., a ship at some country *without* Her Majesty's dominions " ' though the intent be to cruise against a friendly state.

" ' 2. It is no offense for *any* person (subject or no subject) to *equip* " ' a ship *within* Her Majesty's dominions if it be *not* done with the " ' intent to cruise against a friendly state.

" ' 3. The mere building of a ship *within* Her Majesty's dominions by " ' any person (subject or no subject) is no offense, *whatever may be* " ' *the intent of the parties*, because the offense is not the *building*, " ' but the *equipping*.

" ' Therefore any ship-builder may build any ship in Her Majesty's " ' dominions, provided he does not equip her within Her Majesty's " ' dominions, and he has nothing to do with the acts of the purchasers " ' done *within* Her Majesty's dominions without his concurrence, or " ' without Her Majesty's dominions even with his concurrence.' " — [BULLOCK's *Secret Service of the Confederate States*, vol. i. pp. 65–67.]

It is an amazing courtesy which attributes to the eminent counsel a complete ignorance of the object and purpose for which their weighty opinion was sought in the construction of British law. Such ignorance is feigned and not real, and the pretense of its existence indicates either on the part of the author or the counsel a full appreciation of the deadly consequences of that malign interpretation of England's duty for which two illustrious members of the English Bar were willing to stand sponsors before the world. Conceding, as we fairly may concede, that the decision in the case of the *Alexandra* is confirmatory of the opinion given by these leaders of the British bar, the result was simply the establishment and administration of the Naval Department of the Confederacy in England. There was its chief, there were its financial agents, there its workshops. There were its vessels armed and commissioned. Thence they sailed on their mission of destruction, and thither they returned to repair their damages and to renew their supplies. Under formal contracts with the Confederate Government the colonial ports of Nassau and the Bermudas were made depots of supplies which were drawn upon with persistent and successful regularity. The effects of this thoroughly organized system of so-called neutrality that supplied ports, ships, arms, and men to a belligerent which had none, are not matters of conjecture or exaggeration; they have been proven and recorded. In three years fifteen million dollars' worth of property was destroyed, — given to the flame or sunk beneath the waters, — the shipping of the United States was reduced one-half, and the commercial flag of the Union fluttered with terror in every wind that blew, from the whale-fisheries of the Arctic to the Southern Cross.

With this condition of affairs, permitted and encouraged by England and France, our distinguished minister at Paris was justified in saying to the Government of Louis Napoleon on the reception of the

Confederate steamer *Georgia* at Brest, in language which though but the bare recital of fact was of itself the keenest reproach to the French Government: —

"The *Georgia*, like the *Florida*, the *Alabama*, and other scourges "of peaceful commerce, was born of that unhappy decree which gave "the rebels who did not own a ship-of-war or command a single port "the right of an ocean belligerent. Thus encouraged by foreign "powers they began to build and fit out in neutral ports a class of "vessels constructed mainly for speed, and whose acknowledged mis-"sion is not to fight, but to rob, to burn, and to fly. Although "the smoke of burning ships has everywhere marked the track of the "*Georgia* and the *Florida* upon the ocean, they have never sought a "foe or fired a gun against an armed enemy. To dignify such vessels "with the name of ships-of-war seems to me, with deference, a mis-"nomer. Whatever flag may fly from their mast-head, or whatever "power may claim to own them, their conduct stamps them as pirati-"cal. If vessels of war even, they would by this conduct have justly "forfeited all courtesies in the ports of neutral nations. Manned by "foreign seamen, armed by foreign guns, entering no home port, and "waiting no judicial condemnation of prizes, they have already "devastated and destroyed our commerce to an extent, as compared "with their number, beyond any thing known in the records of "privateering."

It would seem impossible that such a state of things could be the result of the impartial administration of an honest neutrality. It must be attributed to one of two causes; — either the municipal law of foreign countries was not sufficient to enable the governments to control the selfishness or the sentiment of their people, — to which the reply is obvious that the weakness and incompetence of munici-pal law cannot diminish or excuse international obligations: or it must have been due to a misconception of the obligations which international law imposes. How far there may have been a motive for this misconception, how far the wish was father to the thought of such misconstruction, it is perhaps needless now to inquire. The theory of international law maintained by the foreign Powers may be fairly stated in two propositions: —

1. That foreign Powers had the right, and in due regard to their own interests were bound, to recognize belligerency as a fact.

2. That belligerents once recognized, were equals and must be treated with the same perfect neutrality.

It is not necessary to deny these propositions, but simply to ascertain their real meaning. In its primary and simple application, the law of belligerency referred to two or more belligerents, equally independent. Its application to the case of insurgents against an established and recognized government is later, involves other and in some respects different considerations, and cannot even now be regarded as settled. To recognize an insurgent as a belligerent is not to recognize him as fully the equal of the government from which he secedes. This would be simply to recognize his independence. The limitation which international law places upon this recognition is stated in the English phrase, "the right to recognize belligerency "as a fact;" — that is, to recognize the belligerent to the extent of his war capacity but no farther. The neutral cannot on this principle recognize in the belligerent the possession of any power which he does not actually possess, although in the progress of the contest such power may be developed.

The Southern Confederacy had an organized government and great armies. To that extent its power was a fact. But when foreign governments recognized in the insurgents the rights of ocean belligerency, they went beyond the fact. They were actually giving to the Confederacy a character which it did not possess and which it never acquired. For the Confederacy had not a ship or an open port. Whenever an insurgent power claims such right, it must be in condition to assume and discharge the obligation which such rights impose. When any power, insurgent or recognized, claims such right, — the right to fly its flag, to deal in hostility with the commerce of the world, to exercise dangerous privileges which may affect the interests and complicate the relations of other nations, — it must give to the world a guaranty that it is both able and willing to administer the system of maritime law under which it claims such rights and powers, by submitting its action to the regular and formal jurisdiction of Prize Courts. Strike the Prize Court out of modern maritime law and the whole system falls, and capture on the sea becomes pure barbarism, — distinguished from piracy only by the astuteness of a legal technicality. The Southern Confederacy could give no such guaranty. Just as it undertook to naturalize foreign seamen upon the quarter-deck of its roving cruisers, so it undertook to administer a system of maritime law which precluded the most solemn and important of its provisions — a judicial decision — and converted the humane and legal right of capture into an absolute and a ruthless decree of destruction. No neutral has the right to make or accept such an interpolation into the recognized and essential principles of the law of maritime warfare.

The application of this so-called neutrality to both the so-called belligerents was not designed nor was it practicable. In referring to the obligation of the neutral to furnish no assistance to either of the belligerents, one of the oldest and most authoritative of international law writers says: "I do not say to give assistance equally "but to give no assistance, for it would be absurd that a state "should assist at the same time two enemies. And besides it would "be impossible to do it with equality: the same things, the like "number of troops, the like quantity of arms and munitions fur-"nished under different circumstances are no longer equivalent "succors." Assistance is not a theoretical idea; it is a plain, practical, unmistakable fact. When the United States had, at vast cost and by incredible effort, shut the Southern Confederacy from the sea and blockaded its ports against the entry of supplies, when that government had no resources within its territory by which it could put a ship upon the ocean, or break the blockade from within, then it was that England allowed Confederate officers to camp upon her soil, organize her labor, employ her machinery, use her ports, occupy her colonial stations, almost within sight of the blockaded coast, and to do this continuously, systematically, defiantly.

By these acts the British Government gave the most valuable assistance to the South and actually engaged in defeating the military operations of the United States. There was no equivalent assistance which Great Britain could or did render to the United States. They might have rendered other assistance, but none which would compensate for this. Let it be supposed for one moment that Mexico had practiced, on the other side of the Rio Grande, the same sort of neutrality, — that she had lined her bank of the river with depots of military supplies; that she had allowed officers of the Confederate army to establish themselves and organize a complete system for the receipt of cotton and the delivery of merchandise on her territory; that her people had served as factors, intermediaries, and carriers, — would any reasonable interpretation of international law consider such conduct to be impartial neutrality? But illustration does not strengthen the argument. The naked statement of England's position is its worst condemnation. Her course, while ingeniously avoiding public responsibility, gave unceasing help to the Confederacy — as effective as if the intention had been proclaimed. The whole procedure was in disregard of international obligation and was the outgrowth of what M. Prévost-Paradol aptly characterized as a "malignant neutrality."

It cannot be said in reply that the Governments of England and France were unable to restrain this demonstration of the sympathy, this exercise of the commercial enterprise of their people. For the time came when they did restrain it. As soon as it became evident that the Confederacy was growing weaker, that with all its marvelous display of courage and endurance it could not prevent the final success of the Union, there was no longer difficulty in arresting the building of iron-clads on the Mersey; then the watchfulness of home and colonial authorities was quickened; then supplies were meted out scantily; then the dangers of a great slave empire began to impress Ministerial consciences, and the same Powers prepared to greet the triumph of the Union with well-feigned satisfaction. But even if this change had not occurred the condition of repressed hostility could not have lasted. It was war in disguise — not declared, only because the United-States Government could not afford to multiply its enemies, and England felt that there was still uncertainty enough in the result to caution her against assuming so great a risk. But the tension of the relation was aptly described by Mr. Seward in July, 1863, when he said, —

"If the law of Great Britain must be left without amendment
"and be construed by the government in conformity with the rulings
"of the chief Baron of the Exchequer [the *Alexandra* case] then
"there will be left for the United States no alternative but to protect
"themselves and their commerce against armed cruisers proceeding
"from British ports as against the naval forces of a public enemy.
". . . British ports, domestic as well as colonial, are now open under
"certain restrictions to the visits of piratical vessels, and not only
"furnish them coals, provisions, and repairs, but even receive their
"prisoners when the enemies of the United States come in to obtain
"such relief from voyages in which they have either burned ships they
"have captured, or have even manned and armed them as pirates
"and sent them abroad as auxiliaries in the work of destruction.
"Can it be an occasion for either surprise or complaint that if this
"condition of things is to remain and receive the deliberate sanction
"of the British Government, the navy of the United States will

"receive instructions to pursue these enemies into the ports which
"thus in violation of the law of nations and the obligations of
"neutrality become harbors for the pirates? The President very
"distinctly perceives the risks and hazards which a naval conflict
"thus maintained will bring to the commerce and even to the peace
"of the two countries. But he is obliged to consider that in the
"case supposed, the destruction of our commerce will probably
"amount to a naval war, waged by a portion at least of the British
"nation against the government and people of the United States—
"a war tolerated although not declared or avowed by the British
"Government. If through the necessary employment of all our
"means of national defense such a partial war shall become a general
"one between the two nations, the President thinks that the respon-
"sibility for that painful result will not fall upon the United States."

The truth is that the so-called neutral policy of foreign Powers
was the vicious application of obsolete analogies to the conditions
of modern life. Because the doctrine of belligerent recognition had
in its origin referred to nations of well established, independent
existence, the doctrine was now pushed forward to the extent of
giving ocean belligerency to an insurgent which had in reality no
maritime power whatever. It was an old and recognized principle
that the commercial relations of the neutral should not be interfered
with unless they worked positive injury to the belligerent. The
new application made the interests of neutral commerce the supreme
factor in determining how far belligerent rights should be respected.
The ship-building and the carrying-trade of England were to be
maintained and encouraged at any cost to the belligerent. Under
the old law, a belligerent had the right to purchase a ship and a
cargo, or a neutral might run a blockade, taking all the risk of
capture. By the new construction, power was to be given to a
belligerent to supplement its territory by the annexation of foreign
ports, to transfer the entire administration of its naval service to
foreign soil, and to create and equip a navy which issued from
foreign waters, ready not for a dangerous journey to their own
ports of delivery, but for the immediate demonstration of hostile
purpose. No such absurd system can be found in the principles or
precedents of international law; no such system would be permitted

by the great powers of Europe if to-morrow they should engage in war.

The principle of this policy was essentially mercenary. It professed no moral sense. It might be perfectly indifferent to the high or the low issues which the contest between the belligerents involved; it was deaf to any thing which might be urged by justice or humanity or friendship; it was the cynical recognition of the truth of the old proverb that "It is an ill wind which blows good to no "one." It was the same principle upon which England declares with audacious selfishness that she cannot sacrifice that portion of her Indian revenue which comes from the opium trade or the capital which is invested in its growth and manufacture, and that China must therefore take the poison which diseases and degrades her population. But selfish as is this market-policy, it is a policy of circumstance. It may be resisted with success or it may be abandoned because it cannot succeed. It creates bitterness; it leads to war; it may in its selfishness cause the destruction of a nation, but it does not necessarily imply a desire for that destruction. But there was in the foreign policy of Europe towards the United States during the civil war the manifestation of a spirit more intense in its hostility, more dangerous in its consequences. It was the spirit of enmity to the Union itself, and the emphatic demonstration of this feeling was the invasion of Mexico for the purpose of converting that republic by force into an empire. Louis Napoleon's enterprise was distinctly based on the utter destruction of the American Union.

The Declaration of Independence by the British Colonies in America was something more than the creation of a new sovereignty. It was the foundation of a new system both of internal government and foreign relation, a system not entirely isolated from the affairs of the Old World but independent of the dynastic complications and the territorial interests which controlled the political conflicts of Europe. At first, with its material resources undeveloped, its territorial extension limited and surrounded by the colonies of the great Powers, this principle although maintained as a conviction, could not manifest itself in action. But it showed itself in that abstinence from entangling alliances which would avoid the dangers of even a too friendly connection. In time our territory expanded. The colonies of foreign nations following our example became independent republics whose people had tne same aspirations, whose governments were framed upon the same basis of popular right. The rapidity of communicatio.1, supplied by the railroad and the telegraph, facilitated and concentrated this political cohesion, and there had been formed from the borders of Canada to the Straits of Magellan a complete system of republics (to which Brazil can scarcely be considered an exception) professing the same political creed, having great commercial interests in common, and which with the extinction of some few jealousies, were justified in the anticipation of a prosperous and peaceful future. There was not an interest or an ambition of a single one of these republics which threatened an interest or an ambition of a single European power.

It needs no argument to show that the central element of the stability of this system of American republics was the strength of the Federal Union, its growth into a harmonious nationality, and its ability to prevent anywhere on the two continents the armed intervention of foreign Powers for the purpose of political domination. This strength was known and this resolution publicly declared, and it is safe to affirm that before 1861 or after 1865 not one nor all of the European Powers would have willingly challenged this policy. But the moment the strength of the Union seemed weakened, the moment that the leading Republic of this system found itself hampered and embarrassed by internal dissensions, all Europe — that Europe which upon the threatening of a Belgian fortress, or the invasion of a Swiss canton, or the loss of the key to a church in Jerusalem, would have written protocols, summoned conferences, and mustered armies — quietly acquiesced in as wanton, wicked, and foolish an aggression as ever Imperial folly devised. The same monarch who appealed with confidence to Heaven when he declared war to prevent a Hohenzollern from ascending the throne of Spain, appealed to the same Heaven with equal confidence and equal success when he declared war to force a Hapsburg upon the throne of Mexico.

The success of the establishment of a Foreign Empire in Mexico would have been fatal to all that the United States cherished, to all that it hoped peacefully to achieve. The scheme of invasion rested on the assumption of the dissolution of the Union and its division into two hostile governments; but aside from that possibility, it threatened the United States upon the most vital questions. It was at war with all our institutions and our habits of political life, for it would have introduced into a great country on this continent, capable of unlimited development, that curious and mischievous form of government, that perplexing mixture of absolutism and democracy, — imperial power supported by universal suffrage, — which seems certain to produce aggression abroad and corruption at home, and which must have injuriously influenced the political growth of the Spanish-American Republics.   Firmly seated in Mexico, it would have spread through Central America to the Isthmus, controlling all canal communications between the two oceans which were the boundaries of the Union, while its growth upon the Pacific Coast would have been in direct rivalry with the natural and increasing power of the United States.   Commanding the Gulf of Mexico it would have controlled the whole commerce of the West-Indian Islands and radically changed their future.   Bound by dynastic connection, checked and directed by European influence, it could not have developed a national policy in harmony with neighboring States, but its existence and its necessary efforts at expansion would have made it not only a constant menace to American Republics but a source of endless war and confusion between the great Powers of the world.   The policy signally failed.   But surely European statesmen, without miraculous foresight, might have anticipated that its success would have been more dangerous than its defeat, and that the conservative strength of the Union might be even to them an influence of good and not of evil.

In 1859 Lord Palmerston wrote to Lord John Russell: "It is plain "that France aims through Spain at getting fortified points on each "side of the Gut of Gibraltar which in the event of war between "Spain and France on the one hand and England on the other "would by a cross fire render that strait very difficult and dangerous "to pass and thus virtually shut us out of the Mediterranean. . . . "The French Minister of War or of Marine said the other day that "Algeria never would be safe till France possessed a port on the "Atlantic coast of Africa.   Against whom would such a port make "Algeria safe?   Evidently only against England, and how could such "a port help France against England?   Only by tending to shut us "out of the Mediterranean."   Later in the same year writing to the same colleague, he says, "Till lately I had strong confidence in the "fair intentions of Napoleon towards England, but of late I have "begun to feel great distrust and to suspect that his formerly de- "clared intention of avenging Waterloo has only lain dormant and "has not died away.   He seems to have thought that he ought to lay "his foundation by beating with our aid or with our concurrence or

"our neutrality, first Russia, then Austria, and by dealing with them
"generously to make them his friends in any subsequent quarrel
"with us. . . . Next he has been assiduously laboring to increase his
"naval means, evidently for offensive as well as for defensive pur-
"poses, and latterly great pains have been taken to raise throughout
"France and especially among the army and navy, hatred of Eng-
"land and a disparaging feeling of our military and naval means."

Is it not strange that, even with such apprehensions, the destruction of the Union was so welcome in England that it blinded the
eyes of her statesmen and her people? They should surely have
seen that the establishment of a Latin Empire under the protection
of France, in the heart of the Spanish-American Republics, would
open a field far more dangerous to British interests than a combination for a French port in Africa, and that in pursuing his policy the
wily Emperor was providing a throne for an Austrian archduke as
a compensation for the loss of Lombardy. There was a time when
Lord Palmerston himself held broader and juster views of what
ought to be the relations between England and the United States.
In 1848 he suggested to Lord John Russell a policy which looked to
a complete unification of the interests of the two countries: "If as I
"hope," said His Lordship, "we shall succeed in altering our Naviga-
"tion Laws, and if as a consequence Great Britain and the United
"States shall place their commercial marines upon a footing of
"mutual equality with the exception of the coasting-trade and some
"other special matters, might not such an arrangement afford us a
"good opportunity for endeavoring to carry in some degree into
"execution the wish which Mr. Fox entertained in 1783, when he
"wished to substitute close alliance in the place of sovereignty and
"dependence as the connecting link between the United States and
"Great Britain? A treaty for mutual defense would no longer be
"applicable to the condition of the two countries as independent
"Powers, but might they not with mutual advantage conclude a
"treaty containing something like the following conditions: —
"1. That in all cases of difference which may hereafter unfor-
"tunately arise between the contracting parties, they will in the
"first place have recourse to the mediation of some friendly Power,
"and that hostilities shall not begin between them until every
"endeavor to settle their difference by such means shall have
"proved fruitless.
"2. That if either of the two should at any time be at war with

"any other Power, no subject or citizen of the other contracting
"party shall be allowed to take out letters of marque from such
"Power under pain of being treated and dealt with as a pirate.
"3. That in such case of war between either of the two parties
"and a third Power, no subject or citizen of the other contracting
"party shall be allowed to enter into the service naval or military of
"such third Power.
"4. That in such case of war as aforesaid, neither of the con-
"tracting parties shall afford assistance to the enemies of the other
"by sea or by land, unless war should break out between the two
"contracting parties themselves after the failure of all endeavors to
"settle their differences in the manner specified in Article 1."

At the time Lord Palmerston expressed these opinions, we had
just closed the Mexican war, with vast acquisition of territory and
with a display of military power on distant fields of conquest which
surprised European statesmen. Our maritime interests were almost
equal to those of the United Kingdom, our prosperity was great, the
prestige of the Nation was growing. In the thirteen intervening
years between that date and the outbreak of the Southern Rebellion
we had grown enormously in wealth, our Pacific possessions had
shown an extraordinary production of precious metals, our population had increased more than ten millions. If an alliance with
the United States was desirable for England in 1848, it was far
more desirable in 1861, and Lord Palmerston being Prime Minister
in the latter year, his power to propose and promote it was far
greater. Is there any reason that will satisfactorily account for His
Lordship's abandonment of this ideal relation of friendship between
the two countries except that he saw a speedier way of adding to
the power of England by conniving at the destruction of the Union?
His change from the policy which he painted in 1848 to that which
he acted in 1861 cannot be satisfactorily explained upon any other
hypothesis than that he could not resist the temptation to cripple
and humiliate the Great Republic.

This brief history of the spirit rather than the events which
characterized the foreign relations of the United States during the
civil war, has been undertaken with no desire to revive the feelings
of burning indignation which they provoked, or to prolong the dis-

cussion of the angry questions to which they gave rise. The relations of nations are not and should not be governed by sentiment. The interest and ambition of states, like those of men, will disturb the moral sense and incline to one side or the other the strict balance of impartial justice. New days bring new issues and old passions are unsafe counselors. Twenty years have gone by. England has paid the cost of her mistake. The Republic of Mexico has seen the fame and the fortunes of the Emperors who sought her conquest sink suddenly — as into the pits which they themselves had digged for their victims — and the Republic of the United States has come out of her long and bitter struggle, so strong that never again will she afford the temptation or the opportunity for unfriendly governments to strike at her National life. Let the past be the past, but let it be the past with all the instruction and the warning of its experience.

The future safety of these continents rests upon the strength and maintenance of the Union, for had dissolution been possible, events have shown with what small regard the interests or the honor of either of the belligerents would have been treated. It has been taught to the smaller republics that if this strength be shattered they will be the spoil of foreign arms and the dependent provinces again of foreign monarchs. When this contest was over, the day of immaturity had passed and the United States stood before the world a great and permanent Power. That Power can afford to bury all resentments. Tranquil at home, developing its inexhaustible resources with a rapidity and success unknown in history, bound in sincere friendship, and beyond the possibility of hostile rivalry, with the other republics of the continents, standing midway between Asia and Europe, a Power on the Pacific as well as on the Atlantic, with no temptation to intermeddle in the questions which disturb the Old World, the Republic of the United States desires to live in amicable relation with all peoples, demanding only the abstinence of foreign

---

NOTE. — In the foregoing chapter the term "piratical" is used without qualification in referring to the Southern cruisers, because it is the word used in the quotations made. It undoubtedly represented the feeling of the country at that time, but in an impartial discussion of the events of the war the word cannot be used with propriety. Our own Courts have found themselves unable to sustain such a conclusion. Looking to the future it is better to rest our objections to the mode of maritime warfare adopted by the Confederacy upon a sound and enduring principle; viz., that the recognition of ocean belligerency, when the belligerent cannot give to his lawful exercise of maritime warfare the guaranty of a prize jurisdiction, is a violation of any just or reasonable system of international law. The Confederacy had the plea of necessity for its course, but the justification of England for aiding and abetting the practice has not yet been presented.

intervention in the development of that policy which her political creed, her territorial extent, and the close and cordial neighborhood of kindred governments have made the essential rule of her National life.

Note. — Her Britannic Majesty's principal ministers of state in 1861-2, — at the time of the correspondence touching the *Trent* affair, referred to in the preceding chapter, — were as follows: —

Premier — Lord Palmerston.
Lord High Chancellor — Lord Westbury.
Lord President of the Council — Earl Granville.
Lord Privy Seal — The Duke of Argyll.
Secretary for Foreign Affairs — Lord John Russell.
Secretary for the Colonies — The Duke of Newcastle.
Secretary for the Home Department — Sir George Grey.
Secretary of State for War — Sir G. C. Lewis.
Secretary of State for India — Sir Charles Wood.
Chancellor of the Exchequer — Rt. Honorable W. E. Gladstone.
Secretary for Ireland — Rt. Honorable Edward Cardwell.
Postmaster-General — Lord Stanley of Alderney.
President Board of Trade — Rt. Honorable Charles Pelham Villiers.

The same Ministry, with unimportant changes, continued in power throughout the whole period of the Rebellion in the United States.

ADDENDUM.

THE Tenth chapter of this volume having been given to the press in advance of formal publication, many inquiries have been received in regard to the text of Judge Black's opinion of November 20, 1860, referred to on pp. 231, 232. The opinion was submitted to the President by Judge Black as Attorney-General. So much of the opinion as includes the points which are specially controverted and criticised is here given — about one-half of the entire document. It is as follows : —

. . . "I come now to the point in your letter which is probably of the greatest practical importance. By the Act of 1807 you may employ such parts of the land and naval forces as you may judge necessary for the purpose of causing the laws to be duly executed, in all cases where it is lawful to use the militia for the same purpose. By the Act of 1795 the militia may be called forth 'whenever the laws of the United States shall be opposed, or the execution thereof obstructed, in any State by combinations too powerful to be suppressed by the ordinary course of Judicial proceedings, or by the power vested in the marshals.' This imposes upon the President the sole responsibility of deciding whether the exigency has arisen which requires the use of military force, and in proportion to the magnitude of that responsibility will be his care not to overstep the limits of his legal and just authority.

"The laws referred to in the Act of 1795 are manifestly those which are administered by the judges, and executed by the ministerial officers of the courts for the punishment of crime against the United States, for the protection of rights claimed under the Federal Constitution and laws, and for the enforcement of such obligations as come within the cognizance of the Federal Judiciary. To compel obedience to these laws, the courts have authority to punish all who obstruct their regular administration, and the marshals and their deputies have the same powers as sheriffs and their deputies in the several States in executing the laws of the States. These are the ordinary means provided for the execution of the laws ; and the whole spirit of our system is opposed to the employment of any other, except in cases of extreme necessity arising out of great and unusual combinations against them. Their agency must continue to be used until their incapacity to cope with the power opposed to them shall be plainly demonstrated. It is only upon clear evidence to that effect that a military force can be called into the field. Even then its operations must be purely defensive. It can suppress only such combinations as are found directly opposing the laws and obstructing the execution thereof. It can do no more than what might and ought to be done by a civil posse, if a civil posse could be raised large enough to meet the same opposition. On such occasions, especially, the military power must be kept in strict subordination to the civil authority, since it is only in aid of the latter that the former can act at all.

"But what if the feeling in any State against the United States should become so universal that the Federal officers themselves (including judges, district attorneys, and marshals) would be reached by the same influences, and resign their places ? Of course, the first step would be to appoint others in their stead, if others could be got to serve. But in such an event, it is more than probable that great difficulty would be found in filling the offices. We can easily conceive how it might become altogether impossible. We are therefore obliged to consider what can be done in case we have no courts to issue judicial process, and no ministerial officers to execute it. In that event troops would certainly be out of place, and their use wholly illegal. If they are sent to aid the courts and marshals, there must be courts and marshals to be aided. Without the exercise of those functions which belong exclusively to the civil service, the laws cannot be executed in any event, no matter what may be the physical strength which the Government has at its command. Under such circumstances, to send a military force into any State, with orders to act against the people, would be simply making war upon them.

"The existing laws put and keep the Federal Government strictly on the defensive. You can use force only to repel an assault on the public property and aid the Courts in the performance of their duty. If the means given you to collect the revenue and execute the other laws be insufficient for that purpose, Congress may extend and make them more effectual to those ends.

"If one of the States should declare her independence, your action cannot depend upon the rightfulness of the cause upon which such declaration is based. Whether the retirement of the State from the Union be the exercise of a right reserved in the Constitution, or a revolutionary movement, it is certain that you have not in either case the authority to recognize her independence or to absolve her from her Federal obligations. Congress, or the other States in Convention assembled, must take such measures as may be necessary and proper. In such an event, I see no course for you but to go straight onward in the path you have hitherto trodden — that is, execute the laws to the extent of the defensive means placed in your hands, and act generally upon the assumption that the present constitutional relations between the States and the Federal Government continue to exist, until a new code of things shall be established either by law or force.

"Whether Congress has the constitutional right to make war against one or more States, and require the Executive of the Federal Government to carry it on by means of force to be drawn from the other States, is a question for Congress itself to consider. It must be admitted that no such power is expressly given ; nor are there any words in the Constitution which imply it. Among the powers enumerated in Article 1, Section 8, is that 'to declare war, grant letters of marque and reprisal, and to make rules concerning captures on land and water.' This certainly means nothing more than the power to commence and carry on hostilities against the foreign enemies of the nation. Another clause in the same section gives Congress the power 'to provide for calling forth the militia,' and to use them within the limits of the State. But this power is so restricted by the words which immediately follow that it can be exercised only for one of the following purposes : 1. To execute the laws of the Union ; that is, to aid the Federal officers in the performance of their regular duties. 2. To suppress insurrections against the State ; but this is confined by Article 4, Section 4, to cases in which the State herself shall apply for assistance against her own people. 3. To repel the invasion of a State by enemies who come from abroad to assail her in her own territory. All these provisions are made to protect the States, not to authorize an attack by one part of the country upon another ; to preserve the peace, and not to plunge them into civil war. Our forefathers do not seem to have thought that war was calculated 'to form a more perfect Union, establish justice, insure domestic tranquillity, provide for the common defense, promote the general welfare, and secure the blessings of liberty to ourselves and our posterity.' There was undoubtedly a strong and universal conviction among the men who framed and ratified the Constitution, that military force would not only be useless, but pernicious, as a means of holding the States together.

"If it be true that war cannot be declared, nor a system of general hostilities carried on by the Central Government against a State, then it seems to follow that an attempt to do so would be *ipso facto* an expulsion of such State from the Union. Being treated as an alien and an enemy, she would be compelled to act accordingly. And if Congress shall break up the present Union by unconstitutionally putting strife and enmity and armed hostility between different sections of the country, instead of the domestic tranquillity which the Constitution was meant to insure, will not all the States be absolved from their Federal obligations? Is any portion of the people bound to contribute their money or their blood to carry on a contest like that?

"The right of the General Government to preserve itself in its whole constitutional vigor by repelling a direct and positive aggression upon its property or its officers cannot be denied. But this is a totally different thing from an offensive war to punish the people for the political misdeeds of their State Government, or to enforce an acknowledgment that the Government of the United States is supreme. The States are colleagues of one another, and if some of them shall conquer the rest, and hold them as subjugated provinces, it would totally destroy the whole theory upon which they are now connected.

"If this view of the subject be correct, as I think it is, then the Union must utterly perish at the moment when Congress shall arm one part of the people against another for any purpose beyond that of merely protecting the General Government in the exercise of its proper constitutional functions.

"I am, very respectfully, yours, etc.,

"J. S. BLACK."

ERRATUM.

IN Chapter VIII. there is some inaccuracy in regard to the number of killed in the John Brown raid at Harper's Ferry. According to the official report of Colonel Robert E. Lee, U.S.A., who commanded the military force that relieved Harper's Ferry, the insurgents numbered in all nineteen men, — fourteen white, five colored. Of the white men, ten were killed; two, John Brown and Aaron C. Stevens, were badly wounded; Edwin Coppee, unhurt, was taken prisoner; John E. Cooke escaped. Of the colored men, two were killed, two taken prisoners, one unaccounted for.

THE APPENDICES.

THE progress of the country, referred to so frequently in the text, is strikingly illustrated and verified by the facts contained in the several appendices which follow.

The appendices include a variety of subjects, and they have all been selected with the view of showing the progress and development of the Nation in the different fields of enterprise and human labor.

The tabular statements as to the population and wealth of the country will be found especially accurate and valuable. The statistics relating to Education and the Public Schools, to Agriculture, to Railways, to Immigration, to the Army, to Shipping, to the Coal and Iron Product, to National and State Banks, to the Circulation of Paper Money, to the price of Gold, and to the Public Debt, will be found full of interest.

Thanks are due and are cordially given to Mr. Joseph Nimmo, Jr., Chief of the Bureau of Statistics, and to Mr. Charles W. Seaton, Superintendent of the Census, for valuable aid rendered in the preparation of the appendices.

For courtesies constantly extended, and for most intelligent and discriminating aid of various kinds, the sincerest acknowledgments are made to Mr. Ainsworth R. Spofford, the accomplished Librarian of Congress.

APPENDIX A.

POPULATION OF THE UNITED STATES AT EACH CENSUS, FROM 1790 TO 1880 INCLUSIVE.

[From the Reports of the Superintendents of the Census.]

States and Territories.	1790.	1800.	1810.	1820.	1830.	1840.	1850.	1860.	1870.	1880.	States and Territories.
Alabama				127,901	309,527	590,756	771,623	964,201	996,992	1,262,505	Alabama.
Arkansas				*18	30,388	97,574	209,897	435,450	484,471	802,525	Arkansas.
California				14,255			92,597	379,994	560,247	864,694	California.
Colorado								34,277	39,864	194,327	Colorado.
Connecticut	237,946	251,002	261,942	*100 } 275,148	297,675	309,978	370,792	460,147	537,454	622,700	Connecticut.
Delaware	59,096	64,273	72,674	72,749	76,748	78,085	91,532	112,216	125,015	146,608	Delaware.
Florida					34,730	54,477	87,445	140,424	187,748	269,493	Florida.
Georgia	82,548	162,686	252,433	340,985	516,823	691,392	906,185	1,057,286	1,184,109	1,542,180	Georgia.
Illinois			12,282	55,162	157,445	476,183	851,470	1,711,951	2,539,891	3,077,871	Illinois.
Indiana		5,641	24,520	147,178	343,031	685,866	988,416	1,350,428	1,680,637	1,978,301	Indiana.
Iowa						43,112	192,214	674,913	1,194,020	1,624,615	Iowa.
Kansas				*182				107,206	364,399	996,096	Kansas.
Kentucky	73,677	220,955	406,511	564,135	687,917	779,828	982,405	1,155,684	1,321,011	1,648,690	Kentucky.
Louisiana			76,556	*484 } 152,923	215,739	352,411	517,762	708,002	726,915	939,946	Louisiana.
Maine	96,540	151,719	228,705	*66 } 298,269	399,455	501,793	583,169	628,279	626,915	648,936	Maine.
Maryland	319,728	341,548	380,546	407,350	447,040	470,019	583,034	687,049	780,894	934,943	Maryland.
Massachusetts	378,787	422,845	472,040	*128 } 523,159	610,408	737,699	994,514	1,231,066	1,457,351	1,783,085	Massachusetts.
Michigan			4,762	*131 } 8,765	31,639	212,267	397,654	749,113	1,184,059	1,636,937	Michigan.
Minnesota							6,077	172,023	439,706	780,773	Minnesota.
Mississippi		8,850	40,352	75,448	136,621	375,651	606,526	791,305	827,922	1,131,597	Mississippi.
Missouri			20,845	*29 } 66,557	140,455	383,702	682,044	1,182,012	1,721,295	2,168,380	Missouri.
Nebraska								28,841	122,993	452,402	Nebraska.
Nevada								6,857	42,491	62,266	Nevada.
New Hampshire	141,885	183,858	214,460	*139 } 244,022	269,328	284,574	317,976	326,073	318,300	346,991	New Hampshire.

	1	2	3	4	5	6	7	8	9	10	
New Jersey	1,131,116	906,096	672,035	489,555	373,306	320,823	*149 / 277,426	245,562	211,149	184,139	New Jersey.
New York	5,082,871	4,382,759	3,880,735	3,097,394	2,428,921	1,918,608	*701 / 1,372,111	959,049	589,051	340,120	New York.
North Carolina	1,399,750	1,071,361	992,622	869,039	753,419	737,987	638,829	555,500	478,103	393,751	North Carolina.
Ohio	3,198,062	2,665,260	2,339,511	1,980,329	1,519,467	937,903	*139 / 581,295	230,760	45,365	. . . .	Ohio.
Oregon	174,768	90,923	52,465	13,294	. . . .	. . . .	. . . .	. . . .	. . . .	. . . .	Oregon.
Pennsylvania	4,282,891	3,521,951	2,906,215	2,311,786	1,724,033	1,348,233	*1,951 / 1,047,507	810,091	602,365	434,373	Pennsylvania.
Rhode Island	276,531	217,353	174,620	147,545	108,830	97,199	*44 / 83,015	76,931	69,122	68,825	Rhode Island.
South Carolina	995,577	705,606	703,708	668,507	594,398	581,185	502,741	415,115	345,591	249,073	South Carolina.
Tennessee	1,542,359	1,258,520	1,109,801	1,002,717	829,210	681,904	*52 / 422,771	261,727	105,602	85,691	Tennessee.
Texas	1,591,749	818,579	604,215	212,592	. . . .	. . . .	. . . .	. . . .	. . . .	. . . .	Texas.
Vermont	332,286	330,551	315,098	314,120	291,948	280,652	*15 / 235,966	217,895	154,465	85,425	Vermont.
Virginia	1,512,565	1,225,163	1,596,318	1,421,661	1,239,797	1,211,405	*250 / 1,065,116	974,600	880,200	747,610	Virginia.
West Virginia	618,457	442,014	. . . .	. . . .	. . . .	. . . .	. . . .	. . . .	. . . .	. . . .	West Virginia.
Wisconsin	1,315,497	1,054,670	775,881	305,391	30,945	. . . .	. . . .	. . . .	. . . .	. . . .	Wisconsin.
Total, States	49,371,340	38,115,641	31,183,744	23,067,262	17,019,641	12,820,868	*4,631 / 9,600,783	7,215,858	5,294,390	. . . .	Total, States.
Arizona	40,440	9,658	. . . .	. . . .	. . . .	. . . .	. . . .	. . . .	. . . .	. . . .	Arizona.
Dakota	135,177	14,181	4,837	. . . .	. . . .	. . . .	. . . .	. . . .	. . . .	. . . .	Dakota.
District of Columbia	177,624	131,700	75,080	51,687	43,712	39,834	33,039	24,023	14,093	. . . .	Dist. of Columbia.
Idaho	32,610	14,999	. . . .	. . . .	. . . .	. . . .	. . . .	. . . .	. . . .	. . . .	Idaho.
Montana	39,159	20,595	. . . .	. . . .	. . . .	. . . .	. . . .	. . . .	. . . .	. . . .	Montana.
New Mexico	119,565	91,874	93,516	61,547	. . . .	. . . .	. . . .	. . . .	. . . .	. . . .	New Mexico.
Utah	143,963	86,786	40,273	11,380	. . . .	. . . .	. . . .	. . . .	. . . .	. . . .	Utah.
Washington	75,116	23,955	11,594	. . . .	. . . .	. . . .	. . . .	. . . .	. . . .	. . . .	Washington.
Wyoming	20,789	9,118	. . . .	. . . .	. . . .	. . . .	. . . .	. . . .	. . . .	. . . .	Wyoming.
Total, Territories	784,443	442,730	259,577	124,614	43,712	39,834	33,039	24,023	14,093	. . . .	Total, Territories.
On the public ships	. . . .	. . . .	. . . .	. . . .	6,100	5,318	. . . .	. . . .	. . . .	. . . .	On the public ships.
In U.S. Service	. . . .	. . . .	. . . .	. . . .	. . . .	. . . .	*4,631	. . . .	. . . .	. . . .	In U.S. Service.
Total, U.S.	50,155,783	38,558,371	31,443,321	23,191,876	17,069,463	12,866,020	9,638,822	7,239,881	5,308,483	3,929,214	Total, U.S.

* All other persons, except Indians, not taxed.

APPENDIX B.

APPORTIONMENT AMONG THE STATES OF REPRESENTATIVES IN CONGRESS AFTER EACH CENSUS.

STATES.	Admitted to the Union.	By Constitution, 1789.	By 1st Census, 1790.	By 2d Census, 1800.	By 3d Census, 1810.	By 4th Census, 1820.
RATIO OF REPRESENTATION	..	30,000.	33,000.	33,000.	35,000.	40,000.
Alabama	1819	..	..	..	..	3
Arkansas	1836	..	..	..	..	..
California	1850	..	..	..	..	..
Colorado	1876	..	..	..	..	..
Connecticut	—	5	7	7	7	6
Delaware	—	1	1	1	2	1
Florida	1845	..	..	..	..	..
Georgia	—	3	2	4	6	7
Illinois	1818	..	..	..	..	1
Indiana	1816	..	..	..	..	3
Iowa	1846	..	..	..	..	..
Kansas	1861	..	..	..	..	..
Kentucky	1792	..	2	6	10	12
Louisiana	1812	..	..	..	..	3
Maine	1820	..	..	..	..	7
Maryland	—	6	8	9	9	9
Massachusetts	—	8	14	17	20	13
Michigan	1837	..	..	..	..	..
Minnesota	1858	..	..	..	..	..
Mississippi	1817	..	..	..	..	1
Missouri	1821	..	..	..	..	1
Nebraska	1867	..	..	..	..	..
Nevada	1864	..	..	..	..	..
New Hampshire	—	3	4	5	6	6
New Jersey	—	4	5	6	6	6
New York	—	6	10	17	27	34
North Carolina	—	5	10	12	13	13
Ohio	1802	..	..	..	6	14
Oregon	1859	..	..	..	..	..
Pennsylvania	—	8	13	18	23	26
Rhode Island	—	1	2	2	2	2
South Carolina	—	5	6	8	9	9
Tennessee	1796	..	..	3	6	9
Texas	1845	..	..	..	..	..
Vermont	1791	..	2	4	6	5
Virginia	—	10	19	22	23	22
West Virginia	1863	..	..	..	..	..
Wisconsin	1848	..	..	..	..	..
		65	105	141	181	213

APPENDIX B—*Concluded.*

APPORTIONMENT AMONG THE STATES OF REPRESENTATIVES IN CONGRESS AFTER EACH CENSUS.

STATES.	By 5th Census, 1830.	By 6th Census, 1840.	By 7th Census, 1850.	By 8th Census, 1860.	By 9th Census, 1870.	By 10th Census, 1880.
RATIO OF REPRESENTATION	47,700.	70,680.	93,423.	127,381.	131,425.	154,325.
Alabama	5	7	7	6	8	8
Arkansas	..	1	2	3	4	5
California	..	..	2	3	4	6
Colorado	..	..	..	..	1	1
Connecticut	6	4	4	4	4	4
Delaware	1	1	1	1	1	1
Florida	..	..	1	1	2	2
Georgia	9	8	8	7	9	10
Illinois	3	7	9	14	19	20
Indiana	7	10	11	11	13	13
Iowa	..	..	2	6	9	11
Kansas	..	..	..	1	3	7
Kentucky	13	10	10	9	10	11
Louisiana	3	4	4	5	6	6
Maine	8	7	6	5	5	4
Maryland	8	6	6	5	6	6
Massachusetts	12	10	11	10	11	12
Michigan	..	3	4	6	9	11
Minnesota	..	..	2	2	3	5
Mississippi	2	4	5	5	6	7
Missouri	2	5	7	9	13	14
Nebraska	..	..	..	1	1	3
Nevada	..	..	..	1	1	1
New Hampshire	5	4	3	3	3	2
New Jersey	6	5	5	5	7	7
New York	40	34	33	31	33	34
North Carolina	13	9	8	7	8	9
Ohio	19	21	21	19	20	21
Oregon	..	..	1	1	1	1
Pennsylvania	28	24	25	24	27	28
Rhode Island	2	2	2	2	2	2
South Carolina	9	7	6	4	5	7
Tennessee	13	11	10	8	10	10
Texas	..	..	2	4	6	11
Vermont	5	4	3	3	3	2
Virginia	21	15	13	11	9	10
West Virginia	..	..	..	..	3	4
Wisconsin	..	..	3	6	8	9
	240	223	237	243	293	325

APPENDIX C.

PUBLIC DEBT OF THE UNITED STATES, 1791–1883.

STATEMENT OF OUTSTANDING PRINCIPAL OF THE PUBLIC DEBT OF THE UNITED STATES
ON THE 1ST OF JANUARY OF EACH YEAR FROM 1791 TO 1842 INCLUSIVE; AND ON THE
1ST OF JULY OF EACH YEAR FROM 1843 TO 1883 INCLUSIVE.

THE amount given for the year 1791 represents the debt of the Revolution under the Funding Bill of Alexander Hamilton, Secretary of the Treasury. The debt had decreased to a considerable extent by the year 1812. In consequence of the war with Great Britain, which began that year, there was a rapid increase, the maximum being reached in 1816. Thenceforward, with the exception of the years 1822, 1823, and 1824, — a period of extreme financial depression, — the debt was steadily decreased, until in the year 1835, under the Presidency of General Jackson, it was extinguished, — the total amount outstanding being only $37,000 in bonds which were not presented for payment. The creation of a new debt, however, began at once, and was increased in the years 1847, 1848, and 1849 by the Mexican war. This, in turn, was quite steadily reduced until the financial panic of 1857, when, during the administration of Mr. Buchanan, there was another increase. The debt was about eighty millions of dollars in amount when the civil war began.

Year.	Amount.	Year.	Amount.	Year.	Amount.	Year.	Amount.
1791	$75,463,476 52	1815	$99,833,660 15	1839	$3,573,343 82	1863	$1,119,772,138 63
1792	77,227,924 66	1816	127,334,933 74	1840	5,250,875 54	1864	1,815,784,370 57
1793	80,352,634 04	1817	123,491,965 16	1841	13,594,480 73	1865	2,680,647,869 74
1794	78,427,404 77	1818	103,466,633 83	1842	20,601,226 28	1866	2,773,236,173 69
1795	80,747,587 39	1819	95,529,648 28	1843	32,742,922 00	1867	2,678,126,103 87
1796	83,762,172 07	1820	91,015,566 15	1844	23,461,652 50	1868	2,611,687,851 19
1797	82,064,479 33	1821	89,987,427 66	1845	15,925,303 01	1869	2,588,452,213 94
1798	79,228,529 12	1822	93,546,676 98	1846	15,550,202 97	1870	2,480,672,427 81
1799	78,408,669 77	1823	90,875,877 28	1847	38,826,534 77	1871	2,353,211,332 32
1800	82,976,294 35	1824	90,269,777 77	1848	47,044,862 23	1872	2,253,251,328 78
1801	83,038,050 80	1825	83,788,432 71	1849	63,061,858 69	1873	2,234,482,993 20
1802	86,712,632 25	1826	81,054,059 99	1850	63,452,773 55	1874	2,251,690,468 43
1803	77,054,686 30	1827	73,987,357 20	1851	68,304,796 02	1875	2,232,284,531 95
1804	86,427,120 88	1828	67,475,043 87	1852	66,199,341 71	1876	2,180,395,067 15
1805	82,312,150 50	1829	58,421,413 67	1853	59,803,117 70	1877	2,205,301,392 10
1806	75,723,270 66	1830	48,565,406 50	1854	42,242,222 42	1878	2,256,205,892 53
1807	69,218,398 64	1831	39,123,191 68	1855	35,586,858 56	1879	2,245,495,072 04
1808	65,196,317 97	1832	24,322,235 18	1856	31,972,537 90	1880	2,120,415,370 63
1809	57,023,192 09	1833	7,001,698 83	1857	28,699,831 85	1881	2,069,013,569 58
1810	53,173,217 52	1834	4,760,082 08	1858	44,911,881 03	1882	1,918,312,994 03
1811	48,005,587 76	1835	37,513 05	1859	58,496,837 88	1883	1,884,171,728 07
1812	45,209,737 90	1836	336,957 83	1860	64,842,287 88	...	...
1813	55,962,827 57	1837	3,308,124 07	1861	90,580,873 72	...	...
1814	81,487,846 24	1838	10,434,221 14	1862	524,176,412 13	...	...

APPENDIX D.

SHOWING THE HIGHEST AND LOWEST PRICE OF GOLD IN THE NEW-YORK MARKET EVERY MONTH, FROM THE SUSPENSION OF SPECIE PAYMENT BY THE GOVERNMENT IN JANUARY, 1862, UNTIL RESUMPTION IN JANUARY, 1879, A PERIOD OF SEVENTEEN YEARS.

MONTH.	1862.		1863.		1864.		1865.		1866.		1867.	
	Highest.	Lowest.	Highest.	Lowest.	Highest.	Lowest.	Highest.	Lowest.	Highest.	Lowest.	Highest.	Lowest.
January	103⅝	100	160¾	133⅝	159¾	151½	233¾	198¼	144⅝	129	137⅞	132
February	104¾	102⅛	172½	152¼	161	157¼	216½	196⅝	140⅝	135⅞	140½	135¼
March	102⅝	101¼	171¾	139	169¾	159	201	148¼	136¼	125	140⅝	133⅜
April	102¼	101	157⅞	145¼	184½	166½	153⅝	144	129⅝	125½	142	132⅝
May	104⅛	102⅛	154¾	143¼	190	168	145⅝	128⅝	141½	125⅛	138⅝	134⅞
June	109½	103¾	148⅝	140½	250	193	147⅞	135⅞	167¾	137⅞	138⅜	136½
July	120½	108¾	145	123⅛	285	222	146	138⅜	155⅜	147	140⅝	138
August	116⅛	112¼	129¾	122⅛	259½	231¼	145⅜	140¼	152¼	146¼	142⅜	139⅞
September	124	116½	143⅛	126⅞	254⅛	191	145	142⅝	147⅛	143¼	146¾	141
October	133½	122	156⅜	140⅜	227¾	189	149	144¼	154⅝	145¼	145⅝	140¼
November	133¼	129	154	143	260	210	148¾	145⅞	148⅝	137¼	141½	138⅜
December	134	128½	152¾	148½	243	212¾	148¼	144⅝	141¾	131¼	137⅞	133

MONTH.	1868.		1869.		1870.		1871.		1872.		1873.	
	Highest.	Lowest.	Highest.	Lowest.	Highest.	Lowest.	Highest.	Lowest.	Highest.	Lowest.	Highest.	Lowest.
January	141⅞	133¼	136⅝	134⅝	123¼	119⅝	111¼	110½	110¼	108½	114¼	111⅝
February	144	139⅜	136⅛	130⅞	121½	115	112½	110¾	111	109½	115⅞	112⅞
March	141⅝	137⅜	132½	130¼	116⅞	110¼	112	110⅜	110⅝	109¾	118½	114⅝
April	140⅝	137¾	134⅜	131¼	115⅝	111½	111¾	110⅜	113¼	109¾	119¼	116¼
May	140½	139⅛	144⅞	134⅝	115¼	113¾	112¼	111	114⅜	112¼	118⅝	116⅝
June	141⅝	139⅛	139⅝	136¼	114⅜	110⅞	113⅛	111⅜	114⅜	113	118⅛	115
July	145¼	140⅜	137⅞	134	122⅜	111¼	113¾	111⅝	115¼	113¼	116⅜	115
August	150	143½	136⅝	131¼	122	114⅜	113⅛	111⅝	115⅝	112¼	116¼	114⅜
September	145⅝	141⅛	162⅝	130⅜	116½	113	115⅝	112¾	115¼	112⅝	116⅛	110⅞
October	140⅝	133⅜	132	128⅛	114¼	111⅛	115	111½	115¼	112¼	111¼	107⅝
November	137	132⅛	128⅝	121¼	113¼	110	112⅝	110½	114¼	111⅜	110½	106⅛
December	136¾	134¼	124	119½	111¼	110½	110⅜	108½	113⅜	111⅛	112⅝	108⅝

APPENDIX D—*Concluded.*

Month.	1874.		1875.		1876.		1877.		1878.	
	Highest.	Lowest.	Highest.	Lowest.	Highest.	Lowest.	Highest.	Lowest.	Highest.	Lowest.
January . . .	112⅛	110⅛	113⅜	111¾	113¼	112½	107⅛	105¼	102⅞	101¼
February . . .	113	111⅜	115⅜	113¼	114⅛	112¾	106⅛	104⅝	102⅜	101⅝
March	113⅝	111¼	117	114	115	113¾	105⅜	104¼	102	100¾
April	114⅜	111¾	115½	114	113⅞	112½	107⅞	104¾	101¼	100⅛
May	113⅛	111⅞	116⅜	115	113¼	112¼	107⅜	106¼	101¼	100⅜
June	112¼	110½	117½	116¼	113	111⅞	106⅜	104¾	101	100⅝
July	110⅞	109	117¼	111¾	112½	111⅜	106⅛	105⅛	101½	100⅜
August	110¼	109¼	114¾	112⅝	112⅛	109¾	105½	103⅞	100¾	100½
September . .	110¼	109⅜	117⅜	113¾	110⅜	109¼	104	102⅞	100½	100⅛
October . . .	110⅜	109¾	117⅝	114½	113¼	108⅞	103⅜	102½	101⅜	100¼
November . .	112⅜	110	116⅜	114⅛	110⅛	108⅛	103⅜	102½	100½	100⅛
December . . .	112⅜	110½	115¼	112⅛	109	107	103⅜	102½	100½	100

Table showing the Total Amount of Gold and Silver Coin issued from the Mints of the United States in each Decennial Period since 1790.

Period.	Gold.	Silver.	Period.	Gold.	Silver.
1793–1800 . .	$1,014,290 00	$1,440,454 75	1851–1860 . .	$330,237,085 50	$46,582,183 00
1801–1810 . .	3,250,742 50	3,569,165 25	1861–1870 . .	292,409,545 50	13,188,601 90
1811–1820 . .	3,166,510 00	5,970,810 95	1871–1880 . .	393,125,751 00	155,123,087 10
1821–1830 . .	1,903,092 50	16,781,046 95	1881–1883 . .	204,076,239 00	84,268,825 65
1831–1840 . .	18,756,487 50	27,309,957 00			
1841–1850 . .	89,239,817 50	22,368,130 00	Total . .	$1,337,179,561 00	$376,602,262 55

APPENDIX E.

The following statement exhibits the total valuation of real and personal estate in the United States, according to the Census Returns of 1850, 1860, 1870, and 1880.

Both the "true" and "assessed" valuation are given, except in 1850, which gives only the "true." The disparity between the actual property and that which is assessed for taxation is very striking.

The effect of the war and the consequent abolition of slavery on the valuation of property in the Southern States is clearly shown by the figures.

In all comparisons of value between the different periods, it must be borne in mind, that, in 1870, gold was at an average premium of 25.3 per cent. To equate the valuation with those of other years, there must be a reduction of one-fifth on the reported valuation of 1870, both "true" and "assessed."

The four periods exhibit a more rapid accumulation of wealth in the United States than was ever known before in the history of the world.

APPENDIX E—*Concluded.*

STATES AND TERRITORIES.	1850. True Value.	1860. Assessed Value.	1860. True Value.	1870. Assessed Value.	1870. True Value.	1880. Assessed Value.	1880. True Value.	STATES AND TERRITORIES.
Alabama	$228,204,332	$432,198,762	$495,237,078	$155,582,595	$201,855,841	$122,867,228	$428,000,000	Alabama.
Arizona	....	....	....	1,410,295	3,440,791	9,270,214	41,000,000	Arizona.
Arkansas	39,841,025	180,211,330	219,256,473	94,528,843	156,394,691	86,409,364	286,000,000	Arkansas.
California	22,161,872	139,654,067	207,874,613	269,644,068	638,767,017	584,578,036	1,343,000,000	California.
Colorado	....	....	....	17,388,101	20,243,303	74,471,693	240,000,000	Colorado.
Connecticut	155,707,980	341,256,976	444,274,114	425,433,237	774,631,524	327,177,385	779,000,000	Connecticut.
Dakota	....	....	....	2,924,489	5,599,752	20,321,530	118,000,000	Dakota.
Delaware	21,062,556	39,767,233	46,242,181	64,787,223	97,180,833	59,951,643	136,000,000	Delaware.
District of Columbia	14,018,874	41,084,945	41,084,945	74,271,693	126,873,618	99,401,787	220,000,000	District of Columbia.
Florida	22,862,270	68,929,685	73,101,500	32,480,843	44,163,655	30,938,309	120,000,000	Florida.
Georgia	335,425,714	618,232,387	645,895,237	227,219,519	268,169,207	239,472,599	606,000,000	Georgia.
Idaho	....	....	....	5,292,205	6,552,681	6,440,876	29,000,000	Idaho.
Illinois	156,265,006	389,207,372	871,860,282	482,899,575	2,121,680,579	786,616,394	3,210,000,000	Illinois.
Indiana	202,650,264	411,042,424	528,835,371	663,455,044	1,268,180,543	727,815,131	1,681,000,000	Indiana.
Iowa	23,714,638	205,166,983	247,338,265	302,515,418	717,644,750	398,671,251	1,721,000,000	Iowa.
Kansas	....	22,518,232	31,327,895	92,125,861	188,892,014	160,891,689	760,000,000	Kansas.
Kentucky	301,628,456	528,212,693	666,043,112	409,544,294	604,318,552	350,563,971	902,000,000	Kentucky.
Louisiana	233,998,764	435,787,265	602,118,568	253,371,890	323,125,666	160,162,439	382,000,000	Louisiana.
Maine	122,777,571	154,380,358	190,211,600	204,253,780	348,155,671	235,978,716	511,000,000	Maine.
Maryland	219,217,364	297,135,238	376,919,944	423,834,918	643,748,976	497,307,675	837,000,000	Maryland.
Massachusetts	573,342,286	777,157,816	815,237,433	1,591,983,112	2,132,148,741	1,584,756,802	2,623,000,000	Massachusetts.
Michigan	59,787,255	163,533,005	257,163,983	272,242,917	719,208,118	517,666,359	1,580,000,000	Michigan.
Minnesota	....	32,018,773	52,294,413	84,135,332	228,909,590	258,028,687	792,000,000	Minnesota.
Mississippi	228,951,130	509,472,912	607,324,911	177,278,890	209,197,345	110,628,129	354,000,000	Mississippi.
Missouri	137,247,707	266,935,851	501,214,398	556,129,969	1,284,922,897	532,795,801	1,562,000,000	Missouri.

Montana				9,043,411	15,184,522	18,609,802	40,000,000
Nebraska		7,426,949	9,131,056	54,584,616	69,277,483	90,585,782	385,000,000
Nevada				25,740,973	31,134,012	29,291,459	156,000,000
New Hampshire	103,652,835	123,810,089	156,310,860	149,065,290	252,624,112	164,755,181	363,000,000
New Jersey	200,000,000	296,682,492	467,918,324	624,868,971	940,976,004	572,518,361	1,305,000,000
New Mexico	5,174,471	20,838,780	20,813,768	17,784,014	31,349,793	11,363,406	49,000,000
New York	1,080,309,216	1,390,464,638	1,843,338,517	1,967,001,185	6,500,841,264	2,651,940,006	6,308,000,000
North Carolina	226,800,472	292,297,602	358,739,399	130,378,622	200,757,244	156,100,202	461,000,000
Ohio	504,726,120	959,867,101	1,193,898,422	1,167,731,697	2,235,430,300	1,534,360,508	3,258,000,000
Oregon	5,063,474	19,024,915	28,930,637	31,798,510	51,558,932	52,522,084	154,000,000
Pennsylvania	722,486,120	719,253,335	1,416,501,818	1,313,236,042	3,808,340,112	1,683,459,016	4,942,000,000
Rhode Island	80,508,794	125,104,305	135,337,588	244,278,854	296,965,646	252,536,673	400,000,000
South Carolina	288,257,694	489,319,128	548,138,754	183,913,337	208,146,989	133,560,135	322,000,000
Tennessee	201,246,686	382,495,200	493,903,892	253,782,161	498,237,724	211,778,638	705,000,000
Texas	52,740,473	267,792,335	365,200,614	149,732,929	159,062,542	320,364,615	825,000,000
Utah	986,083	4,158,020	5,596,118	12,565,842	16,159,995	24,775,279	114,000,000
Vermont	92,205,049	84,758,619	122,477,170	102,548,528	235,349,553	86,806,775	302,000,000
Virginia	430,701,082	657,621,336	793,249,681	365,439,917	409,588,133	308,455,135	707,000,000
Washington	Included	4,394,735	5,601,466	10,642,863	13,562,164	23,810,693	62,000,000
West Virginia		Included	in Virginia.	140,538,273	190,651,491	139,622,705	350,000,000
Wisconsin	42,056,595	185,945,489	273,671,608	333,209,838	702,307,329	438,971,751	1,139,000,000
Wyoming				5,516,748	7,016,748	13,621,829	54,000,000
Total for U. S.	$7,135,780,228	$12,084,509,005	$16,159,616,068	$14,178,986,732	$30,068,518,507	$16,902,993,543	$43,642,000,000

APPENDIX F.

OWNERSHIP AND LOCATION OF PROPERTY.

In the following table, the column headed "Location" gives the valuation of the property located in each State and Territory, by the Census of 1880. The column headed "Ownership" gives the value of property owned by the residents of the several States and Territories, wherever that property may be located. Some interesting results are shown. Residents of New York own thirteen hundred millions of property not located in their State; residents of Pennsylvania, four hundred and fifty millions. Many of the States show a large proportion of their property owned elsewhere. Considerably more than half the property of Nevada is owned outside the State. The whole table presents one of the most interesting deductions of the Census Bureau.

STATES AND TERRITORIES.	Ownership.	Location.	STATES AND TERRITORIES.	Ownership.	Location.
Alabama . . .	$378,000,000	$428,000,000	Montana . . .	$29,000,000	$40,000,000
Arizona	23,000,000	41,000,000	Nebraska . . .	290,000,000	385,000,000
Arkansas . . .	246,000,000	286,000,000	Nevada	69,000,000	156,000,000
California . . .	1,430,000,000	1,343,000,000	New Hampshire,	328,000,000	363,000,000
Colorado . . .	149,000,000	240,000,000	New Jersey . .	1,433,000,000	1,305,000,000
Connecticut . .	852,000,000	779,000,000	New Mexico . .	30,000,000	49,000,000
Dakota	68,000,000	118,000,000	New York . . .	7,619,000,000	6,308,000,000
Delaware . . .	138,000,000	136,000,000	North Carolina .	446,000,000	461,000,000
Dist. of Columbia,	223,000,000	220,000,000	Ohio	3,301,000,000	3,238,000,000
Florida	95,000,000	120,000,000	Oregon	126,000,000	154,000,000
Georgia	554,000,000	606,000,000	Pennsylvania. .	5,393,000,000	4,942,000,000
Idaho	12,000,000	29,000,000	Rhode Island . .	420,000,000	400,000,000
Illinois	3,092,000,000	3,210,000,000	South Carolina .	296,000,000	322,000,000
Indiana	1,499,000,000	1,681,000,000	Tennessee . . .	666,000,000	705,000,000
Iowa	1,415,000,000	1,721,000,000	Texas	725,000,000	825,000,000
Kansas	575,000,000	760,000,000	Utah	67,000,000	114,000,000
Kentucky . . .	880,000,000	902,000,000	Vermont . . .	289,000,000	302,000,000
Louisiana . . .	422,000,000	382,000,000	Virginia . . .	693,000,000	707,000,000
Maine	501,000,000	511,000,000	Washington . .	48,000,000	62,000,000
Maryland . . .	869,000,000	837,000,000	West Virginia .	307,000,000	350,000,000
Massachusetts .	2,795,000,000	2,623,000,000	Wisconsin. . .	969,000,000	1,139,000,000
Michigan . . .	1,370,000,000	1,580,000,000	Wyoming . . .	20,000,000	54,000,000
Minnesota . . .	638,000,000	792,000,000			
Mississippi . . .	324,000,000	354,000,000			
Missouri . . .	1,530,000,000	1,562,000,000		$43,642,000,000	$43,642,000,000

APPENDIX G.

THE following table exhibits the amount of revenue collected at the Custom Houses on foreign imports each year, from 1789 to 1883, under the various tariff laws; also the amount of internal revenue collected each year, from the foundation of the government to 1883. The separate table gives the amount collected each year under the income-tax while in force, and the total amount received from the tax on spirits and beer for twenty-one years after it was first levied in 1862.

RECEIPTS OF THE UNITED STATES FROM MARCH 4, 1789, TO JUNE 30, 1883.

YEARS.	From Customs.	From Internal Revenue.	YEARS.	From Customs.	From Internal Revenue.
1789–1791 . .	$4,399,473 09	. . .	1823	$19,088,433 44	$34,242 17
1792	3,443,070 85	$208,942 81	1824	17,878,325 71	34,663 37
1793	4,255,306 56	337,705 70	1825	20,098,713 45	25,771 35
1794	4,801,065 28	274,089 62	1826	23,341,331 77	21,589 93
1795	5,588,461 26	337,755 36	1827	19,712,283 29	19,885 68
1796	6,567,987 94	475,289 60	1828	23,205,523 64	17,451 54
1797	7,549,649 65	575,491 45	1829	22,681,965 91	14,502 74
1798	7,106,061 93	644,357 95	1830	21,922,391 39	12,160 62
1799	6,610,449 31	779,136 44	1831	24,224,441 77	6,933 51
1800	9,080,932 73	809,396 55	1832	28,465,237 24	11,630 65
1801	10,750,778 93	1,048,033 43	1833	29,032,508 91	2,759 00
1802	12,438,235 74	621,898 89	1834	16,214,957 15	4,196 09
1803	10,479,417 61	215,179 69	1835	19,391,310 59	10,459 48
1804	11,098,565 33	50,941 29	1836	23,409,940 53	370 00
1805	12,936,487 04	21,747 15	1837	11,169,290 39	5,493 84
1806	14,667,698 17	20,101 45	1838	16,158,800 36	2,467 27
1807	15,845,521 61	13,051 40	1839	23,137,924 81	2,553 32
1808	16,363,550 58	8,190 23	1840	13,499,502 17	1,682 25
1809	7,257,506 62	4,034 29	1841	14,487,216 74	3,261 36
1810	8,583,309 31	7,430 63	1842	18,187,908 76	495 00
1811	13,313,222 73	2,295 95	1843	7,046,843 91	103 25
1812	8,958,777 53	4,903 06	1844	26,183,570 94	1,777 34
1813	13,224,623 25	4,755 04	1845	27,528,112 70	3,517 12
1814	5,998,772 08	1,662,984 82	1846	26,712,667 87	2,897 26
1815	7,282,942 22	4,678,059 07	1847	23,747,864 66	375 00
1816	36,306,874 88	5,124,708 31	1848	31,757,070 96	375 00
1817	26,283,348 49	2,678,100 77	1849	28,346,738 82	. . .
1818	17,176,385 00	955,270 20	1850	39,668,686 42	. . .
1819	20,283,608 76	229,593 63	1851	49,017,567 92	. . .
1820	15,005,612 15	106,260 53	1852	47,339,326 62	. . .
1821	13,004,447 15	69,027 63	1853	58,931,865 52	. . .
1822	17,589,761 94	67,665 71	1854	64,224,190 27	. . .

APPENDIX G. — *Concluded.*

RECEIPTS OF THE UNITED STATES, ETC. *Concluded.*

YEARS.	From Customs.	From Internal Revenue.	YEARS.	From Customs.	From Internal Revenue.
1855	$53,025,794 21	. . .	1871	$206,270,408 05	$143,098,153 63
1856	64,022,863 50	. . .	1872	216,370,286 77	130,642,177 72
1857	63,875,905 05	. . .	1873	188,089,522 70	113,729,314 14
1858	41,789,620 96	. . .	1874	163,103,833 69	102,409,784 90
1859	49,565,824 38	. . .	1875	157,167,722 35	110,007,493 58
1860	53,187,511 87	. . .	1876	148,071,984 61	116,700,732 03
1861	39,582,125 64	. . .	1877	130,956,493 07	118,630,407 83
1862	49,056,397 62	. . .	1878	130,170,680 20	110,581,624 74
1863	69,059,642 40	$37,640,787 95	1879	137,250,047 70	113,561,610 58
1864	102,316,152 99	109,741,134 10	1880	186,522,064 60	124,009,373 92
1865	84,928,260 60	209,464,215 25	1881	198,159,676 02	135,264,385 51
1866	179,046,651 58	309,226,813 42	1882	220,410,730 25	146,497,595 45
1867	176,417,810 88	266,027,537 43	1883	214,706,496 93	144,720,368 98
1868	164,464,599 56	191,087,589 41			
1869	180,048,426 63	158,356,460 86			
1870	194,538,374 44	184,899,756 49	Total . .	$5,072,240,329 60	$3,098,575,330 71

YEARS.	From Income Tax.	From Distilled Spirits.	From Fermented Liquors.
1863	$2,741,858 25	$5,176,530 50	$1,628,933 82
1864	20,294,731 74	30,329,149 53	2,290,009 14
1865	32,050,017 44	18,731,422 45	3,734,928 06
1866	72,982,159 03	33,268,171 82	5,220,552 72
1867	66,014,429 34	33,542,951 72	6,057,500 63
1868	41,455,598 36	18,655,630 90	5,955,868 92
1869	34,791,855 84	45,071,230 86	6,099,879 54
1870	37,775,873 62	55,606,094 15	6,319,126 90
1871	19,162,650 75	46,281,848 10	7,389,501 82
1872	14,436,861 78	49,475,516 36	8,258,498 46
1873	5,062,311 62	52,099,371 78	9,324,937 84
1874	139,472 09	49,444,089 85	9,304,679 72
1875	232 64	52,081,991 12	9,144,004 41
1876	588 27	56,426,365 13	9,571,280 66
1877	97 79	57,469,429 72	9,480,789 17
1878	. . .	50,420,815 80	9,937,051 78
1879	. . .	52,570,284 69	10,729,320 08
1880	. . .	61,185,508 79	12,829,802 84
1881	3,021 92	67,153,974 88	13,700,241 21
1882	. . .	69,873,408 18	16,153,920 42
1883	. . .	74,368,775 20	16,900,615 81
Total	$346,911,760 48	$979,232,561 53	$180,031,443 95

APPENDIX H.

IMPORTANT CROPS.

THE following table exhibits the aggregate production in the United States, for a series of years ending with 1882, of certain crops which contribute largely to the national wealth. The total acreage, the yield per acre, and the value per acre, are given in each case.

CORN.

YEARS.	Bushels.	Acres.	Yield per Acre.	Value.	Value per Acre.
1849	592,071,104	. . .	. .	. . .	. . .
1859	838,792,742	. . .	. .	. . .	. . .
1866	867,946,295	34,306,538	25	$591,666,295	. . .
1867	768,320,000	32,520,249	23	610,948,390	. . .
1868	906,527,000	34,887,246	25.9	569,512,460	$16 32
1869	760,944,549	. . .	. .	. . .	. . .
1870	1,094,255,000	38,646,977	28.3	601,839,030	15 57
1871	991,898,000	34,091,137	29.1	478,275,900	14 02
1872	1,092,719,000	35,526,836	30.7	435,149,290	12 24
1873	932,274,000	39,197,148	23.8	447,183,020	11 41
1874	850,148,500	41,036,918	20.7	550,043,080	13 40
1875	1,321,069,000	44,841,371	29.4	555,445,930	12 38
1876	1,283,827,500	49,033,364	26.1	475,491,210	9 69
1877	1,342,558,000	50,369,113	26.6	480,643,400	9 54
1878	1,388,218,750	51,585,000	26.9	441,153,405	8 55
1879	1,754,591,676	62,368,504	28.1	. . .	. . .
1880	1,717,434,543	62,317,842	27.6	679,714,499	10 91
1881	1,194,916,000	64,262,025	18.6	759,482,170	11 82
1882	1,617,025,100	65,659,546	24.6	783,867,175	11 91

WHEAT.

YEARS.	Bushels.	Acres.	Yield per Acre.	Value.	Value per Acre.
1849	100,485,944	. . .	. .	. . .	. . .
1859	173,104,924	. . .	. .	. . .	. . .
1866	151,999,906	15,424,496	10	$333,773,646	. . .
1867	212,441,400	18,321,561	11.5	421,796,460	. . .
1868	224,036,600	18,460,132	12.1	319,195,290	$17 29
1869	287,745,626	. . .	. .	. . .	. . .
1870	235,884,700	18,992,591	12.4	245,865,045	12 94
1871	230,722,400	19,943,893	11.5	290,411,820	14 56
1872	249,997,100	20,858,359	11.9	310,180,375	14 87
1873	281,254,700	22,171,676	12.7	323,594,805	14 59

APPENDIX H—*Continued.*

WHEAT—*Concluded.*

YEARS.	Bushels.	Acres.	Yield per Acre.	Value.	Value per Acre.
1874	309,102,700	24,967,027	12.3	$291,107,895	$11 66
1875	292,136,000	26,381,512	11	294,580,990	11 16
1876	289,356,500	27,627,021	10.4	300,259,300	10 86
1877	364,194,146	26,277,546	13.9	394,695,779	15 08
1878	420,122,400	32,108,560	13.1	326,346,424	10 16
1879	459,483,137	35,430,333	13	. . .	. . .
1880	498,549,868	37,986,717	13.1	474,201,850	12 48
1881	383,280,090	37,709,020	10.2	456,880,427	12 03
1882	504,185,470	37,067,194	13.6	444,602,125	12 00

POTATOES.

YEARS.	Bushels.	Acres.	Yield per Acre.	Value.	Value. per Acre.
1849	65,797,896	. . .	. .	. . .	. . .
1859	111,148,867	. . .	. .	. . .	. . .
1866	107,200,976	1,069,381	100	$72,939,029	. . .
1867	97,783,000	1,192,195	82	89,276,830	. . .
1868	106,090,000	1,131,552	93.7	84,150,040	$74 36
1869	143,337,473	. . .	. .	. . .	. . .
1870	114,775,000	1,325,119	86.6	82,668,590	62 38
1871	120,461,700	1,220,912	98.6	71,836,671	58 83
1872	113,516,000	1,331,331	85.2	68,091,120	51 14
1873	106,089,000	1,295,139	81.9	74,774,890	57 73
1874	105,981,000	1,310,041	80.9	71,823,330	54 82
1875	166,877,000	1,510,041	110.5	65,019,420	43 05
1876	124,827,000	1,741,983	71.6	83,861,390	48 14
1877	170,092,000	1,792,287	94.9	76,249,500	42 54
1878	124,126,650	1,776,800	69.9	73,059,125	41 12
1879	169,458,539	. . .	. .	. . .	. . .
1880	167,659,570	1,842,510	91	81,062,214	44 00
1881	109,145,494	2,041,670	53.5	99,291,341	48 63
1882	170,972,508	2,171,636	78.7	95,304,844	43 84

HAY.

YEARS.	Tons.	Acres.	Yield per Acre.	Value.	Value. per Acre.
1849	13,838,642	. . .	. .	. . .	. . .
1859	19,083,896	. . .	. .	. . .	. . .
1866	21,778,627	17,668,904	1.22	$317,561,837	. . .
1867	26,277,000	20,020,554	. .	372,864,670	. . .
1868	26,141,900	21,541,573	1.21	351,941,930	$16 33
1869	27,316,048	. . .	. .	. . .	. . .
1870	24,525,000	19,861,805	1.23	338,969,680	17 06
1871	22,239,400	19,009,052	1.17	351,717,035	18 50
1872	23,812,800	20,318,936	1.17	345,969,079	17 02
1873	25,085,100	21,894,084	1.14	339,895,486	15 52

APPENDIX H — *Concluded.*

HAY — *Concluded.*

YEARS.	Tons.	Acres.	Yield per Acre.	Value.	Value. per Acre.
1874	24,133,900	21,769,772	1.11	$331,420,738	$15 22
1875	27,873,600	23,507,964	1.18	342,203,445	14 55
1876	30,867,100	25,282,797	1.22	300,901,252	− 11 90
1877	31,629,300	25,367,708	1.24	271,934,950	10 72
1878	39,608,296	26,931,300	1.47	285,543,752	10 60
1879	35,150,711	30,631,054	1.15	. . .	. . .
1880	31,925,233	25,863,955	1.23	371,811,084	14 38
1881	35,135,064	30,888,700	1.14	415,131,366	13 43
1882	38,138,049	32,339,585	1.18	369,958,158	11 45

TOBACCO.

YEARS.	Pounds.	Acres.	Yield per Acre.	Value.	Value per Acre.
1849	199,752,655	. . .	. .	. . .	. . .
1859	434,209,461	. . .	. .	. . .	. . .
1866	388,128,684	520,107	746	$53,778,888	. . .
1867	313,724,000	494,333	631	41,283,431	. . .
1868	320,982,000	427,189	751	40,081,942	$93 82
1869	262,735,341	481,101	569	32,206,325	66 94
1870	250,628,000	330,668	757	26,747,158	80 88
1871	263,196,100	350,769	750	25,901,421	73 84
1872	342,304,000	416,512	821.8	35,730,385	85 78
1873	372,810,000	480,878	775	30,865,972	64 19
1874	178,355,000	281,662	633.2	23,362,765	82 94
1875	379,347,000	559,049	678.5	30,342,600	54 27
1876	381,002,000	540,457	705	28,282,968	52 33
1877	440,000,000	. . .	. .	. . .	. . .
1878	392,546,700	542,850	723.1	22,137,428	40 78
1879	472,661,157	638,841	739.9	. . .	. . .
1880	446,296,889	602,516	740.7	36,414,615	60 44
1881	449,880,014	646,239	696.1	43,372,336	. . .
1882	513,077,558	671,522	764	43,189,951	64 18

APPENDIX I.

THE following table exhibits in a condensed and perspicuous form the operations of the Post-Office Department, from the foundation of the government. The very rapid increase in the revenue of the department since 1860 will be noted.

YEARS.	No. of Post-Offices.	Extent of Post-Routes in Miles.	Revenue of the Department.	Expenditure of the Department.	AMOUNT PAID FOR	
					Salaries of Post-masters.	Transportation of the Mail.
1790	75	1,875	$37,935	$32,140	$8,198	$22,081
1795	453	13,207	160,620	117,893	30,272	75,359
1800	903	20,817	280,804	213,994	69,243	128,644
1805	1,558	31,076	421,373	377,367	111,552	239,635
1810	2,300	36,406	551,684	495,969	149,438	327,966
1815	3,000	43,748	1,043,065	748,121	241,901	487,779
1816	3,260	48,673	961,782	804,422	265,944	521,970
1817	3,459	52,089	1,002,973	916,515	303,916	589,189
1818	3,618	59,473	1,130,235	1,035,832	346,429	664,611
1819	4,000	67,586	1,204,737	1,117,861	375,828	717,881
1820	4,500	72,492	1,111,927	1,160,926	352,295	782,425
1821	4,650	78,808	1,059,087	1,184,283	337,599	815,681
1822	4,709	82,763	1,117,490	1,167,572	355,299	788,618
1823	4,043	84,860	1,130,115	1,156,995	360,462	767,464
1824	5,182	84,860	1,197,758	1,188,019	383,804	768,939
1825	5,677	94,052	1,306,525	1,229,043	411,183	785,646
1826	6,150	94,052	1,447,703	1,366,712	447,727	885,100
1827	7,003	105,336	1,524,633	1,468,959	486,411	942,345
1828	7,530	105,336	1,659,915	1,689,945	548,049	1,086,313
1829	8,004	115,000	1,707,418	1,782,132	559,237	1,153,646
1830	8,450	115,176	1,850,583	1,932,708	595,234	1,274,009
1831	8,686	115,486	1,997,811	1,936,122	635,028	1,252,226
1832	9,205	104,466	2,258,570	2,266,171	715,481	1,482,507
1833	10,127	119,916	2,617,011	2,930,414	826,283	1,894,638
1834	10,693	119,916	2,823,749	2,910,605	897,317	1,925,544
1835	10,770	112,774	2,993,356	2,757,350	945,418	1,719,007
1836	11,091	118,264	3,408,323	3,841,766	812,803	1,638,052
1837	11,767	141,242	4,236,779	3,544,630	891,352	1,996,727
1838	12,519	134,818	4,238,733	4,430,662	933,948	3,131,308
1839	12,780	133,999	4,484,657	4,636,536	980,000	3,285,622
1840	13,468	155,739	4,543,522	4,718,236	1,028,925	3,296,876
1841	13,778	155,026	4,407,726	4,499,528	1,018,645	3,159,375
1842	13,733	149,732	4,546,849	5,674,752	1,147,256	3,087,796
1843	13,814	142,295	4,296,225	4,374,754	1,426,394	2,947,319
1844	14,103	144,687	4,237,288	4,296,513	1,358,316	2,938,551

APPENDIX I — *Concluded*.

YEARS.	No. of Post-Offices.	Extent of Post-Routes in Miles.	Revenue of the Department.	Expenditure of the Department.	AMOUNT PAID FOR	
					Salaries of Post-masters.	Transportation of the Mail.
1845	14,183	143,940	$4,289,841	$4,320,732	$1,409,875	$2,905,504
1846	14,601	152,865	3,487,199	4,084,297	1,042,079	2,716,673
1847	15,146	153,818	3,955,893	3,979,570	1,060,228	2,476,455
1848	16,159	163,208	4,371,077	4,326,850	. . .	2,394,703
1849	16,749	163,703	4,905,176	4,479,049	1,320,921	2,577,407
1850	18,417	178,672	5,552,971	5,212,953	1,549,376	2,965,786
1851	19,796	196,290	6,727,867	6,278,402	1,781,686	3,538,064
1852	20,901	214,284	6,925,971	7,108,459	1,296,765	4,225,311
1853	22,320	217,743	5,940,725	7,982,957	1,406,477	4,906,308
1854	23,548	219,935	6,955,586	8,577,424	1,707,708	5,401,382
1855	24,410	227,908	7,342,136	9,968,342	2,135,335	6,076,335
1856	25,565	239,642	7,620,822	10,405,286	2,102,891	6,765,639
1857	26,586	242,601	8,053,952	11,508,058	2,285,610	7,239,333
1858	27,977	260,603	8,186,793	12,722,470	2,355,016	8,246,054
1859	28,539	260,052	8,668,484	15,754,093	2,453,901	7,157,629
1860	28,498	240,594	8,518,067	19,170,610	2,552,868	8,808,710
1861	28,586	140,139	8,349,296	13,606,759	2,514,157	5,309,454
1862	28,875	134,013	8,299,821	11,125,364	2,340,767	5,853,834
1863	29,047	139,598	11,163,790	11,314,207	2,876,983	5,740,576
1864	28,878	139,171	12,438,254	12,644,786	3,174,326	5,818,469
1865	20,550	142,340	14,556,159	13,694,728	3,383,382	6,246,884
1866	23,828	180,921	14,386,986	15,352,079	3,454,677	7,630,474
1867	25,163	203,245	15,237,027	19,235,483	4,033,728	9,336,286
1868	26,481	216,928	16,292,601	22,730,593	4,255,311	10,266,056
1869	27,106	223,731	18,344,511	23,698,131	4,546,958	10,406,501
1870	28,492	231,232	19,772,221	23,998,837	4,673,466	10,884,653
1871	30,045	238,359	20,037,045	24,390,104	5,028,382	11,529,395
1872	31,863	251,398	21,915,426	26,658,192	5,121,665	15,547,821
1873	33,244	256,210	22,996,742	29,084,946	5,725,468	16,161,034
1874	34,294	269,097	26,477,072	32,126,415	5,818,472	18,881,319
1875	35,547	277,873	26,791,360	33,611,309	7,049,936	18,777,201
1876	36,383	281,798	27,895,908	33,263,488	7,397,397	18,361,048
1877	37,345	292,820	27,468,323	33,486,322	7,295,251	18,529,238
1878	39,258	301,966	29,277,517	34,165,084	7,977,852	19,262,421
1879	40,855	316,711	30,041,983	33,449,899	7,185,540	20,012,872
1880	42,989	343,888	33,315,479	36,542,804	7,701,418	22,255,984
1881	44,512	344,006	36,785,398	39,251,736	8,298,743	23,196,032
1882	46,231	343,618	41,876,410	40,039,635	8,964,677	22,846,112
1883	47,863	353,166	45,508,692	42,816,700	10,315,394	23,870,666

APPENDIX J.

THE following table exhibits the number of miles of railroad in operation, and the number of miles constructed each year, in the United States, from 1830 to 1883 inclusive. It will be observed that nearly three-fourths of the total mileage have been constructed since 1860.

YEAR.	Miles in Operation at the End of each Year.	Miles Constructed each Year.	YEAR.	Miles in Operation at the End of each Year.	Miles Constructed each Year.
1830	23	. . .	1857	24,503	2,487
1831	95	72	1858	26,968	2,465
1832	229	134	1859	28,789	1,821
1833	380	151	1860	30,635	1,846
1834	633	253	1861	31,286	651
1835	1,098	465	1862	32,120	834
1836	1,273	175	1863	33,170	1,050
1837	1,497	224	1864	33,908	738
1838	1,913	416	1865	35,085	1,177
1839	2,302	389	1866	36,801	1,716
1840	2,818	516	1867	39,250	2,449
1841	3,535	717	1868	42,229	2,979
1842	4,026	491	1869	46,844	4,615
1843	4,185	159	1870	52,885	6,070
1844	4,377	192	1871	60,293	7,379
1845	4,633	256	1872	66,171	5,878
1846	4,930	297	1873	70,278	4,107
1847	5,598	668	1874	72,383	2,105
1848	5,996	398	1875	74,096	1,713
1849	7,365	1,369	1876	76,808	2,712
1850	9,021	1,656	1877	79,089	2,281
1851	10,982	1,961	1878	81,776	2,687
1852	12,908	1,926	1879	86,497	4,721
1853	15,360	2,452	1880	93,545	7,174
1854	16,720	1,360	1881	103,334	11,142
1855	18,374	1,654	1882	114,930	11,591
1856	22,016	3,642	1883	119,937	6,608

APPENDIX K.

THE following table gives the number of miles of railroad in operation in each State and Territory in the United States during the years 1865, 1870, 1875, 1877, 1879, 1880, 1881, and 1882 respectively.

STATES AND TERRITORIES.	1865.	1870.	1875.	1877.	1879.	1880.	1881.	1882.
Maine	521	786	980	989	1,009	1,004	1,027	1,056
New Hampshire	667	736	934	964	1,019	1,014	1,021	1,038
Vermont	587	614	810	872	873	916	918	920
Massachusetts	1,297	1,480	1,817	1,863	1,870	1,915	1,959	1,967
Rhode Island	125	136	179	204	210	211	212	212
Connecticut	637	742	918	922	922	922	959	962
New England	3,834	4,494	5,638	5,814	5,903	5,982	6,096	6,155
New York	3,002	3,928	5,423	5,725	6,008	6,062	6,332	7,037
New Jersey	864	1,125	1,511	1,661	1,663	1,692	1,781	1,870
Pennsylvania	3,728	4,656	5,705	5,902	6,068	6,166	6,331	6,857
Delaware	134	197	272	272	280	275	275	282
Maryland and Dist. of Columbia,	446	671	929	944	966	1,005	1,030	1,063
West Virginia	365	387	615	638	694	691	706	813
Middle States	8,539	10,964	14,455	15,142	15,679	15,891	16,455	17,922
Virginia	1,407	1,449	1,608	1,635	1,672	1,897	2,224	2,446
Kentucky	567	1,017	1,326	1,509	1,595	1,592	1,734	1,807
North Carolina	984	1,178	1,356	1,426	1,446	1,463	1,622	1,759
Tennessee	1,296	1,492	1,630	1,656	1,701	1,845	1,902	2,067
South Carolina	1,007	1,139	1,335	1,406	1,424	1,427	1,479	1,517
Georgia	1,420	1,845	2,264	2,339	2,460	2,438	2,540	2,874
Florida	416	446	484	485	519	557	702	973
Alabama	805	1,157	1,800	1,802	1,832	1,845	1,859	1,909
Mississippi	898	990	1,018	1,088	1,140	1,133	1,188	1,309
Louisiana	335	450	466	466	544	675	937	1,032
Southern States	9,129	11,163	13,287	13,812	14,333	14,872	16,187	17,693
Ohio	3,331	3,538	4,461	4,878	5,521	5,824	6,321	6,931
Michigan	941	1,638	3,446	3,477	3,673	3,981	4,326	4,654
Indiana	2,217	3,177	3,963	4,057	4,336	4,020	4,406	5,018
Illinois	3,157	4,823	7,109	7,334	7,578	7,900	8,309	8,752
Wisconsin	1,010	1,525	2,566	2,701	2,896	3,169	3,471	3,824
Minnesota	213	1,092	1,990	2,194	3,008	3,390	3,577	3,974
Dakota Territory	. .	65	275	290	400	1,320	1,733	2,133
Iowa	891	2,683	3,850	4,134	4,779	5,401	6,165	6,968
Missouri	925	2,000	2,905	3,198	3,740	3,964	4,206	4,500
Indian Country	. .	. .	275	275	275	279	285	350
Arkansas	38	256	740	767	808	889	1,033	1,533
Texas	465	711	1,685	2,210	2,591	3,257	4,926	6,007
Nebraska	122	705	1,167	1,286	1,634	1,949	2,273	2,494

APPENDIX K — *Concluded*.

STATES AND TERRITORIES.	1865.	1870.	1875.	1877.	1879.	1880.	1881.	1882.
Kansas.	40	1,501	2,150	2,352	3,103	3,446	3,655	3,866
Colorado	. .	157	807	1,045	1,208	1,576	2,193	2,772
New-Mexico Territory	. .	. .	. .	. .	118	745	1,034	1,076
Wyoming Territory	. .	459	459	465	472	500	564	613
Idaho Territory	. .	. .	. .	. .	220	182	251	472
Utah Territory	. .	257	506	506	593	747	782	967
Montana Territory	. .	. .	. .	. .	10	110	267	659
Western States and Territories	13,350	24,587	38,254	41,169	46,963	52,649	59,777	67,563
Nevada	. .	593	601	627	720	738	894	948
California	214	925	1,503	2,080	2,209	2,201	2,315	2,643
Arizona Territory	. .	. .	. .	. .	183	401	549	765
Oregon	19	159	248	248	295	561	627	807
Washington Territory	. .	. .	110	197	212	250	434	434
Pacific States and Territories,	233	1,677	2,462	3,152	3,619	4,151	4,819	5,597

RECAPITULATION.

	1865.	1870.	1875.	1877.	1879.	1880.	1881.	1882.
New-England States	3,834	4,494	5,638	5,814	5,903	5,982	6,096	6,155
Middle States	8,539	10,964	14,455	15,142	15,679	15,891	16,455	17,922
Southern States	9,129	11,163	13,287	13,812	14,333	14,872	16,187	17,693
Western States and Territories .	13,350	24,587	38,254	41,169	46,963	52,649	59,777	67,563
Pacific States and Territories .	233	1,677	2,462	3,152	3,619	4,151	4,819	5,597
Grand Total	35,085	52,885	74,096	79,089	86,497	93,545	103,334	114,930

APPENDIX L.

THIS table exhibits the total amount of pensions paid by the government from its foundation, including those to soldiers of the Revolution, war of 1812, Mexican war, war of the Rebellion, and the various Indian wars.

YEAR.	Pensions.	YEAR.	Pensions.	YEAR.	Pensions.
1791	$175,813 88	1823	$1,780,588 52	1855	$1,477,612 33
1792	109,243 15	1824	1,499,326 59	1856	1,296,229 65
1793	80,087 81	1825	1,308,810 57	1857	1,310,380 58
1794	81,399 24	1826	1,556,593 83	1858	1,219,768 30
1795	68,673 22	1827	976,138 86	1859	1,222,222 71
1796	100,843 71	1828	850,573 57	1860	1,100,802 32
1797	92,256 97	1829	949,594 47	1861	1,034,599 73
1798	104,845 33	1830	1,363,297 31	1862	852,170 47
1799	95,444 03	1831	1,170,665 14	1863	1,078,513 36
1800	64,130 73	1832	1,184,422 40	1864	4,985,473 90
1801	73,533 37	1833	4,589,152 40	1865	16,347,621 34
1802	85,440 39	1834	3,364,285 30	1866	15,605,549 88
1803	62,902 10	1835	1,954,711 32	1867	20,936,551 71
1804	80,092 80	1836	2,882,797 96	1868	23,782,386 78
1805	81,854 59	1837	2,672,162 45	1869	28,476,621 78
1806	81,875 53	1838	2,156,057 29	1870	28,340,202 17
1807	70,500 00	1839	3,142,750 51	1871	34,443,894 88
1808	82,576 04	1840	2,603,562 17	1872	28,533,402 76
1809	87,833 54	1841	2,388,434 51	1873	29,359,426 86
1810	83,744 16	1842	1,378,931 33	1874	29,038,414 66
1811	75,043 88	1843	839,041 12	1875	29,456,216 22
1812	91,402 10	1844	2,032,008 99	1876	28,257,395 69
1813	86,989 91	1845	2,400,788 11	1877	27,963,752 27
1814	90,164 36	1846	1,811,097 56	1878	27,137,019 08
1815	69,656 06	1847	1,744,883 63	1879	35,121,482 39
1816	188,804 15	1848	1,227,496 48	1880	56,777,174 44
1817	297,374 43	1849	1,328,867 64	1881	50,059,279 62
1818	890,719 90	1850	1,866,886 02	1882	61,345,193 95
1819	2,415,939 85	1851	2,293,377 22	1883	66,012,573 64
1820	3,208,376 31	1852	2,401,858 78		
1821	242,817 25	1853	1,756,306 20		
1822	1,948,199 40	1854	1,232,665 00		$724,658,382 78

APPENDIX M.

THE following table shows the distribution of the tonnage of the United-States merchant-marine employed in the foreign trade, the coasting trade, and the fisheries, from 1789 to 1883 inclusive.

YEAR ENDED	Foreign Trade.	Coasting Trade.	Whale Fisheries.	CodFisheries.	Mackerel Fisheries.	TOTAL MERCHANT MARINE.
	Tons.	Tons.	Tons.	Tons.	Tons.	Tons.
Dec. 31, 1789	123,893	68,607	. . .	9,062	. .	201,562
1790	346,254	103,775	. . .	28,348	. .	478,377
1791	363,110	106,494	. . .	32,542	. .	502,146
1792	411,438	120,957	. . .	32,062	. .	564,457
1793	367,734	122,071	. . .	30,959	. .	520,764
1794	438,863	162,578	4,129	23,048	. .	628,618
1795	529,471	184,398	3,163	30,933	. .	747,965
1796	576,733	217,841	2,364	34,962	. .	831,900
1797	597,777	237,403	1,104	40,628	. .	876,912
1798	603,376	251,443	763	42,746	. .	898,328
1799	657,142	246,640	5,647	29,979	. .	939,408
1800	667,107	272,492	3,466	29,427	. .	972,492
1801	630,558	274,551	3,085	39,382	. .	947,576
1802	557,760	289,623	3,201	41,522	. .	892,106
1803	585,910	299,060	12,390	51,812	. .	949,172
1804	660,514	317,537	12,339	52,014	. .	1,042,404
1805	744,224	332,663	6,015	57,465	. .	1,140,367
1806	798,507	340,540	10,507	59,183	. .	1,208,737
1807	840,163	349,028	9,051	70,306	. .	1,268,548
1808	765,252	420,819	4,526	51,998	. .	1,242,595
1809	906,855	405,103	3,777	34,487	. .	1,350,282
1810	981,019	405,347	3,589	34,828	. .	1,424,783
1811	763,607	420,362	5,299	43,234	. .	1,232,502
1812	758,636	477,972	2,930	30,459	. .	1,269,997
1813	672,700	471,109	2,942	19,877	. .	1,166,628
1814	674,633	466,159	562	17,855	. .	1,159,209
1815	854,295	475,666	1,230	36,937	. .	1,368,128
1816	800,760	522,165	1,168	48,126	. .	1,372,219
1817	804,851	525,030	5,224	64,807	. .	1,399,912
1818	589,954	549,374	16,750	69,107	. .	1,225,185
1819	581,230	571,058	32,386	76,078	. .	1,260,752
1820	583,657	588,025	36,445	72,040	. .	1,280,167
1821	593,825	614,845	27,995	62,293	. .	1,298,958
1822	582,701	624,189	48,583	69,226	. .	1,324,699
1823	600,003	617,805	40,503	78,255	. .	1,336,566
1824	636,807	641,563	33,346	77,447	. .	1,389,163
1825	665,409	640,861	35,379	81,462	. .	1,423,111
1826	696,221	722,330	41,984	73,656	. .	1,534,191
1827	701,517	789,159	45,992	83,939	. .	1,620,607
1828	757,998	842,906	54,801	85,687	. .	1,741,392
1829	592,859	508,858	57,284	101,797	. .	1,260,798
1830	537,563	516,979	39,705	61,556	35,973	1,191,776
1831	538,136	539,724	82,797	60,978	46,211	1,267,846
1832	614,121	649,627	73,246	55,028	47,428	1,439,450

APPENDIX M — *Concluded*.

YEAR ENDED	Foreign Trade.	Coasting Trade.	Whale Fisheries.	Cod Fisheries.	Mackerel Fisheries.	TOTAL MERCHANT MARINE.
	Tons.	Tons.	Tons.	Tons.	Tons.	Tons.
Dec. 31, 1833	648,869	744,199	101,636	62,721	48,726	1,606,151
1834	749,378	783,619	108,424	56,404	61,082	1,758,907
Sept. 30, 1835 (nine months)	788,173	797,338	97,649	77,338	64,443	1,824,941
1836	753,094	873,023	146,254	63,307	46,424	1,882,102
1837	683,205	956,981	129,137	80,552	46,811	1,896,686
1838	702,962	1,041,105	124,860	70,084	56,649	1,995,640
1839	702,400	1,153,552	132,285	72,258	35,984	2,096,479
1840	762,838	1,176,694	136,927	76,036	28,269	2,180,764
1841	788,398	1,107,068	157,405	66,552	11,321	2,130,744
1842	823,746	1,045,753	151,990	54,805	16,097	2,092,391
June 30, 1843 (nine months) . . .	856,930	1,076,156	152,517	61,224	11,776	2,158,603
1844	900,471	1,109,615	168,614	85,225	16,171	2,280,096
1845	904,476	1,223,218	190,903	76,991	21,414	2,417,002
1846	943,307	1,315,577	187,420	79,318	36,463	2,562,085
1847	1,047,454	1,488,601	193,859	77,681	31,451	2,839,046
1848	1,168,707	1,659,317	192,613	89,847	43,558	3,154,042
1849	1,258,750	1,770,376	180,186	81,756	42,942	3,334,016
1850	1,439,694	1,797,825	146,017	93,806	58,112	3,535,454
1851	1,544,663	1,899,976	181,644	95,617	50,539	3,772,439
1852	1,795,650	2,055,873	193,798	110,573	72,546	4,138,440
1853	1,910,471	2,134,258	193,203	109,228	59,850	4,407,010
1854	2,151,918	2,322,114	181,901	111,928	35,041	4,802,902
1855	2,348,358	2,543,255	186,848	111,915	21,625	5,212,001
1856	2,302,190	2,247,663	189,461	102,452	29,887	4,871,653
1857	2,268,196	2,336,609	195,842	111,868	28,328	4,940,843
1858	2,301,148	2,401,220	198,594	119,252	29,594	5,049,808
1859	2,321,674	2,488,929	185,728	129,637	27,070	5,145,038
1860	2,379,396	2,644,867	166,841	136,653	26,111	5,353,868
1861	2,496,894	2,704,544	145,734	137,846	54,795	5,539,813
1862	2,173,537	2,606,716	117,714	133,601	80,596	5,112,164
1863	1,926,886	2,960,633	99,228	117,290	51,019	5,155,056
1864	1,486,749	3,245,265	95,145	103,742	55,499	4,986,400
1865	1,518,350	3,381,522	90,516	65,185	41,209	5,096,782
1866	1,387,756	2,719,621	105,170	51,642	46,589	4,310,778
1867	1,515,648	2,660,390	52,384	44,567	31,498	4,304,487
1868	1,494,389	2,702,140	71,343	83,887*	. .	4,351,759
1869	1,496,220	2,515,515	70,202	62,704	. .	4,144,641
1870	1,448,846	2,638,247	67,954	91,460	. .	4,246,507
1871	1,363,652	2,764,600	61,490	92,865	. .	4,282,607
1872	1,359,040	2,929,552	51,608	97,547	. .	4,437,747
1873	1,378,533	3,163,220	44,755	109,519	. .	4,696,027
1874	1,389,815	3,292,439	39,108	78,290	. .	4,800,652
1875	1,515,598	3,219,698	38,229	80,207	. .	4,853,732
1876	1,553,705	2,598,835	39,116	87,802	. .	4,279,458
1877	1,570,600	2,540,322	40,593	91,085	. .	4,242,600
1878	1,589,348	2,497,170	39,700	86,547	. .	4,212,765
1879	1,451,505	2,598,183	40,028	79,885	. .	4,169,601
1880	1,314,402	2,637,686	38,408	77,538	. .	4,068,034
1881	1,297,035	2,646,010	38,551	76,136	. .	4,057,734
1882	1,259,492	2,795,777	32,802	77,862	. .	4,165,933
1883	1,269,681	2,838,354	32,414	95,038	. .	4,235,487

* After 1867 the tonnage engaged in mackerel fisheries is included in this column.

APPENDIX N.

THE following table exhibits the immigration into the United States by decades from 1821 to 1880.

COUNTRIES.	1821 to 1830.	1831 to 1840.	1841 to 1850.	1851 to 1860.	1861 to 1870.	1871 to 1880.	1881.
England	14,055	7,611	32,092	247,125	251,288	440,961	76,547
Ireland	50,724	207,381	780,719	914,119	456,593	444,589	70,909
Scotland	2,912	2,667	3,712	38,331	44,681	98,926	16,451
Wales	170	185	1,261	6,319	4,642	6,779	1,316
Great Britain, not specified	7,942	65,347	229,979	132,199	349,766	7,908	7
Total British Isles	75,803	283,191	1,047,763	1,338,093	1,106,970	989,163	165,230
Austria	. .	. .	. . .	. . .	9,398	69,558	21,437
Belgium	27	22	5,074	4,738	7,416	7,278	1,939
Denmark	169	1,063	539	3,749	17,885	34,577	8,951
France	8,497	45,575	77,262	76,358	37,749	73,301	5,653
Germany	6,761	152,454	434,626	951,667	822,007	757,698	249,572
Hungary	. .	. .	. . .	. . .	488	13,475	6,756
Italy	408	2,253	1,870	9,231	12,982	60,830	20,103
Netherlands	1,078	1,41.	8,251	10,789	9,539	17,236	10,812
Norway and Sweden	91	1,201	13,903	20,931	117,798	226,488	82,859
Russia and Poland	91	646	656	1,621	5,047	54,606	14,476
Spain and Portugal	2,622	2,954	2,759	10,353	9,047	9,767	464
Switzerland	3,226	4,821	4,644	25,011	23,839	31,722	11,628
All other countries in Europe	43	96	155	116	234	1,265	451
Total Europe, not British Isles,	23,013	212,497	549,739	1,114,564	1,073,429	1,357,801	435,101
Total Europe	98,816	495,688	1,597,502	2,452,657	2,180,399	2,346,964	600,331
China	2	8	35	41,397	68,059	122,436	20,711
All other countries of Asia	8	40	47	61	385	632	64
Total Asia	10	48	82	41,458	68,444	123,068	20,775
Africa	16	52	55	210	324	221	37
British North American Provinces,	2,277	13,624	41,723	59,309	184,713	430,210	95,188
Mexico	4,817	6,599	3,271	3,078	2,386	5,164	244
Central America	105	44	368	449	96	229	33
South America	531	856	3,579	1,224	1,443	1,152	85
West Indies	3,834	12,301	18,528	10,660	9,698	14,461	1,009
Total America	11,564	33,424	62,469	74,720	198,336	451,216	96,559
Islands of the Atlantic	352	103	337	3,090	3,778	10,121	1,287
Islands of the Pacific	2	9	29	158	235	11,421	910
All other countries, not specified	32,679	69,801	52,777	25,921	15,236	1,684	146
Aggregate	143,439	599,125	1,713,251	2,598,214	2,466,752	2,944,695	720,045

NOTE. — Grand total, 1789 to 1881 inclusive, 11,435,521. Prior to the year 1820 no official records of the arrivals of alien passengers were kept. It is estimated however that the total number arrived in the United States from the foundation of the government to the year 1820 was 250,000 — about 8,000 per annum. The large growth of our population for the first thirty years of the Republic was almost wholly from natural increase.

APPENDIX O.

COAL AND IRON PRODUCT.

THE following table exhibits the quantity of coal produced in each State and Territory of the United States during the census years ended May 31, 1870, and 1880, and the calendar years 1876, 1877, 1878, 1879, and 1881 (weight expressed in tons of 2,240 pounds).

STATE OR TERRITORY.	1870.	1876.	1877.	1878.	1879.	1880.	1881.
Anthracite.	Tons.	Tons.	Tons.	Tons.	Tons.	Tons.	Tons.
Pennsylvania .	15,648,437	21,436,667	23,619,911	20,605,262	26,142,689	28,640,819	28,500,016
Rhode Island . .	14,000	14,000	14,000	14,000	15,000	6,176	10,000
Virginia . . .	. . .	. . .	. . .	. . .	. . .	2,817	. . .
Bituminous.							
Pennsylvania .	7,800,386	11,500,000	12,500,000	13,500,000	14,500,000	18,425,163	20,000,000
Illinois	2,624,163	3,500,000	3,500,000	3,500,000	3,500,000	6,115,377	6,000,000
Ohio	2,527,285	3,500,000	5,250,000	5,000,000	5,000,000	6,008,595	8,250,000
Maryland . . .	2,345,153	1,835,081	1,574,339	1,679,322	1,730,709	2,228,917	2,261,918
Missouri . . .	621,930	900,000	900,000	900,000	900,000	556,304	1,750,000
West Virginia .	608,878	800,000	1,000,000	1,000,000	1,250,000	1,839,845	1,500,000
Indiana	437,870	950,000	1,000,000	1,000,000	1,000,000	1,454,327	1,500,000
Iowa	263,487	1,500,000	1,500,000	1,500,000	1,600,000	1,461,116	1,750,000
Kentucky . . .	32,938	650,000	850,000	900,000	1,000,000	946,288	1,100,000
Tennessee. . .	133,418	550,000	750,000	375,000	450,000	495,131	750,000
Virginia . . .	61,803	90,000	90,000	75,000	90,000	43,079	100,000
Kansas	150,582	125,000	200,000	300,000	400,000	771,142	750,000
Oregon	. . .	200,000	200,000	200,000	200,000	43,205	300,000
Michigan . . .	28,150	30,000	30,000	30,000	35,000	100,800	100,000
California . . .	. . .	600,000	600,000	600,000	600,000	236,950	600,000
Arkansas . . .	. . .	. . .	. . .	. . .	. . .	14,778	30,000
Montana . . .	. . .	. . .	. . .	. . .	. . .	224	. . .
North Carolina .	. . .	. . .	. . .	. . .	. . .	350	. . .
Alabama . . .	11,000	100,000	175,000	200,000	250,000	323,972	375,000
Nebraska . . .	1,425	30,000	50,000	75,000	75,000	200	75,000
Wyoming . . .	. . .	500,000	100,000	100,000	175,000	589,595	375,000
Washington . .	. . .	100,000	150,000	150,000	170,000	145,015	175,000
Utah	. . .	45,000	45,000	60,000	225,000	. . .	225,000
Colorado . . .	. . .	250,000	300,000	367,000	400,000	462,747	700,000
Georgia. . . .	. . .	. . .	. . .	. . .	100,000	154,644	150,000
Total bituminous . . .	17,648,468	27,569,081	30,688,339	31,525,322	36,665,709	42,417,764	48,816,918
Total anthracite . . .	15,662,437	21,436,667	23,619,911	20,605,262	26,142,689	28,649,812	28,510,016
Total anthracite and bituminous .	33,310,905	49,005,748	54,308,250	52,130,584	62,808,398	71,067,576	77,326,934

APPENDIX O — *Concluded.*

The following table shows the quantity of pig-iron produced, imported, exported, and retained for consumption in the United States, from 1867 to 1882, expressed in tons of 2,240 pounds.

Calendar Year.	Production.	Year Ended June 30,	Imports.	Total Production and Imports.	Exports, Foreign and Domestic.	Retained for Home Consumption.
	Tons.		*Tons.*	*Tons.*	*Tons.*	*Tons.*
1866	1,205,663	1867	112,042	1,317,705	628	1,317,077
1867	1,305,023	1868	112,133	1,417,156	282	1,416,874
1868	1,431,250	1869	136,975	1,568,225	273	1,567,952
1869	1,711,287	1870	153,283	1,864,570	1,456	1,863,114
1870	1,665,178	1871	178,139	1,843,317	3,772	1,839,545
1871	1,706,793	1872	247,529	1,954,322	2,172	1,952,150
1872	2,548,713	1873	215,496	2,764,209	2,818	2,761,391
1873	2,560,963	1874	92,042	2,653,005	10,152	2,642,853
1874	2,401,262	1875	53,437	2,454,699	16,193	2,438,506
1875	2,023,733	1876	79,455	2,103,188	7,241	2,095,947
1876	1,868,961	1877	67,922	1,936,883	3,560	1,933,323
1877	2,066,594	1878	55,000	2,121,594	6,198	2,115,396
1878	2,301,215	1879	87,576	2,388,791	3,221	2,385,570
1879	2,741,853	1880	754,657	3,406,510	2,607	3,493,903
1880	3,835,191	1881	417,849	4,253,040	6,811	4,246,229
1881	4,144,254	1882	496,045	4,640,299	9,519	4,630,780

QUANTITY OF IRON AND STEEL RAILROAD BARS PRODUCED, IMPORTED, EXPORTED, AND RETAINED FOR CONSUMPTION IN THE UNITED STATES, FROM 1867 TO 1882, EXPRESSED IN TONS OF 2,240 POUNDS.

Calendar Year.	Production.			Year Ended June 30,	Imports.	Total Production and Imports.	Exports, Foreign and Domestic.	Retained for Home Consumption.
	Iron.	Steel.	Total.					
	Tons.	*Tons.*	*Tons.*		*Tons.*	*Tons.*	*Tons.*	*Tons.*
1866	384,623	. . .	384,623	1867	96,272	480,895	159	480,736
1867	410,319	2,277	412,596	1868	151,097	563,693	710	562,983
1868	445,972	6,451	452,423	1869	237,704	690,127	564	689,563
1869	521,371	8,616	529,987	1870	279,766	809,753	885	808,863
1870	523,214	30,357	553,571	1871	458,056	1,011,627	1,341	1,010,286
1871	658,467	34,152	692,619	1872	531,537	1,224,156	4,484	1,219,672
1872	808,866	83,991	892,857	1873	357,631	1,250,488	7,147	1,243,341
1873	679,520	115,192	794,712	1874	148,920	943,632	7,313	936,319
1874	521,847	129,414	651,261	1875	42,082	693,343	14,199	679,144
1875	447,901	259,699	707,600	1876	4,708	712,308	13,554	698,754
1876	417,114	368,269	785,383	1877	30	785,413	6,103	779,310
1877	296,911	385,865	682,776	1878	11	682,787	8,426	674,361
1878	288,295	499,817	788,112	1879	2,611	790,723	7,127	783,596
1879	375,143	618,851	993,994	1880	152,791	1,146,785	2,363	1,144,422
1880	440,859	864,353	1,305,212	1881	302,294	1,607,506	4,274	1,603,232
1881	436,233	1,210,285	1,646,518	1882	295,666	1,942,184	4,190	1,937,994

APPENDIX P.

THE following table shows the number of men called for by the President of the United States, and number furnished by each State, Territory, and the District of Columbia, both for the Army and Navy, from April 15, 1861, to close of the war.

STATES AND TERRITORIES.	AGGREGATE.				Aggregate Reduced to a Three-Years' Standard.
	Quota.	Men Furnished.	Paid Commutation.	Total.	
Maine	73,587	70,107	2,007	72,114	56,776
New Hampshire	35,897	33,937	692	34,629	30,849
Vermont	32,074	33,288	1,974	35,262	29,068
Massachusetts	139,095	146,730	5,318	152,048	124,104
Rhode Island	18,898	23,236	463	23,699	17,866
Connecticut	44,797	55,864	1,515	57,379	50,623
New York	507,148	448,850	18,197	467,047	392,270
New Jersey	92,820	76,814	4,196	81,010	57,908
Pennsylvania	385,369	337,936	28,171	366,107	265,517
Delaware	13,935	12,284	1,386	13,670	10,322
Maryland	70,965	46,638	3,678	50,316	41,275
West Virginia	34,463	32,068	. . .	32,068	27,714
District of Columbia	13,973	16,534	338	16,872	11,506
Ohio	306,322	313,180	6,479	319,659	240,514
Indiana	199,788	196,363	784	197,147	153,576
Illinois	244,496	259,092	55	259,147	214,133
Michigan	95,007	87,364	2,008	89,372	80,111
Wisconsin	109,080	91,327	5,097	96,424	79,260
Minnesota	26,326	24,020	1,032	25,052	19,693
Iowa	79,521	76,242	67	76,309	68,630
Missouri	122,496	109,111	. . .	109,111	86,530
Kentucky	100,782	75,760	3,265	79,025	70,832
Kansas	12,931	20,149	2	20,151	18,706
Tennessee	1,560	31,092	. . .	31,092	26,394
Arkansas	780	8,289	. . .	8,289	7,836
North Carolina	1,560	3,156	. . .	3,156	3,156
California	. . .	15,725	. . .	15,725	15,725
Nevada	. . .	1,080	. . .	1,080	1,080
Oregon	. . .	1,810	. . .	1,810	1,773
Washington Territory	. . .	964	. . .	964	964
Nebraska Territory	. . .	3,157	. . .	3,157	2,175
Colorado Territory	. . .	4,903	. . .	4,903	3,697
Dakota Territory	. . .	206	. . .	206	206
New-Mexico Territory	. . .	6,561	. . .	6,561	4,432
Alabama	. . .	2,576	. . .	2,576	1,611
Florida	. . .	1,290	. . .	1,290	1,290
Louisiana	. . .	5,224	. . .	5,224	4,654
Mississippi	. . .	545	. . .	545	545
Texas	. . .	1,965	. . .	1,965	1,632
Indian Nation	. . .	3,530	. . .	3,530	3,530
Colored Troops*	. . .	93,441	. . .	93,441	91,789
Total	2,763,670	2,772,408	86,724	2,859,132	2,320,272

* Colored troops organized at various stations in the States in rebellion, embracing all not specifically credited to States, and which cannot be so assigned.

APPENDIX P — *Continued.*

REDUCED TO PERIODS OF SERVICE ONLY, THE FOLLOWING AGGREGATES FOR THE DIF-
FERENT PERIODS IN THE ARMY AND NAVY APPEAR: —

Periods of Enlistment.	Number.	Periods of Enlistment.	Number.
60 days	2,045	1 year	393,706
3 months	108,416	2 years	44,400
100 days	85,807	3 years	2,028,630
4 months	42	4 years	1,042
6 months	26,118		
8 months	373		
9 months	89,899	Aggregate enlistments	2,780,478

THE NUMBER OF INDIVIDUALS WHO SERVED DURING THE WAR IS ESTIMATED AS
FOLLOWS: —

Number who died during the war	304,360
Number who were discharged for disability	285,545
Deserters (less those arrested and 25 per cent. additional)	128,352
One-third of those serving terms of less than one year (estimated that two-thirds thereof re-enlisted)	104,134
One-half of those serving more than one year and less than two years (estimated that one-half re-enlisted)	224,053
Number in the service May 1, 1865	1,000,516
Total	2,046,969
Add number in regular army at commencement of the war	16,422
Aggregate number of different individuals who served during the war	2,063,391

There are no records which give with accuracy the number of men in the Confederate Army. The general aggregate for the four years is, upon the best authority attainable, placed at one million one hundred thousand men (1,100,000). The maximum number of men on the Confederate Army rolls at any one time is estimated at five hundred thousand. The irregular manner in which the men were conscripted during the last two years of the war, taken in connection with the loss of records, makes it impossible to give accurate statements of the numbers furnished by the several States.

APPENDIX P—*Concluded.*

REGULAR ARMY.

The following table shows the actual strength of the regular army of the United States at different periods, from 1789 to 1883 (retired officers not included).

Date.	Officers.	Men.	Total.	Date.	Officers.	Men.	Total.
1789–90 . . .	50	672	722	1864	1,813	19,791	21,604
1795 . . .	212	3,228	3,440	1865	1,605	20,705	22,310
1800 . . .	248	3,803	4,051	1866	2,020	31,470	33,490
1805 . . .	196	2,534	2,730	1867	2,853	53,962	56,815
1810 . . .	466	6,488	6,954	1868	2,835	48,081	50,916
July, 1812 . . .	301	6,385	6,686*	1869	2,700	34,074	36,774
Feb., 1813 . . .	1,476	17,560	19,036*	1870	2,541	34,534	37,075
Sept., 1814 . . .	2,395	35,791	38,186*	1871	2,105	26,848	28,953
Feb., 1815 . . .	2,396	31,028	33,424*	1872	2,104	26,071	28,175
Dec., 1820 . . .	712	8,230	8,942	1873	2,076	26,576	28,652
1825 . . .	562	5,157	5,719	1874	2,080	26,364	28,444
1830 . . .	627	5,324	5,951	1875	2,068	23,250	25,318
1835 . . .	680	6,471	7,151	1876	2,151	26,129	28,280
1840 . . .	733	9,837	10,570	1877	2,178	21,767	23,945
1845 . . .	826	7,523	8,349	1878	2,153	23,365	25,818
1850 . . .	948	9,815	10,763	1879	2,127	24,262	26,389
1855 . . .	1,042	14,710	15,752	1880	2,152	24,259	26,411
1860 . . .	1,108	15,259	16,367	1881	2,181	22,994	25,175
1861 . . .	1,004	15,418	16,422	1882	2,162	23,024	25,186
1862 . . .	1,720	21,450	23,170	1883	2,143	23,335	25,478
1863 . . .	1,844	22,915	24,759				

The following summary shows the total number of soldiers serving in the various wars in which the United States was engaged prior to the Rebellion.

Soldiers of the War of the Revolution, 1775 to 1783	289,715
Indian War, General Wayne, 1794	2,843
Indian War, 1811	650
War with Great Britain, 1812 to 1815, number of soldiers, sailors, and marines serving 12 months or more	63,179
Number of militia serving 6 months or more	66,325
" " " " 3 " " "	125,643
" " " " 1 month " "	125,307
" " " " less than 1 month	147,200
	527,654
Number of soldiers serving in Seminole War, 1817–18	5,911
" " " " " Black-Hawk War, 1831–32	5,031
" " " " " South-western disturbances, 1836	2,803
" " " " " Cherokee Country disturbances, 1836–37	3,926
" " " " " Creek disturbances, 1836–37	13,418
" " " " " Florida War, 1836–42	41,122
" " " and sailors serving in Mexican War, 1846–47	105,454
" " " serving in New-York frontier disturbances, 1838–39	1,128
" " " " " Aroostook disturbances, 1838–39, 2 regiments	1,430

* Second war with Great Britain.

APPENDIX Q.

THE following table exhibits the school age, population, and enrollment of the States and Territories in 1881, with salaries paid to teachers, and total expenditure for schools.

STATES.	School Age.	School Population.	No. Enrolled in Public Schools.	Aggregate Salaries Paid to Teachers.	Total Expenditure.
Alabama	7-21	422,739	176,289	$384,769	$410,690
Arkansas	6-21	272,841	98,744	. . .	388,412
California	5-17	211,237	163,855	2,346,056	3,047,605
Colorado	6-21	40,804	26,000	. . .	557,151
Connecticut	4-16	143,745	119,381	1,025,323	1,476,691
Delaware	6-21	37,285	29,122	138,819	207,281
Florida	4-21	88,677	39,315	97,115	114,895
Georgia	6-18	461,016	244,197	. . .	498,533
Illinois	6-21	1,002,222	701,627	4,722,349	7,858,414
Indiana	6-21	714,343	503,855	3,057,110	4,528,754
Iowa	5-21	594,730	431,513	3,040,716	5,129,819
Kansas	5-21	348,179	249,034	1,167,620	1,976,397
Kentucky	6-20	553,638	238,440	. . .	1,248,524
Louisiana	6-18	271,414	62,370	374,127	441,484
Maine	4-21	213,927	150,067	965,697	1,089,414
Maryland	5-20	319,201	158,909	1,162,429	1,604,580
Massachusetts	5-15	312,680	325,239	4,130,714	5,776,542
Michigan	5-20	518,294	371,743	2,114,567	3,418,233
Minnesota	5-21	300,923	177,278	993,997	1,466,492
Mississippi	5-21	419,963	237,288	644,352	757,758
Missouri	6-20	723,484	476,376	2,218,637	3,152,178
Nebraska	5-21	152,824	100,776	627,717	1,165,103
Nevada	6-18	10,533	8,329	59,194	140,419
New Hampshire	5-15	60,899	63,235	408,554	577,022
New Jersey	5-18	335,631	203,542	1,510,830	1,914,447
New York	5-21	1,662,122	1,021,282	7,775,505	10,923,402
North Carolina	6-21	468,072	240,716	342,212	409,659
Ohio	6-21	1,063,337	744,758	5,151,448	8,133,622
Oregon	4-20	61,641	34,498	234,818	318,331
Pennsylvania	6-21	1,422,377	931,749	4,677,017	7,994,705
Rhode Island	5-16	53,077	44,920	408,993	549,937
South Carolina	6-16	262,279	133,458	309,855	345,634
Tennessee	6-21	545,875	283,468	529,618	638,009
Texas	8-14	230,527	186,786	674,869	753,346
Vermont	5-20	99,463	74,646	366,448	447,252
Virginia	5-21	556,665	239,046	823,310	1,100,239
West Virginia	6-21	213,191	145,203	539,648	761,250
Wisconsin	4-20	491,358	300,122	1,618,283	2,279,103
Total for States	. .	15,661,213	9,737,176	$54,642,716	$83,601,327

APPENDIX Q — *Concluded.*

TERRITORIES.	School Age.	School Popula-tion.	No. Enrolled in Public Schools.	Aggregate Sala-ries Paid to Teachers.	Total Expendi-ture.
Arizona	6–21	9,571	3,844	. . .	$44,628
Dakota	5–21	38,815	25,451	. . .	314,484
District of Columbia	6–18	43,558	27,299	$295,668	527,312
Idaho	5–21	7,520	6,080	38,174	44,840
Montana	4–21	9,895	5,112	52,781	55,781
New Mexico	7–18	29,255	4,755	28,002	28,973
Utah	6–18	42,353	26,772	113,768	199,264
Washington	4–21	23,899	14,754	94,019	114,379
Wyoming	7–21	4,112	2,907	25,894	28,504
Indian :					
Cherokees	. .	3,715	3,048	. . .	52,300
Chickasaws	. .	900	650	. . .	33,550
Choctaws	. .	2,600	1,460	. . .	31,700
Creeks	. .	1,700	799	. . .	26,900
Seminoles	. .	400	226	. . .	7,500
Total for Territories	. .	218,293	123,157	$648,306	$1,510,115
Total for States	. .	15,661,213	9,737,176	54,642,716	83,601,327
Grand total	. .	15,879,506	9,860,333	$55,291,022	$85,111,442

APPENDIX R.

The following table gives some interesting and important statistics respecting colleges in the United States.

STATES AND TERRITORIES.	No. Universities and Colleges.	No. Instructors in Preparatory Department.	No. Students in Preparatory Department.	No. Instructors in Collegiate Department.	No. Students in Collegiate Department.	No. Volumes in College Libraries.	Value of Grounds, Buildings, and Apparatus.	Income from Productive Funds.	Receipts for the last Year from Tuition Fees.
Alabama	3	2	20	18	314	8,200	$300,000	$24,600	$8,000
Arkansas	4	10	564	28	271	2,286	114,000	1,000	8,300
California	11	36	1,178	131	602	47,750	1,380,200	105,116	91,014
Colorado	3	2	113	23	45	11,000	230,000	1,282	366
Connecticut . . .	3	. .	. .	62	959	148,155	472,884	120,776	114,128
Delaware	1	. .	. .	8	54	6,000	75,000	4,980	500
Georgia	6	2	70	54	554	30,100	652,300	43,493	10,650
Illinois	28	58	2,901	224	1,887	130,630	2,511,550	95,229	116,844
Indiana	15	58	1,793	128	1,329	76,591	1,298,000	50,029	29,646
Iowa	18	46	1,697	168	1,614	51,022	789,000	51,382	42,568
Kansas	8	21	889	75	431	24,178	523,000	5,500	5,400
Kentucky	14	18	594	97	1,178	45,076	673,000	38,443	37,060
Louisiana	9	22	1,022	68	174	57,995	837,000	15,100	21,060
Maine	3	3	45	32	422	59,371	863,500	39,000	22,000
Maryland . . .	11	18	325	160	1,385	49,922	892,500	181,734	45,705
Massachusetts . .	7	7	192	151	1,865	292,626	1,250,000	276,131	166,851
Michigan	9	22	1,361	114	1,166	59,690	1,344,942	89,290	75,351
Minnesota . . .	5	1	279	44	408	21,600	421,196	50,900	8,340
Mississippi . . .	3	7	557	21	320	8,400	446,000	32,643	8,275
Missouri	16	37	1,101	196	1,695	108,315	1,127,220	63,005	135,294
Nebraska	5	11	360	16	216	8,000	205,000	2,359	682
Nevada	1	1	40	. .	. .	. .	. .	. .	. .
New Hampshire .	1	. .	. .	15	247	54,000	125,000	25,000	16,000
New Jersey . . .	4	. .	. .	73	677	60,600	1,150,000	86,615	20,770
New York . . .	27	113	2,662	426	3,495	294,437	7,480,540	472,413	462,059
North Carolina . .	9	8	616	69	590	31,250	549,000	10,000	37,096
Ohio	36	120	3,726	284	2,612	286,411	3,156,744	180,661	101,775
Oregon	8	21	785	38	458	9,420	257,000	20,600	15,950
Pennsylvania . .	27	70	1,877	288	2,367	163,718	4,744,850	239,499	250,105
Rhode Island . .	1	. .	. .	18	251	53,000	. . .	36,099	30,869
South Carolina . .	8	8	358	42	304	17,450	340,000	22,869	5,194
Tennessee . . .	19	33	1,122	148	1,876	51,708	1,498,250	80,475	39,720
Texas	9	18	1,075	58	540	10,411	335,000	775	55,150
Vermont	2	. .	. .	18	93	33,000	440,000	16,328	6,082
Virginia	8	6	73	69	889	102,000	1,558,000	22,200	20,540
West Virginia . .	4	7	134	32	201	5,800	295,000	8,469	5,592
Wisconsin . . .	8	15	786	88	658	48,765	890,300	101,556	56,702
Dist. of Columbia .	5	9	359	43	222	47,411	900,000	1,957	1,165
Utah	1	3	202	3	. .	2,735	30,000	. . .	3,147
Washington . . .	2	7	83	11	90	3,200	100,000	500	4,500
Total	362	820	28,959	3,541	32,459	2,522,223	$40,255,976	$2,618,008	$2,080,450

APPENDIX R — *Continued*.

STATISTICS RESPECTING SCHOOLS OF SCIENCE IN THE UNITED STATES.

Part I. — Institutions endowed with National Land-Grant.

STATES.	Number of Schools.	PREPARATORY DEPARTMENT.		SCIENTIFIC DEPARTMENT.		No. Volumes in General Libraries.	Value of Grounds, Buildings, and Apparatus.	Income from Productive Funds.	Receipts for the last Year from Tuition Fees.
		No. Instructors.	No. Students.	No. Instructors.	No. Students.				
Alabama	1	1	47	11	135	2,000	$75,000	$20,280	. . .
Arkansas	1	. . .	. . .	2	14	200	170,000	10,400	$2,000
California	1	0	0	26	101	. . .	. . .	. . .	. . .
Colorado	1	. . .	. . .	5	57	150	55,000	. . .	. . .
Connecticut	1	. . .	. . .	25	185	5,000	200,000	29,212	17,798
Delaware	1	. . .	. . .	. . .	. . .	. . .	. . .	. . .	. . .
Florida	0	. . .	. . .	. . .	. . .	. . .	. . .	10,004	. . .
Georgia	5	16	877	19	182	3,500	164,000	17,914	1,800
Illinois	1	3	77	24	303	12,942	545,000	21,398	10,619
Indiana	1	2	141	9	140	2,065	250,000	17,000	2,029
Iowa	1	2	15	20	211	6,000	500,000	45,000	0
Kansas	1	. . .	. . .	13	267	3,050	99,525	31,225	426
Kentucky	1	2	. . .	13	182	. . .	85,000	9,900	1,500
Louisiana	1	1	40	9	29	17,000	400,000	14,500	0
Maine	1	. . .	. . .	8	110	4,105	145,000	7,500	. . .
Maryland	1	. . .	6	7	49	. . .	100,000	6,975	825
Massachusetts	2	. . .	. . .	45	517	5,300	520,727	30,672	53,107
Michigan	1	0	0	12	227	6,250	274,380	20,517	0
Minnesota	1	. . .	. . .	. . .	. . .	. . .	. . .	. . .	. . .
Mississippi	2	10	437	9	102	2,830	300,000	11,679	. . .
Missouri	2	2	25	15	209	1,750	46,660	7,680	1,300
Nebraska	1	. . .	. . .	. . .	. . .	. . .	25,000	. . .	. . .
Nevada	1	. . .	. . .	. . .	. . .	. . .	. . .	. . .	. . .
New Hampshire	1	. . .	. . .	10	44	1,200	100,000	4,800	. . .
New Jersey	1	. . .	. . .	14	54	. . .	. . .	. . .	. . .
New York	1	0	0	52	259	. . .	253,509	. . .	. . .
North Carolina	1	0	0	7	24	2,000	. . .	7,500	. . .
Ohio	1	7	93	13	124	1,600	500,000	33,923	3,798
Oregon	1	. . .	. . .	3	60	. . .	10,000	5,000	. . .
Pennsylvania	1	5	45	12	44	3,000	532,000	30,000	0
Rhode Island	1	. . .	. . .	. . .	. . .	. . .	. . .	. . .	. . .
South Carolina	2	. . .	. . .	4	58	26,500	25,000	11,508	. . .
Tennessee	1	. . .	. . .	. . .	. . .	. . .	. . .	25,410	. . .
Texas	1	0	0	18	127	1,090	212,000	14,280	4,191
Vermont	1	0	0	9	23	. . .	. . .	8,130	. . .
Virginia	2	1	108	33	320	2,200	521,080	23,500	100
West Virginia	1	. . .	. . .	. . .	. . .	. . .	. . .	. . .	. . .
Wisconsin	1	0	0	18	124	. . .	200,000	15,322	18
Total	46	52	1,911	465	4,281	109,732	$6,308,881	$491,229	$99,511
U.-S. Military Academy	1	0	0	52	228	28,208	2,500,000	0	0
U.-S. Naval Academy	1	0	0	65	261	22,629	1,292,390	0	0
Grand total	48	52	1,911	582	4,770	160,569	$10,101,271	$491,229	$99,511

APPENDIX R — *Concluded.*

STATISTICS RESPECTING SCHOOLS OF SCIENCE IN THE UNITED STATES — *Concluded.*

PART II. — INSTITUTIONS NOT ENDOWED WITH NATIONAL LAND-GRANT.

STATES.	Number of Schools.	PREPARATORY DEPARTMENT.		SCIENTIFIC DEPARTMENT.		No. Volumes in General Libraries.	Value of Grounds, Buildings, and Apparatus.	Income from Productive Funds.	Receipts for the Last Year from Tuition Fees.
		No. Instructors.	No. Students.	No. Instructors.	No. Students.				
California	1	2	34	5	68	300	. . .	. . .	. . .
Colorado	2	. .	. .	8	83	600	$15,000	. . .	$1,500
Georgia	1	. .	. .	.	. .	. .	. . .	. . .	. . .
Indiana	1	. .	. .	. .	. .	900	135,000	$15,000	. .
Massachusetts	5	. .	. .	103	224	6,200	188,500	72,755	10,050
Michigan	1	. .	. .	3	7	. . .	. . .	. . .	. .
Missouri	1	5	249	17	153	. . .	125,000	. . .	. .
New Hampshire	2	. .	. .	16	50	2,000	1,700	11,000	2,160
New Jersey	2	. .	. .	29	156	5,000	650,000	43,450	19,780
New York	5	. .	. .	84	2,586	24,393	2,000,000	43,495	44,100
Ohio	3	. .	. .	6	. .	. . .	100,000	9,734	. . .
Pennsylvania	8	. .	7	89	2,268	42,468	594,000	6,050	. . .
Vermont	1	. .	. .	10	20	4,000	20,000	. . .	1,000
Virginia	3	. .	. .	8	123	550	400,000	1,200	7,000
District of Columbia	1	. .	. .	. .	. .	. . .	. . .	. . .	. . .
Total	37	7	290	378	5,738	86,411	$4,229,200	$202,684	$85,590

GENERAL SUMMARY OF THE FOREGOING STATISTICS RESPECTING SUPERIOR INSTRUCTION.

Adding the statistics of public and private schools of science (i.e. schools endowed and schools not endowed with the public land-grant) to those of universities and colleges, we have the following totals: Number of institutions, 447; number of instructors in preparatory departments, 879, in collegiate and scientific departments, 4,501; number of students in preparatory departments, 31,160, in collegiate and scientific departments, 42,967; income from productive funds, $3,311,921; income from tuition, $2,265,551; volumes in college libraries, 2,769,203; value of grounds, buildings, and apparatus, $54,586,447.

APPENDIX S.

An exhibit of the legal-tender currency in circulation on the first day of January and the first day of July in each year since the first greenback was issued in 1862.

Date.	Amount.	Date.	Amount.
Jan. 1, 1863	$223,108,000	Jan. 1, 1874	$378,401,702
July 1, 1863	297,767,114	July 1, 1874	382,000,000
Jan. 1, 1864	444,825,022	Jan. 1, 1875	382,000,000
July 1, 1864	431,178,671	July 1, 1875	375,771,580
Jan. 1, 1865	447,074,374	Jan. 1, 1876	371,827,220
July 1, 1865	432,687,966	July 1, 1876	369,772,284
Jan. 1, 1866	425,839,319	Jan. 1, 1877	366,055,084
July 1, 1866	400,619,206	July 1, 1877	359,764,332
Jan. 1, 1867	380,276,160	Jan. 1, 1878	349,943,776
July 1, 1867	371,783,597	July 1, 1878	346,681,016
Jan. 1, 1868	356,000,000	Jan. 1, 1879	346,681,016
July 1, 1868	356,000,000	July 1, 1879	346,681,016
Jan. 1, 1869	356,000,000	Jan. 1, 1880	346,681,016
July 1, 1869	356,000,000	July 1, 1880	346,681,016
Jan. 1, 1870	356,000,000	Jan. 1, 1881	346,681,016
July 1, 1870	356,000,000	July 1, 1881	346,681,016
Jan. 1, 1871	356,000,000	Jan. 1, 1882	346,681,016
July 1, 1871	356,000,000	July 1, 1882	346,681,016
Jan. 1, 1872	357,500,000	Jan. 1, 1883	346,681,016
July 1, 1872	357,500,000	July 1, 1883	346,681,016
Jan. 1, 1873	358,557,907	Jan. 1, 1884	346,681,016
July 1, 1873	356,000,000	. . . .	. . . .

APPENDIX T.

THIS table presents the number of national banks each year from the passage of the original Bank Act, with the average capital, deposits, and circulation for each year on or near October 1 = from 1863 to 1883.

YEARS.	No. of Banks.	Capital.	Deposits.	Circulation.
1863	66	$7,188,393	$8,497,682	. . . .
1864	508	86,782,802	122,166,536	$45,260,504
1865	1,513	393,157,206	500,910,873	171,321,903
1866	1,644	415,472,369	564,616,778	280,253,818
1867	1,642	420,073,415	540,797,838	293,887,941
1868	1,643	420,634,511	580,940,821	295,769,489
1869	1,617	426,399,151	511,400,197	293,593,645
1870	1,648	430,399,301	501,407,587	291,798,640
1871	1,790	458,255,696	600,868,487	315,519,117
1872	1,940	479,629,174	613,290,671	333,495,027
1873	1,976	491,072,616	622,685,563	339,081,799
1874	2,027	493,765,121	669,068,996	333,225,298
1875	2,087	504,829,769	664,579,619	318,350,379
1876	2,089	499,802,232	651,385,210	291,544,020
1877	2,080	479,467,771	616,403,987	291,874,236
1878	2,053	466,147,436	620,236,176	301,888,092
1879	2,048	454,067,365	719,737,568	313,786,342
1880	2,090	457,; 53,985	873,537,637	317,350,036
1881	2,132	463,821,985	1,070,997,531	320,200,069
1882	2,269	483,104,213	1,122,472,682	314,721,215
1883	2,501	509,699,787	1,049,437,700	310,517,857

APPENDIX U.

THE following table exhibits the principal items contained in the returns of the State banks of the country, yearly, from 1834 to 1861 : —

YEARS.	No. of Banks.	Capital.	Deposits.	Circulation.
1834	506	$200,005,944	$75,666,986	$94,839,570
1835	704	231,250,337	83,081,365	103,692,495
1836	713	251,875,292	115,104,440	140,301,038
1837	788	290,772,091	127,397,185	149,185,890
1838	829	317,636,778	84,691,184	116,138,910
1839	840	327,132,512	90,240,146	135,170,995
1840	901	358,442,692	75,696,857	106,968,572
1841	784	313,608,959	64,890,101	107,290,214
1842	692	260,171,797	62,408,870	83,734,011
1843	691	228,861,948	56,168,623	58,563,608
1844	696	210,872,056	84,550,785	75,167,646
1845	707	206,045,969	88,020,646	89,608,711
1846	707	196,894,309	96,913,070	105,552,427
1847	715	203,070,622	91,792,533	105,519,766
1848	751	204,838,175	103,226,177	128,506,091
1849	782	207,309,361	91,178,623	114,743,415
1850	824	217,317,211	109,586,585	131,366,526
1851	879	227,807,553	128,957,712	155,165,251
1852	914	247,858,036	137,255,794	150,619,015
1853	950	267,908,519	145,553,876	146,072,780
1854	1,208	301,376,071	188,188,744	204,689,207
1855	1,307	332,177,288	190,400,342	186,952,223
1856	1,398	343,874,272	212,705,662	195,747,950
1857	1,416	370,834,686	230,351,352	214,778,822
1858	1,422	394,622,799	185,932,049	155,208,344
1859	1,476	401,976,242	259,568,278	193,306,818
1860	1,562	421,880,095	253,802,129	207,102,477
1861	1,601	429,592,713	257,229,562	202,005,767

APPENDIX V.

MAP SHOWING THE TERRITORIAL GROWTH OF THE UNITED STATES.

THE annexed map is designed to show, clearly and accurately, the territorial extent of the United States as established by the Treaty of 1783, with the various additions since made, by purchase, conquest, or voluntary annexation.

The ma is intended to illustrate many parts of the text, and, in connection with the various Appendices, will exhibit within small compass the expansion of free institutions, the growth of population, and the increase of material wealth with which the Republic has been blessed.